Rebel Rebel

Rebel Rebel

Chris O'Leary

Winchester, UK
Washington, USA

First published by Zero Books, 2015
Zero Books is an imprint of John Hunt Publishing Ltd., Laurel House, Station Approach,
Alresford, Hants, SO24 9JH, UK
office1@jhpbooks.net
www.johnhuntpublishing.com
www.zero-books.net

For distributor details and how to order please visit the 'Ordering' section on our website.

ISBN: 978 1 78099 244 0
Library of Congress Control Number: 2014948079

A CIP catalogue record for this book is available from the British Library.

Design: Stuart Davies

Printed and bound by CPI Group (UK) Ltd, Croydon, CR0 4YY, UK

CONTENTS

Introduction

The rock musician sat down for an interview. It was the early Eighties, barely midway through his half-century career: he would still be releasing new albums in 2014. "Part of me is kinda like an actor," he said. "If I don't have something happening directly about my life, I can take from experiences around me and then by way of becoming another person, another persona, I can express a buncha fuckin' feelings." That was Neil Young. And here's Mick Jagger, interviewed in the early Seventies. "If you're a method actor, you always stay in character—[my character] has changed a lot. It's not just one change...every six months, another person."

Pop music is acting: it always has been. Yet only David Bowie got the rap for being rock's pantomime artiste, its greatest pretender. He happily owned up to the charge, calling himself "The Actor" on the sleeve of *Hunky Dory,* "the faker" in "Changes." Today, with Bowie a cross-national cultural icon (one can imagine his face on a Euro note someday), it may be hard to believe he was once considered the epitome of weedy English decadence. That he was seen as a fraud, as an affront to the "realness" of Sixties rock and roll. That he was suspect.

He agreed with his critics, of course. There had never been so self-conscious an act as Bowie's in pop before. In part this was because he'd had such a lengthy incubation, as a marginal act in the mid-Sixties—it's still strange to realize his first single predates *A Hard Day's Night*—and as a struggling folkie and rocker at the turn of the decade. Bowie spent the Sixties in the audience, standing in the corner of a club or perched off stage, always taking mental notes. There was something unique about Bowie, in his assimilative capabilities (and his pack-rat instincts), in his way of imagining himself as his own audience, and so working to entertain himself, first and foremost. And his long internship made him a consummate pro, ready to grab opportunities. The writer Nick Kent said that at Bowie's London debut as Ziggy Stardust in 1972, there was an equipment malfunction just as the show began, creating "a sudden agonizing silence [that] was instantly felt through the hall." Not missing a beat, Bowie "pointed to each flamboyant article of clothing he was adorned in and recited the name of its designer in an exaggerated camp accent." When the band finally tore into "Hang Onto Yourself," the audience was already tight in Bowie's grasp.

Despite the hack reporter's line about Bowie being a changeable musical chameleon, there was a deep continuity to his music. Riffs, chord progressions, phrases, lyrical subjects, amateur saxophone, sped-up Laughing Gnome voices: all reappear in his songs, even in the present decade. This book attempts to see how Bowie's songs worked, how they were assembled, how they changed upon performance. Because Bowie was so consumed by whatever he chanced upon (books, SF films, underground newspapers, salsa records, Nazi documentaries), I wound up writing some potted cultural histories of 20th Century odds and ends. It was unavoidable: to get a grip on Bowie, you have to have a sense of his times. Only the prosperous, youth-heady, pop music emporia that was Britain and America in the Sixties and Seventies could have produced Bowie the rock musician. Had he come early in the 20th Century, he would have been a painter or a music hall performer; had he come today, he'd likely be writing for Image Comics.

But if this book seems an effort to reveal a magician's tricks, that's not my intent. Consider it a travel atlas. By keeping to the ground and going through Bowie's records song by song, you can slowly get a sense of the scale of Bowie's achievement—a body of work that holds up as well as anything from his era. Julie Welch, witnessing a Ziggy Stardust concert in 1973 at Earls Court (which the future Sid Vicious also attended), wrote that Bowie on stage "was utilizing his most splendid gift—his sense of largeness and glory." As this book focuses on Bowie's music, it has little room to examine other pieces of his oeuvre: his album covers, his photographs, his promotional videos and films, his costumes. Still, the music offers largeness and glory in spades.

What Is This Book?

This book is a guide to Bowie's songs, from his first single, released in 1964, to the *Station to Station* album, released in January 1976. Our survey includes both released and (if I managed to hear them) unreleased songs. Feel free to zip around to find whichever songs you like. Or if you're of a more chronological bent, read it as a narrative, starting with the first entry. This book presumes a small amount of familiarity with David Bowie and his music. But if you have no clue about Bowie, no worries: all you'll need is in the following few paragraphs.

David Bowie was born David Robert Jones, in Brixton in January 1947. He was the only son of Peggy Burns and Haywood "John" Jones, a publicity man who'd once (disastrously) run a nightclub. Haywood had married before, both he and Peggy had children from previous entanglements, and David symbolized their much-delayed entry into lower-middle-class life. Unsurprisingly, David lacked for little in his youth. He went to Bromley Tech (the Bowies had moved to Bromley, a suburb of London, in the early Fifties) and left school in 1963. He wanted to be a famous pop musician and spent the Sixties in pursuit of that ambition, burning through a set of bands, record labels and managers in the process, with no commercial success.

Disillusioned with and considering abandoning professional music, Bowie got a novelty hit ("Space Oddity") in late 1969. He struggled to follow it up. Finally, thanks to the acumen of his wife (Angela Barnett), his ruthless manager (Tony Defries), a sympathetic producer (Ken Scott), a brilliant guitarist/arranger (Mick Ronson) and the full flowering of his songwriting, Bowie became a British rock star with the release of *The Rise and Fall of*

Ziggy Stardust and the Spiders From Mars in June 1972. Soon to follow were #1 albums, Top 10 hits, headlining the Hammersmith Odeon and Radio City Music Hall.

Memories of his post-"Space Oddity" limbo had made Bowie craftier and he discarded the Ziggy Stardust image at its peak of fame, playing his last show as Ziggy in July 1973 and soon afterward breaking up his band. Looking for an American hit (he'd had good press in the US but weak sales), he left Britain for America in 1974. He began exploring soul and R&B while becoming vigorously addicted to cocaine; he got a US #1 hit ("Fame"), a starring role in a film, *The Man Who Fell to Earth,* and acquired enough celebrity to sing a medley of pop hits with Cher on her variety show. This volume concludes with the songs of *Station to Station,* the album Bowie recorded in Los Angeles at the end of 1975, and his departure from America for Europe in the spring of the following year.

Bowiesongs

When referring to "song," I mean any piece of music written, recorded and/or performed by Bowie, with the critical distinction that at least one recording of it exists and is circulating ("circulating" = available on bootleg vinyl, CD or torrent or up on YouTube.) For example, Bowie performed a feedback-laden version of Gustav Holst's "Mars: The Bringer of War" on stage in 1966 but as there are no recordings of these performances, "Mars" is consigned to the appendix. By contrast, Bowie sang James Brown's "If You Don't Work, You Can't Eat" on stage in 1972. A recording of a performance exists, so the song gets its own entry.

I've also used "song" as a changeable object, so whenever Bowie has revisited and re-recorded a song, I address its later incarnations in the same entry. So the entry for "I Feel Free" covers its multiple lives: a live performance by the Spiders from Mars in 1972, an aborted studio take in 1980 and a studio take Bowie recorded in 1992 for *Black Tie White Noise*. This hopefully will prove less confusing in the book than it may seem here.

Song are listed in the rough order of their creation, with some alterations for the sake of narrative. For example "The London Boys" and "Silly Boy Blue," songs Bowie wrote and demoed in 1965, are held back until the 1966 chapter because it made far more thematic sense to place them there. When I lacked information about recording order, I arranged the songs in a scheme that follows (hopefully) some logic. So Bowie's *Pin Ups* covers are in the chronological order of the original singles' release.

This book revises the blog "Pushing Ahead of the Dame," which I started in late July 2009 (http://bowiesongs.wordpress.com). I've rewritten, corrected and, with hope, improved all of the entries, as the blog offered many blunders of interpretation, fact and taste. In many cases, improvements came from my insightful commenters—I have tried to credit them wherever possible, but please consider this a general thank-you.

Much of this book's insights (should you find any) is derived from the work of interviewers, photographers, concert tapers, biographers and researchers who have preceded me. Most of all, Nicholas Pegg and Kevin Cann have wrought order from Bowie chaos. Without their labors, this book could not have existed. I also obviously owe its general scheme to the late Ian MacDonald's chronological song-by-song study of the Beatles, *Revolution In the Head*.

My perspective is that of my age and region: I'm an American writing about a British artist whom I first knew as the "Let's Dance"-era Bowie, and doubtlessly some cultural nuances have escaped me. All facts in the following book have been verified to the best of my abilities; all opinions are my own. As we stop at 1976 in this volume, there's obviously a ways to go: there will be a sequel in the near future.

Chris O'Leary
Easthampton, 2014

Acknowledgements

Thanks owed to:

Manuscript readers: Ian McDuffie, Phil Sandifer, Stephen Thomas Erlewine, Amy Granzin, Alfred Soto, Ned Raggett and Alex Abramovich. Most of all, Stephen Ryan, who reviewed every word of this book with a keen eye (his labors in verifying the spelling of Emir Ksasan's name alone were colossal) and who provided much-needed pushes during various slogs of despair. And Nicholas Currie, aka Momus, who offered theories, sharp quotes, insights and even photographed a band score at the Library of Scotland for me.

Owen Hatherley and Agata Pyzik are the godparents of this book. Tom Ewing was the first to give the blog any notice, for which I remain grateful. I'd also like to thank Andy Zax, Lisa Jane Persky, Jack Womack and Douglas Wolk for various kindnesses and for nice things they've said about the blog in public. I thank Zero and Tariq Goddard for the opportunity and their rather incredible patience.

On musical theory: Jeff Norman and Larry Hardesty. On theory, piano and guitar: Dave Depper and Greg Smith. On bass: John Kringle. On Sixties British culture: Anthony Heague. On Buddhism: Janna White and Andy Rotman. Thanks to Toby Seay, of Drexel University, for letting me hear some *Young Americans* tapes.

For decades of friendship: Mike Slezak and Iyassu Sebhat, Morgan and Corey Griffin (& Ada and Alice), Kristen and Joe Holmgren, Bill Madden-Fuoco, Christopher George, Mark Leccese, Adam Zucker and the rest of The Writers' Mill of Florence, MA. For hosting the Philadelphia research leg: Taije Silverman and Zachary Lesser. Robb and Emily Sandagata and the rest of my very extended family. Thanks to my ever-supportive parents, to the rascals Lucy and Jake, and lastly, to

Sarah Platanitis, whom I met two weeks after I started the blog and who has been the very patient witness of its long transformation into this book.

Chapter 1

The Junior Visualizer (1964-1966)

I never wanted to be a rock star. "'onest, guv, I weren't even there." But I ***was*** *there, that's what happened.*
David Bowie, 1974.

I think he sounds terrible, but he must be some good because he's made a record.
Haywood "John" Jones, David Bowie's father, 1964.

David Bowie sweated away for years on a Sunday, with nobody, repeat nobody, coming to see him.
Harold Pendleton, owner of the Marquee Club.

A meaningless simplification of the blues with all the poetry removed and the emphasis on white, and by definition inferior, performers...unsubtle, unswinging, uncoloured music.
George Melly, on early rock & roll, *Revolt Into Style*.

I was taken on as a "junior visualizer," which means I was a sort of stick-and-paste artist for all the other buggers there who had proper art school training.
Bowie, on his short-lived advertising career.

Liza Jane

(Conn). ***Recorded****: ca. early May 1964, Decca Studios, 165 Broadhurst Gardens, West Hampstead, London. David Bowie: lead vocal, tenor saxophone; Roger Bluck: lead guitar, backing vocal?; George Underwood: rhythm guitar, backing vocal; Dave Howard: bass; Robert Allen: drums. Produced: Leslie Conn; engineered: Glyn Johns;* ***(remake, unreleased)*** *(basic tracks) July 2000, Sear Sound Studios,*

353 W. 48th St., NYC; (overdubs) ca. October-early November 2000, The Looking Glass Studios, 632 Broadway, NYC. Bowie: lead vocal, harmonica?; Earl Slick: lead guitar; Gerry Leonard: rhythm guitar; Mike Garson: keyboards; Cuong Vu: trumpet; Mark Plati: rhythm guitar; Gail Ann Dorsey: bass, backing vocals; Sterling Campbell: drums; Holly Palmer, Emm Gryner: backing vocals. Produced: Bowie, Plati; engineered: Pete Keppler.

***First release**: (as "Davie Jones with the King Bees") 5 June 1964 (Vocalion Pop V.9221). **Broadcast**: 6 June 1964, Juke Box Jury; 19 June 1964, Ready Steady Go!; 27 June 1964, The Beat Room. **Live**: 1964, 2004.*

On the night of 5 June 2004, on stage at an amphitheatre off the Garden State Parkway, David Bowie was winding down what remains his last concert in America. It was also the 40th anniversary of the release of his first single, a song called "Liza Jane." Bowie, who was a sentimental man at the time, marked this milestone by singing a verse of the song. As a preface, he called his debut single "absolutely dreadful" and "excruciating," which was a fair description of the sludgy blues fragment he offered that night. Not that it mattered to the audience, the majority of whom had never heard "Liza Jane" before and never would again. Not that it mattered to Bowie, for whom the song was a memento of being young, hapless and obscure.

Back

"Liza Jane" wasn't quite his first professional recording. In the summer of 1963, Bowie and his band the Kon-Rads had auditioned for Decca, taping four tracks that included his co-composition "I Never Dreamed" (see appendix). Decca passed on the Kon-Rads. Bowie soon ditched them for the King Bees, who were a trio of older Fulham boys—Robert Allen, Roger Bluck and Dave Howard—and a fellow Kon-Rad, his school friend George Underwood, who two years before had struck Bowie in the eye in a fight over a girl, leaving Bowie's left pupil permanently dilated.

After a handful of months, with only rehearsals in Fulham and talent nights at pubs to their credit, the King Bees cut a single for a subsidiary of Decca, one of the two labels that ruled British pop. In 1964, this trajectory wasn't unusual. It was a gold rush. The British pop music industry was generating £100 million annually. Some 20,000 beat groups had formed in Britain by 1963; some twenty of them auditioned for labels each week.

British pop music was the property of a London-based affiliation of cynical older men, many of whom had come up in musical theatre: they had contempt for the acts they marketed, the teenagers who bought them and likely themselves. But now a Liverpudlian beat group managed by a record store chain owner was the biggest act in the country. In the summer of 1964, the Beatles set about claiming the rest of the world; in their wake, everything was up for the taking. Every would-be manager, every grubbing concert promoter thought they were the next Brian Epstein. (A few were.) Waiting for them was a generation of boys with guitars; it was if they'd been seeded across Britain overnight.

Leslie Conn was a record plugger, remembered for his persistence (the entertainer Max Bygraves said Conn "could set fire to a bucket of sand") and his bad timing. He managed two of the biggest British pop stars of the early Seventies (Bowie and Marc Bolan) in the mid-Sixties. He learned of David Bowie when the latter wrote to a washing machine tycoon, John Bloom, asking for a few hundred pounds to buy new gear and promising that Bloom could make a fresh million if he backed the King Bees. An amused Bloom passed on the note to Conn, a friend, who was soon converted. Where the Beatles had won over doubters with their wit, Bowie impressed with his unmoored confidence. Conn signed a management contract with Bowie, agreed to manage the King Bees on a non-contractual basis (neatly severing singer from band) and booked them to play Bloom's anniversary party at a

Soho nightclub. The King Bees opened with Muddy Waters' "Got My Mojo Working" and appalled the guests. Bloom ordered the band offstage after two songs; Bowie wept. An unperturbed Conn used the debacle as a hook for the King Bees' introductory press release. Leveraging his contacts as a freelance A&R man for Decca, he landed a recording session with a label subsidiary, Vocalion.

For the single, Conn selected "Louie Louie Go Home." The proposed B-side was a number the band had played live: "Little Liza Jane." Though Bowie and Underwood knocked together a new arrangement for "Liza Jane," Conn wound up credited as sole composer. He later justified his appropriation by saying he'd improved upon the "six-bar blues that everyone uses." The song itself was a cloudy thing, of unknown provenance. Underwood once said it was an "old Negro spiritual" he and Bowie had picked up somewhere.

Further Back

"Liza Jane," or "Little Liza Jane," wasn't a spiritual. It wasn't a six-bar blues, either. It was a party song, a game song, a child's song that adults made filthy. It was barely a song, really, more of a musical weed. You could sing anything that scanned in the verses as long as you threw in a "lil' Liza Jane" every once in a while.

It came out of the mid-19th Century, from the lower South, possibly a slave song later adopted by minstrel shows. An ex-slave named Marshal Butler recalled singing "Little Liza Jane" Saturday nights on the Collar plantation in Georgia, drinking lemonade and whiskey, men plucking at fiddles with broom straws. The father of Sam Chatmon, one of the Mississippi Sheiks, played "Little Liza Jane" as a plantation work song. "He'd go along and make up things and holler it out in the fields where the old boss man could hear...'Hey Liza, Little Liza Jane,'" Chatmon said. By the 1880s, the song had moved up to tidewater

Virginia, where it was part of a game called "Stealin' Partners." A man standing in the middle of a circle of dancers was the lead ("come my love and go with me"), the dancers his chorus ("little Liza Jane!").

"Little Liza Jane" never kept still: the chanting man in the circle would give it fresh lines, just as Sam Chatmon's father had (by the 1910s, there were signs of upward mobility: "I got a house in Baltimo'/L'il Liza Jane!/Brussels carpet on the flo'..."). Then in 1916, one Countess Ada de Lachau copyrighted it, taking full composer's credit for what she termed a "southern dialect song." Soon "L'il Liza Jane" was a stage hit, the smash number of a cheery racist musical called *Come Out of the Kitchen.*

This was the song's first pop moment: recorded as a jazz side in 1917, its sheet music sent to American army camps preparing for the Western Front. Keeping company with soldiers soon coarsened it: in 1918, folklorist Vance Randolph found an Arkansas man who sang him a version he'd picked up in army camp ("I come once but I come no more—Little Liza Jane!/I come once an' my pecker got sore—Little Liza Jane!"). While "Liza Jane" was often a boast ("Ise gotta gal and you got none," the de Lachau version began), some variants had the singer willing to share Liza Jane with whoever's game ("I'll tell my gal to give you some").

"Liza Jane" followed a split track. Whites came to regard it as a country standard, recorded by the likes of Bob Wills and the "Cackling" DeZurik Sisters; this line would cross over to Britain as a skiffle song, recorded by Lonnie Donegan in 1958. For black audiences, it was an old familiar. Black string bands like the Mississippi Sheiks kept "Little Liza Jane" in their repertoire, as they played for both white and black audiences and found "Liza Jane" worked as a crossover piece. Which is how Huey "Piano" Smith and the Clowns considered the song a generation later.

Smith had grown up in New Orleans and knew "Little Liza Jane" as something the kids in his neighborhood sang in the street. He and his band played it for white audiences, like the fraternity row of LSU. (Not so much the black clubs of New Orleans. "You saw them looking at us like this (sitting, crossed arms)," Smith told his biographer John Wirt. "They weren't moved by "Liza Jane" and stuff like that.") With a session coming up for Ace Records, Smith was looking for something fresh. He grabbed "Liza Jane," believing it was in the public domain and unaware he'd violate the copyright of the Countess Ada de Lachau.

He told his band to think "bluegrass music. That's the session." They were putting a spin on a corny old white song. Smith had his saxophonist Lee Allen play a melody from Dvořák's "Humoresques" popular with Dixieland jazz bands but adding some honking twists. "It was hipper because it was Lee playing, not no bunch of Dixieland front men," Mac Rebennack, aka Doctor John, told Wirt. "Huey was catching the real second line on "Little Liza Jane." Smith purged "Little Liza Jane" of any residual corniness. No more verses about houses in Baltimore or frogs or mules. It was about girls, and it was a rock 'n' roll song.

Smith's "Little Liza Jane" was a regional hit, prompting the competition (including Fats Domino, who shamelessly stole Smith's arrangement) to cut their own versions. Dale Hawkins picked it up in 1959, flavoring Smith's revision with cues from older country versions by the Carlisles and Bob Wills. A Texan teen idol, Scotty McKay, cut a "Liza Jane" with a killer rock 'n' roll line buried in it: "I would stay longer but I stayed too long." This was enough of a ferment for the rock 'n' roll "Liza Jane" to make it over to Britain, where five teenagers from Fulham and Bromley thought it was a "Negro spiritual."

Forward

"Their stuff is homemade music," Cliff Richard said of the Beatles in February 1964, just as the band toppled him as Britain's biggest pop act. "Anybody who can shout can be a Beatle." He was right: it was the moment for amateurs. Fifties British rock 'n' roll had been the work of slumming jazz musicians but now the kids in the stalls were playing it. Cue the King Bees.

Instead of the "little Li-za *Jane*" refrain that went back to Ada de Lachau, the King Bees sang a salacious "OHHHH lit-tle *LI-*ZA!," slavering on the long vowels. (The standard refrain became the eight-bar refrain.) Theirs wasn't a courting song, like Smith's. Bowie already has the girl, he has too much of her, she's driving him crazy. His lines are the desperate brags of a boy upturned by lust.

Though it kicked off with a three-chord guitar riff, almost note-for-note the opening of the Yardbirds' take on "Smokestack Lightning," the track's main hook was Bowie's overdubbed tenor saxophone, which zipped around, wasp-like. (His limitations as a saxophone player and Conn's as an arranger collided mercilessly here, as Bowie plays the same descending phrase over and over again, breaking character only on refrains.) Bowie's voice seemed constituted of adenoids and spit. "Well I gotta *girl* thassa GOOD to me!"he screams, with little mystery as to how—the band groan along on refrains. "Now *she* ain't more than-uh five-foot-*three*!" (Liza loses an inch later in the song.) The refrain was the title slurred four times. The second verse was incomprehensible: "Ah gotta girl whooza *guh* to *GUH*!" His voice cracking hard by the last verse, Bowie battled to cloak his accent, but "Jane" soon became "Jayne" and in the fade he snapped that Liza was "coming back to me lurve!" Bluck's 12-bar guitar solo fell apart after six; Allen slammed the backbeat on his snare as if trying to catch someone's attention.

Conn didn't produce the record as much as he got out of its way. Despite having future master engineer Glyn Johns behind the console, the single was misshapen, murky-sounding, as Johns had spent much of the session just trying to adequately mike Allen's cheap, tape-patched drums. "Liza Jane" was voted down on *Juke Box Jury*, got no airplay in the few hours the BBC allotted to pop music and it died. So did the King Bees.

Further Forward

Their singer managed to keep at it. Bowie's brief live revival of "Liza Jane" in 2004 drew upon a much finer remake he'd cut in the studio for his self-covers album *Toy*, which his label in 2001 had refused to release. This "Liza Jane" was a slow-groove exhumation, the song taken at a loping amble, with seemingly every instrument in the mix distorted: Earl Slick and Gerry Leonard's guitars; the jazz trumpeter Cuong Vu, who sounds as if he's playing through a metallic cloud; a Bowie vocal, likely piped through an effects pedal, that suggested Tom Waits' trademark abuse of megaphones and trumpet mutes.

That night in New Jersey, the 57-year-old Bowie had treated "Liza Jane" like an embarrassing joke. His teenage self had known better. Maybe he'd sensed the song was far bigger than him. He didn't care. He broke it open, he made it work.

Louie Louie Go Home

(Revere/Lindsay). ***Recorded****: ca. early May 1964, Decca Studios. Bowie: lead vocal; Bluck: lead guitar, backing vocal; Underwood: rhythm guitar, backing vocal; Howard: bass; Allen: drums. Produced: Conn; engineered: Johns.*

First release*: 5 June 1964 (Vocalion Pop V.9221).* ***Live****: 1964.*

Leslie Conn had scrabbled in the British music industry long enough for many people to owe him favors, including the Beatles' publisher, Dick James, so Conn had dibs on the latest American releases. For the King Bees, he nabbed an acetate of Paul Revere and the Raiders' "Louie Go Home," which conveniently was published by Dick James.

The Raiders and their Pacific Northwest rivals, the Kingsmen, had cut versions of "Louie Louie" in 1963 but the Kingsmen got the national hit with it. So "Louie Go Home" (the King Bees doubled Louie) was the Raiders' rebound. Where "Louie Louie" has a sailor pining for his girl back home, "Louie Go Home" finds the sailor, having ditched his wife and child, left with a bad conscience: "I'm going home—back to where they need me."

The song was little more than a string of audience-baiting maneuvers, a call-and-response chorus and a long breakdown with a "little bit softer now, little bit louder now" routine à la the Isley Brothers' "Shout." It was the sideshow tent: Mark Lindsay's bleating saxophone and Revere on piano, with his left-hand comping and right-hand flourishes, doing his best Huey Smith. Fitting for the King Bees, it was also the sound of "a bunch of white-bread kids trying to sound black," as Lindsay recalled.

Told to learn the song in a few days, the King Bees struggled to fit "Louie Go Home" into their narrow scope. Lacking a pianist, they shifted the riff to Dave Howard's bass and kicked up the tempo at the expense of swinging, with Robert Allen discarding the original's intricate ride cymbal work to stick with time-keeping 8th notes. Where on "Liza Jane" the King Bees attempted the hard R&B sound of the London clubs, with the Yardbirds, Pretty Things and the Downliners Sect as particular inspirations, their "Louie Louie Go Home" was a fumbled bid for pop radio play (the wayward backing vocals essay Beatles harmonies, especially "Money").

Lacking the manic glee of the Raiders' Lindsay, who did violence to each phrase he came across, Bowie kept the song together until the breakdown, where the King Bees fell to pieces: off-key harmonies, anemic drum fills, Bowie quacking "back back back" until the fadeout came as a mercy. Hearing the playbacks, Conn realized "Louie Louie Go Home" was a bungle and gave a battlefield promotion to "Liza Jane" as the single's A-side, to no avail.

I Pity the Fool

(Malone). ***Recorded:*** *15 January 1965, IBC Studios, 35 Portland Place, Marylebone, London (Studio A). Bowie: lead vocal, alto saxophone;*

Paul Rodriguez: tenor saxophone, trumpet; Woolf Byrne: baritone saxophone; Johnny Flux: rhythm guitar; Jimmy Page: lead guitar; Bob Solly: organ; John Watson: bass; Mick White: drums. Produced: Shel Talmy; engineered: Johns.

***First release**: (as "The Manish Boys") 5 March 1965 (Parlophone R 5250). **Broadcast**: 8 March 1965, Gadzooks! It's All Happening. **Live**: 1964-1965.*

Before Bowie left the King Bees, he'd already begun singing with a sextet from Maidstone called the Manish Boys. Leslie Conn made the introductions, promising the Manish Boys a hot R&B singer, one whom they assumed was black until Bowie came through the French doors of saxophonist Paul Rodriguez's home, "a Belsen-like refugee figure with blondish hair down to his shoulders." Pallor aside, Bowie soon convinced the band to take him on thanks to his look (he favored thigh-length buckskin boots and buckskin waistcoats at the time), his record collection (he introduced them to James Brown's *Live at the Apollo*) and Conn's vague promise of a record contract and American tour. The now seven-strong Manish Boys worked the southeast England circuit in the autumn of 1964, playing US Air Force bases and early Mod havens Eel Pie Island and The Scene. It was the first serious touring Bowie had done and it toughened him as a performer: he learned to use the microphone, smashed maracas on stage. The band's peak was landing an opening slot on the last dates of a Gene Pitney/Gerry and the Pacemakers/Kinks tour, where Bowie first met Ray and Dave Davies.

Conn was courting Shel Talmy, an expatriate American independent producer on a hot streak. Talmy had helmed the Kinks' #1 "You Really Got Me" and would soon cut the Who's "I Can't Explain." Though more intrigued by Bowie's original songs (see "Take My Tip") than he was with the Manish Boys, Talmy agreed to produce their first single. He pushed the band to learn Bobby "Blue" Bland's "I Pity the Fool," giving them an acetate and telling them to hone the song on the Pitney tour. Hedging his bets, he angled to have session musicians replace the Manish Boys' guitarist and drummer. While Talmy didn't get his way, a favorite hired gun, the 21-year-old Jimmy Page, doubled on lead guitar.

Bobby Bland had been a blues shouter until a tonsillectomy reduced his upper register, forcing him to adapt: he started singing behind the beat while expanding his effects arsenal to include a soft, buttery purr, spooky melismatic moans and cello-like low passages. On "I Pity the Fool," Bland opened with dismissive coolness, taking his time on the descending title phrase. He can't be bothered to wonder where his ex-lover is now, but this is just bluster: when the song moved to its bridge, Bland howled. He was still entwined with her and the shame of it was killing him. Backed by a righteous horn section, he boiled in self-hatred: "LOOK at the PEOPLE!!...They just STANDIN' there, watching you make a FOOL of ME!" When he tried to resume the ease of his "I pity the fool" refrain, the horns wouldn't let him rest, hounding him until the fade.

Talmy had made a good pick, as the song's emotional conflict carried on a teenager's wavelength: strutting, oblivious arrogance; raw anger; the fear of being shamed in public. The band also liked the song, calling it a "builder." Yet as the Manish Boys only had time for a quick run-through in a nearby coffee bar and were allowed a mere two takes to cut it, their "I Pity the Fool" wound up being a shoddy reduction of Bland. They opened the song with a blatant ape of the guitar line on the Rolling Stones' recent #1, "Little Red Rooster." While confident in his verse phrasing, Bowie came off peevish and callow in refrains. It didn't help that the saxophone players—Bowie (on alto), Rodriguez and Byrne—were crude company, lacking the dexterity of Bland's six-man section (the latter was also timbrally diverse, its saxophones positioned between trombone and two trumpets playing in unison). Talmy had little experience writing horn charts and the band later complained that he'd made a hash of it, erasing a counter-riff from the Bland arrangement and mixing the saxophones so prominently that they overpowered the song.

Even had Talmy painstakingly followed Bland's arrangement, the Manish Boys were too ungainly and unseasoned to craft "I Pity the Fool" into a hit in 1965. They sounded passé. Despite Conn touting their "sax sound" in press releases as a successor to Merseybeat, the band's triple-sax attack was as creaky as Bill Haley. There was another way: Jimmy Page had just gotten a fuzzbox (most likely a Maestro Fuzz Tone) for his Fender Telecaster and was eager to try it out. Bob Solly recalled its tone sounding like "someone walking through impacted snow." Had Talmy used Page's fuzzbox as a brass substitute, as Keith Richards soon would on "Satisfaction," the track would have had much more of a kick. Packing up his gear, Page said he didn't think "I Pity the Fool" was a hit. He was right. The single cratered despite Conn and Bowie's best shtick and Bowie left the Manish Boys four months later.

Take My Tip

Recorded: *15 January 1965, IBC Studios. Bowie: lead vocal, alto saxophone; Rodriguez: tenor saxophone; Byrne: baritone saxophone; Flux: lead guitar; Page: rhythm guitar; Solly: organ; Watson: bass; White: drums. Producer: Talmy; engineer: Johns.*

First release: *5 March 1965 (Parlophone R 5250).* ***Live***: *1964-1965.*

Bowie's first sole original composition to be recorded, "Take My Tip" opens with John Watson's walking, distorted bass until Bob Solly stabs out a descending four-chord progression. There's a nasal hipster slyness in Bowie's delivery despite his struggles to keep pace with his syllable-choked lyric ("here's the news you are but one fish in her back-garden sea" is crammed into little over a bar). He may have come up with the top melody on his saxophone, as evidenced by the saxes echoing him note-for-note in the refrain and bridge. Jimmy Page turns up on rhythm guitar. After the brief pummeling of a chorus, the process repeats once more for cruelty.

Meager as it was, "Take My Tip" sold Shel Talmy on Bowie's songwriting potential. It was fitting as Bowie's debut composition, as American jazz had been among his first musical loves. He aspired to Mose Allison coolness in the verses, where he warned of a local *femme fatale*, but the more obvious influence was Georgie Fame, whose "Yeh Yeh," with its word-jammed verses and saxophone shadowing the vocal melody, was topping the UK pop charts when Bowie cut the track.

"Take My Tip" is also first evidence of Bowie's idiosyncratic approach to songwriting. "Davie could never work out chord sequences," Solly recalled. "He knew exactly what he wanted but he couldn't play it." None of his bands thought much of his original material and Bowie struggled to promote his songs over playing covers. With scant musical training, Bowie pieced together songs by overhearing his guitarists practice or from melodies that he coaxed from his saxophone. Playing guitar, he'd use random fingerings as a means to sound out ideas, having a strong ear for following a "logical"-sounding progression down the frets, regardless of whether the chords he fingered through were in the same key. (Because Bowie's songs were so oddly-rigged, his bands found them hard to learn.) He'd have his guitarists run through chords until he heard a "cool-sounding" one (Phil Lancaster of the Lower Third recalled playing piano until Bowie stopped him, intrigued by a passing run of chords).

So the opening progression of "Take My Tip," an F# chord shifting to an F major, may have come about when Bowie (or his guitarist Johnny Flux) played F# and then moved the chord shape down a fret to sound F major. It was songwriting via inspired collisions, falling in the line of John Lennon, who'd build a song around any new chord he learned, and Paul McCartney, who admitted his and Lennon's songs were "just dripping with chords that weren't supposed to be there anyway."

That's Where My Heart Is

Recorded: *ca. spring-summer 1965, IBC Studios. Bowie: lead vocal, acoustic guitar. Producer/engineer: Talmy.*

First release: *30 July 1991,* ***Early On (1964-1966)*** *(Rhino R2 70526).*

Shel Talmy was looking to corner the market on young British rock & roll songwriters. With Pete Townshend and Ray Davies already in his stable, he set aside occasional studio time for Bowie, whom he considered a viable, if rough prospect. These demo sessions, hailing around the time Bowie left the Manish Boys and joined the Lower Third, produced nothing of remote commercial appeal, something that Talmy realized at the time ("it was weird music"). He stowed away the tapes for decades until licensing them to Rhino for their 1991 *Early On* compilation. The tracks are mostly of interest as documents of Bowie's mid-1965 forays into a softer pop sound. With two flop singles under his belt, he was wondering if playing straight R&B was a dead end. It would take him another year to realize it was.

While they're the start of a trail that leads to "Sell Me a Coat" and *Hunky Dory*, the demos are generally derivative, grim fare. "That's Where My Heart Is" took as a blueprint Gene Pitney singles like "I'm Gonna Be Strong" and "Yesterday's Hero," whose near-conversational verses built to manically-sung choruses. So Bowie pegged his verse melody to the rigid down-strums of his guitar, gave a touch of Petula Clark to his looser-phrased pre-chorus and then shot for the heights in his refrains, where his ambition was at odds with his vocal abilities. The lyric is hokum (in one refrain, Bowie sings a line the grammatically correct way ("shining so bright*ly*") and then audibly realizes he's made a hash of his rhyme with "night" by doing so. See also the first appearance of the Bowie baritone at :50). Its bridge was the work of an even more fledging songwriter, suggesting it was an older piece that Bowie wedged into "That's Where My Heart Is" to pad out the song.

I Want My Baby Back

***Recorded**: ca. spring-summer 1965, IBC Studios. Bowie: lead and harmony vocal, guitar. Producer/engineer: Talmy.*

***First release**: 30 July 1991, **Early On**.*

Another demo, "I Want My Baby Back" finds Bowie attempting more intricate vocal harmonies beyond the roughneck call-and-responses of his first singles. Double-tracked throughout, with an additional Bowie lead vocal for the refrains, the demo is a modest effort riddled with popped "p" sounds. The song needed a catchier guitar riff, a new bridge and a complete lyrical rewrite (its verses marry clichés with lines like "I tried to phone her but the cable was broke by a storm") to go anywhere further; it didn't.

Bars of the County Jail

***Recorded**: ca. spring-summer 1965, IBC Studios. Bowie: lead and harmony vocals, acoustic guitar, handclaps. Producer/engineer: Talmy.*

***First release**: 30 July 1991, **Early On**.*

A fan of American Westerns since childhood (he took his stage name from slave smuggler, land speculator and Alamo martyr Jim Bowie, as played by Richard Widmark in the 1960 John Wayne-directed *The Alamo*), Bowie had wanted the King Bees to play country & western songs and even sport cowboy outfits on stage. So his cod-Western ballad "Bars of the County Jail" didn't come out of the blue. He took the scenario of a man in jail the night before his hanging from an English composition that he'd written at Bromley Tech; he'd further develop the idea in "Wild Eyed Boy From Freecloud" (see Ch. 3) and, decades later, "I Have Not Been to Oxford Town."

While in the vein of the Everly Brothers' "Take a Message to Mary," "Bars of the County Jail" is more camp and strange, a musical-hall cowboy song complete with crowd-coaxing opener ("gather you all and listen here") and false ending. Bowie intones "on the morrow I will HANG" with a ringing guitar chord, pauses for a breath, then plows into another jaunty wordless refrain, now with shakily-overdubbed handclaps. Inspirational verse: "I was to marry a very rich girl/I loved her as only I can."

You've Got a Habit of Leaving

***Recorded**: ca. early July 1965, IBC Studios. Bowie: lead vocal, harmonica; Denis Taylor: lead guitar, backing vocals; Nicky Hopkins: piano; Graham Rivens: bass; Phil Lancaster: drums. Producer: Talmy; engineer: Johns; **(remake)** July 2000 (basic tracks, vocals), Sear Sound; October-November 2000 (overdubs), Looking Glass. Bowie: lead vocal; Slick: lead guitar, acoustic guitar; Plati: rhythm guitar, acoustic guitar; Garson: piano; Dorsey: bass, backing vocals; Campbell: drums; Lisa Germano: violin; Palmer, Gryner: backing vocals. Produced: Bowie, Tony Visconti; engineered: Keppler, Visconti.*

***First release**: (as "Davy Jones") 20 August 1965 (Parlophone R 5315); (remake) 3 June 2002, "Slow Burn" (Columbia/ISO 672744 2). **Broadcast**: 27 August 1965, Friday Spectacular (Radio Luxembourg). **Live**: 1965-1966.*

Bowie first met Pete Townshend when the former's new band, the Lower Third, opened for the Who in Bournemouth, Dorset on 20 August 1965. Stopping at the Lower Third's soundcheck to hear them bash through songs like "You've Got a Habit of Leaving" (released as a single that very day), Townshend innocently asked whose songs they were playing. Upon hearing they were "Dave's songs," he snapped that they sounded a bit like his.

Bowie and Townshend started recording at the same time and shared a producer in Shel Talmy but that was as far as the parallel went. By late summer 1965, when the Who had released "I Can't Explain" and "Anyway Anyhow Anywhere" and had "My Generation" in the pipeline, Townshend had vaulted past

Bowie, who was reduced to echoing him. Some of this was a matter of age which, in Sixties British pop, neatly determined rank. In 1965 John Lennon, at 25, was the vanguard; Paul McCartney was 23 and Mick Jagger, 22; Ray Davies was 21; Townshend and Eric Clapton were 20. Bowie was only *18* and felt every bit of it.

Townshend also could play off three other distinct personalities. The vocals on Who tracks—Roger Daltrey's growl, Townshend's reedy tenor, John Entwistle's baritone (or near-countertenor)—were like the strands of a single voice, much as how the band swapped musical roles: Keith Moon played rhythm guitar lines on his drums, Entwistle played guitar solos on French horn, Townshend worked as the beleaguered rhythm section.

By contrast, Bowie had the Lower Third, whose ambition was to sound like the Who. The Lower Third were from Margate, Kent. Having worked up an R&B set playing sideshows and seaside resorts, the band moved to Pimlico in May 1965 in search of, consecutively, a lead singer, better gigs and a record contract. Bowie heard of them during his daily politicking at the Giaconda coffee house on Denmark Street and quickly auditioned, beating out his friend Steve Marriott. Guitarist Denis Taylor said he chose Bowie greatly because he most looked the part of a pop singer (on first sight, Taylor had thought Bowie was the Yardbirds' singer Keith Relf). Bowie and the Lower Third's relationship began as a mutual misunderstanding. As Marriott later said, the band thought they were getting a singer, Bowie a backing band.

For their debut single, Bowie and the Lower Third took "You've Got a Habit of Leaving," an older Bowie composition, and beat it until it resembled a Who single. Using the structure of the Kinks' recent "Tired of Waiting for You" (chorus built on a two-chord shift, brief verse, despondent bridge: repeat), they shoehorned a Who/Yardbirds-style rave-up into the middle of it. The rave-up in "You've Got a Habit of Leaving" has some kick, thanks to Bowie's Relf imitation on harmonica and Graham Rivens' throbbing bass (Phil Lancaster also thickened the sound of his kick drum by draping his tweed coat over it). But it's so in hock to the Who's "Anyway Anyhow Anywhere" that Townshend must have cracked up when hearing it performed. The band cut off after 14 bars as if the neighbors were complaining and fumbled their way back to the refrain.

Bowie's vocal, a Roger Daltrey mimicry woeful enough for the single's press release to apologize for it, didn't help. That said, his maudlin, pitying tone had an authentic adolescent feel, one perhaps a bit too authentic for teenagers at the time. (He remade the song for *Toy* in 2000, a recording he later released as a B-side: it was a museum piece of Sixties teenage pique, complete with cutesy quotes from "Do You Wanna Know a Secret." Sterilizing the song did little to improve it, though Bowie sang it well and it ended in a fine howling coda where Lisa Germano's violin contended with a battery of guitars.) "You've Got a Habit of Leaving" marked the end of Bowie's time with Talmy, Parlophone and Leslie Conn who, at a loss at where to go with Bowie, amicably ended his management contract.

Baby Loves That Way

Recorded*: ca. early July 1965, IBC Studios. Bowie: lead vocal, harmonica; Taylor: lead guitar, backing vocal; Hopkins: piano; Rivens: bass, backing vocal; Lancaster: drums, backing vocal; Johns, Talmy: backing vocals. Producer: Talmy; engineer: Johns;* ***(remake)*** *July 2000 (basic tracks, vocals), Sear Sound; October-early November 2000 (overdubs), Looking Glass. Bowie: lead vocal; Slick: lead guitar, acoustic guitar; Plati: rhythm guitar, acoustic guitar; Garson: piano; Dorsey: bass, backing vocals; Campbell: drums; Germano: violin; Palmer, Gryner: backing vocals. Produced: Bowie, Plati; engineered: Keppler.*

First release*: 20 August 1965 (Parlophone R 5315); (remake) 16 September 2002, "Everyone Says 'Hi,'" (Columbia 673134 5).* ***Live:***

1965-1966.

Freed from national service, earning in a month what their fathers had made in a year, sexually avaricious and rewarded, the British rock aristocracy considered themselves a liberated generation. Yet when it dawned on these boys that their appetites were shared by liberated girls, this was a problem. Not all male British rock stars were as accepting as the Kinks' Dave Davies, who happily tumbled into bed with seemingly anyone who asked, man or woman, and with few regrets. There was a hard provincial chauvinism under the shine of Swinging London: "men" could be libertine but libertine girls were cheap heartbreakers. See the slumming upper-class girls who populate Rolling Stones songs or the Beatles' set of callous independent women ("The Night Before," "Norwegian Wood," "I'm Looking Through You," "Girl," "Run for Your Life"). Or see Julie Christie's first major film roles. As Liz in *Billy Liar,* introduced walking along a high street to some rhythm in her head, "she goes where she feels like. She's crazy. She just enjoys herself." "There've been others. Is that okay?" she asks Tom Courtenay's Billy, in a tone that says it's certainly been okay for her. Yet as the title character of *Darling,* her boyfriend calls her a whore: "Your idea of fidelity is not having more than one man in the bed at the same time."

So this was the context of Bowie's "Baby Loves That Way," the superior B-side of "You've Got a Habit of Leaving" (it was a concept single: Mod cuckold laments life), its tone suspended between resentment and delusion. Again in debt to the Kinks, the key song here was their "Nothin' in the World Can Stop Me Worryin' 'Bout That Girl," where Ray Davies fears his girlfriend's cheating, finds out that she is and stays with her, in part from disbelief that she's still lying to him. There was a touch of masochism in it, Davies torturing himself by replaying his humiliations.

Where the Kinks track was built on acoustic guitar and light percussion, Bowie set a similar scenario to a three-chord hook-filled beat song, with a machine-gun guitar-and-snare opening salvo and booming block harmonies for its refrains, with everyone in the studio, including Shel Talmy and Glyn Johns, roped in to sing along. It's such a slab of sound that Bowie, parrying against the chorus singers, soon grew strained. Still his wan timbre, close to that of "Take My Tip," fit his character here. He's a Bromley hipster who didn't take the tip, a boy reduced to a delusive hope his wandering girl will settle for him one day.

Half a lifetime later, Bowie re-recorded "Baby Loves That Way" for *Toy*, slowing the tempo, offering an ember of a vocal. He sang the title refrain with resignation, as if unable to imagine it being otherwise. Quotes from the Beatles' "All You Need Is Love" in the backing vocals and bassline made his remake a requiem for a decade whose promises of liberation were often just stage dressing.

I'll Follow You

Recorded*: ca. July-September 1965, IBC Studios. Bowie: lead vocal, lead guitar?; Taylor: lead guitar?, rhythm guitar, backing vocal; Ravens: bass; Lancaster: drums. Producer: Talmy; engineer: Johns?*

First release*: 30 July 1991,* ***Early On****.*

After the release of "You've Got a Habit of Leaving" in August 1965, Bowie and the Lower Third played London-area shows, traveling (and sometimes bunking) in a second-hand ambulance. Bowie also picked up a new manager, Ralph Horton, a chronically impecunious former road manager for the Moody Blues. The Lower Third was in and out of studios during this period, demoing songs for bands like the Pretty Things (a common industry practice of the time, as touring bands had scant time to cut albums). They also recorded a few Bowie compositions. One full-band recording, likely produced by Talmy at IBC Studios around the time of, if not during the same session as, "You've Got a Habit of Leaving," was the stalker pledge "I'll Follow You." Its sentiments range from cloying to menacing ("you can't lose my trail on you/JUST YOU TRY! JUST YOU TRY!"), its progress interrupted by the most half-assed guitar solo recorded in the Sixties.

Glad I've Got Nobody

Recorded: *ca. July-September 1965, IBC Studios. Bowie: lead vocal; Taylor: lead guitar, backing vocal; Ravens: bass; Lancaster: drums. Producer: Talmy; engineer: Johns?*

First released: *30 July 1991,* ***Early On.***

"Glad I've Got Nobody" is a simulacrum of beat music, the sort of thing piped through a teenage character's prop radio on a sitcom of the period. As on "You've Got a Habit of Leaving," Phil Lancaster tries to thrash the song to life with some snare fills; Denis Taylor is a cut-rate Pete Townshend.

Baby That's a Promise

Recorded: *(unreleased) ca. late August 1965, R.G. Jones Studio, London Road, Morden Manor, Surrey. Bowie: lead vocal; Taylor: lead guitar, rhythm guitar, backing vocal; Ravens: bass; Lancaster: drums. Producer: unknown (Ralph Horton?).*

Live: *1965.*

"Baby That's a Promise" was cut at R.G. Jones Studio, one of the oldest independent studios in Britain. Located in the back room of a house on the grounds of Morden Manor, the studio boasted one of the UK's first four-track machines. Bowie would soon record there embryonic versions of his major Sixties compositions "The London Boys" and "Silly Boy Blue." "Baby, That's a Promise" wasn't quite on their level, with its lumbering bassline and a sullen rhythm guitar that thrashes its way towards ska in the bridge. Bowie thought the song had potential, including it in the set-list of his (unsuccessful) BBC audition in November 1965. Notable for Bowie's vocal on the circulating demo: supple and strong, even when submerged in bootleg murk and having the first capture on tape (1:48) of the falsetto he'd develop by *Young*

Americans.

Can't Help Thinking About Me

Recorded: *ca. early December 1965, Pye Recording Studios, 40 Bryanston Street (ATV House), Marble Arch, London. Bowie: lead vocal, tambourine?; Taylor: 12-string acoustic guitar, lead guitar, backing vocal; Rivens: bass, backing vocal; Lancaster: drums, backing vocal; Tony Hatch: piano. Produced: Hatch;* ***(remake, unreleased)*** *July, October 2000, Sear Sound, Looking Glass. Bowie: lead vocal; Slick: lead guitar; Leonard: rhythm guitar (?); Garson: keyboards; Plati: rhythm guitar; Dorsey: bass, backing vocals; Campbell: drums; Palmer, Gryner: backing vocals. Produced: Bowie, Plati; engineered: Keppler.*

First release*: (as "David Bowie with the Lower Third") 14 January 1966 (Pye 7N 17020).* ***Broadcast****: 4 March 1966, Ready Steady Go!; 23 August 1999, VH1 Storytellers; 25 October 1999, The Mark and Lard Show.* ***Live****: 1965-1966, 1997, 1999.*

The first of three singles Bowie cut for Pye Records, "Can't Help Thinking About Me" was also the closest that he came to a hit before "Space Oddity," with the former briefly in the lower reaches of some charts. Bowie's manager Ralph Horton leveraged an acquaintance with Tony Hatch to sign Bowie to Pye. Hatch, a producer and A&R man for the label, was up to his neck composing, arranging and producing songs for Pye's headline pop acts Petula Clark and Sandie Shaw, as well as arranging music for the Coldstream Guards. Bowie's book of self-penned songs eliminated one job and sold Hatch on producing him. Having little experience with hard rock, Hatch attempted to capture the buzz-bomb sound of the Lower Third's sets at the Marquee Club, but in Pye's cupboard of a studio. The result was a single as murky-sounding as "Liza Jane."

Pye rejected Bowie's first song offering, "The London Boys," allegedly because of a line about taking pills (see Ch. 2) though Hatch later said it was because the song "[took] too long to get going." So "Can't Help Thinking About Me" was a rewrite of "The London Boys" with more drama, no drugs and a bigger beat. It kicked off a run of Bowie songs in which a suburban kid comes to London to sample its pleasures ("Maid of Bond Street," "I Dig Everything," "London Bye Ta-Ta").

His earliest lyrics generally had been earnest bouts of teenage self-pity (there was little of the sexual bravado of other Mod R&B bands). "Can't Help Thinking About Me" was finally a turn to the defiant; its blunt title phrase and petulant lines like "I *wish* that I was sorry this time" bear the stamp of snotty narcissistic youth. It had a pull and a vigor despite a lyric that barely scans (see "my girl calls my name, 'Hi Dave!'," horrifically rhymed with "way again"), owed to Bowie, having forgotten his lyric book, being forced to recall lines from memory in the studio.

It was his first suburban middle-class anxiety song and he picked through his Bromley life for stray details. His disapproving mother scowled in the opening verse while its climactic railway station setting was likely Sundridge Park, a few minutes' walk from his house on Plaistow Grove. "Can't Help Thinking About Me" was also Bowie's own *Billy Liar* (who had plenty of "dishonor": Billy steals from his employer and is engaged to two girls at once), with an altered ending so that Bowie could stay on the train to London with Julie Christie instead of trudging home, as Billy did, to a life of provincial desperation.

Structured tightly (Hatch likely gave pointers), "Can't Help" was quick to showcase its hooky, suspense-building 12-bar refrain, with its second verse halved and refrains broken up only by a measly four-bar bridge. Over a gradual shading of C major into F minor, Bowie's verse melody is a John Lennon-like hovering on a single note, closing off phrases with stepwise rises ("dis*honor*") or drops ("*fam'ly* name"). He was freer in the refrains, in jubilant F major: the long-held notes on "guilty!," the chromatic downward fall on "sorry this time," the deflated movement in the title line. With Hatch's piano and Denis Taylor's shimmering acoustic guitar charged with keeping the rapid harmonic rhythm, Graham Rivens' bass became the lead instrument. The latter played so fast he sometimes outpaced the song, sounding agitated runs of 16th notes whenever he was stuck waiting out a bar. The tambourine player (Bowie?) was a menace, striking off beat and bungling transitions from verse to refrain.

Bowie revived the song in 1999 for a few dates on the "Hours" tour, taking delight in tapping into a vein of gawky teenage defiance after so many years of living seriously. In late 1965, "Can't Help Thinking About Me" was the strongest composition he'd yet written, and its commercial failure had ill consequences: estranging him from his band, sapping his confidence and leading him to chase after whims.

And I Say to Myself

Recorded: *ca. early December 1965, Pye Studios. Bowie: lead vocal; Taylor: lead guitar, backing vocal; Rivens: bass, backing vocal; Lancaster: drums, backing vocal. Produced: Hatch.*

First release: *14 January 1966 (Pye 7N 17020).*

"And I Say to Myself" beats a retreat from the territorial advance of "Can't Help Thinking About Me," reflecting that the song was an older composition than its flipside. Another in the sad sack line of "Take My Tip" and "Baby Loves That Way," its narrator has a girl who once again isn't true to him—he's in a pack of hopeful losers who orbit her. He tries to talk himself out of seeing her until admitting defeat with each refrain.

The track opened with élan: an octave-spanning Bowie vocal supported only by Graham Rivens' slowly rising bass (as on the A-side, the track's defining instrument) and a clever structural feint where a refrain variant was deftly folded into the verse. Inspirations soon petered out—the verse/refrain feint was repeated twice more to diminishing returns, while the refrain itself was a factory-setting Fifties progression. The vocal harmonies were beyond the Lower Third's talents: see the unintentionally comic second bridge, where Bowie says to "sing after me: I'm a fool" and the sullen-sounding Third intone "I'm a fool" as if he's their ESL instructor.

Do Anything You Say

Recorded: *7 March 1966, Pye Studios. Bowie: lead vocal; John "Hutch" Hutchinson: lead guitar, backing vocal; Derek "Dek" Fearnley: bass, backing vocal; John "Ego" Eager: drums, backing vocal; Derek "Chow" Boyes: organ, backing vocal; Hatch: piano. Produced: Hatch.*

First release: *(as "David Bowie") 1 April 1966 (Pye 7N 17079).* ***Live:*** *1966.*

Two weeks after the release of "Can't Help Thinking About Me," Bowie split with the Lower Third. His manager Ralph Horton considered him a solo artist and had run an open campaign to estrange Bowie from his group. After weeks of tension, on 29 January 1966, just before a concert, Horton refused to pay the band their back wages. Denis Taylor said he wouldn't go on, Horton happily fired him, the rest of the group took their gear and followed Taylor out the door. Bowie paced outside, waiting for the bloodletting to be over.

Despite their limitations, the Lower Third had been a capable supporting band who'd built a following among Mods. At recent gigs in Paris, audiences had raved while the band improvised through their sets, ending with feedback-laden versions of "Mars, The Bringer of War." Yet while Horton, as possessive of Bowie as he was inept in promoting him, deserved the controlling share of blame for the split, he was also doing Bowie's dirty work.

Solitary and shy by nature, greatly living in an imagination fed by books like Frank Edwards' *Strange People* and Colin Wilson's *The Outsider*, Bowie was unable to submerge his personality within a larger unit. "I felt often, ever since I was a teenager, so adrift and so not part of everyone else," he recalled in 2002. Seemingly everyone whom he met—managers, producers, bandmates—told him how unique he was. It was true enough of his songs: the odd chord progressions, neatly written on little sheets of paper that he tucked in his cigarette packs; his untrained, ambitious vocal melodies, which often pulled him out of his comfortable range; the protean nature of his developing voice itself, which would venture from Mockney to "Transatlantic" soul belter in the course of a set.

The purging of the Lower Third marked the moment when Bowie rejected the singular "we" that the Beatles had made their public image and which had become the standard frame for mid-Sixties pop. "He wanted to get away from home. And he wanted to get away from being in a band in exactly the same way," Derek Fearnley recalled. Instead Bowie would be a throwback to a pre-Beatles type of entertainer. He'd cultivate the studied eccentricity of an Anthony Newley or Alan Klein (see "Rubber Band"), making a similar move as Scott Walker, who was about to leave the Walker Brothers to begin his own mood suite of a solo career.

In the meantime, Bowie needed another band, so he and Horton assembled one via *Melody Maker* advertisements. Bowie gave nicknames to members of "The Buzz," while Horton kitted them in Carnaby Street clothes and got them proper Mod haircuts. Their sound was beside the point: they were thrown on stage after one rehearsal. While guitarist John "Hutch" Hutchinson and bassist Fearnley would become key Bowie collaborators, the Buzz were second-rate, with the single they cut with Bowie, "Do Anything You Say," the weakest of his Pye releases.

Demoed for Tony Hatch in late February, a fortnight after Bowie and the Buzz had first performed together, "Do Anything You Say" got the nod for the next Pye A-side. The product of an apparent songwriting lull on Bowie's part, the song managed to be frenetically monotonous, lacking any contrasting bridges or solos and only a piano tag for relief. Its would-be soul groove (John Eager slamming his snare on each beat, Motown-style) attempted the driving "hard" R&B sound of contemporary singles like the Spencer Davis Group's version of "Keep On Running," but the latter's fuzz-toned guitars and deep low end made Bowie's single sound third-rate by comparison.

The Buzz proved little improvement over the Lower Third for vocal harmonies, a problem in this case given that the few hooks of "Do Anything You Say" were sung by the chorus, who sound as if they're being held at gunpoint in the vocal booth. The Buzz's collective glumness made Bowie, singing in his high register and ornamenting phrases with grace notes, seem grandiose. No one was on their game: the band, hearing the final mix, thought Hatch had snuffed out whatever glimmers of life they'd heard at playback. One of Bowie's last soul-inflected compositions of the Sixties, "Do Anything You Say" was among the least of his singles. Rather than consolidate the strengths of "Can't Help Thinking About Me," it sandbagged him and Pye began looking to cast Bowie loose.

Good Morning Girl

***Recorded**: 7 March 1966, Pye Studios. Bowie: lead vocal; Hutchinson: lead guitar; Fearnley: bass; Eager: drums; Boyes: organ. Produced: Hatch.*

***First release**: 1 April 1966 (Pye 7N 17079). **Live**: 1966.*

Here lies the remains of jazz hipster Bowie, a rarely-glimpsed incarnation (see "Take My Tip"). The swing-pop "Good Morning Girl" has more dash and charm than its flip side, if just as much a stylistic dead end. A raw processing of passing fancies, "Good Morning Girl" nabbed its title from the Yardbirds (an age-appropriate revision of "Good Morning Little Schoolgirl") and some chords and organ melodies from the Dave Clark Five's "I Need Love." Its highlight, two bridges where Bowie scats along to John Hutchinson's lead guitar, suggested the Spencer Davis Group's summer 1965 single "Strong Love," where Steve Winwood sang the guitar line in breaks. The Buzz's rhythm section had played in jazz bands and convincingly delivered the piece's swing rhythms, with John Eager enlivening the scat breaks with his fills and cymbal work. A curio, but a fun one: Bowie never sounded this ebullient again.

I Dig Everything

***Recorded**: **(first version, unreleased)** 6 June 1966, Pye Studios. Bowie: lead vocal; Hutchinson: lead guitar; Fearnley: bass; Eager: drums; Boyes: organ; Andy Kirk: trumpet; Pete Sweet: tenor saxophone; Graham Livemore?: trombone?; Madeline Bell, Kiki Dee, Lesley Duncan: backing vocals. Produced: Hatch; **(single)** 5 July 1966, Pye Studios. Bowie: lead vocal; unknown musicians: lead guitar, Hammond organ, flute, bass, drums, congas, guiro, backing vocals. Produced: Hatch; **(remake, unreleased)** July 2000 (basic tracks, vocals) Sear Sound, October 2000 (overdubs) Looking Glass. Bowie: lead vocal; Slick: lead guitar; Leonard: rhythm guitar; Garson: keyboards; Dorsey: bass, backing vocals; Plati: bass, rhythm guitar; Campbell: drums; Palmer, Gryner: backing vocals. Produced: Bowie, Plati; engineered: Keppler.*

***First release**: 19 August 1966 (Pye 7N 17157). **Broadcast**: 27 June 2000, An Evening With David Bowie (BBC). **Live**: 1966, 2000.*

While its opening Hammond organ riff has aged into a reeking Sixties cliché, "I Dig Everything" still has a taste of the bright hot summer of 1966, London's high-water mark: Britain winning the World Cup at Wembley; the opening of the Indica Gallery in St. James's; Joe Orton's *Loot* playing in Holborn; Pink Floyd and the Small Faces at the Marquee; *Revolver* and *Aftermath* on turntables; "Sunny Afternoon" and the Alan Price Set on Radio London and Radio Caroline; Diana Rigg on ABC; Terence Stamp, Michael Caine and Julie Christie onscreen.

A boy fresh arrived in London makes the city his stage, its residents his supporting players (except the policemen, the only adults left in town). Where "Can't Help Thinking About Me" built up the journey to London, "I Dig Everything" finds the kid set up in squalor there, having more friends than food, smoking and laughing at the squares all trudging off to work. Lyrical inspiration came from the beehive London of Colin MacInnes' *Absolute Beginners* and Bowie's stays at Ralph Horton's Manchester Street apartment, where bill collectors often rang the doorbell and Horton once shimmied down a manhole to reconnect the switched-off electric. There's an edge in the song—the singer's unemployed and broke, sometimes desperately lonely (he's calling the automated "time-check girl" on the hour)—but his genial pothead indifference to bad news gave "I Dig Everything" a sweetness without being cloying.

The single's easy feel belied its difficult birth. Bowie and the Buzz had tried to record the song in an ambitious session on 6 June 1966 that included the brass section of Dave Anthony's Moods and the singers Kiki Dee, Lesley Duncan and Madeline Bell. Bowie and Dek Fearnley hadn't bothered to rehearse their arrangement and the Moods turned out to be a bad fit (Eager: "they were okay playing soul music but that's not what we wanted"). Tony Hatch pulled the plug after a few disastrous takes. Although Bowie and the Buzz retreated to R.G. Jones Studio to better craft the arrangement, a frustrated Hatch booked a set of reliable London musos for the remake, bringing Bowie in solely for lead vocals.

Centering the revised take on organ and percussion (it was the best percussion track Bowie would have until the Seventies), with a flute countermelody in the second verse, Hatch made the song light and fresh, better suited to the carefree youth singing it. Yet where Hatch's greatest collaborator, Petula Clark, was "fiercely loyal to [her] one great octave," Bowie was hell-bent on writing melodies he could barely sing, like the two-octave excursion here. For every confident phrase he pulled off (the loosely-held long "IIIIs" that swing open the first and third verses), there was a stumble. Taking the descending phrase "everything" into his lower register in particular vexed him and he struggled to sound the low notes (esp. at :44 and 1:31).

Released to general indifference at the end of the summer, "I Dig Everything" finished off Bowie's time with Pye, as Hatch was pressured by label highers-up to dump him. It was the close of one of Bowie's most frustrating periods. Hatch was a subtle, inspired arranger and fundamentally ill-suited for a 19-year-old Mod theatrical still assembling himself. The best they'd achieved had been their first go, "Can't Help Thinking About Me." With each subsequent single, "we were getting further away from what we had [then], rough as it was," Hatch said decades later.

I'm Not Losing Sleep

***Recorded**: 5 July 1966, Pye Studios. Bowie: lead vocal; unknown musicians: lead guitar, rhythm guitar, bass, Hammond organ, drums, flute, guiro, congas, tambourine, backing vocals. Produced: Hatch.*

***First release**: 19 August 1966 (Pye 7N 17157). **Live**: 1966.*

Petula Clark once said Tony Hatch helped her find out what she really was. Theirs was a marriage of strengths—Clark's hard-won professional optimism and pure vocal "presence" on record, Hatch's knack for finding innovations in conventional tonality and pop arrangements. By contrast, Bowie ended his time with Hatch less knowable than when he began it.

Bowie's Pye singles had failed in part because his songwriting still wasn't up to par (by the end, Hatch was pushing him to do covers) but also because Hatch was unable (and Bowie unwilling) to establish an identifiable sound for him. Bowie's singles lacked the "trademark" of a contemporary like Chris Farlowe or the emotional narrative in Clark's string of hits. His Pye records were more stillborn laboratory hybrids—soul records with music-hall inflections.

"I'm Not Losing Sleep," the B-side of "I Dig Everything," was one last hard collision. Bowie came off as a pilled-up Sandie

Shaw imitator, with Hatch gamely playing along (the "too bad!" fifth-descending backing vocal line nicked the vocal hook of "Downtown"). The result was a fascinating mess, a lyric of class resentment and Dylan-esque character assassination as sung by a stage dandy ("though I live in *slums* I'm purer than *you my friend!*"). It was working-class defiance punctuated with flute trills, an Anthony Newley-style stage piece with fuzz-toned guitar to shadow the bassline and a guiro-accented beat.

Bowie's *sui generis* approach to songwriting was in there as well: see the verse's trench warfare between tonic chord and minor second or the jarring key change in the bridge. Taking parting shots at the Rolling Stones ("I can *get* my satisfaction," he snipped in the last verse) and the Beatles (the run of chords that close the verses), "I'm Not Losing Sleep" came off as Bowie's dramatic reading of a resignation letter from rock. His accumulated failures had made him more cunning, if more desperate, and he began plotting a deviant course. In its cracked way, "I'm Not Losing Sleep" was a blueprint for how Bowie would survive the rest of the Sixties: keeping to his corner, costumed and made up, looking to steal cues.

Chapter 2

Gnome Man's Land (1966-1968)

Advertising is not a game which can be played by the rules. Advertising is total war and we must play with any weapons that come to hand.
Zissell (David de Keyser), *Catch Us If You Can.*

Scratch any apparently 'normal' British person and you'll find, somewhere deep inside them, a lunatic, an invert or child who believes in gnomes, elves and fairies. Bowie knew that. (He even pretended to be a fairy for several years.)
Momus.

Coming back to Britain [from being abroad] is also, in many respects, like going back to the nursery. The outside world, the dangerous world, is shut away; its sounds are muffled...
Lindsay Anderson.

I became a Beatles fan, and I started to have fun, and it made things worse at home, because when I would go back home my parents couldn't understand why I was enjoying myself.
French teenager, interviewed by Richard Mills.

I stumbled into the Buddhist Society in London when I was about seventeen. Sitting in front of me at the desk was a Tibetan lama, and he looked up and he said "Are you looking for me"? He had a bad grasp of English and in fact was saying "Who are you looking for?" But I ***needed*** *him to say "You're looking for me."*
David Bowie.

Rubber Band

***Recorded:* (single)** *18 October 1966, R.G. Jones Studio. David Bowie: lead vocal, acoustic guitar?; Derek Boyes: piano; Derek "Dek" Fearnley: bass; John Eager: drums; Chick Norton: trumpet; unknown musicians: tuba, oboe. Produced: Bowie, Fearnley;* **(album remake)** *25 February 1967, Decca Studio 2. Bowie: lead vocal; Boyes: piano; Fearnley: bass; Eager: drums; unknown musicians: tuba, trumpet, oboe; arranger: Arthur Greenslade. Produced: Mike Vernon; engineered: Gus Dudgeon.*

First release: *(single): 2 December 1966 (Deram DM 107); (remake) 1 June 1967,* ***David Bowie*** *(Deram DML/SML 1007).*

Even by his future standards of transformation, "Rubber Band," Bowie's first Deram single, was so sharp a change that it essentially rewrote his life.

Stymied by the failure of his Mod singles and sick of playing second-rate ballrooms, Bowie cast about for a new set of influences, centering on the singer Anthony Newley. He'd come across Newley in the latter's *The Strange World of Gurney Slade*, a 1960 BBC serial that opened with Slade (Newley), who plays a character in a dull sitcom, walking off the set only to have the camera follow him into the street. He overhears thoughts of passersby, talks to dogs and statues, romances a vacuum cleaner ad model who's come to life. *Slade* was suburbia as a place of stultifying ritual but populated by quietly surreal souls, much the same landscape as Bowie's first album. A liberating figure for Bowie, who appropriated his phrasings and his Cockney singing voice, Newley delighted in artifice. "On stage or off, he vibrates in an electric state of perpetual performance," noted a *Life* magazine profile. Newley said what separated him from British rockers was that "I could afford to be silly and they couldn't. The whole rock 'n' roll thing was so desperately serious."

Bowie was tired of being serious. His weekly residency at the Marquee Club in 1966 found him playing to about a dozen fans and occasionally his parents, while most in the room kept their backs to the stage. Attempts to shake up his act with light shows and sound effects tapes had failed. Members of the Buzz scrawled WE HATE SOUL on their touring van; Bowie's manager Ralph Horton wrote to Kenneth Pitt, who would soon replace him, that Bowie "hates ballrooms and the kids."

So Newley was his escape route. Bowie soon found other ones, like the songwriter Lionel Bart (*Oliver!*) and the singer/composer Alan Klein, whose 1964 *Well at Least Its* (sic) *British*, a collection of blues, folk, Beat poetry, skiffle and rock & roll pastiches, was the secret parent of Bowie's debut album. Kenneth Pitt had represented Klein; Decca producer and A&R man Hugh Mendl (who signed Bowie) had signed Klein; Mike Vernon, who would produce Bowie's debut, had recorded *British*. Klein was their common language. Brought together to negotiate an album deal for Bowie and Decca, the three likely had *British* in mind as to what they could do with Bowie's songs.

Bowie acutely timed his costume change. By autumn 1966, the center of gravity in pop music had shifted to San Francisco and Los Angeles, leaving London provincial again. There'd been signs of this even at the peak of Mod. "I love old things. Modern things are so cold," claimed Barbara Hulanicki, founder of the hip Kensington boutique Biba, when interviewed in 1965 by the *Daily Telegraph*."With everything around her so fast, so uncertain, [Hulanicki] needs to go home to...the comfort of dark red wallpaper and Edwardiana. It makes her feel safe."

Having willed itself into a global brand for style and modernism, Britain now began to consume itself. London pop singers and fashion designers took the trappings of Californian psychedelia to indulge in what the critic George Melly called a "cool, if deep chauvinism...as it is impossible to think of England as having no past, this is dealt with by treating history as a vast boutique full of military uniforms, grannie shoes and spectacles..." Out were streamlined Italian-cut suits, in were brigadier moustaches and polka-dotted impersonations of Edwardian dress coats. It was England as The Village in Patrick

McGoohan's *The Prisoner*. There were caftans, deerstalker hats and flapper dresses in shops like I Was Lord Kitchener's Valet on the Portobello Road, a street Cat Stevens archly sang about in 1967: "Cuckoo clocks and plastic socks...Nothing's the same: if you see it again/it'll be broken down to litter." British psychedelia was a game of dress-up. It treasured *Alice in Wonderland* (see the trippy 1966 BBC adaptation scored by Ravi Shankar, or the Cale Street boutique Hung On You, whose customers descended, Alice-like, through a hole in the floor to reach the showroom) and *The Wind in the Willows*, chapters of which, respectively, inspired "Lucy in the Sky With Diamonds" and titled Pink Floyd's first album.

Again, Alan Klein factored in. In 1966 he was touring in a Twenties pastiche group, the New Vaudeville Band, which had a cross-Atlantic hit single with "Winchester Cathedral." "Winchester Cathedral" set the stage for Bowie's "Rubber Band" as the latter preceded *Sgt. Pepper's Lonely Hearts Club Band*. Even the Rolling Stones cut lysergic vaudeville numbers like "Something Happened to Me Yesterday" and "Cool, Calm, Collected," which has a kazoo solo.

So this was the context of "Rubber Band," Bowie's pastiche of Edwardian pop (sounding nothing like actual Edwardian popular music), with a sadly chipper five-verse lyric in which a man trots off to the Great War and loses his love to a bandleader back home. Drawing on family memories of his grandfather Jimmy Burns (who had a renowned moustache, fought in the war and later in life was a busker), Bowie was also playing with a cultural cliché: that the summer before the war was a noontime hour of brass bands and teatime tunes, the last time the world was young. (Many 50th anniversary Great War retrospectives of the mid-Sixties had pushed this line.) As similar clichés would soon apply to the fading Sixties youth culture, this gave "Rubber Band" a displaced sense of melancholy.

Taken at a drill-march pace, "Rubber Band" strode through a

maze of tempo shifts, arrangement variations and a series of minor keys, trotting from A minor opening verses through a B minor trumpet solo to a C-sharp minor last verse before expiring with an E-flat minor coda. Its cut-budget brass band arrangement cast a tuba as its lead actor, dragging to a stop like a dying locomotive. A single trumpet was allotted eight bars to soar over the tuba's protests; Bowie sang a wailing moan in the coda, not having shaken all of the soul out of him yet.

Financed by Pitt, the "Rubber Band" single landed Bowie an album deal with Deram, a newly-founded Decca subsidiary label. As Decca chairman Sir Edward Lewis regarded rock as one would a persistent rash, Deram aimed to give rock a pedigree, offering "exotic" pop singles and "conceptual" albums (the Moody Blues' *Days of Future Passed*) that catered to audiophiles, with chamber and full orchestral arrangements captured by state-of-the-art "Deramic" engineering. The quintessential Deram track was Procol Harum's "A Whiter Shade of Pale," which married Bach fugues to marijuana reveries.

"Rubber Band" quickly died as a single and Bowie re-recorded it in early 1967 for his album. Arthur Greenslade, arranging the remake, did little more than tighten the players (the brass more smoothly intoned their notes and John Eager's drums were a more eager participant) and slacken the tempo: the LP cut is twenty seconds longer than the single despite having the same structure. Bowie ventured into the histrionic by the second verse and stayed in his shaky upper register. By the time he shot a promo film for the remade "Rubber Band" in 1969, it came off as a private joke indulged, a parody of a soured novelty song.

The London Boys

Recorded:* *("Now You've Met the London Boys," unreleased) *25 November 1965, Pye Studios. Bowie: lead vocal; Denis Taylor: lead guitar; Graham Rivens: bass; Phil Lancaster: drums; Tony Hatch:*

piano. Produced: Hatch; ***(single)*** *18 October 1966, R.G. Jones. Bowie: lead vocal; Boyes; organ; Fearnley: bass; Eager: drums; Norton: trumpet; unknown musicians: tuba, oboe. Produced: Bowie, Fearnley;* ***(remake, unreleased)*** *(basic tracks) July 2000, Sear Sound Studios, (overdubs) October 2000, Looking Glass Studios. Bowie: lead vocal; Earl Slick: lead guitar; Gerry Leonard: rhythm guitar; Mark Plati: lead, rhythm guitar; Mike Garson: organ; Gail Ann Dorsey: bass, backing vocals; Sterling Campbell: drums; Holly Palmer, Emm Gryner: backing vocals; unknown musicians: oboe, trumpets, violins, violas, celli (arr.: Tony Visconti). Produced: Bowie, Plati; engineered: Pete Keppler.*

First release*: 2 December 1966 (Deram DM 107).* ***Broadcast****: 27 June 2000, An Evening With David Bowie.* ***Live****: 1965-1966, 2000.*

Pop records of the Sixties are littered with runaways. The Kinks alone had a set: "Little Miss Queen of Darkness," living in a discotheque; Polly Garter, a provincial who slinks home after being debauched; the nameless girl of "Big Black Smoke" who sleeps in cafes and whose "every penny…was spent on purple hearts and cigarettes.""I knew a girl who was like that. She ran our first fan club. She died of junk," Ray Davies told Jon Savage.

In Bowie's "The London Boys," a 17-year-old runaway's working into the Mod scene, taking uppers and living rough. Originally "Now You've Met the London Boys," an early incarnation of the song was in Lower Third live sets by autumn 1965 (Bowie grubbed for cheers by dropping local names—Soho! Wardour Street!). A possible starting point was Them's "You Just Can't Win," Van Morrison's dig at an ex-lover who's moved up in the London scene. Recorded as Bowie's proposed debut single for Pye in November 1965, "London Boys" was rejected, whether due to risqué lines (his claim) or its dragginess (Tony Hatch's).

Feeling he'd made a breakthrough, Bowie spent a year tinkering with the song, during which the melancholy drag of the Kinks' "Where Have All the Good Times Gone" and "See My Friends" seeped in. He now opened "London Boys" in the East End, in the grey dawn after a speed-fueled night ("Bow bell strikes another night"). Recorded as the B-side of the "Rubber Band" single, "London Boys" was carried for long stretches by Derek Boyes' spectral organ and Dek Fearnley's bass, while trumpet, oboe and tuba (the same pit orchestra from "Rubber Band") worked as a chorus: the trumpet played a wan reveille in the first verse; the tuba and oboe's duets were the singer's hopes of joining the gang. Alternating between F major and E-flat major via quick-change shuffles through F-sharp, F minor and F major chords ("*cares* about *you*...oh, the first time"), the song rose to a rousing A major in its last refrain, the bone-weary mood brightening into a Judy Garland-esque finale, with Bowie's strongest singing to date (listen to the grit in his voice on "out there BOY"). The coda, with Bowie's "now you've met the London Boys" harmonized with tuba and oboe, completed the move from "street" to stage. It was as if the London Boys were freezing in a tableau, the curtain about to fall.

As Bowie was living in Bromley, fed and clothed and funded by his parents, "London Boys" can seem like a suburban correspondent filing a story from the field. It's not surprising he could easily convert another "Mod boys in London" song into the Tibetan Buddhist ode "Silly Boy Blue." Still, there was a frankness and beauty in "London Boys," carried in its sharp details, its lack of subterfuge, its emotional sympathy with its subject.

Considering "London Boys" one of his few Sixties songs worth salvaging, Bowie planned to re-record it in 1973 for *Pin Ups*, interspersing verses between covers of old Mod anthems. He held off for another 25 years. Reviving the song at the Roseland Ballroom in June 2000, he soon cut a studio take for *Toy*. Singing as if he'd summoned his teenage self from a depth and trapped him in his voice, there was also a wry sadness in the performance, suggesting the vastness between the boy he'd imagined being in 1965 and the man he thought he'd become. Or as the Go-Betweens once sang: "started out Oliver/ended up Fagin."

Over the Wall We Go

***Recorded*: (demo, unreleased)** *ca. autumn 1966 (1965?), R.G. Jones Studio? Bowie: lead and backing vocal, acoustic guitar, footstomping, baritone saxophone (?);* **(Oscar single)** *ca. early January 1967. Oscar Beuselinck: lead vocal; Bowie: backing vocals; unknown musicians: acoustic guitar, horns, strings, bass, drums, percussion. Produced, arranged: Nicky Welch.*

First release: *(Oscar) 30 January 1967 (Reaction 591012).*

Bowie may have written "Over the Wall We Go" as early as summer 1965, where Kevin Cann dates its demo. If so, he showed little interest in developing the song for more than year until Kenneth Pitt offered it to the impresario Robert Stigwood in early January 1967. Other sources like Nicholas Pegg cite the demo as hailing from roughly a year later, which seems more likely given the song's thematic links to *David Bowie* tracks: the use of nursery rhymes, like "Pop Goes the Weasel" and "Widecombe Fair" here, the various accents that Bowie adopts and its use of sound effects. Stigwood gave the song to his client Oscar Beuselinck, whose cover (with easily identifiable Bowie backing vocals) got airplay on pirate radio and in a few London clubs in spring 1967.

"Over the Wall We Go" was part novelty Christmas song, part topical commentary on the vogue for prison breakouts in Britain at the time, with some *Carry On*-style "queer" jokes in a verse of the Oscar version and a refrain that plays off the East End taunt "all coppers are bastards!" The Goons were a primary influence, with the Oscar single quoting from the George Martin-produced Spike Milligan single "Wormwood Scrubs Tango." The demo, where Bowie seemed to be auditioning for voice work opportunities, came off as a sketch for a radio play, a format he'd further exploit on his debut album (see "We Are Hungry Men" and "Please Mr. Gravedigger").

Uncle Arthur

Recorded: *14 November 1966, Decca Studios. Bowie: lead vocal,* *handclaps; John Renbourn: acoustic guitar; Boyes: piano; Fearnley: bass, backing vocals; Eager: drums; unknown musician(s): shawm, oboe; arrangers: Fearnley, Bowie. Produced: Vernon; engineered: Dudgeon.*

First release**: 1 June 1967,* ***David Bowie.

Released on the same June morning as *Sgt. Pepper's Lonely Hearts Club Band,* Bowie's self-titled debut album was an anthology of underground comic strips: cross-dressing soldiers, cannibal proles, gravediggers, ready-made hipsters, maiden uncles, shabby bombardiers. It didn't sell and he soon wrote the record out of his life. Asked about *David Bowie* in 1972, he dismissed it as having been done on "a very semi-professional basis. I was still working as a commercial artist then and I made [it] in my spare time, taking days off work and all that. I never followed it up, did any stage work or anything. I just did an album 'cause I'd been writing…sent my tape into Decca and they said they'd make an album. Thought it was original."

This was some inspired self-revision. Bowie had quit his advertising job years before he made the album and *David Bowie* was far from something he'd pieced together over sick days and weekends. Rather, it was the work of months in one of Decca's main studios, with a supporting cast that included string, horn and woodwind players from the Royal Philharmonic Orchestra and two of London's most in-demand session guitarists. Still, one thing rang true in Bowie's fable: *David Bowie* was very much "semi professional" from its arrangements to its compositions. It was a work of dedicated amateurism ("It is a weird album. I can't believe it was actually released," its engineer, Gus Dudgeon, recalled in 1993).

So rather than hire an arranger, Derek Fearnley and Bowie acquired Freda Dinn's *Observer's Guide to Music,* a pocket-sized primer of the histories, types and tones of orchestral instruments. They chose instruments based on Dinn's descriptions and had producer Mike Vernon find the appropriate musician, for whom Fearnley, who was barely musically literate, wrote baffling charts: stuffing five quarter notes into a 4/4 bar or scoring a trumpet part above the instrument's range.

Dudgeon recalled getting the first work sheets for the album, "this weird list of instruments like bass flute, contrabassoon, bass drum [but] it was the early days of the Deram label and we used to do some pretty odd sessions." Pop acts were constantly attempting to trump each other with "new" sounds. So the sitar ("See My Friends," "Norwegian Wood") was answered by dulcimer ("Lady Jane") in turn by electric banjo ("Stop Stop Stop") to be countered by bass harmonica ("Wouldn't It Be Nice") and reversed guitar ("I'm Only Sleeping") and recorder ("Ruby Tuesday") and steel drums ("Carrie Anne") and theremin ("Good Vibrations") and so on. There was a side-game with sound effects—the clangs and whistles of "Yellow Submarine," stamping feet on the Hollies' "Crusader," the bullwhip and antic percussion of Dave Dee, Dozy, Beaky, Mick and Tich's "Legend of Xanadu." Bowie would add his own noises to a growing pile.

The Loneliness of the Long-Distance Uncle

David Bowie found its composer trying to break his habit of writing first-person love laments with third-person narratives ("the idea of writing sort of short stories, I thought was quite novel at the time," he said in 1976). He was following the lead of Lennon and McCartney, who had started writing "comedy" songs ("Drive My Car") and character sketches ("Doctor Robert") out of exhaustion with standard love lyrics. Often Bowie simply stole plots of novels or short stories he'd read. One of the first tracks recorded for his album, "Uncle Arthur" had some ties to Bowie's personal life, as its Batman-loving title character was allegedly a portrait of Dek Fearnley, both an uncle and, to Bowie, old (Fearnley was 27). But "Uncle Arthur" was far more a rewrite of Alan Sillitoe's "The Disgrace of Jim Scarfedale," a story collected in *The Loneliness of the Long-Distance Runner*. Like

Arthur, Sillitoe's Jim is a mother's boy who meets a girl, whom he marries against his mother's wishes. The marriage fails; Jim, like Arthur, comes home to mother again.

Bowie keenly edited his filched material, excising Sillitoe's naturalism to make the story more surreal. "Uncle Arthur" is a character study by someone vaguely familiar with human beings: an extraterrestrial or a child (Bowie had spent summer 1966 babysitting Fearnley's nieces). It's a boy's imagining of Sillitoe's story and it runs on a boy's logic. Uncle Arthur shuns girls as any proper nine-year-old boy would; "Uncle Arthur left Sally because he didn't like her cooking" is a boy's theory why a marriage failed.

A shawm, grand medieval ancestor of the oboe, opened the song by playing Arthur's theme, a seesawing nine-note phrase spanning the range of a fifth and ending on the root note of the home chord, A: a movement Bowie paralleled in the verses. Rising stepwise with Arthur's travels ("climbs across his *bike* and *he's a-*"), he sinks back to the root note ("-way"), as Arthur's excursions lead him nowhere but home. One return tellingly lands on "mother." Escape comes in the eight-bar bridge, where the shawm duetted with oboe (Arthur and his wife Sally's union), with an elated move up to B major midway through when Arthur (shawm) plays a bass line for Sally's dance (oboe). But in the last verse Arthur and Sally go bust. The shawm is left to sing alone in the coda, where the refrain, only three lines until now, at last got a fourth ("follows mother"), closing the cadence, Arthur's life and his song.

She's Got Medals

Recorded: *14 November 1966, Decca Studios. Bowie: lead vocal, handclaps; Renbourn: acoustic guitar; Boyes: piano, organ, backing vocal?; Fearnley: bass, backing vocal; Eager: drums, backing vocal?; unknown musicians: shawm, oboe; arrangers: Fearnley, Bowie. Produced: Vernon; engineered: Dudgeon.*

***First release**: 1 June 1967, **David Bowie**.*

"She's Got Medals" is a dirty joke from a drunken evening: "she's got medals" means "she's got balls," near-literally here. A woman cloaks herself as a man to join the army during the war until, tired of "picking up girls...and shaving her curls," she deserts under fire and reclaims her original sex. Bowie sang in a wry stage-Cockney voice, with his conversational verse melody and shuttling five-chord progression likely taken from Love's "Hey Joe" and "7 and 7 Is."

As with "Uncle Arthur," cut on the same evening, "She's Got Medals" winked that behind every old neighborhood figure lies scandal. The two songs had similar arrangements, with woodwinds (again, likely a shawm) coloring over a spare rhythm track while Derek Boyes on piano dutifully pounded chords. An undercooked song whose refrain is a group-sung title phrase affixed to the end of verses, it came to life in its bridge, with its brief feints at B minor and F major and some triumphant organ to celebrate Mary/Tommy's escape, punctuated by woodwinds and thumping drums. Hinting at future Bowie gender-blends like "Rebel Rebel," the track's spirit was more that of the comedians Sid James and Tony Hancock and the grotesque caricatures of "Over the Wall We Go." Its garage-rock heart made "She's Got Medals" among the few *David Bowie* songs to survive its time, as a fine punk version by the band White Fence in 2013 attests.

Join the Gang

***Recorded**: 24 November 1966, Decca Studios. Bowie: lead vocal, sound effects; "Big Jim" Sullivan: sitar, acoustic guitar; Boyes: piano, organ; Fearnley: bass; Eager: drums; Dudgeon: sound effects; arrangers: Fearnley, Bowie. Produced: Vernon; engineered: Dudgeon.*

***First release**: 1 June 1967, **David Bowie**.*

When *Time* ran a cover story on Swinging London in April 1966, the city had reached knowing self-parody: some Carnaby Street shops had *Have You Helped to Keep London **Swinging** Today?*

signs in their windows. Mod London had been opportunistic from the start, the fabrication of art dealers, fashion designers, hairdressers, pop music moguls and magazine editors. Now after three years of ferment, it was exhausted. The British economic boom was deflating, record sales had cratered, the top groups were breaking up or no longer touring and the drugs were more preoccupying (it was the high tide of LSD for the hip set). London "had produced a lot of heavy talent in one flurry and now it had nothing left in the bag," the journalist Nik Cohn wrote. "Everything slowed down, everything petrified...groups spent more time in discotheques than they did on the road."

"Join the Gang," which Bowie allegedly wrote in a half-hour while sitting in a Clapham café for a photo shoot, is a past-peak boom song, with its clique of bright young things desperately on the make—an acid-damaged top model, an existential sitarist who plays celebrity parties and a professionally lunatic rock singer likely modeled on Arthur Brown. He'd never written so cutting a lyric before, reflecting a growing cynicism about the pop music business, his discovery of Frank Zappa's hippie lampoon LP *Freak Out!*, the obscene level of snobbery in Swinging London (case in point, the club Sibylla's, so exclusive that some of its paid members weren't invited to its opening party) and the influence of Kenneth Pitt, a Tory who warned his charge about becoming famous too quickly. Singing briskly, with a crisp timbre, Bowie sent his characters off on their orbits with stepwise runs over a fifth ("let me introduce you to the *gang*!"). There was an acrid taste of envy. Satirist or no, Bowie still had his nose pressed against the glass, watching the banquet unfold: "It's all a big illusion, but at least you're in."

The track was sewn through with contemporary clichés: a funky drummer intro, a manic sitar in the opening verse, Derek Boyes' barrelhouse piano (much like the Who's "A Legal Matter") and, in the fourth verse, a nose-tweak at the soul-inflected pop Bowie had abandoned: as he touts a club called The Web ("this month's pick"), Boyes and Fearnley play a soporific take on the Spencer Davis Group's "Gimme Some Lovin'."

In keeping with its nervy cast of characters, "Join the Gang" changed keys five times in as many verses: Johnny the sitarist's in E major, Molly the model moves up to G and raving Arthur jumps to A. The only break in the pattern was a five-bar bridge with an obtrusive E-flat chord (on "big illusion") and a bar of 6/4 as a breath before diving into another verse. High-strung from the start, "Join the Gang" closed with a nervous breakdown, half a minute of what Gus Dudgeon described as the sounds of "a Hoover, farts and munching" and as such comparable to "serious" psychedelic tracks of 1967 like the Rolling Stones' "Sing This All Together (See What Happens)."

Did You Ever Have a Dream

***Recorded**: 24 November 1966, Decca Studios. Bowie: lead vocal; Sullivan: banjo; Boyes: harpsichord; Fearnley: bass; Eager: drums; unknown musicians: trumpets; arrangers: Fearnley, Bowie. Produced: Vernon; engineered: Dudgeon.*

***First release**: 14 July 1967 (Deram DM 135). **Broadcast:** 27 February 1968, 4-3-2-1 Musik Für Junge Leute.*

Recorded in the second session for *David Bowie*, "Did You Ever Have a Dream" was buried as the B-side of "Love You Till Tuesday" despite being one of the catchiest songs cut for the album. Touting the joys of astral projection and lucid dreaming, it served as first notice of Bowie's interest in occult practices, with a lyric that seemed commissioned as a recruitment pitch for teenagers (he was the son of a PR man, after all). He hustled from talk of everyday dreams of power and flight in the verse to the promise of having out-of-body experiences in the refrain: "You can walk around in New York while you sleep in *Penge!*"

Set in D major, its verses and refrains smoothly closing on the home chord (the verse moving downward, the refrain upward), "Did You Ever Have a Dream" is music-hall spiritualism. Bowie's pitch is introduced by Derek Boyes' tipsy walk across the keyboard and whisked along by the whippet strums of "Big Jim" Sullivan's banjo. So slight a composition that Bowie had to repeat a bridge and the entire last verse just to hit the two-minute mark, "Did You Ever Have a Dream" chased its closing D major chord with the sound of breaking glass, courtesy of engineer Gus Dudgeon, who was becoming Bowie's devoted noisemaker.

There Is a Happy Land

Recorded*: 24 November 1966, Decca Studios. Bowie: lead vocal; Renbourn: acoustic guitar; Boyes: piano, electric organ; Fearnley: bass; Eager: drums; unknown musicians: French horn, vibraphone; arrangers: Fearnley, Bowie. Produced: Vernon; engineered: Dudgeon.*

First release*: 1 June 1967,* ***David Bowie****.*

British psychedelia took as its central theme childhood, considering the child's mind an ideal state that the use of LSD could try to recreate. By liberating one's mind from the dulling habits accrued by adulthood, one could be as "open" as a child again. LSD could cleanse perceptions, undamming streams of creativity. The psychedelic generation considered children to be innate surrealists, which they are. Recall how as a child you might wake up in a different house than where you fell asleep, or that inanimate objects and dogs spoke to you.Yet as much as the psychedelic artists idealized childhood, they also perverted it, diminishing childhood to fit adults. This was inevitable. Those in their twenties (as much of this group were) mourn for a childhood they no longer recall. Having spent a long adolescence waging war against childhood, upon victory they misremember a world they've dispatched.

An exception was David Bowie who, at age 19, seemed still able to perceive the world as a child would, and apparently without chemical assistance. Songs like "When I'm Five," "Silver Tree Top School for Boys" and "There is a Happy Land" are some of the more unnerving depictions in pop of how a child regards the world. The songs convey what the novelist Keith Waterhouse once wrote: that "every child is an 'only child' in the sense that he occupies a private world, and is unwilling or unable to convey a great many of his thoughts to anyone else."

"There is a Happy Land" was Bowie's take on Waterhouse's 1957 novel of the same title, for which Waterhouse had used memories of growing up in Depression-era Leeds. Bowie took from *There Is a Happy Land* a sense of childhood being a separate order, with alliances, languages, songs and legends unknown by adults. "You've had your chance and now the doors are closed sir," as he sang in the last verse. The lyric is set in a field ("the rhubarb fields" near a Leeds council estate, the main location of the novel) near dusk, the hour before dinner, when the empire of children is at its height. Replacing Waterhouse's names with his own (including "Tiny Tim," who later showed up in *Ernie Johnson*: see Appendix), Bowie conveyed the squirrely movement of Waterhouse's prose by a zig-zag of a vocal and rapid harmonic rhythms, the key a blur of G major and C major. Bowie hinted at but didn't disclose the novel's horrific climax: a girl is found raped and murdered in the fields, an older child arrested for the crime. He just sings "there's a special place in the rhubarb fields, *underneath the leaves*," a suspended chord troubling "underneath."

It had a solemn, labored arrangement: an intro of vibraphone/piano and strummed acoustic guitar; competing melodies on piano and French horn, pieces of each resurfacing as motifs; occasional graceful fills like a tiny waterfall of piano notes (kissed at the end by a vibraphone note) in the penultimate bar of each bridge. Bowie countered long, slowly-sung phrases for his child characters with curt four-note interjections to the adult world. The coda's move to a set of grand major seventh chords, with Bowie scatting along to Derek Fearnley's exuberant bass and Derek Boyes' raindrop-spatters of piano, lightened the ominous cast. It was a bright defiance of reality, one worthy of a child.

We Are Hungry Men

Recorded: *24 November 1966, Decca Studios. Bowie: lead vocal, sound effects; Renbourn: acoustic guitar; Boyes: organ; Fearnley: bass; Eager: drums; unknown musicians: trumpets; Vernon: "Nazi" voice; Dudgeon: announcer's voice, sound effects; arrangers: Fearnley, Bowie. Produced: Vernon; engineered: Dudgeon.*

First release: *1 June 1967,* ***David Bowie****.*

"We Are Hungry Men" opens with an announcer (Gus Dudgeon) bewildered by cities overpopulating by the hour, builds to a Nazi (Mike Vernon) rant and Bowie, chanting like a Dalek, advocating mass abortion and infanticide, and closes with teeming masses eating, with great slurps, their would-be messiah leader. On the perversely-sequenced *David Bowie*, this cannibal dystopia sat between "There Is a Happy Land" and "When I Live My Dream."

Alternating between eugenics-promoting leader in the verses and cannibal masses in the refrains, the lyric sketched a set of future Bowie scenarios: collapsed cities, mad technocrats, new messiahs, supermen, celebrity fascists. Where the usual rock & roll take on politics was from the street, Bowie generally identified with power. He had an actor's sense of who got the best lines. It wasn't until "Five Years" that he'd write one of his doomsdays from a commoner's viewpoint.

He'd absorbed science fiction since childhood, from TV serials like *Quatermass* and *Doctor Who* to the British SF magazines *New Worlds* and *Impulse.* Where postwar American SF was full of can-do positivism, postwar British SF was a system of shattered worlds: John Christopher's *The Death of Grass* (grains fail, civilization falls); John Wyndham's *Day of the Triffids* (plague kills nearly everyone, plants finish them off) and *The Midwich Cuckoos* (your children will kill you); the great dystopian Brian Aldiss, whose novels reduced humanity to the prey of giant insects (*Hothouse*) and offered a dry world with no children, only the aged (*Greybeard*).

So "We Are Hungry Men" was Bowie claiming a plot in a well-tilled field. He was riffing on a headline topic of the mid-Sixties, the soon-approaching global overpopulation and mass starvation prophesized in Paul Ehrlich's *The Population Bomb* and using for a backdrop the overpopulated, blighted world of Harry Harrison's *Make Room! Make Room!*, serialized in the August-October 1966 issues of *Impulse*.

Originally called "We Are Not Your Friends," "We Are Hungry Men" started life on acoustic guitar and an earnest folkie sensibility remains beneath the cartoon voices and shrieking trumpets, while its bright A major key made the gruesome scenario gleeful, aided by Bowie's crackpot performance and Derek Boyes' B-movie organ. The song was as bizarre as it was prophetic: of Bowie's future, not, as of yet, the world's.

Sell Me a Coat

Recorded: *8-9 December 1966, Decca Studio 2. Bowie: lead and backing vocal; Renbourn: acoustic guitar; Fearnley: bass; Eager: drums; unknown musicians: French horn, cello; arrangers: Fearnley, Bowie. Produced: Vernon; engineered: Dudgeon;* ***(promo remake)*** *25 January 1969, Trident Studios, 17 St. Anne's Court, Soho, London. Hermione Farthingale, John Hutchinson: backing vocals. Produced: Jonathan Weston.*

First release*: 1 June 1967,* ***David Bowie****; (remake) 13 May 1984,* ***Love You Till Tuesday*** *(Castle Music Videos CMV 1010).* ***Live****: 1967-1969.*

"Sell Me a Coat" is as lovely and austere as its wintry subject, with a nursery-rhyme refrain inspired by the Victorian illustrator Randolph Caldecott's children's books (see "Come and Buy My Toys"). Mooted as a single before the album sessions began, the song's craftsmanship and grace made it stand out like a church spire amid *David Bowie*'s collection of grotesques.

Set in G major, with the tonic chord as hearthstone of verse and refrain, "Sell Me a Coat" has a Bowie vocal that wistfully spans a sixth in the verses while a French horn repeats a descending four-note line shadowed by cello. In the refrains, Bowie held onto a single note through a run of short phrases (like the consonant "little patch pockets") while the cello embroidered a tapestry of a countermelody.

His conceit of comparing a formerly temperate girl to her current frigid incarnation had little connection to his child's rhyme of a refrain except a winter theme. Any regret was tempered by irony—take how Bowie lovingly he sings "and when she smiles, the ice forgets to melt away," which isn't a compliment. The fact that his first line was identical to that of Simon and Garfunkel's "I Am a Rock," another winter breakup song, likely wasn't a coincidence. The bridge toyed with the song's fixation on its tonic chord, moving to a G major suspended chord for two beats ("memo-*ry of a*") before escaping at last to the dominant (D major) for the rest of the bridge ("...day").

With John Renbourn's sympathetic acoustic guitar and John Eager ringing his cymbal bell as though he's in a parade march, "Sell Me a Coat" would have been an inspired, if melancholy choice for a single, but it was passed over for the more crass "Love You Till Tuesday." Remixing the track for Bowie's promotional film *Love You Till Tuesday* in early 1969, the producer Jonathan Weston tried to sweeten "Sell Me a Coat" by having Hermione Farthingale and John Hutchinson (see "Ching-a-Ling") trace over the horn and cello counter-melodies. He then mixed their underwhelming vocals to drown out Bowie's lead and the exquisite instrumentation of the original.

Little Bombardier

***Recorded**: 8-9 December 1966, Decca Studio 2. Bowie: lead vocal; Boyes: harpsichord; Fearnley: bass; Eager: drums; unknown musicians: accordion, tuba, violins, violas; arrangers: Fearnley, Bowie. Produced: Vernon; engineered: Dudgeon.*

***First release**: 1 June 1967, **David Bowie**. **Broadcast**: 18 December 1967, Top Gear (BBC).*

David Bowie complemented its childhood songs with those of men who, as John Updike wrote, turned out as failed boys. Like "Uncle Arthur," "Little Bombardier" has a lonely man fumbling a chance at happiness (it's another joyful union portrayed via instrumental break—here, tuba answered by violin) but it's a grubbier and bleaker song, with its title character a drunken veteran run out of town on suspicion of being a pedophile. Again Bowie raided an Alan Sillitoe story: "Uncle Ernest," in which a sad veteran dotes on two girls until being warned off by the police. Where Sillitoe's Ernest was guilty of nothing but loneliness, Bowie, though offering exaggerated sympathies by wringing his vowels and pushing to a high G ("lines of worry appeared"), gave no clue as to whether his Frankie was guilty of the charge.

One of two waltzes cut in the same session (see "Maid of Bond Street"), "Little Bombardier" had a bandstand arrangement—downward sweeps of strings and tuba to usher along the title phrase, harpsichord and accordion to keep the 3/4 meter. Bowie delighted in his words: take the way he sang the title, forming "lit-tle" with tiny consonant darts, hurling the "bomb" in "bombardier" from the back of his throat. Along with its steeple-chase of a chord sequence, starting in G major and darting off into D minor for the bridge, it all seemed a conspiracy to obscure the sordid business of its lyric, with the last run of harpsichord arpeggios mocking the bombardier's fate (Bowie would rework this coda sequence years later on "Sweet Thing (Reprise))."

Maid of Bond Street

***Recorded**: 8-9 December 1966, Decca Studio 2. Bowie: lead vocal; Sullivan: lead guitar; Boyes: piano; Fearnley: bass; Eager: drums; unknown musicians: accordion, tuba, violins, violas; arrangers: Fearnley, Bowie. Produced: Vernon; engineered: Dudgeon.*

First release: *1 June 1967,* ***David Bowie. Live:*** *1967-1968.*

A verbose jumpy little thing, "Maid of Bond Street" was another knock at the hip London set (see "Join the Gang") though here Bowie had more sympathy for his walking mannequin of a subject. He split his viewpoint between a lonely glamour girl, pasted together from shades of lipstick, magazine covers and movie stills, and an envious boy who yearns to be as famous and empty as her (the song's a distant ancestor to "Star"). The Maid could even be the boy's imaginative twin, his drag persona.

Written on acoustic guitar in early 1966, "Maid" has a witty lyric—a spiritual crisis occurs when the girl rides the short distance on the Tube from Paddington to Oxford Circus (symbolized by shuffling back and forth between E and D chords) and isn't appreciated by the commoners. There's some mild wordplay (the plays on "maid" and "made") and inspired rhymes ("aperitifs" wed to "executives"). Bowie zipped through his lines but struggled with breath control in the bridges: the breakneck "but-she-can't-make-it-with-the-boy-she-really-wants-to-be-with" left him winded. The song's waltzing rhythm was steered by accordion, "Big Jim" Sullivan's guitar and John Eager's brushwork while doughty tuba and palais strings provided upholstering; Derek Boyes' piano threaded bridges to verses.

A run of four verses and two bridges untroubled by a refrain, "Maid" surprisingly turned up the latter at its close: a belter of a C major chorus that offered celebrity as an all-consuming vocation with no time for love. A severe credo for its sunny time, it suggested that Bowie considered stardom something like becoming a monk (see "Silly Boy Blue").

Silly Boy Blue

Recorded: (demo, unreleased) *ca. August 1965, R.G. Jones Studio: Bowie: lead vocal; Taylor: lead guitar; Rivens: bass; Lancaster: drums;*

***(album)** 8-9 December 1966, Decca Studio 2. Bowie: lead vocal; Boyes: piano, backing vocals; Fearnley: bass, backing vocals; Eager: drums, Chinese gong, sticks?, backing vocals; Marion Constable: backing vocals; unknown musicians: violin, cello, trumpets; arrangers: Fearnley, Bowie. Produced: Vernon; engineered: Dudgeon; **(demo)** ca. March-April 1967. Bowie: lead vocal, 12-string acoustic guitar; **(remake, unreleased)** (basic tracks) July 2000, Sear Sound, (overdubs) October 2000, Looking Glass. Bowie: lead vocal; Slick: lead guitar; Leonard: acoustic guitar?; Garson: piano; Dorsey: bass, vocals; Plati: acoustic guitar?; Campbell: drums, percussion; Palmer, Gryner: backing vocals; unknown musicians: violins, violas, celli, flute (arranged: Visconti). Produced: Bowie, Plati; engineered: Keppler.*

***First release**:1 June 1967, **David Bowie**; (1967 demo) 31 May 2012, **The Last Chapter: Mods and Sods**. **Broadcast**: 18 December 1967, Top Gear; 13 May 1968, Top Gear. **Live**: 1965?, 1967, 1999, 2001.*

The gorgeous and stately "Silly Boy Blue" proceeds like a monarch but started life as a Mod. Like its contemporary "The London Boys," the song's original lyric concerned a runaway kid who's fled school to hide out in London. Hard experience has spoiled him. Though he dreams of going home, he's no longer a child ("mem'ries I've seen are all dark in the past") and feels severed from his old life. A letter from home, telling him that someone's died, is a missive from another country.

Bowie and the Lower Third demoed this up-tempo song, with its Bo Diddley guitar fills and Beatles handclaps, in the summer of 1965, possibly on the same date as "Baby, That's a Promise." While considered as a single, "Silly Boy Blue" was more likely earmarked for prospective covers. Bowie went back to it a year later. Retaining its structure (four verses and a bridge), key and its long suspension ropes of verse melodies, Bowie transformed his lyric into a travelogue on Tibetan Buddhist culture, with chelas (disciples of lamas, or spiritual teachers), yak butter statues (sculpted by Tibetan lamas for centuries), the Tibetan capital of Lhasa and the Dalai Lama's winter palace there, the Potala.

His interest in Buddhism dated to his early teens, sparked by Jack Kerouac novels like *The Dharma Bums* and Penguin paperbacks on Zen Buddhism by the British convert Christmas Humphreys. The essential book, Bowie later said, was Heinrich Harrer's *Seven Years in Tibet*, which would be the wellspring of the revised "Silly Boy Blue." Harrer was a German national who'd made his way into Tibet, a country few Westerners had ever visited, and much of his book concerned his stay in Lhasa, his meetings with the young Dalai Lama and his thoughts on life in a Buddhist theocracy.

Bowie began regularly visiting the Tibetan Buddhist Society in late 1965, a time when he was often staying at his manager Ralph Horton's apartment, a five-minute walk from the Society's office in Eccleston Square. There he met and befriended a Tibetan lama in exile, Chime Rinpoche, who became Bowie's spiritual mentor. He would ask Rinpoche and his fellow monks questions about Buddhism that the monks would answer with other questions, a circularity that delighted him.

The more frustrated he became with his pop music career, the deeper his immersion in Mahayana Buddhism: late 1967 and much of 1968, a time when his album had failed and his singles were being rejected by Deram, marked the peak of his self-identification as a Buddhist. He told various people he was "going to chuck it all in" to become a monk, to the point of even visiting a monastery in Scotland and allegedly sleeping upright in a box and keeping to a vow of silence. (It's worth noting the latter practices have nothing do to with Mahayana Buddhism. It suggests an element of fiction in Bowie's tale or that the monastery was extremely unorthodox.)

While Tibetan Buddhism was trendy in late Sixties London (see "Karma Man"), Bowie's Buddhist beliefs were grounded and thorough compared to the average day-tripper's. Central

Buddhist concepts like the ultimate emptiness of self intrigued him. The line "his overself pays the bill" in "Silly Boy Blue" suggested Bowie had read the Tathāgatagarbha Sutras, Mahayana sutras that said within everyone, regardless of their personality or class, was an immortal, transcendental "overself" (a rough equivalent to the Christian concept of the soul, and sometimes referred to as Ātman, or the "Buddha nature"). Yet while almost anyone could be a Buddha, this potentiality was hidden within you, obscured by your own flaws of perception—you wrongly perceived the world, and so wrongly interpreted the world.

This belief would dovetail with Bowie's other main developing religious interest—Christian Gnosticism (see "Quicksand" and "Station to Station"). He considered Buddhism and Gnosticism to share an ethos: that the world as we perceive it is false, but a fragment of the original godhead is within us and, with study and dedication, we can tap into it. Buddhism and Gnosticism would provide a reservoir of imagery for his songs and a belief structure for a curious, self-educated teenager whose ambitions had mainly been to somehow become famous. Through Buddhism, Bowie found a way to identify and channel his desires, to quarry out the artist within a suburban boy from Bromley. "You can only show [people] the way towards it. Buddhism is a process of self-discovery, of discovering the truth for oneself," Bowie told a journalist at the time.

As he'd rearranged Keith Waterhouse and Alan Sillitoe stories on *David Bowie*, he altered the perspective of his source material here. "Silly Boy Blue," while charming in its desire to include Harrer's details about Tibet, was still an alienated Mod song. Its sympathies lay with a young Tibetan monk who can't pay attention, who's unable to pull off an astral projection; a boy at odds with his glorious culture. If Tibet was, to the West, a society in which everyone was religious (even if they really weren't), even in the magic kingdom Bowie cast his sympathies with the heretics.

His fascination with Buddhism led him to be more ambitious in the studio. He'd already wanted the backing chorus of "Baby Loves That Way" to sound like chanting monks. Now "Silly Boy Blue" threw in everything from John Eager's Chinese cymbal to trumpet fanfares to strings (a cello and a single violin, each of which matched Bowie note for note in verses) to another pack of singing "monks" who included the first female singer he'd ever used. Yet he and Dek Fearnley grounded the exoticism in contemporary pop: a Phil Spector-style beat in which Eager played Hal Blaine-esque "on the fours," a Burt Bacharach outro and a bassline in debt to Them's "It's All Over Now Baby Blue." And fitting its imperial tone, "Silly Boy Blue" starts by moving between primary major chords: the tonic, A, its subdominant (IV) and dominant (V) chords, D and E. A shadow falls in the bridge, which opens with an F# minor chord (the vi chord of A), but the song soon builds to its grand sweep up to B major, ushered in by Bowie's fifth-falling "diiiiiiiiieeee" (a high G down to C).

The song blossomed in later renditions. For his two radio performances of "Silly Boy Blue," Bowie and Tony Visconti rearranged the intro, replacing the trumpet fanfare with dreamily arpeggiated electric guitar. Decades later, his studio remake for the *Toy* album was somber and refined, if a bit staid. Better came in February 2001, when Bowie sang "Silly Boy Blue" at a Tibet House benefit at Carnegie Hall. Leading an ensemble that included Visconti, Moby, Philip Glass and (at last!) a legitimate group of Tibetan monks (recruited from the Drepung Gomang Monastic University), Bowie introduced the song by recounting how he'd met Rinpoche. He sang its opening verses slowly, savoring the sway of his phrasings and the richness of the simple rhymes, marveling at his youth's architecture.

Come and Buy My Toys

Recorded: *12 December 1966, Decca Studio 2. Bowie: lead vocal; Renbourn:12-string acoustic guitar; Fearnley: bass. Produced: Vernon; engineered: Dudgeon.*

First release:*1 June 1967,* ***David Bowie***. ***Live***: *1967.*

A minimalist respite on *David Bowie,* "Come and Buy My Toys" is just Bowie's voice, Dek Fearnley's bass and John Renbourn on 12-string acoustic guitar. Another of the album's childhood songs, it kept to the brisk way of "Sell Me a Coat" rather than follow the murkier "There Is a Happy Land." The books Bowie pillaged here were Randolph Caldecott's *The Farmer's Boy* and some collections of children's rhymes he'd read while babysitting. The first verse was a cut-and-pasted 19th Century nursery rhyme, the bridge essentially the folk ballad "The Cambric Shirt"; Bowie filled the rest of the song with some cod-medieval lines of his own.

His rapid seesawing vocal melody in the verses cooled to a more languid phrasing in the bridges, where he slowed to sing two half-notes per bar ("you-shall/own-a/cam-bric/shirt"). Fearnley tacked down the song's G major progression while Renbourn's 12-string acoustic is the miniature sun of the track, playing variations on the opening riff through verses, bridges and refrains. A few months after cutting this, Renbourn formed the English folk revivalist group Pentangle with Bert Jansch. For Bowie, this would be his only dalliance in the style. His folk-inspired songs of the late Sixties were far more in the Beat surrealist line of Bob Dylan than the English neo-traditionalist one of a Pentangle or Fairport Convention. "Come and Buy My Toys" was more an advertisement for its album, with Bowie as a vendor in a market square offering sweets, sours, jewels and baubles.

Please Mr. Gravedigger

Recorded: ***(demo, as "The Gravedigger," unreleased)*** *18 October 1966, R.G. Jones. Bowie: lead vocal, organ;* ***(album)*** *13 December 1966,*

Decca Studio 2. Bowie: lead vocal, sound effects; Dudgeon: sound effects. Produced: Vernon; engineered: Dudgeon.

***First release**: 1 June 1967, **David Bowie**. **Broadcast**: 27 February 1968, 4-3-2-1 Musik Für Junge Leute.*

The last song on *David Bowie* and the last recorded in its primary sessions, "Please Mr. Gravedigger" fittingly kills a child. It's as if having made a record of children's songs, Bowie felt he had to purge himself. Performing a graveyard soliloquy by a murderer, he accompanied his voice with the sounds of thunderclaps, rainfall, tolling bells, shovel scrapes, footsteps, bird chirps and exuberant sneezes. He was a Method sneezer: after his first blast, he kept a snotted-up voice for the rest of the track.

Like "We Are Hungry Men," "Please Mr. Gravedigger" was at heart a radio play, the product of Bowie and Gus Dudgeon plundering Decca's vault of noises. A visitor to Decca during the session found Bowie hunched over the mike as if being drenched by rain while "shuffling about in a box of gravel." In a plot seemingly out of the Fifties horror comic *The Haunt of Fear*, the track's stuffy-nosed murderer stands in a bomb-blasted Lambeth cemetery, watching an old gravedigger at work. He determines to murder the gravedigger, whether for unearthing his crime (the killing of a 10-year-old girl) or for taking a locket of his victim's hair. (The song's title plays off "Please Mr. Postman," another civil servant caught up in someone else's obsession.) Some suggest the lyric references one of the Moors Murders victims, the 10-year-old Lesley Anne Downey (the lurid trial of the sadistic killers Myra Hindley and Ian Brady had taken place in April 1966), but the "Mary Ann" here equally could have been the dead girl in Keith Waterhouse's *There Is a Happy Land*.

More striking was how radical a piece of music "Gravedigger" was, with Bowie's vocal melody removed from any harmonic framing. His narrow-scoped phrases (he's confined to the range of a sixth) provide few clues, as each phrase could fit a variety of chord progressions. All the listener's given at the start is Bowie singing a run of D notes ("there's a little churchyard") that fall a semitone ("just along the way") and leap a fifth ("used to be Lambeth's"). The reappearance of a falling-by-semitones pattern is the closest "Gravedigger" has to a melody ("please-mister-grave-digger" is a falling A-G#-F#-E)). The effect made Bowie's murderer seem even more isolated and deranged, a madman locked outside of his own song.

The Laughing Gnome

Recorded: *26 January, 7, 10 February, 8 March 1967, Decca Studio 2. Bowie: lead vocal, gnome voices; Dudgeon: gnome voices; Pete Hampshire: lead guitar; Boyes, Bob Michaels?: harpsichord; Fearnley: bass; Eager: drums; unknown musicians: bassoon, oboe; arrangers: Fearnley, Bowie. Produced: Vernon; engineered: Dudgeon.*

First release*: 14 April 1967 (Deram DM 123).*

During a state visit to Washington, DC in 1994, Pres. Boris Yeltsin was found dead drunk late one night, standing on Pennsylvania Avenue wearing only his underwear, trying to hail a cab because he wanted to get a pizza. Many consider "The Laughing Gnome" to be something of an equivalent in Bowie's life.

"The Laughing Gnome" is a trump card that anyone who dislikes or has suspicions about Bowie plays in a crucial hand. It's meant to disqualify Bowie, to show up him as a fraud. "A chipmunk-voiced novelty song calculated to make even the staunchest Bowiephile cringe," as Mark Dery described it. At the apex of Bowie's global fame in 1984, Mick Farren (who'd known Bowie in the Sixties) wrote that "whenever [Bowie] comes under discussion and the folks around the bar start to get rapturous, a still, small voice pipes up in the back of my mind to remind me: This is the man who recorded 'The Laughing Gnome.'" When Bowie asked fans to vote for which songs he'd perform on his "greatest hits" tour of 1990, the *NME* launched a write-in campaign to humiliate him by making him sing "Laughing Gnome" on stage.

"The Laughing Gnome" concerns a man who meets a gnome. It has sped-up gnome voices, *à la* Alvin and the Chipmunks, as performed by Bowie (the Laughing Gnome) and engineer Gus Dudgeon (the Gnome's brother, Fred). Bowie and the gnome(s) duet in the refrains. A bassoon is a lead instrument. There are gnome puns, many of them. After "Space Oddity," it was Bowie's best single of the Sixties.

The son of a half-century's worth of British novelty records, from Charles Penrose's "laughing" discs in the Twenties to Anthony Newley's "Pop Goes the Weasel" and "That Noise," "Laughing Gnome" suited the frothy mood of its time, preceding Syd Barrett's "The Gnome" by a few months. It was also Bowie's best Mod soul single: its propulsive 4/4 slammed home by drums, bass, harpsichord and guitar all locked in, the guitar shifting from topping the bassline to biting down hard on each beat. (It was the first of many Bowie attempts to match the drone of the Velvet Underground's "I'm Waiting for the Man.") Even the gnome voices were basically drum fills. His melody, reminiscent of "The Tennessee Waltz," was a rhythm guitar line in a vocal. Bowie started each verse with short upward moves ("I was walk-*ing*, down the *high street*"), took a long stride down an octave ("heard-foot-steps-be-hind-me") echoed by a closing set of short, descending lines ("scarlet and *grey*, chuckling a-*way*"). The refrains were a four-part harmony: soaring oboe, playing whole or half notes; huffing bassoon happy to act like a clown; Bowie's lead vocal and the gnome chorus.

And was the song really just a joke? The musician Nick Currie, aka Momus, suggested that "The Laughing Gnome" was a man losing his mind, a schizophrenic's conversation with himself. Bowie walks down the street, hears a strange voice, has a vision. He has further visions at home. He tries to rally, puts his gnome "on a train to Eastbourne." No such luck. The visions return and multiply—there are two gnomes now! A descent into madness follows. Bowie crows that his gnomes have made him wealthy and famous while he lies curled in a ball on the floor. If you come close you can hear him whisper, "HA HA HA…hee hee hee…"

Bowie and Gus Dudgeon labored on the single for nearly two months (the lengthiest Bowie recording session to date—it took longer to make "Laughing Gnome" than it did the entire *David Bowie* LP). Dudgeon had grown close to Bowie and the two of them spent weeks writing and scrapping "gnome" puns. The audible delight of Bowie's singing (while keeping a straight face in the early verses, he's cracking up by the last refrains) contributed to the sense of happy, bizarre buffoonery. Even the bassoonist closed the last refrain with a honk of satisfaction.

The single's failure to chart and some critical pasting pushed Bowie towards a darker path: soon enough came *Space Oddity* and *The Man Who Sold the World*. This would become his regular maneuver. Whenever he did something too silly (say, *Labyrinth* or the Glass Spider Tour) he'd make amends by dressing as a "serious" artiste for a time. While the cracked, gleeful spirit of the "Gnome" went missing for much of the Seventies, Bowie kept quietly drawing from its stores. The varisped gnome voices returned as ghouls in "After All," "The Bewlay Brothers" and his cover of "See Emily Play," while variations on the chromatic three-octave-descending oboe/bassoon riff are found in tracks like "Fame," "Speed of Life," "Fall in Love With Me," "Scream Like a Baby" and "Real Cool World."

The Gospel According to Tony Day

Recorded: *26 January 1967, Decca Studio 2. Bowie: lead vocal; Hampshire: lead guitar; Boyes: piano; Fearnley: bass, backing vocals; Eager: drums; unknown musicians: bassoon, oboe; arrangers: Fearnley, Bowie. Produced: Vernon; engineered: Dudgeon.*

First release: *14 April 1967 (Deram DM 123).*

He should have doubled down on novelty and made "Over the Wall We Go" the B-side of "The Laughing Gnome," but instead Bowie cut a dippy 10-bar blues vaguely under the influence of Donovan. "The Gospel According to Tony Day" is centered on Derek Fearnley's three-note bassline and the "Laughing Gnome" woodwinds: a querulous bassoon parked in the left channel and a right-mixed oboe passing itself off as a horn section. An inadvertent parody of his label Deram's pretentions, "Tony Day" is a psychedelic blues with baroque-era instruments and a four-verse lyric that Bowie sings half-conversationally, even throwing in some Cockney rhyming slang at the close ("take a close butchers [hook = look]"). Bowie saying "your mind: blow it, blow it" during a bassoon solo is utterly ridiculous, though the *way* he says it, pissily and coldly, as if doing an Old Etonian take on a Timothy Leary "turn on" record, suggests he was in on the joke.

When I Live My Dream

***Recorded**: 25 February 1967, Decca Studio 2. Bowie: lead vocal; Renbourn: acoustic guitar; Boyes: organ; Fearnley: bass; Eager: drums, tambourine?; unknown musicians: vibraphone, trumpet, violins, violas, celli; arranged: Greenslade, Bowie. Produced: Vernon; engineered: Dudgeon; **(remake, proposed single)** 3 June 1967, Decca Studio 3. Bowie: lead vocal; unknown musicians: acoustic guitar, lead guitar, piano, bass, drums, clarinet, oboe, bassoon, tuba, violins, violas, celli; arranged: Ivor Raymonde. Produced: Vernon; engineered: Bill Price; **(unreleased German version, "Mit Mir in Einem Traum")** 29 January 1969, Trident. Bowie: lead vocal. Produced: Weston; (**"Looking Glass Murders" version**) 31 January, 1 February 1970, Leith Theatre, Edinburgh. Bowie: lead vocal; Michael Garrett: electric piano.*

***First release**: 1 June 1967, **David Bowie**; (remake) 13 May 1984, **Love You Till Tuesday**; (Looking Glass) 7 February 2005, **Love You Till Tuesday** (DVD,Universal 0602498233603). **Broadcast:** 18*

December 1967, Top Gear; 1 February 1970, Gateway. ***Live****: 1967-1969.*

Having finished his debut album in mid-December 1966, Bowie cut more tracks two months later to leaven it with some "conventional" pop. The changes were all made to the album's first side. Scrapping a Beat parody ("Bunny Thing") and Pye throwback ("Your Funny Smile") (see Appendix) and demoting "Did You Ever Have a Dream" to a B-side made room for a re-recorded "Rubber Band" and two new prospective singles, "Love You Till Tuesday" and "When I Live My Dream."

The latter had wistful verses marked by slowly descending phrases, Bowie drifting down by a fourth ("gol-den *horse*") or a sixth ("*to* serve *you*") over an unchanging C bass. A set of bridges with a faster harmonic rhythm and some vocal showcase moments (the dramatic leap of a sixth on "you will *find*," Bowie hitting the "middle" note (F) of the underlying E-flat suspended 2nd chord) foreshadowed its grand coda, with a jarring key change from F to A-flat and Bowie hitting high Gs and Fs ("*live* my *dreeeeam...laugh* at *meeeee*") as if he's at a target range, then performing a balance-beam act on his ultimate "dream."

Though his lyric was hobbled by awkward imagery ("the trees will play the rhythm of my dream") and rhymes ("horse" mated with "voice"), Bowie's performance carried the song through. It was a similar character to his various child narrators, suiting the lyric's sad, glossed-up child's imaging of love. (It was also, yet again, the scenario of "Baby Loves That Way"—the singer watches his girl "run to many other men" and hopes she'll come back to him when she's done.) But Bowie's coda vocal was something new: there was an anger in it, a desperate kicking at fate. The performance suggested someone so caught up in a grand vision of himself that he risked seeming like a madman. Even with its Englebert Humperdinck arrangements, the song's truest successor was Bowie's countercultural purge "Cygnet Committee" (see Ch. 3).

Neither of the song's two arrangements quite suited the fragility and weirdness of Bowie's vocal. Arthur Greenslade's work on the album track was as neatly-laid as a garden path, starting minimally (tambourine, distantly-mixed organ, bass and acoustic guitar) to swell to a strings-and-trumpet counter-melody in the bridges, a vibes counterpoint in the last verse and a pizzicato string hook for the coda. Ivor Raymonde's work on the proposed single remake was more crass: an electric guitar prodded the song through its paces, woodwinds took the strings' role in the bridges and a flute tootled the chimes melody. The song's most moving version was its simplest: the "When I Live My Dream" that Bowie performed in the mime telecast *The Looking Glass Murders* in 1970, with only electric organ for support.

Bowie and Kenneth Pitt considered "When I Live My Dream" a possible break-through and flogged it for the rest of the decade, despite a lack of label or popular enthusiasm. Though Deram rejected the remake (proposed as a single in September 1966), Bowie included the song in *Pierrot and Turquoise* and his would-be cabaret act; he cut a German version (his performance accurately described as "barking like Rosa Klebb") and closed his *Love You Till Tuesday* promotional film with it. Its last gasp was in July 1969, when Bowie performed "When I Live My Dream" in a big-band arrangement at Malta's International Song Festival competition and lost to a Spanish child performer named Cristina.

Love You Till Tuesday

Recorded**: (demo, unreleased)** *ca. mid-1966. Bowie: vocal, acoustic guitar;* **(album)** *25 February 1967, Decca Studio 2. Bowie: lead vocal; Renbourn: acoustic guitar; Boyes: piano; Fearnley: bass; Eager: drums; unknown musicians: vibraphone, trumpet, violins, violas, celli; arrangers: Greenslade, Bowie. Produced: Vernon; engineered: Dudgeon;* **(single)** *3 June 1967, Decca Studio 3. Bowie: lead vocal;*

unknown musicians: acoustic guitar, piano, bass, drums, flutes, clarinets, oboes, bassoons, violins, violas, celli. Arranger: Raymonde. Produced: Vernon; engineered: Price; ***(unreleased, German version "Lieb' Dich Bis Dienstag")*** *29 January 1969, Trident. Bowie: vocal. Produced: Weston.*

First release*: 1 June 1967,* ***David Bowie****; (remake) 14 July 1967 (Deram DM 135).* ***Broadcast****: 8 November 1967, Fanclub; 18 December 1967, Top Gear; 27 February 1968, 4-3-2-1 Musik Für Junge Leute.* ***Live****: 1967, 1969.*

"Love You Till Tuesday" was catchy and desperate enough to have been a chart hit in 1967. It could've even been a smash, the single that finally broke Bowie. Instead, despite earning Bowie his best reviews to date, it flopped.

A late album addition, "Love You Till Tuesday" was remade as a single two days after the release of *David Bowie*. Ivor Raymonde's new arrangement had an oppressive cheer and some obvious quotations and Bowie oversold his mildly-clever lyric, singing with an affected nasally tone as if hoping listeners would think the song was from a West End musical. When he cracked up on the mike as he did on "Laughing Gnome," it was a stage laugh. It all came off like an aging Blackpool entertainer's creaky take on free love.

It was the most Alan Klein-influenced of Bowie's songs (there were similarities to Klein's "Will You Ever Come Back Again?") and one of his few full-on Anthony Newley imitations. Written and demoed before the *David Bowie* sessions, "Love You Till Tuesday" was slaved over even as an album track, polished to a shine and fattened with vocal hooks like the "da-da-da-DUM" tags and little "AAH-aah" fills. Set in cheery B-flat major, its verses opened with Bowie displaying his wares, first descending an octave ("just look through your window") then jumping up one ("sits out-*side*!").

The timing seemed right. The "summer of love" and the autumn of love hangover was a period of whimsy and slack for the UK pop charts. Top hits included "All You Need Is Love" and "Hello Goodbye," Englebert Humperdinck's "The Last Waltz" and the San Francisco odes of Scott McKenzie and the Flower Pot Men. "Love You Till Tuesday" could have wormed its way into that set, and arguably only Deram's anemic promotion of the single kept it from charting. You could even imagine an alternate timeline in which "Love You Till Tuesday" hit #2 for weeks, giving Bowie at last a taste of pop stardom: *Sunday Night at the Palladium,* Las Vegas residencies, duets with Petula Clark and Nancy Sinatra, *Bowie Sings Bacharach,* a cabaret show ("Man of Words, Man of Music, Man of Mime") extending well into the Seventies. Instead the single died and Bowie was knocked back to the start of the board, yet again. "Love You Till Tuesday" would be his last Deram release until he became famous on another label.

Waiting for the Man

(Reed). ***Recorded****: 5 April 1967, Decca Studios. Bowie: lead vocal, harmonica; Rod Davies: lead guitar; Bob Evans: tenor saxophone; Butch Davis: piano; Brian "Croak" Prebble: bass, backing vocals; Derek "Del" Roll: drums. Produced, engineered: Dudgeon.*

First release: *31 May 2012,* ***The Last Chapter: Mods and Sods****.* ***Broadcast****: 5 February 1970, The Sunday Show; 25 March 1970, Sounds of the 70s; 11 January 1972, Sounds of the 70s; 18 January 1972, Sounds of the 70s.* ***Live****: 1967, 1972, 1976, 1990-1991, 1996-1997.*

In November 1966 Kenneth Pitt was in New York on a publicity trip. Learning that Andy Warhol was looking for a British promoter for his "house" group, the Velvet Underground, Pitt arranged a meeting at Warhol's Factory. It didn't come to much—Pitt and Warhol were introduced but barely conversed—but Pitt managed to snag an acetate of the VU's debut, *The Velvet Underground and Nico.* Returning to London a month later, he gave the disc to Bowie, who fell in love. In particular with side one, track two: "I'm Waiting for the Man."

Bowie's first impulse was to proselytize. He claimed the day after he heard *Velvet Underground and Nico* he started covering its songs. Exaggeration or no, he *was* the first British musician to perform and record "Waiting for the Man," months before *Nico* even was released in America. ("Now that's the essence of Mod," he later boasted.)

He cut "Waiting for the Man" in an off-the-books recording session in early April 1967 with the Riot Squad (see "Little Toy Soldier"), which sounded as if they were making do with what they'd found in a school music room. Lou Reed and Sterling Morrison's dirty wall of guitars was conveyed by wheezing harmonica (Bowie's, recorded backwards) and Bob Evans' tenor saxophone. Where John Cale's piano had pulsed beneath Reed's blank narration, the piano here was just chirpy accompaniment. Singing in a half-decent attempt to imitate Reed's deadpan New York accent, Bowie threw in some Dylan phrasings as well.

Bowie latched on to "Waiting for the Man" because it felt like a dispatch from the street. It made "London Boys," his own attempt at "street" realism, seem like schoolboy work. Sure, Lou Reed was a middle-class Long Islander and Syracuse English major who'd started out writing knock-off pop songs for a third-string record label, and "Waiting for the Man" was as much owed to Hubert Selby novels as it did Reed's life (something Bowie would have appreciated, had he known it at the time). But by 1967 Reed could sell it: there was no sunlight between his stage persona and his material. It was a trick Bowie needed more years to perfect.

Bowie kept coming back to "Waiting For the Man," cutting it repeatedly for the BBC and making it a staple of the 1972 Ziggy Stardust shows. He intended to *popularize* it, starting by "straightening" out the song. On the VU record, Lou Reed's guitar was down-tuned by a whole tone, so he played the song's E-A-E-A chords as D-G-D-G. Bowie and Mick Ronson played in standard tuning, moving the song up to E major, and also flattened the chords later in the verse ("up to Lexington—125"). Bowie usually began his take by singing wearily, cagily; it was a junkie's blues in line with Reed's original concept for the song. But when the Man showed up he cut loose, moving up an octave ("there he comes!"): he was in love once again. Ronson's lead guitar was glam swagger to replace the VU's sordid jitter. The song became a celebration of The Man, the junkie sidelined in his own story.

His obsessive covering of "Waiting for the Man" (louche funk in 1976, touring holy relic in 1990) suggested he'd never gotten over the song, which he'd played so often in the early Seventies that some of his fans likely thought he'd written it. You could say "Waiting for the Man" was a song Bowie felt he *ought* to have written, and he soaked it into his own compositions: you can hear its rhythms in everything from "The Laughing Gnome" to "'Heroes.'"

Little Toy Soldier

***Recorded:* (demo)** *ca. late March 1967, North London? Bowie: lead vocal, backing vocal; Davies; lead guitar; Prebble: bass;* **(studio take)** *5 April 1967, Decca Studios. Bowie: lead vocal, sound effects; Davies: lead guitar; Davis: organ; Prebble: bass; Roll: drums; Dudgeon: sound effects. Produced, engineered: Dudgeon.*

First release: *31 May 2012,* ***The Last Chapter: Mods and Sods****.* ***Live****: 1967.*

For two months in 1967, Bowie was the secret lead singer of a pop group attempting, late in life, to become avant-garde. This was the Riot Squad, whose earlier incarnation had been label-mates at Pye. In their 20 performances that spring, Bowie and the Riot Squad donned face-paint and masks and played while a police siren flashed throughout their sets. Bowie cracked a whip and stroked the hair of saxophonist Bob Evans, who sported a bowler hat and padded suit (recall it was half a decade before Stanley Kubrick filmed *A Clockwork Orange*). These few scattered nights in places like Harrow and at London's Tiles Club were arguably the birth of glam in Britain.

Bowie and the Riot Squad connected while at loose ends. Bowie was waiting for his album to come out and, lacking a band, couldn't play live; the Riot Squad, who'd been protégés of the producer Joe Meek, were reeling after Meek had killed his landlady and himself in February 1967. They needed a new lead singer, so Evans recruited Bowie. It was openly a short-term fling. Bowie wouldn't let the band use his name (he was called "Toy Soldier" in press releases) while the Squad kept auditioning singers.

Evans wanted Bowie to add stage presence to the band's act, which was straight-up R&B (they'd been offered a slot to back up Wilson Pickett). For their live sets, Bowie contributed "Silly Boy Blue," "I'm Waiting for the Man" and his new Velvet Underground tribute, "Little Toy Soldier." Bowie and the Riot Squad recorded takes of all three at their rehearsal space and in a session at Decca in early April. The latter was likely intended for professional-sounding demos, though it's possible Bowie was trying out VU covers for an assumed sequel LP for Deram.

"Little Toy Soldier" was a wholesale theft of the VU's sadomasochistic "Venus in Furs," with Bowie singing an entire Lou Reed-penned verse during his tale of little Sadie and the toy soldier who binds her "tighter and tighter," offering a parody/homage to Lou Reed's voice. Inspired by Frank Zappa and the Fugs, Bowie ladled on sound effects: cackles, whip-cracks and creaking springs in the verses alone. Where "Little Toy Soldier" originally had a cold ending when the toy soldier killed poor Sadie in a fit of passion, Dudgeon extended the track with a minute-long coda of war whoops, telephone time recordings, explosions, shattering glass, coughs, motorway noise and, as in "Please Mr. Gravedigger," a loudly-blown nose. Though Bowie buried "Little Toy Soldier" (the track only leaked when someone copied Dudgeon's tape in the Eighties), it marked the gruesome end to his run of novelty songs (see "Laughing Gnome," "Over the Wall We Go").

Pancho
Love Is Always

(Albimoor/Giroud/Bowie.) ***Recorded*****: *(demos, unreleased)*** *ca. March-April 1967, Essex Music, Dumbarton House, 68 Oxford Street, London;* ***(single)*** *Andrée "Dee Dee" Giroud: lead vocal; unknown musicians: guitars, flute, trumpets, trombones, saxophones, bass, drums, chimes, backing vocals (arranged, conducted: Albimoor).*

First release*: ("Dee Dee") 10 June 1967 (Palette HT 300128).*

Bowie's occasional translation work for his publisher, Essex Music, was one of his few sources of income in the late Sixties, along with the rare acting gig and stints as a photocopier and housecleaner. After writing lyrics for a batch of Israeli pop songs, Bowie did the same for a pair of songs by the Belgian singer Andrée "Dee Dee" Giroud and her husband, the pianist and composer Willy Albimoor. Bowie erred on the side of camp, transforming their "Pancho" into a motorbike-riding, charismatic thug with a "face lit from inside."

Giroud had performed in Belgium and France as "Bébé Hong Suong" since the early Fifties, and for another three decades she would sing in the Bébé Suong Company in France and the Benelux countries. As for Albimoor, he was a jazz pianist (born Willy de Moor) who backed everyone from Josephine Baker to Chuck Berry and who wrote for anyone breathing in Belgium. His "Jungle Fever," performed by the Chakachas, hit #8 in the US and was banned by the BBC for excessive moaning.

Everything Is You

Recorded**: *(demo, unreleased)*** *ca. March-April 1967, Essex Music. Bowie: vocals, acoustic guitar, footstomps;* ***(Beatstalkers version)*** *27 March, 18 April 1968, CBS Studios, 28-30 Theobalds Road, London. Dave Lennox: lead vocal; Bowie: rhythm guitar, backing vocal; Ronnie*

Smith: rhythm guitar; Eddie Campbell: organ; Alan Mair: bass; Jeff Allen: drums.

First release: *(Beatstalkers) 21 June 1968 (CBS 3557).*

Bowie's galumphing lumberjack love ode "Everything Is You" was a hummable, catchy song (its main guitar riff mirrored by its wordless refrain) hindered by a melodically and harmonically wayward bridge and a bizarre lyric that seemed literally translated from Finnish: "your strength is in the axe I wield." Considered for Bowie's second Deram LP and offered to Manfred Mann's producer John Burgess, "Everything Is You" wound up farmed out to another of Kenneth Pitt's clients, the Scottish quintet the Beatstalkers, whose adaptation butched up the lyric, ventured into ska in the verses and featured Bowie on backing vocal and rhythm guitar. It was issued as the B-side of "Rain-Coloured Roses" in 1968.

Silver Tree Top School for Boys

Recorded*: *(unreleased, demo) *ca. March-April 1967, Essex Music. Bowie: vocal, acoustic guitar, bass?;* ***(as "Silver Tree Top Jam")*** *ca. April 1967, North London. Bowie: lead vocal; Evans: saxophone, flute; Davies: guitar; Davis: keyboards; Prebble: bass; Roll: drums.*

First release: *(The Slender Plenty) 15 September 1967 (Polydor 56189); (The Beatstalkers) 1 December 1967 (CBS 3105); ("Silver Tree Top Jam") 31 May 2012,* ***The Last Chapter: Mods and Sods. Live***: *1967.*

The great lost Bowie song of the Sixties, "Silver Tree Top School For Boys" begins with a boy noting landmarks of his small world—his town, the shopkeepers, the local madman, his school. He zooms in on the school, which is breaking him into a man—he rolls the cricket pitch, runs to a headmaster's call. But in the bridge, he's called out to join "a thousand boys and masters" sitting on the cricket ground sharing joints. It's a sudden moment of cross-generational harmony, reducing the adults to children: the English master thinks he's a purple mouse, while the head "who's usually sad [is] swinging from a tree."

Particularly in its recording by the Slender Plenty, "Silver Tree Top School For Boys" was a study in relentlessness, its syllable-packed verse lines welded to a two-note vocal melody set against a rapid 12/8 meter. The narrative compression of the first verses was furthered by just two bars of descending "yeah yeah yeah yeahs" as breathers between them. More agitators were a guitar hitting on each downbeat and piano and bass descending in lockstep. The conformity finally broke in the bridge, with its longer vocal phrases and leap to falsetto, the liberation furthered by a subsequent empty verse of "la las" (which one interpreter, the Beatstalkers, filled with a guitar solo).

Allegedly inspired by a newspaper article about a pot-smoking bust at a boarding school, Bowie turned the generational struggle into something more benign, the prospect of communal tokes or trips leveling the ground between master and pupil, governors and governed. The spring of 1967 was about the last moment one could imagine this (see also Paul McCartney's loving ode to a meter maid). By the summer the Establishment had turned sharply against the counterculture, banning the pirate radio stations and imposing severe (if soon repealed) jail sentences on Mick Jagger and Keith Richards after a drug raid. A year later, Malcolm McDowell was playing a public school revolutionary in Lindsay Anderson's *If...*, opening fire with an automatic rifle on teachers and alumni.

Bowie worked out "Silver Tree Top School For Boys" during his time with the Riot Squad and in May 1967, Kenneth Pitt sent its demo to producer Steve Rowland. Unusually, there were multiple takers: Glasgow's Beatstalkers (who Pitt managed) and the Slender Plenty, a group of session players assembled by a Polydor A&R man. The latter was the better recording, tightly built upon the strict parameters of Bowie's demo. The Beatstalkers' more free-ranging version found Dave Lennox, who Bowie had tried to coach out of his brogue, stumbling over lines. The Beatstalkers also struggled with harmonies in the bridge, requiring a brutal edit (at 1:00) to punch in vocals sped up to the correct pitch.

April's Tooth of Gold

Recorded: *(demo, unreleased) ca. late 1967-early 1968?, Essex Music. Bowie: vocal, acoustic guitar.*

Long known only as a song title, "April's Tooth of Gold" was finally bootlegged in 2010, revealing itself as a piece of mild psychedelia melodically similar to "Silver Tree Top School for Boys." Driven by a harshly-strummed acoustic guitar reminiscent of the Kinks' "Autumn Almanac," the song concerned strange young people with blue hair and gold teeth and the older generation bewildered by them—it was a first draft of "Oh! You Pretty Things." A minor but appealing song that could've won a place on a second Bowie Deram album.

Let Me Sleep Beside You

Recorded: *1 September 1967, Advision Sound Studios, 83 New Bond Street, London. Bowie: lead vocal; John McLaughlin: lead guitar; Sullivan: acoustic guitar; Tony Visconti: bass; Andy White: drums; Siegrid Visconti: backing vocals; unknown musicians: celli. Arranged, produced: Visconti; engineered: Gerald Chevin;* ***(remake)*** *(basic tracks) July 2000, Sear Sound, (overdubs) October 2000, Looking Glass. Bowie: lead vocal; Slick: lead guitar; Leonard: rhythm guitar; Plati: acoustic guitar?; Garson: keyboards; Dorsey: bass; Campbell: drums; Palmer, Gryner: backing vocals. Produced: Bowie, Plati; engineered: Keppler.*

First release: *6 March 1970,* ***The World of David Bowie*** *(Decca SPA 58); (remake) 17 November 2014,* ***Nothing Has Changed.*** ***Broadcast:*** *20 October 1969, Dave Lee Travis Show.* ***Live***: *1969.*

Tony Visconti, a 23-year-old bass player from Brooklyn, came to Britain in April 1967 to illegally work as an arranger and production assistant. He convinced customs that he was traveling with four guitars because he was a dedicated vacationing musician who had to practice on each daily. In New York he'd caught the eye of British producer Denny Cordell by writing a complete arrangement for a Georgie Fame overdub session in an hour. Once in London, Visconti was put to work on tracks by the Move, scoring woodwinds and strings for their hit "Flowers in the Rain," and Manfred Mann ("So Long Dad").

In July, Visconti first met Bowie at the office of David Platz, who was both Cordell's business partner and Bowie's song publisher. It was an arranged meeting: Platz and Kenneth Pitt had thought the pair would hit it off, as Visconti already had a reputation of being able to work with "weird people," in Platz's words (*i.e.*, Marc Bolan, who Visconti had convinced Cordell to sign). They became fast friends, partly because Visconti "was well into the Tibetan thing," Bowie recalled in 1976. Approved to cut a prospective single for Deram at summer's end, he asked Visconti to arrange and produce it.

So began a partnership that would span, with some large gaps, almost fifty years. Visconti was Bowie's first great collaborator, their relationship building upon what Bowie had started with Gus Dudgeon on "Laughing Gnome." Bowie needed a contemporary behind the console, someone with whom he had mutual interests and who was roughly his same age, rather than hoping an industry pro like Mike Vernon or Tony Hatch could manage to learn his dialect. Visconti would realize Bowie's abstract requests and color his sketches, but he also grounded Bowie with his no-nonsense production style (he worked fast and kept within budget).

Visconti lobbied for Bowie to cut "Let Me Sleep Beside You" as his next single, flattering him by pronouncing the song "almost American." It had a cynical conception. Watching television with Pitt one night, Bowie stood up and announced he was off to write some "Top 10 rubbish." His album and "Love You Till Tuesday" single had failed and he was running out of innings with Deram, so "Let Me Sleep Beside You" was his bald attempt to cash in on the Rolling Stones' "Let's Spend the Night Together" (blunt requests were in vogue). It was the end of his storybook days: he told a virgin ("your lips are void of history") to discard her toys, lock away her childhood and move to the city to be happily corrupted.

Given an identical C major progression for verse and refrain, Visconti had to provide contrasts. He scored lines for celli, providing a sultry relief from the brass- and woodwind-heavy *David Bowie* and "Laughing Gnome," and gave the track a sense of lightness and ease. Andy White's drums worked as accents, the beat kept by the strums of "Big Jim" Sullivan's acoustic guitar, while John McLaughlin's distorted opening guitar riff wasn't allowed to dominate the track, its only repeat coming in the outro. Pushing his own bass high in the mix, Visconti doubled Bowie's vocal hook and recruited his wife Siegrid to sweeten Bowie's harmonies (much as how Ray Davies' wife Rasa was the Kinks' secret weapon, the haunting high end of the three-part harmonies enchanting songs like "Waterloo Sunset").

A rake's proposal in the line of Andrew Marvell or Rod Stewart, "Let Me Sleep Beside You" pitched seduction as a happy means of liberation, Bowie promising that through his efforts she'll enter the circle of womanhood ("wear the dress your mother wore"). In verses he was calm and measured in his phrasing, appraising each syllable ("I will hold a light-ed lamp"), while in the bridge, where he's trying to close the sale, he was double-tracked and sang up an octave. It was the startling, glorious appearance of the high, imperious tone Bowie would use in the Seventies: for a moment, his future winked into view. (A version recorded for Radio One in 1969 was a change of tactics, the song revised into a "build"—the verses were Bowie on a ragged acoustic embellished by Wah-Wahed guitar, while he sang refrains in a raging, strained voice, having dispensed with the cool of the studio take. Mick Wayne's lead guitar, a one-man cello section, led out the song). Openly calculated, the song's real seduction was to convince a listener that a man who'd sung "Come and Buy My Toys" a few months earlier had gone full-out Casanova.

All for naught, as Deram rejected "Let Me Sleep Beside You" for being too risqué, shelving the track until including it on a post-"Space Oddity" cash-in album of Bowie singles and outtakes. Bowie remade the song for *Toy* in 2000. Like much of that record, it was sumptuously performed but rather airless, with multiple-tracked guitars and keyboards in lieu of strings and a hushed Bowie who seemed to be edging towards sleep until roaring awake in the bridge.

Karma Man

Recorded: *1 September 1967, Advision. Bowie: lead vocal; McLaughlin: lead guitar; Sullivan: acoustic guitar; Visconti: bass; White: drums; Siegrid Visconti: backing vocal; unknown musicians: celli. Produced: Visconti; engineered: Chevin;* ***(remake, unreleased)*** *(basic tracks) July 2000, Sear Sound, (overdubs) October 2000, Looking Glass. Bowie: lead vocal; Slick: lead guitar; Leonard: rhythm guitar; Plati: rhythm guitar; Garson: keyboards; Dorsey: bass, vocals; Campbell: drums; Palmer, Gryner: backing vocals; unknown musicians: violins, violas, celli? (arranged: Visconti?). Produced: Bowie, Plati; engineered: Keppler.*

First release: *6 March 1970,* ***World of David Bowie****.* ***Broadcast****: 13 May 1968, Top Gear; 5 February 1970, The Sunday Show.*

All at once, or so it seemed, the British pop aristocracy turned to "Eastern" religion. Pete Townshend found Meher Baba, Dave Davies was reading Vivekananda's *Rajah Yoga*, Donovan and the Beatles discovered the Maharishi Mahesh Yogi's Spiritual Regeneration Movement, an offshoot of Hinduism based on the concept of transcendental meditation.

The mystery is dispelled if you consider that many of these people had taken LSD for years (Tony Visconti and his wife Siegrid tripped once a week for a year, for instance, and Visconti became an ardent Tibetan Buddhist). Eastern teachings resounded with those trying to make sense of a world in which "all limits had been magically removed." In Britain, where Christian observance was in near-collapse among the young, watery varietals of Buddhism and Hinduism sold by celebrity gurus were alluring. Buddhism in particular had no edict-heavy god and its spiritual leaders were best known for protesting war and wearing colorful outfits. Seemingly devoted to the "now," it was misinterpreted as a Pop religion. "I only dig now and I don't know why," as Bowie sang in "Karma Man."

So for weekend Buddhists, Tibet was an Atlantis up in the mountains, a Shangri-La in which everyone was holy and wasn't hung up on material things. The nuanced Tibetan portrait of Heinrich Harrer (see "Silly Boy Blue") gave way to the likes of the 1968 ITC drama *The Champions*, in which secret agents who crash their plane in Tibet are healed and given superpowers by lamas. Yet the fevered political atmosphere of 1968 meant that identifying as a Tibetan Buddhist (and so by default protesting China's occupation) could earn flak from Maoist radicals. Even the apolitical Bowie was heckled by an American Maoist during his pro-Tibet mime performance *Jet-Sun and the Eagle*.

"Karma Man" was Bowie's tribute to monks in exile like Chime Rinpoche. Its title character prays in a carnival tent as one of the exhibits: a metaphor for the lama in the West, a "freak" living ascetically in the world of ice cream cones and sideshow stalls. There was an obvious homage to Ray Bradbury's tattooed *Illustrated Man* ("fairytale skin depicting scenes from human zoos"), the lama as living storybook.

The song was far more fantastic in tone than "Silly Boy Blue," which had the measured tone of a *National Geographic* article by comparison. Bowie had taken to describing Buddhist monks as super-human figures, claiming to the *Melody Maker* that monks could go days without eating, spend months living underground and could live for centuries (there's a trace of this in the later

"Sons of the Silent Age": "they don't die, they just go to sleep one day.") It suggested that Bowie was up on one of the counterculture's heroes, Marvel Comics' *Doctor Strange*. Recall the origin of Doctor Strange: an arrogant alcoholic surgeon stripped of his license (a fine example of the alienated Man of the West—the doctor who kills) who's reborn as a chela to the Ancient One and "spends his days sitting lotus fashion within his tastefully decorated Greenwich Village *pied-à-terre* and tuning into the brainwaves reaching him from across the universe." *Doctor Strange* was full of astral projections, trips to psychedelic bardos and battles with vast dark occult powers like the Dread Dormammu. The comic shed as much light on Bowie's occult beliefs here as his name-dropping of Aleister Crowley would for future songs (see "Holy Holy," "Quicksand").

"Karma Man" itself was a fragile beauty of a construction, its tiptoeing, syllable-stuffed D major verses (the West) calmed by the richly-harmonized B major refrains, whose melody moved up and down in sharps ("slow down, slow down," F#-D#-C#-B, or "Karma Man," B-D#-F#), perhaps Bowie's approximation of "Eastern" music. The song was let down by its recording, the result of a rushed B-side session cut on the same day as "Let Me Sleep Beside You," with obtrusive drumming and a tentative Bowie. Far better was the Visconti-arranged version for the BBC's *Top Gear* in May 1968, so magisterial a performance that it should be considered the song's proper recording.

C'est la Vie

Recorded: *(demo, unreleased) ca. September 1967, Essex Music. Bowie: lead and harmony vocals, acoustic guitar, tambourine, bass?.*

Bowie wrote "C'est la Vie" in summer 1967 and Kenneth Pitt sent demos that October to song publishers and the American singer Chris Montez, to no response. The elaborate tape, which had eight instrumental and vocal versions of the song, with multiple vocal overdubs and prominent clunky bass (apparently

Bowie), suggested Pitt thought "C'est la Vie" one of Bowie's more commercially promising efforts. Considered for Bowie's second Deram album but never taken beyond the demo stage, "C'est la Vie" had a warm melody to suit its lyric's homebody sentiments. Bowie's content to watch the world pass by his window, hoping that time will pass him by in turn. It's a lassitude found in a contemporary interview he gave to *Chelsea News* ("David is contented with contentment: he is a happy loving person with a gentle nature"). He later reworked one line for "An Occasional Dream" ("burns my wall with time") and recycled some of its top melody for "Shadow Man."

Even a Fool Learns to Love

(François/Thibault/Revaux/Bowie). ***Recorded****: (demo, unreleased) 7 or 8 February 1968, 39 Manchester Street, London. Bowie: vocal.*

Geoffrey Heath, a music publisher sharing an office with Bowie's publisher David Platz, returned from Paris in early 1968 with an acetate of the French singer Claude François' "Comme d'Habitude." Heath had a short-term option on the song's British rights, so he needed an English lyric on the double. After some prospects didn't pan out, Heath asked Platz for recommendations and the latter suggested Bowie, who'd done some translations for him (see "Pancho"). Bowie was allegedly "enchanted" with the melody of François' song, which Pitt saw as a way to get his client out of purgatory. Considering Bowie a stronger lyricist than composer, Pitt believed if Bowie wrote "to a strong melody composed by someone else," the result would surely win approval from Deram and could even be a hit at last.

"Comme d'Habitude" was a man finding that his lover only responds to him out of habit, "as usual," and he coolly wonders if the affair's dead. Bowie's translation, clunk-titled "Even a Fool Learns to Love," was full of self-pity and sad clowns, reflecting his recent work in the mime play *Pierrot in Turquoise* (see "The Mask") and a call back to "When I Live My Dream." The play of the "clown and the angel" here also suggested his growing infatuation with the dancer Hermione Farthingale. The song's French publishers rejected Bowie, though more for his obscurity than the sins of his lyric. Soon afterward, Paul Anka heard "Comme d'Habitude" on French television and wrote a lyric for it. Like Bowie's translation, Anka's "My Way" had nothing of the stoicism of François' original; it became the boast of Frank Sinatra's waning years. A piqued Bowie took revenge by grinding up the bones of "Comme d'Habitude" into his "Life On Mars?"

In the Heat of the Morning

***Recorded**: (basic tracks) 12 March 1968 (overdubs, vocals) 29 March, 10, 18 April 1968, Decca Studios. Bowie: lead vocal; Mick Wayne: lead guitar; Visconti: bass; White: drums; unknown musicians: organ, strings. Arranged, produced: Visconti; engineered: Dudgeon; **(remake, unreleased)** (basic tracks) July 2000, Sear Sound, (overdubs) October 2000, Looking Glass. Bowie: lead vocal; Slick: lead guitar; Leonard: rhythm guitar; Garson: keyboards; Dorsey: bass, vocals; Plati: guitar; Campbell: drums; Palmer, Gryner: backing vocals; unknown musicians: violins, violas, celli (arranged: Visconti). Produced: Bowie, Plati; engineered: Keppler.*

***First release:** 6 March 1970, **World of David Bowie**. **Broadcast**: 18 December 1967, Top Gear; 13 May 1968, Top Gear.*

By early 1968, with two of his singles rejected, Bowie's relationship with Deram was precarious. A visit to Selfridges revealed how little the label thought of him: his name wasn't in any promotional materials, his album wasn't available for sale and a clerk couldn't find him listed in the Deram catalog. He was gone from Deram before he'd left it.

He'd assumed he'd make a second album in 1968, to be produced by Tony Visconti. But Visconti, increasingly consumed with Marc Bolan's Tyrannosaurus Rex, wouldn't commit to a recording session date. Deram shared this lack of urgency, suggesting Bowie's record was essentially considered a vanity project. Certainly, had songs like "C'est la Vie" been covered successfully by other musicians, it would have been a far different story. His album may have been something like Laura Nyro's *More Than a New Discovery* or Joni Mitchell's *Ladies of the Canyon*: a songwriter's record of "original" versions of hits. But his songs were only a set of discarded demos. Had an album of them appeared in summer 1968, it would have sold little better than his debut.

The proposed album centerpiece was "In the Heat of the Morning," also intended as Bowie's spring 1968 single. This was Bowie out-Deraming Deram: a piece of florid pop with an organ solo, *tremolando* strings and a lyric full of soldiers catching butterflies, ragged boys racing the wind and senoritas swaying. Despite asking for multiple retakes, the label rejected the single in April and a disgusted Pitt asked Decca's Hugh Mendl to release Bowie from his contract. Bowie had little prospect of getting another record deal. After years of making snap recoveries from commercial disasters, he'd run out of indulgences.

As ambitious as it was slight, "In the Heat of the Morning" suffered from awkward shifts between its stem-winding, octave-spanning C major verses and its assured A minor refrains: take the two bars of wayward humming used as a stalling tactic until the next verse shows up. Despite slaving over his vocal in multiple overdub sessions, Bowie's performance went astray in its more ambitious moments (see the wincing high G on "IIII-love you" at 1:39). No mind: when compared to the forced cheer of "Love You Till Tuesday," "In the Heat of the Morning" at least had some kick, feasting on a fused Hammond organ/guitar hook while Visconti's strings gave it a sensuality its ornamental lyric lacked. The single's rejection was due far more to Deram, in internal disarray, writing off Bowie as a prospect who hadn't panned out and wanting rid of him. "In the Heat of the Morning" was leagues above actually-released 1968 Deram singles like

Whistling Jack Smith's "Only When I Larf" and the London Balalaika Ensemble's "Kalinka." Bowie's remake of the song for *Toy* in 2000 was the labored resurrection of a butterfly.

London Bye Ta-Ta

Recorded: *12, 29 March, 10, 18 April 1968, Decca Studios. Bowie: lead vocal, handclaps; Wayne: lead guitar; Visconti: bass; White: drums, guiro?; unknown musicians: piano, violins, violas, celli. Arranged, produced: Visconti; engineered: Dudgeon;* ***(remake)*** *7,13,15 January 1970, Trident Studios. Bowie: lead vocal, 12-string acoustic guitar; Marc Bolan: lead guitar; Rick Wakeman: piano; Visconti: bass; Godfrey McLean: drums, congas, tambourine; Lesley Duncan, Sue Glover, Heather Wheatman: backing vocals; unknown musicians: strings. Produced: Visconti.*

First release: *(original, alt. take) 25 January 2010,* ***David Bowie*** *(deluxe, Deram 531 792-5); (remake) 19 September 1989,* **Sound + Vision** *(Ryko RCD 2120).* ***Broadcast****: 13 May 1968, Top Gear; 29 January 1970, Cairngorm Ski Night; 5 February 1970, The Sunday Show.* ***Live****: 1970.*

In Victoria Station Bowie overheard a West Indian family calling "London bye ta-ta!" to relatives boarding a train; it titled his song of immigrant London. By the end of the Sixties, London had a growing population of West Indians, Africans and Pakistanis, which bred a fresh strain of reactionary. MP Enoch Powell gave his "rivers of blood" speech, a doom-laden anti-immigration jeremiad ("we must be mad, literally mad, as a nation to be permitting the annual inflow of some 50,000 dependants...It is like watching a nation busily engaged in heaping up its funeral pyre"), days after Bowie finished recording the song.

Blessed with one of his prettiest melodies of the era, "London Bye Ta-Ta" was the latest variation of his provincials-in-London theme ("Can't Help Thinking About Me," "I Dig Everything," "The London Boys") but there was a welcome broadening of perspective. Two young bohemians meet and flirt but they're only ripples in a broadening sea. Everyone's coming to London looking for a new name, face or life, and the city, seemingly overnight, is young and strange again: "The poet in the clothes shop sold me curry for a pound."

Summoned out of little games on acoustic guitar (see the spins off D major in the intro), "London Bye Ta-Ta" developed just as simply, keeping between its D major home chord and its flatted VII chord, C major, until the bridge (where a G chord took its turn playing off D) and a break where the dominant A chord arrived to cook the song to a mid-way peak. Bowie tore through the whole sequence again, like a kid replaying a winning game, but revealed a sad ending to his tale: the two kids quarrel and go broke, the girl whimpers in the mornings when she comes off her high. "I loved her! I loved her!" Bowie pleads but he's out the door all the same.

A curiously ill-fated song, "London Bye Ta-Ta" was cut in the same sessions as "In the Heat of the Morning" and intended as the latter's B-side but its master tape went missing after Deram rejected the single (acetates survived of the master and an alternate take has recently surfaced). It remained a favorite of Kenneth Pitt, who advocated for it as Bowie's follow-up single to "Space Oddity." In January 1970, Bowie re-cut the song with Marc Bolan on lead guitar and a trio of backing singers. Whether the remake's refined bubblegum sound would have hit with audiences is an intriguing but moot question, as Bowie released "The Prettiest Star" instead and shelved "London Bye Ta-Ta" for two decades.

When I'm Five

Recorded**: (demo 1, unreleased)** *ca. January-February 1968, Essex Music? Bowie: lead vocal, 12-string acoustic guitar, bass?;* ***(Top Gear session)*** *Picadilly Studio 1, 201 Picadilly, London. Bowie: lead vocal; McLaughlin: lead guitar; Alan Hawkshaw: organ; Herbie Flowers: bass; Barry Morgan: drums; Visconti, Steve "Peregrin" Took: backing vocals;*

unknown musicians: strings. Produced: Bernie Andrews; engineered: Pete Ritzema, Alan Harris; ***(demo 2, unreleased)*** *mid-April 1969, 24 Foxgrove Rd., Beckenham. Bowie: lead vocal, 12-string acoustic guitar; John Hutchinson: acoustic guitar.*

First release*: (Top Gear) 13 May 1984,* ***Love You Till Tuesday****.* ***Broadcast****: 13 May 1968, Top Gear.* ***Live****: 1968-1969.*

"When I'm Five" is a sung by a child who wants to be a child, a *true* child, a child of five or seven, one who has the business of childhood sorted out. Age gives childhood hierarchies; each year has its own weight. To a four-year-old, a seven-year-old (the year of permanent teeth) is an aspiration, a 10-year-old is a high master, those over 13 cruel fledgling adults.

A thematic sequel to "There Is a Happy Land" (Bowie also recycles its bridge and possibly one of its characters, "Raymond"), "When I'm Five" kept to the confines of a child's mind. It was the culmination of his songs of the past two years, with a vocal astonishing in its weirdness. Bowie sounded like a child piped through a man. Among his eeriest Sixties compositions, "When I'm Five" cleared the path for "Space Oddity," as Major Tom in his isolation was just the same child grown larger.

One of the more autobiographical Bowie lyrics, with references to headaches (which a stressed Bowie endured in 1968-1969), "my Grandfather Jones" and a mother who keeps her secrets tucked away in a drawer, its language was precise enough to avoid any adult condescension. The adult world is one of pleasures arbitrarily denied to children (spitting, laughing in church) while the last verse's prayer to Jesus, a potentially disastrous move, was rescued by its dry humor: the child has seen a "photograph" of Jesus but he might well have seen a photo of a hippie in a newspaper. Intended for Bowie's second Deram album, "When I'm Five" instead wound up with the Beatstalkers, whose bewildered-sounding cover was released in early 1969.

Social Kind of Girl

***Recorded**: (demo, unreleased) ca. June 1968, Essex Music. Bowie: lead vocal, acoustic guitar, stomps, handclaps.*

"Social Kind of Girl," a rewrite of a 1967 composition "A Summer Kind of Love," was a throwback to the likes of "Baby Loves That Way," Bowie obsessing about a "fast" girl who barely knows that he exists. (A possible influence was the Monkees' "She Hangs Out.") The revision darkened but didn't improve the song: "Social Kind of Girl" lacked grace, hooks and, unsurprisingly, interpreters.

Ching-a-Ling

***Recorded**: **(demo, unreleased)** ca. early October 1968, 22 Clareville Grove, South Kensington? Bowie: lead and backing vocal, 12-string acoustic guitar; Tony Hill: lead and backing vocal, acoustic guitar; Hermione Farthingale: lead and backing vocal; **(proposed single)** 24 October (backing tracks, vocals), 27 November 1968 (vocal overdubs), Trident. Bowie: lead and backing vocal, 12-string acoustic guitar, handclaps; John Hutchinson: lead and backing vocal, handclaps?; Farthingale: lead and backing vocal, handclaps; Hill: acoustic guitar, backing vocals; unknown musicians: bass, drums, chimes. Producer: Visconti; **(demo 2, unreleased)** mid-April 1969, 24 Foxgrove Road, Beckenham. Bowie: lead vocal, 12-string acoustic guitar; Hutchinson: lead vocal, acoustic guitar.*

***First release:** 13 May 1984, **Love You Till Tuesday**. **Live**: 1968-1969.*

Having put it off as long as possible, Bowie became a hippie in the summer of 1968. He sat around his manager's apartment naked, tried to mentally contact extraterrestrials during weekly meetings with fellow enthusiasts, cooked macrobiotic meals and formed a folk music trio. By August, he was living at 22 Clareville Grove in South Kensington with his first serious girlfriend, the dancer Hermione Farthingale. They spent much of their time with other couples living nearby, Marc Bolan and his future wife

June Child, Tony Visconti and his girlfriend Liz Hartley. Bowie read constantly, from Brendan Behan to ee cummings to Jean Paul Sartre, and friends would drop by in the evenings to play music. It was a world of genteel bohemianism whose collapse, on various fronts, would inspire the morose *Space Oddity* album in 1969.

The folk trio was Turquoise, soon rechristened Feathers. Bowie founded it with Farthingale, who was a passable singer and guitarist, and the guitarist Tony Hill, who left for more promising opportunities after a few gigs. Soon afterward Bowie reconnected with John "Hutch" Hutchinson, former lead guitarist of the Buzz, who was back from his native Canada with his head full of the new Canadian folk music: Gordon Lightfoot, Joni Mitchell, Leonard Cohen. Visiting Clareville Grove, he was surprised to find the former Mod "into softer things…he didn't need a band to pump it out anymore." And Bowie found in Hutchinson a gentle new influence to absorb.

So in the fall of 1968, following the trade routes of hippie groups past and future, Feathers played a meager circuit of university halls and coffeehouses. It was a passive rebellion on Bowie's part. His manager, desperate and under pressure by Bowie's frustrated father (and financial backer) to find paying gigs, had pushed Bowie to develop a cabaret act and landed him a spot in an ice cream television commercial. While Bowie later described Feathers as a device to spend time with his girlfriend, the group also reflected his estrangement from popular music. He wasn't getting paid anyhow, so why not form a "non-commercial" band? Feathers devised inter-media sets: recited verse from Liverpool poets like Roger McGough (see "Five Years"), recent Bowie compositions like "When I'm Five" and some Jacques Brel and Leonard Cohen covers, interspersed with mime routines set to pre-recorded tapes. "Ghastly," the mime Lindsay Kemp recalled.

The only recording Turquoise made was "Ching-a-Ling," aka

"the Ching-a-Ling Song," which Tony Visconti produced at Trident Studios in late October. Hill's departure required the now-Feathers to re-cut vocals a month later, when Visconti, struggling to replace Hill in the harmonies, angered Hutchinson by pushing him to sing above his comfortable vocal range (a frustrated Visconti eventually mixed in Hill's original vocals).

Its vocal melody inspired by Bowie running an old demo tape backwards on a reel-to-reel player (he'd recycle its bridge in "Saviour Machine"), "Ching-a-Ling" had a sickly charm. Its lyric was a muddle, opening (Bowie's verse) as a "Laughing Gnome" sequel where a little man wants to "blow the doo-dah horn," moving to a Farthingale-sung verse of Tyrannosaurus Rex-style hippie blather and closing with a Hutchinson-sung verse that odes Bowie's current domestic contentment. This was Bowie with all edges smoothed, content and left wide open to the world: it was exactly the sort of thing Kenneth Pitt feared would happen if Bowie indulged his "underground" fantasies too strongly. A song completely of its time, "Ching-a-Ling" floated along like a soap bubble. It was the most depressing thing he recorded in the entire decade.

The Mask

Recorded: *29 January 1969, Trident. Bowie: narrative vocal, sound effects. Produced: Weston.*

First release: *13 May 1984,* ***Love You Till Tuesday***. ***Live***: *1968-1969.*

At the ebb of the Sixties, David Bowie became a semi-professional mime. Another record label was rid of him; everything he'd ever released had failed. Along with the very occasional Feathers gig, he now did the very occasional mime show, whether in stage productions or opening for his friend Marc Bolan's Tyrannosaurus Rex.

What he found in mime was what he'd seen "in such a simple family game as charades, [where] you see these incredible manifestations of personality come out of Uncle Bill or whoever, when he's describing something in mime. That device allows you in an exaggerated form to display who you are." Mime would be as essential to his development as jazz, Buddhism and Lou Reed. It was a foundation of his work. Ziggy Stardust, Halloween Jack, the Thin White Duke, the wan extraterrestrial of the "Berlin" trilogy: all were Bowie's mimetic interpretations of rock stars.

He'd followed the same line as most Sixties British rock singers. He'd left school, played in beat groups, got a manager, cut singles, toured, made a moderately psychedelic LP. So far he'd been basically Steve Marriott without the voice. His mime years altered this pattern, warped his aesthetic. The critique of Bowie being a plastic rocker, a chameleon imitator, starts here. Was Bowie really just a mime who played a rock musician? But when a mime can rock as well as a "real" rock & roll singer, what does it say about the latter?

It began in the summer of 1967 when Bowie met the performer Lindsay Kemp, who'd developed an anarchic form of mime incorporating drag, silent film, absurdist theatre and pop music. Sent a copy of Bowie's debut album by Kenneth Pitt's secretary, Kemp began playing "When I Live My Dream" during shows. As Kemp was apparently the only man in England playing his album, a flattered Bowie soon became part of his circle. By the fall he was taking dance lessons fromKemp, who pushed him to simplify his stage movements, to "exteriorize."

Bowie was taken with Kemp's demimonde of actors, painters, junkies and prostitutes. He was fascinated by Kemp's outrageous persona, his open homosexuality and nocturnal existence, abetted by a flat whose walls were painted black and whose shades were always drawn. "It was everything I thought Bohemia probably was....I joined the circus," Bowie said. He found in Kemp a classroom that led him to composers like John Cage, writers like Jean Cocteau and Jean Genet and German electronic music.

Kemp asked Bowie to perform in a production he was mounting, *Pierrot in Turquoise* (Bowie had suggested "turquoise," the Buddhist symbol for eternity). *Pierrot* featured the standard *commedia del'arte* figures Pierrot, the sad cuckold (Kemp), and Harlequin (the near-blind, massive Jack Birkett), with Bowie as a "protean" narrator named Cloud. The play's short-lived production was a traveling soap opera, with Bowie carrying on simultaneous affairs with Kemp and the troupe's costume designer Natasha Korniloff. Upon discovering the betrayal, Kemp superficially slashed his wrists, which gave an added zing to his performance that night in his blood-stained Pierrot costume.

After *Turquoise,* Bowie danced in a Kemp-choreographed performance of Pushkin's *The Pistol Shot* and by summer 1968 he was performing his own Tibetan Buddhist-inspired mime *Jet-Sun and the Eagle,* backed by "Silly Boy Blue" and some sound effects tapes. His mime never progressed beyond what one spectator, the journalist Geoff Ward, called "conventional sub-Marcel Marceau work: 'Help! I'm trapped in an invisible telephone kiosk with existential overtones.'" Bowie admitted it: "my technique was quite poor, actually, but nobody really knew," he said in 1976. Yet what he'd picked up from his days with Kemp—improved body movement, projection, costuming, stage language, set construction, continuing a performance "off stage"—would be invaluable for what he'd attempt in a few years.

By the time of his Feathers shows in late 1968, Bowie had written a new mime piece called "The Mask," premiering it at 17 November performance at the Country Club in Hampstead.In the vein of Rainer Maria Rilke's *The Notebooks of Malte Laurids Brigge,* the piece began with Bowie finding a mask in a junk shop and donning it to entertain his parents and friends. Soon enough he's winning audiences, getting everything Pitt had wanted for him: "television, films, the lot!" At the height of his triumph, headlining the London Palladium, he finds that he can't remove the mask and his public face smothers him. "Strangled on stage!" Bowie intoned as narrator. It was close to the same fate he'd give Ziggy Stardust.

He shot a performance of "The Mask" for same promo film for which he wrote "Space Oddity." The clips viewed back-to-back are a flip-book take of his Seventies: the spaceman and the mime. In the five minutes of "The Mask," Bowie went through the paces of a future he'd soon commit to living out.

Chapter 3

The Free States' Refrain (1969)

The humanity of the astronaut is a liability, a weakness, irrelevant to his mission. An astronaut, he is not a being: he is an act. It is the act that counts.
Ursula Le Guin, "Science Fiction and Mrs. Brown."

The only truly alien planet is Earth.
J.G. Ballard.

Freaking out and drug culture, anarchist notions of spontaneous freedom, anarchist political action: it all failed. It was defeated. A generation dreaming of a beautiful utopia was kicked—kicked awake and not dead.
Howard Brenton.

Once during the mission I was asked by ground control what I could see. "What do I see?" I replied. "Half a world to the left, half a world to the right, I can see it all. The Earth is so small."
Vitali Sevastyanov, cosmonaut, Soyuz 9, 18.

Their obvious pleasure was to be alone in the sky.
Norman Mailer, on the Apollo astronauts.

Space Oddity

***Recorded**: **(demo 1)** ca. late January 1969, 39 Manchester Street, London? David Bowie: lead vocal, Stylophone; John Hutchinson: lead and harmony vocals, acoustic guitar; **(first studio take)** 2 February 1969, Morgan Studios, 169 High Road, Willesden. Bowie: lead and harmony vocals, 12-string acoustic guitar, ocarina, Stylophone; Hutchinson: acoustic guitar, lead and harmony vocals; Colin Wood:*

Hammond organ, Mellotron; Dave Clague: bass; Tat Meager: drums. Produced: Jonathan Weston; ***(demo 2)*** *ca. mid-April 1969, 24 Foxgrove Road, Beckenham. Bowie: lead and harmony vocal, Stylophone; Hutchinson: lead and harmony vocal, acoustic guitar, electric guitar;* ***(single)*** *20, ca. 23 June 1969, Trident Studios, London. Bowie: lead and harmony vocals, Stylophone, 12-string acoustic guitar, handclaps; Mick Wayne: lead guitar; Rick Wakeman: Mellotron; Herbie Flowers, bass; Terry Cox: drums; unknown musicians: 8 violins, 2 violas, 2 celli, 2 arco basses, 2 flutes. Produced: Gus Dudgeon; engineered: Barry Sheffield; arranged: Bowie, Paul Buckmaster;* ***(Italian version, "Ragazzo Solo, Ragazza Sola")*** *20 December 1969, Morgan Studios. Bowie: lead vocal (Mogol, trans.);* ***(remake)*** *ca. early September 1979, Good Earth Studios, 59 Dean Street, Soho, London. Bowie: lead vocal, 12-string acoustic guitar; Andy Clark: piano; Zaine Griff: bass; Andy Duncan: drums. Produced: Bowie, Tony Visconti.*

First release*: (single) 11 July 1969 (Philips BF 1801, #5 UK); ("Ragazzo Solo") ca. February 1970 (Philips 704 208 BW);(remake) 15 February 1980 (RCA BOW 5); (first studio) 13 May 1984,* ***Love You Till Tuesday****; (demo 2) 19 September 1989,* ***Sound + Vision****; (demo 1) 12 October 2009,* ***Space Oddity*** *(reissue, DBSOCD 40).* ***Broadcast****: 25 August 1969, Doebidoe; 2 October 1969, Top of the Pops; 29 October 1969, Musik Für Junge Leute; 3 November 1969, Hits a Go Go; 5 December 1969, Like Now; 10 May 1970, The Ivor Novello Awards; 22 May 1972, Johnnie Walker Lunchtime Show; 20 October 1973, The 1980 Floor Show; 18 September 1979, Kenny Everett's Video Show.* ***Live****: 1969-1974, 1983, 1990, 1997, 2002.*

So, the beginning: Bowie's first single for Philips/Mercury, his first British Top 5 hit, his first American Top 20 hit and, years later, his first British #1. "Space Oddity" leads off the album it later titled; it leads off Bowie compilations and retrospectives. When he dies, the television tributes will lead off with it.

An odd beginning, though. Its status as the first "classic" Bowie song came circuitously. A novelty single with a sell-by date (the July 1969 moon landing), "Space Oddity" didn't chart until months after the moonshot and its highest chartings were in the mid-Seventies. Some in the Bowie camp thought it a mistake—his friend Tony Visconti refused to produce the single, considering it cheap, a sell-out publicity stunt ("it's not a David Bowie record, it's 'Ernie the Milkman'"). He was right. In hock to the Bee Gees' death bubblegum "New York Mining Disaster 1941" and similar in tone to Zager and Evans' "In the Year 2525," "Space Oddity" is a gimmicky folk song in extravagant garb.

3

In December 1968 Bowie's manager Kenneth Pitt funded *Love You Till Tuesday*, a collection of promotional videos. He hoped to revive a moribund career, with *LYTT* serving as Bowie's visual resume for film and television producers. While there'd be promos shot for *David Bowie* tracks, Deram outtakes, a mime piece and a Feathers song, the film lacked anything fresh, so Pitt asked Bowie to come up with "another strong song." He retreated to his room at Clareville Grove.

Stanley Kubrick's *2001: A Space Odyssey* had opened in London in May 1968 and played for months to the young and the altered. In a typical *2001* screening, Visconti, high from drinking cannabis tea, had to talk down a tripping couple terrified by the film's climactic "Stargate" sequence. Bowie saw *2001* ("out of my gourd...very stoned") several times and was taken by Kubrick's shots: a star-child looming above the Earth; the dead astronaut Frank Poole floating off into space; an astronaut having a stilted one-way conversation with his parents via video-phone.

Like *2001*, much SF of the time suggested humanity's venture into space would drive it mad or transfigure it. Ray Bradbury's "No Particular Night or Morning" had a deranged astronaut hurling himself into the void. In Gordon Walter's "No Guarantee," an astronaut violently hallucinated while talking to Ground Control. An astronaut in Terry Pratchett's "The Night

Dweller" realized "we were in a void with nothing below us...it was cold and empty and hostile."

Clashing against this doom-backdrop were the American astronauts, genial ex-athletes equipped with beautiful wives and sets of healthy children. "NASA was vending space," wrote Norman Mailer, interviewing the Apollo 11 crew before the moonshot. Neil Armstrong, the first man on the moon, was "a salesman with a clear mild modest soft sell." Yet there was something uncanny in the Apollo astronauts as well, something beyond the jokes about astronaut food and golf and the hundreds of tedious tasks they performed, as if they were celestial mechanics. For Mailer, an astronaut like Armstrong had "something close to schizophrenia in his lack of reaction to the dangers about him." The astronauts had an easy familiarity with death; they were salesmen over an abyss. Major Tom's disaster (is it a disaster at all?) voiced the collective dread that the moon landing would go horribly wrong, and on live TV. (The BBC didn't play "Space Oddity" before the landing: a song in which an astronaut doesn't return seemed in questionable taste.)

And the man back on earth, playing his 12-string Hagström acoustic in his room, was nowhere. After four years in pop music, Bowie had no record contract and just a handful of folk and mime gigs. He considered abandoning pop music for mime, musical theatre (he unsuccessfully auditioned for *Hair*), film parts, modeling, Buddhism, anything. Though his most lucrative job of the period was a bit part in a TV spot for Luv Ice Cream, his manager kept telling him work would turn up. So Major Tom is sent into orbit by Establishment figures who monitor him, give him stage directions and need him to do his share of media promotion. The song ends with Major Tom ignoring cues and walking off stage. Bowie was also writing as the first serious relationship of his life crumbled, cutting a studio take of "Space Oddity" the day after his break with Hermione Farthingale. There was a numbness in the song, a longing to sever ties and drift into the void.

Yet though all of this was swirling in the song—a technocrat American astronaut cracking up like he was in a Kurt Vonnegut novel, a failed pop singer writing a letter to his girlfriend out in space—there were pantomime qualities as well. Buried within "Space Oddity" were favorite tunes of his boyhood: Frank Loesser's "Inchworm" (whose semi-tonal melody is in the Stylophone) and "Over the Rainbow." There was the schlocky hand-wringing "she KNOWS!" from Ground Control when Major Tom tells his wife he loves her. Goofy bits like the cod-Italian pronunciation of "most-a pe-cuiliah way." And "Space Oddity" was another child's song (see Ch. 2). Two kids could perform it on walkie-talkies. Bowie used the simplest of rhymes ("can you ***hear***" jump-cuts to "***here*** am I floating...") and favored the kid's word over the bureaucrat's: "spaceship" instead of "rocket," "countdown" instead of "ignition sequence." Even "Major Tom" was an action hero's name, another Dan Dare. The Apollo 11 astronauts called their capsule "the cathedral." But it was just a tin can here: you could see the wires it hung from.

2

He'd never written anything on such a scale before. In a touch over five minutes, there was a faded-in intro, a 12-bar solo verse, a "liftoff" sequence, a duet verse, a bridge, a two-bar acoustic guitar break, a six-bar guitar solo, a third verse, another run of bridge, break and solo and a "Day in the Life"-style outro to the fade.

In 2002, Bowie said he'd been "keen on...writing in such a way that it would lead me into leading some kind of rock musical...[that's] probably what I really wanted to do in the late Sixties. I think I wanted to write a new kind of musical, and that's how I saw my future at the time." He storyboarded the song, each section setting up the next. The spoken "countdown" backing vocal built suspense in the latter half of the opening verse, leading to a D major chord ("God's love be with yoooou") aching to be resolved by the "liftoff" sequence. The acoustic guitar breaks (C-F-G-***A***-***A***, Bowie slamming the last two chords) were stage-clearing.

The chord sequence was the fruit of a year's dabbling in folk music, with John Hutchinson, over a few nights at Clareville Grove, translating Bowie's odder ideas into fret shapes. Having established a base chord sequence on his Stylophone (see below), Bowie fingered through progressions on his 12-string, following the internal "voices" of his guitar—playing chord changes that sounded right to his ear and that were achieved with fleet, easy movements, like converting a F major barre chord ("and I'm") into F minor ("floating in a") by lifting a finger. Later compositions like "Quicksand" shared this tactile sense of movement.

The chord pairings of the intro (a slow dance of Fmaj7/E and E minor) and the first verse's alternating C majors and E minors, presented a division to be exploited. Mick Wayne sounds two guitar harmonics (E and B) while Bowie's Stylophone drones two whole notes a half-step apart (C and B). Before the first verse starts, Major Tom is already high in space, Ground Control far below him.

The song was full of these sort of resonances, its harmonic language telling part of the story. Take the E7 chord that appears in the second verse ("really made the grade") to question the prospective key of C major. It was as dramatic a move harmonically as Bowie's vocal leap on the post-liftoff "this is Ground Control to Major Tom" was melodically. Shifting to E7 instead of the expected E minor brightened the song, expanded it outward. Or take the bridge's "planet earth is blue" section (B-flat major 9th/A minor add9/G major add9/F), a folk-style descending progression whose opening chord (Bbmaj9) was a distance from C major, a move ratifying Major Tom's choice (or doom) to stay out in space.

1

Bowie and Hutchinson cut "Space Oddity" for *Love You Till Tuesday* on 2 February 1969, recording the track the day before its promo film was shot (it's far inferior to the subsequent single, particularly its leaden drumming and a wheezing ocarina solo). Hutchinson, having left Bowie in the spring, was a ghost in the single recording, his absence heightening its feeling of loss and dislocation. Playing "ground control," Hutchinson had been the song's only voice until midway through the second verse, when Major Tom transmits at last: Bowie soaring over a seventh for his opening phrase, a wafting-in "Garfunkel" to supplant Hutch's "Simon." (Because it's a seventh interval rather than an octave, Bowie's first phrase has a yearning, striving quality; it's a goal not quite reached.) With Hutchinson gone, Bowie now sang the opening verse in imitation of him, harmonizing with himself in octaves. (In live performances in 1972, Mick Ronson took some of the high harmonies.)

The *LYTT* "Space Oddity" had downplayed the Stylophone, which Bowie had started playing around Christmas 1968 and on which he started writing the song. A portable synthesizer with two settings, "normal" and "vibrato," the Stylophone was operated by touching a stylus to its tiny metallic keyboard. Bowie worked out a progression on it, a two-note sequence shifted up an octave for the following verse (on "papers want to know," the Stylophone moved between A-flat and G). Heard isolated in the mix, the Stylophone is a futurist police siren. In the outro, as Wayne sent guitar notes into the exosphere, Bowie frantically tapped at the little keyboard as if making a last SOS.

Making the Stylophone central to the "Space Oddity" single gave it a "futuristic" hook and added to its hokey charm. Although recorded at a top studio at a substantial budget (£493.18), there was a winning sense of amateurishness. The orchestral instruments played secondary roles: the strings' massed entrance in the liftoff sequence; the spacewalk of darting flute and moaning celli in the bridges; the bow scrapings in the outro, an apparent homage to György Ligeti's "Atmosphères," used in *2001*. Instead the two synthesizers, meek Stylophone and grand Mellotron (the latter played by Rick Wakeman and held in reserve until the first bridge), bore much of the song's dramatic weight. They were vocal chorus and organ, saxophone and string section.

Gus Dudgeon mapped out its recording like a battle plan. Unable to write music, he used colors (celli were brown) and squiggly lines to mark where he wanted instruments to come in, with Paul Buckmaster helpfully translating his scrawls into charts for the musicians. With only eight tracks at hand, Dudgeon had to be economical, leading to inspired moves like recording Wayne's Gibson ES-335 on the same track as the Stylophone, furthering the sense that the two instruments formed a spectrum: astronaut and home base. Struggling to keep his borrowed Gibson in tune, Wayne cut a take with a flat bass string, "the warped note swamped with reverb," but Dudgeon liked the sound and told him not to retune. Wayne used any trick he could muster, picking between his guitar's bridge and tailpiece, using a chrome-plated cigarette lighter as a bottleneck slide for the takeoff sequence, giving a distorted pressure-drop tag to his first solo (he sounded like a bass synthesizer), moving off his fingerboard for the outro. His two solos, for which Bowie asked him to play like Wes Montgomery ("which meant to play octaves"), were a pair of sweeping orbits, the last escaping Earth's pull.

Herbie Flowers and Terry Cox were the secret movers. Drumming for Pentangle at the time, Cox served the song well—a man with a funkier bent may have struggled with a pop tone poem. Opening with parade-ground snare tattoos, Cox soon developed a pattern to drive the track: for each bar, two sets of kick drum/closed hi-hat eighth notes punctuated by a pounded snare and crash cymbal. (He subtly shifted to ride cymbal 16ths and high toms for the bridges and solos.) Flowers' bassline was the song in miniature. A tolling root-note fixation in the opening verse warmed to a dancing movement in the second and a descending two-octave "spacewalk" to kick off the bridges. Told to ad lib for the outro, the two gave a jazz duet, Flowers playing a roaming, chromatic line that peaked on a high A, Cox hissing his ride cymbal and retorting on his toms.

Liftoff

The world, or at least one small corner of London, first heard "Space Oddity" on 5 July 1969 when it played over the PA system during the Rolling Stones' Hyde Park concert (see "Memory of a Free Festival"). While the BBC reportedly played "Space Oddity" during its moon landing coverage two weeks later (though it more favored "Also Sprach Zarathustra," the official soundtrack of space thanks to *2001*), the single barely charted upon release and sales soon tapered off despite Pitt paying a chart-rigger £140 to get the single into *Record Retailer*.

Here, it seemed, was the maddening last chapter of Bowie's career. The song that his label, manager and friends thought was finally *the one*, the song he felt forced into recording, his big sell-out record, had suffered yet another chart death, performing little better than "Liza Jane." Then he caught a break. With a dearth of new releases in September, Philips' new marketing director set his entire staff to flogging the single and "Space Oddity" rebounded, peaking at #5 in November. (It was the success Bowie might have had in 1967 if Deram had gone to the wall for "Love You Till Tuesday.") It helped that the "serious" rock acts had abandoned the singles charts, clearing room for middle-aged crooners, chancers, sex chansons, celebrity vanity records, cartoons, the occasional reggae masterpiece and a few weird one-offs. "Space Oddity" sounded like nothing else, but it sounded like 1969.

A novelty song for a dying decade, "Space Oddity" should

have faded away, but it kept being called back for encores. It was an American hit in 1973 and two years later RCA reissued it in Britain as a maxi-single. By 1975, with Major Tom no longer an ominous future but a faded keepsake, it hit #1. A breakup song, a child's song, a death song, a prison song, a showbiz song, a Bee Gees song, a first and a last song, "Space Oddity" made Bowie as much as he'd made it.

And he remade it at the end of the Seventies, debuting it on a New Year's Eve telecast, *Will Kenny Everett Ever Make It To 1980?* (he did). Bowie sheared the song down to acoustic guitar, a modest piano, bass and drums. Instead of the liftoff sequence, there were 12 seconds of silence; instead of the spiraling-outward coda, a faded-out snare. "Space Oddity" ended unresolved, the door of the capsule left open; it had suggested some kind of escape was possible, even for a corporate-sponsored "loser" like Major Tom. This violent reduction of the song closed it off: space was empty. Soon afterward Bowie decided to look up Major Tom to see what had become of him (but that's a tale for another book).

"Space Oddity" is nearly half a century old. Born mournful, it's become more so. Bowie had felt something linked the Apollo astronauts (who thought they'd be the opening act of a new age of space exploration and turned out to be one-hit-wonders), the doomed astronauts of science fiction, all of the lost boys of the imploding counterculture. The American space program began an unchecked slide into irrelevance. The year 2001 would be remembered not for Kubrick's Jupiter missions but by fanatics destroying New York skyscrapers. In 2013, when humanity had gone no further into space than it had when "Space Oddity" first charted, a version sung by the Canadian astronaut Chris Hadfield, filmed onboard the International Space Station, went viral. It was a video of a man singing in a tin can many had forgotten was still out in space; Hadfield was a project manager with a glorious view from his office windows.

Bowie once said he considered the fate of Major Tom to be the technocratic American mind coming face to face with the unknown and blanking out. His song was a moonshot-year prophecy that we would lose our nerve and sink back into the old world, that we aren't built for transcendence, that the sky is the limit. Or as Hadfield sang from space: "planet Earth is blue and there's nothing left to do."

Love Song
Life Is a Circus

(Duncan ("Love Song"); Bunn ("Life is a Circus")). ***Recorded:*** *(demos, unreleased) mid-April 1969, 24 Foxgrove Road. Bowie: lead and harmony vocals, 12-string acoustic guitar; Hutchinson: lead vocal ("Love Song"), acoustic guitar, harmony vocals.* ***Live:*** *1969.*

After he and Hermione Farthingale broke up (see "Letter to Hermione"), Bowie folded Feathers, his folk trio with her and John Hutchinson, into a double act, "Bowie & Hutch." Live, Hutchinson played the straight man to Bowie's latest stage character, a chatty, fey persona who cracked up audiences between numbers. Their repertoire was essentially that of Feathers: Bowie songs like "When I'm Five" and "Ching-a-Ling," covers like Jacques Brel's "Amsterdam" and "Au Suivant," Leonard Cohen's "Lady Midnight" and the swing-era standard "A Hundred Years From Today." Recording a 10-song demo for prospective record labels, Bowie and Hutchinson included two covers from their sets on the tape.

"Love Song" was intended to spotlight Hutchinson, who sang lead. Written by Bowie's friend Lesley Duncan, it was a dreamy piece built on finger-picked arpeggios. Elton John cut "Love Song" with her on *Tumbleweed Connection*, one of its roughly 160 covers to date. A quiet influence on Bowie's late Sixties, Duncan was a suburban hippie, living in a series of bedsits, running a UFO-watching/meditation group and serving as a creative godmother for the still-aspiring likes of Bowie. She was a storied pop industry pro, having sung backup on Dusty Springfield and Dave Clark Five records.

Bowie took "Life Is a Circus" from Djinn, a British folk quartet led by the late Roger Bunn. Bunn was a jazz fanatic, a bassist and guitarist who'd played in Hamburg when the Beatles were there and who was deep in the woodwork of Sixties London, working shows with everyone from the Animals to the Soft Machine, cutting demos at Apple Records and briefly playing lead guitar for Roxy Music. In late 1968, Bowie auditioned for Djinn and was rejected, for which Bunn later apologized. An unperturbed Bowie incorporated Bunn's "Life Is a Circus" into his live sets, and he and Hutchinson may have chosen the song for their demo to showcase their (at times shaky) harmonies, with Bowie pushing into a pinched falsetto.

With a family to support, Hutchinson couldn't survive on the occasional meagerly-attended folk gig and in late April 1969 he left for Scotland to work as a draughtsman. He'd have a brief epilogue when he became the rhythm guitarist of the last Spiders From Mars tour in 1973.

Letter to Hermione

***Recorded*: (demo, "I'm Not Quite," unreleased)** *mid-April 1969, 24 Foxgrove Road. Bowie: lead vocal, 12-string acoustic guitar; Hutchinson: acoustic guitar, harmony vocal;* **(album)** *16-17 July 1969, Trident. Bowie: lead vocal, 12-string acoustic guitar?; Keith Christmas, 12-string acoustic guitar; Tim Renwick: acoustic guitar? Produced: Visconti; engineered: Sheffield, Malcolm Toft or Ken Scott.*

First release*: 14 November 1969,* ***Space Oddity*** *(Philips SBL 7912, orig.* ***David Bowie****).* ***Live****: 1969.*

Bowie met Hermione Farthingale, born Hermione Dennis from Edenbridge, Kent, in late 1967 in one of Lindsay Kemp's dancing classes. The following summer they were living together in South Kensington; the following winter, when the two filmed *Love You Till Tuesday*, they broke up, spending their last day as a couple on a soundstage.

These facts impress the songs Bowie wrote about Farthingale (see also "An Occasional Dream") with a stamp of truth. Everyone describes "Letter to Hermione" as being authentic and plaintive, as if the song should rightly be credited to David Jones. It's understandable. Bowie is so unknowable as a person, even today, that any apparent crack in the wall is worth exploring. And his time with Farthingale was the most consuming emotional experience of his young life. The breakup left him wary of being so vulnerable again; he acted as if he was still in recovery a decade later.

To harp too much on the song's "truth," however, can blind one's appreciation of how much artifice and craft it had, how private desolation drove Bowie to create a nearly flawless object. The reality, Bowie disclosed in 2000, was that Farthingale had resumed contact around the time he wrote the song and "obviously we could have gotten back together again." This willful amnesia on his part (he didn't recall receiving her letters for nearly three decades) suggested a deliberate attempt to prolong a state of misery for the sake of a song. It worked. Nothing he'd written to this point had its grace or emotional depth.

He made the song a narrative in three verses, each verse a song in miniature with "verse," "bridge" and "refrain" sections. Bowie begins in delusion (the first verse, where he thinks "Hermione" is as broken as he is), slowly wises up (in the second verse he acknowledges "they" say she's doing fine, but he hopes she cries for him at night) and ends in wistful acceptance. She's better off with her new man and she'd only remember Bowie "just by mistake," a line emphasized by a bar of rapidly-arpeggiated guitars in 7/8 time.

There was a loving attention to detail, in the rhymes—given the conceit of the song being a letter never sent, its rhymes are informal, mainly assonant or consonant ("well/girl," "pain/same," "hide/tired")—and in phrasing. The central phrase of each verse ("what can we do," "well so do I," "just by mistake") is narrow in range, Bowie's voice only rising by a third, suggesting a helplessness, while the closing lines ("I'm not quite sure what...") broaden to the range of a fifth. It's an echo of "Space Oddity," with Bowie a Ground Control watching lost Hermione float away from him (there were some other parallels, like the E minor/C major pairing in the verses).

The track was woven by three acoustic guitars, the most predominant a 12-string (most likely Keith Christmas, who played 12-string in most of the *Space Oddity* sessions), a dry presence strumming eighth chords. Bowie had spun the song out of his 12-string guitar's shadowy tunings and echoing resonances, exploiting this array of tones further via dense augmented chords (many courtesy of Hutchinson): an opening E7sus4, a C major seventh with a G root note (on "tear my soul to ease the pain"), an F major seventh chord with an added sharp 11th. The latter was another "Space Oddity" chord made thornier, closing the song in resolute doubt.

With Hutchinson gone, the two six-string acoustic guitars, mixed left and center, had to serve as the supporting singers, answering Bowie's scatted phrases. While the right-mixed guitar paralleled the left for a time (both played natural harmonics in the refrains, tensing lines like "I can see it's not okay"), it took a divergent course once Bowie's delusions collapsed in the second verse. Soon it was playing an octave higher than the left-mixed guitar and it ended as a high counterpoint to Bowie's last, wistful scatting.

The demo, called "I'm Not Quite," had a more intimate feel, mainly owed to its dim sound quality: it sounded like a literal bedsit lament. By the time Bowie recorded "Letter To Hermione," possibly completing the track on the first day of the *Space Oddity* sessions, he'd refined away any rawness. With his measured tones fraying to a rasp by the second verse, he gave a performance of such sad perfection that it made further extensions on this "confessional" line pointless.

An Occasional Dream

***Recorded**: **(demo)** mid-April 1969, 24 Foxgrove Road. Bowie: lead vocal, 12-string acoustic guitar; Hutchinson: acoustic guitar, lead and harmony vocal; **(album)** 16-17 July 1969, Trident Studios. Bowie: lead and harmony vocal, 12-string acoustic guitar?; Christmas: 12-string acoustic guitar; Renwick: lead acoustic guitar?, recorder, clarinet; John Lodge: bass; John Cambridge: drums; Visconti: recorder. Produced, arranged: Visconti; engineered: Sheffield, Scott or Toft.*

***First release**: 14 November 1969, **Space Oddity**; (demo) 12 October 2009, **Space Oddity**. **Broadcast**: 5 February 1970, The Sunday Show. **Live**: 1969.*

"An Occasional Dream" attempted the intimacy of "Letter to Hermione" with a more purple lyric: a hundred days of passion, sheets of summer, gently weeping nights, Swedish rooms of Hessian and wood, ashes of time. It was Bowie under the sway of Scott Walker's solo albums, with their sad bohemians mourning lost love from apartment terraces, as well as Walker's inspiration Jacques Brel. Though any hope of a Gallic sensibility—Bowie examines a dead love affair, pins it to a card, cases it up—went lost in the song's oddly chipper studio recording.

Its demo by Bowie and John Hutchinson had a fragile beauty, with Hutchinson confidently negotiating the song's byzantine chord sequence while providing sympathetic harmony vocals. As with "Space Oddity," "An Occasional Dream" lay in the shadow of Simon and Garfunkel, most noticeably a closing arpeggio similar to the opening of "The Sound of Silence."

For *Space Oddity*, Tony Visconti opened up the "Bowie & Hutch material" for use by a full band, leaving only "Letter to Hermione" in its original form. "An Occasional Dream," one of the first songs completed for the album, was a casualty of cloudy intentions, increased in tempo (the fastest on the album, nearly double the tempo of sister "Hermione") and given a garish woodwind arrangement. While clarinet doubling the lead acoustic guitar melody was a nice touch (1:16), the jaunty recorders undermined portentous lines like "in our madness." The rapid tremolo on the recorders after "gently weeping nights" (1:44) was another thematic mismatch, while the cheerful clarinet/recorder melody after "dance you far from me" made Hermione's departure seem like a lark. The guitars were two tracks of 12-string acoustic and a lead acoustic guitar that played a crablike octave-scaling melody, while the rhythm section met quiet steadiness (John Cambridge, keeping to side stick and bass drum) with fluid, if thin-sounding exuberance (John Lodge, often playing up an octave on bass).

Bowie embellished his lyric's worst moments, hissing "TIME" like a sibyl, indulging in plenty of Robin Gibb-esque vibrato and singing Hutchinson's harmonies as clunky overdubs: a half-bar-delayed echo of his lead vocal, pitched a third below. For the coda, Bowie inflated the title phrase higher with each repeat until he expired by holding on a D note through four bars. The chastened performance of "An Occasional Dream" for a BBC session in February 1970—the last time he'd ever play the song—was that of a hung-over romantic.

Janine

Recorded*: (demo, unreleased)** *mid-April 1969, 24 Foxgrove Road. Bowie: lead vocal, 12-string acoustic guitar; Hutchinson: acoustic guitar, backing vocal;* ***(album) *16-17 July 1969, Trident. Bowie: lead vocal, kalimba, handclaps?; Christmas: 12-string acoustic guitar; Wayne: lead guitar; Renwick: rhythm guitar, down-tuned acoustic guitar; Lodge: bass; Cambridge: drums, tambourine. Produced: Visconti; engineered: Sheffield, Scott or Toft.*

First release*: 14 November 1969,* ***Space Oddity. Broadcast****: 20 October 1969, Dave Lee Travis Show; 5 February 1970, The Sunday Show.* ***Live****: 1969-1970.*

The liveliest track of a dour album, "Janine" was mooted as the follow-up single to "Space Oddity" and unlike most of *Space Oddity* it stayed in the repertoire of Bowie's first glam rock group in 1970. Written concurrently with the "Hermione" songs, "Janine" cut the exotic, unattainable "Hermione" figure down to size. Her incarnation as Janine sounds like a better time: "you're fey, Janine, a tripper to the last," Bowie sang with a bluffer's admiration.

Its lyrical thrust—Bowie complaining that a girl doesn't get him, that he's too far ahead of her—was more garage-rock bravado than folkie introspection. "Janine" wasn't just a respite from the melancholy "Hermione" songs, it was Bowie rejecting "confessional" singer/songwriter music. He blustered his way through the performance, doing an Elvis Presley impersonation with Continental flavors (the vaguely French pronunciation of "dzah-neen"). Janine wants him to bare his soul, to "collocate" (to arrange, like books on a shelf) his mind, but he knows he's denied his true self so much that he's become a complete mask: "If you take an axe to me/you'll kill another man, not me at all."

Solidly in D major, "Janine" genially repeated a verse-verse-refrain structure. Opening with short, parallel phrases ("my-love/Ja-nine," etc.) whose rhythm was pegged to a one-long, two-short strum pattern on the 12-string acoustic, the verses took off on antic vocal runs (see the 20-note dash starting with "scares me into gloom") filled with buried rhymes: take how "Polish wanderer" is echoed by "travel ever onward."

Its refrains grew crowded with electric guitars reinforcing the 12-string chords, drums fattened by handclaps and tambourine 16ths and, as on "An Occasional Dream," John Lodge playing an aggressive lead bass, querying the vocal line with long rambles up an octave. A raucous mix included studio chatter, an open-D tuned acoustic guitar clattering in the verses, a Bowie harmony vocal bellowing a fifth over his lead and the occasional clangs of a kalimba, an African "thumb piano" he'd found in a box in the

Trident control room. He used it to ape the movements of Mick Wayne's lead guitar, whose slowly descending lines were channeled through a volume pedal.

Having envisioned some sort of rousing coda for the song (in its demo Bowie used the "Hey Jude" na-na-NA-na hook as a place-filler), Bowie instead let "Janine" trail off, expiring in a two-chorus jam on the album take and in guitar solos for its two radio performances. The 1970 BBC performance was part of Mick Ronson's first-ever live appearance with Bowie, and you can hear traces of "Width of a Circle" in some of Ronson's closing lines.

Conversation Piece

Recorded*: (demo, unreleased)** *mid-April 1969, 24 Foxgrove Road. Bowie: lead vocal, 12-string acoustic guitar; Hutchinson: acoustic guitar, backing vocal;* ***(single) *ca. late July-early September 1969, Trident. Bowie: lead vocal; Christmas: 12-string acoustic guitar; Wayne: lead guitar; Lodge: bass; Cambridge: drums; unknown musicians: cello, oboe. Produced, arranged: Visconti; engineered: Sheffield, Scott or Toft;* ***(remake)*** *(basic tracks) July 2000, Sear Sound Studios, (overdubs) October 2000, Looking Glass Studios (strings) late 2000? Bowie: lead vocal; Earl Slick: lead guitar; Mark Plati: rhythm guitar; Lisa Germano: mandolin, backing vocals; Mike Garson: piano; Gail Ann Dorsey: bass; Sterling Campbell: drums; Holly Palmer, Emm Gryner: backing vocals; Elena Barere: lead violin; unknown musicians: violins, violas, celli (conducted, arranged: Visconti). Produced: Bowie, Plati; engineered: Pete Keppler, Visconti.*

First release*: (single) 6 March 1970 (Mercury MF 1135); (remake) 11 June 2002,* ***Heathen*** *(bonus disc, ISO/Columbia 508222 9).* ***Live:*** *1969.*

"Conversation Piece" was one of Bowie's freshest compositions when he and John Hutchinson cut their demo, as Hutchinson called it "a new one" and Bowie had to prompt him the opening chords. Hearkening back to the character sketches of *David Bowie*, "Conversation Piece" was Bowie mining the recent past for material, setting the lyric in a thinly-veiled depiction of his manager Kenneth Pitt's Manchester Square apartment, where Bowie lived off and on, filling his room with scattered papers and scads of tape recorders and amplifiers.

Bowie rewrote his life as a frustrated musician into a portrait of a failed writer or academic, the sort of man who wanders the streets begrudging life, the sort who'd even write a rock opera about a suicide party (see "Ernie Johnson," Appendix). While the lyric hints at suicide as resolution—in the three refrains, Bowie moves from the street to a bridge to "the water"—its chords offered a happier story. Having shifted between A minor verses and C major refrains, a move to A major in the last verse finds Bowie reveling in his florid isolation and suggesting it's all been a bit of stagecraft.

Simon and Garfunkel were a crushing influence on the "Bowie & Hutch" era and the obvious inspiration here was "I Am a Rock," with which "Conversation Piece" shared a narrator using books as a shield, C major/A minor key shifts and, in the demo, plaintive vocal harmonies in the refrains. On the studio take, Bowie's yearning vocal ("a melody that rips your heart out," Mike Garson called it decades later) was paired with a sighing guitar line, likely Mick Wayne's guitar played through a volume-tone pedal and deepened by cello, a marriage of sounds to impersonate a slide guitar. Along with John Cambridge's steady rim hits, the guitar/strings fusion gave a "country" melancholy to the track, while the oboe countermelody linked it to reveries like "An Occasional Dream." Cut from the album and issued a year later as a B-side, it would be one of Bowie's finest obscurities; the early Belle and Sebastian albums are a collective tribute to it.

Bowie revived "Conversation Piece" in 2000, recording a remake for *Toy* that wound up issued on a *Heathen* bonus disc two years later. It was the jewel of the sessions. Staying in his lower register, Bowie sang in near-conversational detachment, a Visconti-scored cello haunting the verses and Mike Garson's piano offering idle thoughts. *Toy* often seemed like an older man trapped in a juvenile's songs and vainly picking at the lock. Here, sung by a man in his winter years, blankly cataloging the last room in which he'll ever live, the self-pity of "Conversation Piece" seemed hard-earned. He's not walking back from the bridge this time.

Wild Eyed Boy From Freecloud

Recorded*: (single)** *20 June 1969, Trident Studios. Bowie: lead vocal,12-string acoustic guitar, handclaps; Paul Buckmaster: arco bass. Produced: Dudgeon; engineered: Sheffield;* ***(album) *ca. late July-August 1969, Trident. Bowie: lead vocal, 12-string acoustic guitar; Visconti: bass; Cambridge: drums, temple block?, woodblocks?; Mick Ronson?: guitar?, handclaps?; unknown musicians: violins, violas, celli, cor anglais, French horn, trumpets, trombones, flutes, clarinets, oboes, bassoons, harp, timpani, vibraphone. Arranged: Bowie, Visconti. Produced: Visconti; engineered: Sheffield, Scott or Toft.*

First release*: (single) 11 July 1969 (Philips BF 1801); (album) 14 November 1969,* ***Space Oddity. Broadcast****: 5 February 1970, The Sunday Show; 25 March 1970, Sounds of the 70s.* ***Live****: 1969-1970, 1972-1973.*

Bowie's Tibetan songs end with a fable, "Wild Eyed Boy From Freecloud," a song seemingly written for a puppet show or a mime piece. It came out of his 1968 mime *Jet-sun and the Eagle*, in which he'd played a Tibetan boy, and "Wild Eyed Boy From Freecloud" still seems scored for actors' movements, its lyric a set of stage directions: the hangman folds the rope into its bag, the village "dreadful yawns." "As the night...begins for ONE!" as the hangman exits stage left.

Another influence was a book he'd read in spring 1969, Jean-Marc Gaspard Itard's *The Wild Boy of Aveyron*. A doctor in Napoleonic France, Itard had domesticated a "feral" boy, Victor, who'd been found living in the woods. Despite Itard's efforts, Victor never learned to talk, let alone read or write, and he died, savage and obscure, around the age of 40.

As the critic Roger Shattuck suggested, it's possible Victor had suffered some form of schizophrenia which had driven him into the woods, where his tenacity of spirit and innate intelligence (as Bowie sang, "it's the madness in his eyes"—"Freecloud" was the real precursor of "All the Madmen") had kept him alive and happier than he'd ever be in town. Bowie's "Wild Boy" channeled this reading, devising an outsider figure, possibly suffering from mental illness, who's hated by the world he's rejected. Bowie described his Wild Boy as having "a beautiful way of life" up on his mountain. Determining to hang the boy for some unknown offense, the villagers in the valley below bring down the mountain's wrath.

Its lyric was a grab-bag that took its setting of a night before a hanging from the Child Ballads or, more likely, Western ballads (see "Bars of the County Jail"), its retribution levied upon a damned town from Brecht/Weill's "Pirate Jenny," its lofty lines describing Freecloud ("where the eagle dare not fly") from JRR Tolkien. Its harmonic structure was a game of diversions based on twists of the D major chord and carried on a descending chromatic bassline. The tantalizing appearances of a C major chord right before the close of each verse ("breaks the night to cry—") gave a glimpse of escape that, after a "bridge" section rich in internal rhymes, occurred in the final, catastrophic C major verse. Yet as the boy picks his way home through the rubble, the original D major progression and descending bassline reappear. He's just won a respite, doomed to repeat it all again the following night on stage (though the closing chord is a defiant C major).

Bowie wrote "Freecloud" around May 1969 and unveiled it a month later to Gus Dudgeon as a B-side for "Space Oddity" (Dudgeon had never heard the song before). He cut the master take in 20 minutes, singing along to his 12-string acoustic guitar while Paul Buckmaster bowed an arco bass in support. (Hired to write a score, Buckmaster had only completed the cello part by the time of the session, so Bowie simply had him play it.)

A full orchestral version was cut for *Space Oddity* about a month later. Calling Dudgeon's "Freecloud" a "throwaway" and hearing "a Wagnerian orchestra in my head," Tony Visconti made his arrangement an extended piece of one-upmanship. Where Dudgeon had used eight tracks, Visconti had 16. Where Dudgeon had a baker's dozen string and flute players for "Space Oddity," Visconti hired a 50-piece orchestra (for an album cut, no less) and scored parts for vibraphone, cor anglais, harp and timpani.

With so many to shoehorn into a five-minute track, Visconti wasn't content to follow the dramatic arc of the song, as established by Buckmaster on the single: spare opening verses (Buckmaster didn't start bowing until the second) build to a diva spotlight bridge and mountain-trembling final verse. Instead Visconti staggered in musicians in the track's opening seconds. The six-bar intro alone had descending lines by bassoon, oboe and cor anglais, while a vibraphone cued a harp glissando and pizzicato strings as trombones established a C chord. Some players were given pieces of the lyric to act: trombones shrouded "imprisoned," flutes and clarinets twirled 16th notes on "smoke into the room," the mountain was announced by massed trumpets and trombones; the eagle dared not fly over flute, oboe and clarinet triplets. Far more often, the score was bloated: the townsmen debate over thwacked woodblock, a chromatic rising string line and dancing flutes and clarinets. As if stacked up in tower blocks, the players began to entertain themselves: oboes and bassoons played octaves in the first verse, vibraphone and harp sang parallel rising melodies in the second.

So when the song moved to its peak ("really you and really me"), the orchestra became a din. All at once there were snare drums and timpani, the harpist playing octave glissandi and armies of woodwinds and strings travelling parallel arcs. The mountain's revenge via avalanche merited a similar onslaught. Yet all this "Wagnerian" rage accomplished was to distract the ear from the fact that Bowie's vocal was weaker than the single take, his voice cracking on the last "Freecloud" (possibly due to nerves, as Visconti had set Bowie, with his footstool and 12-string guitar, dead center in his orchestra while having time for only a single take). Wearying and lacking dramatic intelligence, Visconti's arrangement fell far short of his typically nuanced scores, let alone those of London contemporaries like Robert Kirby, whose Delius-inspired arrangements warmed Nick Drake's *Five Leaves Left*, or Joe Boyd's "Tudor" woodwinds on Vashti Bunyan's *Just Another Diamond Day*.

A reclamation effort came in the last Ziggy Stardust shows of 1973, when Bowie sang the opening verses of "Wild Eyed Boy From Freecloud" over piano and acoustic guitar (John Hutchinson, retrieved from the past) and Mick Ronson's gorgeous low-line on guitar. He brought the song back to the stage, which had birthed it; he made "Freecloud" the black fable it was always meant to be. And when he threw it aside at its peak to break into a righteous "All the Young Dudes," it was a triumph: his lost boy had found home at last.

Don't Sit Down

***Recorded**: ca. August-September 1969, Trident. Bowie: guide vocal; Wayne: lead guitar; Renwick: rhythm guitar; Lodge: bass; Cambridge: drums. Produced: Visconti; engineered: Sheffield, Scott or Toft.*

***First release**: 14 November 1969, **Space Oddity**.*

"Don't Sit Down" is a squib, a 40-second jam with a simple melody from a cracking-up Bowie. Its inclusion on *Space Oddity* was part of the deliberate informality of late Sixties albums, many of which kept sounds that would have gotten an engineer reprimanded in 1964. See Jimi Hendrix coughing at the start of "Rainy Day, Dream Away," Bob Dylan asking whether the tape's rolling on *Nashville Skyline* or the Beatles' "White Album," which is riddled with mutters, coughs, false starts and control room chatter. Listed as a separate track on the original Philips release, "Don't Sit Down" was deleted from the sleeve and label of RCA's 1972 reissue and appended without notice to "Unwashed and Somewhat Slightly Dazed." A restored independence, courtesy of Ryko's *Space Oddity* reissue, was short-lived: the 40th anniversary CD merged it with "Unwashed" again.

God Knows I'm Good

***Recorded**: ca. early August-16 September 1969, Trident. Bowie: lead vocal, acoustic guitar?; Christmas: 12-string acoustic guitar; Wayne or Renwick?: lead acoustic guitar. Renwick: acoustic guitar. Produced: Visconti; engineered: Sheffield, Scott or Toft.*

***First release**: 14 November 1969, **Space Oddity**. **Broadcast**: 5 February 1970, The Sunday Show. **Live:** 1969-1970.*

Mercury head Lou Reizner didn't want his new signing to produce another hodgepodge like *David Bowie*, so given Bowie's current tastes, making a "folk" album seemed the most feasible goal. Tony Visconti placed a 12-string acoustic guitar dead center in the mix of nearly every track and took sequencing cues from Bob Dylan's first records, where songs of personal experience were complemented by what Dylan once called "finger-pointin' songs."

"God Knows I'm Good" was among the latter for Bowie. A social commentary piece popular in his weekly sets at the Arts Lab he co-founded in Beckenham, it filtered empathy (for an elderly shoplifter) through smugness (scorning the "honest, rich and clean" bourgeois who watch her downfall). Inspired by an article in a local newspaper, Bowie set a four-verse narrative in a soulless modern supermarket (the kind whose "cash machines" are spitting and shrieking) and stacked the deck further by making his woeful protagonist blind, starving, old and broke. Slipping a can of stewing steak into her handbag, the old woman hopes God will forgive her transgression, as if He'll turn a blind eye to a longtime employee nicking from the till. Having endured countless political conversations at his Arts Lab, Bowie regurgitated a few talking points: the oppressive System, the growing power of the Machine.

The artless lyric wouldn't matter so much if the song wasn't such a chore, sung by Bowie in a busker's whine. As in "Letter to Hermione," with which it shared a G major key, its arrangement was two "commenter" acoustic guitars mixed left and right while a centered 12-string guitar played chords. A sprightly Bo Diddley-inspired riff on open strings capped by a C chord was the closest thing "God Knows I'm Good" had to a hook and it was pressed into service nearly every time Bowie took a breath. It compensated for the refrain, a three-note repetition of the title phrase stretched across two bars of 3/4 and a lurch back to 4/4. Among his dreariest efforts, Bowie wouldn't attempt this sort of grim "protest" naturalism again until the Tin Machine years.

Unwashed and Somewhat Slightly Dazed

***Recorded**: ca. late August-16 September 1969, Trident. Bowie: lead vocal, 12-string acoustic guitar?; Christmas: 12-string acoustic guitar; Wayne: lead guitar; Renwick: rhythm guitar; Lodge: bass; Cambridge: drums; Benny Marshall: harmonica; unknown musicians: saxophones, trumpets. Produced: Visconti; engineered: Sheffield, Scott or Toft.*

***First release**: 14 November 1969, **Space Oddity**. **Broadcast**: 20 October 1969, Dave Lee Travis Show; 5 February 1970, The Sunday Show. **Live**: 1969-1970.*

Written while Bowie was planning a festival and burying his father (in late July 1969, Haywood Jones fell ill with pneumonia, dying two days after Bowie returned to Britain from a song festival in Malta), "Unwashed and Somewhat Slightly Dazed" was unsurprisingly chaotic, a snapshot of Bowie caught midway through a shape-shift. Its title, referencing his well-maintained hippie scruffiness, aptly described the track's inchoate feel. It opened with Bowie comfortably in the range of fifth, stringing together rising phrases ("see you see *me*," "through your win*dow*") as a 12-string acoustic guitar alternated A minor 7th and A suspended chords. With the occasional appearance by Mick Wayne's tremolo-shrouded lead guitar and John Cambridge's hi-hat, the song looked to be another brooding "Letter to Hermione" piece until things went awry.

Kicked off with two guitars feasting on F major chords, a turbulent 11-bar sequence of shifting time signatures and rapid chord changes knocked the song's A minor key into the sunlight of its relative major, C. Tim Renwick played a simple riff on muted strings, John Lodge's bass rumbled to life and Bowie caught fire, broadening his range, elongating phrases, chewing his vowels: "yoooooou're the gleeeeeam." Unable to fully sustain the whole notes, he was helpfully obscured by a guitar that doubled his voice.

A Bo Diddley beat (Bowie used it whenever he was in a fix on this record) ushered "Unwashed" into its final phase, where the band settled into a mid-tempo blues-rock groove over a meat-and-potatoes rock & roll progression (C-F-C). Veering across the stereo spectrum, Bowie tried to work himself up as a dangerous "street" figure and managed one good line ("I've got a headful of murders") for every three groaners ("got eyes in my backside/that see 'lectric tomatoes!") This "hard rock" finale dispatched the "Hermione" figure at last, casting her as some rotten rich girl with a "red parquet floor" and a Braque painting on the wall (that eats her). No longer the muse of long, weeping nights of hessian and wood, she's just another conquest of Bowie's scruffy would-be revolutionary. (He's all but playing Bertolt Brecht's bohemian seducer Baal, a decade before he would on stage.) Best were its nasty refrains, with Bowie holding on one note and singing in two- or three-syllable bursts as if opening fire at close range. Mick Wayne abetted him by edging up stepwise, slamming his whammy bar to plummet back down.

While a frustrated Bowie griped during a *Space Oddity* session that "it's gotta rock!," he'd hobbled his backing band, Junior's Eyes, with protracted, scattered album sessions, inadequate rehearsals and being unable to work out the songs with them live. The inescapable 12-string acoustic, strumming away yet again here, became musical tryptophan. Sunk in a mix so murky a listener can easily miss when a horn section shows up, the closing jam was nowhere in the league of a Cream or Led Zeppelin, instead falling in the shambolic line of early progressive groups like Family (see their "The Weaver's Answer"). Aided by Hull musician Benny Marshall, who cut scorching lead harmonica in a one-take overdub, the band thrashed the song to its close as best they could, leaving Bowie, groaning encouragements and attempting some Marc Bolan-esque bleating, a bystander in his own would-be liberation.

Cygnet Committee

Recorded*: (demo, "Lover to the Dawn," unreleased)** *ca. mid-April 1969, 24 Foxgrove Road. Bowie: 12-string acoustic guitar, harmony vocal; Hutchinson: lead vocal, acoustic guitar;* ***(album) *ca. late August-early September 1969, Trident. Bowie: lead vocal; Christmas: 12-string acoustic guitar; Wayne: lead guitar; Renwick: rhythm guitar; Wakeman: electric harpsichord; Lodge: bass; Cambridge: drums. Produced: Visconti; engineered: Sheffield, Scott or Toft.*

***First release*:** *14 November 1969,* ***Space Oddity*. *Broadcast*:** *5 February 1970, The Sunday Show.* ***Live*:** *1969-70.*

"Cygnet Committee" was, consecutively, a break-up letter to a communal arts center Bowie co-founded, a scattershot attack on the counterculture and a desperate self-affirmation. Deep in this gnomic, nearly ten-minute screed was a struggle to find a workable design for the years ahead, Bowie pledging himself to a life of creative destruction while keeping clear of professional revolutionaries. It was the sound of Bowie willing himself to become a stronger artist, hollowing himself out to let a greater creative force, for good or ill, take hold in him. The possession took. In fleeting moments, you can hear the apocalyptic, utopian voice of "Five Years" and "Sweet Thing," of "Station to Station" and "'Heroes.'" The man who was able to write those songs had to go through the crucible of "Cygnet Committee" first.

Bowie and his lover/flatmate Mary Finnigan founded the Beckenham Arts Lab in May 1969, one of roughly 50 such Labs in Britain at the time. Along with weekly musical performances at the Three Tuns pub, the Lab (aka "Growth") offered tie-dying lessons, poetry readings, puppet shows, lectures and mime routines. Hoping to attract local kids and subsequently "turn on their parents," the Lab's slogan was "Growth is people, Growth is revolution." Bowie envisioned an escape valve for suburban dreamers; perhaps he saw the Lab as a way to find younger versions of himself. "There was nothing in Beckenham, just television," he told a Dutch journalist at the time. "The lab is for extroverts who wish to express themselves, not for established artists." This was Bowie as proud counter-cultural Beckenhamite, a character out of Hanif Kureishi's *The Buddha of Suburbia,* which would gently satirize this era. In August 1969, interviewed by Finnigan for the *International Times,* Bowie said he hoped "Space Oddity" became a hit because it would mean exposure and capital for the Lab. Using sparkling ad-man copy, he claimed "Arts Labs should be for everybody, not just the so-called turned-on minority. We need energy from all directions, from heads and skin-heads alike." It could be a bit much. Keith Christmas recalled Bowie being "a twerp in those days…strum[ming] a few folk songs in between a lot of crap about changing the world."

Nothing in particular soured Bowie on the Lab, at which he'd play regularly until March 1970. By then he'd assembled a hand-picked artistic community at his house in Haddon Hall and no longer had to publicly recruit followers. Yet he was noticeably estranged early on. Roger Wootton, a Lab regular, recalled Bowie as being an "outsider" in the pot-reeking, student-infested Three

Tuns shows. "He was never really a part of what was going on. He didn't seem to be one of the other people." As the most talented and charismatic figure in the room, Bowie resented the apathetic types the Lab attracted upon its (relative) success. He'd wanted collaborators and got spectators; his encounters with mediocrities in hippie garb spouting "revolutionary" slogans became a drain on him.

As he told the journalist Patrick Salvo, he intended the first harmonically free section of "Cygnet Committee" to symbolize the ideal of the Lab. "It was saying—Fellow man I do love you—I love humanity, I adore it, it's sensational, sensuous, exciting—it sparkled and it's also pathetic at the same time." His players make a staggered entrance, as if plugging in when the mood strikes them. Over a murmuring backdrop of Three Tuns-esque chatter, Bowie sang arcing, eleventh-spanning phrases while Mick Wayne, using a volume pedal, played off a descending chromatic bassline.

The leak of a Bowie & Hutch composition called "Lover to the Dawn," demoed on the same tape as "Space Oddity," revealed Bowie had used "Dawn" as the basis of the opening sections of "Cygnet Committee," from the opening riff and bassline (itself taken from Led Zeppelin's "Your Time Is Gonna Come") through the "they drained her [my] very soul...dry" section. And the long closing section Bowie appended to the reconstituted "Lover to the Dawn" was a bog-standard rock 'n' roll progression, the "Stand By Me" I-vi-IV-V sequence he'd used before (see "And I Say to Myself"). Regardless of its length and furor, "Cygnet Committee" was just a folk number bluntly welded to a rock song.

"Lover to the Dawn" also shed light on what happened in the mutation that created "Cygnet Committee." The original song starred yet another "Hermione" figure, called "bitter girl" in its refrains: a woman weary of the incessant demands of her lovers, who've drained her soul dry. The original refrain had a sympathetic Bowie and Hutch ("you gave too much and you got nothing!") urging the bitter girl to get on with her life—it's something of a hippie "Georgie Girl."

In "Cygnet Committee," Bowie cast *himself* as the bitter girl (not for the last time) and there was no larking Hutchinson to tell him to grow up and out of it. Instead, the self-pity of "Lover to the Dawn" got blown up to widescreen proportions. Bitter Boy isn't just heartbroken, he's set upon by parasites of all shapes; his tragedy isn't personal but that of an entire generation. Its last venomous C major verse became a jeremiad, calling out New Leftists, cult leaders and cult followers, cursing hippie capitalists and their slogans (including "kick out the jams" and "love is all we need," the revolution brought to you by, respectively, Columbia and EMI).

This extended damning of a movement of which Bowie was barely part requires a touch of context. The British underground lived in a bubble. Unlike in France, China and the US, British youth (apart from those in Northern Ireland) were passive and quiet, if discontented, in the late Sixties. There was nothing equivalent to the violence of the Democratic National Convention in 1968 or the May 1968 student riots in Paris. Colin Crouch, the student union president at the London School of Economics, saw the few substantial protests of the time quickly devolve into games of dress-up. British radicals seemed to get stuck on the idea of protest, raising protest "to a position of value in its own right," Crouch wrote. "The sit-in became not so much a part of the sojourn in the wilderness for the chosen people of the revolution, but a trailer for the Promised Land."

Bowie used this failure, the failure of the Arts Lab writ large, as a means to rid himself of the suffocating cant and pretense of the counterculture. In December 1969 he lamented the hippie set as being "the laziest people I've met in my life. They don't know what to do with themselves. Looking all the time for people to show them the way. They wear anything they're told, and listen to any music they're told to." As he sang, *they knew not the words of the Free States' refrain*. He'd spent the last years of the Sixties burying himself in committees ("submerging myself," as he told Mary Finnigan); now he was free.

So with its dead fathers and sons of dirt, the 39-bar-long closing verse of "Cygnet Committee" was the radical faction that took over the whole enterprise. The faceless villains who turned up, busy slitting throats, killing children and betraying friends, predicted the underground's slide into cheap criminality. Yet the lyric, in turns grandiose, mocking (of Dylan's "Desolation Row" among others) and fanatic, was more Bowie purging himself of "taste" and "narrative," ridding himself of the stink of bedsit laments and cabaret, and exploring a inner darkness, calling up images of supermen, ringleaders, wraiths. The "talking man," a summoned demon who gives the singer access to his "many powers," would be the dark muse of *The Man Who Sold the World*.

As on "Unwashed and Somewhat Slightly Dazed," "Cygnet Committee" suffered from an under-rehearsed band, having to master a lengthy, harmonically dense song, that couldn't deliver the searing accompaniment its vocal demanded (if you're going to quote the MC5, you should lay down heavier fire than this, or at least ditch the harpsichord). The production did the song little favors, as the drums sound like paper and John Lodge's bass goes missing towards the close. Bowie gave a more vital, if still ragged performance for a BBC broadcast of the following year. Despite occasionally bungling lines from his ramble of a lyric, he sang with an eerie sense of self-possession. "Cygnet Committee" had spent itself out in its making, its recording the afterimage of some lost primal inspiration. Still, in its tortuous way, it was as critical to Bowie's development as "Space Oddity."

Memory of a Free Festival

Recorded*: 8-9 September 1969, Trident. Bowie: lead vocal, Rosedale electric chord organ; Wayne: lead guitar; Renwick: rhythm guitar;*

Lodge: bass; Cambridge: drums, tambourine; unknown musician(s): baritone saxophone; Visconti, Bob Harris, Sue Harris, Tony Woollcott, Marc Bolan, "Girl": backing vocals. Produced, arranged: Visconti; engineered: Sheffield, Scott or Toft; ***(remake, as "Memory of a Free Festival Pt. 1 & Pt. 2")*** *21, 23 March, 3, 14-15 April 1970, Trident and Advision Studios, London. Bowie: lead vocal, 12-string acoustic guitar, Rosedale organ; Ronson: lead guitar, backing vocal; Ralph Mace: Moog; Visconti: bass, backing vocal; Cambridge: drums; unknown musicians: strings (arr. Visconti). Produced: Visconti.*

First release*: 14 November 1969,* ***Space Oddity****; (single) 26 June 1970 (Mercury 6052 026).* ***Broadcast****: 5 February 1970, The Sunday Show; ca. June 1970, Six-O-One: Newsday; 15 August 1970, Eddy Ready Go!* ***Live****: 1969-1971, 1973-1974.*

The free festival was an open-air concert and fair, held on the Croydon Road Recreation Ground in Beckenham on 16 August 1969 (across an ocean, the Woodstock Festival was underway). Bowie performed, his set allegedly including a reggae version of "Space Oddity," as did groups like the Strawbs. There were puppet shows, Tibetan goods vendors and coconut shies; his new girlfriend Angela Barnett cooked hamburgers in a wheelbarrow. The festival was peaceful and a success, with some 3,000 attending. Beckenham's mayor and chief of police complimented Bowie for pulling it off.

The song he recorded three weeks later, sequenced to close *Space Oddity* as his last word on the Sixties, depicted a golden afternoon in which he wandered through a blissful crowd of flower children, exchanging kisses and greeting passing Venusians. In reality Bowie, who'd buried his father only five days before, had swung between near-catatonia and a foul temper, calling his partners "materialistic arseholes" for profiting off hamburgers and concert posters, complaining about the PA system and skipping the after-party. Mary Finnigan later called Bowie a hypocrite for writing a peace-and-love song for a festival at which he'd been so abrasive.

A contrary set of feelings, a man trying to reconstitute a bad day as the hope it ought to have been, gave "Memory of a Free Festival" depth and even bite, with Bowie making some deprecating asides about the holy tribe: "We claimed the very source of joy ran through/it didn't, but it seemed that way." The warmth, the easy unity, of the Free Festival is already in the past. If the hippies are the "children of the summer's end," they should ready for winter.

Like the Arts Labs, the free concert was a child of the late Sixties. In summer 1968, the promoter Blackhill Enterprises began putting on monthly free rock shows in Hyde Park with the likes of Pink Floyd and the Move. The Rolling Stones hired Blackhill to run their own free Hyde Park concert the following summer (archly described by Richard Neville as "free, courtesy of Blackhill, of Granada's groovy camera team, Marshall's great amplification system and triple-priced Lyon's ice cream.") The Beckenham festival was a homespun version of this and it actually was free, unlike Woodstock, which had been forcibly converted into a free show. The happy chaos of Woodstock, soon followed by the 1969 Isle of Wight concert and the violent chaos of the Stones' free show in Altamont that December, made the free festival yet another fault line between straight and hippie worlds. Parliament soon passed an act banning gatherings of over 5,000 at the Isle of Wight.

"Memory of a Free Festival" opens with Bowie playing a Rosedale electric chord organ that he'd found at Woolworths. As with the Stylophone, he gave a toy instrument dignity. The sole accompaniment of the song's four verses, the organ was his voice's rickety, ecclesiastic complement, making him sound like a wandering sermonizer.

Composing on the organ, even a toy like the Rosedale, liberated Bowie from the guitar's melodic consistency; it foreshadowed the freedom he'd find when writing on the piano a year later. After politely announcing the piece's title, he started by playing variations on E minor while nudging up the bassline stepwise from C to F. Settling into a loose 3/4 time, he sang the first two verses over a descending, nebulous chord sequence, shifting from B minor to B-flat ("felt the Lon/don sky," "source of/joy") while anchored on a D bass. The third verse gained momentum, Bowie singing more hurriedly while mainly keeping on an E note (pushing up slightly on "ecstasy"), slackening at the end of each phrase. A shift to D major ("scanned the skies") marked the peak of the festival: the aliens arrive, the joints get passed around, the revelers "walk back to the [Croydon] road, unchained."

What followed was a free-time interlude of organ swirls, snippets of chatter, laughs and guitar fills while John Cambridge kept loose order with his ride cymbal. A memory so far, the festival shifts to the present, a party as much ominous as joyful. The sequence's real purpose was more practical: it had to glue the "Free Festival" verses to a three-chord (D-C-G) "sun machine" refrain possibly once intended for another song. Having considered using the "Hey Jude" refrain for "Janine," Bowie now made the long coda of "Free Festival" in its image: loops of ragged communal chanting, with Bowie in Paul McCartney's soul cheerleader role.

In early 1970, Mercury's American wing asked Bowie to re-record "Memory of a Free Festival" as a single, requesting a faster tempo and to get to the refrain sooner. The compromise was to cut the track in half, devoting the B-side entirely to the sun machine. This new "Free Festival" found Bowie outshone by his backing band, who tromped in singly during the intro. Even with the Sixties fresh in the grave, there's a feeling of getting down to business. Guitar, bass and drums kick in before the first verse starts, the Moog rolls over the humble Rosedale organ like a Panzer tank, the psychedelic interlude gets deep-sixed, the chanted backing vocals of the refrains could be from a football terrace. Mick Ronson, Tony Visconti's free-flowing bass and

Ralph Mace's Moog used the long fadeout as a preview of coming attractions. "Memory of a Free Festival Pt. 1 and 2" was the sound of *The Man Who Sold the World,* hard glam rock, and a bit too hard and glam for summer 1970, as the single sold dismally.

The Beatles ended the Sixties by breaking up, the last record they made showing them walk single-file off stage. The Stones ended with blood and fire and the sense they'd survive it all (and they would). The Who had a messiah pulled down by his followers, the Kinks emigrated to Australia, Dylan and Van Morrison and a host of others went to ground in the country. Bowie closed a decade in which he'd been a footnote by throwing a party, singing a jaded memory of the summer's end: the fun-fair of the Sixties was just prelude, his work's troubled childhood. His "Memory of a Free Festival," a last gathering of the tribes, had a sad, faded grandeur. Forty-five years on, it can still touch a medieval chord in the soul.

Chapter 4

The Man On the Stair (1970)

Nothing is true, everything is permitted.
Turner (Mick Jagger), *Performance.*

Everybody was just playing a part…just like a bunch of little kids playing.
Charles Manson.

You've got to be drastic and violent to reach the audience now. They've been getting too much ***given*** *to them.*
Pete Townshend.

If you insist on living a dream, you may be taken for mad.
I like my dream.
Mary Morris and Patrick McGoohan, *The Prisoner,* "Dance of the Dead."

The Prettiest Star

Recorded**: **(single)** 8, 13, 15 January 1970, Trident Studios, London. David Bowie: lead vocal, 12-string acoustic guitar; Marc Bolan: lead guitar; Rick Wakeman [?]: Lowrey organ; Delisle Harper, Tony Visconti: bass; Godfrey McLean: drums; unknown musicians: vibraphone, strings. Arranged, produced: Visconti;* ***(remake) *ca. 18-24 January 1973, Trident. Bowie: lead vocal, 12-string acoustic guitar, tenor saxophone?; Mick Ronson: lead guitar, backing vocal; Mike Garson: piano; Trevor Bolder: bass; Woody Woodmansey: drums; Ken Fordham and/or Brian Wilshaw: saxophones. Produced: Ken Scott; engineered: Scott, Mike Moran.*

First release**: (single) 6 March 1970 (Mercury MF 1135); (remake) 13 April 1973,* ***Aladdin Sane *(RS 1001/LSP-4852, UK #1, US #17).*

***Broadcast**: 5 February 1970, The Sunday Show. **Live**: 1970, 1973.*

The success of "Space Oddity" nearly ruined David Bowie. After some hemming and hawing, he cut two options for his next single in January 1970: a remade "London Bye Ta-Ta" and "The Prettiest Star," which he'd written around Christmas for Angela Barnett, whom he'd marry two weeks after its release. He chose the latter, on which his rival and friend Marc Bolan played lead guitar. "The Prettiest Star" was hummable, warm and sweet: it sold less than 800 copies in its first week.

Bowie was indifferent to its fate. He declined to promote it, rarely singing "Prettiest Star" live and playing it just once on a BBC broadcast. Yet even had he spearheaded a promotional push, it wouldn't have done much. "Space Oddity" was such an obvious one-hit-wonder that it almost left Bowie in the bin of discarded Sixties novelties with the likes of the Lemon Pipers and Peter Sarstedt. And while he resisted the obvious and didn't do a SF-themed sequel, his alternative sounded square, its mood treacly and nostalgic. It was a dead end. A month after its release, Bowie was recording heavy metal.

Still, "The Prettiest Star" had a charming lyric, with its easy and dyslexic rhymes ("tried" and "tired") and its tribute to Angela was as much for her professional ambition ("you will rise up high and take us all away") as it was any love pledge. Working in the service of an F major progression with occasional spices from its parallel minor, its arrangement blended a Lowrey organ with a set of violins, but its dragging tempo made its sentimentality leaden (Visconti later overdubbed the bass track, as he felt the bassist he'd hired wasn't up to snuff).

The track was dominated by Bolan's vibrato-saturated lead guitar. Bowie liked Bolan's "totally naive approach to the guitar—a lot of what he played was 'incorrect' but it worked," as he said in 1993. But as "Prettiest Star" would be one of his first notable electric solos (to recruit him, both Visconti and Bowie praised his skills on electric guitar, which he'd recently taken up),

Bolan slaved over his lines on his Fender Stratocaster beforehand. He became cemented in his riff, playing without variation throughout the song, daring only to shift upward just before the fade. Cutting his part in under an hour, Bolan scarpered after his wife June soured the mood in the studio by loudly opining he was the only good thing about the track.

As Bowie remade "The Prettiest Star" with Mick Ronson three years later, it offers a rare A/B comparison of two lead guitarists. At first Ronson seems to concede the game to Bolan, as he keeps well within Bolan's lines, including clashing a vibrato-laden chord against Bowie's peak note in the bridge. Where Ronson overwhelmed Bolan was in his tone and his arranging instincts. He'd plug his '68 Les Paul directly into a cranked-up amp, often using just a sole Cry Baby Wah-Wah pedal set in mid-range, and then fatten the track with precise overdubs. So on "Prettiest Star," Ronson tracked a scratchy, distorted secondary guitar, beginning at the end of the intro. This gave the *Aladdin Sane* take more grit than the single, where Bolan's lead was supported only by Bowie's strummed 12-string acoustic.

It's unclear why Bowie remade "Prettiest Star" in 1973. He may have considered the song to be close to an outtake, given its dismal reception (it was never released in the US), and its mood fit *Aladdin Sane*'s future-nostalgia theme, with its "movies in the past" linking the song to "Drive-In Saturday." Ronson and Bowie gave it judicious edits, perking up the draggy middle section—where two identical refrains had sandwiched a guitar solo—by ditching the solo and slipping the third verse between the refrains. If the first "Prettiest Star" was a valentine, its remake was a rowdy engagement party, complete with doo-wop backing vocals, swinging saxophones and juke-joint piano.

Threepenny Pierrot
Columbine
The Mirror

***Recorded**: 31 January, 1 February 1970, Leith Theatre, Edinburgh. Bowie: lead vocal, 12-string acoustic guitar; Michael Garrett: piano ("Threepenny Pierrot").*

***First release**: 7 February 2005, **Love You Till Tuesday** (DVD). **Broadcast**: 1 February 1970, Gateway: "Pierrot in Turquoise or The Looking Glass Murders."*

In late January 1970, Bowie renewed his connection with the mime Lindsay Kemp, who had relocated his troupe to Edinburgh (see "The Mask"). Readying an updated *Pierrot in Turquoise* for an arts program on Scottish Television, Kemp leapt at the chance to use Bowie, now a national name thanks to "Space Oddity." As he was scheduled to play a few dates in Scotland around that time, Bowie agreed, even bunking with Kemp for a night.

In a letter to Kenneth Pitt requesting Bowie's services (for £60), Kemp wrote that he intended his new *Pierrot* to be "all in color with lots of bits of film and things as well." Retitled *The Looking Glass Murders*, the play was a substantial revision of Kemp's original *Pierrot*, as it had both a narrative and a lead actress, Annie Stainer. She played Columbine, lover of both Pierrot (Kemp) and Harlequin (Jack Birkett) and as such the instigator of the plot.

Kemp wanted some new songs from Bowie, as he'd discarded most of the *David Bowie* songs used in the 1967 *Pierrot* except his favorite, "When I Live My Dream." In particular, he asked Bowie to rewrite "London Bye Ta-Ta" as a song for Pierrot. It proved a simple enough business, Bowie dashing out a new verse over the original's piano melody. At rehearsals on 31 January, Bowie unveiled two other pieces, "Columbine" and "The Mirror," both somber ballads cut from *Space Oddity* cloth. Whether Bowie wrote the songs for Kemp's production or, as seems more likely, he fleshed out pieces begun in the *Space Oddity* sessions, he quickly recorded acoustic guitar and piano backing tracks and (again playing the narrator Cloud) sang the three new songs, along with "When I Live My Dream," in the following day's filming.

The wistful "Columbine" reworked "Unwashed and Somewhat Slightly Dazed," whose acoustic guitar intro turned up slightly altered in the former's verse (Bowie would soon use the guitar line again in "The Width of a Circle"). It was an effort to get back into the mindset of the Deram years, with a "Letter to Hermione"-esque heartbreaker and a sad clown who's "left in clouded dreams." One sharp line ("just in case you're my disguise") pointed to Bowie's future, as did all of "The Mirror," with its impressively-sung vocal and its lyrical musings on makeup, mirrors, disguises and obsessions.

Buzz the Fuzz

(Rose). ***Broadcast****: 5 February 1970 (unreleased), BBC Paris Studio, 4-12 Lower Regent Street, London. Bowie: lead vocal, 12-string acoustic guitar. Produced: Jeff Griffin; engineered: Tony Wilson.* ***Live****: 1969-1971.*

Bowie loved those who crawled further out on the limb then he'd ever venture: eccentrics like Ivor Cutler, Ken Nordine with his *Word Jazz* albums or the odd figure of Paul "Biff" Rose, who Bowie once called the flower-power Randy Newman. Born in New Orleans in 1937, Rose was a banjo-playing comedian folk singer ("the acceptable middle-class hippie," as he described himself decades later) who by the end of the Sixties had written for a revue with George Carlin and was recording for Bill Cosby's Tetragrammaton Records.

Rose's 1968 *The Thorn in Mrs. Rose's Side* would be a reservoir for Bowie, who fished melodies, lyrics, arrangements and even whole songs from it (see "Fill Your Heart"). One track, "Buzz the Fuzz," was Bowie's first public acknowledgement of Rose: he started playing "Buzz" by the end of 1969. An entry-level hippie gag tailored for straights, "Buzz the Fuzz" was the tale of a rookie LA cop and the femme fatale he encounters, Alice Dee (rim shot).

Bowie called it "a Los Angeles song" when playing it at the Friars Club in Aylesbury in September 1971, a performance he introduced by noting Rose hadn't sold any records despite having been on the job for years (at the time, Bowie felt some affinities). As on a BBC performance of "Buzz the Fuzz" the year before, Bowie sang in a string of goon voices, overplaying and occasionally bungling Rose's jokes. In all its surviving recordings, Bowie's cover was a shaky translation from a lost language.

Amsterdam

(Brel/Shuman/Blau). ***Recorded:*** *ca. November 1971, Trident Studios. Bowie: lead vocal, 12-string acoustic guitar; Ronson: acoustic guitar?*

First release: *12 October 1973 (RCA 2424).* ***Broadcast:*** *5 February 1970, The Sunday Show; 21 September 1971, Sounds of the 70s.* ***Live:*** *1968-1972, 1990.*

Jacques Brel composed "Amsterdam" in Roquebrune-Cap-Martin, in a villa overlooking the Mediterranean. He read his lyric to a fisherman friend, who wept while he carved open sea urchins. "Amsterdam" inspired these sort of visceral responses. After Robert Guillaume debuted the English version of "Amsterdam" at the Village Gate in January 1968, there was a "disconcertingly long hush—followed by a roar so damn loud I jumped."

While one of his best-known songs, Brel never recorded "Amsterdam," only singing it on a 1964 concert album. Bowie came to the song indirectly, via Scott Walker's cover on the latter's 1967 debut and via *Jacques Brel Is Alive and Well and Living in Paris,* a revue Bowie saw in London in summer 1968. (Bowie and Walker used that show's translation, by Mort Shuman and Eric Blau.) While avoiding the Brel worship that consumed Walker for a time, Bowie would still fall under Brel's sway, with most of his glam showstoppers basically electrified Brel songs ("Rock and

Roll Suicide," "Time," "Sweet Thing/Candidate").

By late 1968 Bowie was playing "Amsterdam" with his folk trio and he'd keep the song in his stage repertoire until 1972 (he replaced it with Brel's "My Death," which better suited the times). Like "Waiting for the Man," another song Bowie was obsessed with during the glam years, "Amsterdam" offered street life as stage material. Where "Waiting For the Man" was confined to the narrow lens of its junkie narrator, "Amsterdam" was a sprawling Brueghelian canvas: a port overrun with drunk, paunchy sailors who gnaw on fish heads, piss and fight in the street and use the port prostitutes "for a few dirty coins." "Amsterdam" also gave Bowie a primer in how to craft an apocalypse in song, as it opened quietly, with the port waking up, and steadily built to a wild, drunken carnival (it was the template for everything from "Five Years" to "Station to Station.")

After performing the song twice for the BBC, Bowie cut a studio take of "Amsterdam" that was issued as a B-side in 1973. Where Walker's "Amsterdam" had been a reel of accordion, strings and horns, Bowie sang accompanied only by his (and in the studio take, Mick Ronson's) acoustic guitar. In early live recordings Bowie seemed in awe of the song, but by the studio take and his last live performance, he'd developed a saucy tone for the opening verses, boldly inflating and compressing phrases. Yet when he vied to match Brel and Walker in intensity in the last verse, he still audibly strained for effect. His last apprentice work.

The Width of a Circle

***Recorded**: 17 April-22 May 1970, Trident Studios and/or Advision Studios, 23 Gosfield Street, London. Bowie: lead vocal, 12-string acoustic guitar; Ronson: lead guitar, acoustic guitar, banjo?, backing vocal; Visconti: bass, backing vocal; Woodmansey: drums, timpani. Produced: Visconti; engineered: Ken Scott, Gerald Chevin.*

First release**: 4 November 1970,* ***The Man Who Sold the World

(Mercury SR-61325 (US)/ Mercury 6338 041 (UK)). ***Broadcast****: 5 February 1970, The Sunday Show; 25 March 1970, Sounds of the 70s.* ***Live****: 1970-1974.*

Lacking creative equals in the bands he joined and abandoned, Bowie again and again fell back on himself. This bred a creative resilience but also gave his work the lonely intensity of an autodidact. He could sound like a man playing to a mirror. A month into the Seventies, Bowie found Mick Ronson, and everything changed.

Ronson was from Hull. Born in 1946 to a Mormon family (he was a practicing Mormon all his life), he learned piano, violin, cello and recorder until committing to guitar—one reason, he later said, was that he got grief when walking around carrying a violin case. He was in a run of local bands that included the Mariners, the Buccaneers and the Rats (nautical themes were big in Hull), playing in the latter with future Bowie sidemen John Cambridge, Woody Woodmansey and Trevor Bolder. He followed promising leads to London and Scandinavia but came back each time empty-handed to Hull where, at the end of the Sixties, he was a municipal gardener for the City Council: minding sheep, marking rugby pitches.

What defined Ronson's guitar playing was his sheer volume—especially once he'd switched from a Gibson to a '68 Les Paul Custom and acquired a Marshall stack ("with three knobs, all turned to 10," Tony Visconti recalled)—and his ability to massively sustain notes, thanks in part to a deformed fingernail into which he could notch strings. What kept him from a life of grandstanding was an innate melodic sensibility (he had perfect pitch, Ian Hunter recalled) and a genial humility. A born arranger, he valued songcraft and rarely let his soloing derail a track. Everyone had a guitar ace in those days. It was Bowie's great fortune to have one who could read music, score cello lines, arrange vocal harmonies and write and play piano and synthesizer parts.

Cambridge lured Ronson with the promise of a gig with Bowie, driving up to Hull to fetch him. Ronson and Bowie first met on 3 February 1970 at a nightclub called La Chasse. Two days and a few rehearsals later, Ronson backed Bowie at a BBC session, which included the debut of a Bowie composition, "The Width of a Circle."

This had started life as a surreal narrative Bowie had sung over an A major progression on his 12-string acoustic guitar. He was considering having his next album use the structure of Bob Dylan's *Bringing It All Back Home*: one side electric, one side rambling and acoustic, with "Width of a Circle" slated for the latter. But he was tiring of folk music. Undertaking a small tour in late 1969 to promote *Space Oddity*, he was occasionally heckled and once (in Kent) got pelted with empty beer cans and cigarette butts. He was crouched on a stool with his acoustic guitar, meandering through his songs at a time when tastes were coarsening. The Beatles were dead. Led Zeppelin was the biggest band in Britain, with Black Sabbath and Deep Purple right behind them.

So if there was going to be an arms race, Bowie began to stockpile munitions. With a hot lead guitarist in Ronson, Bowie soon formed a hard rock trio: The Hype. Their stage act reworked the Riot Squad shows of 1967 (see "Little Toy Soldier"), with the band sporting costumes: Visconti a superhero, Ronson a gangster, Cambridge a cowboy. In the Hype shows, Bowie's songs mutated into extended set-pieces and worked out in a way the *Space Oddity* songs never were.

The Man Who Sold the World, the album that came out of this period, was Bowie's most adolescent record. "It was all family problems and analogies put into science-fiction form," he recalled in 1976. There's a hot teenage stupidity in the likes of "The Supermen" and "She Shook Me Cold," while "Running Gun Blues" and "Saviour Machine" channel sexual tension into fantasies of violence and dominance. It was the loud, messy repudiation of having once been a child.

In the debut performance of "Width of a Circle," you can hear Ronson, who'd learned the song the day before, thinking aloud—filling in spaces, working out angles. He opened with an ominous riff that sounded like the opening music of the Seventies, emerging tentatively once Cambridge established a kick-drum pattern. His playing is close at times to Jeff Beck's "Beck's Bolero," just one of the steals the barely-rehearsed players threw in: some Bo Diddley riffs crop up as well. After Ronson's solo, the band rumbled to a close in the vein of some *Space Oddity* tracks.

By the time he cut "Width of a Circle" in the studio two months later, Ronson had honed his opening riff into a weapon. After a feedback squall, with reversed reverb echoing in the right channel, he slid a finger along his guitar's A string, making a slow retreat up the neck from seventh to second fret. Soon mirrored by Bowie's acoustic guitar (its two lowest strings tuned in unison) and paced by Woodmansey's closed hi-hat, and further shadowed by Visconti's bass, Ronson took flight when Woodmansey roused to life with a snare-to-middle tom fill. (There's a rich texture to the mix, thanks to Visconti miking the band live in one room at Trident Studios, the drums bleeding into the other tracks.)

Compared to how Marc Bolan flogged his riff to death on "The Prettiest Star," Ronson husbands his goods: his opening riff only appears once more, after the third verse. He dominated by other means, like fast E chord revving for the ends of phrases. His first solo, a 20-bar set of assorted explosions, opened with Ronson notching and bending his guitar's G string as if he intends to snap it off. After a streak of high F-sharps, he devoted four bars to extravagant pull-offs with so much vibrato it sounds as if he's thwanging a giant rubber band. He closed with a vicious pick slide. Ronson's solo was his grand debut: nothing of its like had ever been on a Bowie record.

As the initial "Width of a Circle" had petered out after two verses and a guitar solo, Ronson and Visconti thought it could work on a more epic scale. During a rehearsal, they played what Visconti described as a "spontaneous boogie riff" in D major, which the two liked enough to append it to the existing song. Working the "boogie" riff into a 16-bar verse structure, they asked Bowie to come up with melodies and lyrics for it.

On the studio take, after the band repeats the opening riff sequence, the tempo slows (4:28) for a quick shuffling of players—Bowie's acoustic, smeared in backwards reverb, briefly becomes the lead ("Columbine" winks in here). Ronson reappears with a melody that Bowie sings back to him. This had been the climax of the original. Now came the join, a shift to a juddering 12/8 with a doubling of tempo (5:33) as Bowie descends into hell.

Bowie's original lyric, the product of being drunk under the spell of Friedrich Nietzsche's *Thus Spake Zarathustra* (see "The Supermen"), was a parable for his creative growth. A weak disciple who'd kept to the "straight and narrow" and whose work had suffered for it, Bowie finds his alter ego sitting by a tree; it's the first of several doppelgangers on the record. He chats with his liberated un-self, realizes he's been so under the sway of "masters" that he's lost himself—he's been an old man at a time when even God's young. So he gets laid and sweeps off stage in drag. Salting in a few chic references (the Lebanese poet Khalil Gibran, a favorite of Angela Bowie's and whose *The Prophet* was standard issue for any young hippie's flat), Bowie tied off his transformation with a few triumphant wails.

Needing to come up with more lyrics for the "boogie riff" section, Bowie went for lurid spectacle. Now he wrestles with a demonic lover ("turn around, *go back*!" Visconti and Ronson holler as Bowie falls into the pit, or heads to the back room of the bar), sex so consuming or debasing that it seems like a mental break, Bowie using the imagery (a crack in the ground, a burning pit) of his half-brother Terry's descriptions of his schizophrenic episodes. With its swollen tongues, spitting snakes, puckered lips and leather belts, the lyric coupled Kenneth Anger and L. Sprague de Camp. Bowie sold it like a bawd.

Ronson and Visconti mortared in the cracks, making the boogie section seem a natural extension of the original song. Ronson's second big solo (6:38) was a bluesy elaboration of the dirty riff he'd used to propel the verses, his lead playing now embellished by a possibly equalized acoustic guitar (EMI transcribers call it a banjo) parked low in the right channel. Visconti egged him on with exuberant leaps: his bass was mixed so high and given such massive distortion (Ronson's doing, Visconti claimed) that it's the champion of the coda, tolling under Bowie's last cries. The track concludes with a quotation on timpani from Strauss' "Also Sprach Zarathustra." Given all that's come before, this seems modest.

On stage, Ronson turned "Width of a Circle" into a high mass for the electric guitar. By 1973 he'd solo for nearly ten minutes as Bowie went backstage for a costume change. After Bowie and Ronson split, Bowie rearranged the song for his "Diamond Dogs" tour, distributing many of the guitar parts to flute, saxophone and keyboards. His new guitarist Earl Slick delivered two squalling solos that still ruled the song: Ronson had made a guitarist's feast and Slick wasn't one to abstain.

The Supermen

Recorded**: 23 March, 17 April-22 May 1970, Trident and/or Advision. Bowie: lead and backing vocal; Ronson: lead and rhythm guitar, backing vocal; Visconti: bass, backing vocal; Woodmansey: drums, timpani. Produced, arranged: Visconti; engineered: Scott, Chevin;* ***(remake) *12 November 1971, Trident. Bowie: lead vocal, 12-string acoustic guitar; Ronson: lead guitar; Trevor Bolder: bass; Woodmansey: drums. Produced: Scott.*

First release**: 4 November 1970,* ***The Man Who Sold the World**; (remake) ca. June 1972,* ***Revelations—a Musical Anthology for

Glastonbury Fayre *(Revelation REV 1A-3F).* ***Broadcast:*** *25 March 1970, Sounds of the 70s: Andy Ferris; 3 June 1971, In Concert: John Peel; 21 September 1971, Sounds of the 70s: Bob Harris; ca. 4-6 January 1997, ChangesNowBowie (Radio One); 26 September 1997, CFNY (Toronto); 7 November 1997, Rock & Pop (Argentina).* ***Live:*** *1970-1973, 1997, 2003-2004.*

Never having the sunniest of dispositions, Bowie grew publicly apocalyptic in the Seventies. He knew what was coming, or so he told interviewers: neo-fascism, nuclear war, institutional decadence, civilization's end (he gave the human race 40 years to live, soon cut it down to five). Worse, he was reading Nietzsche, in particular *Thus Spake Zarathustra* and *Beyond Good and Evil,* from which he took the idea of a race of "overmen" supplanting *homo sapiens.* This was a best-case scenario.

Using Nietzsche to reflect the generational turmoil of his own time, Bowie toyed with a metaphor: the children of the Seventies as a mutant strain of humanity that would consume their parents (see "Oh! You Pretty Things"). With Nietzsche as a starting point, he tossed into the brew SF novels like John Wyndham's *The Midwich Cuckoos,* Arthur C. Clarke's *Childhood's End* and Theodore Sturgeon's *More Than Human.* His overmen were also the mutated Buddhist monks of his Sixties songs, Wilder Boys from Freecloud.

While Bowie later said his Nietzsche period was bluster ("the Nietzsche thing was kind of a quick read. I probably liked the cover"), he was selling himself short, as he tended to wind up actually reading the books he bluffed about (as Mick Farren said: "where some people would read a book jacket and bullshit, David would bullshit, then read the book quietly one Sunday afternoon."). He'd imbibed enough Nietzsche for images and lines from *Zarathustra* to haunt *The Man Who Sold the World,* where he conflated Nietzsche's overman (not the Aryan god of Nazi pseudo-mythology, but someone who had escaped the "slavery" of Christianity to be life-affirming and creative) with Buddhism and his developing interest in Aleister Crowley (see "Holy Holy"). This tidal pool created his dominant artistic persona of the early Seventies: an overman space-monk figure who would lead the escape from "the tribal feelgood dope-fug of the 1960s," as Momus said. *MWSTW* shares with *Ziggy Stardust* and even *Station to Station* a common narrative tone: the voice of someone removed, enlightened yet still questing, at times seeming deranged.

"The Supermen" was a "period piece," Bowie said in 1973, although which period, the dawn or end of time, he left open. He set his overmen playing and warring on their "loveless isle" (still rainy England, one assumes). Where Donovan's "Atlantis" had the survivors of ancient Atlantis bestow art and science to the human race, Bowie's supermen are just brutes, articles of force (he later called the song "pre-fascist"). It was a warning: *this* is the liberated self, freed from all ties to humanity, someone who grows so weary of perfection he dreams of murder and rotting flesh ("Saviour Machine" had the same plotline).

Jimmy Page had given Bowie the main riff—a lumbering stride up an octave in F major and G major. It begins in the depths: after an opening fanfare on drums, the riff sounds first on timpani and is taken up by Tony Visconti's bass. The underlying monolithic F and G chords war for dominance. While F major seems to prevail at last in the refrain, "The Supermen" could equally be in the thrall of C major.

Ronson and Visconti set Bowie's lonely gods in an "outrageous sonic landscape" that included timpani, echo-tracked drums, a guitar track devoted to playing feedback-shrouded root notes and a four-part choral harmony that soars over an octave. Ronson's solo, which he spun out of three harmonized guitars (a lead guitar and two others pitched a third and fifth lower), opens with a declaration of war, peaks with a rollicking nine-note phrase repeated across three bars of 7/8 and restores calm with a bar of 6/4.

While impressive, "The Supermen" sounds thin and strange when heard alongside contemporary hard rock records like *Led Zeppelin II* and Black Sabbath's *Paranoid*. Part of it was due to Philips' miniscule budget for *The Man Who Sold the World*, which required Visconti to schedule most sessions on weekends, shuttling between two studios on the graveyard shift (a typical recording session was 1-7 AM, Sunday morning). It was also owed to Bowie's outrageous vocal. He whines, sours vowels, sings in a high nasal burr, forces rhymes with a Mockney accent, pops the mike, wheezes alliterative lines (the larynx-scraping aitches of "heavy hung"). It's as though he's inventing Johnny Rotten. If "The Supermen" was meant to be Bowie's voice of God, it's God as an unhinged android, a camper version of Laurence Olivier's already-shrieking take on King Richard III.

He re-recorded "The Supermen" during the *Ziggy Stardust* sessions, donating one of two completed takes to a compilation LP for the Glastonbury Fayre. The revision suggested a group rethink of the song, similar to the contemporaneous remake of "Holy Holy." In both cases, Bowie replaced eccentricity with hard rock suavity. On the remade "Supermen," he kept a straight face while the arrangement cleanly offset acoustic verses with slamming Ronson-dominated refrains (Ronson now forgoes his solo). Bowie and the Spiders played the refitted "Supermen" in most of their live shows. He'd later exhume the master race in an acoustic rendition for his 50th birthday year, also playing it on some of his later tours.

All the Madmen

Recorded: *17 April-22 May 1970, Trident and/or Advision. Bowie: lead vocal, 12-string acoustic guitar; Ronson: lead and rhythm guitars, recorder; Visconti: bass, recorder; Woodmansey: drums; Ralph Mace: Moog. Produced: Visconti; engineered: Scott, Chevin.*

First release: *4 November 1970,* ***The Man Who Sold the World****.*

***Live**: 1971, 1987.*

Bowie's family, on his mother's side, was riddled with mental illness: his aunt Una was institutionalized after a breakdown and died in her late twenties; another aunt was diagnosed with manic-depressive psychosis and lobotomized; a third had schizophrenic episodes. Then there was his mother's son, his half-brother Terry Burns, who was diagnosed with paranoid schizophrenia. When Bowie recorded *The Man Who Sold the World,* Burns was a regular ward at Cane Hill, a Victorian-era psychiatric hospital in Croydon, and occasionally released to stay at Haddon Hall on weekends.

So Bowie believed he had considerable odds of going mad. The prospect bled into his work—all the lyrics about identity, control and insanity, the devising of various personae as means of escape, writing songs as conduits. "One puts oneself through such psychological damage in trying to avoid the threat of insanity," he recalled in 1993. "As long as I could push these psychological excesses through into my music, into my work, then I could always be throwing it off."

In "All the Madmen," his first overt attempt to grapple with his inheritance, Bowie references Cane Hill ("mansions cold and grey") and the treatments offered there: EST (electroshock therapy), Librium (brand name of the anxiety drug chlordiazepoxide) and "good old lobotomy." And his refrain is a homage to one of Burns' (and his) favorite books, Jack Kerouac's *On the Road*: "The only people for me are the mad ones…the ones who never yawn or say a commonplace thing, but burn, burn, burn like fabulous yellow Roman candles."

The idea that the institutionalized were, in Bowie's words, society's "organic minds kept in a cellar," was becoming common in the Sixties. The psychiatrist R.D. Laing argued much of what was diagnosed madness was instead a sensitive mind's defense against the oppressions of family and modern civilization. In his *The Politics of Experience* (1967) Laing argued the schizophrenic could be the most "sane" person of an insane society, and that behavior labeled schizophrenic was instead a "special strategy that a person invents to live in an unlivable situation." Similarly, the idea of involuntarily confining the insane to a mental institution had come under attack. Ken Kesey's *One Flew Over the Cuckoo's Nest*, Michel Foucault's *Madness and Civilization* and Erving Goffman's *Asylums* depicted the asylum as society's washroom, its bureaucratic means of removing the mad from common life to better enforce cultural norms (like having homosexuals "cured" via shock treatment). Institutionalization created its own self-fulfilling cycle of admittance-treatment-breakdown-readmittance. It was a prison culture. The anti-psychiatric movement, proposing the deinstitutionalization Goffman and other sympathetic writers favored, came out of this ferment. So did "All the Madmen."

That said, the song also had Bowie's mordant sense of humor, his collagist sensibility (Bowie tweaks the Beatles' "You Better Hide Your Love Away" and "Fool on the Hill" in his lyric) and his taste for shock and ghoulishness. He mingles "The Laughing Gnome" ("he followed me home Mum, can I keep him?" he pips in a sped-up "kid" voice) with Friedrich Nietzsche. Like "Width of a Circle," Bowie used the "Tree on the Hill" chapter of *Thus Spake Zarathustra*, in which Zarathustra encounters a young man who desperately yearns for transcendence, who wants to free the dogs from his "cellar" so that he can climb the heights. The closing Dadaist-inspired line ("zane zane zane, ouvre le chien (open the dog)") referenced this: "thy wild dogs want liberty, they bark for joy in their cellar when thy spirit endeavoureth to open all prison doors." More prosaically, if you break open your own asylum, you'll unleash your basest instincts along with your nobler aspirations.

Given this backdrop, it's fitting that "All the Madmen" was Bowie's most harmonically radical piece on the album. Opening with shifts between E minor and augmentations of the E major chord, the verse soon establishes two spheres of influence: E major and F major ("the far side of town"), while the arrival of a G major chord ("heavy as can be") in the pre-chorus offered another candidate. With E major, F major and G major vying for control, "All the Madmen" feels chaotic, as those chords don't coexist in any key, a conflict never resolved (see "Station to Station"). But as E, F and G are chords often used in flamenco, Ronson and Visconti, in an inspired response, wrote a "bolero" style accompaniment for Ronson's solo (starting at 3:07).

One of the first songs recorded for the album sessions, "All the Madmen" began with Bowie on his 12-string acoustic, slowly panned left to right. A brusque performance with ringing open strings, Bowie keeps a constant low E as a bassline while in a closing bar of 5/4, he's topped by a "violining" C note from Ronson. After a second acoustic verse marked by a descant recorder duet (Ronson and Visconti) and Woodmansey ringing on his cymbal bell, Ronson kicks into the refrain with a distorted power chord; soon he's off on a two-harmonized-guitar solo. After a spoken interlude by Deram-era Bowie, with its newscasters and eerie children, "All the Madmen" became Ronson's show again. He rips through the last verse with pick scratches as if mocking the recorders' tippling accompaniment (they're soon swapped out for Ralph Mace's Moog, which acts as a string section).

After dabbling for much of its length, "All the Madmen" commits to madness. It closes with Bowie chanting "ouvre le chien" in descending phrases while voices swirl around him and echoed handclaps sound him out. One of his most brilliant compositions to date, "All the Madmen" was also the keystone of an inspired musical sequence, the first side of *The Man Who Sold the World*, where "Madmen" douses the spirits of "Width of a Circle" and presages the ashen side-closer "After All."

After All

Recorded: *late April-22 May 1970, Trident and/or Advision. Bowie: lead and backing vocals, 12-string acoustic guitar, Stylophone; Ronson: lead guitar, 12-string acoustic guitar, recorder; Visconti: bass, double bass?, recorder; Woodmansey: drums, orchestral bass drum; Mace: Moog. Produced: Visconti; engineered: Scott, Chevin.*

First release: *4 November 1970,* ***The Man Who Sold the World***.

The Man Who Sold the World is extremities: devils, supermen, supercomputers, madmen, serial killers, sex maniacs. Bowie once described it as a landscape in which the human element had been erased. The high exception was "After All," the album's one broken human element, its E minor key shading into its parallel (E) and relative (G) majors, its lyrical perspective that of a disintegrating personality who shifts between "I," "we" and "they."

With Bowie putting off writing his lyrics until the eleventh hour, this perversely gave his songs unity: *Man Who Sold the World* was a more coherent concept album than either *Ziggy Stardust* or *Diamond Dogs*. Sharing thematic similarities and imagery (climbing, for instance), the songs mirror and answer each other. "After All" was the obverse of "The Supermen" (both tracks were side closers). Rather than gods, humanity is a group of children at play, those who daub their faces and dress like stars and the sadder, older children who mistake weariness for insight. It's mankind as a sad clown and a crawling child, a figure so hapless that Bowie has to intercede for them with a disappointed God ("please trip them gently, they don't like to fall"; in the last verse he apologizes for wasting the deity's time). His narrator here had his own sinister overtones, tying Buddhist reincarnation ("live 'till your rebirth") to Aleister Crowley's mantra "do what thou wilt."

The last of his psychedelic lullabies (see "There Is a Happy Land," "When I'm Five"), "After All" also bid farewell (for a time) to two of his Sixties trademarks. The varisped choir of grotesques in the refrains—a trio of treated voices spanning three octaves, alternating between "high" and "low" sets of "children"— was the "Laughing Gnome" as ghoul-show, while the Stylophone of "Space Oddity" crept in to drone. (At the same time "After All" looked ahead to generational manifestos like "All the Young Dudes," with its sense of a war brewing between older hippies and their younger siblings.)

Opening with Bowie singing in a near-whisper over two tracks of acoustic guitar, one strumming chords while the other needles them, his progress unsettled by the "oh-by-jingo!" refrains. Moving to G major ("painting our faces"), Bowie manages a smoother, more conjunct phrasing, while later verses introduce Visconti's distorted bass (sounding like a foghorn), a ruminative Ronson lead guitar and Ralph Mace's shadow bassline on Moog. A four-bar F-sharp minor interlude was a haunted calliope: recorders and Moog impersonated a pipe organ, supported by pizzicato double bass and Woodmansey pounding an orchestral bass drum. Unusually for the album, Bowie had recorded his vocal and acoustic guitar tracks first, leaving the rest of the song to Visconti and Ronson: the bridge was mostly their doing, with each trying to top the other in overdubs. The track doesn't feel overdone: if anything, there's a cold absence at its heart, heard in the decaying beauty in Bowie's title phrase, whose last note is swallowed in gloom.

She Shook Me Cold

***Recorded**: ca. 1-22 May 1970, Trident and/or Advision. Bowie: lead vocal; Ronson: lead guitar; Visconti: bass; Woodmansey: drums. Produced: Visconti; engineered: Scott, Chevin.*

***First release**: 4 November 1970, **The Man Who Sold the World**.*

Leading up to *The Man Who Sold the World*, Bowie ran through chord progressions and song structures with Mick Ronson and Tony Visconti in the basement rehearsal space at Haddon Hall. Once in the studio, however, he often let Visconti and Ronson develop the songs. ("David would suggest a chord sequence,

Mick and I would leap on that...and embellish it. Maybe write a bridge," Visconti recalled.) They came up with arrangements, cut rhythm tracks and solos and overdubs; they even named songs ("Black Country Rock"). Only towards the end of the sessions, even into the mixing stage, did Bowie write most of his lyrics and cut his vocals. It goes too far to claim that Bowie was an absentee landlord on the album and that Ronson and Visconti wrote most of it, but the argument rings true for "She Shook Me Cold": the sound of a long-struggling provincial guitarist given the run of Trident Studios to make a homage to Cream.

Ronson had built a power trio in Cream's image. Having ousted the affable John Cambridge for the more intense Woody Woodmansey, Ronson encouraged Visconti to emulate Cream's Jack Bruce, even convincing Visconti to use Bruce's favored Gibson short scale bass for the sessions. Pioneered by Cream, the Who and the Jimi Hendrix Experience, the power trio was the child of technology—higher-wattage amps like the Marshall Major (1967), effects pedals like the Wah-Wah, Octavia and Uni-Vibe (1966-1968), with overdubs more easily done on eight- and 16-track decks (1968 for the latter). Dispensing with the rhythm guitarist slot, a role suited for songwriters, meant lead guitarists had to double as nuts-and-bolts men. This was fine if you had Jimmy Page but it often meant taking shortcuts, settling for "a degradation of texture and a decline in musical subtlety...an excuse to replace songs with riffs and discard nuance for noise," as Ian MacDonald wrote.

So it's a credit to Ronson and Visconti that "She Shook Me Cold" wasn't just a grind-fest (it helped that both were arrangers). Opening with a homage to Hendrix's "Voodoo Child (Slight Return)," Ronson plays power chords under Bowie's stop-start vocal melody: a rising three-note phrase ("we-met-uh-"), a longer-held hinge note ("-PON") underscored by a hard-strummed chord and a root note plucked on bass, and two descending notes ("a hill"). Beneath this, Woodmansey is in turmoil with crash cymbal hits and triplet tom fills.

The bridge, with its freer vocal, finds Visconti and Ronson as co-conspirators in noise, both massively distorted against the hissing backdrop of Woodmansey's cymbals. At one point in Ronson's exuberant solo, he bends a string behind the nut before tearing off on a run of 32nd notes. After a spray of triplets, a Jeff Beck-esque "exotic" riff (starting at 3:26) and a free-time section where he lords over Woodmansey's kick drum, Ronson swaps roles with Visconti, holding the bottom end with a two-note pattern while the liberated bassist vaults octaves. Upon hearing the takes, Bowie gleefully joined the festivities with a suitable *al fresco* sex magic scenario that naturally climaxed in a verse of moaning (this also meant one less verse for him to write). The sonic barrage proved so exhausting, however, that Bowie's return for a post-coital verse was overkill.

Saviour Machine

***Recorded**: ca. 4-22 May 1970, Trident and/or Advision. Bowie: lead vocal, 12-string acoustic guitar; Ronson: lead guitar, rhythm guitar; Visconti: bass; Woodmansey: drums; Mace: Moog. Produced: Visconti; engineered: Scott, Chevin.*

***First release**: 4 November 1970, **The Man Who Sold the World**.*

"Saviour Machine" was a nightmare of the Great Society (along with global overpopulation, see "We Are Hungry Men") in which giant computers conquer and threaten to exterminate the human race. The exponential growth of government between 1940 and 1970 and the parallel rise of mainframe computer networks (the idea of a "personal computer" was far-fetched to all but a few cranks) had one logical outcome: only a super-computer would be able to keep things running one day. Patrick Troughton's and Jon Pertwee's *Doctor Who* often took place on near-future Earths in which various Controllers and Supervisors run mega-computers that control everything from moon colonies to the weather.

Opening with a technocrat “President Joe” elected on a platform of installing a computer called “The Prayer” to end war and hunger (one wonders what his opponent’s platform was), much of “Saviour Machine” was devoted to an extended rant by The Prayer, in keeping with how *The Man Who Sold the World* had a taste for the deranged. Bowie’s jumpy mid-range third-person verse was the warm-up routine for his performance as a histrionic, easily bored computer. In the bridges he starts each phrase by bloating notes (usually the rhyming syllable: “***fea***si-ble, “be-l***ieve,*** “a-g***ree***”) and closes with a wailing moan. While the Prayer easily handles its job, perfection bores it enough to consider sending new plagues to keep its human subjects occupied. Chastising like an officious Old Testament God, it winds up begging to be unplugged.

In a rollicking 12/8 established by Woody Woodmansey’s hi-hat and emphasized, on the last three beats of each bar, by a unison Tony Visconti and Mick Ronson, “Saviour Machine” quickly dispenses with its verse to slalom through a set of bridges, guitar solos and refrains. A reappearing B-flat chord appeared, apparently to nudge the vaguely A minor key into F major, but the bridges instead veered into F-sharp minor.

Given its harmonic and structural oddities and that Ronson played the melody of “Ching-a-Ling” for his first solo, “Saviour Machine” was likely one of the *MWSTW* tracks Bowie was most involved in. That said, the lyric came from an overnight cram session spurred by Visconti’s deadline (the idea of a pushy computer imposing its will on humanity had some slight personal resonances). What made “Saviour Machine” was the group’s performance, conveying a churning violence beneath Bowie’s computer blues. Visconti challenged Ronson throughout the latter’s second solo, pushing his distorted bass higher and higher while Ronson bent notes and played descending patterns in triplets. Recovering in the coda, Ronson was soon harried by Woodmansey’s ride cymbal. But the most dexterous performer of

"Saviour Machine" was Ralph Mace, whose Moog was a gallery of musicians—a buzzing root-note tone for the intro, a "string section" spanning two octaves at breakneck speed in the bridges, a "trumpet" to close out Ronson's solo and herald its own, in which the synthesized trumpet plays the "Ching-a-Ling" melody over synthesized piano and bass, joined by a whistling ghost-in-the-machine arpeggio the second time around.

Running Gun Blues

***Recorded**: ca. 4-22 May 1970, Trident and/or Advision. Bowie: lead vocal, 12-string acoustic guitar; Ronson: lead guitar, slide guitar, backing vocal; Visconti: bass, backing vocal; Woodmansey: drums, tambourine; Mace: Moog. Produced: Visconti; engineered: Scott, Chevin.*

***First release**: 4 November 1970, **The Man Who Sold the World**.*

An early entrant in the distinguished "crazy Vietnam veteran" genre, "Running Gun Blues" found Bowie attempting to sound unhinged in the verses, where his octave-ranging, sing-song vocal suggested his gag work on "Buzz the Fuzz." He up-shifted to menace in the refrains, where he ranted about slicing up "gooks" (the title was a play on the Viet Cong epithet for American soldiers, "running dog"). Inspired by articles on the My Lai massacre and Charles Whitman's mass shootings at the University of Texas in 1966, Bowie wrote the lyric during an afternoon in which he kept being interrupted for press interviews, which might be why he rhymed "promote oblivion" with "plug a few civilians."

A ghastly holdover from his "protest" material of 1969 and raggedly assembled (with a bar of 7/8 to close out refrains), "Running Gun Blues" came close to being axed from *The Man Who Sold the World*. (Perversely, once Bowie decided to spare the track, he led off the LP's second side with it.) As with "Saviour Machine," the band lifted the song higher than it had any right to be. Mick Ronson, playing both slide guitar and a distorted lead, gives blood to the D-C-G riff Bowie had opened on double-tracked acoustic; Tony Visconti carries the world on his back; Woodmansey, after a reverbed kick drum intro and an opening verse playing tambourine 16ths, shifts to tom fills and wild abuse of his crash and ride cymbals for the refrains. As on "Saviour Machine," Ralph Mace broke the Moog into a cast of characters, including a "sine wave" vibrato-shrouded sound (playing, in the first verse, a variant of the "Space Oddity" Stylophone line, with a two-octave leap on "oblivion"), a synthesized bassline glowering an octave beneath Visconti and even some weedy-sounding "harmonica" fills.

Black Country Rock

Recorded: *ca. 1-22 May 1970, Trident and/or Advision. Bowie: lead vocal; Ronson: lead and rhythm guitars, piano; Visconti: bass; Woodmansey: drums, tambourine, shaker; Mace: Moog. Produced: Visconti; engineered: Scott, Chevin.*

First release*: 4 November 1970,* ***The Man Who Sold the World****.*

Tony Visconti and Mick Ronson worked up a barely-there Bowie sketch, an E major verse/refrain and a C major bridge, and provisionally called it "Black County Rock." Pressed for a lyric, Bowie played off the title for the verse, wrote four desperately-rhymed ("point of view/fond adieu") lines for the bridge and that was that. While intended as album filler, "Black County Rock" was far better: one of the album's best ensemble performances and a testament to Ronson's economic arranging skills.

Ronson was pointillist in his use of little riffs and motifs to assemble "Black Country Rock," for which he taped at least six separate guitar tracks. After an arpeggiated intro bar, he plays a bold ascending riff (0:04) across three octaves via two guitars and Visconti's bass, and gave a sharp, needling response (0:08) of four descending bent notes arrested by a leap up a third to sound an E#, the last note given heavy doses of vibrato and winking out with a grace note. He cycled these riffs through the verse/refrains, playing the descending motif on the third beat of every bar and having the ascending one cap each verse. The bridge had another pairing: a low-end riff (0:43), again echoed by bass, that trudges down to the cellar to stop on a low A, and a flurry of notes Ronson wrung from a single string to close out the bridge (0:51) and twice used to kick off a 16-bar solo.

Strengthened by two months of live performances, rehearsal time at Haddon Hall and nights jamming in the studio, the "power trio" of Ronson, Visconti and Woody Woodmansey proved to be leagues ahead of the shambling *Space Oddity* guitar jams. Doubled by Ralph Mace's Moog (in the solos, Mace kept sounding a distorted low A note like a system overload warning), Visconti was free to play roaming, exuberant lines—take how he excitedly spans a twelfth in each bar of the solo or how in the coda he pips in little high notes between playing eighth-note roots. Woodmansey's galvanizing kick drum and tom fills were shadowed by tambourine in the verse/refrains and a shaker in the bridges. Once Ronson's roadhouse-style piano is flown in at 3:07, it's as though the band gets a shot of amphetamine to take them to the fade.

While their title suggested Ronson and Visconti were having a go at the heavier sound then coming out of Birmingham, in the vocal booth Bowie trained his sights on Marc Bolan, making the last bridge a merciless Bolan imitation ending in a grotesquely-bleated "fond adieuuuuuuuuuu" and a satyr's gargled "ahh!" Visconti thinned the vocal tracks with an equalizer to make them a better match: the "my friend" in the last refrain is uncanny.

The Man Who Sold the World

***Recorded**: late April-22 May 1970, Trident and Advision. Bowie: lead vocal, 12-string acoustic guitar; Ronson: lead guitar, organ, vocal; Visconti: bass; Woodmansey: drums, guiro, woodblock, maracas. Produced: Visconti; engineered: Scott, Chevin;* **(Lulu take)** *16 July 1973, Château d'Hérouville, Hérouville, Val d'Oise, France; ca. early*

December 1973 (saxophone overdubs), Olympic or Trident Studios, London. Lulu: lead vocal; Bowie: alto saxophone, baritone saxophone, backing vocal; Ronson: lead guitar; Mike Garson: piano; Bolder: bass; Aynsley Dunbar: drums; Geoff MacCormack: backing vocal, conga. Produced: Bowie, Ronson; engineered: Andy Scott; **(remake)** *ca. October 1995. Bowie: lead vocal; Brian Eno: synthesizer; Reeves Gabrels: lead and rhythm guitar; Erdal Kizilcay? Gail Ann Dorsey?: bass; Mike Garson: piano, synthesizer; Sterling Campbell or Joey Barron: drums. Mixed: Eno.*

First release**: 4 November 1970,* ***The Man Who Sold the World*; (Lulu) 11 January 1974 (Polydor 2001 490, UK #3); (remake) November 1995 (RCA/BMG 74321 32940 2).* ***Broadcast****: 15 December 1979, Saturday Night Live; 23 November 1995, MTV Europe Music Awards; 2 December 1995, Later...With Jools Holland; 19 January 1996, Det Kommer Mera; 26 January 1996, Taratata; ca. 4-6 January 1997, ChangesNowBowie; 27 June 2000, An Evening With David Bowie.* ***Live****: 1995-1997, 2000, 2003-2004.*

Bowie planned to call the album *Metrobolist*, playing off Fritz Lang's *Metropolis*. *Metrobolist* was also the title of Mike Weller's cover illustration, in which a man, whose image Weller took from a photo of John Wayne in a film annual, walks past Cane Hill Asylum shouldering a rifle. A piece of his head is exploding, as if the "Running Gun Blues" sniper has picked him off. In a (last?) speech bubble, he says: ROLL UP YOUR SLEEVES, TAKE A LOOK AT YOUR ARMS. Mercury, which released the album in America half a year before it would in Britain, erased the bubble for its alleged heroin reference and for good measure changed the album's title, without Bowie's consent, to *The Man Who Sold the World*.

On the last day mixing the album, Bowie had yet to write a lyric for a track cued up on the deck. While Tony Visconti waited, tapping his fingers on the console, Bowie sat in the reception area of Advision Studios to scratch out some lines on paper. He ran into the booth, taped his lead vocal, cut overdubs. Visconti flanged the vocal, mixed the track in a few hours and sent the tapes off the same night.

You'd expect something like "Black Country Rock" from these straitened circumstances but instead Bowie wrote "The Man Who Sold the World," his most sublime lyric of the record. Mercury was right: "The Man Who Sold the World" was the album's real title, its prime mover. We should take Visconti's story with a grain of salt, as it's likely Bowie had written some lines before that night in Advision (though some do scan like a first draft: "I gazed a gazely stare"). But much of it feels improvisatory. It's a sleep-walker's memory, a piece of automatic writing.

A pair of verses and a four-line refrain, Bowie's lyric had a score of absent fathers. Its title came from Robert Heinlein's *The Man Who Sold the Moon*, its opening lines from Hughes Mearns' poem "Antigonish" (or, more likely, the Forties song taken from it, "The Little Man Who Wasn't There"). The idea of a man meeting his double also came from Mearns (he'd based his poem on tales of a ghost haunting the stairwell of a house in Nova Scotia), though the idea was stock German Romanticism, later filtered through science fiction (see Ray Bradbury's "Night Meeting," where a man and Martian cross paths in the deserts of Mars one night, each convinced the other hails from the distant past). There was also *The Image*, a 1967 short film Bowie had co-starred in, in which an artist paints a picture of a young man (Bowie) who turns up at his door and who, despite soon being killed, keeps returning to plague the artist. Upon destroying the painting, the artist falls dead, having killed himself along with his alter ego.

Bowie passes a man on the stair (who's going up, who's going down?). He's not really present—he could be asleep, dead, gone astray from his own time. Whatever led him to the stair, he finds the man he meets far stranger. "I thought you died *alone*, a long, long time ago,"he says. The other answers in a refrain: "Oh *no*, not *me*" and, as if extending his card, announces he's the Man

Who Sold the World, the greatest of the extremities this strange record has offered. He could be just what he says he is: a Major Tom who never lost contact with Ground Control; a man who never let his imagination take him where it would; the man who kept his dogs in the cellar (see "All the Madmen"). Just common David Jones, living out a quiet life in Bromley, rebuking a divergent self.

On "Width of a Circle," meeting his doppelganger inspired Bowie to liberate himself. The encounter here promises nothing and yields less. His lines have the coldness of an old riddle and he delivers them in stage actions, singing a descending phrase two bars before the verse proper begins ("we passed upon the..."), starting most of his phrases with a verb ("spoke," "said," "died," "searched," "gazed"). If the first verse is Now, the second verse was Afterward; a cut from the stairwell to the world, where Bowie wanders in exile, passing thousands of others who've had their own encounters on their own stairs.

There's a stillness in "Man Who Sold the World," the eye of its album. Apart from Mick Ronson's processed electric guitar, it's an acoustic track with light percussive colors: woodblock and croaking guiro in the verses, maracas in the refrains. Visconti eschewed his usual octave-leaping to provide a steady floor, while Ronson's riff was simple enough to be a first guitar lesson. As could the refrain: first Visconti on bass, then Ronson on guitar climb the same path, playing scales as if they're pupils in a band class—first the C major scale, then F major. (A B-flat minor chord casts a brief shadow of doubt.)

Like "All the Madmen," the song had three tonal centers vying for control: A major (the opening chord of intro and verse), D minor and F major (the key of the refrain). Bowie sang and Ronson played across all of them, strangers moving through a moving landscape. The ominous coda, with its wordless melody that becomes a three-part choral round, sank further and further into D minor but didn't seem to find any rest there.

Made My Way

Sometime in the late Eighties Chad Channing, a drummer in Seattle, bought a used *The Man Who Sold the World* LP and dubbed it onto cassette. He played the tape when he drove around his bandmates, Kurt Cobain and Krist Novoselic. Cobain soon picked up on the title song and was surprised to learn it was by David Bowie (recall this was the "Glass Spider" Bowie era). A few years later, when Cobain and Novoselic's band began what would be their final tour, they went to New York to play a set for *MTV Unplugged*. Nirvana didn't do an acoustic "Smells Like Teen Spirit" (defeating the purpose of the show, which was to make Starbucks-ready versions of your hits) and devoted half of their set to relatively obscure covers: three Meat Puppets songs, a Vaselines hymn, a Leadbelly blues and "The Man Who Sold The World," which, as far as MTV was concerned, might as well have been a Bowie outtake.

After Cobain killed himself six months later, the songs he sang that night were forced into new shapes. "All Apologies" became a self-requiem, "Where Did You Sleep Last Night" a last curse, "Plateau" and "Lake of Fire" visions of the afterlife. And "Man Who Sold the World" became his ghost song. Singing it that night in 1993, Cobain came off as a emptied man, floating on a slight wave of disgust (with himself, with whoever he found on the stair), his voice catching on lines like "he said I was his friend." He kept "Man Who Sold the World" in sets throughout the subsequent Nirvana tour, including their last show in Italy. Then he made his way back home to Seattle, where he died alone.

Back Home

Before Cobain had claimed a stake in "Man Who Sold the World," Bowie had only revisited the song twice. In 1973, he turned it into glam disco for the Scots belter Lulu, building her track on a fresh Ronson riff and his own piercing saxophone overdubs. Lulu sang the hell out of it (Bowie had her smoke cigarettes before takes to abrade her voice), dressed in a gangster suit for the promo film. Her "Man Who Sold the World" was loud, captivating, distorted; it made the Bowie original seem like a demo and it charted higher (#3 UK) than nearly all of his Seventies singles.

On one of the last weekends of the Seventies, Bowie went Lulu one further. Someone turning on *Saturday Night Live* that night could have thought a European avant-garde theater troupe had commandeered the show. Wearing a giant Dadaist tuxedo, Bowie was hoisted onstage like a placard by the singers Klaus Nomi and Joey Arias, two vampires in crimson and black dresses. Bowie sang "Man Who Sold the World" as a riddle he hadn't puzzled out, while Nomi and Arias' countertenors, especially in the astonishing coda, soared over Bowie. The performance had a severity; it was a final aria, one of Bowie's set of farewells to the Seventies.

Maybe he'd never have played it again. But Nirvana's cover, aired throughout 1994 (MTV sat shiva for Cobain by running *Nirvana Unplugged* seemingly around the clock), brought the song back into the light. Despite Cobain's introductions on stage that "this is a David Boooie song," many kids thought Cobain had written it. Bowie was in a spot. If he revived "Man Who Sold the World," it could seem as though he was cashing in on a dead star. Yet Cobain had made the song *current*. It couldn't be ignored.

A year later, Bowie made his move. He responded to Cobain's annexation by winding the song into itself, erasing everything familiar—the vocal melody, Ronson's riff, the chorus scales—as if it was the speech bubble of Mike Weller's cartoon (much as how he'd deconstructed "Space Oddity" in 1979). Singing recitative over a minimalist electronic beat, he was still out in the world alone, he'd never made it back to the stair. This deliberate estrangement didn't last for long. By the end of the century, and particularly in his last tour of 2003-2004, Bowie sang "The Man Who Sold the World" in its "classic" version, with a touch of

Cobain. It was now part of the canon, up there with "Changes" and "Jean Genie" and "Let's Dance." He'd reclaimed a child stolen from him, but it wasn't his anymore.

Tired of My Life

Recorded: *(demo, unreleased) ca. spring-summer 1970, Haddon Hall, Beckenham? (Trident?). Bowie: lead and harmony vocal, 12-string acoustic guitar; Ronson [?]: harmony vocal?.*

A song of maudlin potential considered for *The Man Who Sold the World*, "Tired of My Life" exists only as a demo, one most likely cut at Haddon Hall though it could be a studio run-through. It's a return to the folk ruminations of *Space Oddity*, with a more pronounced Crosby, Stills & Nash influence in the vocal harmonies (by a multi-tracked Bowie or with Mick Ronson). Bowie shelved it for a decade, then recycled its bridge for "It's No Game" on *Scary Monsters*, where the line "put a bullet in my brain and it makes all the papers" acquired a new, horrific context after John Lennon's murder.

Holy Holy

Recorded: ***(single)*** *9 November, 13-16 November 1970, Island Studio 2, 8-10 Basing Street, London. Bowie: lead vocal, 12-string acoustic guitar; Alan Parker: lead guitar; Herbie Flowers; bass; Barry Morgan: drums. Produced: Flowers;* ***(remake)*** *ca. October/November 1971, Trident Studios. Bowie: lead vocal; Ronson: lead and rhythm guitar; Bolder: bass; Woodmansey: drums. Produced: Scott.*

First release: *15 January 1971 (Mercury 6052 049); (remake) 14 June 1974 (RCA APBO 0293).* ***Broadcast***: *18 January 1971, Six-O-One Newsday.*

Bowie's third straight flop single, "Holy Holy" marked the end of his time with Philips/Mercury. As with "The Prettiest Star," its commercial failure was helped by his apparent disinterest in the single, with Bowie singing it once on a Granada TV show and apparently never playing it live. He cut "Holy Holy" during a period in late 1970 when he'd squandered whatever progress he'd made with *The Man Who Sold the World*. He'd split with Tony Visconti and, temporarily, with Mick Ronson and Woody Woodmansey (frustrated by lack of work, they'd gone back to Hull). So "Holy Holy" was a pick-up job, with Bowie's new manager Tony Defries hiring the bassist Herbie Flowers to produce and arrange a session. Flowers brought in most of Blue Mink, a studio group with a pair of hit singles. "Holy Holy" even was hyped as the start of a Bowie/Blue Mink partnership.

Flowers didn't think much of it ("some things don't gel," he later said), as Blue Mink had to hold together a half-written song—a single alliterative verse, a pre-chorus and a refrain. Bowie had just picked a few pieces from recent compositions: dueling E major and F major chords from "The Supermen," flamenco guitar from "All the Madmen." More notable were a few open references to Aleister Crowley. As he'd soon expand on his Crowley obsession in "Quicksand," it's worth briefly delving into Crowley's appeal to the British rock scene at the dawn of the Seventies.

Born in 1875, Crowley was a polymath, occultist, mountaineer, logorrheic writer (publishing over 400 books—his autobiography alone was six volumes) and long-distance sexual athlete, attempting to seduce every woman and man he encountered, with each of his wives unsurprisingly committed for insanity. He cultivated a reputation as the most evil man in England but as with most notable degenerates, the rumors of his villainy surpassed his actual life, though not for lack of effort. His sex-saturated existence, his colossal estimation of his talents, his consumption of drugs by the barrelful, his dandified style (as a young man he wore "pure silk shirts and great floppy bow-knotted ties"; he aged into a Superman villain) and his necromantic obsessions would captivate a generation of British rockers. A notable disciple was Jimmy Page, collector of Crowley memorabilia and alleged member of one of Crowley's magic societies, the Ordo Templi Orientis.

What Page (and Bowie) found in Crowley wasn't the crude Satanist of public imagination but a Gnostic sage, one whose primary teaching was to liberate the self from all restraints (societal, psychological) to fulfill one's God-bestowed potential. Bowie had found a similar message in Nietzsche; others had found it in LSD. The appeal of this sort of ecstatic self-liberation was obvious in a prosperous, celebrity-mad age. "A man's progress depended on personal prowess," Crowley wrote. "No doubt this is philosophically absurd but I still maintain that it is practical good sense." Bowie and Page, both of whom had been on the margins for much of the Sixties, believed that following Crowleyian ritual had paid off ("it works," Page once said of Crowley's system)—it was a dark prosperity gospel with lots of sex.

"Holy Holy" is entry-level Crowley, with an emphasis on "sex magick." The goal was to channel the primal life force generated by sex, the peak power of orgasm, to charge talismans with magic power and gain insight into one's magical potential. ("Crowley's discovery of sex magic...united his two central aims: to be a magician and be a sexual athlete," Colin Wilson wrote.) Sex magick entailed "using sexual intensity as a ladder to ascend to still greater heights of intensity, focusing on the illumination." This was basically Tantric Yoga, into which Karl Kellner, founder of the OTO, had been initiated. Crowley went at it like a trooper in the 1910s, with one of his male partners believing he'd been possessed by the god Apollo upon orgasm.

So Bowie's crass come-on in the E major verse (it makes "Let Me Sleep Beside You" seem ornate) is elevated into a promise of sexual enlightenment in the A major refrain. Any chance of this being taken seriously was undermined by his dotty singing, a performance that didn't suggest Crowley as much as it did Anthony Powell's Kenneth Widmerpool, an aging peer who winds up cavorting in a hippie cult. (In 1997, Bowie told the *NME*

"I always thought Crowley was a charlatan.")

As with "The Prettiest Star" and "The Supermen," Bowie remade "Holy Holy" with the Spiders from Mars. Given some well-landed edits to lop a minute off the original's length and with Ronson seemingly inventing Brian May in the process, the revised "Holy Holy," with an echoed, menacing Bowie, was worthy of *Ziggy Stardust*. Instead it was released as a B-side three years later. So much a piece of its time, its time never came.

Chapter 5

Moon Age (1971-1972)

Yours is the last generation of **homo sapiens***...In a few years it will all be over, and the human race will have divided in twain. There is no way back, and no future for the world you know...You have given birth to your successors, and it is your tragedy that you will never understand them.*
Arthur C. Clarke, *Childhood's End.*

He stands there thinking, the kids keep coming, they keep crowding you up.
John Updike, *Rabbit, Run.*

[Dandyism] is the joy of astonishing others and the proud satisfaction of never oneself being astonished.
Charles Baudelaire, *The Painter of Modern Life.*

It all amounts to having faith in your manipulators.
Vince Eager.

The Nazz never did nothin' simple. When He laid it, He laid it.
Lord Buckley, "The Nazz."

Oh! You Pretty Things

Recorded**:** ***(demo, unreleased)*** *ca. March 1971, Radio Luxembourg Studios, 38 Hertford Street, London. David Bowie: lead vocal, piano;* ***(album)*** *21 June-late July 1971, Trident Studios, London. Bowie: lead vocal, piano, handclaps; Mick Ronson: harmony vocal, handclaps; Trevor Bolder: bass; Woody Woodmansey: drums; unknown musician: cello (arr. Ronson). Produced: Bowie, Ken Scott; engineered: Scott.*

First release*: 17 December 1971,* ***Hunky Dory*** *(RCA LSP 4623/*

SF 8244, UK #3). ***Broadcast****: 3 June 1971, In Concert: John Peel; 21 September 1971, Sounds of the 70s: Bob Harris; 7 February 1972, The Old Grey Whistle Test; 22 May 1972, Johnnie Walker Lunchtime Show.* ***Live****: 1971, 1973.*

We open at a recital, a prelude in F-sharp major: Bowie alone at a piano, keeping to its bass end and mainly to black keys, playing a querying three-note figure with his right hand, bass octaves with his left. Starting in an easy 2/4, he uses a waltz bar to propel into 4/4, where he stiffly plays a set of quaver chords. It sounds like a faulty player piano. He shifts into a higher key; the song "proper" begins.

"Oh! You Pretty Things," which opens with a man rousing someone for breakfast on a fresh, apocalyptic morning, was among the first songs he composed on piano. After Tony Visconti moved out of Haddon Hall in the summer of 1970, Bowie brought a grand piano (the gift of a neighbor) into Visconti's former room, making it his conservatory. He wrote much of *Hunky Dory* and *Ziggy Stardust* in there, with its chaise lounge and cut-rate art nouveau screen, an overflowing ashtray on the piano and tall windows that let out into the garden. He was free to do nothing but write. His manager Tony Defries had secured him an advance from his new publisher. Now he wanted Bowie off the road and out of the studio until he got a new record contract.

Given the wide range of tones within one's reach, songs composed on piano tend to be more harmonically adventurous, as songwriters can rig together chords and sound out progressions more easily than using the narrow voices of a guitar. Hence the freewheeling "Oh! You Pretty Things," a song that feels like it could go anywhere and soon enough does, roaming out of G major upon the arrival of B7/D# and D# diminished chords (which coincide with the first signs of apocalypse in the lyric). The tag bars between verses alone are a foxing run of chords that briefly revert to the intro's key and 2/4 time.

Bowie's phrasings were equally loose, with his sudden shifts in tone, internal rhythms and emphases, as if he was voicing all parts of a whirling conversation. In the first verse alone, he moves from holding on one note ("wake up you sleepyhead") to range across progressively larger melodic intervals, both sinking ("put another log on the fire for me" drops a sixth, from G to B) and rising ("and it looks as though they're here to stay" is a long clamber up an octave). "*Homo su*-perior" naturally tops out on an operatic high C.

It felt as if he'd captured the song in the wild, and in a way he had. The song appeared fully-formed in his mind one night, leaving him unable to sleep until he got up and found the chords on his piano. Feeling he had a potential hit, Bowie asked his publisher Bob Grace to double-book a session at Radio Luxembourg to cut a demo (on which his jangling bracelets were audible). Grace offered it to the producer Mickie Most and a few weeks later, Bowie played piano on a take by ex-Herman's Hermit Peter Noone, whose single reached #12 in the UK charts, Bowie's first pop presence since "Space Oddity."

Recorded in early summer 1971 for *Hunky Dory*, Bowie's take was a minimalist response to Noone's hit. It was the composer's cut. He dispensed with acoustic guitar, which Most had used to help the chord changes fall easier on the ear, and restored the song's original "recital" framework (Noone's single was bookended by refrains). Further, he played "composer's piano" instead of using Rick Wakeman, pianist for most of the album. Recorded dryly by Ken Scott, the piano in the verses was a restless force uninterested in supporting the vocal line (if anything, the vocal tries to impose order on a chaotic piano). Only in the refrain did "Oh! You Pretty Things" blossom into a modest pop production, with echoed handclaps and a slowly-descending cello line scored by Mick Ronson (his only contribution besides backing vocals). The refrain was the song's sunny public face, so hummable and sprightly ("it had that plodalong bassline that was very much a Paul McCartney thing," Bowie recalled), that it distracts from the strange business of its lyric: the supplanting of *homo sapiens* by a more evolved species.

Where "The Supermen," Bowie's first draft of this scenario, was a brutish epic, "Oh! You Pretty Things" had a charming domesticity. He took from Arthur C. Clarke's *Childhood's End,* a 1953 SF novel in which aliens called the Overlords come to Earth, end war and hunger and are revealed as midwives, having come to supervise the birth of the next species of humanity. The novel closes with the last *homo sapiens* living out their days in empty peace while their *homo superior* children roam the stars.

Bowie was inspired by the beautiful boys and girls he saw on parade at the Sombrero club in London each night, the coming race of bisexual fashion plates, but the song's emotional resonance came more from his use of Nietzschean SF trappings as a metaphor for how any generation regards its successor: with longing, wariness and resentment. It's an ode to paternal anxiety by a man about to become a father. After all, by reproducing, you bring home an alien being whom you'll serve and who will replace you (see "Kooks").

There's more acceptance than dread in the song, whose only harsh note is "the earth is a bitch," an image of the ground itself birthing a litter of super-children (Noone and Most replaced the line with "beast"). Bowie sang with the unflappable calm of a Gurney Slade walking through the world of Marvel Comics' *The X-Men*. Sung in anguish, "all the nightmares came today/and it looks as though they're here to stay" could be a Black Sabbath lyric. But Bowie sang it lightly, giving a rolling purr to the last words; he greeted the apocalypse with a shrug. Why struggle? What's the point? We're born obsolete and the world is so eager to leave us behind. "Oh! You Pretty Things" praises the beautiful and revolutionary children, our oblivious displacers, but takes quiet comfort in knowing they'll suffer the same fate. It ends as it began: a piano recital, the sound of a child's diligent success.

How Lucky You Are (Miss Peculiar)

***Recorded:* (demo, unreleased)** *ca. late December 1970, Radio Luxembourg Studios?. Bowie: lead vocal, piano; unknown musicians: bass, drums;* **(2nd demo, unreleased)** *ca. late April 1971, Trident. Mickey King: lead vocal; Bowie: backing vocal, piano?; Herbie Flowers: bass; Barry Morgan: drums; unknown musicians: horns.*

"How Lucky You Are" (also called "Miss Peculiar" on bootlegs) hailed from the composition binge that produced "Oh! You Pretty Things" and "Right On Mother," both of which Peter Noone recorded. It's hard to imagine Noone singing this one, however, Bowie's cracked embellishment of "Under My Thumb": "when you walk, you follow—two steps behind!" Its waltz rhythms suggested a cabaret influence, that the song had started life as one of Bowie's Jacques Brel pastiches (and there's a touch of the Beatles' "Happiness Is a Warm Gun" in its bridge). After offering the song to Tom Jones, who unsurprisingly passed on it, Bowie reworked it in April 1971 for would-be singer Mickey King (see "Rupert the Riley"), giving it a faster tempo and a horn arrangement impersonating John Barry's work. While "Miss Peculiar" went no further, Bowie reused its coda a decade later in "Revolutionary Song" and its opening verse in *Heathen*'s "A Better Future."

Right On Mother

***Recorded:* (demo, unreleased)** *9-10 March 1971, Radio Luxembourg. Bowie: lead vocal, piano.*

"Right On Mother" answers "Oh! You Pretty Things," bridging the latter's generation gap while using similar piano quaver chords and handclaps in its refrain. It was also a cheerier remake of "Uncle Arthur," in which the mother welcomes her son's new relationship; it suggests a ceasefire between Bowie's mother and his wife Angela. A bizarre lyric finds a boy elated that his mother knows he's having sex ("I'm a MAN!" he squeaks), though in the last verse he drops off his girl ("Siobhan," drawl-rhymed with "morn") so that he can spend the night with Mum instead. Peter Noone cut a version during his "Oh! You Pretty Things" session, with Bowie again playing piano, and released it as a dud single in late 1971.

Hang Onto Yourself

***Recorded*: (demo, unreleased)** *13 February 1971, Tom Ayres' house, Los Angeles. Bowie: lead vocal, guitar, bass;* **(Arnold Corns single)** *25 February 1971, Radio Luxembourg. Bowie: lead vocal, acoustic guitar?; Mark Pritchett: acoustic guitar, electric guitar; Peter de Somogyi: bass; Tim Broadbent: drums, tambourine;* **(album)** *8-11 November 1971, Trident Studios. Bowie: vocals, 12-string acoustic guitar; Ronson: lead and rhythm guitar; Bolder: bass; Woodmansey: drums; all: handclaps. Produced: Bowie, Scott; engineered: Mike Stone, Dennis MacKay.*

First release: *(Corns) 7 May 1971 (B&C CB 149); (album) 6 June 1972,* ***The Rise and Fall of Ziggy Stardust and the Spiders From Mars*** *(RCA SF 8287/ LSP 4702, UK #5).* ***Broadcast***: *11 January 1972, Sounds of the 70s: John Peel; 18 January 1972, Sounds of the 70s: Bob Harris; 16 May 1972, Sounds of the 70s: John Peel; 17 September 2003, Last Call With Carson Daly.* ***Live***: *1971-1973, 1978, 1983, 2003-2004.*

On 23 January 1971 David Bowie came to America for the first time. His former manager Kenneth Pitt had wanted Bowie's cross-Atlantic debut to be like Oscar Wilde's, alighting upon a New York City dock and met by a mob of reporters eager for witticisms. Instead Bowie, sporting a Lauren Bacall haircut and a "Universal Witness blue fur coat," flew into Dulles International Airport, where he was detained by customs agents, who searched him and sniggered at him. The only people to greet him were Mercury publicist Ron Oberman and his immediate family. Bowie spent his first night in the United States at Oberman's parents' house. He ate at a kosher deli in Silver Spring, Maryland, and went to a keg party, so covering the gamut of the

American experience.

Although he had a green card thanks to his American wife, he couldn't perform professionally thanks to the American Federation of Musicians, whose rules confined him to making radio and personal appearances to promote *The Man Who Sold the World*. So he turned his trip into research. With his acoustic guitar, a satchel of notebooks and a few dresses, he made his way north and west, from Washington DC to New York (where he saw the Velvet Underground play the Electric Circus) to Detroit to San Francisco and Los Angeles. In LA, he met DJ/scenester Rodney Bingenheimer and RCA producer Tom Ayres, who told him he should switch labels because RCA's cash cow Elvis Presley could only live so long.

He'd come to a fantastically prosperous country that had gone to war with itself. ("They've got lots of murders," Bowie said of the US to an audience in Aylesbury later that year. "It's kind of inbred in them to murder and kill...they come up with original ways of killing people.") Some of the violence was political. Around the time of Bowie's visit in early 1971, there was the Attica prison riot; in Michigan, the KKK dynamited school buses and tarred and feathered an integrationist high school principal; the Weather Underground bombed the Capitol; a pair of would-be eco-terrorists planned to poison Chicago's water supply. Much more of it was random street improvisations. Bowie got a taste outside of a Houston radio station, when a man drew a gun and said to kiss his ass. Despite this, Bowie traveled across America in absorption, gorging on new records, cases of which he shipped home to Britain (in San Francisco, Bowie bought the Stooges' *Fun House*). He was set to a boil. On sheets of hotel stationery he sketched ideas for a fabricated rock star whose name he coined from two new finds, Iggy Pop and the Legendary Stardust Cowboy.

"Hang Onto Yourself," a little tensor muscle of a song—a single verse and refrain over a rockabilly-style acoustic guitar riff—was his first musical response. He cut a demo at Ayres' home studio, which Gene Vincent was using at the time, and in Mod style debuted the song the following night at a Valentine's Day party. Days after his return to Britain, Bowie slated the song for the earliest of his "plastic rock star" ventures. Unable to record under his own name at the time because of his manager's negotiations, Bowie instead distributed new songs via false storefronts. He'd write and produce singles for a Dulwich College band called Rungk. Intrigued by the idea of corrupting "a bunch of public schoolboys," Bowie renamed them the Arnold Corns, in honor of Syd Barrett (a play on Pink Floyd's "Arnold Layne"), and gave them a cherubic lead singer, the stylist Freddi Burretti. As Burretti wasn't much of a singer, a bad situation made worse by Burretti's bout of performance anxiety in the studio, Bowie wound up doing the lead vocals.

The Corns' "Hang Onto Yourself" was a blend of old songs—its rhythms derived from the Velvet Underground's "Sweet Jane," its riff from Eddie Cochran's "Something Else," its chorus from "Please Please Me." Bowie's vocal was a beatnik-mumble take on Lou Reed and Dylan. Foreshadowing one of *Ziggy Stardust*'s concerns—the business of fabricating rock stardom—the original lyric read like a struggling band's indie promo effort. "Come on! we really got a good thing goin'!" the singer urges, telling his girl to keep the radio on until she hears his song.

Revising "Hang Onto Yourself" in late 1971 for *Ziggy Stardust,* Bowie toughened it up, quickening its tempo, moving it up in key (to D major) and bringing in a predatory groupie ("she's a funky-thigh collector"). Now he spoke-sung the verse and insinuated the refrain, rather than belting them out as on the Corns single, while the backing vocals conspired an octave beneath him. (Singing "Hang Onto Yourself" live, Bowie went back to belting out the song so he could be heard over his band.) The Spiders made the track sing. Trevor Bolder plays hammer-ons and syncopated lines in the verses, going full-tilt but managing to swing. Woody Woodmansey's pulsebeats are fattened by handclaps, while Mick Ronson said he just strapped on his guitar "and thrashed it to death, basically," though he also perfected the slide guitar hook Mark Pritchett had clunked through on the Corns single. Ronson became more outrageous the more he played "Hang Onto Yourself" live: by a May 1972 performance for the BBC, his final solo sounds like he's using a band saw.

Made to frenzy a crowd, "Hang Onto Yourself" was the first song that Bowie played for the first Spiders from Mars performance (for John Peel on 11 January 1972), the bruising set opener on most nights of the following tour and one of the few hard rock tracks on *Ziggy Stardust*, a record on which rock & roll often occurs off stage, like naval battles in Shakespeare's plays.

Moonage Daydream

Recorded**:** ***(Arnold Corns single)*** *25 February 1971, Radio Luxembourg. Bowie: lead vocal, piano; Pritchett: acoustic, electric guitar, backing vocals; de Somogyi: bass; Broadbent: drums, tambourine;* **(album)** *12 November 1971, Trident. Bowie: lead vocal, 12-string acoustic guitar, piccolo?, baritone saxophone; Ronson: lead guitar, piano, piccolo?; Bolder: bass; Woodmansey: drums; unknown musicians: violins, violas, celli. Arranged: Bowie, Ronson. Produced: Bowie, Scott; engineered: MacKay, Stone.*

First release*:(Corns) 7 May 1971 (B&C CB 149); (album) 6 June 1972,* ***Ziggy Stardust*****.** ***Broadcast****: 16 May 1972, Sounds of the 70s: John Peel.* ***Live****: 1972-1974, 1995-1997, 2002.*

It opens in shock. Two D major power chords—BAM*BAMM*—*I'm-an-ALL-UH-****GA****-TOR!*—two F# power chords with venom in them—BAM-***BAMM***!—*I'm-a-MAMMAPAPPACOMIN-FOR****YOU****!!!!!!,* the excitement fed by silent beats between each volley. (It's a rewrite of the Stooges' "TV Eye," which had opened with Iggy Pop screaming as though he'd been gored while Ron Asheton ignited his guitar.) But after only four bars, "Moonage Daydream" stills itself. Bowie's 12-string acoustic assumes control, Mick Ronson disappears. A melancholy B minor verse spools into a wistful piano-led refrain. The first solo isn't the presumed Ronson rave-out but a duet between a piccolo and baritone saxophones.

So "Moonage Daydream" is rock 'n' roll of delayed anticipation, a game of bluffs. (The guitarist Mark Pritchett once described the song as "Brechtian": "like a funfair with camp overtones"). As with "Hang Onto Yourself," Bowie crafted a lyric from whatever he found in his head, "busting out my brains for the words": ray guns and space faces from *Beano* and *New Worlds*; "far outs" and "freak outs" from favorite Frank Zappa ("come on, you Mothers!" Bowie yelled on the song's first version, the Arnold Corns single); "the church of Man-love" could even spoof Thomas Paine.

The Arnold Corns "Moonage Daydream" began with a thudding drum intro and a verse that made the listener do the imaginative heavy lifting: *lay the real thing on me,* a fraudulent singer implores on stage, *make me jump into the air*. Revising "Moonage Daydream" for *Ziggy Stardust,* Bowie saw he needed to build this up, that his character needed an opening holy-shit fanfare before he could make any demands. So he pushed the "lay the real thing" verse behind the refrain and sang a fresh opening verse in a rock 'n' roll stage dialect. The phonemes of *yer s**qu**aw**k**ing-li**k**e-a-pin**k**-mon**k**ey-birrrd!* were like stabs of a penknife.

He was exacting in what he wanted, considering "Moonage Daydream" as much a visual object as a record: it exemplified the producer Mike Leander's line that glam records "were constructed to be seen." On the Arnold Corns take, Bowie sat down at the drum kit to show Tim Broadbent precisely how to play a section. On *Ziggy Stardust,* Bowie sketched Ronson's climactic guitar solo, drawing a straight line that became "a fat megaphone-type shape, and ended as sprays of disassociated and broken lines." Ronson translated this into a run of vibrato-saturated notes that build to fast bends, spiking up to high F#s, with his Les Paul's tone tainted at the fade by washes of phased glissando strings. It's one of his definitive recorded moments, sounding as if a satellite had picked it up from deep space.

Along with nailing a rhythm track that took 10 takes to achieve (an eternity for the *Ziggy Stardust* sessions), Trevor Bolder was a secondary voice throughout, his descending bassline mirroring Bowie and Ronson's harmonies in the refrain. His light touch was an adaptation: Ken Scott had close-miked and directly injected his bass into the recording console, so if Bolder had plucked his stings too hard, he'd have broken up his tone. Woodmansey was an agitation—take how his low and medium tom fills shake up the refrain's closing bars, or how his snare triplets enfilade the solos. Ronson's scoring for strings added a fresh voice in the third refrain, with blissful rising notes on violins and violas countered by celli underscores (see "freak out" at 2:40).

By the time Bowie and the Spiders played their last concert at the Hammersmith Odeon in July 1973, "Moonage Daydream" had become a dreamsong: teenagers in the audience sang its refrain with their hands clasped to their faces. "Every night you knew that 'Moonage Daydream' was going to be the one that really lifted them," Bolder recalled in 1976. "Then we'd go and follow on from there to the end."

Rupert the Riley

Recorded*: (unreleased) 23 April 1971, Trident. Mickey King: lead vocal; Bowie: tenor saxophone, backing vocal, piano?; Pritchett: lead guitar; Flowers: bass; Morgan: drums. Produced: Bowie; engineered: Scott.*

The most endearing of Bowie outtakes, "Rupert the Riley" is an ode to his cars. With its purring engine of saxophone, piano, bass, sound effects and hummed backing vocals (the last reminiscent of Fairport Convention's "Cajun Woman"), "Rupert the Riley" was another go at creating a "fake" rock & roll singer, here a character who was part of the Bowie circle in the early Seventies. Known variously as Mickey, Sparky or Nick King, he was, in Bowie's words, "a 'club boy' who I encouraged to sing." King lived brightly, dangerously and not long—he was stabbed to death around 1974. He left behind this happy ghost of a song, whose "beep beep" hook Bowie recycled in "Fashion."

Lightning Frightening (The Man)

Recorded*: 23 April 1971, Trident. Bowie: lead vocal, tenor saxophone, piano?; Pritchett: lead guitar; Flowers: bass; Morgan?: drums; unknown musicians: harmonica (Benny Marshall?), piano. Produced: Bowie.*

First release*: 30 January 1990,* ***The Man Who Sold the World*** *(Ryko RCD 10132/ EMI CDEMC 3573).*

Cut in the same session as "Rupert the Riley," "Lightning Frightening," originally called "The Man," appeared two decades later as a bonus track on Rykodisc's *The Man Who Sold The World*. A blues-rock trudge over three chords, the track was mainly devoted to a set of 16- and 32-bar solos for harmonica (possibly Benny Marshall, who was around for some of the post-*MWSTW* sessions), saxophone and guitar, none distinguished. Along with its dullness, the track's subsequent obscurity was owed to the fact that Bowie's borrowings were just too blatant, as "Lightning Frightening" plagiarizes Crazy Horse's "Dirty Dirty" from their self-titled LP released in February 1971.

Man in the Middle

(Pritchett). ***Recorded****: 17 June 1971, Trident. Pritchett: lead vocal, lead guitar; Bowie: harmony vocal, acoustic guitar?; Ronson: rhythm guitar; Bolder: bass; Woodmansey: drums. Produced: Bowie, Roy Thomas-Baker.*

First release*: 11 August 1972 (B&C CB 189).*

"Man In the Middle," the proposed B-side of the second

Arnold Corns single, was a blurred carbon of the Velvet Underground in which Mark Pritchett, credited as songwriter, offered a decent mimicry of Doug Yule's voice, circa *Loaded*. Soon after cutting the track, Bowie abandoned the Arnold Corns to focus on *Ziggy Stardust*, whose title figure is presaged in some of the (likely co-written) lyric.

Looking for a Friend

Recorded*: (demo, unreleased)** *ca. spring 1971, Radio Luxembourg? Bowie: vocal, acoustic guitar?; unknown musicians: lead guitar (Pritchett?), bass (de Somogyi?), drums (Broadbent?), tambourine;* ***(Arnold Corns single, unreleased, two takes) *17 June 1971, Trident. Bowie: lead vocal, piano?; Pritchett: lead guitar, lead vocal; Freddi Burretti: vocal?; King: vocal?; Geoffrey MacCormack: vocal?; Ronson: rhythm guitar, vocal, piano?; Bolder: bass; Woodmansey: drums. Produced: Bowie; engineered: Thomas-Baker;* ***(Ziggy Stardust outtake, unreleased)*** *ca. early November 1971, Trident? Bowie: lead vocal, acoustic guitar?; Ronson: lead guitar; Bolder: bass; Woodmansey: drums. Produced: Bowie, Scott?*

First release*:** *(broadcast take): 26 September 2000,* ***Bowie at the Beeb *(EMI 7243 5 28629 2 4).* ***Broadcast*:** *3 June 1971, In Concert: John Peel (Bowie, Pritchett: vocals).* ***Live*:** *1971.*

In the summer of 1971, Bowie briefly fancied himself a starmaker, assembling a ragbag collection of would-be pop singers and "celebrities" in the vein of Andy Warhol's Factory. The Arnold Corns and Bowie's recruitment of Mickey King ("Rupert the Riley") were the first of these designs. When Bowie came to the Paris Cinema Studio on 3 June 1971 for a radio broadcast with John Peel, he went the whole hog. Despite this being his first radio appearance in over a year, and instead of showcasing songs from *The Man Who Sold the World* (released two months earlier), Bowie instead played covers and unreleased songs and brought along four other singers—the Corns' Mark Pritchett and friends Geoffrey MacCormack, George Underwood and Dana Gillespie—for a glam hootenanny.

Unveiled at the Peel session was "Looking For a Friend," which Bowie had demoed for consideration as an Arnold Corns single (he cut a studio take two weeks after the broadcast). A blues-by-numbers rocker in the Crazy Horse or Rolling Stones line, it starts by spoofing Dylan's "Times They Are a-Changin'" and its refrain is a cruising anthem for someone with catholic tastes: "don't have to be a big wheel/don't have to be the end." In the BBC take, Mick Ronson played a guitar line, doubled on Trevor Bolder's bass, that wound up on "Ziggy Stardust," while some of the lyric ("face-to-face with the spaceman on the wall") suggests Bowie had his mind on his new concept. Its best performance was one of its studio takes, where a roomful of revelers (including Bowie, Pritchett, Ronson, possibly King and MacCormack) pass the mike, each pretending to be Freddi Burretti, the Corns' alleged lead singer.

Almost Grown

(Berry). ***Broadcast****: 3 June 1971, In Concert: John Peel. MacCormack: lead vocal: Bowie: backing vocal; Pritchett: lead guitar, backing vocal; Ronson: rhythm guitar, backing vocal; Bolder: bass; Woodmansey: drums.* ***Live****: 1971.*

First release*: 26 September 2000,* ***Bowie at the Beeb****.*

At Bowie's June 1971 BBC performance, his friend Geoffrey MacCormack sang Chuck Berry's "Almost Grown." Berry was back in vogue, part of a rock 'n' roll revival coinciding with the rise of glam: Marc Bolan closed T. Rex's "Get It On" quoting Berry's "Little Queenie" and Berry himself got a cross-Atlantic #1 in 1972 with the atrocious "My Ding a Ling."

"Almost Grown" hymned middle-class respectability: a teenager's got a job and a car, he's doing okay in school and by the last verse he's domesticated. Finely attuned to his audience's moods, Berry saw by the end of the Fifties that many were graduating, getting drafted or married and having children. So in "Almost Grown" Berry flattered them, told them adulthood hasn't snuffed them out yet. He sang his aspirational middle-class narrative over a dirty jump blues, winking that beneath the kid's vows of responsibility are dreams about sex (Berry leers "got my eye on a little gurrrrl") and spending money.

The BBC session was the first time Bowie, Mick Ronson and Woody Woodmansey had played together in over a year and it was Trevor Bolder's first-ever (nerve-wracked) performance with Bowie—he bungles a few transitions and gets taken by surprise when Ronson and Mark Pritchett plow into a second solo chorus. A third-rate performance when compared with Berry's single (which, to be fair, boasted backing vocals by the Moonglows, Etta James and Marvin Gaye), the BBC broadcast documents a band listening to itself and working out kinks. While Bowie and the Spiders would play "Almost Grown" at a few gigs in 1971, they soon swapped it out for Berry's more raucous "Around and Around," whose stop-time structure they used in the last verse.

Song for Bob Dylan

***Recorded**: 8 June-6 August 1971, Trident. Bowie: lead vocal, 12-string acoustic guitar; Ronson: lead guitar, 12-string acoustic guitar?; Rick Wakeman: piano; Bolder: bass; Woodmansey: drums. Produced: Bowie, Scott; engineered: Scott.*

***First release**: 17 December 1971, **Hunky Dory**. **Broadcast**: 3 June 1971, In Concert: John Peel (George Underwood: vocal). **Live**: 1971-1972.*

The music critic Ralph J. Gleason was the sort of man—earnest, middle-aged, bohemian—who was most deranged by the counterculture. By the end of the Sixties, his columns in *Rolling Stone* invoked rock & roll prophets who, although currently in hiding, would return to offer deliverance, "program[s] for improvement of the young people of the world." In his bleaker hours, Gleason wrote the hippie Book of Revelation: "Out of it will come the programs. Out of it will come the plans. When the time is right."

Gleason mainly was writing about Bob Dylan. The latter had lived up in the Catskills since the mid-Sixties, though in 1970 he'd moved his family to New York City, hoping for greater anonymity (it didn't work out—"scholars" were soon digging through his garbage). Dylan's public absence since 1966 had coincided with the full flowering of youth culture, from which he was disengaged. "The events of the day, all the cultural mumbo jumbo were imprisoning my soul—nauseating me...I was determined to put myself beyond the reach of it all," he wrote decades later. He wasn't in Chicago, he wasn't in Berkeley, he wasn't at the march on the Pentagon; he'd even skipped out on Woodstock, held in his backyard. His new records were just as absent from the times: he sang country songs, domestic odes, Gordon Lightfoot covers. In 1971, after issuing a topical "George Jackson" single to get the radicals off his case, Dylan fell silent for what would be years. His goodbye note was another single, "Watching the River Flow," which cheekily began: "What's the matter with me? I don't have much to say..."

Against this backdrop came Bowie's "Song for Bob Dylan," a plea for an absent sentinel to return to his post. The lyric wasn't his perspective, Bowie said. He was writing in character, in the voice of his friend George Underwood (who sang "Bob Dylan" in Bowie's BBC broadcast) or a disappointed hippie pleading to a record sleeve. There was also some opportunism afoot. Bowie starts by referencing Dylan's own succession piece "Song to Woody," as if to promote himself as Dylan's heir presumptive for the Seventies. "It was at that period that I said, 'Okay, Dylan, if you don't want to do it, I will.' I saw that leadership void...if there wasn't someone who was going to use rock 'n' roll, then I'd do it," he said in 1976.

A companion piece to other "songs about people" Bowie was writing at the time, "Song For Bob Dylan" sat at the intersection of artistic "honesty" and fakery. His use of Dylan's real name, only becoming common knowledge around 1970, was an apprentice self-craftsman's homage to a master. Where John Lennon, in his post-Beatles rant "God," screamed he didn't believe "in ZIMMERMAN," Bowie found Dylan's professional disguise inspiring. He took heart that the Voice of Truth "Dylan" had been a fiction all along.

Still, something was off in this lethargic and padded song (though the *Hunky Dory* take blessedly has two fewer refrains than the BBC debut). Bowie struggled with "Song For Bob Dylan" throughout the *Hunky Dory* sessions, finally cutting a master take on the last day of recording. Its long evolution in the studio transferred some melodic weight from guitar to piano: Rick Wakeman amplified the vocal line in the verses, so when Bowie sings a descending phrase ("rather be scared") Wakeman slinks two octaves down his keyboard. Filigrees aside (see also Mick Ronson's acoustic arpeggios), the song suffered from harmonic drudgery, with its step-by-step retreats from subdominant to tonic chord in the E major verses (A-G#m-F#m-E) and an equally slogging advance through A major in its refrains.

There was also a lyrical disconnect: the refrains, with their painted ladies bursting like the goddess Athena from superbrains, have nothing to do with the sad hippie and wayward prophet of the verses, suggesting verse and refrain hailed from different songs. (It did connect with "Andy Warhol," however, with Dylan being called a painter). Even Bowie's vocal was more Elvis parody (see "Janine") than any Dylan burlesque. Underwood's performance had better matched Dylan's cadences.

Ronson, whose guitar intro (which he elaborated into an eight-bar solo) had a taste of Mick Ralphs' riff on "All the Young Dudes," went on to play with Dylan in the mid-Seventies, serving as the linchpin of the Rolling Thunder Revue. Little is known of Bowie and Dylan's sporadic encounters, apart from Dylan once allegedly telling Bowie he hated *Young Americans*.

Andy Warhol

***Recorded**: ca. early July 1971, Trident. Bowie: lead vocal, 12-string acoustic guitar; Ronson: lead acoustic guitar; Woodmansey?: whip; Scott: ARP synthesizer. Produced: Bowie, Scott; engineered: Scott.*

***First release**: 17 December 1971, **Hunky Dory**. **Broadcast**: 3 June 1971 (Dana Gillespie: vocal), In Concert: John Peel; 21 September 1971, Sounds of the 70s: Bob Harris; 23 May 1972, Sounds of the 70s: Bob Harris; ca. 4-6 January 1997, ChangesNowBowie. **Live**: 1972, 1996-1997.*

Hunky Dory's first side was Bowie as bright young composer, while on the flip he homaged his elders. Of these Andy Warhol was his newest influence. Having first heard of Warhol when Kenneth Pitt met him in 1966, Bowie likely saw Warhol's major retrospective at the Tate Gallery in March 1971. That August Bowie hobnobbed with the London cast of Warhol's *Pork* and met the "real" Warhol the following month in New York.

By 1971 Warhol was little more than a walking trademark or signature (for him, this was a triumph). His major paintings were a decade old; his films were boring exploitations; he'd gone from promoting avant-garde bands like the Velvet Underground to designing LP covers for the Rolling Stones, a premonition of how he'd become the "court painter to the 1970s international aristocracy." Not that it mattered: Warhol had drafted the concept of the Seventies back at the Factory in 1964. "Everybody wanted to be a star and nobody really wanted to play backup for anybody," he wrote of his Sixties "superstars." All he wanted to do was photograph, film and tape-record them. To be a star, one merely had to convince enough people; this would be the working philosophy of Bowie's manager Tony Defries and of Bowie himself. And Warhol's need for new markets, to continually build out his "brand"—in a decade he'd gone from painting to films to books to plays to pillows (even being shot by a deranged hanger-on in 1968 seemed like a performance)—paralleled Bowie's own "cross-media" ambitions.

Bowie wrote "Andy Warhol" with Dana Gillespie in mind: she debuted the song at his June 1971 BBC session and recorded it a few weeks later. Its two verses had Warhol as a paper doll against a set of changing backdrops, noting Warhol's absent reactions, clucking at the tedium of his life (Warhol had said making art is boring). The refrain rewords a Warhol statement that by attending his exhibits, he became the exhibit. The song was Warhol as he'd view himself: at a distance, without emotion, with a faint sense of bemusement.

After its public debut, Bowie revised "Andy Warhol" to differentiate his take from Gillespie's. Her BBC performance has a rumbling Jefferson Airplane feel, with Gillespie giving a brooding cast to her lines. Freed from the draggy drum pattern of the BBC take, the *Hunky Dory* "Warhol" goes at a faster clip (168 bpm) and is a more austere performance, its accompaniment just two Mick Ronson acoustic guitar tracks, Bowie's 12-string acoustic chording and a whip snapped on the off beats. There was also a fresh opening guitar hook, Ronson playing a scale starting on an open low E string; it was lifted, barely altered, from Ron Davies' "Silent Song Through the Land" (see "It Ain't Easy"). (The other guitar hook, a four-note stepwise descending phrase (on "for show" or "gallery," marking a brief shift into 2/4), hails from the BBC performance.) Bowie sang in a dry, observational tone, icily alliterating and syncing emphases with guitar lines. Take the fifth-descending "put you all inside my show" to echo the descending notes Ronson's just sounded. In the refrain, doubling himself up an octave, Bowie kept to a narrow range until breaking loose with closing yawns of "wallll" and "allll."

After finally cutting a satisfactory take, Bowie and Ken Scott set about framing "Bob Dylan," prefacing it with fifty seconds of studio "*verité*": two tracks of ARP synthesizer burble while Bowie checks that he's in tune and corrects Scott's pronunciation. "It's War-hol, actually...as in hols." Though it seems like studio banter in line with "Don't Sit Down," it was pure construct. Scott first recorded the synthesizer tracks, then spliced in dialogue from another take, switching between playback and Sel-Sync to jump-cut and echo Bowie's voice. "Andy Warhol" had a false ending, too. After a closing A major chord, there's a sharp cut to an E minor postlude in which Ronson and Bowie's guitars sound as cut-up as Bowie's voice had been in the intro. On one track, Ronson shifts a chord shape up and down his fretboard, stopping seemingly at random; on the other he plays off-beat harmonics. It concluded with its players applauding themselves, true Warholians.

During his visit to Warhol's Factory, Bowie let Warhol film and photograph him, performing a mime routine for the camera. He played a tape of "Andy Warhol," which reportedly drove Warhol to leave the room in embarrassment. Warhol hated the song; when Bowie left, Warhol asked his assistants if Bowie should have to pay him royalties for using his name. Their subsequent meetings were few and formal. Warhol died in 1987 and Bowie caricatured him on screen (wearing one of Warhol's own wigs) in Julian Schnabel's *Basquiat*, which coincided with Bowie's revival of "Andy Warhol" for his Outside tour.

Queen Bitch

***Recorded**: ca. 20 June-mid-July 1971, Trident. Bowie: lead and backing vocal,12-string acoustic guitar; Ronson: lead and rhythm guitars; Bolder: bass; Woodmansey: drums. Produced: Bowie, Scott; engineered: Scott.*

***First release**: 17 December 1971, **Hunky Dory**. **Broadcast**: 3 June 1971, In Concert: John Peel; 11 January 1972, Sounds of the 70s: John Peel; 18 January 1972, Sounds of the 70s: Bob Harris; 7 February 1972, The Old Grey Whistle Test. **Live**: 1971-1972, 1976, 1990, 1997, 2004.*

It starts with him unable to sit still, pacing the narrow length of his room on the eleventh floor of some cheap hotel, drawn back to the window again and again so he can watch his lover pick up someone on the street. What's galling isn't the cheating—that's old bipperty-bopperty hat—but just how low his man's sinking. *Oh God, I could do* ***better*** *than* ***that!*** He could be a more discerning john, a finer grade of prostitute.

"Queen Bitch," Bowie's Velvet Underground tribute ("sister Flo" working alongside "Sister Ray"), doesn't imitate the VU as much it annexes and streamlines them, from the scraping, cutting tone of Mick Ronson's double-tracked guitars to the compressed rigor of the rhythm section. It's like an electric folk memory of the band. When Lou Reed duetted with Bowie on "Queen Bitch" at Bowie's 50th birthday concert, he looked bemused, as if trying to recall whether he'd written the song. In a way, he had.

The main guitar riff (a non-VU steal: it's from Eddie Cochran's "Three Steps to Heaven") gathered mass over an eight-bar intro. Bowie first plays it on his 12-string Hagström acoustic, muting his strings to give the riff a kick. Ronson roars in with his fuzzed–up Les Paul (the drums and bass piling right after him) and four bars later he tracks in a second guitar mixed left, this one played through an overdrive pedal. His guitars are a clattering personality throughout the track: the left-mixed guitar is raw, Ronson playing gobby smears of tones instead of chords; the right-mixed one imposes itself on the acoustic, doubles the bassline in the build-ups to the refrain. Trevor Bolder is kinetic energy via four strings: not content to play root notes, he jumps octaves and darts up the G scale in the verses.

As with "Andy Warhol," Bowie's studio recording of "Queen Bitch" was a corrective swerve from its debut at the June 1971 BBC session. There Bowie had kept the main riff to his acoustic while Ronson played a whinnying countermelody (heard in the studio take's refrain), and he'd sung "Queen Bitch" in a deadpan Lou Reed imitation. He's far less butch on *Hunky Dory*: "satin and tat" was one of the mime Leslie Kemp's favorite phrases; "bipperty-bopperty hat" is a camp take on Dylan's leopard-skin pillbox hat. So Bowie turns one of Reed's "street" narratives into a stage aria of resentment, a drag queen's cry of vengeance, much as how in "Bombers" he tarted up Neil Young.

He takes his time, starting out with a semi-spoken patter, keeping on one note until, on "walk out of her heart," he grudgingly offers a fifth-spanning melody. His indignation builds in the later verses; he moves up higher ("she'll lay him *right* down") as if he's unable to let the accumulating slights go. He lies down, he jolts up. The band rides along with him—Woodmansey rebuking his cymbals, Ronson throttling his guitar—as Bowie pounds his hands against the wall, words punctuating his blows ("***down***! on the ***street!*** so I ***throw!*** both his ***bags!*** down the ***hall!***") until he howls out a curse: *"IT COULD'VE BEEN MEEEE—WHYDIDNTISAAAAAY."* There's blood and glitter in this song; it's as good as anything Bowie ever made.

Bombers

***Recorded**: **(demo, unreleased)** ca. May-June 1971, Radio Luxembourg? Trident? Bowie: vocal, piano; **(album)** 9 July 1971, Trident. Bowie: lead vocal, piano; Ronson: lead guitar, backing vocals; Wakeman: harpsichord; Bolder: bass; Woodmansey: drums. Produced: Bowie, Scott; engineered: Scott.*

***First release**: 30 January 1990, **Hunky Dory** (Ryko RCD 10133/ EMI CDEMC 372). **Broadcast**: 3 June 1971, In Concert: John Peel.*

The grotesque "Bombers" is a throwback to the psychedelic comic-strip songs of Bowie's first album, with a lyric out of the *Fabulous Furry Freak Brothers*: pilots bomb a wasteland occupied by an old man; when the smoke clears he's still sitting there unscathed, so they keep bombing him. The Pentagon and the Queen get involved; the army drops enough nukes to crack open the earth; the old man survives, at least celestially.

Bowie called it "kind of a skit on Neil Young...it's quite funny" in a 1972 radio interview. It mainly tweaks "After the Gold Rush" and "Don't Let It Get You Down" (Young's "old man standing by the side of the road" goes off in the bomb-blasted wasteland here), with Bowie doing a doleful Young imitation in his last verse ("nuhhthing lehhhft to view"). It's not only Young getting knocked, though: it's the whole noble tradition of protest folk. Crimes that the likes of Joan Baez would've lamented—the insane carpet bombing of innocents, the rape of the environment—are played for laughs, with Bowie turning in an outrageous camp vocal. As with "Queen Bitch," he queers a po-faced American genre, mocking folk "realism" (his bomber crew is a Gilbert and Sullivan company in Vietnam) and his own past pretensions. Where the old woman in "God Knows I'm Good" was meant to evoke pity, the old man here is a winking imp. The final verse, with Bowie teetering up to squawk a high C, even spoofs his solemn post-apocalyptic coda for "Wild Eyed Boy from Freecloud."

He debuted "Bombers" on piano at his BBC session in June 1971, a staid performance compared to its studio take, with doo-wop bassman harmonies, clattering harpsichord (courtesy of Rick Wakeman) and its cat-yowl of a lead vocal. (The refrain progression—C, G, B-flat, F—is mainly piano chords formed by playing every other white key, suggesting Bowie wrote much of it by shifting his hand, holding the same chord shape, across the keyboard (see "Changes")).Originally slated for *Hunky Dory*, "Bombers" possibly got the chop because "Fill Your Heart" and "Kooks" had filled the album's whimsy quota. Rykodisc dug up "Bombers" for its 1990 *Hunky Dory* reissue but chose a trebly, inferior mix than the oft-bootlegged "Bowpromo" one: see the fumbling snare drum punch-ins (see 0:23 and 1:12) in the Ryko mix that hobble an already ungainly song.

It Ain't Easy

(Davies.) ***Recorded**: 9 July 1971, Trident. Bowie: lead vocal, 12-string acoustic guitar; Ronson: lead guitar, piano, harmony vocals; Wakeman: harpsichord; Bolder: bass; Woodmansey: drums; Gillespie: harmony vocals. Produced: Bowie, Scott; engineered: Scott.*

***First release**: 6 June 1972, **Ziggy Stardust**. **Broadcast**: 3 June 1971 (lead vocal with Alexander and Underwood), In Concert: John Peel. **Live**: 1971.*

"It Ain't Easy" was written by Ron Davies, a born Louisianan from the Pacific Northwest. A prodigy songwriter who'd penned an album's worth of songs for local heroes the Wailers while still 17, Davies signed to A&M three years later. His first album, *Silent Song Through the Land*, with its ruminations on nature and loss, suggested a gruffer Nick Drake; Davies' strangled singing voice was close to Bowie favorites Neil Young and Biff Rose.

Unlike the Rose songs that Bowie performed, "It Ain't Easy" was far from obscure, as Three Dog Night, Mitch Ryder and Long John Baldry had covered it before Bowie sang it at his June 1971 BBC session. There "It Ain't Easy" was a group finale: Bowie, Geoff MacCormack and George Underwood each took a verse and harmonized with Dana Gillespie in the song's cavernous refrains. The BBC performance aped the feel of the rock & roll circuses of the time, like Delaney & Bonnie & Friends or Joe Cocker's Mad Dogs & Englishmen revue. Bowie briefly entertained the idea of assembling a similar troupe of musicians, including Underwood, MacCormack and Gillespie, to caravan around Britain with him.

He cut "It Ain't Easy" in the studio a month later, considering it for *Hunky Dory* but ultimately sequencing it as the first-side closer of *Ziggy Stardust*, an alleged concept record on which it has no role. With its singalong refrains and its verses offering spiritual and carnal satisfaction, it gave *Ziggy* a mid-sequence respite of competent blues-rock in steady A major. (You could ret-con it as the sort of thing Ziggy played before the annunciation.) Perhaps Bowie included the song as a tip of the hat to its composer, who'd contributed, if unknowingly, to his recent work (see "Andy Warhol").

Bowie's "It Ain't Easy" ditched the bottleneck slide and harmonica of Davies' original and ignored the solos Three Dog

Night and Baldry had wedged between the second and third verses. Woody Woodmansey's kick drum and Trevor Bolder's bass mainly served to demarcate bars while Bowie's 12-string acoustic and Rick Wakeman's harpsichord chimed alternating chords. The refrains flew in a two-tracked Ronson electric guitar and a barely-audible piano. Singing in an approximation of Davies' raspy tone, Bowie was liberal with the lyric, mangling and rewriting nearly every line: "the help of the good Lord" and "love of a hoochie-coochie woman" were his own would-be Americanisms, while he promoted Davies' "go ahead when you're going down" tag to "get to heaven."

Kooks

Recorded*: *(demo, unreleased)** *ca. early June 1971, Radio Luxembourg? Trident? Bowie: vocal, 12-string acoustic guitar, bass?;* ***(album) *ca. early July 1971, Trident. Bowie: lead vocal, 12-string acoustic guitar; Ronson: lead guitar; Wakeman: piano; Bolder: bass, trumpet; Woodmansey: drums; unknown musicians: strings (arr. Ronson). Produced: Bowie, Scott; engineered: Scott.*

***First release*:** *17 December 1971,* ***Hunky Dory*. *Broadcast*:** *3 June 1971, In Concert: John Peel; 21 September 1971: Sounds of the 70s: Bob Harris.*

On 30 May 1971, David Bowie was at home listening to Neil Young's *After the Gold Rush* when someone from Bromley Hospital rang to tell him he was a father. After a 30-hour labor which cracked her pelvis, Angela Bowie had given birth to a son, whom the Bowies named Duncan Zowie Haywood Jones. For his part, Bowie finished a song he'd been kicking around, debuting "Kooks" at a BBC performance four days after Duncan's birth. Fittingly, the song was in debt to Neil Young, with its jaunty piano and trumpet all but transposed from Young's "Till the Morning Comes." "For Small Z.," Bowie wrote on the LP sleeve.

The modest tradition of rock & roll fatherhood songs is one of genial blessings: take Bob Dylan's "Forever Young" or the Kinks'

"Wonderboy." Bowie's was a bit more pointed. "The baby was born and it looked like me and it looked like Angie, and the song came out like—if you're gonna stay with us, you're gonna grow up bananas," he wrote in a promo sheet for *Hunky Dory*. So "Kooks" is an apology to his infant son for the sorry condition of his parents. By being born into this family, Zowie's joined the circus and should brace for the worst (between the song's BBC debut and its studio recording, Bowie changed "what to say to people *if* they pick on you" to "*when* they pick on you"). In its romping way, "Kooks" ended a tale Bowie had started in his first compositions. Having worked through his childhood, having undergone a moody adolescence on *The Man Who Sold the World*, he found himself at the last turn of the wheel, now a father responsible for beginning yet another cycle.

Opening with and ruled by its refrains, its two 12-bar verses serving more as bridges, "Kooks" begins with Bowie alternating between D major and D suspended fourth chords (just moving his finger between two frets on his guitar's high E strings), a game of tension and release broken by a resounding C major on "we believe in you." The busy arrangement (in 12/8) doubled up Trevor Bolder on bass and trumpet: the latter knots together verse and refrain with an echo of the vocal melody and gets a five-note cameo upon its mention in the verse. Rick Wakeman's piano is the family's tipsy uncle. And after Mick Ronson's echo-laden intro, which adds a slight layer of suspense by playing the mediant notes of each passing chord, Ronson spent the rest of the song in his arranger's cap. His celli mirror Bolder's bassline, he hangs his strings like drapes across the refrains and gracefully sweeps them up an octave for the key change to E major.

So a new father cops to his son that he'll be no good at beating up dads, that family's something of a curse, that school will be a disaster. Take some consolation in being an oddball: it's preferable to normal life (in the BBC "Kooks," Bowie proposed going downtown to "watch the crazy people race around"). A piece of community came with the backing vocals, pitched a third above Bowie's lead; another vocal track, pitched a sixth higher, became a frenzied voice in the last refrain. Yet Bowie always sang the line "we believe in you" alone, stressing the long vowels. While "Kooks" promises a collective of misfits, its heart is a pledge from father to son. Whatever his father's qualms, Duncan Jones seems to have had a fine life, as lives go.

Fill Your Heart

*(Rose/Williams).**Recorded**: ca. late June-early July 1971, Trident. Bowie: lead vocal, tenor saxophone; Wakeman: piano; Bolder: bass; Woodmansey: drums; unknown musicians: violins, violas, celli, trumpets, saxophone? (arr. Ronson). Produced: Bowie, Scott; engineered: Scott.*

***First release**: 17 December 1971, **Hunky Dory**. **Broadcast**: 5 February 1970, The Sunday Show; 21 September 1971, Sounds of the 70s: Bob Harris. **Live**: 1970-1971.*

"Fill Your Heart," written by Biff Rose and Paul Williams, was in Bowie's live sets by early 1970 and he started the second side of *Hunky Dory* with it, his first cover performance on record since "I Pity the Fool." Where "Buzz the Fuzz," the other Rose song that Bowie performed, was a hippie drug joke, "Fill Your Heart" was a psychedelic mantra with Rose as demented master of ceremonies, his spiel peaking with a shakily-incanted "fear is in your head, *only in your head* so *forget your head*." Your past shames aren't real, the past has no hold on you, it's just residue you can flush out by flooding your mind with free, universal love. The song was sequenced well on *Hunky Dory* as the balm for the tortured mind of "Quicksand."

As often with Rose, you're not clear how far the joke goes, or whether it's a joke at all. The singer of "Fill Your Heart" could be deluded, witless or a true prophet (likely all). Rose sang as though he believed every word of his sermon; Bowie sang as if could hardly bear the weight of his newfound wisdom. Piecing together his singing voice from the likes of Anthony Newley, Scott Walker and Rose, Bowie took from the latter the courage to let his voice fly where it would, even if the results (the piercing high B on "fa-REEE") had only a passing familiarity with pitch.

Mick Ronson wrote the dance-band arrangement for horns and strings, taking much of it, from the swinging brass to the violin-and-piano dance, from Arthur G. Wright's score for Rose's track. Although Bowie graciously credited Wright on the LP sleeve, Rose took offense upon meeting Bowie at a Max's Kansas City show in 1973 ("[Bowie] stared smiling like a corpse stuck up the Cheshire cat...and I told him 'Hey thanks for doing Fill Your Heart but did you have to cop the whole arrangement...I mean couldn't you have done your own treatment of it.' He couldn't, being as he's an imitation...like Bruce Springsteen's initials."). Bowie's cover was a talent-show performance, a night of provincial music-hall hippie-isms, skipping to the same 12/8 time as "Kooks" and doubled from Rose's tempo. His saxophone solo was a novice's reduction of the one on Rose's track while Woodmansey on snare brushes lacks the proper Dixieland snap. Yet where Rose had ended with a shrug, Bowie gave a show-biz finale: a three-octave descending showcase for Rick Wakeman, a "yeah yeah yeah" refrain and a final goose of piano and echo-laden horns that segue directly into "Andy Warhol."

Quicksand

***Recorded:* (demo)** *ca. June 1971, Trident. Bowie: vocal, 12-string acoustic guitar;* **(album)** *14 July 1971, Trident. Bowie: lead and backing vocal, 12-string acoustic guitar; Ronson: 12-string acoustic guitar?, recorder, backing vocal; Wakeman: piano; Bolder: bass; Woodmansey: drums; unknown musicians: violins, violas, celli, vibes. Arranged: Bowie, Ronson. Produced: Bowie, Scott; engineered: Scott.*

First release*:** *17 December 1971,* ***Hunky Dory*; (demo) 30 January 1990,* ***Hunky Dory*** *(Ryko).* ***Broadcast*:** *ca. 4-6 January 1997, ChangesNowBowie.* ***Live*:** *1973, 1997, 2004.*

A peak of Bowie's astonishing run of compositions on *Hunky Dory*, "Quicksand" is a lushly-arranged song of despair and delusion whose refrain implores its listeners to give up hope of knowledge and wait for death for answers. Cut before the release of John Lennon's "Imagine," it seems a pre-emptive response. Where "Imagine" flatters its listeners by inviting them to join the elect, those who have no need of God or countries or possessions, "Quicksand" makes no attempt at connection, offers no points of entry. To imagine here is to be lost and alone. If Bowie's "Changes" is a man watching his life from the outside, "Quicksand" is one sifting through the wrack of his mind.

A quarter century after he made "Quicksand," Bowie recalled the man who'd written it. "My knowledge had to be the only important knowledge," he said, adding that he'd reject anyone trying to impart new information to him. "I wouldn't own up to the fact that I didn't know it all." An obsessive reader and moviegoer, deeply shy, quickly bored, the 24-year-old who wrote "Quicksand" spent much of his days living in his mind. Still absorbing what he'd found on his American trip, and with songs now pouring out of him as though he'd unstopped a current, he was wary of calming his mental tumult: after all, it was working. But you can hear in "Quicksand" a fear that he was becoming "a collection of other people's ideas." That by keeping in a state of flux to fuel his creativity, he risked losing his identity.

Bowie opens by referencing Aleister Crowley (see "Holy Holy") and Crowley's first magic society, the Hermetic Order of the Golden Dawn. Crowley had advocated the liberation of the will, employing a "uniform of imagery" that Bowie would use on "Station to Station." But what comes after you're free? Once loosed from all mental and cultural restraints, what's next? A life of refined egotism, Heinrich Himmler's "sacred realm of dream-reality," life as stylized as a silent film? As Bowie sang, he felt "torn between the light and dark," excited by where his imagination was taking him, worrying that it was walling him off from everyday existence.

Yet as he nears the abyss, "Quicksand" proposes limits. In the fatalistic refrain he held back until midway through the song, he says nothing can be proven true, that the life of the mind is a pit from which only death provides escape, whether by revealing another world or reincarnation or just by ceasing its labors at last. A chastened last verse offers equanimity: Bowie's blinded by dint of being human but knows that a fragment of the whole is within him ("a mortal with potential of a superman"). It's the first sign of a Gnosticism that, in various colors, would appear throughout his work (see "Station to Station"). He ends with a nod to his Buddhist days: if I'm wrong, tell me on the next bardo, the antechamber between reincarnations, where your karma ripens and your next rebirth is determined.

Two years before, Bowie would have sung his obscurantist lyric over some Puritan acoustic guitar (see "Cygnet Committee") and spare backing. "Quicksand" went down easily. He and Ken Scott sweetened the song: compare the harsh strumming of the demo to the sinuous guitar patterns on the album take, or the double-tracked arpeggiating on the verse's climactic lines. Scott recently had engineered overdubs for George Harrison's *All Things Must Pass*, which Phil Spector had produced, so for "Quicksand" he used the Spectorian method of massively overdubbing instruments, here the acoustic guitars. Foreshadowing what Tony Visconti would do for Bowie's voice on "'Heroes,'" Scott arranged for sets of double-tracked guitars to "open" as the song progressed. From a lone guitar in the intro, "Quicksand" swells to a six-guitar complement by the later refrains, ebbing back to a single guitar in the outro. The guitars-within-guitars nesting made tangled harmonies: in the arpeggiated bars, a supplementary guitar, up a sixth from a lead guitar, will fall a beat later to playing notes a third under the lead.

There were soft touches throughout the track: the vibes—

playing a two-note sequence like the Stylophone on "Space Oddity"—that dance beside Bowie's guitar strums in the intro; the barely-audible recorder (or Mellotron? at 1:16 and in the outro); a little guitar flourish on "superman"; Woody Woodmansey dashing out triplets on his ride cymbal like fleeting thoughts. Ronson's string arrangement used a favorite gesture of having an ascending line on celli swept up by violins a bar later. Rick Wakeman's piano was an unaligned voice, free to ramble where it cares to, then returning to accompany a descending vocal or adorn a violin phrase. In a song of the caprices and snares of the mind, Wakeman is thought at its most happily anarchic.

Bowie contrasted the simple movements of the verses (cloudy C major added 9th chords which resolve to the G major home chord, with a subtle modulation to A major in the second verse) with more harmonically vexing refrains, full of sharp or diminished chords that resolve in contrary directions: a D# diminished chord moves up to E major ("deceive with belief"), a B-flat diminished sinks to a B minor seventh ("comes with death's release"), a D# diminished wrenches back to the A major tonic chord (the first run of "aahs"). These were remnants of the song's tough birth on acoustic guitar; there's a sense of hard-won movement in "Quicksand," a physical presence, to ground its lyrical fancies.

Bowie starts by stressing, often by moving up a fifth, the key words of his opening verses (imagery, reality, destiny, symmetry) then dramatically falls on "I'm sinking"; at times he'll stand back from the mike to give his consonant rhymes (living/portraying, realm/dream, dark/target) more presence in the ear. Like the guitar overdubs, he and Ronson sang a maze of harmonies—their closing set of "ahhs" sometimes mirror the lead vocal, sometimes are down an octave. It's all in keeping with how the singer of "Quicksand" asserts that something's settled and then slackens his grip. A magnificent song: a portrait of the artist as a young mind.

Changes

Recorded*: (demo, unreleased)** *ca. May-June 1971, Radio Luxembourg? Bowie: vocals, piano, handclaps;* ***(album) *ca. early-mid July 1971, Trident. Bowie: lead vocal, tenor and alto saxophone; Wakeman: piano; Bolder: bass; Woodmansey: drums; unknown musicians: violins, violas, celli (arr. Ronson). Produced: Bowie, Scott; engineered: Scott;* ***(remake)*** *December 2003, Compass Point Studios, Nassau, Bahamas (Bowie vocal). Butterfly Boucher: lead and harmony vocal, piano?; Bowie: lead and harmony vocal; unknown musicians: piano?, bass, drums, saxophones, strings, synthesizer. Produced: (track) Boucher, Brad Jones, Robin Eaton; (Bowie vocal):Tony Visconti.*

First release**: 17 December 1971,* ***Hunky Dory*; (remake) 7 June 2004,* ***Shrek 2 OST*** *(Dreamworks 9862698).* ***Broadcast****: 22 May 1972, Jonnie Walker Lunchtime Show; 15 June 2002, A&E Live By Request; 10 October 2002, Live With Regis & Kelly; 20 April 2004, The Ellen DeGeneres Show.* ***Live****: 1971-1974, 1976, 1990, 1999-2000, 2002-2004, 2006.*

"Changes" is Bowie's teenage anthem, a song where a cold, unknowable artist meets his adolescent audience halfway. Or so it seemed to me at age 16, in part because John Hughes had used a few angst-ridden lines from it as the preamble of *The Breakfast Club*. In its unsettled way, "Changes" still seemed current in 1988. It wasn't a hippie remnant like "Both Sides Now" or "You Can't Always Get What You Want" (it even seemed anti-Baby Boomer: "Where's your shame? You've left us up to our necks in it!," though Bowie had aimed the line at his father's generation). In regular rotation on "classic rock" radio, "Changes," whenever it appeared between slabs of hard rock and hair metal, sounded blithe, otherworldly. Somehow his most Anthony Newley-inspired song since the Deram days, with its piano, saxophone, bass, modest strings and modest drums, had sneaked into the rock canon.

"All the Young Dudes" was better suited as an adolescent hymn: there's room for anyone in the song; it speaks to the crowd. "Changes" is more a transcribed internal monologue of someone you will never meet. Its handful of lines that make it "universal" ("don't tell them to grow up and out of it!") are bait, like the hooks that distract from the strangeness of much of the song, from its chord progressions to its top melodies.

Just take the piano-and-strings intro, which starts on a C major 7th chord (the tonic chord) and moves up by semitones: D-flat added 6th, D minor 7, Eb7, F7. The critic Wilfrid Mellers was struck by Bowie's audacity, calling the intro "near-anarchic," a set of chord changes that violate "orthodox musical grammar." Yet Bowie didn't try to violate tonality: he'd written a progression a child could have found. He starts by playing four consecutive white keys (Cmaj7: C-E-G-B), shifts his fingers over once, still playing four white keys (Dm7: D-F-A-C) and does it again, four more white keys (F7: F-A-C-E), getting his passing chords by moving a finger or two to black keys (Eb7: Eb-G-Bb-Db). This was quintessential Bowie: a chord progression, found by random movement, that sounded "right" despite being technically "wrong." And as if to reassure the listener that, no worry, it's going to be a pop song, Bowie drums up a bar's worth of anticipation ("oh yeah!' and pounded piano/kick drum eighth notes) before rolling out a big fat hook: a rising eight-note melody played by saxophone, bass, strings and piano. Just as quickly, he takes it away: the hook won't return until after the refrain and that's the end of it.

This dance between the conventional and strange is there throughout the song. While the verse chord progressions are straightforward—an ambling movement through C major—the top melody has a bizarre shape. The first verse alone is a single run-on sentence that Bowie drags over seven bars and breaks into nine disjunct phrases. He expands and contracts each phrase at whim, sometimes staying flat, sometimes jolting up ("running *wild*," the stepwise lift of "not-so-*sweet*"), sometimes sinking ("waiting **for**"). This suits the free-wheeling lyric, with its rhymes made out of hints: slant rhymes like "leave"/"stream," consonant rhymes ("glimpse/test," "quite aware," "warm impermanence"). Sometimes his lines don't even scan—Bowie swallows the "the" in "how others must see the faker" and squeezes "fascinating me" into four syllables. (Playing it live, Bowie recited the verses like beat poetry over Mike Garson's free-form piano.) Rick Wakeman's piano and Trevor Bolder's bass converse in the background, perking up on the last beat of each bar—Bolder often shifting up an octave, Wakeman dealing in fragments.

And although he loaded the refrain with hooks—the stuttered title phrase (saturating the mix when a five-tracked Bowie sings it in full), a harmony vocal that deftly becomes the lead, Bolder's two-octave-descending bassline—he also made it a steeplechase of shifting times, with moves to 2/4 ("different man," "necks in it") and four whirling bars of 3/4 (a different chord on each beat) barely held together by Woody Woodmansey's snare fills.

"Changes" made for a musical autobiography of sorts. Bowie recounts his career's dead-end streets, his false hopes; in the second verse he tries to get a fix on his current state, as if plotting a cloud's progress on a map. Like "Life On Mars?," it was his retort to "My Way." "Changes" is "a credo song, and the credo is 'turn and face the strange' rather than 'I did it my way,' so there's a much more fragmented sense of identity," Momus said. Bowie's managers and labels in the Sixties had tried to make him commit to a line, whether soul, hard rock, folk or cabaret. Here Bowie, who once compared rock & roll to factory work, commits to a life of constant revision.

The last refrain's dig at aging rock and rollers put Bowie just where he wanted to be in the Seventies: a beat behind the waning pop aristocrats. If he'd never top Pete Townshend or John Lennon at their peaks, if he was fated to stay in their shadow, now he was happy to be there. The shadows gave him cover. There's a photograph of Nick Drake by Keith Morris, used for the back cover of *Five Leaves Left*. Drake stands against a wall while a man speeds towards him, the man's body an arrowed motion. "Changes" is its musical analogue: Bowie betting on a life of movement, not a still life of a Drake, who had sounded his depths.

Bowie performed "Changes" in the studio again, at what (for a time) seemed like the end of his recorded life (he was co-singing with Butterfly Boucher a version for the *Shrek 2* soundtrack in 2004). There was triumph in his voice, even if time had eroded its register. He still sang "pretty soon now, you're gonna get older!" like a kid's taunt.

It had become his theme song. Countless TV retrospectives have scored Bowie clip montages to the "Changes" refrain. It's hard to believe "Changes" has an ending, but it does, slowly coming to a stop in a postlude, a five-note Bowie tenor saxophone solo. Like "Oh! You Pretty Things," the song ends with its introduction; only here the progression moves in reverse, like a film getting rewound. "Changes" closes on the C major 7th that it started on, with all of its warring voices—Bowie's saxophone, Ronson's strings, Bolder's bass, Wakeman's skylarking piano—now a coalition.

Eight Line Poem

***Recorded**: ca. early-mid July 1971, Trident, London. Bowie: lead vocal, treated piano; Ronson: lead guitar. Produced: Bowie, Scott; engineered: Scott.*

***First release**: 17 December 1971, **Hunky Dory**. **Broadcast**: 21 September 1971, Sounds of the 70s: Bob Harris. **Live**: 1971.*

Bowie and Mick Ronson's creative partnership in miniature, "Eight Line Poem" is a 15-bar instrumental duet, a 16-bar "poem" and a nine-bar instrumental outro, performed by Bowie on treated piano and Ronson on his Les Paul. Ronson takes the melodic lead in instrumental sections, Bowie in the verse. In the intro and outro, the two generally stick to competing chords, with Ronson leading on the tonic chord, C major, while Bowie's piano is on shifts to F major. Ronson opens starting on his guitar's low E string and slowly dances up two octaves. He plays two descending phrases, each echoed by Bowie's piano chords, and heralds the verse by moving down the neck on his B string, picking and bending notes as he goes.

The lyric section is what the title promised: an eight-line blank verse. Starting with a rich set of internal rhymes ("t*act*f**u**l *cact***us**," "s*ur*v***ey***s *the* pr***ai***rie"), Bowie soon slackens to freer lines. He's narrating a painting or, better, he's dictating a shooting script. The first line's an establishing shot (cactus on a windowsill surveys its owner's apartment); lines two to four are interiors; lines five, seven and eight are exteriors (the cactus turns its attention to the street); line six is a close-up (the cactus has a brief existential crisis). Bowie tried on voices like hats—Henry Higgins-like elocution for "Clara" (a cat who puts her head between her paws, conveyed by Bowie singing notes between pounded piano chords); a cowboy drawl on "AWWWL the cack-ti"; "collision" hollered as if he's falling down an elevator shaft. In the outro Ronson returns to run the show, Bowie content to support him. In the *ritardando* bar that ends the track, both play a C major chord, echoing the unified front that had closed "Changes." Minor compared to the tracks bookending it on *Hunky Dory*, "Eight Line Poem" has the beauty of an arranged conversation.

The Bewlay Brothers

***Recorded**: 30 July 1971, Trident. Bowie: lead vocal, 12-string acoustic guitar; Ronson: lead guitar, acoustic guitar; Bolder: bass. Produced: Bowie, Scott; engineered: Scott.*

***First release**: 17 December 1971, **Hunky Dory**. **Broadcast**: 18 September 2002, David Bowie, Live and Exclusive. **Live**: 2002, 2004.*

One of the last songs cut for *Hunky Dory*, "The Bewlay Brothers" was also the only song on the album Bowie wrote primarily in the studio. Decades later, he described its creation as being emetic: "I had a whole wad of words that I had been writing all day. I had felt distanced and unsteady all evening, something settling in my mind." He recorded "Bewlay Brothers" alone on guitar (Mick Ronson and Trevor Bolder apparently cutting their overdubs later), then went out drinking at the Sombrero.

He was dismissive of "Bewlay Brothers" while he was making it, calling it a song for the American market. He told Ken Scott that as Americans enjoyed looking for clues on LP sleeves and in lyrics, he'd written something to put them to work (God knows what he would have made of this book); in his press notes for *Hunky Dory* he mocked the song as being "*Star Trek* in a leather jacket." Even when he finally sang "Bewlay Brothers" live in 2002, he groaned at his lyric's demands, saying it had more words than *War and Peace*, sounding like a man who wouldn't recognize his younger self if he passed it on the street. This cumulative belittling was a protracted feint, Bowie rubbishing a song to hedge his audience from getting too close to it, much as how he alternated lines with the sting of memory with those full of obscure wordplay.

At the heart of "Bewlay Brothers" was Bowie's half-brother Terry Burns (he's been frank about this, telling a radio interviewer in 1977 that song was about him and Terry). Even the title itself, allegedly inspired by a London tobacconist chain down the street from Trident Studios, is a syllabic and near-consonant rhyme of "Bowie." The half-brothers' relationship had hung on Burns' mental condition. A fairly stable Burns had stayed at Haddon Hall in 1970 but he'd begun to deteriorate at the time of *Hunky Dory*. The two were growing apart, an estrangement that soon became a break. Yet to consider "Bewlay Brothers" to be directly autobiographical, to parse each line for clues about a summer Bowie and Terry spent together, for example, is to misread the role "Terry Burns" plays in Bowie's elegy. He's more a spent muse than a lost sibling. The break at the center of "Bewlay Brothers" is necessary:

the lost brother needs to die so the singer can live.

The sequencing of *Hunky Dory*'s "tribute" side mapped a series of battles. Starting with the genial Biff Rose ("Fill Your Heart"), whose influence on Bowie was light and superficial, the sequence continues through figures Bowie found progressively more difficult to assimilate: Andy Warhol's flatness, Bob Dylan and Lou Reed's dense self-mythologies. And the side closes with "Bewlay Brothers," where Bowie grappled with the psychic power that Burns held over him.

Later in life, Bowie told an interviewer he was "never quite sure of what real position Terry [who had killed himself in 1985] had in my life, whether Terry was a real person or whether I was actually referring to another part of me." Bowie had cast himself as Burns' reflection, introducing himself as "Terry's brother" to Haddon Hall visitors. Burns was, as Bowie said, his doppelganger. "I wonder if I imbued my stepbrother with more attributes than he really had," he said. He wanted Burns to be something he wasn't. "As long as I believed that's what they were, it gave me the energy to be convinced I was worth doing it for."

A primary influence of his childhood and early adolescence, Burns embodied everything non-bourgeois, non-suburban and non-British for a lower-middle-class child in Fifties Bromley (and as his mother's illegitimate son, Burns was also out of sorts in the Jones household: he and Bowie's father greatly disliked each other). Burns introduced his brother to Buddhism, the Beats, jazz, science fiction, R&B; he'd essentially programmed "David Bowie." In "All the Madmen," the other major song inspired by Burns, Bowie had pledged solidarity to those like Terry whom society had driven to the margins, while acknowledging a thin line separated him from the insanity that had plagued much of his family.

"Bewlay Brothers" is more distant, its sympathies more guarded. It's tall tales from a sordid boyhood, the brothers as a gang ("the moon boys," "kings of oblivion") whose outlaw status is built up with lines hinting at the gay underground ("real cool traders," with Bowie raiding a favorite novel, John Rechy's *City of Night* (see "Fascination")). Set against them are agents of the Establishment. Like Ray Davies' "people in grey," these brawny close-cropped "good men of tomorrow" have, in Bowie's wonderful line, "bought their positions with saccharine and trust."

Yet by the second verse, something's gone astray. The brother's weakening: he's "wax" to the singer's "stone," he's more impressionable to the world's blows. Bowie closes the last verse with a last act of generosity: he fuses stone and wax, turning his brother into a "chameleon, comedian, Corinthian and caricature," letting him escape into art and memory. Bowie's left behind in the world, taking stock of a broken estate of fragments: faces on cathedral floors, passwords whispered in dreams, names of lost paintings. The whale of a lie like they hoped it was, like the hope it was.

As if to make amends for his verbosity and his vocal, rivaling "Changes" in its frenetic movements, Bowie made "Bewlay Brothers" compact. After an intro of 12-string acoustic guitar and Ronson's tremolo-shrouded Les Paul (which sounds like an organ), the song plays out across three 16-bar verses, three 16-bar choruses and a coda. The chord progressions advance in the verses, retreat home in refrains; the arrangement is two acoustic guitar tracks, two electric guitar tracks and a bass that wakes up in the refrains. (Singing "Bewlay Brothers" live in 2004, Bowie brought in drums on the last verse, which came across like a boorish latecomer at a wake.) Apart from the fuzzed-up B minor chords to prod the song into its refrains, Ronson is content to haunt the Bewlays, constellating notes above Bowie's voice or ruminating in empty corners of the song.

Its mournfulness is thrown over in the coda, when a gargoyle chorus shows up (Bowie's multi-tracked voice, sped up and down to span over an octave). Like "After All," it's the Laughing Gnomes as specters. Having stolen this final melody from Marc Wilkinson's theme for the 1971 British horror film *The Blood on Satan's Claw,* Bowie ended song and album on a fine grotesque note. As the track fades out, you hear a scream.

Life On Mars?

Recorded**:** ***(demo, unreleased)*** *ca. May-June 1971, Haddon Hall? Radio Luxembourg? Bowie: vocal, piano;* ***(album)*** *8 August 1971, Trident. Bowie: lead vocal; Ronson: lead guitar, recorders; Wakeman: piano; Bolder: bass; Woodmansey: drums; unknown musicians: violins, violas, celli, string basses (arr. Ronson). Produced: Bowie, Scott; engineered: Scott.*

First release*: 17 December 1971,* ***Hunky Dory****.* ***Broadcast****: 5 September 1980, The Tonight Show; 23 August 1999, VH1 Storytellers; 21 September 2002, Parkinson.* ***Live****: 1972-1973, 1976, 1983, 1990, 1999-2000, 2002-2005.*

"Life On Mars?" is the *Citizen Kane* of Bowie songs: young man's bravura. It came to Bowie easily ("being young is easy," he said at age 61). Like "Oh! You Pretty Things," the song seemed to fall upon him. Sitting in a Beckenham park, he began humming a melody; soon enough he'd run home to his piano at Haddon Hall, where over an afternoon he wrote much of it.

One reason the song came so easily was because Bowie carved it out of "My Way." Having had his English lyrics for Claude François' "Comme d'Habitude" (see "Even a Fool Learns to Love") rejected, Bowie endured Paul Anka converting the song into a Frank Sinatra grandiosity, which Bowie found smug and crass. So using "Comme d'Habitude" as the starting point for "Life On Mars?" wasn't theft, he felt. More a statement of rightful ownership. He was brazen enough to put "Inspired by Frankie" on the LP sleeve.

Its conception was quick, its recording deliberate. Bowie and Ken Scott saved "Life On Mars?" until the end of the *Hunky Dory* sessions. Believing it could be "the Big One" (it wasn't quite, though it would hit #5 in Britain once Bowie broke with *Ziggy Stardust*), they debated how to render the song, considering Dudley Moore to play piano on it. In the end "Life On Mars?" was immortalized by Rick Wakeman's piano, a string arrangement Mick Ronson wrote in the Trident Studios toilet and Bowie's astonishing vocal, the work of half a decade's efforts to expand his vocal range.

A sullen teenage girl goes to the movies, gets stood up by her friend and dejectedly takes her seat. She's the subject of the song, not the typical rock 'n' roll object of beauty or lust or distraction. In a few lines, Bowie captures a teenager's life, its slights, its cosmic sense of injustice, its losing war against tedium, its restlessness (he starts nearly every line with a conjunction), its uneasy cynicism. The movie screen flickers to life, showers the girl with images. The song becomes the screen, its pre-chorus is an extended trailer—soaring strings, thunderous piano, ascending chords—for the refrain, one of the most shameless, gorgeous melodies he ever wrote.

As with "Quicksand," Bowie's first American trip fed his lyric. You could say Bowie, frustrated songwriter and suburban misfit, goes in drag as the mousy-haired "anomic heroine," while the B-movie reel is the alluring, crass promise of America. "I think [the girl] sees that although she's living in the doldrums of reality, she's being told there's a far greater life somewhere, and she's bitterly disappointed that she doesn't have access to it," he said in 1997, adding that where he'd empathized with the girl back then, he felt sorry for her at age 50. The film won't relent until she does. The suburban realism of the first verse disintegrates in the second, the lyric devolving into a string of jokes ("Mickey Mouse has grown up a cow" made Trevor Bolder and Woody Woodmansey crack up in the studio), esoteric references and gibberish. It's the perspective of the movie screen, reeling itself out to the girl in frames, intercutting Britain— workers on strike (a common Seventies condition, though here it's for fame), holiday-goers scurrying to tourist traps, whether Continental (Ibiza) or domestic (the Norfolk Broads)—with America. Mickey Mouse, "Alley Oop" ("look at those cavemen go!"), cops and robbers. As the verse ends, the director breaks the fourth wall: you overhear Bowie asking the girl to focus on the screen, as if he's framing her in close-up until another reel starts.

It starts with a cold opening—a single piano note, a rest, two sung notes to kick-start the verse (*"It's a*/god-awful"), the latter becoming a rhythmic motif (*"But her*/friend is...," *"She could*/spit"). A harmony vocal appears, a third below Bowie's lead; Bolder deepens "sunken dream" with a bass fill. By the pre-chorus, a sense of movement has become relentless. All of its players are conscripted: strings and bass slam downbeats; Rick Wakeman's piano drums out chords; Bowie vaults from a D to a high B-flat ("fo-cus on/SAI-LORS") as a last flourish. Yet the refrain plays another game of suspense. After his opening gymnastic, Bowie feigns as if he's losing strength, as he hits the next Bb briefly ("***OH*** man") and his next leap is a shorter interval, from E to B (**"***law*-man"). It's all a ruse: his final jump is his grandest—holding a three-bars-long Bb on "***MARS!***" The whole song is a clockwork. Everything has led up to this glorious indulgence. All that's left to do is replay the whole sequence and close with fireworks.

There's a parallel game in the song's structure. The verses are comfortably in F major, with a C7 chord ("told her to go") shuttling back home to F ("but her friend") but at the close, a now-C9 chord jarringly leads to A-flat chords ("lived it ten times"). The pre-chorus becomes a battle for control between waning F major and B-flat, which assures its victory with a triumphant B-flat that opens the refrain as Bowie leaps to sing its root note. Bolder's bass prepares the ear: in the pre-chorus, his rising chromatic line (inching up from Eb to E, from F to Gb) heralds the transition; in the refrain he tacks things down, keeping to the roots of the newly-established Bb key.

The accompaniment was a set of overlapping conversations. Ronson based his cascading string arrangement (the whirling violin octave drops on "sailors," the chromatic cello descent on "freakiest show") from the bassline Bolder worked out in rehearsals. Woodmansey in turn answers the strings, playing a snare-medium tom fill to echo a descending violin line. Playing the same piano that Paul McCartney used for "Hey Jude," Wakeman made little dancing responses, like the sinking triplet after Bowie's "freakiest show." The second verse's bittersweet double-recorder line sweeps downward from Ibiza to the swamps back home. After Ronson's vibrato-saturated solo of generous perfection, the track gets an MGM ending: grand sweeps of strings until deadened toms invoke the *2001* tympani. It's not over yet; the last reel keeps spinning on the projector. You hear Wakeman's piano off in the distance, playing his chorus melody. A phone rings, the song's manufacturers grumble, we're left awake and alone.

Shadow Man

Recorded*: *(unreleased) *15 November 1971, Trident. Bowie: lead vocal, 12-string acoustic guitar; Ronson: lead guitar, piano; Bolder: bass; Woodmansey: drums. Produced: Bowie, Scott; engineered: MacKay, Stone;* ***(remake)*** *(basic tracks) July 2000, Sear Sound Studios, (overdubs) October 2000, Looking Glass Studios, New York, (strings) late 2000? Bowie: lead vocal; Earl Slick: "ambient" guitar; Mark Plati: acoustic guitar; Mike Garson: keyboards; Gail Ann Dorsey: bass, vocals; Sterling Campbell: drums; Lisa Germano: violin; unknown musicians: strings (arr. Visconti). Produced: Bowie, Plati; engineered: Pete Keppler.*

***First release*:** *(remake) 3 June 2002, "Slow Burn" (ISO Columbia/COL 672744 2).*

While recording *Hunky Dory*, Bowie was at work on its sequel. He was essentially programming two records at once, shuttling "domestic" numbers to *Hunky Dory* and "performance" tracks (by mid-1971, he'd written the title track, "Star," "Lady Stardust," "Moonage Daydream" and "Hang Onto Yourself") to *Ziggy Stardust*. Despite this *Ziggy Stardust* took a long time to gel, its track list a blur even its last days of recording and mixing. The final sequence owed as much to Ken Scott (who arranged LP sides based on track length) and the demands of RCA executives as it did to Bowie. Nearly a side's worth of proposed tracks wound up culled (see "Round and Round," "Amsterdam," "Velvet Goldmine").

Another *Ziggy Stardust* outtake, recorded on the same day as the unreleased "It's Gonna Rain Again" (see appendix) and the master take of "Five Years," "Shadow Man" worked through Bowie's favorite themes of identity and doubling ("it's a reference to one's own shadow self," he said in 1989). Its studied melancholia was that of *Space Oddity*, suggesting the song dated to 1969 or mid-1970, around the time of "Tired of My Life." It may have begun as a rewrite of his "C'est la Vie" (Bowie also reused the "really you, really me" vocal tag from "Wild Eyed Boy From Freecloud" towards the fade). Its outside influences were just as discernible: Neil Young's voice is in the bridge (the doleful descending melody of "he'll show you tomorrow/he'll show you the sorrows") and from Biff Rose's "The Man" Bowie took everything from lyrics to phrasings.

The circulating *Ziggy Stardust* "Shadow Man" doesn't seem like a final take (Woody Woodmansey seems to have just heard the song for the first time, as he's flailing all over the place). There's no record of any further remakes attempted in 1971 or 1972, suggesting that Bowie was tentative about the song and hadn't seriously considered it as an album contender. "Shadow Man" came off like a student's work: it was the sort of song the narrator of "Conversation Piece" could have written.

Bowie revised "Shadow Man" during the *Toy* sessions of 2000 and released it two years later as a B-side. He slowed the tempo to a crawl, leaving space for a Tony Visconti string section and for Earl Slick to weave a cloud of feedback. These elements, along with the delayed echo on his voice and Mike Garson's narrative piano, gave "Shadow Man" a dreamy, languid atmosphere, a far remove from its more prosaic 1971 incarnation.

Ziggy Stardust

Recorded**:** ***(demo)*** *ca. late February 1971, Radio Luxembourg. Bowie: vocal, 12-string acoustic guitar;* ***(album)*** *11 November 1971, Trident. Bowie: lead vocal, 12-string acoustic guitar; Ronson: lead guitar, rhythm guitars; Bolder: bass; Woodmansey: drums. Produced: Bowie, Scott; engineered: MacKaye, Stone.*

First release*: 6 June 1972,* ***Ziggy Stardust****; (demo) 11 June 1990,* ***Ziggy Stardust*** *(Ryko).* ***Broadcast****: 11 January 1972: Sounds of the 70s: John Peel; 18 January 1972, Sounds of the 70s: Bob Harris; 16 May 1972: Sounds of the 70s: John Peel; 15 June 2002, A&E Live By Request; 27 June 2002, Friday Night with Ross and Bowie; 29 November 2003, Parkinson.* ***Live****: 1972-1973, 1978, 1990, 2000, 2002-2003.*

His finest conceit came together during his first American trip. Bowie saw the Velvet Underground in New York and mistook the singer/bassist Doug Yule for the departed Lou Reed. Learning of his error, he considered that he'd enjoyed meeting the "fake" Reed just as much as he would have the real one. This was the kernel of Ziggy Stardust, plastic spaceboy rocker: a rock star as mistaken identity, as an assumed identity. By the time the actor Tony Zanetta (future MainMan executive and Bowie biographer) visited Haddon Hall in September 1971, Bowie had drafted the role. Ziggy Stardust would be the lead character of a musical play. When he grew tired of the part, another actor could take his place. Two months later, Bowie tinned his stage show into an album.

While Bowie took the character's name from two fresh American discoveries, the feral rocker Iggy Pop and the unhinged novelty act the Legendary Stardust Cowboy, Ziggy Stardust had needed the whole of his life to come into being. The domestic spaceman angle came from Bowie childhood favorites the *Quatermass* serials and *The Flowerpot Men*; the spaceman-messiah angle from Robert Heinlein's *Stranger in a Strange Land*, whose Martian charismatic founds a Church of Man-Love and gets lynched for his troubles. There was Buddhist cyclicality and its echoes in British science fiction, particularly Michael Moorcock's ambiracial/bisexual rocker-assassin Jerry Cornelius. There were Andy Warhol's statements on identity as an exhibit and a refreshable brand, with Warhol having younger, handsome actors "play" him in personal appearances. Bowie also stewed Ziggy from combustible personalities he'd known, like the rocker Vince Taylor, who Bowie once found on his knees on a London sidewalk mapping out UFO landings, and the rock & roll casualties he'd only read about: Jim Morrison, dead in a Parisian bathtub like Marat; Brian Jones floating in his swimming pool; Eddie Cochran strewn across a Chippenham street.

Ziggy Played...

Ziggy Stardust has been called a "cartoon" rock & roller, but that's not quite right. Cartoons have weight and presence, hold entrenched positions in the memory: think of the eternal Charlie Brown or Superman. Ziggy is far vaguer, with Bowie using the counterculture's myths as sketch paper. "He played left hand" referenced recently-dead Jimi Hendrix and allegedly-dead Paul McCartney. "Stardust" also suggested the refrain of Joni Mitchell's "Woodstock," "we are stardust," a pop Gnostic line soon revised as a hook by Carl Sagan. Ziggy was a pictograph, a flipbook of images: his ghost pallor, his screwed-down hairdo, his Japanese spaceman outfits, his "god-given ass."

Even by the meager standards of rock "concept" records, *The Rise and Fall of Ziggy Stardust and the Spiders From Mars* is a thin business. Its songs include recycled Arnold Corns singles and a cover from the *Hunky Dory* sessions; its unifying lyrical theme consists of having the word "star" in a few songs. Bowie wrote much of the *Ziggy* story after he made the album, having just sketched out a few plot points in a notebook ("4. How [Ziggy] knew how to out-hip those queens and get into the role oh so well"). As he told William S. Burroughs in 1973, the album begins with the world ending ("Five Years"), which is the cue for the arrival in Greenwich Village of a black-hole-jumping alien race (or they're sentient black holes, it's rather unclear). These are "the infinites" (see the Overlords of Arthur Clarke's *Childhood's End* or the Nova Mob of Burroughs' *Nova Express*), who make a drugged-out rock singer called Ziggy Stardust their herald. He sings about them ("Starman"), becomes a messiah figure for his doomed generation. In the finale ("Rock & Roll Suicide") Ziggy is torn to pieces on stage by the black-hole jumpers who then, as Bowie said, "take his elements and make themselves visible." This was Bowie ransacking *Nova Express* to make an SF parody of Christ's annunciation and betrayal, in the vein of the "hippie Christ" musicals of the time (*The Godspell, Jesus Christ Superstar*). One tell is Ziggy being called "the Nazz," a reference to the comedian Lord Buckley's "hipster" nickname for Christ: Ziggy as beatnik spaceman messiah.

The crackpot story is beside the point: *Ziggy Stardust*'s concerns lay with its potential buyers. To believe Bowie was somehow playing a con on the British (and later American) public with his "plastic rocker" is to belittle his target audience's sophistication. This was the first generation who'd grown up with rock and the counterculture as givens. These were teenagers whose first memories of pop were the Beatles, whose various incarnations (moptops in 1964, psychedelic bandleaders in 1967, estranged brothers in 1970) had appeared like fresh editions of a magazine. John Lennon and Bowie had been stunned when they first heard Elvis and Little Richard: it had no precedent in their lives ("rock and roll was real, everything else was unreal,"

Lennon said). The first rock and rollers had been extraterrestrials. To a child in Bromley, Elvis Presley was a starman. But Ziggy Stardust came later in the game. The kids in 1972 had watched rockers rise and fall; they'd come to expect one would flame out and be replaced by another, slightly more outrageous version. Pop was becoming demystified; you could guess the upcoming plots. So *Ziggy Stardust* let kids in on the story, made them co-authors.

At the heart of Ziggy, at the heart of glam rock, was collective performance. Glam, like its successor punk, was participatory: the crowd fed the stage act which fed it straight back to the crowd. It was a reaction to something like George Harrison's Bangladesh benefit concert. There, after Ravi Shankar promised the audience that "your favorite stars" would soon appear, the worshipful screams for the likes of Harrison, Bob Dylan and even Ringo Starr suggested rock & roll had become a liturgical service in which mystical figures appeared on stage and played songs to each other. At the Bangladesh concert, there's a wall between crowd and stars; Harrison might as well be shown on a video monitor. It was sanctimonious boredom. "The fans are fed up with paying to sit on their hands while watching musicians who clearly couldn't care less about the customers," as Noddy Holder of Slade said.

Ziggy Stardust, like T. Rex and Mott and Slade, cared about the customers. Take how its songs are from the perspective of the crowd or the radio listener. Only a few tracks are sung in Ziggy's voice and then in the context of him on-stage ("Hang Onto Yourself," "Moonage Daydream," the discarded "Sweet Head"). Even his death song, "Rock 'n' Roll Suicide," ends as a piece of children's theater. In his *The Performing Self,* Richard Poirier wrote that the Beatles and Dylan had created "an emanation of personality, of a self that is the generous master but never the creature of its audience." *Ziggy Stardust* scrapes against that conceit. Ziggy *is* the creature of his audience, they write him into being.

...*Guitar!*

As for "Ziggy Stardust" itself, you have to start with the riff. Two bars long, it repeats four times in the intro, twice after the first refrain, three-and-a-half times at the close. Each pass takes about five seconds: a slammed G major chord, a fanfare in D and some tough connective tissue, Ronson arpeggiating three augmented or slash chords (Cadd9, G/B, Am7), to set up the subsequent G chord. The demo reveals Bowie's responsible for its basic shape while Ronson added some colors, like the arpeggiating. It's like Bowie's take on Handel's "Arrival of the Queen of Sheba": each time the riff plays, the band stops to pay homage (Woodmansey plays martial-sounding snare and tom fills). While Ronson gave "Ziggy Stardust" great ornamentation—the double-tracked crunching chromatic bass figure (under "Spiders From Mars," for example) that pulls the song from tonic to dominant chord, the spiky harmonics on "became the special man," the vicious root chords in the refrains—the memory recalls him only playing the riff over and over again.

The lyric was a pocket history of Ziggy, his band and his fall, coming off as a parody of a folk ballad. It lacks a definable narrator: the singer could be a kid in the audience recalling Ziggy years later, like the Christian Bale character in *Velvet Goldmine*; he could be one of Ziggy's bandmates or even the disassociated memories of Ziggy himself. Bowie sang like he was running down a ghost, using as a phrasing template his earlier "In the Heat of the Morning." He closed his tale with a bellowed, descending "played gui-TAAAAR" that Ronson buffeted with a stinging run of triplets, while a last harmonic ended the track with a stratospheric high G. "Ziggy Stardust" was only the score: Bowie and his audience would be its cumulative performance.

Star

***Recorded*: (demo, "Rock 'n' Roll Star," unreleased)** *Radio Luxembourg, ca. April-early May 1971: Bowie, vocal, lead guitar,* *piano; Ian Ellis: bass; Harry Hughes: drums;* **(album)** *11 November 1971, Trident. Bowie: lead and backing vocal; Ronson: lead guitar, slide guitar, piano; Bolder: bass; Woodmansey: drums. Produced: Bowie, Scott; engineered: MacKay, Stone.*

First release*: 6 June 1972,* ***Ziggy Stardust****.* ***Live****: 1978, 1983.*

An ingénue's opening number, the manically aspirational "Star" could be sung on *Glee* today. Written for a Princes Risborough band fittingly named Chameleon, "Star" pits rock stardom against competing trades, whether it's starving in an artist's garret in Beckenham or fighting in Northern Ireland (as a Nationalist or a Brit) or in Parliament, with a nod to the late Labour politician Aneurin Bevan. "Someone has to build the buildings/someone has to tear them down," as its second verse originally started. It's all performance, so why not be a rock & roll singer? It's an easy enough role.

Having demoed "Rock 'n' Roll Star" for Chameleon in spring 1971, Bowie promptly forgot about the song until reminded of it at his Aylesbury gig that September. He trimmed its title, rewrote its lyric and put it in contention for *Ziggy Stardust*, where "Star" was part of the album's most inspired sequencing: "Lady Stardust" is Ziggy recalled by his audience; "Star" flashes back to when he only sang to the mirror; "Hang Onto Yourself" cuts to the "present," with a stage-eye view of the crowd.

Like much of *Ziggy Stardust*, "Star" rummages through the pop past for trinkets, its would-be star making a demo reel from other people's songs. The multi-tracked backing vocals, up an octave from Bowie's lead, ape Beatles and Who harmonies (Bowie claimed "Lovely Rita" as an inspiration and there's "Happy Jack"-style "la la la las" in the bridge). Like the Velvet Underground's "Sweet Jane," the lyric sets characters who live in the "real world" against the singer who's in a rock & roll band, or at least dreams that he is.

It opened at a sprint: Mick Ronson hammering quaver chords on piano, Trevor Bolder thudding runs of root notes, Woody

Woodmansey's rapid-fire patter between snare and crash cymbal, Bowie's high G aaahs hanging above the fray. Five bars into the verse, the fever broke with a downshift to E minor, but there was little time for rest: a tag bar of 2/4 hustles in the following verse. "Star" moved in jump cuts, like the skip from the refrain to a three-bar F major "rock" interlude in 6/4: Bowie howls "get it on!" while the band plays a T. Rex stomp (it's the only track on *Ziggy Stardust* that doesn't have an acoustic guitar). There's a quick cut back to "reality": an eight-bar bridge in which Bowie assesses his dreams ("I could do with the money") over runs of triplets on guitar, bass and drums (Woodmansey even sneaks in a tiny snare fill). Ronson, a rival actor, takes Bowie's place for half the following verse, tracking two slide guitars separated by an octave.

After zipping through the whole sequence again, the players cut the tempo in half for an exhausted coda. Liberated from his galley slave role on piano, Ronson plays a few dancing notes and his double-tracked guitar returns while Bowie sings a bouncing vocal hook he'd soon give Lou Reed for "Satellite of Love." "Star" ends safely back home on a last G major chord. At the fade, Bowie whispers "just watch me now!" (another "Sweet Jane" quote) while, overdubbed, he hums the Richard Strauss tympani line he'd used on "Width of a Circle" and "The Supermen." No orchestra required—everything he needs is in his head.

Velvet Goldmine

Recorded*: 11 November 1971, Trident. Bowie: lead and backing vocal, 12-string acoustic guitar; Ronson: lead guitar, piano, backing vocal; Bolder: bass; Woodmansey: drums. Produced: Bowie, Scott; engineered: MacKay, Stone.*

First release*: 26 September 1975, "Space Oddity" (RCA 2593).*

"Velvet Goldmine," after which Todd Haynes named his 1998 glam fantasia movie, was slated for *Ziggy Stardust*'s second side until Bowie recorded a last batch of songs in early 1972. In a contemporary radio interview, Bowie said he cut "Velvet Goldmine" because its lyrics were "a little bit too provocative." This doesn't seem the whole of it. While "Sweet Head," the other major *Ziggy* outtake, may have been too racy, "Velvet Goldmine" isn't any bawdier than "Suffragette City." Theories that Bowie thought the song too overtly gay don't hold water either, as Bowie publicly disclosed his alleged homosexuality soon after he cut it and he'd release a "bisexual anthem" ("John, I'm Only Dancing") the following summer.

Perhaps he scrapped it because he felt the track hadn't gelled, with its transitions between guitar-stomp verses and goose-stepping refrains, the latter complete with thumping Weimar piano (it's a precursor of Roxy Music's "Triptych.") Or maybe it was just bad timing. Its quirkiness better suited the conservatory feel of *Hunky Dory*; *Ziggy Stardust* was crafted for broader public consumption. Still, "Velvet Goldmine" offers so many pleasures that its eventual release (as a B-side of a reissued "Space Oddity" in 1975) justified its status as a lost Bowie classic. Among the highlights: Bowie's salacious lyric ("I'll be your king volcano," "heal ya head with my own"); the eerie D minor refrain, with its near-spoken backing vocals; Mick Ronson's high glam solo, whose "underwater" tone he derived from a phaser and by setting his Wah-Wah pedal midway as a tone control; the goon-squad outro with its massed hummed melodies, whistles, stage laughs and moans.

Sweet Head

Recorded: *11 November 1971, Trident. Bowie: lead vocal, 12-string acoustic guitar; Ronson: lead guitar, rhythm guitar; Bolder: bass; Woodmansey: drums. Produced: Bowie, Scott; engineered: MacKay, Stone.*

First release: *11 June 1990,* ***Ziggy Stardust*** *(Ryko RCD 10134/ EMI CDEMC 3577).*

Unlike "Velvet Goldmine," few beyond the Bowie inner circle

knew the phenomenal "Sweet Head" even existed until it turned up on Rykodisc's 1990 reissue of *Ziggy Stardust*. Even Ken Scott, who presumably recorded it, said he had no memory of the track, perhaps because it was cut in a frenzied session at which "Velvet Goldmine" and other *Ziggy* master takes were recorded. "Sweet Head" nearly stayed non-existent, as Bowie initially vetoed its inclusion on the reissue.

Far from some studio trifle, "Sweet Head" rivaled "Hang Onto Yourself" and "Suffragette City" as the most pile-driving rocker of the *Ziggy Stardust* sessions. It even fit the album concept, as it's the only song besides "Ziggy Stardust" to even mention the title character. Blame its exile on its lyric, too outré even by the collapsing standards of popular music in 1972 ("it was about oral sex, and it was one I don't think RCA particularly wanted,"Bowie told *Musician* in 1990), from racial slurs in its opening verse to the refrain, which stars "my guitar and Mr. Fag."

The song moves between a power chord/arpeggiated guitar riff (Mick Ronson hitting on A major, then hammering out an A6 chord) and an express-train E to A progression (taken from the Velvet Underground's "Sweet Jane") that hits like blood being pumped into the heart. A B minor bridge gave Bowie and Ronson a breath: the latter played harmonics, the former vowed to "lay you, one and all." This was Ziggy as a traveling preacher, espousing a gospel of violence and bisexual liberation like some twisted reincarnation of Pete Townshend's Tommy. Half of its lines could open a novel: "before you had rock, you only had God"; "I had 99 tales of murder-called-life." It's Bowie mining the coalface of rock 'n' roll and flinging whatever he's dug out. He calls down Jerry Lee Lewis, sires Johnny Rotten (the scornfully rolled "rrrs" in "rubber peacock") and closes with a line worthy of his idol Little Richard: "I got pretty shoes and I'm kid and proud/ I'm street-side out with my ear to the crowd."

Round and Round

*(Berry). **Recorded**: 8-11 November 1971, Trident. Bowie: lead vocal; Ronson: lead guitar; Bolder: bass; Woodmansey: drums. Produced: Bowie, Scott; engineered; MacKay, Stone.*

***First release**: 6 April 1973, "Drive-In Saturday" (RCA 2352). **Live**: 1971, 1973.*

"Round and Round" (Bowie's diminution of Chuck Berry's "Around and Around") nearly made *Ziggy Stardust* and nearly even titled the album. Sequenced to follow the annunciation of "Moonage Daydream," the song was essentially footage of the Spiders in action. By the time Bowie returned to Trident Studios in early 1972 to finish the album, he'd worked up "Suffragette City." As the latter sounded like Chuck Berry lost in a William Burroughs novel, it made an actual Berry cover redundant. Bowie stockpiled "Round and Round" for a future B-side.

Born from a jam and likely to expire in one, "Around and Around" had come from Berry hanging out before a concert with some "on-the-ball musicians...playing standard sweet songs to gut-bucket rock and boogie." Issued as the B-side to "Johnny B. Goode" and included on the 1959 LP *Chuck Berry Is On Top*, "Around and Around" was in the repertoire of any half-competent British beat group. (In June 1964 the Rolling Stones, in an act of competitive worship, cut a version of it at Chess Studios in front of Berry himself.) It was audience bait: its stop-time verses tantalizing dancers, its chorus releasing them. Offering the sweet promise of a club that's never heard of closing time (until the cops kick in the doors), "Around and Around" was Mod solidarity: there are no girls to impress, no boys making a scene.

Where the Stones' and the Animals' covers had prominent piano, the Bowie/Spiders take hangs entirely on Ronson's distorted Les Paul and Trevor Bolder's bassline. Ken Scott recalled the track needing the fewest overdubs of any *Ziggy Stardust*-era cut. With little hope of matching Berry's rhythms, the band set about clobbering the song, pushing up the tempo, knocking the guitar solo back until after the second verse, letting the track expire in a Ronson fusillade. It was the template for how Bowie and Ronson would record *Pin Ups* the following year.

Lady Stardust

Recorded*: (demo, "Song for Marc" or "He Was Alright")** *9-10 March 1971, Radio Luxembourg. Bowie: lead vocal, piano;* ***(album) *12 November 1971, Trident. Bowie: lead vocal, 12-string acoustic guitar; Ronson: piano, backing vocals; Bolder: bass; Woodmansey: drums, tambourine. Produced: Bowie, Scott; engineered: MacKay, Stone.*

First release**: 6 June 1972,* ***Ziggy Stardust*; (demo) 11 June 1990,* ***Ziggy Stardust*** *(Ryko);* ***Broadcast****: 11 January 1972, Sounds of the 70s: John Peel; 23 May 1972, Sounds of the 70s: Bob Harris; ca. 4-6 January 1997, ChangesNowBowie.* ***Live****: 1972.*

Bowie and Marc Bolan's relationship in the early Seventies played out as name-dropping, boasts and complaints in the music press. Bowie would quote T. Rex lines and riffs in his songs, use the band as a reference in "All the Young Dudes" (which Bolan considered a subtle insult), while Bolan acted as if Bowie didn't exist. Which, you could argue, was true enough. Bowie's singles charted lower than T. Rex, the Sweet or Slade, and he never came close to T. Rex's mercury run of hits in 1971-1973: "Hot Love," "Get It On," "Jeepster," "Telegram Sam," "Metal Guru" (so confident it's a smash that it starts with its outro), "Children of the Revolution," "20th Century Boy." Morrissey described Bolan as someone who "didn't seem to have any life other than his songs."

Bowie bided his time, watching Bolan's progress, and planned to outflank him. He courted the music press, who began writing up Bowie's work as being more sophisticated and intelligent than the teen-pop of T. Rex. Bolan's overweening ego and his quick creative depletion did the rest. The king of his moment, Bolan was left entombed in it. By the end of 1973, he was a spent commercial force and had split with Tony Visconti, architect of his hits. Their last album together, *Zinc Alloy and the Hidden Riders of Tomorrow,* was received (a bit unjustly) as a *Ziggy Stardust* rip-off. By then Bowie had pulled far ahead of Bolan, never to look back.

That was the future. "Lady Stardust," Bowie's "Song for Marc," was a portrait of Bolan at the dawn of his reign. Where its brother "Ziggy Stardust" sails in on its titanic guitar riff, "Lady Stardust" opens with the after-hours musings of Mick Ronson's piano, a quiet 12-string acoustic guitar and the rhythm section as discreet backdrop. It's pieced together from scraps of old songs: Leonard Bernstein's "Maria" is in the intro, the psychedelic Stones appear in the second verse ("I smiled sadly"). Its A major setting grew unsettled in the refrain, when the dominant E major chord is usurped by an E minor seventh, briefly casting the lady in shadow ("awful nice...really quite out of sight").

Addressed throughout as "he," the Lady is a drag queen, a subject of abuse who blossoms into an object of androgynous wonder, enchanting both femmes fatales and rowdy boys ("Look: come closely now," the Lady winks in an aside at the close). There's something of fallen medieval royalty about him, more obvious in an early draft of the lyric: "Lady Stardust sang his songs of rebels, kings and queens." As Phil Sandifer wrote, the drag queen typically gets his performance as a woman *wrong* in some way ("drag transgresses, but is willfully blind to its own failure to "pass" such that its transgression is always obvious"). Here the Lady sings death ballads with a smile, withering into a black memory while still on stage. Bolan's effusive "yes," his promise of a world far away from drab midcentury Britain, is nowhere to be found. Instead "Lady Stardust" rings with old betrayals, from Oscar Wilde ("a love I could not obey") to Christ. In its demo, Bowie sang "I ***lied*** when they asked if I knew his name" in the D major bridge, referencing the Apostle Peter's triple denial of Jesus. He deconsecrated the line to "sighed" on the album take.

Mick Ronson translated Bowie's sung opening melody (as heard on the demo) into a piano line, lowering the top note of each chord by a semitone and deepening them by doubling the bass root notes at the octave. He played flights of fancy in the verses—the little fill after "creature fair," the arcing low-end phrase before "boy in the bright blue jeans," the scatter of notes that herald Lady Stardust's arrival. And Bowie's vocal, a blithe assimilation of Elton John's tone and phrasings, starts out by keeping on root notes, C# ("stared") and F# ("hair") and gathers ambition by the refrain, where he squeaks out a high B on "out of sight" and "paradise," a note as tenuous and as fleeting as his subject.

Soul Love

***Recorded**: 12 November 1971, Trident. Bowie: lead and backing vocal, 12-string acoustic guitar, baritone saxophone, handclaps; Ronson: lead guitar, rhythm guitar, backing vocal; Bolder: bass; Woodmansey: drums, conga. Produced: Bowie, Scott; engineered: MacKay, Stone.*

***First release**: 6 June 1972, **Ziggy Stardust**. **Live**: 1973, 1978, 1983.*

"Soul Love" shows up love as being amoral and ruinous, sweeping over "cross and baby" like a plague or an infestation. Its three verses were three indictments. A mother kneels at her son's tombstone (the son's been killed in a war, having died "to save the slogan"), her "stone love" resolute, his entombed. Two teenagers are so consumed by infatuation they think they're inventing a new language. After a move up to A major, a priest kneels at an altar, blindly in love with a possibly absent God.

So the song was a rising movement, love ascending from a primal state (a mother's love for her child) through teenage lust to close at its most abstract, the union of God and man. Each section of the path lies in blindness; in each "love" is the hand that takes. Bowie's verse vocal worked in parallel: he starts on a whole D note ("stone"), goes up a fourth to G ("brave") and peaks on the octave D ("eyes"). A single-note high harmony is the unattainable object of desire, hanging an octave above Bowie's lead, which never reaches it (the closest he gets is a fourth beneath the harmony note). Playing a fifth below Bowie's climactic note and an octave below the harmony note, Ronson is the solid earth.

It's unknown when Bowie wrote "Soul Love," which had little to do with the Ziggy Stardust concept. Its pairing with "Five Years" on *Ziggy Stardust* suggests the two songs were written close to the same time or that Bowie had spun one out of the other, as they share a drum intro, a near-identical verse progression and a sense of pity for a mass of desperate, doomed people ("love descends on those defenseless"). Sequenced back to back, the songs came off as different-tempo variations of the same work, two preludes before Ziggy Stardust appears in the album "opener," "Moonage Daydream."

It opens with Woody Woodmansey playing rapid 8ths on his closed hi-hat and a kick-rimshot-kick pattern, garnished with handclaps and conga, Bowie's rapidly-strummed 12-string acoustic guitar (muting a strum on the third of every four strokes) and Trevor Bolder's vaguely Latin bassline. The verses' rhythmic skip (a bar of 2/4 pops in midway through) has a counterpart in the harmonic dislocations of the refrains, where Bowie swaps an E major for an expected E minor ("sweeping over") and upturns a triumphant C major dominant chord ("defenseless," "inspirations") by cooling it to a C minor ("all I have"), celebrating the coup by singing an E-flat note.

A dissenter from the song's schematics was Bowie's baritone saxophone, first heard harrying things along in the second verse and then taking over for a verse, reversing the top melody and then veering off from it, following a long, sloping phrase with a sharply arcing one, not-quite-executing a two-note volley and ringing through a few rising triplets to transition the key change.

And though Ronson's double-tracked guitars war against Bowie's vocal line in the refrains, he surrenders: his coda guitar solo plays Bowie's verse melody note for note, with Bowie soon appearing to sing him out.

Five Years

***Recorded**: 15 November 1971, Trident. Bowie: lead vocal, 12-string acoustic guitar; Ronson: piano, autoharp, backing vocal; Bolder: bass; Woodmansey: drums; unknown musicians: violins, violas, celli, basses (arranged: Ronson). Produced: Bowie, Scott; engineered: MacKay, Stone.*

***First release**: 6 June 1972, **Ziggy Stardust**. **Broadcast**: 18 January 1972, Sounds of the 70s: Bob Harris; 7 February 1972, The Old Grey Whistle Test; ca. 8-12 February 1976, Dinah! **Live**: 1972-1973, 1976, 1978, 2003-2005.*

Of all the apocalyptic Bowie songs, "Five Years" is the most unsettling. It's in the details, what Bowie discloses and what he doesn't—that is, *why* the world's going to end. The planet's just received a terminal prognosis. The singer stays on the street, watching those who, having heard the news (the same news that "all the young dudes" are carrying, Bowie later said), despair and debase themselves. Yet there's a joy in the five (naturally) refrains of "five years!!" that ring out the song. It's a last jubilee. The end is coming, but not quite yet; in the meantime, dance and slough off the old world. Held back for nearly three minutes, the refrain is a relief after having endured a pair of long, despairing verses anchored by Woody Woodmansey, who tried, via a terse dialogue of snare, kick and closed hi-hat, to put "hopelessness into a drumbeat."

"Five Years" is Bowie as doom millenarian, which put him in a popular key of his time. The fear, or hope, that Western civilization teetered on the brink of ruin was everywhere, the backdrop of the *Planet of the Apes* franchise and the BBC1 series *Doomwatch*. There were doomsayers across the political spectrum, from soured hippies, overpopulation eco-kooks and anti-urbanists like Robert Allen, an associate editor for *The Ecologist* who wrote admiringly of how the Khmer Rouge had cleansed Cambodian cities, to those on the right who crowed about the bloody collapse of welfare states and who regarded as documentaries the likes of *Dirty Harry*, whose contemporary San Francisco—a cesspool of perverts and killers and the milquetoast government that enables them—seemed post-apocalyptic.

And it felt as though time was running at a Benzedrine pace. You could imagine human civilization might end in five years, as it seemed as though we'd burned through an epoch in the previous five. By 1972, 1967 was a lost childhood and 1957 had apparently occurred on another planet. The future was always coming, hungry to dispatch the present.

The difference was that Bowie didn't take his doomsday quite so seriously. "The whole thing was to try and get a mocking angle at the future. If I can mock something and deride it, one isn't so scared of it," he told Charles Shaar Murray in 1972. He crafted "Five Years" as a stage piece. Lyrical inspiration came from Roger McGough's poem "At Lunchtime: A Story of Love," which Bowie had recited during his Feathers and Arts Lab shows (the poem concerns bus riders who, upon learning the world will end at lunchtime, happily embark on orgies.) His opening line even offered a theater location—the Market Square in Aylesbury, home of the Friars Club (the only club he could sell out at the time). The street reactions he documents are bits of underground "action" theatre: policemen kneeling to priests, teenage girls trying to kill children, "queers" and blacks as moral consciences and cultural critics.

The central chord progression of both verse and refrain (G-E minor-A-C) was a twist on a hoary jazz/pop sequence: it's the end of the world as paced to "I Got Rhythm" or "Heart and Soul." (See also the occasional Americanisms: "TV" instead of "telly," or the drawled "thawwwt of Maw" before the refrain.)

Bowie's narrator grows tongue-tied and nonsensical, his doomsday imagery more word collisions ("all the fat-skinny people.") "My brain hurt like a warehouse," he complains, much like how he'd busted out his brains for the words on "Moonage Daydream."

Still, "Five Years" mostly wore its mourner's mask, its verses beginning with Bowie's somberly falling vocal and Mick Ronson strumming a double-tracked autoharp to broaden a piano chord. Trevor Bolder nudges up to help each turnaround while sneaking in octave jumps and drops whenever the piano falls quiet. (As on "Life On Mars?" Ronson wrote his score with Bolder's bassline in mind: upon their arrival in the second verse, the celli are in thrall to Bolder.) In the bridge, as Bolder plays glissandos and rapid little fills, Bowie makes a dramatic sweep, singing dominant notes ("telephones, opera house") and then, as with "Soul Love," makes an ascending stepwise movement, rising from a D ("and it rained") to an F# ("your face! your race!") to a high G ("I kiss you!"). As with his "hopelessness" drum pattern, Woodmansey was the track's dramatist: the three snare hits that punctuate "somebody," the crash cymbal in the second verse, the two-triplet fill that triggers the refrain.

The throat-shredding refrain, which drove Bowie to weep in the vocal booth (you can hear him in the last sets of "five years!"), needed a second take so Ken Scott could reset the microphone levels. The outro, with its massed strings and trellis-like ascending violins, descends into the maelstrom, soon bringing in Ronson's "whinnying" guitar (heard again on "Time"), bow scrapes and phased strings.

"I thought of my brother and wrote 'Five Years,'" Bowie wrote in an autobiographical fragment in 1976. Even if Terry Burns was once again a muse (see "Bewlay Brothers"), "Five Years" wasn't as mournful as "All the Madmen" or "Bewlay Brothers." It's the end of the world as carnival, the ecstatic promise of the end of days. "People are so incredibly serious and scared of the future that I would wish to turn the feeling the other way, into a wave of optimism," as he told Shaar Murray. With "Five Years" and "Rock 'n' Roll Suicide," Bowie bookended *Ziggy Stardust* with a pair of joyful deaths.

Suffragette City

***Recorded**: 4 February 1972, Trident. Bowie: lead vocal, 12-string acoustic guitar; Ronson: lead and rhythm guitar, piano, ARP synthesizer, backing vocals; Bolder: bass; Woodmansey: drums. Produced: Bowie, Scott; engineered: MacKay, Stone.*

***First release**: 28 April 1972 (RCA 2199). **Broadcast**: 16 May 1972, Sounds of the 70s: John Peel. **Live**: 1972-1974, 1976, 1978, 1990, 2003-2004.*

The first thing you hear after the engine-revving guitar and synthesizer is "HEY MAN": flat, stoned-sounding, insistent. Buzzing from left to right speaker, the voice disrupts the singer's flow, flusters him. It coils "Suffragette City" into a ball of agitation. It's a complaint by someone who's sure he'll get laid if only things would somehow work out, if his deadbeat roommate would just get *out of the house* for once, if his boyfriend wouldn't mind if he just brought this girl over for a bit. It's a "Queen Bitch" who's desperately on the make but just as aggrieved.

Having offered the song to Mott the Hoople, who rejected it, Bowie reclaimed "Suffragette City" in the last *Ziggy Stardust* sessions of early 1972. It was a rock & roll simulacrum: Jerry Lee Lewis-style pounded eighth-note chords, synthetic saxophones that seem ready to break into Frankie Ford's "Sea Cruise," a bright piano line that calls back to the Beatles' "Back in the USSR." Even the false ending's in quotations. Bowie said he took "wham! bam! thank you ma'am!" from a track on Charles Mingus' *Oh Yeah* but he just as likely nicked it from the Small Faces.

A run of rehearsals, TV/radio spots and live gigs in January 1972 hardened the Spiders into a crack unit, giving "Suffragette

City" a muscular performance to suit its no-minor-chords-allowed structure. Mick Ronson's opening riff is as spare in design (he's mainly sliding along his two lowest strings) as it's thick in power. As on "Moonage Daydream," Ronson lays low in the verses after an opening double-tracked barrage, roars to life in the refrains and runs rampant over the outro. Trevor Bolder sounds as if he's demonstrating a heart attack via bass strings; Woody Woodmansey's drums are scattered across the stereo spectrum like batteries of artillery. His kick is panned half-left, his snare half-right, his cymbals mixed low—the latter because Ken Scott disliked cymbals and pushed up Bowie's 12-string acoustic guitar to supplement them. (Scott got a livelier drum sound on the *Ziggy Stardust* sessions by using gaffer's tape and "sometimes a small piece of sponge on the drum head to get rid of some of the ring of the drums.")

Bowie wanted to have a wall of saxophones, a desire thwarted by the limits of his saxophone skills. Rather than hiring session players, Scott brought in an ARP 2600 synthesizer, monkeyed with it until he got a facsimile of a tenor saxophone sound and let Ronson do the rest. The ARP made "Suffragette City" sound like a rock 'n' roll oldie reproduced by a mainframe. It was a serpentine presence in the outro, descending to a root note and leaping up to a high C#, adding another spot of tension to a performance already on the verge of a nervous breakdown.

A last-minute influence was Stanley Kubrick's *A Clockwork Orange* (which the Bowie entourage saw mid-January), both lyrically ("say droogie don't crash here!") and sartorially (the band's stage outfits would be based on the film's droog-wear, which Bowie later called a "terrorist we-are-ready-for-action look"). But "Suffragette City" was far more sex comedy than any incitement to violence. No charismatic menace like Malcolm McLaren's Alex in *Clockwork Orange*, the singer's just a hot mess, stammering through the first verse, unable to finish his thoughts (Bowie had wanted to sing it in a phone booth when performing live). Bowie uses tics and fumbles to jar up the song: his run of "she *said she*...*but she*...and *then she*" hit like drum fills. He's at the mercy of everyone around him, from his roommate/lover ("Henry") to the nameless woman who's disposed of him in an afternoon. Getting to "Suffragette City" would be a masochistic dream: a brave new world of liberated women to torture him. This sense of aggrieved bisexuality would soon get a sequel with "John, I'm Only Dancing."

Rock 'n' Roll Suicide

Recorded: *2-4 February 1972, Trident. Bowie: lead vocal, 12-string acoustic guitar; Ronson: lead and rhythm guitars, ARP, backing vocal; Bolder: bass; Woodmansey: drums; unknown musicians: 2 trumpets, 2 trombones, 2 tenor saxophones, baritone saxophone, 8 violins, 4 violas, 2 celli, 2 double basses (arranged: Ronson). Produced: Bowie, Scott; engineered: MacKay, Stone.*

First release: *6 June 1972,* ***Ziggy Stardust***. ***Broadcast***: *23 May 1972, Sounds of the 70s: Bob Harris.* ***Live***: *1972-1974, 1978, 1990.*

Ziggy Stardust's grand finale "Rock 'n' Roll Suicide" lacks death and rock 'n' roll. In the first run of Ziggy Stardust shows, the band typically closed sets with Velvet Underground covers ("White Light/White Heat," "Waiting For the Man") so there was a need for Bowie to have his own curtain piece. His wife Angela told him to write a song in which he urged the audience to rush the stage and reach out to him, a "spontaneous" act that employees of his management company (and Angela) would push fans to do at shows.

The result was a mongrel, a gushy Fifties pop ballad fused with a *chanson*, possibly written with an eye on replacing a cover of Jacques Brel's "Amsterdam" that had been slotted as the last track of *Ziggy Stardust*. Bowie's lyric was a dog's dinner of Brel: "oh no, love! you're not alone!" is from Brel's "Jef" ("Non, jef, t'es pas tout seul") and "Les Vieux" (which Bowie raided later for "Sons of the Silent Age") inspired lines about the clock waiting patiently and "when you've lived too long." Yet beneath this was a ticking doo-wop heart in 12/8, obvious once Mick Ronson started arpeggiating a tremolo-thinned line in the second verse. Its progression strode confidently from C to G major only to putter out on an A minor chord ("you forget," "hurry home"). Moving away from its austere opening—a close-miked Bowie and 12-string acoustic, capped off by thudding door-knocks from Woody Woodmansey's kick drum—the song ventured into more bathetic waters, melodically referencing Judy Garland's take on "You'll Never Walk Alone" and lyrically spoofing Gerry and the Pacemakers "Don't Let the Sun Catch You Crying." By the last verse, there was Trevor Bolder (who celebrates that "the day breaks" by popping a few high notes but plays a doleful Shadows bassline for much of the song), Woodmansey's full kit and baritone saxophones as a chorus: a three-note "snarling," some honking E octaves on "the road."

"Rock 'n' Roll Suicide" starts as the ember of a life, some forlorn soul wandering through the streets (say, the morning after he's learned we've only got "Five Years" left), no longer young, cashed out. Given its title and its verses, one assumes there'll be a body on stage at some point. That's what *Ziggy Stardust*'s been building up to: the pop idol has to die as a closer. Nik Cohn's fascist pop-star Johnny Angelo (another Ziggy Stardust influence) went out in a hail of bullets. "I dream about him a lot but they're always horrid dreams 'cos he always dies in the end," a teenage fan says of Paul Jones' pop idol in the film *Privilege* (see "Somebody Up There Likes Me"). And Bowie apparently *had* intended for Ziggy to die: he'd been taken with the idea of a pop singer being killed on stage for years (see "The Mask"). In the "black-hole Bacchantes" scenario he described to William Burroughs, Ziggy was meant to be torn to pieces.

But ending in blood wasn't glam at all. So "Rock 'n' Roll Suicide" instead ended like a production of *Peter Pan,* when children are asked to clap Tinkerbell back to life: "Give me your *hands*! 'Cause you're *wonderful*!" This was such an ecstatic bit of theatre that Bowie fainted while singing the refrain in New York on Valentine's Day, 1973 (a fan on the bootleg recording wonders aloud if he's dead). In 1974 Bowie reveled in "Rock 'n' Roll Suicide," embracing its shamelessness; in his 1978 shows, he often bade goodbye to Ziggy at its close, a winking farewell to childhood. That should have been the end: a last revival for his "greatest hits" tour of 1990 often came off as a soulless obligation.

Having dumped his *chanson* for a Judy Garland-style finale, Bowie now drew from James Brown, whose "Try Me" and "I Lost Someone" on Bowie's treasured *Live At the Apollo* were a set of instructions of how to bend an audience to one's will. In proper Brown style, "Rock 'n' Roll Suicide" ends with three "beg" refrains, each progressively wilder. In the first, the arpeggiated guitar is doubled-tracked, the horns comment from the wins (lurching up an octave on "you're all tangled up!"), the massed strings tense on a single note. A chromatic rise of violins heralds the second refrain and a wrenching move to E-flat minor, with Bolder's arcing bassline answered by celli. Bowie's "you're NOT alone!" now peaks at a high B-flat, the crowning note of "Life On Mars?," and sung here as if he's torn his larynx. And an *a cappella* "you're NOT ALONE" drop-kicks the song into its last refrain and key (D-flat major), with Ziggy bowing out with one final push for applause. Ronson gives the crowd a final blessing, intoning "wonderful" as the horns soar upward, then leads the way to the exits with a bonsai guitar solo and scoring a last D-flat for celli.

Starman

Recorded: *4 February 1972, Trident. Bowie: lead vocal, 12-string acoustic guitar, handclaps; Ronson: lead guitar, rhythm guitar, backing vocal, handclaps; Bolder: bass; Woodmansey: drums; unknown musicians: violins, violas, celli, double bass (arr. Ronson). Produced:*

Bowie, Scott; engineered: MacKay, Stone.

First release*: 28 April 1972 (RCA 2199/ 74-0719, UK #10).* ***Broadcast****: 22 May 1972, Johnnie Walker Lunchtime Show; 15 June 1972, Lift Off With Ayshea; 5 July 1972, Top of the Pops; 23 June 2000, TFI Friday; 15 June 2002, A&E's Live By Request.* ***Live****: 1972-1973, 1990, 2000, 2002-2004.*

"Starman" is Bowie's Christmas carol, promising the human race's redemption by a higher power with a refrain crafted for a crowd to sing. It finally broke him: "After 'Starman,' everything changed," Woody Woodmansey recalled in 2008. Yet while *Ziggy Stardust*-era Bowie is remembered for his gift for outrage, the song that made his name was warm, reassuring and, most of all, familiar.

For most British pop listeners in the summer of 1972, David Bowie was still the oddball who'd had the song about Major Tom back in the Sixties. Here he was back at last, with another astronaut song, a sunnier "Space Oddity." Where in the latter a frail human being went lost in space, in "Starman" space was domesticated. The alien comes to visit *us* in our suburban homes, whispering through our radio speakers, promising revelations if we're good, as if he's Santa Claus. No longer is planet earth is blue and there's nothing we can do. Now an alien tells us human life "is all worthwhile." Variations on this theme of extraterrestrial altruism played throughout the Seventies, from Erich von Däniken's theories that aliens were responsible for human civilization to the benevolent star-children of *Close Encounters of the Third Kind* to Jon Pertwee-era *Doctor Who*, in which the time-and-cosmos-traveling Doctor is comfortably exiled in near-future Britain and freelances for the military.

"Starman" wasn't intended for *Ziggy Stardust*. After hearing a mix of the album, RCA made the typical complaint of not hearing a single; Bowie's manager Tony Defries agreed. So like "Space Oddity," another song owed to managerial imposition, Bowie went off to grind out a hit. He came back with a song that RCA's contemporary music VP Dennis Katz loved so much he demanded it appear on the album.

It was Bowie softening his image, brightening his eerie children's songs (the Starman would offer that "There is a Happy Land" without irony), even subtly revising "All the Madmen," given one possible inspiration: David Rome's story "There's a Starman in Ward 7." Rome's narrator, an institutionalized schizophrenic who believes he's a child, wakes to find the Starman, a new inmate in Ward 7 who says he's from Alpha Centauri ("he says nobody believes him, that's why he's here") and who offers freedom ("Not just me!! He's going to cure EVERYBODY!!!"). In reality an insane "quack head-doctor," the Starman encourages an inmate uprising that lands the narrator in the heavier-policed Ward 8. The Starman has vanished but the narrator watches the sky from his cell, wondering if he'll see the Starman's ship "coming down...like a silver angel."

So: liberation, madmen, community, aliens. "Starman" celebrates the world that pop music creates, its secret societies. The key line's in the second verse, when Bowie learns that his friend's carrying the news, too. In a parallel the harmony vocals, starting a third above Bowie's lead, directly echo Bowie at the peak of the refrain ("it's all worthwhile!"). The Starman's a voice on the radio, a cosmic DJ whispering secrets late at night, and the track itself was a pulp of radio hits. Its guitar-piano hook was from the Supremes' "You Keep Me Hangin' On" or Glen Campbell's "Wichita Lineman" (another song where voices sing through the wires) while its "LA-la-la-la-LA" outro is the coda of T. Rex's "Hot Love."

For all of its assurances, "Starman" opens in hesitation, Bowie humming while he strums his 12-string acoustic, shuffling between two major seventh chords (Bbmaj7 and Fmaj7) with ringing open strings and picking bass notes with his thumb. Another acoustic guitar makes impatient interjections while Mick Ronson bides his time, playing a few reverb-shrouded root notes on his Les Paul. This collective meandering keeps you on edge, wondering when the song will break, until a Woodmansey fill (medium toms to snare) and a faint breath of violins kick off the verse. Once jump-started "Starman" tears off: Bowie closes out verses with dashes of rapid-fire strums while Woodmansey reverses course with snare-to-tom fills. The "Wichita Lineman" hook sets up the refrains, where Ronson's scoring celebrates Bowie's peak moments: celli gracefully ascend on "starman," violins skitter up on "all worthwhile."

Bowie didn't oversell it. He keeps to the comfortable middle of his range and barbs the ends of phrases with descending three-note hooks ("low-oh-oh," "nigh-high-height"). Ronson's guitar solo is as restrained: as on "Moonage Daydream" he plays the mediant note of each chord on downbeats and worries a few notes with finger vibrato and string bends.

There's an easy confidence. The refrain comes seemingly out of nowhere, as if you'd just picked up its frequency on your radio. Like "Life On Mars?" it opens with an octave leap, but here so obvious a lift from "Over the Rainbow" ("some-*where*/ Star-*man*") that Bowie cheekily merged the songs one night at the Rainbow Theatre in August 1972.

Released two months before *Ziggy Stardust*, "Starman" made a slow trek up the charts, but thanks to the buzz that Bowie's live shows were generating, it hit the Top 10 in late June. Two television appearances were the last touch. The first was *Lift Off with Ayshea*, whose performance stunned the 13-year-old Steven Morrissey ("Bowie is detached from everything, yet open to everything; stripped of the notion that both art and life are impossible") while fellow Mancunian Marc Riley, later of the Fall, recalled his grandmother shouting insults at the television ("something she usually saved for Labour Party broadcasts,"he told David Buckley). *Top of the Pops*, filmed on 5 July 1972 and broadcast the following day (and repeated at Christmas), took care of the rest. Bowie's fellow Bromleyite Susan Ballion, soon to call herself Siouxsie Sioux, watched it while in hospital recovering from colitis; ten-year old Dave Gahan in Basildon, 14-year old Gary Numan in West London and 13-year old Ian McCulloch in Liverpool were other converts. Bowie was a window, opening upon a life they didn't know was conceivable.

Bowie's *TOTP* performance has become totemic (there's been a book and a TV retrospective devoted to it) but it's worth noting that its impact wasn't immediate. At the time, no reporters noticed anything of interest in the *TOTP* broadcast, nor did any of Bowie's first-wave biographers consider it even worth mentioning. David Buckley's 1999 biography, for which he interviewed the likes of Numan, Riley and McCullough about the *TOTP* performance, established the legend.

It's not surprising that "Starman" resonated most with those born in the late Fifties and early Sixties: it was propaganda for the coming race. "The older people have lost all touch with reality and the kids are left on their own to plunder anything," as Bowie said to William S. Burroughs. (It's telling that Bowie stopped playing "Starman" live once the single had done its work. It was a hard-to-sing piece that risked seeming corny to the older audiences he drew on tour.) The kids might not be able to go to Bowie's shows but they could watch him on TV, with his copper-colored mullet and his spaceman leotard (much like the one Peter Cook had worn as Satan-as-pop star in *Bedazzled*). Brimming with charisma, Bowie twirled his finger at the camera while singing "you-ooh-oooh" and hooked every susceptible child in Britain. He sold futures. The essential part of the *TOTP* broadcast is when Bowie starts the first refrain and Ronson tentatively approaches the mike. Bowie sweeps his arm over Ronson's shoulder, pulling him close. It's a sweet moment of inclusion, the alien embracing the rocker and, by proxy, all of the nation's misfits. "Starman" left community in its wake; its promise came true.

Chapter 6

Ziggy in Nixonland (1972-1973)

The victor's trophy—a silver gilt figure of odious design, symbolizing Fame embracing Speed.
Evelyn Waugh, *Vile Bodies.*

I am a sublimated Aladdin, the thousand and second knight.
T.E. Lawrence.

Violence and glamour and speed, splendour and vulgarity, gesture and combustion—these were the things that he valued, none else, and his tours turned into full-scale odysseys, and Johnny himself was seen almost as a messiah, whose message was a single word: excess.
Nik Cohn, *I Am Still the Greatest Says Johnny Angelo.*

America is the noisiest country that ever existed.
Oscar Wilde, *Impressions of America.*

You Got to Have a Job (If You Don't Work, You Can't Eat)/ Hot Pants

("Job," Brown/Reed;"Hot Pants," Brown/Wesley). David Bowie: vocal, tenor saxophone; Mick Ronson: lead guitar; Trevor Bolder: bass; Woody Woodmansey: drums; Nicky Graham: piano?

***Live**: 1972.*

The first tour of Ziggy Stardust and the Spiders from Mars, which ranged across Britain from February to July 1972, was a series of small insurrections. It kicked off at the Toby Jug pub in Tolworth, Surrey, with Angela Bowie working the lights. Bowie wore his "combat suit" from the *Ziggy Stardust* cover shoot; the band wore denim. His ambition was greater than his audiences:

aping Iggy Pop one night at Imperial College, Bowie tried to be carried aloft by the crowd, which was spread too thin. He crashed to the floor.

The tour was a traveling workshop. After each gig, Bowie, Angela and his manager Tony Defries autopsied the performance: which songs worked best, how to choreograph and light them. Bowie quickly got a reputation among students (like Imperial College alumni Roger Taylor and Brian May, who attended that show) and a growing rank of misfits. "This was no...drag act full of lisping gestures and limp hands," the *Melody Maker* wrote of the Imperial College show. Instead, Bowie was "queening his way through old and new songs" with charismatic shamelessness.

Allegedly touring in support of the just-issued *Hunky Dory*, Bowie only played four songs from it. His sets instead comprised of songs from the unreleased *Ziggy Stardust* and covers: Chuck Berry's "Around and Around," two Velvet Underground standards, Jacques Brel's "Amsterdam" and a medley of James Brown's "Hot Pants" and "You Got to Have a Job (If You Don't Work, You Can't Eat)."

Brown had turned a mid-tempo single, "You Got to Have a Job," that he'd co-written and produced for James Crawford into a scorching duet with Marva Whitney, with Brown and Whitney circling around each other, grappling for advantage. Bowie most likely based his cover off Bobby Byrd's version of the song, a piece of tight funk minimalism. A bizarre interpreter for a bootstrapping communiqué to the African-American community, Bowie's inclusion of "Got to Have a Job" reflected his tentativeness about how to present the still-developing Ziggy Stardust character. Playing a heavy R&B number, even if leadenly, could at least keep the interest of audiences who didn't know any of his songs besides "Space Oddity" (on bootlegs, there are some crowd whoops on the shift to "Hot Pants"). It was also a well-worn stage routine for him, as he'd sung a James

Brown medley back with the Manish Boys and Lower Third in 1965. Bowie would fashion his glam persona out of Brown's stage costumes and routines, with Brown's prolonged set of farewells on "Please Please Please" in the blood of "Rock 'n' Roll Suicide."

Mick Ronson tempered embarrassment by compressing the Byrd single's guitar-horns interplay into a guitar riff over a resilient Trevor Bolder bassline. The weak links, at least in the Kingston recording, were Woody Woodmansey as funk antimatter and Bowie, whose tortuous six-chorus saxophone solo deserved some hurled tomatoes. He considered reviving the Brown combination for his 1974 "Soul Dogs" tour until going with another medley: "Footstompin'" and "I Wish I Could Shimmy Like My Sister Kate" (see Ch. 9).

I Feel Free

(Bruce/Brown). ***Recorded****: (live, 1972) Bowie: vocal; Ronson: lead guitar; Bolder: bass; Woodmansey: drums; Graham: piano;* ***(studio take, aka "Is There Life After Marriage," unreleased)*** *ca. May 1980, Power Station, New York. Carlos Alomar: rhythm guitar; George Murray: bass; Dennis Davis: drums. Produced: Tony Visconti;* ***(remake)*** *ca. May-June 1992, Mountain Studios, Montreux, and The Hit Factory, New York. Bowie: lead vocal; Ronson: lead guitar; Nile Rodgers: rhythm guitar; Richard Hilton, Dave Richards, Philippe Saisse, Richard Tee: keyboards; Barry Campbell: bass; Poogie Bell and/or Sterling Campbell: drums; Fonzi Thornton, Tawatha Agee, Curtis King, Jr., Dennis Collins, Brenda White-King, Maryel Epps: backing vocals. Produced: Rodgers, Bowie; engineered: Jon Goldberger.*

First release*: (live, 6 May 1972) May 1995,* ***RarestOneBowie*** *(GY 014); (remake) 5 April 1993,* ***Black Tie White Noise*** *(Arista 74321 13697 2, UK #1, US #39).* ***Live****: 1972.*

If "You Got to Have a Job" was Bowie tapping an influence, his cover of Cream's "I Feel Free" tried to exorcise one. A mid-set crowd-pleaser of the first Spiders shows, "I Feel Free" also served as intermission music, with Mick Ronson soloing at length to give

Bowie time to change outfits. Enough of a Cream devotee to have made *The Man Who Sold the World* in tribute to them, Ronson had lobbied for the cover, though the Spiders' "I Feel Free" thudded more than it glided. It was gone from the set by the end of their first British tour.

On stage, "I Feel Free" gave Ronson a rare chance to indulge himself. His solos sometimes bloated over a hundred bars, as if he hoped to erase the memory of Eric Clapton's concise soloing by sheer duration. His amp cranked and his notes ballooned with sustain, Ronson recycled riffs and effects from "Width of a Circle," a song that would soon replace "I Feel Free" in set-lists. Ronson was an overwhelming figure in the early Spiders shows, drowning out his bandmates and forcing Bowie to quickly master mike technique: he'd almost swallow the mike to ensure he got heard. Soon enough roadies tampered with Ronson's amps so that when he cranked up to ten, he was only at eight.

"I Feel Free" had some resonance for Bowie as well. His half-brother Terry Burns had been a Cream fan and had suffered a schizophrenic episode outside a hall where the band was playing. Bowie would toy with recording "I Feel Free" for over two decades, slating it for both *Pin Ups* and *Scary Monsters*. In the latter's sessions, his band cut a rhythm track that switched up the verse's chord changes. He declined to develop this further but used the track as a blueprint for a genteel dance-pop "I Feel Free" cut a decade later for *Black Tie White Noise*. This last icy incarnation, with Bowie bobbing along the groove and singing in a weighty baritone, was a last bow for Ronson, whose solo was one of his last recorded performances. Sadly, it was barren compared to the fecundity of his 1972 solos. Ronson died of cancer at age 47, mere weeks after the album's release.

White Light/White Heat

(Reed). ***Recorded: (live, Hammersmith Odeon, 3 July 1973)*** *Bowie: lead vocal, 12-string acoustic guitar; Ronson: lead guitar, backing*

vocal; John Hutchinson: rhythm guitar; Mike Garson: piano; Bolder: bass; Woodmansey: drums; Geoffrey MacCormack, Tony Visconti: backing vocals. Produced: Ken Scott; engineered: Scott, Mike Moran; ***(studio backing track)*** *9-31 July 1973, Château d'Hérouville, Pointoise, France. Ronson: lead and rhythm guitars; Garson: piano; Bolder: bass; Aynsley Dunbar: drums; Bowie: rhythm guitar? Produced: Bowie, Scott; engineered: Dennis Blackeye.*

First release*: (live) 24 October 1983,* ***Ziggy Stardust: The Motion Picture*** *(RCA PL-84862/RCA CPL2-4862, UK #17, US #89); (backing track) January 1975,* ***Play Don't Worry*** *(Ronson, RCA APL1 0681).* ***Broadcast:*** *16 May 1972, Sounds of the 70s: John Peel; 23 May 1972, Sounds of the 70s: Bob Harris; ca. 4-6 January 1997, ChangesNowBowie.* ***Live****: 1972-1973, 1983, 1987, 1990, 1996-1997, 2002-2004.*

As Bowie and the Spiders honed their live act, they swapped out the likes of "Andy Warhol" for more pummeling stuff like the Velvet Underground's "White Light/White Heat." A set regular by May 1972, "White Light/White Heat," with its lean A major chord structure and its drone rhythms, presaged the feel of Bowie's next two singles. His only crack at it in the studio, however, was a rhythm track cut during *Pin Ups* that Mick Ronson used as the chassis of his own version, on 1975's *Play Don't Worry*.

Though "White Light/White Heat" hymns the joys of speed, with John Cale's off-time, two-note outro bassline a sonic methamphetamine injection, it was also an occultist song. Lou Reed was singing about Alice Bailey's *A Treatise on White Magic*, a 1934 tome that instructs how to attempt an astral projection "down a stream of pure White Light." As Bowie had written an astral projection song ("Did You Ever Have a Dream") and would subsist on books like Bailey's during his time in Los Angeles in the mid-Seventies, it was fitting that "White Light" would be his longest-running cover (he played it in the majority of his tours, ranging from 1972 to 2004).

Boosting "White Light/White Heat" and "Waiting for the Man" brought Reed into Bowie's sphere of influence. The two were on the same label and when Bowie offered to produce a follow-up after Reed's solo debut had failed to sell, Reed and RCA's Dennis Katz grabbed a lifeline. In July 1972, Reed played his first-ever British concert as Bowie's guest. Angela Bowie soon had him in appropriate leather and make-up, with Reed favoring a white pallor/black mascara combination to play up his "New York cool" image—he wanted to look bloodless, he later said.

Bowie and Ronson produced Reed's *Transformer* over two frenzied weeks in August, working with Reed during the day, rehearsing for Bowie's Rainbow Theatre shows at night. While the pace proved exhausting (Bowie was once found in the studio bathroom weeping), there was a delicacy in Bowie's contributions: the gorgeous multi-tracked high harmonies on "Satellite of Love"; the catty co-lead vocal on "New York Phone Conversation." And although Reed found Ronson's Hull accent indecipherable, Ronson did the lion's share of arranging. He was "the man on the floor" during the sessions, bassist Herbie Flowers recalled, even tuning Reed's guitar for him. Ronson's fingerprints are everywhere on *Transformer*, from the oom-pah brass accompaniment of "Goodnight Ladies" to "Perfect Day," where Ronson liberated the song from Reed's guitar and bestowed it on his own wistful piano and soaring strings. Listening to the isolated string tracks of "Perfect Day" decades later for a documentary, Reed blissed out for a moment, then blankly stared at the camera: "Boy, Ronson's good."

All the Young Dudes

Recorded**: *(Mott the Hoople)*** *14 May 1972, Olympic Studios, 117 Church Road, Barnes, London. Ian Hunter: lead vocal, piano; Mick Ralphs: acoustic guitar, lead guitar, backing vocals; Verden Allen: Hammond organ, backing vocals?; Overend Watts: bass, backing vocals?; Dale Griffin: drums, tambourine, backing vocals; Bowie:*

backing vocals, acoustic guitar?; Stan Tippins: vocals; Stuey George, Nicky Graham: handclaps. Produced: Bowie, Ronson; engineered: Keith Harwood; ***(Bowie)*** *7-10 December 1972, RCA Studios, New York. Bowie: lead and backing vocal, tenor saxophone?; Ronson: lead guitar, backing vocals; Garson: piano; Bolder: bass; Woodmansey: drums; Ken Fordham, Brian "Bux" Wilshaw: tenor saxophone. Produced: Bowie, Scott; engineered: Mike Moran.*

First release*: (Mott) 28 July 1972 (CBS 8271, #3 UK, #37 US); (Bowie) May 1995,* ***RarestOneBowie****; (Mott track w/ Bowie guide vocal) 14 September 1998,* ***All the Young Dudes: The Anthology*** *(Sony/Columbia 491400 2).* ***Live****: 1972-1974, 1992, 1996-1997, 2003-2004.*

Why did Bowie give away his best song? Mott the Hoople, as he played them "All the Young Dudes" on acoustic guitar in his publisher's Regent Street office, found his generosity bewildering. Asked if they wanted the song, "we broke our necks to say yes," Mott's drummer Dale Griffin said.

Mott got "All the Young Dudes" thanks to inventory overload (Bowie had cut back-to-back albums and had a fresh single, "John, I'm Only Dancing," lined up), because his manager wanted to bring Mott into his stable of acts, because Bowie still considered himself as much a songwriter as a performer and, most of all, because he was a fan. He romanticized the band, acting as if a quintet of gruff circuit veterans from Herefordshire were the motorcycle gang from *The Wild One*. And as Mott had turned down an earlier-proffered "Suffragette City," his competitive streak drove him to write something they couldn't refuse.

After four poor-selling records and a financially ruinous tour, Mott were considering breaking up. Mott's Overend Watts found Bowie's "Suffragette City" demo and called him to ask if he knew anyone in need of a bassist. Upset to learn Mott was splitting, Bowie said he had a song that could save them, though he'd only written its chorus.

So "All the Young Dudes" was a bequest: it's a gang's song, a ballad of a band's self-mythologies that's soaked in their private language. Mott gave it a gang performance: Mick Ralphs' ringing arpeggiated riff; Verden Allen's organ; Ian Hunter sparring against his bandmates, then turning to pick out faces in the crowd. He took his closing harangue—"Hey ***you!*** With the ***glasses!*** I want you! I want you in the ***front***!...I want it ***right here***!..I've wanted to do this for ***years***!"—from a dressing-down he'd just given a heckler; it was a come-on and a threat.

Bowie's lyric was his society pages, listing the gang at the Sombrero Ballroom: his friends Freddi Burretti and Wendy Kirby turn up by name. While relishing the odd detail, Hunter turned the song outward. Bristling with contempt, he made the song a manifesto, proposing a dream of secession to the younger Baby Boom kids from their hippie older siblings. It's telling that the hippie brother's sitting around at home with his Beatles and his Stones, lost in someone else's revolutionary fantasies, while the Young Dudes are out on the streets. Their revolution, if they even want one, is the amoral one D.H. Lawrence had proposed in his "A Sane Revolution" ("it would be fun to upset the apple-cart/and see which way the apples would go a-rolling"), a poem Mott reprinted on the sleeve of their last great album. "You have to try and kill your elders," Bowie recalled to Paul DuNoyer in 2002. "We had to develop a completely new vocabulary...The idea was taking the recent past and re-structuring it in a way that we felt we had authorship of. My key 'in' was things like *Clockwork Orange*: that was *our* world, not the bloody hippy thing."

A descendent of Bowie's 'lost boys' pieces ("London Boys," "When I'm Five"), "All the Young Dudes" has a vein of sadness running through it. Its verses begin on a D major chord but soon sink into a run of B minor and F# minors; its D major key frays apart in the refrain as the vocal harmonies, which open the refrain with a triumphant rising phrase, become despondent, their final "carry the news" a somber falling sixth. This feeling of collapse suits the "news" the dudes are carrying: the knowledge that the world's going to end, Bowie later said. The world's last children, the Dudes spend their days in happy revolt, a life of petty crimes and sharp costumes.

It sounded like a smash from the start ("we knew we were singing a hit," Hunter said): the single hit #3 in Britain and cracked the US Top 40, becoming a staple of American FM radio. His publisher Bob Grace thought Bowie had blundered by not releasing the song first, believing it could've been his first chart-topper. Yet Bowie's own recording, provisionally intended for *Aladdin Sane*, was a shell of Mott's version and quickly scrapped. Lowered in key and tempo (Hunter wrote in his diary "to be honest, I prefer our version...this seems too slow"), pointlessly extended and diffidently sung, the Bowie track stuck Mick Ronson with aping Ralphs' lead riff, while saxophones subbed for Mott's harmonies. Singing "All the Young Dudes" live, Bowie was more inspired: see the "cabaret" version from his 1974 tour or his performance at the last Ziggy Stardust concert.

John, I'm Only Dancing

***Recorded**: 24 June 1972, Trident, and/or 26 June 1972, Olympic Studios, London. Bowie: lead vocal, 12-string acoustic guitar; Ronson: lead guitar; Bolder: bass; Woodmansey: drums; Lindsay Scott: violin?; Ian McLagan?, Ron Wood?, Ronnie Lane?, Kenney Jones?: handclaps. Produced: Scott (24 June), Bowie (26 June); engineered: Harwood (26 June); **(first remake, unreleased)** 7 October 1972, RCA Studios, Chicago. Bowie: lead vocal, acoustic guitar?; Ronson: lead guitar; Bolder: bass; Woodmansey: drums; Lou Reed?: rhythm guitar?, vocals?; **(second remake)** 18-23 January 1973, Trident. Bowie: lead vocal, 12-string acoustic guitar, saxophone; Ronson: lead guitar; Garson: piano; Bolder: bass; Woodmansey: drums, tambourine; Wilshaw, Fordham: tenor, baritone saxophones. Produced: Bowie, Scott; engineered: Scott.*

First release**: 1 September 1972 (RCA 2263, #12 UK); (2nd* *remake) April 1973 (RCA 2263).* ***Live: *1972-1973, 1990.*

More than forty years on, it's still Bowie's most notorious interview, with *Melody Maker*'s Michael Watts: "David's present image is to come on like a swishy queen, a gorgeously effeminate boy. He's as camp as a row of tents, with his limp hand and trolling vocabulary. 'I'm gay,' he says, 'and always have been, even when I was David Jones.'"

His self-outing was as deliberate as a Boris Spassky chess move. Enough ground had been cleared: homosexuality had been decriminalized in Britain five years before; the British wing of the Gay Liberation Front was founded in 1970. His admission, approved by Tony Defries and Angela Bowie, was shocking enough to make news (the story was picked up by the *London Evening Standard* and the other music trades), not shocking enough to ruin his career. Bowie was a relative unknown, his public image still coalescing; he had few fans who deserted him and he gained twice as many through the notoriety. He'd wanted to be a star his whole life. Now he gambled on a last desperate throw and won a stake.

The only thing was, Bowie wasn't gay. While from the vantage point of 2015, it appears that he was a mild bisexual who chose only women for long-term relationships, the *Melody Maker* interview solidified a general public perception of Bowie as being gay or bi. Kenneth Pitt had laid the groundwork by having Bowie grant a (non-disclosing) interview to the gay magazine *Jeremy* and Watts noted that when Bowie played a club in Hampstead in late 1971 "about half the gay population of the city turned up to see him." A few months after the interview, *The Gay News* said it hoped Bowie's popularity would give "gay rock a potent spokesman," Looking back in 1980, Jon Savage recalled that "the spice in [Bowie's] image was gayness."

Bowie played a tight game: he did little to dispel the impression of being gay but from the start took pains to say he "doesn't have much time for Gay Liberation...a particular movement he doesn't want to lead," as he told Watts, who noticed a "sly jollity" in Bowie's pronouncement. He rarely said he was gay or bisexual again, his last time during a 1976 Cameron Crowe interview filled with so many other bizarre statements that it was likely overlooked. This tacit denial became, in a 1983 *Rolling Stone* interview, his public denial that he'd ever been bisexual, let alone gay.

His self-outing to *Melody Maker* was part of the blithe sexual innocence of his milieu and likely reflected a legitimate questioning of his sexuality at the time. And being a publicly-identified homosexual was also the nervy culmination of his outsider affectations, the next step beyond identifying as a Mod or a hippie or a Buddhist. Homosexuality "seemed to be the one taboo that everyone was too afraid to break. I thought—well, if there's one thing that's going to put me on the edge, this is it," he recalled to Tony Parsons in 1993. He flattered and inspired a culture in which he was trafficking at the time. "Gay clubs really became my lifestyle and all my friends were gay," he said. "I really opted to drown in the euphoria of this new experience which was a real taboo with society. And I must admit I loved that aspect of it." In 1972, everything Bowie touched seemed to be gay: "All the Young Dudes" was taken up as a rallying cry and Lou Reed's *Transformer* included "Make Up," with its post-Stonewall "we're coming out of our closets...out on the streets" refrain. Yet "Queer David," as the writer John Gill would call him, remained far more a hypothetical figure—one glimpsed only in his mock-fellatio stage routines with Mick Ronson (which embarrassed Ronson so much that he nearly quit the group) and in a handful of tracks, some shelved (*e.g.*, "Sweet Head").

So although "John, I'm Only Dancing," the follow-up single to "Starman," was among Bowie's most gay-indentified songs, there's not much in it to justify the claim despite its composer's boast that it was "my attempt to do a bisexual anthem." It charted without incident in the UK, hitting #12, and it wasn't released in

America as much for Bowie's poor sales history than any lyrical controversy. "John, I'm Only Dancing" lacks the polemical urgency of Tom Robinson's "Glad to Be Gay," the empathy of Bronski Beat's "Small Town Boy." It's more shadow and strut, a mood captured in Mick Rock's promo film that intercut a writhing male-female pair of dancers with Bowie and the Spiders, who look as if they've stepped out of Kenneth Anger's *Scorpio Rising*.

It's far more "Son of Suffragette City" (or "Daughter of Queen Bitch"), a song starring another man in a vaguely-defined relationship flirting with/obsessed with someone else. A clue as to its title came from the drummer John Cambridge. Watching Bowie cavort with a group of boys at a Haddon Hall party, he said Bowie had winked to him at one point, as if to signal he only planned to dance.

With a simple structure—verse, refrain, verse, extended refrain—and a G major key that shifts to its relative minor in refrains, "John, I'm Only Dancing" found Bowie, with five months of concerts under his belt, working in a streamlined hard rock style that would soon lead to "Jean Genie." The Spiders sounded more dynamic here than on *Ziggy Stardust*, particularly Ronson, whose guitar was mixed to knife out of the speakers ("a guitar like sawing through metal," Ian Rankin described it in *Black and Blue*). Ronson took his verse riff from the Yardbirds' take on "Pontiac Blues," gave a siren wail to the refrains and ended his coda solo by flicking his Les Paul's toggle switch to make staccato feedback bursts. Woody Woodmansey, who used mallets to get the "hollow"-sounding beats Bowie wanted, cut his first-ever drum overdub, tracking a few tom fills. And Trevor Bolder's refrain bassline, a saunter up the E minor scale followed by an aneurysm of octave root notes, was the track's fattest hook.

Bowie was never satisfied with the song. Having recorded it twice in three days in July 1972, he spent the next year cutting further remakes, including a session in Chicago with Lou Reed (not bootlegged) and another in London during the *Aladdin Sane* sessions, where he brought in a saxophone section. (A more radical revision in 1974, "John I'm Only Dancing (Again)," is covered in Ch. 9). On the *Aladdin Sane* remake, Bowie reduced the gawkiness of his original vocal—the screeched "touch me!s" in the coda, the spat-out "ever cared"—but kept a phrasing in which he sang a tone above the bassline, building a subtle tension released in the refrain, with its exuberant leap up a fifth on "dancing."

He may have come out for the publicity or to court a voting coalition. Whatever his motives, he still came out and so opened up a world. "For gay musicians, Bowie was seismic. To hell with whether he disowned us later," Tom Robinson said, while Gill wrote that "I belong to a generation that probably has to thank Queer David for the comparative ease with which we came out…[his] clever (if ultimately meaningless) packaging of sexual outrage created a safe space where many of us, gay, bi or straight, could play out games and experiment with difference." The essential moment of "John, I'm Only Dancing" is when Bowie sings, with lust and longing, another man's name in the refrain.

My Death

(Shuman/Blau/Brel). Bowie: vocal, 12-string acoustic guitar; ***(1973 live recordings)*** *Garson: piano.*

First release: *(live, 3 July 1973) 24 October 1983,* ***Ziggy Stardust: The Motion Picture****; (live, 20 October 1972) 25 April 1994,* ***Santa Monica '72*** *(GY 002); (live, 28 September 1972) May 1995,* ***RarestOneBowie****.* ***Broadcast****: 17 January 1973, Russell Harty Plus Pop; 15 October 1997, GQ Man of the Year Awards.* ***Live****: 1972-1973, 1995-1997.*

After an accident-plagued trip to Cyprus in June 1972, Bowie had a shaky flight home, fearing the plane would crash. This led him to refuse to fly for years, sharpened an already-keen sense of mortality and inspired him to sing Jacques Brel's "My Death" in his first shows upon his return to Britain. These were his self-financed debutante balls, the three Rainbow Theatre shows of August 1972, with choreography by Lindsay Kemp, a set rigged with ladders and catwalks and Andy Warhol-style projections of the faces of stars, from Elvis to a shot of Lou Reed fresh from the ongoing *Transformer* sessions.

"Brel was a reflection of the times I was going through—all sorts of dark images, which I associated with [him]," recalled Scott Walker, whose recording of "My Death" on his 1967 debut album haunted Bowie's take on the song. As with Brel's "Amsterdam," Bowie first encountered the song refracted through Mort Shuman, who translated "La Mort" for the revue *Jacques Brel Is Alive and Well and Living In Paris*. Like Walker, Bowie had to contend with Shuman's translation, which was as crass (Brel's "death waits in your bright hands" becomes "my death waits there between your thighs") as it was inane (Brel's "death waits behind the leaves/Of the tree that will make my coffin" becomes "my death waits there among the leaves/in magicians' mysterious sleeves").

Walker and Elly Stone (who performed it in the *Jacques Brel* revue) had sung "My Death" as a reverie, growing a degree more obsessive with each verse, and singing over intricate arrangements: Stone's piano-centered recording had solo passages for flute, mandolin, ominous horns and choral interjections; Walker's swaying folk-rock version had harpsichord, tympani and dissonant strings. Bowie recast "My Death" as an acoustic guitar ballad, hanging the song on the chords and strum patterns of his own "After All." Debuting his take on the song at the Rainbow, Bowie began tentatively: he sang with more reserve than Walker, almost speaking the end phrases Walker had clouded with vibrato; the jolt to a fervid pitch in the last verse seemed cued by a prompter. By the time of his Santa Monica concert in October 1972, Bowie had an ownership stake in the song: there was a cold luster in his singing.

"My Death" in Bowie's 1972-1973 shows was a *memento mori* plonked into the middle of a rock concert; it was an existential sermon for teenagers. He'd had an "acoustic" interlude since the first Spiders shows (usually playing "Space Oddity" and "Andy Warhol" with Mick Ronson) but the inclusion of "My Death" toughened the show's "folk" portion, which had been a last remnant of the Arts Lab Bowie. While some stage recordings of "My Death" of the era are tiresome, the Santa Monica performance is entrancing and D.A. Pennebaker's film of its performance at the last Ziggy Stardust concert documents a charismatic whose skeletal features and ghost-white stage makeup, shining blue in the stage lights, make him resemble the song's title character. Bowie swings his strumming arm like a scythe.

The Jean Genie

Recorded: *6 October 1972, RCA Studio D, New York. Bowie: lead vocal, harmonica, rhythm guitar, maracas?; Ronson: lead guitar, backing vocal; Bolder: bass; Woodmansey: drums, tambourine, maracas? Produced: Bowie; engineered: Moran.*

First release: *24 November 1972 (RCA 2302, #2 UK).* ***Broadcast***: *3 January 1973, Top of the Pops; 20 October 1973, The 1980 Floor Show.* ***Live***: *1972-1974, 1976, 1978, 1983, 1987, 1990, 1996-1997, 2000, 2003.*

Somewhere between Cleveland, where he played his first concert in the United States, the following gig in Memphis and the ride back to New York, Bowie started writing "The Jean Genie." Someone (the most likely candidates are Mick Ronson and Bowie's friend George Underwood) was playing acoustic guitar in the back of the bus, strumming through Chuck Berry and Bo Diddley songs and doing variations on the Yardbirds' "I'm a Man" that the tour entourage took up ("Bus, bus, bus, we're goin' bussin'!"was one refrain, the roadie Will Palin recalled). This sparked Bowie to bluff a song out of the "I'm a Man" riff; he finished the lyric in Cyrinda Foxe's apartment in

New York ("Watch That Man") and recorded the song the following week.

Cutting "Jean Genie" in RCA's New York studio was a quick deal: one take; a few percussion, vocal and harmonica overdubs; the whole thing done in under two hours. It helped that it was such a blatant rewrite of "I'm a Man" that Trevor Bolder could just play the Yardbirds' bassline with some extra runs. A day after cutting it, Bowie premiered "Jean Genie" in Chicago as an encore tribute to Iggy Pop ("He's not here tonight so it's for you here," he told the crowd). Mixed in Nashville a week later, "Jean Genie" was released in late November and became Bowie's highest-charting UK single to date.

Even more than "John, I'm Only Dancing," "Jean Genie" was just muscle and sinew. Its verses, driven by two guitars that play muted riffs (likely Bowie) and power chords over Bolder's thudding, root-heavy bassline, shift between E major and E suspended fourth chords: the first three sets of beats of each 12/8 bar are over E chords, the last begins on Esus4 then flicks back to E. Singing a word-packed, rhyme-soaked lyric, Bowie's voice was a competing rhythm to the bass/guitar stomp, using descending fifths for emphasis ("off to the CIT-y," "talkin' 'bout MON-roe"). Over this he tracked a squalling harmonica—meant to sound like Mick Jagger's harp on the first Rolling Stones LP—and percussive colors: constant tambourine fourths, handclaps to double the tambourine in refrains, rattlesnake maracas as scene-changers.

The B major refrain loosed the verses' knots—its sermon was "let yourself go!" though the band managed to keep things tacked down until the third verse, where Bowie's harmonica and Ronson's guitar buzzed triplet 16ths as if stringing lines of barbed wire. Bowie gets snagged on "loves to be loved," skipping back again and again until Ronson elbows him aside for a double-tracked solo that closes in a run of three-note jabs.

Bowie's glam singles have a generosity to them—their focus,

from "Life On Mars?" to "Rebel Rebel," is on someone the singer's appraising, who's caught his fancy, who he's boosting up. Glam offered a democratic aristocracy, one you could enter by wearing your mother's old coat and pasting on some glitter bought at Woolworths. All that was required of you was to be properly outrageous. In "Jean Genie" Bowie gave a primer how: he turned Iggy Pop into a future legend, incarnated here as some American primitive, "an Iggy-type character...a white-trash, kind of trailer-park kid thing—the closet intellectual who wouldn't want the world to know that he reads." Bowie had found a simpatico soul in Pop: both were both suburban misfits who tore themselves up on stage (Pop easily, Bowie deliberately). The Jean Genie was also Ziggy Stardust "as a kind of Hollywood street rat," and an American denim-clad edition of Alex from *Clockwork Orange*—a thug who loves Beethoven, or an avant-garde revolutionary club kid (hence the title's pun on the playwright Jean Genet, which Bowie claimed wasn't intentional, blaming his subconscious).

"Jean Genie" at heart was a Mod blues purist's song, which perhaps was why it was kept from hitting #1 by the Sweet's "Blockbuster." The latter had nearly the same guitar riff but bigger hooks—ringing klaxons, tympani fills, baying vocals, goofy asides by bassist Steve Priest. "Blockbuster" was simply better at being a pop record. Still, "Jean Genie" did the job enough. It widened Bowie's audience, winning him the working-class vote for a time. In Belfast, Bobby Sands dressed in denim in homage.

Drive-In Saturday

Recorded: *9-10 December 1972, RCA Studios, New York. Bowie: lead and harmony vocal, 12-string acoustic guitars, tenor saxophone, ARP synthesizer, handclaps, finger clicks; Ronson: lead guitar, harmony vocal, handclaps; Garson: piano; Bolder: bass; Woodmansey: drums, tambourine. Produced: Bowie, Scott; engineered: Scott, Moran.*

***First release**: 6 April 1973 (RCA 2352, #3 UK). **Broadcast**: 17 January 1973, Russell Harty Plus Pop; 23 August 1999, VH1 Storytellers; 25 October 1999, Mark Radcliffe. **Live**: 1972-1974, 1999.*

Sometime around 1972, various radio and TV programmers, screenwriters and stage producers invented"The Fifties." *American Graffiti* and *That'll Be the Day* were in cinemas; Chuck Berry had a cross-Atlantic #1 single and Elvis and Rick Nelson charted; the last two UK #1 albums of 1972 were "golden oldies" compilations; *The Rocky Horror Show* was playing the West End and *Grease* was on Broadway. The timing was right: the teenagers of the Fifties were now old enough to feel old, and the era was remote enough to have a slight mystery for the young. The Fifties became a false collective memory of some lost suburban Eden, a chaste rebuke to the open sexuality of the early Seventies.

Nostalgia was once considered an ailment (it was a medical term for debilitating homesickness), the nostalgic person "unfit for life in modern society, for they lacked the prized characteristic of adaptability." The early 20th Century, with its emigrations, urbanizations, deportations and ethnic cleansings, its bloody erasures of borders and countries, had needed a measure of coldness to get through it. It wasn't safe to dwell on the past. Postwar, with the pace of cultural change now at a breakneck tempo (for a teenager in 1972, 1962 seemed Victorian) and with a national mass media at work, a market for "comfortable" nostalgia emerged. This was nostalgia deprived of anything that could lead one to question the past. Rather, nostalgia was something one could consume, like a dietary supplement.

While you can find glimpses of Fifties nostalgia at the crumbled end of the Sixties (see the Beatles' *Let It Be* sessions, with their plodding takes on Buddy Holly and Larry Williams numbers), glam was rock's first self-conscious "nostalgia" movement. Sha Na Na at Woodstock, where the band came off like alien beings singing "At the Hop" in a failed attempt to communicate with hippies, was arguably the first mass-media glam performance. Glam rockers dressed as the past's idea of the future, looking like extraterrestrials who'd fashioned their looks from postwar movies and glamour magazines. Their songs, filled with purloined Chuck Berry riffs and honking saxophone solos, were cracked reflections of Fifties pop. It was the sort of music you'd expect to hear in a moon colony in some Fifties SF movie.

"Drive-In Saturday" was Bowie's layer-cake pastiche of the Fifties (its chord structure, BBC Light Programme saxophones and doo-wop backing vocals) and the Sixties, with Mick Jagger and Twiggy cast as erotic instructional figures. Its scenario came from an overnight train ride Bowie made from Seattle to Phoenix on 2 November 1972. Unable to sleep as the train was crossing the desert at night, he spied a row of enormous silver domes in the distance and naturally assumed they were secret government laboratories or post-nuclear-war staging facilities. From this establishing shot he built a post-apocalyptic world ("probably the year 2033, which is a good year") where "radiation has affected people's minds and reproductive organs." The society has forgotten how to have sex, so its warders, the "strange ones in the dome," make the kids watch Rolling Stones promo films and Mod movies in the hopes they'll pick up a lost language. (There's a buried joke in calling the kids "ravers," a slang term for middle-class day-tripper jazz fans.) As on "Oh! You Pretty Things," Bowies' SF narrative doubles for a human predicament—here, how teenagers have to improvise their way through sex using second-hand knowledge, with film and pop stars as instructions (or aids) to completion (and recall that Noel Coward described a Beatles concert he attended as "a mass masturbation orgy").

Bowie wrote "Drive-In Saturday" on acoustic guitar, playing a few wistful, glum versions in his late November 1972 concerts, chirping out a line—"his name was always Bud-dee"—that in the studio he'd make a roaring affirmation: "BUD-DAY!!" Recording the song in New York, he firmed up its 12/8 meter and tracked in nickelodeon harmonies, girl-group percussion (finger-clicks and handclaps) and a tenor saxophone doubled at the octave with a "violin" courtesy of the ARP 2600 synthesizer. This was Bowie meeting the challenge of Roxy Music, who had opened for him that summer and whose "Virginia Plain" made his singles seem ordinary. "Drive-In Saturday" was a quick assimilation of Roxy's sound: the horror-movie ARP (first heard spooking up "the strange ones in the dome") is in line with Brian Eno's squiggles, the saxophone is an Andy Mackay impersonator and Bowie's vocal—straight-faced yet emotive—rivals Bryan Ferry's takes on torch ballads ("Chance Meeting") and country-western ("If There Is Something").

The A major verses (the intro builds on the dominant (E major) chord until swooning homeward to A to start the verse) slide, at the end of the pre-chorus, into a shadowy new key, either an elated leap to C major (the teenagers' success) or a resigned sigh to G major. The latter move suggested the middle-aged man, "Jung the foreman," of the second verse, who works in the dome on the teenagers' behalf while mourning his own lost virility ("once had raged a sea that raged no more"). Like "Life On Mars?," it's a cut from a girl in the stalls to the screen that's playing films for her.

With the track's foundation a double-tracked Bowie 12-string acoustic, Mick Ronson's two electric guitars are decorative: after his arpeggiated opening, he's content to interject once a bar in the verses and play a distortion-riddled countermelody in refrains. The backing vocals orbit Trevor Bolder's bass, singing three-note fills to close out bars and taking parallel downward steps in the long outro ("driii-iii-iive-in"). At first singing the title line softly, Bowie opens up in later refrains, hitting a high G on his ultimate "drive." He goes out echoing the saxophone, doubling the latter in two-note descending runs at the fade.

While offered to, and rejected by, Mott the Hoople, "Drive-In Saturday" was quickly kitted up as Bowie's leadoff single for

Aladdin Sane. It was an inspired choice, a bolt from the bluesy minimalism of his previous two singles into a subtler mood picture. Although it peaked at #3 in Britain, "Drive-In Saturday" was wrongly consigned to the second tier of Bowie hits though it's one of his finest singles: a counter-stroke in which Bowie, at the height of glam, conceived a world beyond it.

Watch That Man

***Recorded**: ca. 18-23 January 1973, Trident. Bowie: lead vocal, tenor saxophone?; Ronson: lead guitar, rhythm guitars; Garson: piano; Bolder: bass; Woodmansey: drums; Juanita "Honey" Franklin, Linda Lewis, MacCormack: backing vocals; Fordham and/or Wilshaw: tenor saxophone. Produced: Bowie, Scott; engineered: Scott.*

***First release**: 13 April 1973, **Aladdin Sane**. **Live**: 1973-1974.*

Having considered releasing a "Ziggy Stardust in America" live record, Bowie soon had enough new songs from his ongoing US tour to convert the idea into a studio album, *Aladdin Sane*. He was finding inspiration on the road and bouncing ideas off his band, and as his tour's erratic itinerary would sometimes leave him stranded in a city for a week, he had enough free time to write. The songs of this period were generally rockers with modulating, "shadowy" keys and common subjects: charismatics losing their hold, decrepit celebrities. Cutting tracks upon his return to London in January 1973, with Ken Scott better capturing Woody Woodmansey and Trevor Bolder ("the drum sound was much, much more live," Scott recalled) and the pianist Mike Garson as a new spice in the mix, Bowie crafted a hard music that made the vanguard bands of the Sixties seem played out.

Mostly written in late September 1972 while Bowie was holding court in New York, "Watch That Man" chronicles a New York Dolls concert after-party. The stars that night were Angela Bowie and the model Cyrinda Foxe (appearing as "Lorraine" here, with Bowie lovingly alliterating her two-line description), who danced together and who would mirror each other once

Angela dyed her hair platinum blonde.

Bowie was taken by the Dolls, catching two of their shows at the Mercer Arts Center in the Lower East Side. He regarded them as the rightful heirs of the Rolling Stones. The Dolls mixed the lurid stage presence and volume of the Stooges with the gossipy snap of Warhol's Factory (many Warhol "superstars" were Mercer Arts regulars). Dolls shows were fashion orgies in which "it was hard to tell who was in the band and who wasn't," the photographer Bob Gruen recalled. The Dolls made British glam bands seem as if they were play-acting. Bowie soon got a taste of real street life: while Bowie was walking on the Bowery with the band, David Johansen provoked a passing trucker into a fight as a horrified Bowie begged him to stop.

With the Stones outmatched by the Dolls, Bowie planned his own assault in "Watch That Man," his lead-off track for *Aladdin Sane,* for which he retrieved a guitar riff from "Suffragette City" and pressed it into even bloodier service. It worked: even the critic Lester Bangs, while calling Bowie "that chickenhearted straw man of suck rock you love to hate so much," admitted Bowie had blown away the Stones with the track. Its mix was *Exile on Main St.*-style murk, with Bowie's lead vocal buried within the saxophone section, fighting to be heard over Mick Ronson's three electric guitars and the singers Juanita Franklin and Linda Lewis. His voice blends into the instruments—his rise of a fifth on "the mirrors in sha-hame" is the treble end of Trevor Bolder's parallel leap on bass, and his "watch! that! man!" is a staccato flavor in the guitar and piano chords. As Bowie never attended mixing sessions, this was Ken Scott's doing (the track "just seemed to have more power that way," he said). While MainMan and RCA each requested a cleaner "up-vocal" mix, each eventually approved Scott's original. (The Stones settled matters by releasing the enervated *Goats Head Soup* four months after *Aladdin Sane* and a month after the Dolls' debut.)

A volatile marriage of G major (intro and refrains) and A

major (the verses, which end in deceptive cadences), "Watch that Man" changes keys with a jolt on the last beat of its title phrase. Garson raps out chords and does a few comic illustrations, like a lunge down to the bass end of the keyboard after the Reverend Alabaster kneels. The octave-descending saxophone line in the refrain is a deflating presence, like the catty "it was so-so" rejoinders of the verses.

Reading Evelyn Waugh's *Vile Bodies* on his voyage home to Britain (see "Aladdin Sane"), Bowie added to his partygoers some waspish members of the New York music press, a self-stigmatized Benny Goodman fan (an old veteran from the last round of pre-war decadence), John Lennon ("lemon in a bag") and cast himself as the Waughian "Reverend Alabaster." The hi-fi's blasting, the champagne bottles and cocaine mirrors are on the table and a gaggle of drunks hang in a corner. The only game that matters is status: someone's quietly dominating the room and it's getting to Bowie. Whether it's Shakey the host or the party's nameless drug connection or a thinly-disguised David Johansen, the "Man" of the title takes Bowie off his game. By the last verse he can't keep up his end of the conversation and flees the party, heading down to the street, "looking for information." The backing singers leave with him but they sound as captivated by his rival as he is.

Panic In Detroit

Recorded: *ca. 18-24 January 1973, Trident. Bowie: lead vocal, rhythm guitar?; Ronson: lead guitar, rhythm guitars; Bolder: bass; Woodmansey: drums; Franklin, Lewis: vocals; MacCormack: vocals, congas, maracas, handclaps. Produced: Bowie, Scott; engineered: Scott;* ***(remake)*** *ca. early September 1979, Looking Glass Studios, London. Bowie: lead vocal, 12-string acoustic guitar; Zaine Griff: lead guitar; Andy Clark: piano; Tony Visconti: bass; Andy Duncan: drums. Produced: Visconti.*

First release: *13 April 1973,* ***Aladdin Sane***; *(remake) 22 May*

1992, ***Scary Monsters*** *(RCD 20147/EMI CDP 79 9331 2).* ***Live****: 1973-1974, 1976, 1990, 1997, 2004.*

The leading man of "Panic In Detroit" is a fading revolutionary/sex symbol whose last act is suicide, though he graciously leaves behind a last autograph. Inspired by Iggy Pop's stories of the 1967 Detroit riots and the rise of the White Panther Party, flavored with a pinch of Michael Moorcock's Mod assassin Jerry Cornelius, the song's last main ingredient was Bowie's encounter at his Carnegie Hall show with a former classmate from Bromley Tech. This nondescript British kid had become a drug dealer operating out of South America; he'd flown his private plane to the show.

"Panic In Detroit" came as the New Left was devolving into celebrity personality-cult terrorism. The White Panthers' John Sinclair (former jazz critic and the MC5's former manager, commemorated by John Lennon on *Some Time in New York City*) and the late world-trotting revolutionary Che Guevara (whose Korda photograph, once an icon for radicals, now hangs in dorm rooms) were just the starting round. Now there was the Weather Underground, whose internal politics were those of a touring, squabbling rock group; Germany's Baader-Meinhof Gang (Baader, who owned a Che poster, paid a designer to make his group's machine-gun-and-star logo), and California's Symbionese Liberation Army, whose kidnapping of the heiress Patty Hearst in 1974 was one of America's most popular TV programs. "Such movements are almost wholly intellectual and see no immediate prospect of attracting even a minority mass base," Richard Clutterbuck wrote in 1977. Political violence was a means of self-expression; revolutionary cells became performance artists, their various alliances with criminal groups a form of patronage.

This sort of media-savvy pop revolution was catnip for Bowie. In "Panic In Detroit," he gave his provincial Che (late of the National People's Gang) a backdrop of riot-torn streets and bloodless authority, the latter embodied by a cringing teacher and a student who runs to smash a slot machine in the chaos. It was an America Bowie had spied through bus and limo windows and from hotel balconies: a country of empty spaces and fallen cities. "There were snipers all over America, on tops of buildings," he recalled in 1990. His imagined dystopian worlds had turned out to be real places: in Texas, Los Angeles and New York, he'd been harassed and even attacked by strangers. "It was really happening. Suddenly my songs didn't look out of place," he said.

"Panic in Detroit" made "Five Years," cut the year before, seem like a genteel middle-class apocalypse. Opening with a power chord riff, its monstrous-sounding tone soon tracked with another Wah-Wahed guitar, Ronson shadows Bowie with bombing runs down the scale that end with thick clots of E chordal figures. In the refrain he needles Bowie's vocal with lines that expire in clouds of feedback. Given leave to solo in the bridge, he sneers.

Working on Ronson's behalf are a rockabilly Trevor Bolder bassline and a mesh of percussion. Emboldened by his conversion to Scientology and bitter about his paltry wages, Woody Woodmansey refused to play a Bo Diddley-esque shuffle Ronson and Bowie had requested, saying it was corny. Instead he played 16ths on his medium toms and punctuated chorus phrases with his crash cymbal (phased, like the backing vocals). So Bowie brought in his friend Geoff MacCormack to play congas and maracas to cook up a Diddley-style "swamp" groove. The track's central pulse is MacCormack's moves between high and low congas, occasionally muting the high conga for effect, as on the title phrase. Gliding between B minor and D major, "Panic In Detroit" descends into the maelstrom for its minute-plus coda, with Ronson's pick scratches, Woodmansey's crashes, MacCormack's congas and the wails of Juanita Franklin and Linda Lewis sounding like a collective murder.

Cracked Actor

***Recorded**: ca. 18-23 January 1973, Trident. Bowie: lead vocal, harmonica; Ronson: lead guitar, rhythm guitar, backing vocal; Bolder: bass; Woodmansey: drums, tambourine. Produced: Bowie, Scott; engineered: Scott.*

***First release**: 13 April 1973, **Aladdin Sane**. **Broadcast**: 16 November 1999, Late Night with Conan O'Brien; 21 November 1999, Musique Plus; 30 November 1999, Later With Jools Holland; 23 June 2000, TFI Friday; 27 June 2000, Bowie at the Beeb. **Live**: 1973-1974, 1983, 1999-2000.*

Bowie spent two weeks in Los Angeles in late October 1972. As his manager said you had to spend like a star to become one, Bowie brought his 46-person entourage (including Mike Garson's family and Iggy Pop) to the Beverly Hills Hotel on Sunset Boulevard and turned the Polo Lounge into "Max's Kansas City's back room." They spent afternoons by the pool, nights at Rodney's English Disco on the Sunset Strip, charged limousines to their rooms. To complete the LA experience, some took a course at the Scientology Celebrity Centre (Garson, a Scientologist, had converted Woody Woodmansey and a bodyguard by proselytizing on the tour bus). By the time they left LA, Bowie and company had racked up a $20,000 hotel bill.

He wrote "Cracked Actor" during his stay, inspired by what he saw on a tour of Hollywood Boulevard and at Rodney's—barely-teenage girls in Shirley Temple and dominatrix outfits, popping Quaaludes; people shooting heroin in the bathrooms. Bowie said he couldn't tell the prostitutes and runaways apart from the slumming rich girls and would-be starlets. He took the persona of a debauched aging film star whose life is a series of coarse transactions, another old performer, as in "Panic in Detroit," who's "stiff on his legend." He's a walking corpse.

The lyric was a sour mash of drug slang ("bad connection," "since he pinned you, baby," *i.e.*, since he got you hooked on smack), showbiz puns ("show me you're real/your reel,"

"Hollywood highs" (Heights)), homonyms ("Oh say!" moaned like "Jose!") and single-entendres, with the refrain hammered through with harsh, plosive sounds ("crack," "smack," "suck") given a treble-tracked Mick Ronson escort. Ronson opened "Cracked Actor" with brutal chording overhung by a guitar track so devoted to feedback and so distorted by his Wah-Wah and fuzzbox that it's a grey blear of noise. Bowie's harmonica, played through Ronson's cranked-up Marshall amp, Bolder's antic chromatic bassline and a thundering Woodmansey (his snare hits echoed by tambourine) made the track slam and sing.

Its tonality was cracked as its title. Its verses, in a loose alliance of A major and A minor, cut to a refrain, full of suspended fourths, in a sickly G major. "Cracked Actor" dies after its second refrain (1:40) but Ronson's guitars and Bowie's harmonica drag its corpse through another four refrains and start a fifth at the fade. With a callback to "The Bewlay Brothers," with Bowie wailing "stay for a day," it's life as a perpetual nightmare.

For his 1974 Diamond Dogs tour, Bowie took "Cracked Actor" off the casting couch and staged it as a tableau of an actor's mind. On stage he was a Bel Air Hamlet, complete with cape, sunglasses and a skull to croon to (and French kiss). (Recreating this routine in his 1983 tour, he came off as an animatronic Disneyland exhibit.) A curse on Los Angeles, "Cracked Actor" would rebound on Bowie: it would title a documentary that chronicled his life in LA when he was a jittery husk of a human being.

Time

Recorded*: (demo, "We Should Be On By Now," unreleased)** *ca. June-July 1971, Advision Studios. George Underwood: vocal; Bowie: acoustic guitar?, vocal?; Ronson: guitar; Rick Wakeman: piano; other musicians?;* ***(album) *ca. 18-23 January 1973, Trident. Bowie: lead and backing vocal, 12-string acoustic guitar, tenor saxophone?; Ronson: lead and rhythm guitars, backing vocal; Garson: piano; Bolder: bass; Woodmansey: drums; Fordham: tenor saxophone?; Wilshaw: flute.*

Produced: Bowie, Scott; engineered: Scott.

***First release**: 13 April 1973, **Aladdin Sane**. **Broadcast**: 20 October 1973, The 1980 Floor Show. **Live**: 1973-1974, 1987.*

Just as Bowie perfected glam rock, he turned to writing sprawling mood pieces crafted for his pianist Mike Garson. He got to know Garson on the road: the two would occasionally duet on standards like "My Funny Valentine" in hotel bars after shows. Much as how he trusted Mick Ronson to come up with riffs and string arrangements to adorn a top melody/chord sequence, Bowie found he could offer Garson any abstract idea and see it turned into a piano line.

Garson grew up in Brooklyn. He intended to become a rabbi and turned out a pianist, working in the Catskills with Jackie Mason and was a regular in New York jazz clubs (he also once backed Martha and the Vandellas). In September 1972, Garson heard that a British band was looking for a touring pianist. Like most Americans, he had no idea who Bowie was. He walked into a room full of rainbow-haired men wearing circus outfits and got the gig after playing eight bars of "Changes" from Ronson's chord sheets.

During a tour hiatus in New Orleans in November 1972, Bowie began revising a song, "We Should Be On By Now," that he'd written for George Underwood the previous year. A central image was "time" as a stage manager who makes mortal actors hop to his capricious orders; it was inspired by his lighting man, who he saw each night in the wings or pacing overhead on a catwalk, whispering "senseless things" into his headset. Bowie kept piling on the metaphors. In a single verse, time molted from director to whore (who "falls wanking to the floor," suggesting a mime sequence blessedly never performed) to drug dealer to Death to a sniper (see "Panic In Detroit"). The run vaguely worked—each was a profession tied to the clock—but the lyric tottered with all of these lunges for effect and the song nearly collapsed when Bowie gave bathos to a Chuck Berry quote:

"well, I looked at my watch/it says nine twenty-five..." After keeping a tense vigil on the mediant note of each chord ("Time...in Quaa-ludes and...), he devolved into Living Theater shrieks ("SCREAM with boredom").

D.A. Pennebaker, who filmed the last Ziggy Stardust concert, said the audience had been as poised as actors, yelling at the stage on cue: chanting "wham! bam! thank you ma'am!" or hollering "MEE!" upon Bowie singing "behind the door is..." in "My Death." Showing Bowie fans a rough cut of his film in Edinburgh later that year, he found the moviegoers did the same group performance, now talking back to the screen on cue. It foreshadowed the audience rituals of *The Rocky Horror Picture Show*, where some of the glam spirit would flee in the mid-Seventies.

So "Time" works when keeping this audience in mind. Compared to the solemnity of Pink Floyd's (contemporaneous) "Time," Bowie's song seems garish and tasteless, a pantomime set of neuroses, but there's a bloody zest for life in it. It's a nose-tweak at mortality: it elegies the New York Dolls' drummer Billy Murcia, who Bowie had met two months before. The surging army of Bowie voices, with their endless "LI-li-li-lis," suggest Simon and Garfunkel's "The Boxer." They're the twisted backbone of an ominous coda where Trevor Bolder whimsies on bass while a low-mixed flute and a submerged saxophone swell the ranks. As Marcello Carlin wrote, Bowie's line "we should be on by now!" wasn't just "the understandable cry of the touring artist, but something more, a recognition that he too has travelled from the sixties, but that too many people did not find their way out, were still not doing so." ("Aladdin Sane," a fractured portrait of, among others, Syd Barrett, was its sister song.)

A dark recitative piece, "Time" forgoes refrains for extended verses, a wordless bridge and a long outro, all pitched in a rollicking sway between A minor and C major. The verse is in three parts: an eight-bar opening anchored by Garson's stylized "stride" piano ("a little left field, with an angle") and built over the intro's chord changes, a foggy four-bar transition to introduce Ronson and Woodmansey and a last full-band section that's essentially the song's refrain. Like the not-quite-right "Fifties" of "Drive-In Saturday," "Time" offers fake-Weimar Berlin jazz, stride in quotations. The alienation was heightened by Ken Scott's mix, which set Garson to the far right of the stereo spectrum and jump-cut to him playing a grand piano upon Bowie's opening "time!"

Garson staked his claims everywhere: chromatic falling octaves on "senseless things," rocketing fourths on "Quaaludes"; conversing with Trevor Bolder's bassline in the bridge; a lightning run of quintuplets that peaks on a high E-flat (2:28). But "Time" was ultimately Ronson's song. First appearing in triplicate, each of his guitar tracks sounding a different note of the underlying chord, he soon sets about topping Garson. He meets the latter's rainfall of notes after "so many dreams" with a waltzing line and responds to Garson's doom-laden C major chord with one of his most outrageous solos on record: three whinnying, vibrato-bloodied descending phrases that sound like a horse convulsing. Lacing in melody after melody, raiding Pachelbel's Canon (3:10) and the "Ode to Joy" from Beethoven's Ninth (3:20), Ronson wins control of the song by the sheer power of his tone, a mastery furthered in his 1973 live performances. "Time" fittingly shuffles off with a nod to the past (a hissed "time!" calls back to "An Occasional Dream" and the lost bedsit world of Bowie and Hermione). It would be the centerpiece of Bowie's most flamboyant tours. In 1974, he sang it sitting cross-legged behind an enormous black hand; on his 1987 Glass Spider tour, he sang while wearing fiberglass angel wings and standing atop the infamous spider sculpture.

Aladdin Sane (1913-1938-197?)

Recorded: *ca. 4-10 December 1972, RCA Studios; ca. 18-23 January*

1973, Trident Studios. Bowie: lead vocal, 12-string acoustic guitar; Ronson: lead guitar, rhythm guitar; Garson: piano; Bolder: bass; Woodmansey: drums; Fordham: tenor saxophone. Produced: Bowie, Scott; engineered: Scott.

***First release**: 13 April 1973, **Aladdin Sane**. **Broadcast**: ca. 4-6 January 1997, ChangesNowBowie. **Live**: 1973-1974, 1996.*

Bowie took a cruise ship, the *R.H.M.S. Ellinis,* home to Britain in mid-December 1972. During the voyage he read Evelyn Waugh's *Vile Bodies* and, finding some of his life in the novel, he soon got a song out of it.

At a London press conference the summer before, Bowie was playfully unnerved by his success. "People like Lou [Reed] and I are probably predicting the end of an era," he said. "Any society that allows people like Lou and me to become rampant is pretty well lost. We're both pretty mixed-up, paranoid people—absolute walking messes. If we're the spearhead of anything, we're not necessarily the spearhead of anything good."Once there'd been well-groomed boys in matching suits on *Top of the Pops*. Now there was Roxy Music, who seemed like extraterrestrials, and Slade and Roy Wood, hill trolls in Halloween costumes, and the Sweet, a malevolent bubblegum group. Pop had turned absurd.

Waugh's novel opens on a cross-Channel ship, shuttles through a length of parties, after-parties, *soirées* and movie sets, peaks at an auto race and ends on a battlefield. The speed of the narrative was that of its composition—Waugh wrote it in a few months in 1929, while his marriage was falling apart. His intention, as he wrote in *Labels*, was to "catch the flavour of the period, how will this absurd little jumble of antagonising forces, of negro rhythm and psycho-analysis, of mechanical invention and decaying industry, of infinitely expanding means of communication and an infinitely receding substance of the communicible...how will this ever cool down and crystallise out?" His hapless protagonist, who loses and gains an illusory £1,000 throughout the novel, shuffles from being an aspiring novelist to a fabulist gossip columnist to an indifferent soldier.

The song Bowie wrote to answer *Vile Bodies* lacked Waugh's tart sense of his time, his taste for the vernacular of the popular press. Instead of the mayfly slang Waugh's characters use, Bowie's lyric is the effete imagery of some hothouse civilization: faded roses, glissando strings, fountains, sake (only "motor sensational" and "passionate bright young things" borrow from Waugh). He took some of it from Aleister Crowley's "Tale of Archais" ("Are the roses dead to-day?/Is the wine spilt?...Has the dancer danced away?"). "Aladdin Sane" himself, starting with the name's weak punning, was a flimsy creation: he existed primarily as Brian Duffy's seven-color LP photograph. Bowie later would claim that Ziggy Stardust's final incarnation in spring-summer 1973, with his Japanese robes, gold makeup and chakra, was Ziggy metamorphosed into "Aladdin Sane," but the Aladdin of his song wasn't such a peacock. A passive nonentity, drowning in a decadent world, he's more a cartoon version of Syd Barrett, who by 1973 was one of rock's foremost acid casualties and notorious recluses (see "See Emily Play").

With fifteen years of economic depression and global war as its long epilogue, *Vile Bodies* came off as a last whirl for modernity (the Twenties were a disappointed Sixties). Bowie thought his era would end the same way, that glam would be a last dance before some awful retribution came. Most likely a nuclear holocaust, though he was happy to entertain other nightmares. Hence the title parenthetical—(1913, 1938, 197?)—each the last year before a cataclysm. Bowie seemed to believe that the world would end before 1980. When it didn't, his work was never the same: those are the breaks when you make apocalypse a muse.

Got a Message From the Action Man

"Aladdin Sane" is built of sets of nine—a nine-bar intro, two nine-bar verses, two nine-bar refrains and Mike Garson's 45-bar piano solo, or five nine-bar refrains. Its opening chords, a set of ninths and suspended seconds that suggest a B minor key, create a sense of unease while Mick Ronson's descending four-note scale (F#-E-D-B) previews Bowie's vocal melody tag ("you'll-make-it"). Trevor Bolder's bass, spiking up and sliding down over two bars, is a secondary movement; Bowie's 12-string acoustic chords and Woody Woodmansey's hi-hat provide weak order. Garson's first motif, a topsy-turvy set of octaves shadowed by suspended chords on the bass end of his piano, foreshadows his role to come.

At Trident, Bowie asked Garson, sitting at the same Bechstein grand piano Rick Wakeman had played on *Hunky Dory*, to solo over a rhythm track of 4/4 drums, Bolder's root notes (a quarter note and eighth note for each chord) and his own acoustic strums, with the chords just repeated two-beat shifts between A and G major. Offering no guidelines, he quickly shot down Garson's first two tries (a blues and a Latin-tinged solo), telling him to go further out. On tour, Garson had told stories of the Sixties New York avant-garde jazz scene and free jazz hierophants like Cecil Taylor. Go there, Bowie said. So Garson played, off the top of his head and in a single take, one of the most outrageous rock piano solos ever recorded.

The jazz critic Ekkehard Jost wrote that for Cecil Taylor, *energy* was everything. The speed at which Taylor hit notes, the dynamism and interplay of his bass and treble end figures, how he constantly decelerated or accelerated tempos: these were as important to Taylor as developing a melodic phrase or a chord progression. Applying calculus-level rhythmic concepts, Taylor was a drummer with 88 piano keys and three pedals at his disposal. So Garson took what he heard in Taylor and broadcast it, as if he was a gramophone horn. The result was stunning. Ian MacDonald wrote of the Beatles' "Revolution 9" that it was "the world's most widely distributed avant-garde artefact." Garson's solo on "Aladdin Sane" was much the same: "Aladdin Sane" is likely the only piece of avant-garde piano jazz that tens of thousands own.

Garson's solo starts by dispatching a rival. In the opening nine-bar refrain (2:02 to 2:20), he shares the stage with Ken Fordham's tenor saxophone, the latter committed to a wending, low melody. Rather than accompany Fordham, Garson is hell-bent on driving him out, playing jarring five-note clusters (quintuplets in sextuple time) to disrupt the saxophone's musings. By the fifth bar Fordham's reduced to two or three notes per bar and soon departs. Garson responds with a triumphant run of dodecuplets and a flurry of notes played so fast the ear can scarcely differentiate them in pitch.

In the second refrain (2:21-2:40) Garson, after some swooping octave-leaping dashes across the keyboard (with some high G# notes to clash against the underlying G chord), kites out lines with his right hand and tersely responds with his left: a transcription of the notes he plays is a jumbled city skyline in dots. The third refrain (2:41-2:57) is the storm's eye, a respite with a few quotations—"Rhapsody In Blue" (2:48) and "Tequila" (2:52), a hint of "On Broadway," which Bowie sings in the outro. The fourth (2:58-3:15) kills that indulgence when Garson pounding two bars of dodecuplets (in undecuple time, why not?) undergirded by bass octaves—it's as if he's bludgeoning the song with his fists. After Garson's last lightning round across the treble end, with runs of grace notes and triplets, Fordham's saxophone calmly pushes back in, signaling an end to the fun. Garson protests, shattering chords and making a thick paste of a note cluster. He offers a last extravagance (which bridges into the start of the fifth and final refrain (3:14-3:31)): a chromatic parallel climb up three octaves across the bass and treble ends of his piano. All that's left is a return to earth. Midway through the last refrain, Garson boxes himself into a simple rhythmic figure: bass octaves and a dashing three-note phrase on every other beat.

If the solo wasn't enough, "Aladdin Sane" ended about as

wildly. Like "Panic In Detroit" and "Cracked Actor," it bleeds out, fading in a two-minute din of saxophones, Ronson's fuzz-distorted guitar, Bowie singing the chorus of "On Broadway" and Garson settling into making small trouble. All that's left in its last seconds is Garson rationed to a handful of notes and Ronson as a ghost of amp feedback and the buzzing noise of his pickup switch. It's as good a guess as any of what an exhausted civilization sounds like as it dies, but it also suggests a palette scoured free of colors, a fresh start in the ruins.

Let's Spend the Night Together

*(Jagger/Richards). **Recorded**: ca. 4-11 December 1972, RCA Studios, New York?; ca. 18-23 January 1973, Trident. Bowie: lead vocal, ARP; Ronson: lead and rhythm guitar, backing vocal; Garson: piano; Bolder: bass; Woodmansey: drums. Produced: Bowie, Scott; engineered: Scott.*

***First release**: 13 April 1973, **Aladdin Sane**. **Live**: 1972-1973.*

While it would become one of the Rolling Stones' hammiest satyr songs live, the original "Let's Spend the Night Together" was a mildly psychedelic record, built over a drone of piano (even the backing singers are vocalizing piano chords) and organ, the stasis only breaking with a *Pet Sounds*-influenced middle section, a swirl of vocal harmonies and truncheon claves, the latter courtesy of policemen visiting Olympic Studios.

Bowie unfurled his cover of "Let's Spend the Night Together" as a show-opener for his "welcome home" concerts in Britain at the end of December 1972. He kicked it up in key (from G to A), increased its tempo and let Mick Ronson and Mike Garson off the leash. In the studio, he added to the fun with some squiggles and squeals on the ARP 2600.

Although inspired by a then-clandestine relationship with Marianne Faithfull, Mick Jagger's lyric was hypothetically lustful, sung by someone whose hope outweighs his experience (Jagger was always a good actor). Jagger sings the title phrase by tentatively emphasizing "night" and drawing out "together." He dithers, hems and haws, fills in spaces with "my my my my" and other tics, plumbs vowels and even admits "this doesn't happen to me every day!" When he gets past his last moment of doubt (the ominous bridge), he takes on the last verse with gusto, the backing singers cheering him on.

Bowie instead delivered the refrains like royal edicts, keeping to a four-note range and being mostly single-tracked. Sprinting through the verses as if he had a stopwatch in the vocal booth, he sounds hoarse at times and put odd emphases on phrases, as though it hardly mattered how he words his seduction. His contribution was a new spoken verse, closing with a breathy declaration that while they've said "our kind of love is *no fun*" (a hat-tip to the Stooges) he doesn't care: "our love comes from *above*....let's make...*lurve*." Cue Ronson's whining slide guitar: the nightmare shrieks of "Time" now those of a rutting beast.

If the Bowie cover was a gay liberation of the Stones' pure-heterosexual original, it was at the expense of the original's humanity. But it was far more the sort of plastic rock 'n' roll Ziggy Stardust allegedly played: a junked-up, pilled-up demolition of a Sixties "standard." It's loud, tacky and pointless and it fits well on *Aladdin Sane*, serving as the Sixties counterpart to the Fifties pastiches "The Prettiest Star" and "Drive-In Saturday." Along with "Watch That Man," it was a shot across the bow to the Stones, serving notice that Bowie was playing their music better than they were. Later Stones performances of "Let's Spend the Night Together" used Bowie's version as a template, with Jagger chasing a glam spoof of himself.

Lady Grinning Soul

Recorded*: ca. 18-24 January 1973, Trident. Bowie: lead vocal, 12-string acoustic guitar; Ronson: lead acoustic guitar, lead and rhythm guitars; Garson: piano; Bolder: bass; Woodmansey: drums; Fordham, Wilshaw: baritone saxophones. Produced: Bowie, Scott; engineered: Scott.*

***First release**: 13 April 1973, **Aladdin Sane**.*

"Lady Grinning Soul" is a lost James Bond theme song, its closing line ("your living end") a finer title than the Bond films of the past thirty years have had; its coda is Shirley Bassey's "Goldfinger" under an assumed name. Bowie seemed to have raided a film library for the song, whose verse melody has traces of Quincy Jones' "On Days Like These" from *The Italian Job* and whose octave leaps and stepwise falls echo those of Max Steiner's "Tara's Theme" in *Gone With the Wind*.

Its goulash of a lyric—French cologne, Uruguayan card games, German cars and American credit for a Lady who's stateless, rootless, all-conquering— argues for the song's muse being not the singer Claudia Lennear (as consensus has it) but the actress/model/singer Amanda Lear, cover star of Roxy Music's *For Your Pleasure*, host of Bowie's *1980 Floor Show* and his lover at the time. A longtime companion of Salvador Dali, Lear was adept at making her life a mystery, offering a few different birthdates and sets of parents, claiming variously that she had English, French, Vietnamese, Transylvanian, Chinese, Russian and Indonesian heritage and not denying rumors that she was a hermaphrodite or a transsexual. (She also may have driven a Volkswagen Bug.) The Lady of Bowie's song (Aretha Franklin's *Lady Soul*, now grinning like a death's head) is both muse and sexual vampire ("she comes, she goes") and "represents absolute sexual difference, not the misty blurred ground of gender experiment that Bowie normally traverses," as Camille Paglia wrote.

Written soon before, if not during, the *Aladdin Sane* sessions in London, "Lady Grinning Soul" was a last-minute addition to the album, bumping off the "John, I'm Only Dancing" remake as a closer and so shoring up a weak LP side. It hymns an abstraction, its key line "how can life become her point of view?": another clue that Lear was its subject. She once told an interviewer Bowie had fallen in love with her image on the cover of *For Your Pleasure*, not the "real" her, which admittedly she took great pains to obscure.

With a bewildering B major verse chord progression built on flatted and relative minor chords that shifts to a bitter G# minor refrain, with a secretive move back to B major for the outro, "Lady Grinning Soul" also has traces of parody. Take Mike Garson as a florid maestro. In the intro, he foreshadows the vocal melody with a leaping set of F# octaves and makes exuberant scuttles across the keyboard. He settles into playing sets of trickling arpeggios, intended to sound "French, with a little Franz Liszt thrown in" but coming off more as an tribute to Liberace. Bowie later described Garson's performance as evoking a 19th Century aesthete's gauche attempt at playing "exotica." His own *a cappella* entrance, a slow ascent that spans an F# octave, is as stunning as it's a touch campy—a grand dame drifting down from a catwalk. "Lady Grinning Soul" gave *Aladdin Sane* a closing dose of "Continental" schlock, a sweet chaser after all of the album's grimy Americanisms.

The band, who appear in the long breath between Bowie's first and second phrases, offer restraint—Woody Woodmansey, who plays hi-hat 8ths and an off-beat kick pattern throughout—and tasteful exuberance (Bolder's long, striding basslines). Mick Ronson's spotlight moment is a eight-bar "Spanish" acoustic guitar solo, dryly recorded and percussively picked, that sings the vocal melody, develops into a run of triplet thirds and peaks with three rising lines, the last spiking to a high F# to rattle the underlying B major suspended fourth chord.

Still, even Ronson was just a supporting player. "Lady Grinning Soul" hangs on Bowie, whose hypnotically slow pacing deepens the sumptuousness of the melody— he often allows only two or three notes per bar and ends verses by severing the last line in two, the first phrase a graceful fall of fifths, the second a swaying melody that blissfully expires ("soul") on the root note. He savors the tumbling syllables of "canasta," the melodious depths of "cologne;" he sounds like a man who swallowed a dream. The postlude finds him hitting the absolute ceiling of his vocal range (the G#5 at 3:20 is the highest note he ever sang on record). Having perfected the song in the studio, Bowie saw no need to ever perform it live.

This Boy
Love Me Do

(Lennon/McCartney). ("This Boy") Bowie: lead vocal; Ronson: lead guitar, harmony vocal; Bolder: bass; Woodmansey: drums; ("Love Me Do")(1973) Bowie: vocal, harmonica; Ronson: rhythm guitar; Jeff Beck: lead guitar; Bolder: bass; Woodmansey: drums; (1974) Earl Slick: lead guitar; Herbie Flowers: bass; Tony Newman: drums; (2000) Slick: lead guitar; Mark Plati: rhythm guitar; Gail Ann Dorsey: bass, harmony vocal; Sterling Campbell: drums.

***Live**: ("This Boy") 1972, ("Love Me Do") 1973-1974, 2000.*

At an otherwise undistinguished show at the Locarno in Bristol, on 27 August 1972, Bowie threw the Beatles' "This Boy" into his set. He likely played it in a few other shows around this time but the Bristol set is its only recording. Cut for the B-side of "I Wanna Hold Your Hand," "This Boy" was the Beatles essaying doo-wop, with huddled-close three-part harmonies over 12/8 (John Lennon was channeling his treasured Miracles records, doing his best Smokey Robinson in the bridge). Reducing the song to a fragile-sounding solo vocal, with Ronson giving occasional harmonies, Bowie's "This Boy" came across like a lullaby recalled from childhood. It was the seed that grew into "Drive-In Saturday" later that year.

Covering Lennon/McCartney also predicted that there would soon be a Ziggymania to rival Beatlemania. While in the US Bowie had weak sales, no radio hits and ill-attended shows, Tony Defries ensured these details didn't trouble the British press. By late spring 1973, after a second, better-calibrated US tour and a triumphant run in Japan, Bowie had become a rock star in Britain, with *Aladdin Sane* his first #1 LP.

The Spiders show was now on a broader canvas. John Hutchinson returned to play rhythm guitar; Geoff MacCormack sang backup; the two-man saxophone/flute section of *Aladdin Sane* came aboard. The costumes were grander—in Japan, Bowie got a set of new duds from Kansai Yamamoto, including a billowing white robe and a kimono to be stripped off him on stage (it had to be stitched anew after every performance). His stage presence was more dominating and physical. This all came at the expense of the camaraderie of the early Spiders shows. Bowie and Defries planned to sack Trevor Bolder and Woody Woodmansey while Woodmansey was considering quitting. Swayed by Defries' promise of a solo career, Ronson had turned on his bandmates. By the end of the spring 1973 American tour, the band's only glimpses of Bowie came on stage and, at a distance, in after-parties. He even gave his old friend Hutchinson the cold shoulder.

In Japan, the MainMan crew was still provoking crowd reactions, encouraging kids to rush the stage at the end of the show (which once caused a near-riot). But when Bowie returned to Britain in early May 1973, there was no need: the mania he'd prophesized in Bristol had come true. Haddon Hall was overrun by fans. There were fistfights and couplings, perhaps by the same people, in the back rows of Green's Playhouse in Glasgow, while an Edinburgh show at the Empire Theatre found the stage "in a constant state of siege, as Bowie slowly and remorselessly worked the audience up to a state of total sensory overload," Charles Shaar Murray reported.

His voice was giving out—he'd started doing medleys of older songs like "Life On Mars?" and Quicksand" because "I've found that I can't sing half the rest of the show after I've done them," he said—and he was unnerved by the violence. He saw a security guard karate-chop a fan; at another gig a bouncer hurled a girl off stage. He was shedding weight. Freddi Burretti's costumes, which were getting worn and frayed, now drooped over him.

Whether Bowie truly felt he was becoming Ziggy Stardust and losing his identity or if that was a legend he later pushed to justify his career moves, his decision to scrap further tours, break up the band and retire Ziggy Stardust was his most precisely-timed piece of theater. In part done for financial reasons (RCA wasn't funding the next American tour, so it would've been cut-rate or done at a huge cost to MainMan), the move also reflected how keenly Bowie had studied pop. He'd reached the Beatlemania stage, at least in Britain, and now there was nowhere to go but down, as Marc Bolan was learning.

During their last British shows, the Spiders extended "Jean Genie" for over ten minutes, during which, cued by Bowie's harmonica, they'd segue into "Love Me Do." It was an expedition up to the source. "Love Me Do," the first Beatles single, had been a raw, modern-sounding record upon its release, all expectation and promise. At the final Ziggy show at the Hammersmith, with Jeff Beck on lead guitar, Bowie sang "Love Me Do" simply, letting his audience finish the chorus phrases. After a time, he crept back into his own song. The show ended, Bowie broke up the band. Looking for an escape route, he ducked into the past.

Chapter 7

The Anxiety of Influence (1973)

[He] was made restless by the thought he had missed it, that authority had drained from the figures he most admired and from the aesthetics he most wanted to master.
George W.S. Trow, "Eclectic, Reminiscent, Amused, Fickle, Perverse."

He becomes an echo of someone else's music, an actor of a part that has not been written for him.
Oscar Wilde, *The Picture of Dorian Gray.*

He's been looking back to appreciate forward motion more.
Biff Rose, "Shell of a Man."

Everything's Alright

(Crouch/Konrad/Stavely/James/Karlson). ***Recorded****: 9-31 July 1973, Château d'Hérouville, Hérouville, Val d'Oise, France. David Bowie: lead vocal, tenor saxophone; Mick Ronson: lead guitar, backing vocal; Mike Garson: piano; Trevor Bolder: bass; Aynsley Dunbar: drums; Geoff MacCormack: backing vocal; Ken Fordham: baritone saxophone. Produced: Ken Scott, Bowie; engineered: Dennis Mackay ("Denis Blackeye").*

First release*: 19 October 1973,* ***Pin Ups*** *(RS 1003/APL1-0291, UK #1, US #23).* ***Broadcast****: 20 October 1973, The 1980 Floor Show.*

Six days after the death of Ziggy Stardust and the Spiders from Mars, David Bowie and a small entourage made their way by cross-Channel boat and train to Pointoise, a city northwest of Paris. Over three weeks at a refurbished chateau in the nearby village of Hérouville, Bowie cut an album. It was one of a pack of obligations, including a photo shoot for *Vogue*, a prospective single with Lulu and a batch of press interviews.

While RCA wanted a new Bowie LP in the shops for Christmas, Bowie was exhausted from touring and creatively spent. His manager Tony Defries was haggling with his publisher for better rates (he would win, increasing Bowie's stake in his songs to 75%) and discouraged Bowie from recording any new compositions until negotiations were done. The solution was obvious: dash out cover versions of a dozen "oldies" and call it an album. This was *Pin Ups*, the runt of Bowie's Seventies albums; it was a man settling assorted debts and rewriting the past.

Bowie had been a tertiary figure in Sixties pop. Had he quit making records in 1968, his Deram LP and Pye singles would be hipster obscurities at best today, with the occasional track turning up on a Wes Anderson soundtrack. So in *Pin Ups* he recast mid-Sixties British pop, giving himself a starring role and infesting the songs with the sounds of the glam era. Its title suggested David Bailey's *Box of Pin-ups,* a 1965 collection of black & white headshots of London's pop royalty, an assemblage that David Jones never could have joined. *Pin Ups* is also a fan's record, if one made by a fan who thought he was hipper than the bands he saw at the Marquee and the Ricky Tick. "In those days I was an audience," Bowie told Charles Shaar Murray during the sessions. "But I never dressed like anybody that was in the rock business."

Of his cover selections, only the Yardbirds, the Kinks, Pink Floyd and the Who qualified as influences on his music, and they were minor compared to those whose songs weren't on *Pin Ups*: Anthony Newley, the Velvet Underground, Scott Walker and Jacques Brel. He didn't intend any sort of autobiography. He mainly covered his jobbing contemporaries, the bands for whom he'd opened, the bands who'd beat the Manish Boys and the Lower Third on the charts, the bands he had outlasted.

He confined his picks to British (mostly) rock singles cut between 1964-1967, his research consisting of going through a stack of 45s in his rooms at the Hyde Park Hotel before leaving for France. Casting a vote was the musician Scott Richardson, a Pretty Things fan who lobbied Bowie to cover two of their songs. After making his picks, Bowie summoned Mick Ronson and Trevor Bolder for a quick run-through hearing. While he later said he'd chosen "more obscure songs" to have greater license to monkey with their arrangements, the songs weren't that obscure and many of his arrangements clung to those of the originals. Bowie's idea of rehearsing a song was to play the band the 45 a few times, then start recording.

He'd chosen his songs to serve each end of the cross-Atlantic market. For Britain, where his selections had all charted, *Pin Ups* was a nostalgia record for the washed-out mood of late 1973: the album stayed at the top for five weeks, tying with *Aladdin Sane* for his longest-reigning #1. For America, where only three of the original singles had reached the Top 40, *Pin Ups* was essentially a new Bowie album.

In America, it wound up extending an argument opened by Lenny Kaye's *Nuggets* garage rock compilation, released in fall 1972. An "official" history of rock 'n' roll was being drafted, a narrative in which rock 'n' roll emerges from some lost hinterland of blues, R&B and country music, erupts with Elvis, matures with the Beatles and Bob Dylan and crystallizes into something like *The Dark Side of the Moon*. It's an evolution from primitive teenage dance music up to "relevance" and "complexity," with the occasional refreshing dip into "roots" music for sustenance. This story still remains with us. *Nuggets*, and now *Pin Ups*, offered what would be the punk rebuttal, knocking the myth of musical progress, prizing the trashy single over the concept LP, the high school dance over the hippie festival, inspired mistakes over chops.

That said *Pin Ups* wasn't quite in *Nuggets*' revivalist spirit. *Nuggets* was reverent, with Kaye curating his garage rock 45s like holy relics. Bowie was more impish. He tarted up butch odes to lust, shrieked refrains like some pantomime Dracula. The album's scattershot feel, its lack of a coherent style, reflects the schizophrenia of its creation. Its sessions were idyllic—cut during a fine summer in the French countryside, with overflowing dinners at the Chateau's refectory table and nightly limousine trips to Paris nightclubs—and tense. Bolder, who Bowie had wanted to replace with Jack Bruce, accurately believed he was unwanted, so he laid down his bass tracks early and went home (Woody Woodmansey already had been sacked via phone on his wedding day). Ken Scott was distracted by his concerns for his pregnant wife, who gave birth midway through the sessions, and was under pressure by his management company to stop working for Bowie because MainMan wasn't paying royalties. Mick Ronson drowned himself in work. "He did everything in the studio, he tuned everybody's instruments, he worked on all the arrangements," Richardson recalled. Ronson had "a tremendous burden on him...he worked all the time [and] I think he was completely at sea about his future. Because that band [the Spiders] had a real integrity. And they were gone." Bowie's increasingly remote and truculent attitude in the studio didn't help matters.

* * *

The oldest track Bowie covered was the Mojos' "Everything's Alright," which hit #9 in Britain in April 1964. Its inclusion reflected one of his aims for the record: making a fan's testimony. The Mojos' lead singer Stu James, who had been at the Liverpool Institute a few years behind Paul McCartney and George Harrison, was an obsessive fan of the Beatles, all but living at the Cavern Club. The Beatles had made a new reality for him: "This thing was actually happening with some guys who'd been in our Fifth Form," he recalled.

James won a songwriting competition that landed him a publishing deal and a tape recorder. His five-piece Mojos came together quickly and by the end of 1963 they had taken their idols' path and were playing the Star Club in Hamburg. Like Davie Jones and the King Bees, the Mojos got a contract with Decca; unlike the King Bees, they got a national hit. Recorded in Hamburg, "Everything's Alright" started as James' attempt to rewrite Art Blakey's jazz standard "Moanin'" by riffing some lines over the piano hook. The band sewed in more bits: some "Twist and Shout," some Tony Sheridan-style backing vocals. The C major verses were just come-ons for the G major refrain, with its thrice-chanted "let me hold your HAND, be your LOVIN' man," James holding back until the last repeat to give a climactic howl. "Everything's Alright" seemed held together by twine: there was a gimcrack feel to its construction, from the jerking chromatic stomps in and out of the barely-there F major bridge to its sudden collapse of an ending, the final "everything's alright" a post-coital sigh.

In Bowie's cover, Mick Ronson claimed the Mojos' piano hook while Aynsley Dunbar on drums swapped out the original's ride cymbal 16ths for thundering cross-channel tom fills. An oddly-muted Mike Garson declined to elaborate on the original's Jerry Lee Lewis-isms (the hard-pounded 8ths in the refrains) while the solo break, just a few flashy piano runs on the Mojos single, was now Ronson, Garson and Bowie's honking saxophone trading twos.

The vocal arrangement bracketed Bowie's sneering Elvis imitation between goofy marginal voices mixed far left and right (Bowie and Geoff MacCormack). It was Bowie playing both the star and the gawky fans singing along to the record in their bedrooms. This premise fared better on record than in the song's one live outing, on Bowie's "1980 Floor Show" TV broadcast, where his alleged soul trio the Astronettes derailed the performance with flailing vocals and dance moves.

I Wish You Would

*(Arnold). **Recorded:** ca. 9-31 July 1973, Château d'Hérouville. Bowie: lead vocal, harmonica, Moog; Ronson: lead and rhythm guitars; Bolder: bass; Dunbar: drums; Michel Ripoche: electric violin. Produced: Scott, Bowie; engineered: MacKay.*

***First release**: 19 October 1973, **Pin Ups**.*

Born in Depression-era Chicago, Billy Boy Arnold was a journeyman in the city's postwar blues scene and a collaborator of Bo Diddley's (he played harp on Diddley's "I'm a Man"). In 1955, itching to cut his own records and on the outs with Chess Records owner Leonard Chess, Arnold went to rival label Vee-Jay to cut "I Wish You Would," an overnight rewrite of his "Diddy Diddy Dum Dum." Though Arnold considered himself a bluesman, "I Wish You Would" sold, pushing him into playing rock & roll.

"I Wish You Would" was a rock & roll record with a fatalistic blues heart. Arnold opened with standard lines: his woman's left him, she's going around town, can't love me and another man too. In the second verse he widened the lens. She left him because he was drinking, because he mistreated her and he's deserved what he's gotten. Arnold didn't sound too bothered. She might come back, he might change, she might cheat again: it was as circular as Jody Williams' agitated guitar riff. The track was fresh (reportedly the first Chicago blues single to feature electric bass), a city boy's song, with Arnold and Williams picking apart the blues to find a few shiny bits.

Arnold's record was taken up a decade later by the British R&B stylists the Yardbirds, who were an ocean and a lifetime removed from him (their drummer was a former stockbroker). Played in their earliest sets, "I Wish You Would," being one of the poppiest songs in their repertoire that still passed muster with resident purist Eric Clapton, was issued as their debut single in May 1964. The Yardbirds straightened the Arnold single's snaky, clattering beat, excised the man's part in the mess (now it's the woman who's been drinking) and made the song an excuse for a thrashing rave-up. Keith Relf sang sullenly, talking back himself on his harp. "We just sounded young and white," Clapton recalled. While "I Wish You Would" didn't chart, it bowled over the likes of the King Bees and the Manish Boys. It helped that the song, a one-chord stomp, was easy to play: mastering it was an early milestone for any R&B pretenders.

Bowie and Mick Ronson quickened the tempo even more than the Yardbirds had and kicked the song up to A major. Ronson, while keeping Williams' original guitar figure, replaced the harp riff with twin-tracked guitar, smoothing the riff's rhythm from the two-beat/triplet/two-beat chugging harp pattern to a four 8th notes/two quarter notes pulse, the last note bent. A homage to Clapton's raga-influenced Yardbirds replacements, Jeff Beck and Jimmy Page, came from the electric violinist Michel Ripoche, who doubled Bowie's harp solo and finished off the track with a 16-bar dervish. Along with Ronson's needle-sharp picking, Aynsley Dunbar's punk drumming (future Sex Pistol Paul Cook used the album as a clinic), a "haunted house" Moog bassline rumbling through the mix and a convincing, single-tracked Bowie, Ripoche made "I Wish You Would" one of *Pin Ups*' better realizations.

Rosalyn

(Duncan/Farley). ***Recorded:*** *ca. 9-31 July 1973, Château d'Hérouville. Bowie: lead vocal; Ronson: lead and rhythm guitars; Bolder: bass; Dunbar: drums, shaker. Produced: Scott, Bowie; engineered: MacKay.*

First release*: 19 October 1973,* ***Pin Ups****.*

The Pretty Things were beatnik guitarist Dick Taylor, seemingly the only bearded man in Britain at the time, the dashing, indifferent Brian Pendleton (in group photos he looked like their lawyer), the brutish near-twins Phil May and John Stax and Vivian "Viv" Prince, a lunatic drummer who sported a bowler. In 1964, they released two singles on Fontana that should have gotten them arrested. May sang "Rosalyn," their debut 45, like he was tearing into a hunk of meat, rolling "Roh-sa-LYNN" around in his mouth, rhyming its last syllable with a sneered "BIN" and screaming "YEAH-GOTTA-KNOW! YEAH-GOTTA-KNOW!" while his band thrashed out an amphetamine strain of the Bo Diddley beat.

It was so primal a performance that Bowie and Mick Ronson's only option was to play "Rosalyn" louder. Ronson tracked a Bo Diddley-ghosting rhythm guitar (itself double-tracked) with a drop-D-tuned slide guitar mixed in the left channel, but the rhythm section let down the side, with Trevor Bolder's stepwise descending bassline turfed in the mix and Aynsley Dunbar plagued by good taste, offering surgically precise fills in lieu of the lopsided thunks Viv Prince had clobbered across the last verse. Dunbar also declined Prince's cymbal-drunk attack (Prince would play snare beats on his ride cymbal) to play a muted kick and tom pattern garnished by a shaker. While Bowie unnervingly channeled May's voice, getting all the howls and slurs right, his consistent "HEY"s neglected the crucial distinction of May's interjections—an on-the-make "YEAH Rosalyn" and a sated "OH Rosalyn." As "Rosalyn" was sequenced as the lead-off track on *Pin Ups*, some of its buyers likely wondered just whose record they'd purchased.

Don't Bring Me Down

(Dee). ***Recorded:*** *9-31 July 1973, Château d'Hérouville. Bowie: lead vocal, rhythm guitar?, harmonica; Ronson: lead and rhythm guitar; Bolder: bass; Dunbar: drums, tambourine. Produced: Scott, Bowie; engineered: MacKay.*

First release*: 19 October 1973,* ***Pin Ups****.*

A benign pop song that the Pretty Things put to disreputable ends, "Don't Bring Me Down" was written by an obscure singer known as Johnny Dee. The band turned it into two minutes of mating calls. It would be their biggest hit. Built on four descending major chords (E-D-C-A), its rhythm shrugging between stop-start bother and guitar-mad 4/4, the song opened with May as a rolling stone, looking for trouble ("don't bring me down, man"). Upon finding a girl he likes, he grew domestic: "I got this *PAD*/jus' like a *CAVE*." Soon enough he's laid her on the ground, a line that got the single banned by some American radio stations.

As with "Rosalyn," Bowie was content with a higher-wattage imitation. Aynsley Dunbar was in better form here, replacing the tambourine/handclaps of the Pretty Things' stop-start sections with a menacingly-hissed hi-hat, and he slammed his way through the refrains. The solo was a hash, the mix championing Bowie's amateur harmonica over Mick Ronson's guitar, which admittedly was no match for Dick Taylor, who'd rung out notes like a fire alarm in his solo. Bowie's vocal, a shadow of May's performance, offered nothing to top May's final tonsil-tearing "MAAAN."

I Can't Explain

*(Townshend). **Recorded**: **(unreleased studio take)** 24 June 1972, Trident. Bowie: lead vocal, rhythm guitar?; Ronson: lead guitar; Bolder: bass; Woodmansey: drums. Produced: Scott; (**album**) 9-31 July 1973, Château d'Hérouville, ca. mid-August 1973, Trident. Bowie: lead vocal, tenor saxophone, rhythm guitar?; Ronson: lead guitar, backing vocal; Garson: piano; Fordham: baritone saxophone; Bolder: bass; Dunbar: drums, tambourine; MacCormack: backing vocal. Produced: Scott, Bowie; engineered: MacKay.*

***First release**: 19 October 1973, **Pin Ups**. **Broadcast**: 20 October 1973, The 1980 Floor Show. **Live**: 1972, 1983.*

After an acerbic first meeting in 1965, at which Pete Townshend noted Bowie was ripping off his songs (see "You've Got a Habit of Leaving"), the two mellowed into acquaintances, enough that Townshend felt comfortable leaving his eight-year-old brother in Bowie's care during a Who concert in 1969. Four summers later, both men were revising their Sixties. Bowie covered two of the Who's Mod singles on *Pin Ups* at the same time the Who was recording Townshend's Mod opus *Quadrophenia*. The albums were released within weeks of each other, *Pin Ups'* dominance of the top of the chart keeping the Who out.

Bowie would appropriate pieces of an artist's persona into his own but he could never piece out Townshend, a closet playwright who wrote three-minute psychodramas, whether a cad gleefully dumping his pregnant girlfriend ("A Legal Matter"), a kid so fraudulent he may not exist ("Substitute"), masturbation to centerfolds as cross-generational bonding ("Pictures of Lily") or "I'm a Boy," a pop single worthy of Philip K. Dick. Townshend's perspective was typically that of *another*. He was an evangelist whose audience wound up converting him; he closed *Tommy*, his record of false messiahs, with a hymn to the mob. And the Who, as he described them, was "a fairly simple form of Pop Art" who only existed in performance. "Off stage, the group get on terribly badly."

Townshend had a near-breakdown writing *Tommy*'s sequel, an opera whose audience would input their vital statistics—height and weight, star sign—into a computer, which would convert the data into a personalized musical signature. Once the tabulations were finished, all of these signatures, sounded simultaneously on quadraphonic speakers, would make one "universal" note or chord. Ridiculous as the idea may seem to our jaded age, it was consistent with Townshend's belief that the audience was responsible for carrying its share of the weight in a rock performance ("audiences are very much like the kids in Tommy's Holiday Camp: they want something without working for it," he once said). Finding universal communion via rock music was about as far as one could get from the defiantly singular Bowie, whose songs were unmistakably *his* perspectives. "I'm very selfish as an artist. I mean, I really do just write and record what interests me," Bowie said in 2002. He and Townshend were of irreconcilable minds, of irreconcilable worlds, and perhaps that got to Bowie, who so capably had absorbed so many other influences.

Is this why Bowie's cover of the Who's first major single, "I Can't Explain," was one of his most grotesque interpretations? He bled the song of anything that had given it power—Keith Moon's whirlwind drumming, the surf group backing vocals—and hung around waiting for it to die. Obviously this was intentional: Bowie played a Mod gone sour, one bloated with pleasure, and "I Can't Explain" was rock 'n' roll as a flyblown corpse. With the song moved down in key (from E major to C major) and its pilled-up tempo nearly halved, Mick Ronson did his part by swapping out Townshend's 12-string Rickenbacker solos, jangly excursions full of bends and grace notes, with a mash-up of a solo that quoted Joe Moretti on Johnny Kidd's "Shakin' All Over." Bowie's bronchial saxophone, yet another deflation of the original's spirit, was the sound of a third-rate dance band on an off night.

"I Can't Explain" is sung by a kid who's never been in love, who's maybe never even been attracted to another person before, but suddenly it's *happening* and nothing makes sense anymore. He's trying to trap the unsayable in words (Townshend later described "I Can't Explain" as him trying to write what songs were doing to him.) Bowie sang his lines coolly, teasing out and lingering on phrases like some cabaret vamp. He's appalling in his confidence, offering smugness cloaked as sexiness. Corrupt intentions aside, Bowie mainly committed the capital Mod sin of being dull. He brought back "I Can't Explain" a decade later for his "Serious Moonlight" tour, where the song continued to elude him.

Anyway, Anyhow, Anywhere

(Townshend/Daltrey). ***Recorded:*** *9-31 July 1973, Château d'Hérouville. Bowie: lead vocal; Ronson: lead and rhythm guitars,*

backing vocal; Garson: piano; Bolder: bass; Dunbar: drums; MacCormack: backing vocal. Produced: Scott, Bowie; engineered: MacKay.

First release*: 19 October 1973,* ***Pin Ups****.*

With "Anyway Anyhow Anywhere," the Who wanted "to achieve the sound we get on the stage at present…show what we're really trying to do," Pete Townshend said at the time. After two refrains and a bridge, there was a 45-second steeplechase where Townshend, his 12-string Rickenbacker stuffed with paper, used his toggle switch "to make the guitar sound like a machine gun when it was feeding back" while Keith Moon set off bombs underneath him. The lyric's pure Pop aspirations—I can do anything I want, at any time; the past means nothing (Townshend wrote it while listening to Charlie Parker)—came off as brassy ambition when voiced by Roger Daltrey, all blustery arrogance of youth. Bowie, whose Daltrey imitation was as uncanny as his take on Phil May on "Rosalyn," sang the lines as hard statements of fact. He matched Daltrey in back-of-the-throat yelps and outlasted him for a bar on the last held "anywhere."

The rest of Bowie's version was able mimicry. Mike Garson played Nicky Hopkins' lilting piano line as if reading from a transcription while Trevor Bolder kept up John Entwistle's brooding on the E string of his bass. A muted Mick Ronson dutifully flicked his pick-up switch and played a few random bottleneck slides (1:47) but he ceded much of the solo to Aynsley Dunbar, whose tom fills and phased crash cymbals were panned across the mix. It's a powerful performance that you hear Dunbar thinking all the way through.

Here Comes the Night

(Berns). ***Recorded*** *9-31 July 1973, Château d'Hérouville. Bowie: lead vocal, alto saxophone; Ronson: lead guitar, backing vocal; Garson: electric piano, Mellotron; Fordham: baritone saxophone; Bolder: bass; Dunbar: drums; MacCormack: backing vocals; Ripoche: violin.*

Produced: Scott, Bowie; engineered: MacKay.

First release**: 19 October 1973,* ***Pin Ups*.*

Bert Berns was a mambo dancer and kickabout performer who, after a failed venture to open a nightclub in pre-revolution Cuba, became a producer and songwriter ("Twist and Shout," "Tell Him"). Brought over to London on Decca's dime in 1964, he was set loose on a group of acts managed by the Ulster impresario Phil Solomon. Berns was a chain-smoking anomaly in Decca's studios, which were still run by patrician men in white coats, and he played the "Broadway huckster" for all it was worth. He introduced himself to the Belfast quintet Them, led by one Van Morrison, by walking into the studio, bashing a cymbal and chiding them to get to work. Berns had nearly died of rheumatic fever as a child and had an acute sense of mortality (rightly so, as he would die of a heart attack at 38); he worked fast, with a shameless taste for recycling. So for Them he retrieved a tolling guitar riff from Marv Johnson's "Come On and Stop" and had the session guitarist Jimmy Page shuffle a new song around it, "Here Comes the Night." Morrison choked out the verses as if he was building himself up to commit murder, while in the refrains, he howled down the world: "Here it ***COMES***! HERE COMES THE NIIIIHHHIIIIIIIIGHT!"

Them first released another Berns production, "Baby Please Don't Go," and assumed "Here Comes the Night" would be their follow-up single. To their irritation, a second-guessing Decca had Berns rework the song for Lulu. He dressed "Here Comes the Night" as a somber mood piece. Where Morrison was consumed with rage, Lulu was self-loathing. She spies her old boyfriend walking with someone new and soon enough she's imaging them necking or worse, while remembering how she'd fallen just as easily. Lulu made the verses a chutes-and-ladders game, building up a tension she only released on the last phrase ("cryyy," "guyyy") *"Here it is,"* she sang with beatific resignation. The single was a florid downer in the beat-mad atmosphere of 1964, and it flopped. So Them got the go-ahead to issue their version, which sold 16,000 copies on its first day of release, peaked at #2 in the UK and cracked the US Top 40 in the summer of 1965.

Bowie halted the *Pin Ups* sessions in mid-July 1973 to cut a Lulu single (versions of his "The Man Who Sold the World" and "Watch That Man") with the same musicians but without his producer. He'd met Lulu after a show in Sheffield the month before and promptly initiated both an affair and a career makeover plan with her. She was impressed at the pace at which Bowie worked, later describing the atmosphere at the Chateau as being like a boarding school. Perhaps planning the Lulu session had brought "Here Comes the Night" to mind as a possible cover, though one can't imagine Lulu was overly fond of the song.

Sequenced to erupt out of "Rosalyn" with a Mick Ronson pick-slide as segue, Bowie's "Here Comes the Night" was pure *Rocky Horror Show*, Bowie swooning out the title phrase. While raiding both the Lulu and Them singles, the arrangement was mainly Bowie and Ronson's invention, from the intro baritone saxophone that plays the verse melody (the saxophone later subs for the guitar riff in one refrain) to the violin that holds a high E note throughout the last verse. The most bewildering moment was Bowie's eight-bar alto saxophone solo, a fumbling performance aptly described as "asthmatic." Given that Bowie had Ken Fordham on hand to play a proper solo, his choice to go it alone reflected both arrogance and a growing dissatisfaction with the easy comforts of "pro" musicianship. It foreshadowed *Diamond Dogs*, where he'd offer similarly abrasive results on lead guitar.

Where Have All the Good Times Gone?

(Davies). ***Recorded:*** *9-31 July 1973, Château d'Hérouville. Bowie: lead vocal, tenor saxophone; Ronson: lead and rhythm guitar, backing vocal; Garson: piano; Bolder: bass; Dunbar: drums; MacCormack: backing vocal. Produced: Scott, Bowie; engineered: MacKay.*

***First release:** 19 October 1973, **Pin Ups**.*

"Where Have All the Good Times Gone," the B-side of the Kinks' "Till the End of the Day," reflected a growing melancholy in Ray Davies' writing. In Davies' earlier songs the future held promise, if a provisional one ("Something Better Beginning"), while the present was full of pleasures ("All Day and All of the Night"). "See My Friends," a piece of psychedelic alienation from the summer of 1965, was an early sign that things were going wrong. "Where Have All the Good Times Gone" was the first Davies composition to sound his major theme for the rest of the decade: "ordinary" English people lost in a world they no longer understood. A kid meets sadness for the first time in his life, which turns him inward to mourn a youth he'd discarded the day before; it's enough to make him empathize with his parents.

"Where Have All the Good Times Gone" also doubled as a commentary on the Kinks' current state (broke, feuding and blacklisted) and on the 1965 British pop scene, which had gone from the Liverpool docks to the Hollywood Bowl and was sifting winners from losers, with Davies predicting he was headed for the latter pile. He sent up the song that symbolized this divide, the Beatles' precious, world-weary "Yesterday." "Let it be like *yesterday,"* Davies groaned in the second verse, with a feint to A minor, while the start of his concluding verse was taken nearly word-for-word from Paul McCartney. (The Stones also got a nod with "time was on my side.")

While he could have picked a Kinks barn-burner for Mick Ronson, Bowie chose wisely here, sequencing "Where Have All the Good Times Gone" as an album and an era closer, eulogizing Bowie's Mod London as well as the fast-decaying glam scene. Its lyric was the only one reprinted on the LP sleeve to emphasize the point. Ronson imported Dave Davies' sliding G-F guitar lick from the Kinks' "Tired of Waiting for You," undergirded by Trevor Bolder's bass. A low-mixed saxophone offered a threadbare countermelody in the refrains, Mike Garson piano fills wink in the left channel and a dynamic Aynsley Dunbar gave presence and depth to a song whose original recording was ramshackle even by Kinks standards.

Friday On My Mind

(Young/Vanda). ***Recorded:*** *9-31 July 1973, Château d'Hérouville. Bowie: lead and backing vocal, baritone saxophone?; Ronson: lead and rhythm guitars; Fordham: baritone saxophone;; Bolder: bass; Dunbar: drums; MacCormack: backing vocal. Produced: Scott, Bowie; engineered: MacKay.*

First release: *19 October 1973,* ***Pin Ups****.*

The Easybeats' "Friday On My Mind," a UK #6 from late 1966, was one of the last triumphs of Bowie's former producer Shel Talmy. A 2:45 teenage manifesto and one of a string of tough working-class pop songs in the mid-Sixties, "Friday On My Mind" was loaded with hooks—the band singing guitar fills, the bassline as a factory clock—that swept out the dreariness of the working week (the E minor verses) for the liberation of the weekend (the A major chorus).

The nadir of *Pin Ups*, Bowie's take was similar to his goof-job on "Everything's Alright" but more crass: his and Geoff MacCormack's harmony vocals are dirty scribbles in the margins. The Easybeats' Stevie Wright had bounded from resentment to comedy, steadily building to the elation of the refrains. His was a generous, winning performance (the way he sing "my girl, she's so pretty!" as if he's pointing her out to the world). Bowie played cartoons: a squicked-out "BUGS ME"; gasping attempts to hit a high E; a gargled-up Anthony Newley impression; the zeppelin-crash of his "toniiiiiiights" in the refrains. You could say this was a snotty little brother's response to a teenage dream song, a scrawl in his brother's love letters: yet another revenge plot by the Young Dudes.

Where the Easybeats' Harry Vanda sounded as if he was

plucking ship's cables in the intro, a checked-out Ronson nagged at his guitar strings. The only remotely interesting piece of the arrangement was using baritone saxophones as chaperones in the second refrain, while Trevor Bolder earned acquittal with some epileptic bass fills.

Sorrow

(Feldman/ Goldstein/Gottehrer). ***Recorded:*** *9-31 July 1973, Château d'Hérouville. Bowie: lead and backing vocal, 12-string acoustic guitar, tenor saxophone; Ronson: lead guitar, backing vocal; Garson: piano; Bolder: bass; Dunbar: drums; MacCormack: backing vocal; Fordham: baritone saxophone; unknown musicians: violins, violas, celli (arr. Ronson). Produced: Scott, Bowie; engineered: MacKay.*

First release: *12 October 1973, RCA 2424 (UK #3).* ***Broadcast:*** *20 October 1973, The 1980 Floor Show.* ***Live:*** *1974, 1983.*

Weeks before Bowie recorded *Pin Ups* in France, Bryan Ferry cut a covers album in London. This was Ferry's first solo record, made as his band Roxy Music was entering a less anarchic second edition without Brian Eno. Learning that Bowie was doing his own covers album, Ferry grew agitated, reportedly calling *Pin Ups* "a rip-off," a charge with some heft, given that Bowie would steal the look of Roxy Music's saxophonist Andy Mackay for the album sleeve. Though Ferry allegedly considered having his label file an injunction to prevent *Pin Ups* from being issued before his record, the reality was more polite. After some negotiations between managers, Bowie called Ferry, allegedly to ask permission to record a Roxy Music song but also to drop the news about *Pin Ups*. "He'd heard that I was doing this thing and that he was going to do something similar," Ferry told David Buckley. Ferry had to admire what Mick Rock called Bowie's "marvelous street instinct." "There doesn't seem to be any great self-doubt there," Ferry said. "Whereas I'm always riddled with doubts and self-criticism and God-knows-what."

Ferry needn't have worried. *These Foolish Things* is what *Pin*

Ups could have been: bolder in ambition and scope (Ferry took on the heavyweights: Elvis, Bob Dylan, Smokey Robinson, the Beatles and the Rolling Stones), its arrangements fresher, its execution more consistent. Ferry considered his covers as Dadaist "readymades," interpreting each song in a glam rococo style, singing in what Greil Marcus called his "Dracula-has-risen-from-the-grave voice" and backed by a female chorus seemingly recruited from an Andy Williams session. It wasn't cheap parody. Ferry strove to keep each song's dignity intact within its new casing (his "It's My Party" is *tragic*). Where Bowie stuck with the point of view of the macho teenage Mod, Ferry was catholic in tone, singing from female and male perspectives, elevating "trashy" songs and lowering "serious" ones. He made "Sympathy for the Devil" a Vegas revue number and sang "A Hard Rain's a-Gonna Fall" at a gallop, filling it with "grand camp gestures that the song just had to lie down and take," as Robert Forster wrote, and left the Dylan original in flames. Ferry closed the record with its title song, a straight cover of Maschwitz/Strachey's standard. It was the legend to his map: a song of how the ephemeral contains the eternal.

The *Pin Ups* track most worthy of *These Foolish Things*, and the only enduring piece of music from its sessions, was Bowie's version of "Sorrow." Like "I Wish You Would," it was a second-generation interpretation (Bowie covering the Merseys' take on the McCoys' original), a Romantic revision of a grungy teenage blues.

Written in 1965 by Richard Gottehrer, Bob Feldman and Jerry Goldstein, "Sorrow" was the B-side of "Fever," a single from the McCoys, an Indiana garage band led by Rick Derringer. It wasn't much of a song, a clichéd lyric over three chords that Derringer sang sheepishly, swallowing "sorrow" like a pill. Tony Crane and Billy Kinsley, as the Merseys, transformed the song when covering it the following year. Opening the track with a bowed bass, the Merseys met insistence— jangling guitar and piano—

with a hollowed-out longing. Crane and Kinsley, singing close harmonies, let the last syllable of "sorrow" hang in the air and circled obsessively over two phrases, the title line and "your long blonde hair." The Merseys' "Sorrow" hit #4 in Britain and was treasured by the likes of George Harrison, who quoted its opening lines in his "It's All Too Much."

Mick Ronson's arrangement for Bowie's "Sorrow" took the choicest bits of the Merseys' and subtly improved them. He made the Merseys' bowed bass a solitary violin, in line with how the opening verse was just Bowie, his 12-string acoustic guitar (its only appearance on the album) and Mike Garson's processed piano. The Merseys' half-bar-delayed harmony vocals became a hall of Bowie mirrors. Their piping trumpets and trombones became a ruminative saxophone break: a baritone harmonic base and a tenor melodic line. Ronson's scoring for strings rivaled his work on *Hunky Dory*, from the long-held high notes in the ultimate verse (matching Bowie's gorgeous leap of an octave) to the waltz patterns that sweep through the last refrain. As a last pip, Bowie's "Sorrow" had a thirty-second F major outro, where Garson on electric piano worked on a new melody until the fade consigns him to silence. It paralleled how Bowie had moved the lyric to the past tense—the disaster's over and he's left trying to pick up the pieces.

Shapes of Things

(Samwell-Smith/McCarty/Relf). ***Recorded:*** *9-31 July 1973, Château d'Hérouville. Bowie: lead vocal, tenor and alto saxophone, Moog; Ronson: lead and rhythm guitars; Bolder: bass; Dunbar: drums; MacCormack: backing vocal; unknown musicians (Ripoche?): violins, violas (arranged: Ronson). Produced: Scott, Bowie; engineered: MacKay.*

First release*: 19 October 1973,* ***Pin Ups****.*

Cut in Chicago at the end of 1965 as a response to the Who's "Anyway Anyhow Anywhere," the Yardbirds' "Shapes of

Things" was a piece of sonic adventurism built in stages: a bassline that Paul Samwell-Smith took from Dave Brubeck's "Pick Up Sticks"; a chord structure of shifts between G major and F major (resolving on a D chord); a top melody and lyric that Keith Relf scratched out overnight. Told to do whatever he wanted for the 16-bar rave-up, Jeff Beck mainly kept on the G string of his 1954 Fender Esquire, whose tone was cloaked by his homemade fuzzbox, and played an Indian-inspired line that sounded like a distorted violin. Beck closed out the song with staggered bursts of feedback, providing instructions that Mick Ronson would later follow in "John, I'm Only Dancing."

One of the first heavy-metal records, "Shapes of Things" essentially created the atmosphere in which *Ziggy Stardust* and *Aladdin Sane* breathed. Ronson's playing is inconceivable without it. So Bowie, never one for reverence, paid his respects by singing it like an East End drag queen, reminiscent of his piss-take on high Sixties pop in "I'm Not Losing Sleep." Subverting the original's melodic flow and pace, Bowie gave grandiose lines even more grandiose pronunciations ("PAH-sing haaands!" "Heeeeeeeyuhhh! with-in-my lone-luh FRAYME") and bizarre emphases ("MY eyes!"), with phased backing vocals that swarmed around him in the refrains. Meanwhile a stepwise ascending violin line in the first verse devolved into eerie bitonality by the last; a Moog generated square waves in the intro, then impersonated a flute in the din of backwards-mixed saxophones and guitars in the refrains. Ronson's take on Beck's guitar solo was assured mastery in place of further invention, with his harmonized pair of guitar tracks slowly falling out of sync. The *ritardando* feedback-bloodied outro sounded as if Ronson meant to kill off the Sixties for good.

See Emily Play

(Barrett). ***Recorded:*** *9-31 July 1973, Château d'Hérouville. Bowie: lead and backing vocal, Moog; Ronson: lead guitar, backing vocal; Garson:*

organ, piano, harpsichord; Bolder: bass; Dunbar: drums; unknown musicians: violins, violas, celli, double basses (arranged: Ronson). Produced: Scott, Bowie; engineered: MacKay.

***First release**: 19 October 1973, **Pin Ups**.*

Syd Barrett's masterpiece "See Emily Play" was among the last songs he wrote for Pink Floyd. Its Emily was a lost girl, a modern *Alice in Wonderland*; its setting, like the Beatles' near-synchronous "Strawberry Fields Forever," came from a childhood playground—a copse near Cambridge where Barrett and Roger Waters once had rambled. Its refrain was an eerie nursery rhyme and its arrangement was a nursery's worth of clatter, from Richard Wright's sped-up ragtime piano to Barrett's "Hawaiian" guitar.

Indulging in LSD had frayed Barrett's already fragile mind (David Gilmour, his soon-to-be replacement, visited Abbey Road Studios during the single's recording and was unnerved by Barrett's glass-eyed stare), although Barrett's departure from Pink Floyd was as much owed to him losing a battle for creative control with Waters as it was due to any nervous breakdown. The song's muse, the sculptor Emily Young, had a perspicacious view of it: that Barrett had used his idea of her, a psychedelic schoolgirl lost in the woods, "as a vision of his own delicate, "feminine" creativity." "See Emily Play" is full of portents, with the end of its last verse ("float on a river, forever and ever") suggesting a collapse of the ego, of someone relinquishing their claim on reality and wandering where they would. "Even then [Barrett] knew he was in danger," Young said. "["See Emily Play"] was a warning to himself, which he could not heed."

Bowie had spent the turn of the Seventies writing similar warnings to himself. He saw in Barrett a creative predecessor whose trail, had he followed it, could have led to Cane Hill Asylum. His "See Emily Play" was the odd woman out among the *Pin Ups* set. It's the only single from the utopian year of 1967 and the only true psychedelic song (it's a shame Bowie didn't record a new version of his "The London Boys," as he originally intended: it would have been a fitting bookend). While singing the verses plainly, even languidly, Bowie in the refrain was overtaken by a choir of ghouls (see "The Laughing Gnome" or "The Bewlay Brothers"): his and Mick Ronson's vocals varisped to lurk an octave beneath his lead vocal. It was Barrett's symbolic fate in cartoon form.

Ronson's playing offered another Barrett tribute, his lines suggesting the descending surf-guitar riff of "Lucifer Sam" and the chording of "Astronomy Domine." Bowie used an ARP synthesizer in place of Pink Floyd's analog trickery, Mike Garson alternated between cracked-sounding harpsichord and rock 'n' roll piano while Aynsley Dunbar played rolling sets of snare fills.

Bowie's "See Emily Play" closed with Garson and Ronson offering a potted history of Western music in fragments. Garson played a touch of Mozart's *Magic Flute* overture (3:25) and resurrected the old Bowie favorite, "Also Sprach Zarathustra" (see "The Supermen"). Ronson's string arrangement set history in reverse, opening with shivery atonal progressions in vague tribute to Arnold Schoenberg and closing with a quote from Bach's Partita No. 3 in E. The track faded on soaring, harmonious strings, suggesting that the singer's madness has abated for the moment or, conversely, that he's now stranded in a dream, floating forever. The demonic voices bleeding into the final verse, as though eating away at the song, suggested the latter.

Zion

Recorded: *(unreleased) ca. 18-24 January 1973, Trident?; 9-31 July 1973, Château d'Hérouville? Bowie: guide vocal, piano? Mellotron?; Ronson: lead guitar, Mellotron?; Garson: piano; Bolder: bass?; Dunbar: drums? percussion?; Woodmansey: drums? Produced: Scott, Bowie?; engineered: Scott?*

A black hole of Bowie songs, lacking even a confirmed title, this six-minute unreleased track is known most commonly as

"Zion" though various bootleggers have christened it "A Lad in Vein," "Love Aladdin Vein" and "Aladdin Vein." In his only public reference to the piece, Bowie said it was part of a musical he was developing called *Tragic Moments*.

Mick Ronson and Mike Garson were almost certainly on it and if Trevor Bolder and Aynsley Dunbar are the rhythm section (it's a tough call: the propulsive drum fills in the guitar sections suggest Dunbar, the rigid insistence of the hi-hat in the "theme" sections argue for Woody Woodmansey), this establishes "Zion" as hailing from the *Pin Ups* sessions of July 1973. Further evidence comes from the journalist Martin Hayman's visit to the Château d'Hérouville during the making of *Pin Ups*, where Bowie played Hayman a demo of "perhaps seven minutes of…highly arranged, subtly shifting music with just a touch of vaudeville," with "no vocals on it yet, just my la-la-la-ing." Bowie said the demo was part of "the next project...something I've always wanted to do…I envisage a scenario first, then the music."

The other contending theory has "Zion" being recorded in the *Aladdin Sane* sessions of January 1973 (the reliable Kevin Cann backs this claim), with a main piece of evidence here Charles Shaar Murray's April 1973 *NME* review of *Aladdin Sane*, which mentioned the track having been included in an early sequencing: "a then-incomplete track called 'Zion' has been replaced by 'Lady Grinning Soul'." If so, it's likely the *Pin Ups* sessions were used for further overdubs. Regardless of where "Zion" began, it no doubt was intended for one of number of musical theatre concepts Bowie plotted throughout 1973.

The surviving bootleg recording is Bowie sketching top melodies over a series of piano/guitar figures (the circulating version isn't a studio jam: it has multiple overdubs and appears to have been mixed). There's a 16-bar "theme" carried first by piano, then Mellotron (the latter section similar to the incidental music of the Beatles' *Magical Mystery Tour* film); a ferocious guitar solo section over which Bowie scats a wide-spanning melody, peaking at the high end of his range; and a section with Bowie scatting what may have been intended as a saxophone part, first over a thunking bass and drumline, then over jaunty Garson piano.

While the bootlegged track is an intriguing musical sketchbook, it lacked any development. Instead Bowie repeated each section, with little variation. At an apparent loss for where to go with "Zion," Bowie chopped it up and scattered a few pieces into *Diamond Dogs*, where he used the Mellotron/piano theme in the segue of "Sweet Thing (Reprise)" into "Rebel Rebel."

Growing Up and I'm Fine
Music Is Lethal
Hey Ma Get Papa

(Ronson/Bowie ("Hey Ma Get Papa"), Battisti/Bowie ("Music Is Lethal")). ***Recorded:*** *4 September-4 October 1973, Château d'Hérouville. Ronson: lead and backing vocal, lead and rhythm guitar, acoustic guitar, piano; Garson: piano; Bolder: bass; Dunbar: drums, percussion; David Hentschel: ARP synthesizer ("Hey Ma"); Margaret Ronson, Dennis MacKay: backing vocals; Sid Sax, unknown musicians: strings. Produced, arranged: Ronson; engineered: MacKay.*

First release*: 1 March 1974,* ***Slaughter on 10th Avenue*** *(RCA APL1-0353, UK #9).* ***Live****: 1974 (Ronson, all songs).*

The creative partnership of David Bowie and Mick Ronson, which in three years had produced *The Man Who Sold the World, Hunky Dory, All the Young Dudes, Transformer, Ziggy Stardust* and *Aladdin Sane,* withered and died in the last months of 1973. There's no definitive reason why it happened. "It was very much left up in the air when we split, because I didn't really know what I was going to do," Bowie recalled in 1997.

There were a number of pressures, one of which was Ronson's growing prominence in the MainMan organization. Regarded as

Bowie's rock & roll straight man, in various senses, Ronson was receiving as much fan mail, and getting nearly as much press attention, as Bowie. Tony Defries was grooming him as a solo act to fatten MainMan's thin roster of artists and as insurance against Bowie becoming a commercial has-been (T. Rex singles had started missing the Top 10 in late 1973). Defries cast Ronson in a role for which he was profoundly unsuited: a teen idol guitar hero, with bare-chested promotional pictures, gooey *Teen Beat*-esque confessions in press releases and his face plastered on billboards in LA and Times Square. (Bowie, aware of Defries' plans, slyly introduced Ronson as "Suzi Quatro" in some of the last Spiders shows).

The autumn and winter of 1973 found Bowie enisled in various studios, sketching and recording and scrapping half-formed ideas. Ronson's lead guitar and string arrangements had become so definitive to his sound that Bowie came to regard Ronson as a hindrance. By September 1973, Bowie was downplaying Ronson, calling him "a great technician...[who] knows how to relay message[s] to the other technicians." Decades later, Bowie said Ronson would've been happier playing second guitar with Jeff Beck and that "I just gave up trying to get him to come out and see other bands or listen to interesting musics...If he didn't know the person, he didn't bother to listen...You'd mention something new and his pet phrase was 'don't need to.'" Bowie said this in 1997, a time he was attempting drum 'n' bass and talking up his affiliation with avant-garde painters, so his claims of showing up with something "new by John Cage or Stockhausen or whoever" to be met by Ronson's Philistine indifference are likely colored by the time of their recollection. That said, it's easy to imagine a glum Ronson in Philadelphia cutting *Young Americans* and wondering what the hell Bowie was doing.

For Ronson, he simply wanted to be in a top-rate working band. "I don't want a band that's going to be together for a short time," he said in 1973. As Bowie had dismembered a perfectly good one, Ronson saw his solo album as a way to form a Spiders from Mars II, with Trevor Bolder, Mike Garson, Scott Richardson and Aynsley Dunbar. It didn't happen: Defries lured Richardson away with the (false) promise of a solo career and Bowie wanted Garson on tour with him. Ronson's own UK tour in spring 1974 was a flop, his under-rehearsed band and shaky vocals earning him scathing critical notices. Plans for an American tour were scrapped. "They spent a lot of money on him," Ian Hunter recalled. "They put Mick out there, but Mick wasn't a front man...He couldn't do it. He got too flummoxed."

The tour was in support of Ronson's *Slaughter on 10th Avenue,* cut in September 1973 after a few weeks off from the *Pin Ups* sessions, with Ronson using the same studio and players as on Bowie's album. Bowie agreed to write some new songs and visited the Château d'Hérouville midway through the sessions to work them out with Ronson. Yet where he'd once given away "Oh! You Pretty Things" and "All the Young Dudes," his contributions now were a cut below his typical work.

"Music is Lethal" marked his return to translation (see "Pancho" or "Even a Fool Learns to Love"), with Bowie providing English lyrics for Lucio Battisti and Mogol's 1972 "Io vorrei...non vorrei...ma se vuoi." His translation, though it barely merited the name, was intended to fit the album's loose concept, which Ronson gamely described to the *NME*: "The story's about a guy in the 1980s. He's a layabout...just sort of bums around the streets. He sees this chick and falls in love with her. She's a dancer in a nightclub and a prostitute as well. She falls in love with him in the end and wants to quit and go with him. But her pimp boyfriend finds out. She comes out of this club one night and he shoots her. And I'm left alone without her."

So Bowie merged Jacques Brel's Amsterdam waterfront with images from his own developing Hunger City, having Ronson wander through a cityscape of "mulatto hookers, cocaine bookers, troubled husbands." Given that Ronson already had to strain at the top of his vocal range to hit some of Battisti's notes, it was an act of cruelty to saddle him with lines like "two wet lips of infant leisure," "the long metal dirge" and "your smooth pimp, Piranha, cradles my swimming head," especially as Mogol's original lines, mainly just two or three syllables, had been smoothly crafted to fit Battisti's phrases. To make amends, Ronson kept much of Battisti's arrangement, from the circling string figures in the refrain to the ringing guitar postlude.

The more intriguing "Hey Ma Get Papa" is the unique case of Ronson's music in support of a Bowie lyric, a throwback to his Sixties grotesques: street toughs like "Pigsty Paul" lead Ronson astray and soon enough he's speared someone to death with a fencepost. The jittery verse melody and rhythms were under the spell of Todd Rundgren's bizarre "Zen Archer"; Ronson gave Queen pointers in the refrain; the garish specter of the Beatles' "Maxwell's Silver Hammer" hung over it all. Over a base of Garson's pounded piano chords, David Hentschel's synthesizer roams around pursued by Aynsley Dunbar's drums, while Ronson contributed silvery lead guitar.

While making his album, Ronson imagined a life in which he and his new band would support Bowie on tour and on albums and do solo work in the gaps. "I know that when David has something he wants me to help him with, then I'll adjust my schedule and he'll adjust his," Ronson told a reporter in October 1973. And Bowie was considering using Ronson as his lead guitarist for his *Diamond Dogs* tour. Ronson later claimed he turned Bowie down. Yet a fairly sharp break occurred by early 1974, sparked by Bowie's decision to dispense with Ronson on *Diamond Dogs* and the ignominy of Ronson's solo career, and worsened by Bowie's increased cocaine use and (correct, to be fair) paranoia about his place in the MainMan scheme. Ronson and Bowie soon were sniping at each other in the press and wouldn't speak again until the following decade.

Bowie's last contribution to *Slaughter on 10th Avenue* was his only solo credit on the album. Again vaguely in line with the "layabout falls in love with a prostitute" narrative, "Growing Up and I'm Fine" also referenced a Bruce Springsteen song that Bowie was covering at the time (see "Growin' Up"). A grab bag of recycled lyrics (the smashed slot machine of "Panic in Detroit" shows up again) and chord progressions, like the "Oh! You Pretty Things"/ "Changes" piano line in the chorus, "Growing Up and I'm Fine" wound up being the capstone of its era. It was Bowie's farewell to a man who, as Charlie Parker once said of Dizzy Gillespie, had been his worthy constituent.

Chapter 8

Tomorrow's Double Feature (1973-1974)

What you aspire to as revolutionaries is a master. You will get one.
Jacques Lacan, to students at Centre Universitaire Expérimental de Vincennes, 1969.

The situation in England strikes every month a decadent, yes decadent note. People say, why not get someone else to sort it all out for them...a strong man.
Alec Guinness, 1972.

When you have seen through [this] world you can never become its victim, but can fight it with the only unanswerable weapon—cynical despair.
Sonia Brownell.

Each day the towers of central London seemed slightly more distant, the landscape of an abandoned planet receding slowly from his mind.
J.G. Ballard, *High-Rise*.

When I'm just in my own mind, it's a dangerous neighborhood.
Bowie, 1996.

What the bloody hell are you doing, Bowie, all this mutant crap?
John Lennon, allegedly said while Bowie was working on a model of Hunger City, 1974.

I Got You Babe

(Bono). ***Recorded:*** *20 October 1973, Marquee Club, 90 Wardour Street, London. David Bowie: lead vocal; Marianne Faithfull: lead*

vocal; Mick Ronson: lead guitar; Mark Pritchett: rhythm guitar; Mike Garson: keyboards; Trevor Bolder: bass; Aynsley Dunbar: drums; Geoff MacCormack, Ava Cherry, Jason Guess: backing vocals. Produced: Ken Scott.

***Broadcast**: 20 October 1973, The 1980 Floor Show.*

From 1973 to 1977, David Bowie ran an inadvertent guerrilla war against television, particularly American television. In those years, he appeared on the most popular TV programs of the day and disrupted them. It's not that he meant to. He didn't act outrageously when he showed up on *Dinah!* or *Cher* or *Soul Train* or *The Dick Cavett Show*. If anything, he was gracious, polite, happy to flatter the host. But his emaciated coke-wraith appearance was disturbing merely as a visual, and whether he was sitting on a couch bantering or singing a medley of contemporary hits with Cher, Bowie came across as estranged, distracted, standing at a remove from humanity. He seemed like an extraterrestrial summoned by the cameras, someone who, in turn, had picked up English and facial expressions from watching television.

TV meant to reassure, to be the commons for millions. Bowie couldn't fit properly into its frame. He was tuned to a different key than everyone else on the screen, which made the "normal" TV celebrities jarring. He made Cher inexplicable, Dinah Shore a malevolent cartoon. He broke a basic contract of celebrity, in which the famous and beautiful live in a flat, bright world for our enjoyment, with their celebrity strengthened when they encounter one another on screen, like atoms fusing to form a molecule. Bowie was a celebrity who made no sense; he was a visitation. Television was relieved when he finally left it alone.

It ended with the pairing of Bowie and Bing Crosby for a Christmas special in 1977, the project having reached its limit of absurdity. It started in October 1973 with Bowie's *1980 Floor Show,* a televised stage revue filmed over three days at London's Marquee Club and aired the following month on NBC's *The Midnight Special*.

The *Floor Show* lacked the reserve of Bowie's later TV appearances. Its squalid lighting looked even worse on videotape. He'd chosen the Marquee as his set for nostalgic reasons, as it was the club he'd played the most in the Sixties, but then he had his set directors gut the club to install a new stage and backdrop (perfect symbolism for *Pin Ups*). The *Floor Show* was glam rock as avant-garde theater, a jumble of Bowie's past and future. He sang a muted "Space Oddity" and unveiled "1984"; Mick Ronson and Trevor Bolder were still there, along with the Astronettes, his new vocal trio. Bowie made the *Floor Show* a string of visual shocks, with his body as special effect. He went through a series of costumes designed by Freddi Burretti, including a fishnet body-stocking affixed with gold lamé hands to grip his torso and a Tristan Tzara-derived leotard whose front was an enormous keyhole. It was Ziggy Stardust (never mentioned by name) unraveling.

The closing number found Bowie in ostrich plumes and Marianne Faithfull in a backless nun's habit duetting on Sonny and Cher's "I Got You Babe." Faithfull's voice was ravaged by laryngitis and years of living rough while Bowie, who had what looked like Robert Rauschenberg's stuffed condor strapped to his chest, smirked with malice. Ronson hung back, looking as though he wanted to sneak off stage. Yet as the song rolled on, with Bowie and Faithfull swapping traditional gender roles (Faithfull as the troll-voiced "Sonny" to Bowie's diva "Cher"), they made it work, sounding the song's humble beauties. Crafted for an ill-matched couple, "I Got You Babe" can outlast anything: it's endured UB40 and Beavis and Butthead, it could survive a chemical war. As Dave Marsh wrote, the song boils down to "love redeems everything, no matter how ridiculous, moronic, or grotesque...[it's the] essence of what rock & roll brought to pop music that hadn't been there before…a willingness to reach for effects and worry about decorum later, an understanding of where to find the sublime amidst the trivial." On the Marquee stage, Bowie and Faithfull honored this mandate, crafting a touching performance from outlandish materials.

Growin' Up

(Springsteen). ***Recorded:*** *ca. November-December 1973, Olympic and/or Island Studios, London. Bowie: lead vocal, rhythm guitar?; Ron Wood: lead guitar; Pritchett: rhythm guitar?; Garson: piano; Herbie Flowers: bass; Dunbar: drums; MacCormack: backing vocals, cowbell?. Produced: Bowie; engineered: Keith Harwood?*

First release*: 13 July 1990,* ***Pin Ups*** *(RCD 10136/ CDEMC 3580).*

Freshly arrived in New York to prepare his 1973 US tour, Bowie went to Max's Kansas City on 5 February to catch his favorite oddball Biff Rose. The opening act was a young New Jersey musician who "came on and did this Bob Dylan thing. It was awful, so cringe-making," Bowie recalled in 1987. "He'd sit there with his guitar and be folky, have these slow philosophical raps in between the songs." He was about to leave when Bruce Springsteen stood up, strapped on a Fender Telecaster, brought on a full band and ripped into "Does This Bus Stop at 82nd St.?" It was a revelation. "[He] was like a different performer and he was just marvelous." A few days later, *Greetings From Asbury Park, N.J.* was on Bowie's turntable.

Springsteen's sudden transformation from glum folkie to rock 'n' roll barnstormer rang a sympathetic bell with Bowie. He'd found a kindred spirit, a fellow self-mythologist whose instincts were theatrical. Both Bowie and Springsteen had knocked around the professional music scene for years with little success, both finally had found their niche by becoming "cosmic kids in full costume dress," even if Springsteen's was denim and leather. Both were labeled magpies and imitators by critics, both would age into curators and revivalists. Later in 1973, still besotted by Springsteen, Bowie recorded two songs from *Asbury Park* and had his Astronettes vocal trio cover "Spirit In the Night."

Although his songs were being pushed in Britain by the

publisher Adrian Rudge, Springsteen remained an obscurity. Bowie could add him to his menagerie of American eccentrics with Rose, the Legendary Stardust Cowboy and Ken Nordine, and as with the Velvet Underground, Bowie would be one of the first British artists to cover Springsteen. His takes could possibly be the songs' definitive versions (as Manfred Mann would do with "Blinded by the Light"). But he released none of his Springsteen covers at the time, suggesting that Springsteen was a harder nut to crack than Bowie first considered.

With Ron Wood contributing tasteful lead guitar lines, Bowie cut Springsteen's "Growin' Up" in one of the provisional sessions for *Diamond Dogs*. A piece of American blue-collar exotica in C major, "Growin' Up" was goofball adolescent testimony: half *Mad* magazine feature, half misheard Dylan lyric. Bowie worked his way into the song by moving it up in key and exploring the high end of his range, sometimes singing an octave above Springsteen's original vocal. Mike Garson twisted David Sancious' rapid-fire four-note piano hook into a subtler three-note figure while Aynsley Dunbar was a steadier presence than Springsteen's then-drummer Vinnie Lopez. Though he mustered a decent American approximation for his vocal (until he squawked "she couldn't SAYL" in the second verse), Bowie grew winded by Springsteen's elongated, word-packed phrases, sounding deflated in the last verse.

It's Hard To Be a Saint In the City

*(Springsteen). **Recorded**: ca. November-December 1973, Olympic and/or Trident?; (remake?) 20-24 November 1974, Sigma Sound Studios, Philadelphia. Bowie: lead vocal, 12-string acoustic guitar, lead guitar? rhythm guitar?; Pritchett: lead guitar?; Earl Slick: lead guitar?; Garson: piano; Flowers?: bass; Dunbar?, Tony Newman?: drums; strings: arr. Tony Visconti. Produced: Bowie.*

***First release**: 19 September 1989, **Sound + Vision**.*

Bowie's "teeth-grinding coke mix" (Tony Visconti) of Bruce

Springsteen's "It's Hard To Be a Saint In the City," embossed with a Visconti string arrangement and cooked by digital delay processors and flangers, foreshadowed what Springsteen would do on his *Born to Run* in 1975: broaden his sonic palette to get at the "teenage symphonic" feel of Phil Spector records, to craft what the radical John Sinclair sneeringly called "tales of a mythic urban grease scene."

The swanning "It's Hard To Be a Saint" was a better vehicle for Bowie than Springsteen's "Growin' Up." He used it to survey and extend the borders of his vocal range, taking the verses in his lowest register, moving up for "don't that man look pretty" and repeatedly attempting a thin falsetto in the last chorus. Discarding the bar-band-tuning-up intro of Springsteen's *Asbury Park* version, Bowie kicked off "It's Hard to Be a Saint" with a volley of guitar and drums. Where Springsteen would sheepishly hold back, grinning and slurring his lines over his acoustic guitar and retreating to piano accompaniment in refrains, Bowie gave each line a dramatic reading—see how he gives a precise weight to each swaggered word of "walk like Brando into the sun." He twisted "boy out on the street" into "BO-WIE"; in the bridge, which Springsteen had kept as a quiet epiphany, Bowie whipped his drummer and his string players ahead of him. Bowie's last line, where he ditched the Americanisms to sing in a sneering toff accent and ended with an outrageously sibilated "CITY," was like the moment when a drag queen smears her makeup to end a performance (he'd act this out a few years later on his "Boys Keep Swinging" video).

Bowie finally met Springsteen when the latter came to Sigma Sound on 25 November 1974 during one of the last *Young Americans* sessions. Philadelphia DJ Ed Sciaky brought him along at the request of Visconti, who thought Springsteen would like to hear Bowie's cover of "It's Hard To Be a Saint" and possibly contribute to it. Springsteen at the time was committed to living out his myths. He hitched a ride to Asbury Park, took a Trailways bus to Philadelphia and, upon arriving, hung out with bums in the station until he was picked up. Bowie arrived at the studio an hour after Springsteen. The latter was reserved, while Bowie said years later that he'd been so cracked up on cocaine and worn out by his work routines that it was difficult to relate to anyone. "What do I say to normal people?"he recalled. "There was a real impasse."

Still, the two found common ground by complaining about stage jumpers. Bowie considered cutting a vocal but determined it wasn't late enough yet. He drifted in and out of conversations, perking up when the talk turned to UFOs. Springsteen left at 5 AM. Bowie never played him his version of "It's Hard to Be a Saint," reportedly because he was still uncertain about the track ("I remember chickening out").

Bowie was a Springsteen fan for a while longer (he attended the first of Springsteen's shows at the Roxy Theatre in Los Angeles in October 1975) but he sat on "It's Hard To Be a Saint" for too long. Had he included the track on *Young Americans*, his interpretation could have been definitive, a star's tip of the hat to a cult artist, like the Eagles covering Tom Waits on *On the Border*. Once Springsteen became a household name with *Born to Run*, releasing "It's Hard to Be a Saint" would be seen as Bowie taking on a young heavyweight. So he shelved one of the better covers he ever recorded, finally releasing it in 1989.

Having a Good Time
Things To Do
I Am Divine
People From Bad Homes
I Am a Laser

Recorded:** ca. 26 December 1973-15 January 1974, Olympic. Cherry: lead vocal ("Laser," "People"), harmony vocals; MacCormack: lead vocal ("Divine," "Good Time"), harmony vocals, congas; Guess: lead vocal ("Good Time"), harmony vocals; Bowie: backing vocals?,* *saxophone, ARP?; Mark Pritchett: guitar; Garson: piano, organ, electric piano; Flowers: bass; Dunbar: drums, percussion; unknown musicians: strings ("Divine," arr. Luis Ramirez? Visconti?). Produced: Bowie; engineered: Harwood;* ***("Laser" remake, unreleased) *13-14 August 1974, Sigma Sound Studios, 212 N. 12th Street, Philadelphia. Bowie: lead vocal; Carlos Alomar: rhythm guitar; Garson: piano; David Sanborn: alto saxophone; Willie Weeks: bass; Andy Newmark: drums. Produced: Visconti.*

First release: *16 May 1995,* ***People From Bad Homes*** *(GY 005).*

Bowie spent the last months of 1973 shuttling between London studios, cutting demos and picking at songs with a grab-bag collection of musicians. At the same time he was trying to get a "soul" vocal trio off the ground, writing and producing tracks for them. This was the Astronettes: his girlfriend Ava Cherry, his school friend Geoff MacCormack (aka "Warren Peace") and the unaffiliated singer Jason Guess.

After a month's sessions at Olympic Studios (it was a sign of his and MainMan's profligacy that they used a top London studio as rehearsal space for an unsigned act), Bowie abandoned the project, though he'd incorporate Cherry and MacCormack as backing singers on tour. In January 1974, his own interests—finishing his album and planning his American tour—took precedence, and it was also obvious that the Astronettes material wasn't up to snuff. Had he developed the Astronettes on the road as his opening act and then gone back into the studio with them, the group might have worked. Instead, true to habit, he was content to recycle some oddments from the sessions, rewriting a few Astronettes compositions for later albums. That said, the Astronettes tracks, cut with Mark Pritchett on lead guitar, Bowie on saxophone, Mike Garson on keyboards and a rhythm section of Herbie Flowers and Aynsley Dunbar, were essential sketchwork: he couldn't have made *Young Americans* without these false starts.

Bowie started by running the Astronettes through a few picks from his record collection. Cherry took the lead on Annette Peacock's "Seven Days" (from Peacock's 1972 *I'm the One*) and gave a gorgeous torch song delivery to the Beach Boys' "God Only Knows," graced with mandolins and one of Bowie's livelier saxophone solos. (In tempo and phrasing, Cherry's version was the blueprint for Bowie's lugubrious "God Only Knows" in 1984.) MacCormack offered an am-dram version of Bruce Springsteen's "Spirit In the Night" while Guess bungled through Frank Zappa's "How Could I Be Such a Fool," a doo-wop pastiche from 1966's *Freak Out*. Roy Harper's "Highway Blues" (from his 1973 *Lifemask*) was a strained group effort, and a compassionate engineer would have wiped Cherry and MacCormack's sub-Manhattan Transfer "I'm In the Mood For Love," complete with Garson elaborately farting on synthesizer.

The Astronettes had two rough but compelling lead singers in MacCormack and Cherry and a barely passable harmonizer in Guess. Unable to gel, they made do with parceling out verse lines and hollering over each other in refrains, a situation worsened by Bowie's penchant to write complex vocal pieces for them. MacCormack and Guess managed the canonical harmonies of "Having a Good Time" but "Things To Do" was blighted by off-key singing, with Cherry sharp in the refrains. The latter track was more of interest for being Bowie's first recorded attempt at Latin music, on which he was gorging at the time (he played his collection of Latin records to fellow passengers on a voyage from Hawaii to Japan earlier in 1973). Under the influence of Santana and particularly the Nuyorican bandleader Joe Cuba, "Things To Do" was propelled by MacCormack on congas and Garson offering a playbook salsa montuno. It was also the first mention of God in a Bowie lyric, even quoting the Edwin Hawkins Singers' "Oh Happy Day" and the 23rd Psalm (see "Word On a Wing").

Garson held together Bowie's "People From Bad Homes," whose opening hook is a dog whistle synthesizer. He swung from electric piano in the Cherry-sung verses to grand piano in the group-sung refrains. The track's competing rhythms—MacCormack's flourishes on congas, Bowie's saxophone honking its way in, a tambourine sparking the choruses and Dunbar as flexible bedrock—were as dense as Bowie's vaguely sociopolitical lyric was incoherent. Its title outlived the song, turning up in "Fashion."

More promising was "I Am Divine," with a robust MacCormack lead vocal (he sounds like Chicago's Robert Lamm) enlivened by Cherry's harmonies, in service of a piece of insider braggadocio: "I'm MainMan in my city/Hey Jim (Osterberg?) I'm in control!" With a string arrangement (pizzicato in the opening verses, Philly Soul sweeps in the refrains), scratchy guitar patter by Mark Pritchett and an off-kilter Garson piano solo that trundles through the coda, all "I Am Divine" lacked was smooth transitions between its chatty verses and soaring refrains, something Bowie easily could've rectified. Instead he turned "I Am Divine" into "Somebody Up There Likes Me" (see Ch. 9), retaining from the former some of its chord structure and Cherry's "so divine" vocal tag.

Nothing embodied the potential and the limits of the Astronettes more than "I Am a Laser," a track paced by a Dunbar performance that's a vivid argument between his toms and hi-hat and Pritchett's chicken-scratch guitar. It also has Cherry's finest vocal of the sessions, in which she somehow manages to find dignity and charisma in one of the worst excuses for a lyric Bowie ever wrote. "All your friends can *see* him roasting like a tur*key*," she sings, standing over some conquered DJ. Later she promises you'll "feel my golden shower" and that "they say I'm the black Barbarella."

It would have the most tantalizing afterlife of all. On one of the first nights recording at Philadelphia's Sigma Sound in August 1974, Bowie unveiled a complete revision of the song. "You set a tempo," he told his drummer Andy Newmark as the tape rolled. Newmark, Garson and bassist Willie Weeks play a rollicking New Orleans groove worthy of Professor Longhair, letting Bowie ease into the song. "Let's hear it for the *gouster*," he begins, edging up to and slightly inflating the last word. "Baggy pants and a *watch chain*." Other verses have gun molls ("razor blades in her bra"), old beatniks ("clicking chick-a-boo Lenny Bruce") and gouster fashion choices ("dogtooth or *paisley*?/processed or *straight*?"). Bowie laughs with delight after Garson's piano solo, claps on the off-beats as David Sanborn's alto saxophone responds. "Mirror mirror on the wall, sees all," he sings, working himself into a righteous fervor: "I...am...a...*LASER*! *BURNING* through your *EYES*!" It's a fantastic recording that Bowie shows no sign of ever releasing. All that survived was its mighty span of a chorus melody, which he reused for "Scream Like a Baby" half a decade later.

1984
Dodo

Recorded: ("1984," studio take, unreleased) *ca. mid-January 1973, Trident Studios. Bowie: lead vocal; Ronson: lead guitar; Garson: piano?; Bolder: bass; Woody Woodmansey: drums;* ***("1984/Dodo")*** *ca. early-mid October 1973, Trident. Bowie: lead vocal, baritone saxophone, tambourine?; Ronson: lead guitar; Pritchett: rhythm guitar; Bolder: bass; Dunbar: drums; Garson: piano, electric piano; MacCormack: backing vocals, congas; Cherry, Guess: backing vocals; unknown musicians: violins, violas, cellos (arranged: Visconti). Produced: Bowie, Scott;* ***("1984")*** *ca. late December 1973-mid-January 1974, Olympic and/or Island Studios. Bowie: lead vocal, rhythm guitar?; Alan Parker: lead guitar; Garson: electric piano, harpsichord; MacCormack: backing vocals; Flowers: bass; Dunbar or Newman: drums; unknown musicians: violins, violas, cellos (arranged: Visconti);* ***("Dodo")*** *ca. November 1973-January 1974, Trident and/or Olympic. Bowie: lead vocal, lead guitar, baritone saxophone; Garson: electric piano, piano; Flowers: bass; Newman or Dunbar: drums; unknown* *musicians: trumpets, trombones. Produced: Bowie; engineered: Harwood?*

***First release**: ("1984") 24 April 1974, **Diamond Dogs**; ("1984/Dodo") 19 September 1989, **Sound + Vision**; ("Dodo") 16 October 1990, **Diamond Dogs** (RCD 10137/ CDEMC 3584). **Broadcast**: ("1984/Dodo") 20 October 1973, The 1980 Floor Show; ("1984") 5 December 1974, The Dick Cavett Show. **Live**: ("1984") 1974.*

The album that became *Diamond Dogs* was a salvage job, a collection of pieces from a few stillborn Bowie projects, including a *Ziggy Stardust* musical ("Rebel Rebel," "Rock 'n' Roll With Me"), an *Oliver Twist*-via-William S. Burroughs scenario ("Diamond Dogs," "Future Legend") and his grandest failed ambition, making a musical of George Orwell's *Nineteen Eighty-Four*.

He'd considered the latter for some time, recording an early version of "1984" during the *Aladdin Sane* sessions. After Ziggy Stardust's retirement, the Orwell project, the most coherent option he had at the time, took on steam. In September 1973, the New York producer Tony Ingrassia came to London to co-write the adaptation, which was being mulled as a cross-Atlantic stage production, a movie (a documentary of a performance or possibly a stand-alone film) and a concept/soundtrack album. Bowie, though irritated by Ingrassia's work ethic (at one point he refused to get out of bed), drafted over a dozen songs for the project. He would play the lead role of Winston Smith, Marianne Faithfull was rumored for Julia while Wayne County and Geoff MacCormack were considered for supporting parts.

"It actually was a stone-cold version of *Nineteen Eighty-Four* as a musical," Bowie recalled in 1993. "And it was in fact the first time I was rejected by a literary figure." Orwell's widow and executor, Sonia Brownell Orwell, refused to grant MainMan permission to adapt the book. Bowie lambasted her in the press. "For a person who married a Socialist with Communist leanings, she was the biggest upper-class snob I've ever met in my life," he said in 1976, a characterization clouded by the fact that he'd never met her. Two decades later, Bowie was still griping about her veto. "In so many words, [she] said 'You've got to be out of your gourd. Do you think I'm turning *this* over to *that* as a musical?'"

Some other facts to consider here. Orwell systematically rejected all proposed adaptations and licensing of her late husband's work, not snobbily singling out a rock musician's theatrical conceit. She rejected biographers, documentarians and film producers in keeping with Orwell's wishes: he'd married her because he was dying of tuberculosis and wanted her, a crack editor and organizer, to annotate and safeguard his work (the estate had allowed a few film and TV adaptations of *Nineteen Eighty-Four* in the Fifties, which she'd come to regret). MainMan also bungled its end of the negotiation. Tony Defries and the MainMan staff were sloppy in their proposal, had no contacts in the circles that Orwell moved in and Defries tried to lowball her on licensing fees as if she was some two-bit concert promoter.

Her refusal was a blessing. Given his mayfly attention span, his boatload of commitments and his congenital dislike of writing concept albums, it's hard to imagine Bowie pulling off a professional musical in 1974; it easily could have been a disaster. As it turned out, all he'd needed were a few concepts that he'd appropriate from *Nineteen Eighty-Four* anyhow, without permission. Rather than having to shoehorn songs into some sort of narrative, he could use Orwell's book as a means to channel some fresh experiences.

In late April 1973, Bowie and Geoff MacCormack had taken the Trans-Siberian Express from Vladivostok to Moscow. While the trip was generally pleasant (Bowie spent his time playing acoustic guitar, drinking tea and seducing fellow travelers), there was a growing sense of oppression once the train entered the orbit of Moscow. Passengers grew reserved, even hostile. In the dining car a group of Russians were "staring at us in a way that made us think they were looking for an argument," Bowie said, with one man drawing his hand across his throat as they left the car. At Yekaterinburg station, a man in a trench coat and sunglasses demanded his and MacCormack's film. On a subsequent train from Moscow to Paris, a conductor in Poland tried to batter into their compartment, demanding Bowie show his papers.

Once safe back home, Bowie played up his Iron Curtain stories. Talking to the reporter Roy Hollingworth, he said he knew "who's controlling this damned world. And after what I've seen of the state of this world, I've never been so damned scared in my life." If he wrote about what he'd seen, "it would be my last album ever," he said, darkly intimating he'd be dispatched after recording it. He cultivated his paranoia, feasting on books about life in totalitarian societies. Stacking them in piles, he poured through the likes of Evgenia Ginzburg's *Journey Into the Whirlwind*, a memoir by a Russian Community Party member caught in the Stalinist purges, her life a Kafkaesque series of denunciations, interrogations, sham trials and Siberian exile.

By the end of 1973 Bowie was planning to leave Britain. It was supposed to be a short-term move for income tax reasons but after he left London on 29 March 1974, he would return to Britain sporadically, never again to be a permanent resident. So the last album he recorded in London was a parting curse on his home. If Orwell's Oceania had been a thinly-veiled austerity Britain, with its watery coffee, half-cigarettes and cramped flats, *Diamond Dogs* was the grey paralyzed Britain of late 1973 and early 1974, an anemic reenactment of the war years. Again there was government-mandated rationing (oil and gas restrictions and the Three-Day Week electricity cuts, which lasted until March 1974), again there were bombs going off in London (courtesy of the IRA), again there were some fascist rumblings in the Establishment. Sir William Armstrong, the Head of the Home

Civil Service and PM Heath's right-hand man, stripped off his clothes while attending a government seminar in January, "chain-smoking and expostulating wildly about the collapse of democracy and the end of the world…about moving the Red Army from here and Blue Army from there." The next day Armstrong told a meeting of permanent secretaries "to go home and prepare for Armageddon. The Christmas 1973 *Spectator* gamed the likelihood of a military coup in Britain, quoting a Tory lobby hack that Britain "had seen our last general election, since from now on the Prime Minister would merely need to continue to prolong various states of emergency and elongate the life of this parliament."

The most paranoiac, despondent warnings of the time came from the upper classes, with whom Bowie was now hobnobbing. He'd moved from the hippie manse of Haddon Hall to a chic flat on Oakley Street in Chelsea and was spending his nights at clubs favored by the jet set. It's little surprise that an album as jaundiced and cynical as *Diamond Dogs* came out of this milieu. The endgame now seemed in play. The future wouldn't be the revolution of the radicals or the utopia of the hippies but a quisling culture, one happily relieved from freedom. His Winston Smith wouldn't require conversion—he'd shove his face into a rat cage without prompting. Bowie sang "1984" like a man beseeching a lover; there's a touch of Roy Orbison's obsessive "Leah" in it.

The Man at the Top

At first "1984" was conjoined with another song, "Dodo," which was essentially the former's bridge. Bowie debuted "1984"/"Dodo" at his *1980 Floor Show* in October 1973 and recorded the medley around the same time at Trident Studios. This was the last performance of the two-thirds Spiders From Mars (Mick Ronson and Trevor Bolder) and Ken Scott's last Bowie production. Eventually issued as an outtake, the

"1984"/"Dodo" medley is the sound of an alternate Earth's *Diamond Dogs*, for which Bowie used his *Floor Show* unit, giving the Spiders' aggression richer R&B flavors, like the strings playing a percussive motif and the call-and-response Astronettes vocals that spanned from *basso profondo* to Ava Cherry's soprano.

Besides his taste for irregular meters, Bowie had been rhythmically dull. Many of his songs chugged to the eight-to-the-bar strum of his 12-string acoustic guitar. Now armed with a crack drummer in Aynsley Dunbar and with Mike Garson as always game for any suggestion, Bowie started working through ideas he'd picked up from James Brown, Isaac Hayes and Barry White (whose *I've Got So Much to Give* he kept playing to Ken Scott during the session). On these records the song was subservient to the groove, with harmonic development secondary to rhythmic complexity, with contrapuntal basslines and overlapping drum and percussion figures. (That said, "1984" was a typically knotty Bowie progression, with its D minor verse/refrain wrenched, via a bar of 3/4, into an E-flat major bridge.)

The problem lay with the band. Mark Pritchett, who played rhythm guitar on the medley session, said that "with the first couple takes it became fundamentally clear that all of us, but Mick was the lead musician, weren't black funky." Bowie now wanted "black funky" and he soon decided he had to go to America to find it. That said, the medley intro was still one of the best grooves on a Bowie record to date. Bolder's bass riff is doubled by baritone saxophone and a ska-style off-beat guitar; tambourine, congas and a curlicue piano figure swirl through the mix. Dunbar works his floor tom for brooding emphases, ends verses with slashes of closed hi-hat and uses a detuned kick drum to gut-sinking effect.

This apparently wasn't enough for Bowie. Excising "Dodo," he remade "1984" during the *Diamond Dogs* sessions, having the session guitarist Alan Parker play a Wah-Wah rhythm figure in homage to Charles Pitts' work on "Theme from *Shaft*." Faster in tempo and more streamlined than the medley version, the *Diamond Dogs* "1984" was hooked on Parker's guitar, Dunbar's (or Tony Newman's) 16th-note hi-hat ride pattern, a slinking Herbie Flowers bassline and Garson, who plays a police-siren electric piano in the intro and a harpsichord in the verses. Unlike much of *Diamond Dogs,* Bowie arranged and recorded the song live in the studio, making edits and doing quick rehearsals between takes. The new string arrangement promoted violins over the original version's celli while Bowie now assumed most of the chorus vocals (was the original "1984" too communal an effort for him by now?). Playing it as a show-opener throughout 1974, he kept tightening the song like a guitar peg. By the time of a performance of "1984" on *The Dick Cavett Show* in December, it was as if Bowie was bouncing off his band.

For his lead vocal, Bowie sang with rhythmic feints and odd phrasings, often hitting his highest note on the penultimate beat of a phrase. There's an absurdity at times in the sea-shanty refrains ("come see come see") or in how portentously Bowie sings an ugly rhyme, mating "savage jaw" with "eighty-four." To fill the hole left by "Dodo," Bowie sutured in a new verse that furthered the sense "1984" was as much a dark Sixties retrospective as a future warning ("looking for the treason that I knew in '65").

As for "Dodo," Bowie proposed it as a follow-up single for Lulu (her "Man Who Sold the World" hit #3 in the UK in January 1974). A lesser creature than its medley recording, where sweeps of strings had parried against groaning guitar, the stand-alone "Dodo" was still eerie, claustrophobic funk. Its guitar line sounded percolated, the synthesized dog-whistle from "People From Bad Homes" returned, the horn players came off as bruisers (trombones scowl through the second verse). The track's sickly feel was heightened by a hoarse-sounding Bowie, who to be fair was only providing a guide vocal for Lulu. But its extraction from "1984" exposed a few structural flaws, like how a tension-ridden bridge with a kiting vocal melody thuds right into one of Bowie's dopier refrains ("do-*do*, oh-*no*"). Aptly named, "Dodo" was superfluous on *Diamond Dogs* and waited 15 years to appear a bonus track.

Big Brother

Recorded: *14-15 January 1974 (basic tracks) Olympic, ca. late January-early February 1974 (overdubs), Olympic; poss. March 1974 (overdubs) 9 Melrose Terrace, London. Bowie: lead and backing vocals, 12-string acoustic guitar, rhythm guitar, baritone and tenor saxophone, Mellotron, handclaps, tambourine?; Alan Parker: lead guitar; Flowers: bass; Newman: drums; Visconti: sound effects. Produced: Bowie; engineered: Harwood.*

First release*: 24 April 1974,* ***Diamond Dogs****.* ***Live****: 1974, 1987.*

A love song to submission, a fascist and a cocaine hymn, "Big Brother" was possibly intended to close Bowie's *Nineteen Eighty-Four* adaptation, as little could top it dramatically. Opening in apprehension with a moaning synthetic choir and "trumpet" reveille via Mellotron, after two B minor verses where Bowie sings despairing, fifth-sinking phrases ("a-sylum," "of mayhem"), "Big Brother" gave itself over to power. The conversion starts in the first bridge—"please savior, savior ***show*** us!" Bowie now jumping up a fifth—and crests in the shining D major refrains, where Bowie rises an octave to hit a high A on "*shame* us!" "*blame* us!" Each subsequent refrain offers further enticements and bribes—skittish handclaps, a considered tambourine, a counter-melody via Alan Parker's guitar, a spasmodic snare fill by Tony Newman that predicts Mick Fleetwood's work on "Tusk" by half a decade.

"Big Brother" was built like a flowchart: beyond a certain point you can't go back (after the first bridge, there are no more verses). A pair of saxophones keep things in line. The tenor saxophone sweetens verses with bar-length notes, a baritone saxophone prods you along like a warder. Only the four-bar second bridge, with its scrappily-strummed acoustic guitar and its shaky octave-doubled vocal, is a last moment of doubt.

It's a fragment of the past, the voice of some Arts Lab hippie about to be turned out on the street or packed off to Orwell's Correction Room. "You *know*, you *think* you're *awful square*, but you've *made* everyone and you've *been* everywhere," Bowie chirps, as if in admiration. The squares—the bankers, the landlords, the promoters, the Mr. Joneses of the world—have become the real revolutionaries, ones who make the decadence of Bowie's earlier songs look absurd ("don't talk of dust and roses," or spare us the claptrap of *Aladdin Sane*). The squares (Momus: "brave Apollos to the subcultural Dionysians"), liberated by the freedoms the counterculture fought to give them, will inherit the earth. They were the *homo superior* all along, and by the end of the century their rule would be secure (see "Alternative Candidate").

Are there any signs of resistance? Bowie's 12-string acoustic guitar, running underground for much of the track? His vocal, with his more resonant voice shadowed by a lower-pitched one like a bad conscience? The sense of humor beneath the erotic ode to power? As Nicholas Pegg noted, an ancestor to "Big Brother" is the Bonzo Dog Band's 1969 parody of Charles Atlas ads, "Mr. Apollo." So it's Bowie worshipping a cult leader as if he was some fascist bodybuilder. It's too meager an insurgency in any case. By its last refrains "Big Brother" is in love with its own melodic strength and ends with a simply-sung "we want you Big Brother," segueing without a pause into the tribal celebration of "Chant of the Ever Circling Skeletal Family." It's a broken man brought to his feet and made to dance.

Chant of the Ever Circling Skeletal Family

Recorded: *ca. 14-16 January 1974, Olympic; ca. early March 1974, 9 Melrose Terrace. Bowie: chant vocal, phased electric guitar, Mellotron, Moog, Chamberlin?; Flowers: bass; Newman: drums; Bowie?*

MacCormack?: guiro, woodblock, tambourine; Visconti: sound effects. Produced: Bowie; engineered: Harwood.

***First release**: 24 April 1974, **Diamond Dogs**. **Live**: 1974, 1987.*

Brutish and short, "Chant of the Ever Circling Skeletal Family," coming directly out of "Big Brother," managed to reconcile a few disparate elements of *Diamond Dogs*. The track could be a reprise of the title song, the Dogs dancing around a bonfire on a skyscraper roof in Hunger City; it could be the end of "Rebel Rebel." Its most obvious intention was as Bowie's adaptation of the "Two Minutes Hate" of *Nineteen Eighty-Four*. The Hate, a daily ritual in Orwell's Oceania, begins with a "hideous grinding screech." As the arch-traitor Emmanuel Goldstein speaks on a telescreen over "the dull, rhythmic tramp of soldiers' boots," viewers erupt in anger. "People were...shouting at the tops of their voices in an effort to drown out the maddening bleating voice that came from the screen." Everyone watching, even doubters like Winston Smith, is consumed with fear and rage, the urge to murder and torture. Just as it grows too much to bear, the image of Big Brother fills the screen to restore calm. "The entire group of people broke into a slow, rhythmical chant of "B-B!..B-B!" over a backbeat of stamping naked feet and tom-toms.

So Bowie made a portrait in rhythm. After a 10-second introduction, the "Chant" proper (starting when the drums kick in) begins, six rounds of a 12-bar sequence: two bars of 3/4, a bar of 2/4, a bar of 3/4, and a repeated sequence of 2/4, 3/4, 3/4, 3/4. His octave-doubled vocal and distorted, phased guitar start a percussive ensemble that's joined by tambourine (shaken on the 7th and 11th bars of each sequence), woodblock (appearing in the second sequence and struck either twice or thrice in alternating bars), guiro (starting in the third sequence, played throughout) and a distortion effect that sounds like a jackhammer (beginning with the fifth sequence) that Tony Visconti or Bowie added at the mixing stage with one of Visconti's new toys, the Eventide Instant

Phaser, Digital Delay Generator or the Keypex (see "Diamond Dogs").

It rises in crescendo, with Bowie's lower-pitched voice moving from a conversational echo in the first sequence to a shriek in the last. The chant ends by being boxed into a looped syllable, faded after eight bars of face-stomping 4/4. Mixing the track at Visconti's home studio, Bowie and Visconti wanted to loop the word "brother" but the digital delay unit could only capture Bowie's first syllable. This was even more fitting, as the cycling "bruh-bruh-bruh" sounded like "riotriotriotriot."'

We Are the Dead

Recorded: *ca. 14-16 January 1974, Olympic. Bowie: lead and backing vocals, lead guitar, baritone saxophone; Garson: Fender Rhodes; Flowers: bass; Newman: drums. Produced: Bowie; engineered: Harwood.*

First release*: 24 April 1974,* ***Diamond Dogs****.*

Its title quotes from Orwell's *Nineteen Eighty-Four* but "We Are the Dead" owes more to William S. Burroughs. Having boned up on *Nova Express* and *The Wild Boys* before meeting Burroughs in November 1973, Bowie soon fully embraced Burroughs' "cut-up" method for his own lyric writing.

Conceived by the poet Brion Gysin, cut-up entailed (to give an example) writing lines on paper, cutting the lines into strips, drawing the strips randomly from a hat and pasting the rearranged lines together into a new piece of writing. Bowie learned of the practice possibly though the *International Times*, which ran a Gysin cut-up as its center spread in a April 1967 issue, and certainly at the Arts Lab, which screened Burroughs' 1966 avant-garde short *The Cut Ups*. He dabbled with cut-up as early as *Hunky Dory*, if not earlier: Roger Ferris from the Kon-Rads recalled Bowie cutting up lyric sheets, throwing pieces into the air and "seeing what came out" back in 1963. But on *Diamond Dogs*, Bowie used cut-up more remorselessly than he ever had before. Applying the techniques of abstract expressionist painting to words, cut-up let a writer use blind chance to bypass her habits. Its vogue was part of the counterculture's love of the spontaneous, a credo summed up by Allen Ginsberg: "first thought, best thought." For Bowie, cut-up killed any vestiges of "narrative" in his lyric writing, moving it closer to the spontaneous means through which he'd found chord progressions. Cut-up gave him lines like "dancing where the dogs decay/defecating ecstasy"or"I love you in your fuck-me pumps/and your nimble dress that trails." He later said using cut-up was like throwing the *I Ching* and that the technique had imposed order upon his fragmented way of thinking.

Along with being the most obvious use of cut-up on *Diamond Dogs*, "We Are the Dead" was a nest of echoes and blurs, of distorted wavelengths. Triple-tracked at times, Bowie's lead vocal is echo-shifted to the left stereo channel while a sped-up harmony vocal is up an octave and mixed right. Digital delay was applied to anything that moved in the track, particularly Mike Garson's Fender Rhodes (at 2:42 an "echo" organ appears in the left channel to get a jump on the "proper" Fender). Its G minor verses are soul laments looking for a soul chorus for relief, but instead get two bridge/refrains in a nebulous key, tramping out in alternating 4/4 and 2/4 bars. Keeping mainly to a three-note range, with another voice sweeping by him like a ghost on a stairwell, Bowie's voice has to contend with smears of guitar, phased cymbals and a cancerous-sounding baritone saxophone.

Beyond its title, the lyric has only traces of Orwell ("I hear them on the stairs") but in its way"We Are the Dead" is the truest of Bowie's Orwell adaptations, with the tumbling rhythm of its cut-up verses as counter-code to Orwell's doublespeak. It seems to putrefy as it's performed, leaving strings of words.

Rock 'n' Roll With Me

(Bowie/MacCormack.) ***Recorded:*** *14-15 January 1974, Olympic.*

Bowie: lead vocal, 12-string acoustic guitar, lead guitar, baritone saxophone; Garson: piano, organ; Flowers: bass; Newman: drums, tambourine?; MacCormack: backing vocals, tambourine?. Produced: Bowie; engineered: Harwood.

***First release**: 24 April 1974, **Diamond Dogs**. **Live**: 1974.*

A spot of reassurance on a diseased-sounding record, "Rock 'n' Roll With Me" plays the role reserved for cover songs on Bowie's earlier albums. Considering it a prospective single, Bowie led off *Diamond Dogs'* second side with it despite this making a hash of any "Hunger City"/*Nineteen Eighty Four* album concept.

Co-composed by Geoff MacCormack, who came up with some verse chords, "Rock 'n' Roll With Me" was originally slotted for the sketchiest of Bowie's mid-Seventies plans, a *Ziggy Stardust* musical intended for the stage or TV. Talking to William S. Burroughs, Bowie said the musical would be a "cut-up" performance. He'd write some 40 scenes and then "shuffle [them] around in a hat the afternoon of the performance and just perform it as the scenes come out...it would change every night."

"There are two stars in rock 'n' roll—me and the audience," Bowie said at one of the last Ziggy Stardust concerts in Newcastle, irritated by bouncers hitting a few kids. "And if these stewards don't stop...the stars are going to make this place into a matchbox." A precursor of "We Are the Champions" and other self-congratulatory arena rock standards, "Rock 'n' Roll With Me" is hewn of rock "spiritual" timber—a "Lean On Me" piano intro, a Mike Garson organ hymn for the chorus and a Bowie vocal arc that takes predictable flight. He sings low and confined in the first verse, swoops up an octave for the second, caps things off with some roared refrains and scats ("I'm in *tears*...I'm in *tears*").

What saved "Rock 'n' Roll With Me" from sentimentality was its acerbic take on the coarse relations of audience and actor ("they sold us for the likes of you"). If it's meant to be the voice of Ziggy, it's a Ziggy tartly explaining why he broke up the band and was renting a room somewhere in America to get away from his fans ("I've found a door that lets me out!"). Asked in summer 1974 whether his fans considered him as a leader, Bowie nervously laughed that "Rock 'n' Roll With Me" was his response: "you're doing it to me. Stop it." Much as how Arts Lab hangers-on had bothered him (see "Cygnet Committee"), he was frustrated by fans who were stuck on a persona he'd discarded. They were content to "adopt the stance of a character that didn't exist at all, and a life-style that hadn't been created...they created their own *life-style* for Ziggy," he later said, baffled that anyone had taken him seriously. On stage in 1974, he used performances of "Rock 'n' Roll With Me" to have gnomic dialogues with his audience. In Boston, he broke off midway through to ramble "this one is very much for you, this song…are you people? I'm people."("It's about me and singing," he said during another performance.) On record, he gave the last word to his lead guitar, a corrosive agent that makes growling retorts to the church piano, smears across the second verse, gnaws on pieces of melody for its solos and sags off with a car alarm of a riff.

Rebel Rebel

Recorded: *ca. late December 1973, 14-16 January-late January 1974, Trident and Olympic. Bowie: lead vocal, 12-string acoustic guitar; Alan Parker; lead guitar; Garson: piano; Flowers: bass; Newman: drums, tambourine, cowbell? Produced: Bowie; engineered: Harwood;* ***(single remake overdubs)*** *mid-April 1974, RCA Studios, New York. Bowie: backing vocal, guitars; MacCormack: castanets, congas, guiro, tambourine, backing vocal;* ***(remake)*** *ca. January-March 2003, Looking Glass Studios, New York. Bowie: vocals; Gerry Leonard, Mark Plati and/or David Torn: guitars; Gail Ann Dorsey: bass, vocals; Sterling Campbell: drums; Catherine Russell: backing vocals. Produced: Bowie, Visconti.*

First release: *15 February 1974 (RCA LPBO 05009, UK #5);*

(single remake/remix) May 1974, (RCA APBO 0287, US #64); (remake) 24 June 2003, ***Charlie's Angels: Full Throttle*** *OST (Columbia CK 90132).* ***Broadcast:*** *13 February 1974, TopPop; 30 May 1978, Musikladen; 23 August 1999, VH1 Storytellers; 2 October 1999, Saturday Night Live; 8 October 1999, TFI Friday; 28 October 1999, WB Radio Music Awards; 18 September 2002, Live and Exclusive; 15 October 2002, VH1/Vogue Fashion Awards; 18 October 2002, Later With Jools Holland; 30 October 2002, The Early Show; 23 September 2003, Sessions@AOL.* ***Live:*** *1974, 1976, 1978, 1983, 1985, 1987, 1990, 1999-2000, 2002-2004.*

Glam died swiftly, with great theater. By summer 1974, the top British glam acts had been deposed on their home soil by bubblegum stompers (Mud, the Bay City Rollers) and *opera buffa* rock groups (Sparks, 10cc, Queen). Slade went to the hills to live in exile, Marc Bolan kept pleading with an audience who'd tired of him ("Whatever Happened to the Teenage Dream?" he asked—it missed the Top 10). Mott the Hoople, self-chroniclers to the end, issued as a final single the retrospective "Saturday Gigs," with Mick Ronson in tow. Roxy Music closed each side of *Stranded* with resignation letters, ecclesiastical ("Psalm") and existential ("Sunset," which finds Bryan Ferry sitting in his sports car contemplating the void). By the end of the year, even the shameless likes of Gary Glitter were on their way down.

The end was inevitable ("the really great scenes die," the producer Tom Ayres once noted) and long in coming. Self-parodying from the start, glam died when it lost its wit, descending into farce—see KISS outlasting the New York Dolls—or knees-up shtick. Bowie found he was being crowded out by imitators, with Ziggy Stardust's mantle waved about by the likes of Jobraith and Steve Harvey.

So "Rebel Rebel" is Bowie blessing a movement that he abandoned as it fell. The first wave of punk kids in Britain were former Bowie and Roxy Music fans, and "Rebel Rebel" is Bowie's goodbye and tribute to them (he often sings it like "rabble,

rabble!"). He divides the kingdom, distributes inheritances. The promo video he made for "Rebel Rebel" in Holland taught the future punks style and attitude. Wearing an eye-patch and dressed in thrift-shop motley, Bowie held an unplugged red Hagström Kent with disdain, hardly pretending to play it.

It's a primer of a rock & roll record: easy to play, easy to remember (each of its verses repeat), its arrangement simple as nails, its top melody cut to fit anyone's voice. Bowie keeps to a comfortable four-note span for much of it, his phrasing loose and conversational. There's some David Johansen attitude: "where'dya wanna GO?" A sparring two-chord (D major and E major) verse progression spills over into the refrains, an A major chord finally showing up in the four-bar bridge to referee between them.

Its front-loaded mix, a loop of beats and guitar riffs, was owned by Alan Parker's lead guitar riff, Herbie Flowers' bass (playing constant, subtle variations throughout, with walking lines and scalar passing tones—Flowers makes you able to dance) and a Tony Newman crush-on-every-beat manifesto that's relieved by an occasional modest fill. There are a few lesser players, like Bowie's strummed acoustic guitar parked in the right channel and Mike Garson's piano, buried so deep in the mix that it sounds like another cowbell.

The lead riff's in three parts—a descending fanfare, a centerpiece (two barked-out E chords) and a last hook that starts with a near-two octave jump and ends on a fat D root note to launch another repetition. There were rumors it was Mick Ronson's work, but its tripartite structure was close to the Bowie-penned "Ziggy Stardust" riff, and Bowie singing the notes in the intro suggests it began, as many of his riffs did, as a scatted melody. He had three-fourths of the riff down when he played it on acoustic guitar to Alan Parker, telling him "I want it to sound like the Stones." Parker thought it needed "honing," so he transferred the riff to a Les Paul standard, using a Fender reverb amp with a single Wharfedale speaker, and added a few bends to barb its last piece. Ronson's absence was noticeable in how the riff got run into the ground. In the four-plus minutes of "Rebel Rebel," it's only absent in the two bridges and the "hot tramp" tags.

Bowie's voice is of someone a bit older—someone edging out of the scene, a bit jaded, and who's bemused at first by some tacky cross-dressing kid's antics. "You put them on!": donning a new set of glam gear while tweaking the noses of her parents. (An original line was "your hair's on fire," a call back to Arthur Brown—he also changed "we like dancin' and we like to ball" to "look divine".) The kid's young enough not to know better, Bowie's old enough to care (he whispers "donch'a?" after bellowing his love). As the song piles into a 20-bar coda, Bowie loses whatever reserve's bottled in him. His words keep coming, keep piling up. "Rebel Rebel" slams shut as Bowie watches the kid walk off into her youth, his juvenile successor. It was played every half-hour at Rodney's English Disco in LA, where future Runaways Cherie Currie and Joan Jett were regulars. Their "Cherry Bomb" would be its answer song.

Four and a half minutes on LP, the track's harmonic stasis and its Moebius strip of a guitar riff made it feel longer. As with "Diamond Dogs," the song spread out, as if Bowie couldn't be bothered to rein it in: there was a punishing sense to it. But upon arriving in New York in April 1974, he reworked "Rebel Rebel" to pop on US radio, with Geoff MacCormack adding congas, guiro and castanets to give the track a "Latin" tinge. Bowie trimmed "Rebel Rebel" by nearly two minutes, gutting a set of verses and the second bridge, pushing up the hooks. He led off the track with the "hot tramp" chorus tag, salted in new phased chorus vocals and lowered the lead riff in the mix to give more prominence to Flowers' bass, Garson's piano and his own acoustic guitar. The US edit was the essential "Rebel Rebel," Bowie's single of singles; most of his live versions took off from it.

He played "Rebel Rebel" on every tour until 1990. By then he'd tired of it, telling a reporter that the song meant nothing to him anymore, that it was a relic of a lost time. So when he went back to the song, in a revision that he debuted on stage in 2002 and cut in a studio take for the soundtrack of a *Charlie's Angels* sequel, he started at a distance, singing the opening verse coldly over a four-note guitar line. It's a man wondering what youth has gotten up to over the years; it' s as if his sympathies lie with their mothers now. He's self-effacing on the "they say I'm wrong" line (maybe he's been wrong all along), seems wary that the refrain's coming up. Then the old metal beast of a riff kicks in, and in come the drums, and the ghost of Herbie Flowers' bassline walks, and every lie he'd once believed in his youth is true again.

Future Legend

(Bowie/Rodgers). ***Recorded:*** *ca. mid-late January, early February 1974, Olympic; ca. early March 1974, 9 Melrose Terrace. Bowie: lead and marginal vocals, lead guitar, Moog, Mellotron; Visconti: sound effects. Produced: Bowie; engineered: Harwood, Visconti.*

First release*: 24 April 1974,* ***Diamond Dogs****.*

The one-minute LP opener "Future Legend" is the *Diamond Dogs* "concept." Not for Bowie the librettos of the Who's *Quadrophenia* or Genesis' *The Lamb Lies Down on Broadway*. He just offered fragments. Reciting a paragraph of lurid expository text, helpfully printed on the record's gatefold, he offered a scenario as if throwing out an idea to an improv troupe. Picture a conquered, abandoned city (a first incarnation of the cold Warsaw of Bowie's imagination) in which tribes of mutants of all sorts—even the fleas are gargantuan—prey upon each other and vie to control the coveted roofs of skyscrapers. Go!

As Bowie told William S. Burroughs, who was an obvious influence here, he got distracted easily. He liked the idea of concept records but not the grim business of writing them. As his more ready-made narratives, *Nineteen Eighty Four* and *Ziggy*

Stardust: the Musical, had soured, Bowie had to gin up another idea a few months before he had to tour again. Having written at least some of "Diamond Dogs," Bowie wrote an abstract on the Dogs' Hunger City, intoned it over sound effects, segued "Future Legend" into the title track and he was done. His precedent was the grandfather of concept records, *Sgt. Pepper's Lonely Hearts Club Band,* whose story arc consists of the LP cover, the title song, "With a Little Help From My Friends" and the reprise. The rest of the album was a random set of Beatles compositions stuck together. If the songs told a story, it was because the listener made them do it. "It worked 'cause we *said* it worked," John Lennon later said.

Bowie's lines have some wordplay—"no more big wheels" (*i.e.,* no more ruling class and also no more cars, only the wheels of the Dogs' roller skates); a "Love Me Avenue" instead of a Lonely Avenue—while he may have derived his Darwinian mutant food chain from Ray Bradbury's *Something Wicked This Way Comes* ("rats which fed on spiders which fed, in turn, because they were large enough, on cats"). He narrates as a rolling scrim of synthetic, phased and distorted sounds pass "behind" him in the mix. Inspired by the montage that opened Lou Reed's *Berlin,* "Future Legend" sports a howling air raid siren, spectral children, grumbling zombies, synthesizer washes, pick slides, muttering gnomes, Bowie playing the chorus melody of Rodgers and Hart's "Bewitched, Bothered and Bewildered" on distorted electric guitar, then impersonating Scott Walker singing "Any Day Now." It's a condensed sequel to "We Are Hungry Men," and it's just as juvenile, tasteless and strange. It ends with canned applause and a call to genocide, which seems appropriate.

Diamond Dogs

Recorded: ***(demo, "Diamond Dawgs," unreleased)*** *ca. mid-March 1973, Los Angeles;* ***(album)*** *14-16 January 1974-late January 1974,*

Olympic. Bowie: lead and backing vocal, lead and rhythm guitars, tenor and baritone saxophone; Garson: piano; Flowers: bass; Newman: drums, cowbell? Produced: Bowie; engineered: Harwood.

***First release**: 24 April 1974, **Diamond Dogs**. **Live**: 1974, 1976, 1996, 2004.*

"Diamond Dogs" has never sounded quite right. It's a "classic rock" song overrun by grotesques: amputees in priest's robes, Tod Browning rejects. Bowie's least-successful single since *Hunky Dory*, it topped out at #21 in the UK, went nowhere in the States and is still unassimilable forty years later. It's overlong and sounds used, repurposed, as though Bowie had found a discarded tape and overdubbed various slurs and noises onto it.

Everyone was writing better Rolling Stones songs than the Stones were in 1974 (see Elton John's "The Bitch Is Back" or Aerosmith's "Train Kept a Rollin'"); Bowie was making a specialty of it. Using the Stones' favorite British studio, Olympic, and their engineer, Keith Harwood, Bowie pasted "Diamond Dogs" with Keith Richards guitar riffs and played blatant steals of Bobby Keyes' saxophone line on "Brown Sugar" in the coda. He cloaked the Stones as the gang in *A Clockwork Orange*, rock 'n' roll Droogs. He even stole their cover artist Guy Peelleart, who Mick Jagger had commissioned for *It's Only Rock 'n' Roll*, to design *Diamond Dogs* (and beat the Stones to the shops by half a year). As if to rub it in, when singing "Diamond Dogs" live, he sometimes went into "It's Only Rock 'n' Roll" for its end refrains.

Scrambling for a fresh album concept, Bowie found a new tentpole song with "Diamond Dogs" (originally "Dawgs") which he'd demoed in Los Angeles at the end of his last US tour. It allowed him to keep the "fallen city" idea he'd been developing for the *Nineteen Eighty-Four* musical. The seeds of "Diamond Dogs" were in stories his father had recounted about the founding days of his workplace, the children's charity Dr. Barnardo's Homes, in which Dr. Barnardo and his patron Lord Shaftesbury went around Victorian London rescuing bands of homeless children living on tenement roofs. Bowie also freely raided William Burroughs' novel *The Wild Boys* (while recording *Pin Ups*, he read choice passages from the book aloud and raved about the possibility of a "glitter apocalypse"). He bred Barnardo's Victorian ragged boys with Burroughs' homosexual Bowie-knife-wielding guerillas in rainbow-colored jockstraps to make his "diamond dogs": packs of feral kids camped on high-rise roofs, tearing around on roller skates, terrorizing the corpse-strewn streets they live above. "I was trying to evolve a new kind of street gang and develop a rather glamorous pre-punk collusion of elements," he said in a webchat in 2000. As always, he did a spot of research, tearing through a few books about old teenage gangs from the Peaky Blinders to the Teddy Boys.

Making the Dogs' home base a post-holocaust skyscraper, here a former bank ("Manhattan Chase"), fit the dystopian fashion of the time. The Seventies were the rot of the postwar dream of general prosperity. You could see it in the shabby Art Deco train stations and graffitied Modernist council flats. The city, for both hippies and reactionaries, had become a symbol of the mongrelized, the polluted; it was a sewer, an open-air prison, with Brutalist parking garages used as handy symbols of cultural dysentery. (Bowie's Halloween Jack could have lived atop the Thamesmead South estate where Stanley Kubrick filmed *A Clockwork Orange*.) *Diamond Dogs* was Bowie's own SF urban album, its title track his city song. Hunger City was the place that "Ziggy comes from," he once said, and he described the character he played on the Diamond Dogs tour as "a paranoid refugee of New York City. That [tour] was about the collapse of a major city and I think I was right to be remote." Ziggy Stardust had been a Buddha of suburbia, a hipster who'd left the city to carry the news out to kids in Orpington and Croydon. "Diamond Dogs" took him home.

So if those left behind in the cities were the losers and the discarded, it's fitting how scrapped together "Diamond Dogs" sounds; it's punk music purloined from the gentry. Like the work of another set of marginalized kids in the real-life Bronx of the Seventies, the track starts with a sample, an opening shot of applause from the live Faces record *Overture and Beginners* (a detourned Rod Stewart yells "hey" as Bowie's guitar sneers). "Diamond Dogs" goes on through its Stones steals, Dylan vocal phrasings and Bo Diddley guitar riffs. Roaming over no-frills A major progressions in the verse and refrains, Bowie threw out voices and phrasings willy-nilly ("Tod Browning's freak you was" sinks an octave in a bar). Sometimes he sounded like a sideshow barker, sometimes he sullenly held one note. His two lead guitars (center, right) nosed back and forth like greyhounds, with Bowie wringing bent and slurred notes from their treble strings, while his grunting rhythm guitar (left) shuns full chords in favor of double stops. He mixed them in a paste of sound into which he sunk Mike Garson's piano like an anchor. The pre-choruses ("I'll keep a friend serene") broke apart while being played, with Bowie's lead guitar, smearing a run of bent notes, sounding as if it's losing power while Tony Newman shifts to a "reverse backbeat," hitting his snare on the "1 & 3" beats instead of the "2 & 4" backbeat. A thwacked 4/4 cowbell is more interested in punishment than keeping things moving.

This was rotten music. Bowie's backing vocals sound so distorted that the master tape seems contaminated. Nor does the track ever seem to die, with Bowie throwing in yet another riff at late as 4:50, while its coda drags out for over a minute. "Diamond Dogs" made a playtime from societal collapse. The elevator's shot so Halloween Jack swings by a rope, Tarzan-style, to reach the street.

Candidate 1 (Alternative Candidate)

Recorded: *ca. 1-9 January 1974, Olympic. Bowie: lead and backing vocal, 12-string acoustic guitar, lead guitar; Garson: piano; Flowers: bass; Newman: drums. Produced: Bowie; engineered: Harwood.*

***First release**: 16 October 1990, **Diamond Dogs** (reissue).*

Sharing two lines ("I'll make you a deal," "pretend we're walking home") and a title with the "Candidate" of *Diamond Dogs,* "Alternative Candidate" was either an early draft of the latter or a song derived from the same mother source (a pile of cut-up lines?). Bowie demoed "Alternative Candidate" at Olympic Studios on New Year's Day 1974 and recorded at least one full-band take of it over the following week. A three-verse, three-refrain (a fresh lyric for each refrain) piece in B minor, its foundation was Tony Newman's drums (marked in the intro with a space-distorting detuned snare on the fourth beat, then moving to a shuffle in the refrains), Mike Garson's three-chord piano hook, advancing and retreating, and Bowie's 12-string acoustic guitar shuffling through the song's harmonic cards. After bloodying it with a few electric guitar overdubs, he stowed away the track for 15 years.

Appearing on the Ryko reissue of *Diamond Dogs,* "Alternative Candidate" seemed at first glance a rough draft with a guide vocal and a scratch lyric. Appearances aside, it was an essential Bowie song: a storehouse of his obsessions, a catalog of his themes and motives. It apparently was another refugee from Bowie's scrapped *Nineteen Eighty-Four* musical, though little remains of its origins besides a line that could reference Orwell's Room 101 ("the correction room"). Its opening verse's lusty teenagers (and a poor mother who wishes her son was still a sweet Tommy Tinker ("Tinkrem" here)) hint at a setting: some mingle of Orwell's Anti-Sex League and the erotic film instructionals of his own "Drive-In Saturday."

More of "Alternative Candidate" was an oblique move forward, with Bowie weighing his chances in America and devising a huckster personality for the job. He'd only had provisional success in the US to date. Now in 1974 he aimed to "break" America in the way British acts had been trained to do since the Beatles. "Alternative Candidate," especially once it crawls into its last verses and refrains, is a detached Bowie surveying a field he means to conquer, acknowledging the lunacy of his aims yet so consumed by ego that he doesn't care."Do I have to give your money back when I'm the Führerling?" he winks at the end. "That's not a line written by someone trying to fool and bamboozle us," as Momus said, "but someone pointing out how funny and absurd the whole thing is, and saying: "For God's sake don't trust me!'" (In "Rock 'n' Roll With Me," Bowie said much the same, in more reassuring tones.)

Bowie devised a performing self as an openly corrupt political candidate, a transparent falsehood: *inside this tin is tin...techno-plate*. As in the *Diamond Dogs* "Candidate," he wants to strike a deal: sex for fame, money for notoriety, the future hocked for the present. But the singer of "Candidate" grows desperate in his patter; he knows he's getting behind in the game. The singer of "Alternative Candidate" couldn't care less. His only emphases come with the slight lifts he gives the last words of each phrase. It's as though he considers posing each as a question, then lets each line expire.

You could go further in. By the time Bowie wrote the song, Pres. Richard Nixon was embroiled in the Watergate scandal, whose details—missing audio tapes ("my tongue is taped"), the image of a "cancerous" conspiracy in the center of power—are heard in a few lines. Being a proper British citizen, Bowie considered the American presidency a bizarre office: an elected monarch-salesman to whom a loud democratic country gave colossal powers. The presidency was like a game show that no one could win. In Bowie's memory, American presidents had either wound up being shot or drummed out of office as shattered men.

So Nixon (who turns up by name on "Young Americans" and in shadow in "Somebody Up There Likes Me") was the latest failing idol. By early 1974 he was dying on the road, his records were stiffing and his own master tapes had played a role in his downfall. So Bowie offers himself up as a replacement candidate (it's like the Joker running for mayor of Gotham City). "I'll make you a deal," he sings in the last refrain. I'll pretend I'm from earth, pretend that I'm like you, and you just give me the future. What use do you have for it?

"Alternative Candidate" was the corrosive promise of the transformation of the self, the dream that Bowie offered his fans. He was a nobody from Bromley who'd willed himself into a legend. This ideology of radical personal transformation, so central to the Seventies, was the only ideology left standing. It had snuffed out the old utopian dream of changing society for the better; a revolution in the head was merely a revolution of one ("socialism in one person," as the Yippie Stew Albert once said). If you could hustle yourself free from the past, if you could rewrite yourself, then the nation, the city, the family could go hang. The liberated huckster of this odd little song, someone who can use "gazelle" as a verb, this uncorked id with its deals and side-deals and dirty jokes and jokey Nazi intimations, was Bowie's most disturbing and resonant character. It was his mirror, shone up for the times. The best of his work to come would be increasingly disturbing variations on it.

Sweet Thing—Candidate—Sweet Thing (Reprise)

Recorded: *14-16 January 1974, Olympic. Bowie: lead and backing vocals, 12-string acoustic guitar, lead guitar, baritone and tenor saxophone, Mellotron, Moog; Garson: piano; Flowers: bass; Newman: drums, tambourine. Produced: Bowie; engineered: Harwood.*

First release: *24 April 1974,* ***Diamond Dogs****.* ***Live:*** *1974.*

The "Sweet Thing"-"Candidate"-"Sweet Thing (Reprise)" triptych has only cursory ties to Bowie's Orwell musical or his various Ziggy Stardust-on-roller-skates scenarios. Conceived as a complete work (as a provisional lyric sheet shows), "Sweet Thing" *et al* was fundamental *Diamond Dogs*, the album's black heart. Bowie made the subsequent tour in its image, singing

"Sweet Thing" on a catwalk, preening to an audience he hardly acknowledged, writhing as though being electrocuted. His stage set was a row of skyscrapers (which he and his dancers ripped down at show's end), a papier-mâché version of the world in his head: "my set is amazing, it even smells like a street." The suite had been theater even at its conception. Bowie sang his vocals under a spotlight at Olympic Studios, having switched off all lights save those directly over his microphone.

Using *Diamond Dogs* to fortify himself against glam's collapse and to get out of Britain, Bowie also was moving further inward. He was becoming addicted to cocaine. He had dispensed with the fiction of having a band and had begun keeping vampire's hours—sleeping at dawn, rising in the late afternoon. Real life was a rumor. Wary of how to proceed, he fell back to his reserve lines, back to mime, back to the claret and cabaret world of Scott Walker records and the Living Theatre. The Diamond Dogs owe as much to Lionel Bart's *Oliver!* as they do William Burroughs' *Wild Boys*, and while Bowie claimed Fritz Lang's *Metropolis* and Robert Wiene's *Cabinet of Dr. Caligari* as the forebears of his Hunger City, the Diamond Dogs shows came off like a Depression-era musical (*The Broadway Melody of 1984*).

The album was Bowie in an endless circle of revisions. "There was a lot of backwards and forwards in the recording and in the writing," said Jon Astley, a tape op on the album. Bowie would cut and recut vocal after vocal. He played a saxophone line, erased it, replayed it. He took the hours of recordings he'd made with Herbie Flowers and Aynsley Dunbar and had Tony Newman replace Dunbar's drums, beat for beat. His "Sweet Thing" players were a pit orchestra—just Mike Garson, Flowers and Newman—who doubled as actors. Bowie coached them, telling Newman to play the snare rolls in the opening verse of "Candidate"as if he was a French Revolutionary drummer boy watching his first guillotining. Flowers was a ghost in the walls. Garson provided a few moments of grace and levity, like a winking run of notes after "you're older than me."

The rest of the suite was Bowie in a hundred pieces: synthesizers, saxophones, distorted guitars, vocal impersonations, diva moments. He begins in the depths in a *basso profondo* that sounds like a blighted incarnation of Scott Walker. Eight bars in, he moves up an octave to middle G, now in his usual mask (a scornful "isn't it *me*"); after four increasingly antic phrases, he leaps up to a high G ("will you SEE"). It's much the same movement he'd made on "Rock 'n' Roll With Me," except it sounds like a man putting himself to the rack. Bowie tugs and tears at words, tumbles out phrases in bushels (muttering "where the knowing one says" over three beats). He parcels himself into supporting characters—a Warner Brothers tough guy ("if you wannit, boyz"); a set of grotesques for the A minor refrains, the bass voice overtopped by tenors like a row of gargoyles on a parapet; a croaking voice that seems most prominent when you're half-listening.

The lead role was a hustler out of a favorite novel, John Rechy's *City of Night* (or as Bowie sings here, "seedy young knights"). Rechy's nameless "youngman" narrator moved through fallen cities—New York, Los Angeles, New Orleans—servicing clients (including some S&M transactions, "putting pain in a stranger"). Bowie moves Rechy's hustler into larger realms. Everything is transactional. Hustlers are freelance politicians, "free trade" a governing philosophy. In Hunger City, it's safe to love in a doorway.

The "Candidate" section is a run of 64 bars built over a condensed version of the "Sweet Thing" refrain progression, D minor-A minor-G major. Played live in 1974, "Candidate" had peacocking solos by guitarist Earl Slick and saxophonist David Sanborn, but on record it was just Bowie. He'd spent months getting up to speed on guitar, depriving himself of the ease Mick Ronson could have provided. It was as if he felt too close to the songs, was unwilling to let anyone else touch them (when he had to, he could outsource the work to a pro like Alan Parker, a bloodless financial transaction). There's a self-loathing in Bowie's scraping guitar solos and rhythm figures: you, we, don't deserve better than this, this is all we can afford. Yet the closing solo of "Sweet Thing" sounds as if Bowie had spent nights mapping it out note by note, bend by bend, crafting it like one of his clay set models for Hunger City. It's touched by grace. Keeping mainly to the treble strings, he wrings line after floating line from the guitar. The bluntness of his fingerings, the severity of his bends, grounds the melodies. It makes each leap into orbit the more stunning. The last note hangs in midair. It decays, becomes a corrupted signal, its trebly death mocked by the saxophone that rumbles in to clear the stage for "Candidate."

In "Candidate," the hustler begins confident, sounding glib and conspiratorial as Newman's guillotine snare and a bludgeoning rhythm guitar serve as his muscle. A second voice, pitched on a ledge high above the first, edges in on the sale, starts harrying the mark. The hustler's not closing the sale and he starts to grow desperate (the seesaw up and down an octave on "some make you sing," the chromatic tumble of "put all I had in another bed"). As with the "Sweet Thing" opening verse, Bowie slowly climbs two octaves, though here his peak notes feel like distractions, a means to distract you from what he's doing with his hands: "SO much fun," "BULLET-proof faces." The guitar, at first confined to the right channel, starts bleeding through while Bowie's phrases echo its rhythms. By the last lines, his vocal is a run of slurs, colliding syllables, shadow-rhymes ("shop on"/"papier"). The "Sweet Thing" refrain reappears—time's running out. The hustler cashes out. When it's good, it's good, but now he's gone to pieces. "Candidate" closes with rock 'n' roll suicide: a couple scores, watches a band, jumps in the river.

After a saxophone set change, the single-verse "Sweet Thing (Reprise) begins. The hustler's dead, the actor's left in his place. He looks in the mirror, talks to himself. "Is it nice in your snowstorm?" he wonders. "Do you think that your face looks the same?"—there's pity in his voice here. All that's left is theater, with Bowie making a last push to a gasped high D ("yooouuu") to bring down the curtain. The set's struck—you hear a bit of "Zion" on Mellotron, the opening piano hook of "Changes" on Garson's bass keys, and a minute's worth of grinding guitar panned back and forth across a rhythm loop. Flowers broods over a bass figure while Newman starts hitting his snare on every beat, as if trying to punch his way out of the song. Maybe he got through: just before you escape into the dream of "Rebel Rebel," you hear a shout of relief.

Chapter 9

Campaigner (1974-1975)

With the crooners, and particularly with the later exponents of special styles from America, one is in the world of the private nightmare.
Richard Hoggart, *The Uses of Literacy.*

This pretty gowster is sure pimping his ass off.
Iceberg Slim, *Pimp.*

In America, fame was an absolute value, higher than money.
Hanif Kureishi, *The Buddha of Suburbia.*

I am a lonely visitor, I came too late to cause a stir. Though I campaigned all my life towards that goal.
Neil Young, "Campaigner."

Knock On Wood

(Floyd/Cropper). ***Recorded****: 11 or 12 July 1974, Tower Theater, Upper Darby, PA. David Bowie: lead vocal; Earl Slick: lead guitar; Michael Kamen: organ; Mike Garson: piano; David Sanborn: alto saxophone; Richard Grando: baritone saxophone; Herbie Flowers: bass; Tony Newman: drums; Pablo Rosario: tambourine; Geoff MacCormack, Gui Andrisano: backing vocals. Produced: Tony Visconti; engineered: Eddie Kramer, Keith Harwood.*

First release*: 13 September 1974 (RCA 2466, #10 UK).* ***Live****: 1974.*

In the first minutes of Alan Yentob's *Cracked Actor*, a BBC documentary shot in August-September 1974, Bowie is in the back of a limousine driving through the desert beyond Los Angeles. It's as if Nosferatu is touring Death Valley. Throughout the performance, as it's very much a performance, he keeps picking up on the song playing on the tape deck, Aretha Franklin's "Natural Woman," and wanly singing along. He seems to be using Franklin's voice as a means to keep himself in focus. So begins Bowie's soul era.

His move into R&B in the summer of 1974 was calculated enough for him to enlist as researchers the LA music writer Harvey Kubernik, who mailed him boxes of soul records, and his assistant Corrine Schwab, to whom he gave a list of Latin albums to buy. He watched *Soul Train* religiously. He would record at Sigma Sound Studios in Philadelphia to trade on its atmosphere and, with hope, get an American pop hit at last.

If this was an affectation, it was far from a new one. Bowie had come up as a Mod soul singer, covering Bobby "Blue" Bland on record and Don Covay, Ray Charles and Sam and Dave on stage. In the first Ziggy Stardust shows, he was still singing James Brown. So when Bowie downgraded his grandiose Diamond Dogs tour set in autumn 1974 for a "soul revue" format (exchanging European Art for American Soul, a trade he'd soon enough reverse) and released *Young Americans* in March 1975, it was a return to his first opportunistic principles, another step back after the Mod exhumation of *Pin Ups*.

Marc Bolan already had tried to use soul as an exit ramp out of glam on his *Zinc Alloy and the Hidden Riders of Tomorrow*, having Gloria Jones curse tracks with spectral harmony vocals. Nor was Bowie the first white Brit to record at Sigma Sound, as Dusty Springfield had cut an album there with Kenneth Gamble and Leon Huff in 1969. But Bowie treated soul and funk with little reverence, regarding the music as a new puzzle to master. Asked years later if he'd felt self-conscious coming from England to make "black" music, he said "it honestly never occurred to me. I was so hermetically sealed from everything. I was so in my own universe, that so much didn't occur to me about how other people thought."

Confecting his own version of the "reality" he felt soul singers conveyed, Bowie didn't go the usual route of the white English singer tearing himself up to approximate soul. He channeled the music through his own strange vehicles. Though ostensibly going to Sigma Sound to tap the house vibe, the only Philadelphia musician he used was a conga player. He imported his producer and sidelined the house engineer. It was like a man copying a painting by peering through glass, and it made him a trenchant interpreter, amplifying the anomie and desperation he heard in the lushest Philadelphia soul records. And it worked. "Fame" first hit on R&B radio and Bowie was one of the first white artists to play *Soul Train*.

While he'd dabbled in the Latin and funk scenes during visits to America in 1973, his conversion began once he set foot in New York in April 1974. He was touring that summer with a show he intended to be "remorseless," the culmination of a theatrical vision he'd had since 1971, when he'd sketched ideas for his pet band Arnold Corns to play in a boxing ring surrounded by pillars. His Rainbow Theatre shows of 1972, with their three-tiered catwalks, were a first draft. Now given a blank check from MainMan (because he was funding it himself), Bowie hired Broadway lighting designer Jules Fisher and set designer Mark Ravitz to build his Hunger City: a skyline of 30-foot-tall paper skyscrapers, a motorized bridge with Porsche brakes, a moveable giant star-flecked "fist" and a cherry picker to convey Bowie over the first rows of the floor seats.

Bowie told Fisher to think German Expressionism—Fritz Lang's *Metropolis* and Robert Wiene's *Cabinet of Dr. Caligari*. He told Ravitz to use "power, Nuremberg and Fritz Lang" as organizing concepts, encouraging him to favor violent and totalitarian images. An early set design had Nazi-esque banners rising to the stage. Bowie drilled his dancers (with Toni Basil as his choreographer) and wanted his musicians stationed off-stage and on a strict timetable, with no improvisation allowed. He hired British expat Michael Kamen to run the band; through Kamen he found guitarist Earl Slick and alto saxophonist David Sanborn. Kicking off on 14 June 1974 in Canada, the Diamond Dogs tour was in residence a month later at Philadelphia's Tower Theater, where five of six shows were taped for a prospective live album.

Throughout his months of preparations, Bowie had sneaked up to Harlem with Ava Cherry to see the likes of the Spinners, Marvin Gaye and the Main Ingredient at the Apollo Theater. He knew he'd soon grow bored of the Diamond Dogs show after he pulled it off ("I've a feeling this may be the last big production type of tour that I do," Bowie told a reporter in April, long before the tour started), so these trips were partly field research for his next venture.

The shows were built on *Diamond Dogs* songs, supplemented by stylized versions of *Hunky Dory*, *Ziggy Stardust* and *Aladdin Sane* numbers. But in Philadelphia, Bowie put Eddie Floyd's "Knock on Wood" dead center in the set-lists. The song was a breather for both band and audience ("we're going to do some extras tonight...some silly ones," Bowie said), brightening the mood after the "Sweet Thing" suite, the cabaret "All the Young Dudes" and death's-head "Cracked Actor." This spectacle had kept the audience in their seats (Lenny Kaye, who saw an early concert in Toronto, said the crowd was "watching with near-stunned attention," only getting to their feet for the encore): playing "Knock On Wood" let them get up and dance.

A bar band staple since its release, "Knock On Wood" was soul at its most democratic: easy to sing (suited for Floyd's husky tenor) with a no-frills groove. Cooked up at a Memphis hotel during a thunderstorm, the song came out of Steve Cropper reversing the opening guitar riff of "In the Midnight Hour" while Floyd knocked together a lyric out of "rabbit foots and stuff, the whole superstitious thing." Recorded at Stax the next day, "Knock On Wood" was built by committee. Isaac Hayes wrote the bridge's sprightly horn line, which Floyd thought sounded like a soap opera theme; Al Jackson Jr., recalling the

Fifties R&B hit "Open the Door Richard," came up with the "knock-knock-knock-knock" snare hook.

Bowie would only play "Knock On Wood" on stage, its *David Live* recording issued as a single that made the UK Top 10 due to the last gasp of Ziggy Stardust fandom. He used the Mod tactic of pilling up a soul song until it rattled, gunning the tempo at the expense of swing. His band sounded like a ship's crew trying to ride out a storm. Compare Herbie Flowers' thudding root-fixated bassline to the crafty bass work on the Floyd single, where Donald "Duck' Dunn slipped past downbeats and needled the groove with high notes. While in verses Slick's lead guitar filled in capably for Floyd's horns, letting down the side were Mike Garson's abstract swing piano and the stodgy Sanborn and Richard Grando, whose saxophones were likely studio dubs. His voice worn down by a month of almost-nightly shows, Bowie came off like a student who'd been up all night cramming. A better recording on all fronts was made at the Universal Amphitheatre in Los Angeles on 5 September 1974, with Bowie energized after the first round of *Young Americans* recording sessions.

Here Today, Gone Tomorrow

(Bonner/Harris/Jones/Middlebrooks/Robinson/Satchell/Webster). ***Recorded****: 11 or 12 July 1974, Tower Theater. Bowie: lead vocal; Slick: lead guitar; Kamen: organ; Garson: piano; Sanborn, alto saxophone; Grando: baritone saxophone; Flowers: bass; Newman: drums; Rosario: chimes; MacCormack, Andrisano: backing vocals. Produced: Visconti; engineered: Kramer, Harwood.*

First release*: 16 October 1990,* ***David Live*** *(RCD 10138/39/CDS 79 5362 2).* ***Live****: 1974.*

Considered by its singer, producer and contemporary critics as the worst record Bowie released in the Seventies, *David Live* (Lester Bangs: "a dismal flatulence"; Robert Christgau: "the artiste at his laryngeal nadir, mired in bullshit pessimism and arena-rock pandering"; Tony Visconti: "one of the quickest and shoddiest albums I've ever done") was erratically recorded during Bowie's Philadelphia residency in July 1974. The backing singers/ dancers Geoff MacCormack and Gui Andrisano tended to wander off-mike, requiring them to re-cut vocals in the studio. Even Bowie was inaudible at times during "Space Oddity," which he'd sung into a telephone from his cherry picker roost. Further, Keith Harwood had erratically recorded the shows and had failed to separate instruments, so that bass guitar notes and kick drum beats were a clump of sound on a single track. Not that sound quality mattered a whit to RCA, who just wanted to rush-release a live record before Bowie resumed touring in autumn 1974.

So *David Live* came across as a field recording of some kabuki performance. The horn/woodwind section took more cues from *Cabaret* than it did Stax/Volt, with the opener "1984" kicking off with what sounded like a klezmer melody. Remixing the album in 2004, Tony Visconti re-sequenced Bowie's cover of the Ohio Players' "Here Today and Gone Tomorrow," (Bowie had ditched the conjunction) also debuted in the Philadelphia concerts.

Where "Knock On Wood" was a soul song that even squares knew, "Here Today, Gone Tomorrow" was more obscure, the choice of Bowie the soul 45 crate-digger. One of the first Ohio Players singles, the track was red-earth soul compared to the rakish funk the band played in the mid-Seventies ("Fire," "Sweet Sticky Thing," etc.). Paced by Leroy "Sugarfoot" Bonner's guitar and stately in its progression (its refrain doesn't appear until halfway through the track), "Here Today and Gone Tomorrow" laments a woman who blows through town like a sailor. On Bowie's cover, Earl Slick's guitar (a Gibson SG with an 100-watt Marshall half-stack, with Slick often using an MXR Phase 90 pedal) is hotter than Bonner's, while a dialogue between Michael Kamen's organ and Garson's piano added some light. Compared to "Knock on Wood," Bowie sings more freely, venturing into falsetto in the choruses. Where the Ohio Players original had drifted off in a half-minute coda of resignation, here Bowie kept harping on the chorus, as if repeating the lament long enough would cauterize the wound.

Can You Hear Me

***Recorded**: **(unreleased demo, "Take It In Right")** 1 January 1974, Olympic Studios, London. Bowie: vocal, acoustic guitar?, electric guitar?; **(Lulu single, unreleased)** 25 March 1974, Olympic, 17 April 1974, RCA Studios, New York. Lulu: lead vocal; Bowie: backing vocal?; Carlos Alomar: rhythm guitar; Flowers: bass?; Newman: drums?; **(album)** 13-18 August, 20-24 November 1974, Sigma Sound Studios, Philadelphia. Bowie: lead vocal; Alomar: rhythm guitar; Garson: piano; Sanborn: alto saxophone; Willie Weeks: bass; Andy Newmark: drums; Larry Washington, Pablo Rosario?: conga; Luther Vandross, Ava Cherry, Robin Clark, Diane Sumler?, Anthony Hinton?: backing vocals; unknown musicians: strings (arr. Tony Visconti, recorded Air Studios, London, January 1975). Produced: Bowie, Visconti, Harry Maslin; engineered: Carl Paruolo.*

***First release**: 7 March 1975, **Young Americans** (RCA RS 1006/ APL1-0998, UK #2, US #9). **Broadcast**: 23 November 1975, Cher. **Live**: 1974.*

Bowie wrote "Take It In Right" as a single for Lulu, cutting a studio demo on New Year's Day 1974 and producing Lulu sessions that spring in London and New York. He intended the single as the first piece of what he envisaged as a proper Southern soul album for her, essentially *Lulu In Memphis*. While nothing else came of the idea, a Lulu overdub date in New York would have colossal importance for Bowie, as there he met the guitarist Carlos Alomar.

Alomar, born in Puerto Rico and the son of a Pentecostal minister who moved to New York City to establish a ministry, was playing guitar in the Apollo Theater's house band by his late teens. After stints with James Brown and Wilson Pickett, Alomar joined the funk group the Main Ingredient and became a New York-based session player for their label RCA, which is how he wound up at the Lulu session. The first sight of the session producer shocked him. Bowie was in cadaverous shape, weighing around 100 pounds, his chalk-white skin offsetting his russet hair ("he looked like a fuckin' vampire, come on!" Alomar recalled). However, Alomar found Bowie to be friendly and polite and in earnest to learn about the New York R&B scene. So Alomar invited Bowie to his Queens apartment for what was likely the most substantial meal he'd had in months (at the time, Bowie was subsisting for days on vitamin slushes). Anxious to experience music scenes he'd only read about, Bowie found in Alomar a charming, and well-connected, ambassador. He offered Alomar a gig as his touring guitarist and in the summer of 1974 asked him to come to Philadelphia to make an album.

"Every British musician has a hidden desire to be black. They all talk about 'funky rhythm sections' and their idols are all black blues guitarists," Tony Visconti said in 1974. (Lou Reed put it more bluntly on "I Wanna Be Black," a song he left off *Sally Can't Dance* the same year, finally releasing it in 1977). Bowie had been fascinated by American black culture since he was a teenager (he'd pressed J. Saunders Redding's *On Being Negro In America* upon his bandmates in the Manish Boys) and his delight at meeting Alomar was obvious, to the point of being a bit cringe-making. Days after their meeting, he was effusing to a reporter at a nightclub that he'd found "a really incredible black guy called Carlos."

With Alomar as his inside man, Bowie just needed the right setting. He found it in Philadelphia. Founded by Joe Tarsia in 1968, Sigma Sound Studios had become a R&B/disco hit factory by 1974. It was the home base of the composers and arrangers Kenneth Gamble, Leon Huff and Thom Bell and their various projects: the Stylistics, the Spinners, the O'Jays, the Three Degrees. The studio's relative isolation in Philadelphia let producers operate with less scrutiny by record labels and let them skirt musician union rules. As Sigma's three studios were miniscule by New York standards, musicians were often jammed in together, which cooled egos, heightened interplay and created an "ambient" tone that warmed dozens of Philly Soul singles.

Gorging on Philadelphia International records at the time, Bowie learned about Sigma Sound when Ava Cherry recorded demos there during his Philadelphia residency in July 1974. Michael Kamen recalled Bowie being particularly impressed by the house musicians, MFSB ("he met the guys, these fantastic black guys," Kamen said. "Something really shifted in him"), and Bowie booked time at Sigma for the following month. Yet once in the studio, Bowie didn't use anyone from MFSB except the conga player Larry Washington. Instead he brought in some of his touring band (Mike Garson, David Sanborn) and some New York-based legends Alomar had recruited: the bassist Willie Weeks and drummer Andy Newmark. After a few days of in-studio rehearsals, Bowie flew in Tony Visconti from London to take over production.

Vocals were an issue. Bowie, who'd mainly recorded in Britain, was used to the methods of an Olympic or Trident Studios, whose engineers applied equalizers and compression tools at the point of recording. So when takes were played back, the singer already heard his voice treated with EQ and reverb. By contrast, Sigma Sound favored a "dry" ambience, its engineers capturing the sound of the room flat, using little reverb, and cleaning up flaws and adding effects at the mixing stage. This process unnerved Bowie, who hadn't heard his "naked" voice on tape in years.

Bowie also realized that having a vocal chorus would help mask any flaws in his singing. "My drug problems were playing havoc with my voice, producing a real raspy sound that I fought all the time when I wanted to sing high, swooping into falsetto and such," he said in 2006. By chance, Alomar had brought along for company his wife, the singer Robin Clark, and his childhood friend Luther Vandross. Hearing Vandross and Clark harmonizing as he was sketching in the control room, Bowie quickly got them and Ava Cherry into the vocal booth and deputized them as his chorus singers (see "Young Americans").

"Can You Hear Me," as it was a soul ballad Bowie had in the tank (he'd renamed it "Take It In Right" before the Sigma session), was among the first songs he cut in Philadelphia. On a reel taped the evening of 13 August 1974, Bowie cues the band with "let's do the first one we did." The subsequent take was a lovely, muted version of the song, with Alomar playing gorgeous lead guitar, particularly in the second verse (he foreshadows in tone John McFee's lead playing on Elvis Costello's "Allison"). The take, however, lacked Vandross' vocal arrangement, which would prove central to the song. The rich open harmonies of Vandross, Clark and Cherry's voices, the warm assurance with which they hold notes and their sense for the dramatic (Bowie introduces the "take it in right" hook, the chorus sells it) all serve to anchor Bowie's desperate lead vocal.

Bowie's singing is a study in frustration and perseverance, in sync with how his verses follow advances away from the home F major chord to the dominant chord, C major ("once we were...they understand") with sad retreats back home (a B-flat major to a G minor 7th, "closer than others...I was your...") that are in turn broken by jumps back to C major ("...man"). Bowie opens confidently, with a phrase that rises by a fifth ("once we were *lovers*"), but he soon crabs his ambitions, keeping to the confines of third or even second intervals. There's a slurred nasal phrasing in the second verse ("so many othurrs"), a shaky falsetto in later refrains. Bowie first sings the title phrase low in his range, falls back whenever he manages to hit a new peak. The refrain itself is a slowly-accumulating confidence; it reverses the verse progression ("can you feel me") and, after repeating that move more brightly with major chords ("show your love"), it culminates in a rousing "take it in right!" rung over C major. Bowie's last sustained "*take it in right!*" has a sense of release. He's finally singing above his chorus singers, a man on the high-wire alone (he achieved a similar effect singing "Can You Hear Me" on *Cher,* with Cher holding the bass end of the vocal harmony).

Where "Here Today, Gone Tomorrow" is a man lamenting a wayward lover, "Can You Hear Me" is a player's perspective, someone who goes through "sixty new cities" but "wants love so badly" (there's a similar line in the unreleased "Shilling the Rubes": "fifty new faces, fifty new cities"). Said to be written for Cherry, the track has a studied unease. It's shot through with guilt, its ornate arrangement and small cathedral of voices working to obscure a pathetic man at the heart of the song.

Honed over the first Sigma sessions and polished during a subsequent trip in November, "Can You Hear Me" is sumptuous, its intro alone masterful. Heralded by Newmark's drum fill and Alomar's two-part guitar line (a quick shuffle through the tones of a C chord and a downward-spiraling arpeggio), the band quickly establishes an ominous foundation: Newmark's tympanum imitation on his floor tom, Weeks' bass fills every other bar and Garson pounding bass octaves on piano. In the verses, Visconti entwined strings with Alomar's guitar lines, each elaborating bars (*e.g.*, the spiral of guitar notes after "closer than others"). There's stagecraft in the arrangement. David Sanborn's alto saxophone, kept back until the third verse, becomes a competing vocal line, while a two-beat fill (everyone hitting, from piano to strings) sets up Bowie's spotlight moment on "take it in right."

With its exquisite low end and the banked fire of its vocals, "Can You Hear Me" was a strong opening round for Bowie at Sigma. Unlike the forced antics of "Knock on Wood" and "John I'm Only Dancing (Again)," Bowie sang contemporary R&B here with cool assurance. It was first notice he could credibly pull off his new role.

John, I'm Only Dancing (Again)

***Recorded**: 13-18 August 1974, 20-24 November 1974, Sigma Sound. Bowie: lead vocal; Alomar: rhythm guitar; Garson: Fender Rhodes, clavinet; Sanborn: alto saxophone; Weeks: bass; Newmark: drums; Washington: conga; Rosario: chimes, cowbell; Vandross, Cherry, Clark, Sumler, Hinton: backing vocals, handclaps?. Produced: Visconti; engineered: Paruolo.*

***First release**: 7 December 1979 (RCA BOW 4, UK #12). **Live**: 1974.*

Disco happily ate anything it was fed, so there were disco records built on Beethoven symphonies, swing tunes and Italian police thriller themes, disco sung by cartoons and puppets. Bowie threw glam rock into the pile. One of his objectives in moving into soul and disco was to get an American hit single. For a first go he revised "John, I'm Only Dancing" for the American market. It seemed a canny move. "John, I'm Only Dancing" had hit #12 in the UK but hadn't been released in the US: it was a readymade single that just needed some alterations for 1974.

So retaining its key and refrain, Bowie wrote a new set of verses and upgraded the rhythm section. The original single had a chassis of chugging acoustic guitar strums. Its revision, provisionally called "Dancin'," set Carlos Alomar's needling rhythm guitar against a pulsing eighth-note Willie Weeks bassline welded to Andy Newmark's kick drum. Mick Ronson's guitar riff was handed over to an alliance of Mike Garson's Fender Rhodes and Alomar's phased lead guitar (with some later synthesizer overdubs). David Sanborn's alto saxophone added rowdy patter throughout the track.

Where the original's two verses were miniature character sketches, evoking a world of seedy nightclubs and quick assignations, the remake had five hectoring verses with Bowie as wedding party MC, cracking the occasional joke and dropping hints as to his current state ("got a line on my hand and Charlie on my back") and America's ("president has got the blues"). "John I'm Only Dancing (Again)" comes off in places as a desperate white British burlesque of American black music. It's saved from disgrace by its latter half, when triggered by Garson's shift to clavinet (on early takes, Bowie yelled "get on that, G!" to cue him), the backing singers spar with Bowie while Alomar lets loose with some in-the-pocket rhythm guitar.

Though Bowie played "John (Again)" on tour in autumn 1974, his enthusiasm for it had cooled by the time he returned to Sigma Sound in November. He still kept the song in contention, as his album was mostly ballads and he needed a dance track. After trying out his cover of "Foot Stomping" as a potential replacement, the happy appearance of "Fame" at the eleventh hour finally made "John (Again)" redundant and Bowie shelved it. At the end of 1979, just as disco was peaking, RCA issued "John (Again)" as a stand-alone single. As with the original, the remake hit #12 in the UK and was a commercial nonentity in America.

Young Americans

***Recorded**: 13-18 August, 20-24 November 1974, Sigma Sound. Bowie: lead vocal; Alomar: rhythm guitar; Garson: piano; Sanborn: alto saxophone; Weeks: bass; Newmark: drums; Washington: conga; Vandross, Cherry, Clark: vocals. Produced: Visconti; engineered: Paruolo.*

***First release**: 21 February 1975 (RCA 2523/ GB-10469, UK #18, US #28). **Broadcast**: 4 December 1974,* The Dick Cavett Show; *23 November 1975,* Cher. ***Live**: 1974, 1983, 1987, 1990.*

Americans love flattery and youth, so it's no surprise that Bowie finally cracked the US Top 40 with this song in the spring of 1975. A diatribe whose bite is kissed away by Bowie's backing singers, "Young Americans" had "no story. Just young Americans," he said. "It's about a newly-wed couple who don't know if they really like each other. Well, they do, but they don't know if they do or don't" (compare Sly Stone's "Family Affair": "Newly-wed a year ago, but you're still checkin' each other out"). With a jerry-rigged structure (three verses and refrains, saxophone solo, bridge, breakdown, two more extended verses and refrains), "Young Americans" opens with a young, bewildered couple finding solace in sex, and not much—it takes him minutes, takes her nowhere. They squander their youth, which is all they have going for them.

Its jumble of characters (a greaser rival for the boy crops up in the second verse), vaguely blue-collar setting and garrulous saxophone make "Young Americans" seem lifted off *The Wild, The Innocent & The E Street Shuffle*. But where Bruce Springsteen was in love with his characters, giving pathos even to walk-on roles, Bowie's boy and girl lack names, jobs, histories. They're just paper dolls moved around a stage. If this is Springsteen, it's a Brechtian one. "I feel the American is the loneliest person in the world," Bowie told an interviewer in late 1972. "I get an awful feeling of insecurity and a need for warmth in people here. It's very, very sad. So many people in America are unaware they are living."

Alienation started in the opening line, "they pulled in just behind the fridge." A reference to Peter Cook and Dudley Moore's stage revue *Behind the Fridge,* it's an odd line in the context of the verse. It ought to be "behind the bridge," offering a standard-issue American make-out session in a car parked off the highway. Instead it's American life as a dark British comedy. The boy and girl move in jump cuts, speak as if they're hostages reading from a script. Theirs is "poster love," he's "her breadwinner," she's a talking Barbie doll. Even the chorus hook sounds like Maoist agitprop: She wants the young American! (always a singular "American"—their union's only in the title).

After a set of diversions—David Sanborn saxophone solo, wistful four-bar bridge, guitar/conga breakdown—Bowie returns to tear up his puppets and curse his audience. He scans

America through his picture window,watches a country spool past his limousine as the words spew out of him: Ford Mustangs, Americans carrying razors "in case of depression" (a dark play on the "in case of fire, break glass" warnings that he saw in every hotel), black Americans moving from the backs of buses to driving Cadillacs; Americans blacklisted; whites dancing and Afro-Sheen advertisements on *Soul Train*.

This was American pop as if written by French provocateurs like Jean-Luc Godard ("few films have ever been more hostile to Americans and more devoted to their cars," J. Hoberman wrote of Godard's *Pierrot Le Fou*) and Serge Gainsbourg, in whose "Ford Mustang" he and the singer Madeline Bell seduced each other with American ad tags: *Keep cool! Fluid makeup! Coca Cola!* This was in 1966, when Gainsbourg could tap the hip vitality American imagery had in Europe. "Young Americans" comes nearly a decade later, when the president's just been kicked out of the White House. By its last verse, "Young Americans" has split its seams. The opening line of the Beatles' "A Day in the Life" erupts from nowhere, sung ecstatically by Luther Vandross, Ava Cherry and Robin Clark. They've "*heard* the news today" where John Lennon had "read" it: fact is now rumor.

The sense of things falling apart extends to Bowie, suddenly left alone at the mike, asking for "one damn song to make me…break down and cryyyyyyy." The last phrase skyrockets over an eleventh, peaking on a high D (fittingly on "break"). This was a revision to cook up the dramatics: in earlier takes, Bowie had sung the line somberly, keeping to the middle of his range.

And with that "cry" appears the last American that Bowie channels, the secret muse of the whole venture: Johnnie Ray. One of the first white R&B singers to pass muster with black audiences, a farmboy from Hopewell, Oregon, a failed actor who became a bloodletter of a singer, Ray recorded for Columbia's "black" label OKeh. His "Cry" topped the R&B and pop charts; other of his singles ruled the charts in Britain (where, as Kevin

Rowland sang years later, he "moved a million hearts in mono"). Ray fashioned a bespoke version of black singing and performance: flaying his voice, convulsing in ecstatic weeping on stage. "Women see reflected in me all of the emotion and tenderness that...the American male just doesn't have time for today...people are too crowded inside themselves these days," Ray once said.

Bowie shared with Ray a sense of visitation, of being a man so entranced by a music outside his ken that he bent himself into fantastic shapes to accommodate it. Lester Bangs, watching Bowie perform in Detroit in October 1974, looked and saw a ghost: "I peered and peered, trying to catch the ultimate vibe…Johnny Ray. Johnny Ray on cocaine singing about 1984."

You and Your Idol, Singing Falsetto

While many of songs Bowie recorded at Sigma were built up in the studio, he already had the structure of "Young Americans" worked out in his head. Even in its first takes Bowie had in place the Beatles quote, the bridge (though only a scatted melody, not a lyric yet) and the break sequence, which originally was an Alomar phased guitar solo.

Built of steady movements across the key of C major, the verses end on C's dominant chord, G major ("taken *anything,*" *"fifty more"*) and then slam straight into the refrains, which start still far away from "home" (the F majors and G majors under the "all night!s") until finally falling back to C on the title phrase. (Bowie had also reversed his verse's chord progression to get his refrains in "Can You Hear Me?") The three-part bridge section (saxophone solo, vocal, guitar solo) veers into A minor until Alomar closes with a resounding A major ninth chord to ready the song for the change up to D major for the fourth verse, a modulation that cues Bowie to dump his Springsteenisms for more rolling impressions and prophecies.

Mike Garson's piano line, with its intended "Latin feel, without going over the top into salsa," needed flavoring with a syncopated Alomar guitar line, Larry Washington's conga, Andy Newmark's disco hi-hat and Willie Weeks's root-fat bassline. Two hooks developed in the studio: David Sanborn's alto saxophone intro, whose opening melody stresses a different beat in each bar (Sanborn, who grows to be too much, is down-mixed in later verses), and the chorus refrain harmonized by Vandross, Cherry and Clark in thirds. The latter's a bar-long exaltation ("AAAALLL") punctuated by a higher note ("NIGHT!") and followed by a title phrase sung in three long arcs, the last peaking on a middle E ("*young* American").

Listening to run-throughs of the song at Sigma, Vandross worked up a phrase to play off Bowie's "all right!s," which had been the original chorus hook. He tried it out on Clark: "What if there was a phrase that went *'young Americans, young Americans, he was the young American—all right!'* Now when *'all right'* comes up, jump over me and go into harmony." Overhearing them, Bowie quickly hustled Vandross and his hook into the track.

The song's middle section came out of what Bowie had heard in New York clubs in spring 1974—DJs favoring singles with long "breaks," like Eddie Kendricks' "Girl You Need a Change of Mind," which deployed an old gospel technique. Kendricks' producer told the band "to break it down to nothing, then gradually come in one by one and rebuild to the original fervor of the song." That was seemingly Bowie's intention here after the bridge—cutting things down to Alomar's phased guitar, Washington's moaning conga and a shaker—but the tempo's too slow, the mood too ruminative and the chords too many for the break to be any sort of dance-floor peak. You can even hear the master Andy Newmark trying to come up with a fill to get the break back to the verse.

Still, given a boost by the key change, there's a brio in Bowie's singing, all of the zips up to falsetto, all his reeling loops of words. In the last verse, with his desperate octave-sinking phrases coming every two beats, Bowie sounds like a man so caught up in his rant he can't bother to catch his breath ("YOU! ain't a pimp 'n YOU! ain't a hustler!").

"Young Americans" was a curse on a host country by a tourist who'd never left his car. Playing it live, Bowie smoothed the song, strumming an acoustic guitar as if it was a folk piece. At the height of his fame in the Eighties, Bowie sang "Young Americans" on stage as though he really was covering Springsteen, letting the crowd hand his Johnnie Ray line back to him. On his greatest-hits revue tour of 1990, he used "Young Americans" as a means to ham through a few R&B oldies and that was its last appearance. The song had lost everything he'd ever given it.

Shilling the Rubes

***Recorded**: (unreleased) 13 August 1974, Sigma Sound. Bowie: vocal; Alomar: lead guitar; Garson: piano; Weeks: bass; Newmark: drums. Produced: Visconti; engineered: Paruolo.*

Cut in the first days of the Sigma sessions, "Shilling the Rubes" was one of seven proposed titles for the upcoming album, along with *The Gouster* and *Dancin'*. Using only Carlos Alomar, whose guitar was so distorted by a phaser that it sounded like a clavinet, Mike Garson on piano and the rhythm section of Willie Weeks and Andy Newmark, Bowie cut at least one full take of the song, which was a countershot to "Can You Hear Me" and "It's Gonna Be Me," its lyric the perspective of a woman whose lover has abandoned her.

Its circus metaphors ("It's only a Ferris wheel...ringmaster, cannonball") suited a man fresh off the spectacle of the Diamond Dogs tour. On a 13 August take of "Shilling the Rubes," Bowie references the weariness of touring ("fifty new faces, fifty new days") and of having to wear a mask, with a nod to Smokey Robinson ("gone, like the tears of a clown"). In the chorus, heralded by piano and guitar descending in unison, Bowie repeatedly intones "gone!" to the rumble of Garson's bass keys.

"*Gone!* The day he left town! *Gone!* He was shilling *the* rubes!" The latter was carny slang that Bowie took to mean "fleecing the suckers."One carny would be the "shill" and pose as a customer to convince "rubes" (townies, yokels, what have you) to buy a ticket or patent oil medicine, etc. So it's a huckster (Bowie) using inside shills (African American and Latino musicians) to get rubes to buy his "soul" album.

At this stage the song was mostly potential. Its lyric wasn't finished (Bowie scatted a third verse over Garson's piano), its chorus melody was dull and its rhythms sluggish, with Weeks and Newmark yet to work out a groove. "That's going to be very nice," Bowie said at the end of the take, but he apparently didn't develop the song much further. "Shilling the Rubes" was soon out of contention as an album track: it apparently wasn't mixed and wasn't on the album sequence Tony Visconti drafted at the end of the sessions. Its existence long rumored, its recording never circulating, "Shilling the Rubes" finally leaked in 2009 as a one-minute snippet of the 13 August take, after someone acquired a *Young Americans* reel through dubious means and tried to sell it on eBay. The complete "Shilling the Rubes" is now under Bowie's lock and key.

It's Gonna Be Me

Recorded*: 13-18 August, poss. 20-24 November 1974, Sigma Sound. Bowie: lead vocal; Alomar: lead guitar; Garson; piano; Sanborn: alto saxophone; Weeks: bass; Newmark: drums; Cherry, Vandross, Clark: backing vocals; unknown musicians: strings (arr. Visconti, recorded Air Studios, London, January 1975). Produced: Visconti; engineered: Paruolo.*

First release*: 14 May 1991,* ***Young Americans*** *(reissue).* ***Live****: 1974.*

"It's Gonna Be Me," an epic outtake from *Young Americans*, has a similar frame as "Can You Hear Me": a wayward man wonders if he's left behind a chance at love with someone he's abandoned in a hotel room. Cruder ("I balled just another young girl last night") and stranger than the latter, "It's Gonna Be Me" is Bowie giving himself over to regret and madness, his vocal chorus backing his delusions.

A spare recording, its verses are Bowie singing a rhythmically free melody over Mike Garson's piano and a skeletal rhythm section: Andy Newmark keeping languid 3/4 time with a faint hi-hat and a snare hit on every other downbeat; Willie Weeks playing a single root note to open each bar. The band struggled to pull the song together. Multiple takes recorded on 13 and 14 August document the energy in the room audibly dissipating, with Bowie revising his lyric on each take. He switched from second person to first, played off flubs ("there was no raincheck for me" became "there was no rein to check me"), toyed with end phrases (the second verse once closed with "stallions and lightning won't hold me back!!") and vocal effects (he once tried stuttering out "stammer").

By the time he got a master take, "It's Gonna Be Me" had been sweetened with a Carlos Alomar guitar intro, a David Sanborn saxophone solo, an understated, cello-heavy string arrangement by Tony Visconti (seemingly inspired by Bobby Martin's charts on Harold Melvin and the Blue Notes' "If You Don't Know Me By Now") and a chorus vocal line derived from a melody Mike Garson had played in the verse.

In 1999, Bowie compared his work on *Young Americans* to method acting. "I'd immerse myself...it was a process of becoming, of transforming into the thing you admire and want to be. To find out 'what makes it tick.' Then, hopefully, you've absorbed that knowledge and you move on to something else." The use of the vocal chorus in "It's Gonna Be Me" is Bowie's take on a soul convention. On a typical Al Green track, the vocal chorus is under Green's thumb, waiting for his cue. So in "Let's Get Married," it's only after Green concludes his thought ("I wanna settle down") that the chorus rushes in to sing the title phrase. They're a committee ratifying his decision. Or take how Aretha Franklin, in "Respect" or "Don't Play That Song," makes her chorus her confidant: they back her plays, fuel her indignation.

In "It's Gonna Be Me," the relation between Bowie and singers is more tenuous. Ava Cherry, Robin Clark and Luther Vandross are barely present in the three lengthy verses, appearing only to underline a stray phrase, like "weep over the breakfast tray." They form ranks in the refrains, singing in close harmonies as Bowie scurries beneath them. He can barely bring himself to voice the title line, which at first he nearly mutters, leaving the business of the melody to his singers. There's a narrative of sorts, Bowie's lead is a wandering penitent who's reconciled to community in the refrain, a movement that parallels the song's questing harmonic structure, with the verses and refrains a long ramble away from the tonic chord, C major.

But Bowie seems unwilling to accept his singers' reassurances, his jittery phrasing undermines their solidarity. They push back with a jolting "NO!" in the second verse and whatever dialogue they've had breaks down. Midway through the last verse, with everyone but loyal Garson having abandoned him, Bowie tries to find one of the girls he's deserted. He sees her with "a little tear running down her cheek," a trickle of piano keys as illustration. Distracted by passing cars and "people looking at me," with Bowie seemingly singing with his lips pressed against the mike, he knocks "hard hard hard" on her door and she, on cue, falls into his arms like "a treasured toy." He sings the line as if she's dropped dead. When the singers appear to help Bowie play out the final refrain, they're doing it out of pity.

Bowie debuted "It's Gonna Be Me" in his autumn 1974 live shows and it was slated for *Young Americans*. But along with "Who Can I Be Now?," it was cut to fit in Bowie's two John Lennon collaborations. While its 6:28 length did the track little favors, its last-minute excision also suggested Bowie had second thoughts about releasing such a bizarre antic of a soul confessional.

After Today

***Recorded**: 13-18 August 1974, Sigma Sound. Bowie: lead vocal; Alomar: rhythm guitar; Garson: piano; Sanborn: alto saxophone; Weeks: bass; Newmark: drums. Produced: Visconti; engineered: Paruolo.*

***First release**: 19 September 1989, **Sound + Vision**.*

Once Tony Visconti assumed control at Sigma Sound, Bowie's musicians would show up in the early afternoon to cut overdubs, jam and work out arrangements. Willie Weeks would make the occasional flub until he mastered the song, after which he was note-perfect for however many takes were needed. David Sanborn would hang back, coming in halfway through. Bowie arrived by 10 or 11 in the evening and would work through the following morning. The pace soon took its toll on the musicians (Mike Garson was one of the few who had the stamina to endure the all-nighters; another player recalled routinely falling asleep) and on Visconti, who thought he was having a heart attack leaving the studio one morning.

Upon arriving, Bowie went through the day's tapes, picked what he liked and sang a few takes live in the studio with the band. This improvisatory, freewheeling routine reminded Visconti of the chaotic making of *The Man Who Sold the World*, with Bowie playing fresh songs to the band on acoustic guitar (as he had on *Space Oddity*) and having them flesh the pieces out. Making an album out of jam sessions by a genial set of musicians and with Bowie fans camped outside the studio as his own version of the Beatles' Apple Scruffs (he brought in the kids on the last night to hear rough mixes) was a tonic for him after the isolation of *Diamond Dogs*. Decades later, Bowie told an interviewer he'd loved the communal nature of the Sigma sessions: it temporarily eased a feeling of intense loneliness that was plaguing him.

So "After Today" is a quintessential Sigma track, a song loose enough to work as both a ballad and an up-tempo funk piece. One take of the latter (marked "take 1") was cut on 14 August, on the same reel as takes of "It's Gonna Be Me" and "Can You Hear Me." Another take, with a slightly slower tempo and possibly cut on the same or following evening, was issued on Bowie's career retrospective *Sound + Vision* in 1989. On each take, singing over the syncopated dialogue of Garson's piano and Carlos Alomar's phased guitar in the verses, Bowie offers a vaguely aspirational lyric with an undercurrent of foreboding—the person to whom he's wishing good fortune doesn't merit it. It's a buck-up talk for a faulty actor ("doing the wrong thing/forgetting your lines"). What likely consigned "After Today" to the scrap pile was Bowie's attempts to sing refrains in falsetto, far too ambitious given the state of his voice. In the *S&V* take, Bowie gasps for breath and barely grazes his would-be high Gs and As (he sings the second refrain in a lower register to cut himself a break).

Each take was a clinic by Andy Newmark, who opened with a kick-drum cannonade answered, four bars in, by Weeks' massive bass hook. Newmark, who had played for Sly and the Family Stone and Roxy Music, was so dynamic a player that during an impromptu audition he got a wasted Sly Stone out of bed and dancing. He favored a stripped-down kit—detuned kick, snare, floor tom, hi-hat and a cymbal doing double-duty as a ride and crash—and owed his sharp, cracking tone to a tightly-tuned snare, Remo drumheads and a penchant for rim-shots.

Who Can I Be Now?

***Recorded**: 13-18 August 1974, Sigma Sound. Bowie: lead vocal; Alomar: electric guitar; Garson; piano; Sanborn: alto saxophone; Weeks: bass; Newmark: drums, tambourine?; Cherry, Vandross, Clark: backing vocals. Produced: Visconti; engineered: Paruolo.*

***First release**: 14 May 1991, **Young Americans** (reissue).*

"Who Can I Be Now?," its title an unclaimed gift for Bowie biographers, was the peak of the soul confessionals he recorded in the first Sigma Sound sessions, moving beyond the self-eviscerating "It's Gonna Be Me" into diagnosing a wider-spread malaise. Everyone Bowie sees is "raised in blindness...can feel their chains." By the second verse he's planning an insurrection against heaven, crafting a manmade "star" to steal some of a false heaven's angelic light. It's a pop reduction of a Gnostic teaching: that man, once godlike, has fallen into captivity, trapped by time and mortality, and worships the false god who's imprisoned him (see "Station to Station").

Its refrain, whose melody seems cast in steel, ties this occultism into another well-worn Bowie theme, the fear of losing one's core identity after donning too many masks. "Who can I be now?" sings the man who's just exchanged glam pirate gear for Forties "gouster" suits. "*Now* can I be *now*?...Can I be real?" Unusually for *Young Americans* mixes, the backing vocals are split into two overlapping factions—Cherry and Clark mixed in the left channel, Vandross dominating the right.

Bowie scrapped "Who Can I Be Now?" for apparently the same space-related reason as "It's Gonna Be Me," but the song also (at least in its officially-released version) was leaden, its arrangement overstuffed, with David Sanborn determined to annex any open space, and had a weak low end. Still, the strength of Bowie's singing and his refrain melody put the song leagues above one of its replacements, his cover of "Across the Universe."

Somebody Up There Likes Me

***Recorded**: 13-18 August, 20-24 November 1974, Sigma Sound. Bowie: lead vocal; Alomar: rhythm guitar; Garson: piano, synthesizer; Sanborn: alto saxophone; Weeks: bass; Newmark: drums, tambourine; Cherry, Clark, Vandross: backing vocals. Produced: Visconti; engineered: Paruolo.*

***First release**: 7 March 1975, **Young Americans**. **Live**: 1974*

On "Somebody Up There Likes Me" Bowie inked in what he'd sketched on "Alternative Candidate." It's *homo superior* as celebrity politician ("[he] looked a lot like you and me," much as how Bob Dylan's voice "came from you and me"). The candidate hugs babies, kisses ladies, says everybody's a star and he's the brightest. His campaign hook is his song's title, taken from a Paul Newman boxing film whose tagline was "a girl can lift a fellow to the stars" or a line in Kurt Vonnegut's *The Sirens of Titan* spoken by an amiable twit to account for his good fortune.

Bowie recycled some of the refrain melody and a few lines from his Astronettes composition "I Am Divine" (see Ch. 8). "I Am Divine" was a cocksure singer talking himself up. "Somebody Up There Likes Me" is a product testimonial, the singer as advance handler for the candidate. The backing singers, whose three-part harmonies are panned across the stereo spectrum, pop in like advertisements.

Bowie used Vance Packard's *The Hidden Persuaders* as the meat of the rambling societal diagnoses of his peak cocaine period. Packard had documented a recent trend (in 1957) in which psychologists and social scientists were being recruited by American advertisers. These "persuaders" regarded the populace as "bundles of daydreams, misty hidden yearnings, guilt complexes, irrational emotional blockages...image lovers given to impulsive and compulsive acts." In Detroit in November 1974, the reporter Bruno Stein found Bowie backstage lecturing Ava Cherry and roadies about the media, who were engaged in "cultural manipulation," and ad agencies, "who are killers, man...they're dealing with lives." Rather than selling products to consumers "rationally," say by using market surveys, advertisers with shrinks on retainer would craft campaigns to tap base cravings: oral gratification (candy ads), envy of neighbors or siblings (cars, appliances), delusions of immortality (cigarettes), dreams of sexual prowess/submission (everything).

Packard also had charted the move of "deep researchers" from selling toilet paper into selling political candidates. John Kennedy and Richard Nixon were each packaged like cigarette brands, their campaigns working on a subconscious level. Kennedy signaled youth, sex, glamour; Nixon tapped vast pools of resentment and paranoia. And each man had taken it too far, like Ziggy Stardust: one was shot, the other was fleeing the White House just as Bowie was recording "Somebody Up There Likes Me" in Philadelphia.

That night in Detroit, Bowie turned the conversation to Adolf Hitler, who he called "a marvelous morale booster...a perfect figurehead" but also a dupe, a stalking horse for more powerful forces like the media. "I don't believe [Hitler] was the dictatorial, omnipotent leader that he's been taken for." (It sounds like Bowie had seen Peter Watkins' *Privilege*, a 1967 film where Paul Jones, the lead singer of Manfred Mann, played a pop star used by a fascist church and government to channel the energy of youth into controlled circuits.) In interviews the following year, Bowie gave Hitler more credit. Now he praised Hitler as a media artist, called him the first rock star, with moves like Mick Jagger. "The world will never see his like [again]. He staged a country...He would march into a room to speak and music and lights would come on at strategic moments...girls got hot and sweaty and guys wished it was them up there. That, for me, is the rock 'n' roll experience."

As Bowie was calling fascism a media event and Hitler a pop idol, some of the 20th Century bogeymen, from Nixon to Franco, were dying or falling from power, as if written out *en masse* by an author wrapping up an overlong book. There was a moment in 1974 or 1975 when it seemed that time, a meager but dedicated prosecutor, was ridding the world of its shabby emperors. "Somebody Up There Likes Me" calls out that delusion. For Bowie, the likes of Nixon were clumsy, grasping, analog. Tyranny evolves; it adapts. "Television is the most successful fascist," he said. Movie stars like Rudolph Valentino and pop stars like himself were far better at creating enduring cults of personality than a Hitler, who'd simply wanted it too much. The Nazis needed truncheons behind their propaganda posters. The pop star lets his audience bring the violence, lets them destroy themselves for his ends ("somebody plays my song...[it] makes me stronger for you").

Another of Bowie's key books of the time was *The Immortal*, a novel about an ambitious, amoral Method actor (a thinly-veiled James Dean) who dies young and creates a death cult. This was the winning formula: rock 'n' roll would eventually spawn a fascist Elvis. "There will be a political figure in the not too distant future who'll sweep this part of the world like early rock and roll did," Bowie said. "Somebody Up There Likes Me" was his outline of how it would happen, his "'watch out mate, Hitler's on his way back'...rock 'n' roll sociological bit."

So "Somebody Up There Likes Me" was a series of withheld pleasures, a charismatic toying with his audience. It starts with a minute-long alto saxophone solo whose chords circle through the A major key but avoid any move home to the tonic chord. Bowie gets boxed out by his musicians—twice during the intro, he sounds as if he's about to launch into the verse, only to have David Sanborn break into yet another round. And two of its last three refrains close without letting Bowie complete the title hook ("somebody up there..."), which makes the "...likes me" finally sung at the end of the last refrain seem like a reward.

It was also Bowie's most twisted version of the "Philly Sound." The records Gamble and Huff and Thom Bell had made at Sigma were palaces for an ambitious public. Baseline emotions—fear, despair at the state of the world, a desperate hope to be loved—were set in what the critic Nate Patrin called "high-class, post-Mantovani symphonic arrangements...populist FM radio fare you could listen to in a laundromat." Bowie saw Philly Soul as another of Packard's Hidden Persuaders: an aspirational urban music that toyed with one's deepest cravings.

With Mike Garson's synthesizer for strings, Sanborn's alto saxophone in lieu of a full horn section and a mixed set of "amateur" singers instead of the poised likes of the Three Degrees, "Somebody Up There Likes Me" was like a Philly Soul bootleg. Its graces were Bowie's vocal, ranging across a two-octave span (in the fourth refrain, he opens with a push towards falsetto only to sink to a near-basso in the next bar) and an undercarriage of a fluid Willie Weeks bassline, whose fills are echoed by Garson's synthesizer, and a two-tracked Carlos Alomar for rhythm (sharp chording mixed right) and texture (phased arpeggios mixed left). It's dedication to pleasure, gospel-tinged hedonism put to divine fascist ends.

Right

Recorded*: 14-18 August 1974, 20-24 November 1974, Sigma Sound. Bowie: lead vocal; Alomar: rhythm guitar; Sanborn: alto saxophone; Garson: clavinet: Weeks: bass; Newmark: drums; Washington: conga; Vandross, Clark, Cherry, MacCormack: backing vocals. Produced: Visconti; engineered: Paruolo.*

First release*: 7 March 1975,* ***Young Americans****.*

At the close of the documentary *Cracked Actor,* Bowie is rehearsing a new song at Sigma Sound. Luther Vandross, Robin Clark and Ava Cherry stand in a semi-circle around him, glancing at lyric sheets like actors about to go off book. He guides them through the rapids of his call-and-response bridge and seems abashed and happy when they're done.

The song, "Right," marked a shift. Having begun with "standard" Bowie compositions spiced with R&B or Latin flavors, the Sigma sessions began producing more spare, groove-anchored tracks, likely reflecting the divide between songs Bowie had written beforehand and those he spun out of studio jams (given how the top melody of "Right" is tightly wound to Carlos Alomar's guitar, Bowie may have used Alomar's lines as a starting point). Where "Young Americans" and "Can You Hear Me" have rapid harmonic rhythms, with chords changing at least every bar, "Right" has only two alternating chords, an F major seventh and a E major. While the progression feels like it should move somewhere else, to resolve to C major or A minor, instead the chords keep cycling. This hypnotic stasis is furthered by a structure in which a pair of six-bar refrains alternate, with relief coming only from a vocal breakdown and an Alomar guitar solo, a concisely picked set of lines that he ties up with a sparkling run along his treble strings.

Bowie said he wanted to put "a positive drone over" with "Right," to write a success mantra: *never no turning back, never been known to fail*. For whom? The documentarian Alan Yentob said Bowie would talk about himself in the third person during interviews , and as with "Win," "Right" seems as much intended for its composer as its audience. Bowie sang his positive drone in his lower register while Alomar and Willie Weeks played resounding little fills to pad out bars and usher in fresh refrains—take Weeks' popped notes that close out the fourth refrain (2:35). By comparison David Sanborn's alto saxophone is boorish, even nosing its way into the vocal break.

The latter was a combative dialogue between lead and backing singers. Bowie begins by echoing his chorus ("(WISHING!) *wishing you* (WISHING!) *wishing that...*). He feints at them, pouts, tries out voices. They interrogate him, he pushes back ("*taking you with me!* (SOMETIMES!) *lovin' it!* (RIGHT! TAKE IT!)"). The battle leaves the chorus in a power position for the rest of the song. By the last set of refrains, Bowie's fallen silent.

Foot Stomping/I Wish I Could Shimmy Like My Sister Kate

(("Foot Stomping") Collins;("Sister Kate") Williams/Piron.)
Recorded*: (unreleased versions) 20-24 November 1974, Sigma Sound; ca. 3-5 December 1974, Record Plant, New York?; ca. 12-15 January*

1975, Electric Lady Studios, New York. Bowie: lead vocal; Alomar: rhythm guitar; Slick: lead guitar?; Garson: piano; Sanborn: alto saxophone; Emir Ksasan: bass; Newmark and Dennis Davis: drums; Pablo Rosario: conga; Vandross, MacCormack, Cherry, Clark, Sumler, Hinton: backing vocals. Produced: Visconti; engineered: Paruolo, Maslin.

Released: *(Cavett performance) May 1995,* ***RarestOneBowie****.* ***Broadcast****: 4 November 1974, The Dick Cavett Show.* ***Live****: 1974.*

After a West Coast leg of his tour in September 1974, Bowie took advantage of a few weeks off to scrap most of the Hunger City sets (props were given to a Philadelphia school) and to purge his set lists of the melancholic: "Sweet Thing," "Aladdin Sane," "Time" and "Big Brother" got the chop. Only four songs remained from *Diamond Dogs*, the album Bowie still allegedly was promoting, while he introduced five songs he'd recorded at Sigma Sound.

He also did some recasting for what was being informally called the "Soul Dogs" tour. Bandleader Michael Kamen left, griping that the tour suddenly had become "a third-rate gospel revivalist meeting. The stage was full of large black people going 'Hallelujah' and shaking tambourines." His new bassist Emir Ksasan and drummer Dennis Davis were both suggestions of Carlos Alomar (Bowie and Geoff MacCormack were now the only British members of the tour). The backing singer ranks expanded to Luther Vandross, Ava Cherry, Robin Clark, Diane Sumler and Anthony Hinton, while Earl Slick had to share guitar duties with Alomar, much to Slick's frustration.

Mick Farren, who saw the tour in New York, recalled it being "like a crazed Funkadelic tour with added cocaine paranoia and Scientology...obviously they'd cobbled it together on the fly." It was Bowie indulging a whim on a grand scale. "I like devising shows, I like putting them together and I like the first, say, three or four nights," he said in 2002. "And then I get bored beyond belief of having to do the same damn thing every night." Once there had been countervailing forces. The Tony Defries of 1972 wouldn't have allowed Bowie to dump his expensive sets after three months, nor would the Angela Bowie who'd been tour and lighting director in the first Spiders from Mars days. But with Defries and Angela now both off in their own worlds, in mid-1974 there was no one left to tell Bowie no. (The transformation was also Bowie's first offensive against Defries: scrapping the $400,000 Hunger City set three months after its construction would derail his manager's plans to bring the show to Brazil and Europe in 1975. Defries didn't sweat the change, as the loss ultimately came out of Bowie's pocket.)

Bowie risked alienating his fans as he had some of his musicians. Kids had showed up at the Diamond Dogs shows wearing Ziggy Stardust gear, only to learn they were out of date. And those resilient enough to wear "Continental" decadent gear to a Bowie show in late 1974 instead found *that* look was now passé, as Bowie was now wearing "gouster" suits. With no new album or single to give his audience any indication of his latest whims, his new songs got weak and sometimes hostile receptions, particularly the "Mike Garson Band" (the touring band minus Bowie) opening act. But Bowie enjoyed playing ringmaster to his troupe, reporters noticing his jittery energy and stage patter (Lester Bangs accused Bowie of "posing as a get-down dude"), his often hoarse voice, his glad-handing and crotch-grabbing during songs.

Along with "Knock on Wood," Bowie wanted another uptempo R&B song in the new sets. He hit upon combining the Flares' "Foot Stomping" with the jazz standard "I Wish I Could Shimmy Like My Sister Kate." Debuting the medley during a residency at Radio City Music Hall, he sang it like a diva, flanked by two of his male backing singers (Its performance on the *Dick Cavett Show* a month later is its only "official" recording).

The Flares' "Foot Stomping" had erupted with a saxophone conga line led by session ace Plas Johnson, its biggest hook two bars' worth of tromping, with everyone in the studio contributing their shoes. The bass man carried the lead tenors, who sang with demented ecstasy. A guitar solo, a saxophone break, stomping: it was over in two minutes. For Bowie's revision, Alomar hooked the song on a guitar riff he'd conjured from the Young Rascals' "Jungle Walk" and his own guitar work on the Main Ingredient's "You Can Call Me Rover": a needling line that sounded like a Morse code transmission.

Bowie had heard the other piece of the medley, "Sister Kate," on the Sixties London club circuit. The Beatles had played the song live and fellow Liverpudlians the Remo Four cut it as a single. Bowie used the Olympics' version, "Shimmy Like Kate," a 1960 single (the tell is Bowie using the Olympics' line "north-west-south-east/gonna go west"). Where the Flares seemed to have pulled "Foot Stomping" out of the air, "Sister Kate" had deep roots. Louis Armstrong claimed it was the first song he'd ever written, a bawdy thing called "Take Your Feet Off Katie's Head," and said New Orleans musicians Clarence Williams and Armand Piron had stolen his music.

Despite a few attempts to cut the medley in the studio, nothing took. Bowie was having a last go at the songs in January 1975 when Alomar grafted the "Foot Stomping" guitar riff into a developing jam with John Lennon (see "Fame").

Fascination

(Vandross/Bowie). ***Recorded****: 20-24 November 1974, Sigma Sound?; ca. 3-10 December 1974, Record Plant. Bowie: lead vocal; Alomar: rhythm guitar; Slick?: lead guitar?; Garson: clavinet, piano, organ; Sanborn: alto saxophone; Ksasan: bass; Newmark or Davis: drums; Rosario: cowbell, shaker; Vandross, Clark, Cherry, Sumler, MacCormack, Hinton: backing vocals. Produced: Visconti; engineered: Paruolo, Maslin.*

First release*: 7 March 1975,* ***Young Americans. Live****: (as "Funky Music," via the 'Mike Garson Band') 1974.*

The sessions of August 1974 hadn't made an album. While there were some obvious winners like "Young Americans," other songs hadn't developed and the majority of the completed tracks tended toward the brooding. Playing "Can You Hear Me" and "It's Gonna Be Me" back-to-back had dragged in his concerts; critics lambasted the new material as being turgid and underdeveloped. A collection of seven-minute-long soul torch ballads would have been a hard sell.

So after two months of touring, Bowie, most of his band and Tony Visconti reconvened for a few days at Sigma Sound in late November 1974. Though the session was intended for overdubs and clean-up work, Bowie used the time to cut more uptempo candidates for the album, especially as he was having doubts about "John, I'm Only Dancing (Again)" as LP opener. He struggled to cut an acceptable take of "Foot Stomping" but another inspiration, rewriting a song Luther Vandross was performing in his opening act, proved easier to execute.

Bowie first heard "Funky Music (Is a Part of Me)" during the August sessions, as Vandross would run Robin Clark and Ava Cherry through the song during downtimes. When he asked Vandross for permission to record "Funky Music," the latter was incredulous."What do you mean, 'let' you record it. I'm living in the Bronx in a building with an elevator that barely works and you're asking me to 'let' you record one of my songs."

Bowie had picked up on a tension between Vandross' music, with its ominous, snaking bass hook, and his open-faced lyric. One of Vandross' first compositions, "Funky Music" was a sales pitch for himself, a New York hustle: "I do the singing, just give me a beat!"is pure George M. Cohan. Bowie, who also feared he'd cut too desperate a figure singing something called "Funky Music," rewrote the lyric as "Fascination," curdling Vandross' boosterism into obsession, with the singer now consumed by hunger for cocaine ("I've got to use her"), sex, oblivion, black magic. Swapping a few words, he turned a man walking down the street looking for a good song into one prowling around for a fix.

He kept Vandross' structure, the descending three-chord progression (E minor-D-C) and, in the second verse, most of Vandross' original lines, but Bowie altered the interplay of lead and backing singers. Vandross had sung much of the refrain in lockstep with Cherry and Clark. Bowie instead let his singers take the lead, shakily repeating their words, as though he can barely process them, in a jittery, ashy timbre. At one point he mutters a junkie's agitated "comeoncomeoncomeoncomeon."

"Fascination," cut primarily during sessions at the Record Plant in early December, had nearly every instrument in its mix distorted: the bass (likely Emir Ksasan) is run through a phaser or a Mutron, Carlos Alomar's guitar and Garson's clavinet are heavily phased and David Sanborn's alto saxophone sings through a Wah-Wah pedal, making his accompanying lines sinister. It's a transformation in keeping with the song's: ambition corrupted into desperation.

Win

Recorded*: ca. 20-24 November 1974, Sigma Sound; ca. 3-10 December 1974, Record Plant. Bowie: lead vocal; Alomar: rhythm guitar; Garson: Fender Rhodes; Sanborn: alto saxophone; Ksasan: bass; Newmark or Davis: drums; Vandross, Cherry, Clark, Sumler, MacCormack, Hinton: backing vocals; unknown musicians: strings (arr. Visconti, recorded Air Studios, January 1975). Produced: Visconti; engineered: Paruolo, Maslin.*

First release*: 7 March 1975,* ***Young Americans****.* ***Live****: 1974.*

The finest *Young Americans* ballad, "Win" is the closest Bowie came to the Philly Soul sound, using it to cushion a study of obsession and control. Softening David Sanborn's alto saxophone, which plays dreamy scales throughout, and adding sweeps of low strings, Bowie and Tony Visconti made the track seem swathed in cotton. Along with the promiscuous use of sixth and major seventh chords, the arrangement gave "Win" a narcotic lassitude.

Like "Fascination," "Win" has little in common with the rambling early Sigma Sound recordings —it's the track on *Young Americans* to most foreshadow *Station to Station*, signaling an end to Bowie's American soul project. Bowie said the chord structures in "Win" were "much more of a European thing than an American thing" though they were also apparently a Brooklyn thing, too, as Earl Slick claimed in 2014 that he and Bowie "came up with that whole chord structure" in a hotel one night on tour. It was a standoff between G major and F major in the verses (with an A major posing an unresolved question, rather than moving the song anywhere) and a modulation to D major in the refrain. It may have come from Todd Rundgren's "Hello It's Me," with which "Win" shares a taste for sixth and major sevenths and a rhythmic hiccup: in the latter case, it's two bars of 6/8 capped by a bar of 2/4 at the close of the refrain.

Singing his most inspired lines on the album ("someone like you should not be allowed to start any fires,""Me, I hope that I'm crazy"), Bowie made a vocal in brushstrokes. The Philadelphia DJ Ed Sciaky, who attended the last "Win" session, said Bowie worked by "sing[ing] three lines, then having the engineer play them back, keeping the first line every time...hitting every line the way he wanted." Finishing around seven in the morning, Bowie had the track played back twice, then nodded and pronounced it done.

While on other *Young Americans* tracks, Bowie had been foiled by his backing singers, on "Win" he keeps them in check. He paces them, undermines them (take the threatening "it *ain't* over" that closes the second refrain). The refrain's a set of knife blows, with an organ high in the mix and a Carlos Alomar arpeggio that calls back to the closing guitar figure of the Beatles' "You Never Give Me Your Money." Bowie sings *"all...you've got...to do...is...**win**"* like a piece of extortion, dreamily lingering on the last word (he'd developed the refrain from riffs during live performances of "Rock 'n' Roll Suicide": "you're not alone! All you've got to do is win!"). At the close, Bowie sings "it ain't *over*" in a rising melody over an out-of nowhere E major chord. It's as if "Win" was just prelude so far, that the song's about to move somewhere else, that Bowie's barely exhausted his reserves. The sudden fade comes as a small mercy.

Across the Universe

*(Lennon/McCartney). **Recorded**: ca. 12-15 January 1975, Electric Lady Studios, 52 West 8th Street, New York. Bowie: lead and backing vocals, acoustic guitar? Mellotron?; John Lennon: acoustic guitar, vocal?; Alomar: rhythm guitar; Slick: lead guitar; Ksasan: bass; Davis: drums. Produced: Bowie, Maslin; engineered: Eddie Kramer.*

***First release**: 7 March 1975, **Young Americans**.*

Bowie's cover of the Beatles' "Across the Universe" was a blatant and successful attempt to lure John Lennon into the studio. The two had first awkwardly met in September 1974 in Los Angeles at a party thrown by Elizabeth Taylor. In New York three months later, Bowie invited Lennon and his then-girlfriend May Pang to his hotel, with Tony Visconti enlisted as moral support. Bowie didn't acknowledge Lennon for hours until, cocaine- and Cognac-fueled, the two began sketching caricatures of each other. This finally broke the ice, though Visconti (who years later would marry Pang) recalled the party ending with the group getting into "a dismally dark conversation about 'what does it all mean,' 'it' being life, which left us all staring dejectedly at the floor."

Dismal or no, the party was enough to make Bowie and Lennon regular companions for a few months, a routine severed once Lennon reunited with Yoko Ono in February 1975 and Bowie left for LA soon afterward. About a week into the new year, Bowie called Lennon to say he was in Electric Lady Studios cutting "Across the Universe." This was an obvious ploy, as there was no need for more *Young Americans* tracks. Visconti was in London with the tapes and an 18-page list of Bowie's mixing instructions, writing and recording string arrangements. But Bowie had sounded his man. At the time Lennon was a known "studio hound" at loose ends. Bored and flattered, he agreed to come down and play acoustic guitar on his own song.

Having used "Across the Universe" as bait, Bowie then rammed the track onto *Young Americans*. He couldn't resist the temptation to have his very own Beatle cover-collaboration and there were political reasons as well. Planning to split from his manager, Bowie used the commercial potential of his Lennon collaborations as an enticement to ensure that his label, RCA, would back his move.

"Across the Universe" was the work of a depressed, LSD-blotted Lennon. Bothered by his wife Cynthia talking in bed one night, Lennon channeled his irritation into a meditative song whose self-absorption borders on the ecstatic. Originally slotted as the Beatles' spring 1968 single, "Across the Universe" emerged in the studio as a meek performance with chirping backing vocals courtesy of two teenage Beatles fans recruited from the nearby street. The song was resistant to change, its composer its worst enemy. Lennon second-guessed himself, scrapping vocals, backwards-masked bass and drum tracks, George Martin's contributions on organ and his own Mellotron playing. As the Beatles had to get on a plane to India, they set the track aside and released "Lady Madonna" as a single instead.

Upon his return to Britain, Lennon seemed indifferent to salvaging "Across the Universe." He didn't re-record it during the long "White Album" sessions and while he toyed with the song during the *Let It Be* rehearsals, he didn't cut a suitable remake then either, requiring the Beatles to dust off the 1968 recording for the film soundtrack. For *Let It Be,* Phil Spector brought "Across the Universe" down a semitone and glopped on a choir, a harpist and a string section. The song's canonical version by default, it became the template for Bowie's cover.

Lennon was too close to "Across the Universe"—he'd never been happy with any recording of it, nor did he think much of Bowie's version ("Why *that* song?" he said to Pang)—but he'd also outgrown its sentiments. The man who embarked on a life of pop radicalism with Yoko Ono was no longer the dulled suburbanite who'd written the song. So there was room for Bowie to liberate "Across the Universe." Calling the Beatles original "watery" (no foul there), Bowie said he wanted to mine the song's thin vein of defiance by "hammer[ing] the hell out of it." He gave "Across the Universe" a manic coke extroversion, ditching Lennon's *"jai guru deva om"* mantra for a guitar solo, straightening out Lennon's irregular-meter verses and dispensing with Lennon's syllabic rhythms and creeping semitonal melodies.

He quickly crossed over into boorishness. The childlike textures of the original (Lennon conveying thoughts jostling in a letterbox by shoving a pile of syllables into the line) gave way to broad strokes. He made a gooey caramel of "insiiiide" and even seemed to ululate towards the close (was he paying homage to Yoko?) Going for a cheap bounce by moving up to E major for the final verse, Bowie then added a two-minute coda that required Dennis Davis, in his first appearance on a Bowie record, to give multiple resuscitations via crash cymbals and snare fills. Bowie later told the *NME* he was proud of the track despite the fact "not many people like it."As dreadfully made as it was craftily conceived, it's one of his most utterly tasteless recordings.

Fame

(Bowie/Lennon/Alomar). ***Recorded****: ca. 12-15 January 1975, Electric Lady. Bowie: lead vocal, rhythm guitar, piano, percussion; Lennon: acoustic guitar, backing vocal; Alomar: rhythm guitar; Slick: rhythm guitar; Ksasan: bass; Davis: drums, vibraslap; Jean Fineberg, Jean Millington: backing vocals? Produced: Bowie, Maslin; engineered:*

Kramer.

First release*: 7 March 1975,* ***Young Americans****; (remix, "Fame 90") 26 March 1990 (Rykodisc RCD5 1018, UK #28).* ***Broadcast****: 4 November 1975, Soul Train; 23 November 1975, Cher; 14 October 1997, Live From the 10 Spot; 29 January 1998, Howard Stern Birthday Bash; 27 June 2000, Live at the BBC; 2 June 2002, Top of the Pops 2; 15 June 2002, A&E's Live By Request.* ***Live****: 1976, 1978, 1983, 1987, 1990, 1997, 2000, 2002-2004.*

"Fame," one of Bowie's pair of US chart-toppers, was an inspired fluke. Its groove, so compelling that James Brown stole it, and its Beatles pedigree made it a smash but Bowie could have as easily dumped "Fame" into his pile of outtakes. It was a mutant hybrid of "Foot Stomping," a Mulligan stew of a few hours' studio jamming. Bowie later called "Fame" his least favorite track on *Young Americans*, a sentiment some of his players shared—Andy Newmark dismissed "Fame" (on which he didn't drum) as "just a vamp, a groove" while Luther Vandross called it "shit," telling Carlos Alomar that "Fascination" should've been released in its place.

Ironically (well, for Bowie, fittingly), "Fame" was the polar opposite of his original plans for *Young Americans*. Instead of being a record made in Philadelphia with local musicians, it was a track cut with session pros in New York. No horns, just distorted guitars; no chorus singers, just John Lennon's squeaked "fame" and "Laughing Gnome"-style varisped vocals; no keyboards save traces of a backwards-masked piano. "Fame" was a jumble of vocals, guitars, bass, drums and effects: funk via the cut-up method. Built mainly on one chord (F7), "Fame" is a refrain, a brief B-flat bridge ("it's not your brain") and a reoccurring F minor intro that kicks off in 3/4. It's powered by Emir Ksasan's bass—he mainly plays root 16th notes on off-beats and plays the occasional grace note to chase a downbeat— and Dennis Davis, who rations fills as if he'll be fined for going over his quota. The rest is guitars: at least six tracks by four players

(Bowie, Carlos Alomar, Lennon and Earl Slick) using the widescreen stereo placement of contemporary funk tracks like Lyn Collins' "Rock Me Again & Again & Again & Again."

How "Fame" began requires one to parse a half-dozen people's foggy and self-serving memories. Lennon had come down to Electric Lady to play on "Across the Universe" and hung around afterward. As Bowie's studio band was mainly R&B players, Lennon started playing old Stax/Volt songs with them. Having just knocked off an oldies album (*Rock & Roll)*, during which he'd spent long drunken nights jamming on the likes of "Ain't That a Shame" and "Lucille," Lennon was prepped to pull a song out of an idle jam. One story has Lennon playing Shirley and Company's "Shame Shame Shame" with Alomar, which led them into "Fame." Another has Alomar playing his "Foot Stomping" riff with Lennon joining in, either contributing the title word or singing "shame," which Bowie misheard as "fame."

Lennon and Bowie had been commiserating about the music business (the former recently had written "Steel and Glass," his poison pen letter to ex-manager Allen Klein). Bowie finally had realized he was single-handedly financing Tony Defries' MainMan empire—the promotions for Mick Ronson and Dana Gillespie, the offices in London, New York and LA, the limousines and hotel suites. He'd been a (deliberate) naïf in his financial life and hadn't known that the contract he'd signed with Defries, instead of making him a 50% owner of MainMan as he'd thought, only entitled him to 50% of MainMan earnings less copious expenses. In reality, he was Defries' employee and cash cow. So "Fame" had a specific, galling meaning for Bowie: it was the title of a play about Marilyn Monroe that MainMan (meaning himself) had financed and that had closed, losing reportedly $250,000, after a single night.

Two weeks after cutting "Fame," Bowie began his separation from Defries, a legal jiu-jitsu bout that ended with Bowie escaping Defries at the cost of $800,000 and giving Defries a percentage of all of his earnings until 1982 (and in perpetuity for music of the 1972-1982 period until Bowie bought Defries out in 1998 with his "Bowie Bonds" scheme).

Two rock stars complaining about their managers and the woes of fame would normally be dreadful, but Lennon and Bowie's lines are lurid enough ("loose and hard to swallow") to dodge self-pity for self-contempt. There's poison in how they sing "fame": Bowie elongating the "ay" phoneme while falling a half-step between syllables, while Lennon makes the opposite move. It sounds like a phasing mistake, a blight, or as the comic Mike Myers once said, fame "as an industrial disease of creativity." "What you like is *in the limo*!" sings Bowie, who'd been all but living in a limousine for the past year. Compared to something like Bob Seger's "Turn the Page," where Seger shoulders rock stardom like a sack of grain, "Fame" is catty and ridiculous ("nein! it's mine!"). In the first verse, "fame" is an active possession (it "makes," "puts," "lets"); in the second, Bowie pits "what you like" against "what you get" and "what you need"—a dying Sixties echo, calling back to the Rolling Stones and a Dylan line from "Memphis Blues Again."

"Fame" was credited to Bowie, Lennon and Carlos Alomar. Lennon wrote the intro chord progression, played an acoustic guitar that, reversed, is heard mainly as a suction sound in the intro, supervised the backwards piano track and sang the mocking "fame" hook. While sometimes mistakenly called the song's creative mastermind, Lennon was far more gracious, publicly crediting Alomar for the guitar lick. In turn, Alomar recalled that "Fame" began once Bowie finally pulled the plug on "Foot Stomping," which he'd been trying to cut in the studio for months. "Foot Stomping" just "sounded like a plain, stupid, old rock & roll song,"Alomar told David Buckley. "David didn't even like it. So what he did was to cut it up into blues changes, which is one-four-five-four, which is what "Fame" is. It cut it up so he just had drums, bass and that one guitar line."

Bowie quickly saw he'd bottled lightning with the jam. He'd been looking for a dance single and now suddenly he had one with a John Lennon co-vocal: the "John I'm Only Dancing" remake soon went out the window. The engineer Eddie Kramer recalled an excited Bowie being "very much in charge, he knew exactly what he wanted." Bowie was working on the outro and adding more overdubs after Lennon had gone home.

The primary guitars on "Fame" are two tracks that play Alomar's "Foot Stomping" riff throughout the verses (wide-separated left and right, with the left-mixed guitar using a Wah-Wah pedal) and Bowie's elephant blast of distorted guitar, which "makes the long Wah and the echoed Bomp! sound." It's the track's brass section and second bassline, squashing on Ksasan's notes. There's also a "telephone ringing" guitar fill, Alomar strumming his three highest strings on the sixteenth and seventeenth frets, and some other secondary colors—Lennon's barely-there acoustic; another electric guitar (Slick?) that's a jabbing commentary on the main riff, mixed right. Garnishes included rattlesnake percussion punched in after the third verse and a closing varisped vocal (see "The Bewlay Brothers," "The Laughing Gnome," "After All") that followed the stepwise descent of the "Laughing Gnome" bassoon: a repeated "fame" (Lennon and Bowie) begins in the stratosphere on a high E flat, falls over two octaves in four bars to close on a low D, its gravid conclusion tweaked a beat later by one last high-pitched Lennon "fame!"

Released in August 1975, "Fame" topped the US charts a month later. It was Bowie's passport. It got him on *Soul Train*, where he could barely muster the strength to lip-sync it. James Brown paid tribute by absconding with much of the track—Alomar's riff, the "telephone" guitar fills—for his 1976 single "Hot (I Need to Be Loved, Loved, Loved)." (Some accounts have Brown dropping the needle on Bowie's record and saying "play this" to his band.) For Alomar, who'd once been a Brown sideman, it was a particularly strange turn of the wheel. Bowie chose not to sue, whether out of respect to an idol, the dismal state of his own legal/financial situation or the Brown single's weak performance (#31 R&B). Plagiarized, cocaine-addicted, in litigation and now a #1 hitmaker, Bowie had broken America at last.

Chapter 10

The Man In the Tower (1975-1976)

Creating a work of art is not a harmless thing...There are two choices: either you create black magic to turn people's heads or you create some kind of basic sanity. Those are the two possibilities so you should be very, very careful.
Chögyam Trungpa, *Dharma Art*.

Humanity is estranged from its authentic possibilities…Each sometimes sees the same fragment of the whole situation differently; often our concern is with different presentations of the original catastrophe.
R.D. Laing, *The Politics of Experience*.

I had fragmented myself out of existence.
Alan Burns, on the use of cut-up in his novels.

I'm evolving higher than myself.
Biff Rose, "Evolution."

Of this he was sure: his "present existence" was false, almost entirely the construct of other people's imagery….So he had to make the world's illusions annihilate themselves. His head would fix the universe with its own images.
Brian Vickers, *The Coded Sun Game*.

This is from back in the Seventies. Well, ***my*** *Seventies, they weren't necessarily* ***your*** *Seventies.*
David Bowie, introducing "Station to Station," Atlantic City, 2004.

Golden Years

Recorded: *ca. 21-30 September 1975, Cherokee Studios, 751 North Fairfax Avenue, Los Angeles. David Bowie: lead and backing vocal, handclaps, melodica, Moog; Carlos Alomar: lead and rhythm guitar; Earl Slick: lead and rhythm guitar; George Murray: bass; Dennis Davis: drums, vibraslap; Geoff MacCormack: backing vocal, congas? Produced: Bowie, Harry Maslin.*

First release: *17 November 1975 (RCA 2640/ PB 10441, UK #8, US #10).* ***Broadcast:*** *4 November 1975, Soul Train.* ***Live:*** *1983, 1990, 2000.*

Having spent summer 1975 in New Mexico making *The Man Who Fell to Earth*, Bowie returned to Los Angeles in late August, already under pressure to follow up his #1 single. Unnerved by stories circulating about Bowie's erratic behavior, RCA sent executives to the movie set to check on him. He told them to pack off. As "Fame" had done the trick, Bowie rounded up the same producer, Harry Maslin, and most of the same group—Carlos Alomar and Earl Slick on guitar and the drummer Dennis Davis, with the bassist George Murray recruited from Weldon Irvine's jazz/funk outfit. For a studio, Bowie and Maslin investigated Cherokee, which had opened the previous January in the former MGM studios on Fairfax Avenue. It swiftly became one of LA's premier studios, inheriting MGM clients like Frank Sinatra (see "Wild is the Wind"). Bowie sang in the cavernous Studio One, played a piano chord and said "this will do nicely." Unlike Sigma Sound, Cherokee prided itself on space, tech and amenities—five studio rooms, 24-track consoles, 24-hour sessions, a fully-stocked bar in the lounge.

First order of business was the prospective single, "Golden Years," a song he'd started writing in May before leaving for the film shoot. His friend Geoff MacCormack, for whom Bowie tried out the song, suggested a trombone-like WAH-wah-WAH tag for the refrains. At Cherokee, MacCormack added more embellishments like a "go-oh-oh-old" phrase as a tag for the bridge and a similarly descending "run for the shadows" hook. MacCormack even wound up filling in for Bowie on the falsetto notes in the bridge's backing vocal (at :45, for example), which were torture for him to hit.

The last time Bowie followed up a career-altering hit he'd cut "The Prettiest Star" as a (disastrous) sequel to "Space Oddity." Time had made him sharper and cannier in his approach. "Golden Years" was both a natural sequel to "Fame," keeping the latter's icy disco sound, but also a swerve from the "now" minimalism of "Fame" towards the sounds of his early adolescence. He used the Diamonds' "Happy Years," a 1958 doo-wop hymn to teenagerdom, and two "Broadway" songs—the Drifters' "On Broadway," which Alomar recalled Bowie playing on piano during rehearsals and throwing in a "come buh-buh-buh baby" after each line, and Dyke and the Blazers' "Funky Broadway," which Slick raided for a few riffs. Fittingly, Bowie wrote "Golden Years" with Elvis Presley's vocal range in mind, although he never submitted the song to Elvis, as negotiations with his manager Col. Tom Parker went nowhere.

Yet any golden oldie he used was nearly unrecognizable, as they were blended with the sound of German bands Kraftwerk and Neu!, heard in the conversation of guitars and the cycling progression: an F-sharp chord downshifting to E major on the third beat of each bar. Bowie described his aim years later when he talked of his love of Donna Summer's records: "this incredible sound, half-Kraftwerk, half-American soul. An amazing incongruous juxtaposition."

Cut in roughly ten days at the start of the *Station to Station* sessions, "Golden Years" was issued as a single less than two months later: it charted while Bowie was still at Cherokee finishing the album. Maslin said "Golden Years" came together with little fuss, especially by comparison to the endless number of retakes and overdubs on the rest of the album. The single was mixed full of small pleasures: Dennis Davis' hi-hat lifts (right on the beat in the verse/refrains, he moves to slightly hang behind on the bridges) and other echo-slathered percussion (handclaps, vibraslap, melodica); Bowie and MacCormack's "round-"sounding backing vocals via an old RCA mike Maslin dusted off; the dueling guitars—one right-mixed playing variations on the opening riff throughout while a left-mixed phased guitar (likely Alomar) keeps a gliding rhythm until moving, after the bridges, to a three-chord riff that echoes MacCormack's "WAH-wah-WAH."

Bowie played little games with the song structure by making the bridge either two or six bars. The longer bridge had the song's only real progression, a run from G major ("nothing's gonna touch you") through A minor ("golden") and an E minor seventh ("yeeeears") capped off with a 2/4 bar: Bowie singing the descending "go-oh-oh-ollld" hook shadowed by a Murray bass slide overlaid with Moog. He did the same to his lyric, altering phrasings and rhythms. In the third verse, he moves from a word-packed, near-rap vocal to surge up to an F# on "all the WAY!", then tumbles right into a fresh chorus hook, the harmonized "run for the shadows."

"Golden Years" opens as a blessing, with Bowie and MacCormack cooing the title phrase, and its opening verses are Bowie in huckster mode (see "Right"), singing sharply enunciated syllables stepping down in pitch. There's the bustling consonance of "in walked luck and you looked in time" and an octave leap to "*AN*-gel"matched, four bars later, by a depths-dredging "yuh-uh-unnng."

The promise of "golden years" isn't communal here. The chance is offered just to one person, the hope of being sealed off in a limousine from the street. His life in Los Angeles added to the lyric's anomie—long paranoid days in his mansion, making occasional appearances on TV with the Fonz. Angela Bowie, busy with her own celebrity, said the song was Bowie's blessing for her and perhaps it was, as there was a threat in it. You want fame?

Here, take it: it will eat you up. *Last night they loved you, opening doors and pulling some strings,* Bowie sang, snarling out the gees. The following night, the doors could well be shut. A rap of materialist promises becomes a desperate prayer to God, followed by a murmured warning to run for the shadows. At first caressing the words "golden years," he began to put them to the rack, rattling consonants, rotting vowels—"years" was a strangled curse heard beneath the backing vocals (esp. at 2:58).

Its video complement was Bowie's performance on *Soul Train,* where he's a wraithlike spiv barely able to keep his balance, let alone mime his vocal. It's as though he's hearing the song for the first time, that he's still in character from *Man Who Fell to Earth.* It's his loneliest, saddest television appearance: a crowd of magnificent strangers dance around him, as if communally denying his presence.

TVC 15

Recorded: *22 September-late November 1975, Cherokee. Bowie: lead and backing vocal, tenor saxophone, baritone saxophone?; Alomar: lead and rhythm guitar; Slick: lead and rhythm guitar; Roy Bittan: piano; Murray: bass; Davis: drums; Maslin: tenor saxophone? baritone saxophone?; MacCormack: backing vocal. Produced: Bowie, Maslin.*

First release*: 23 January 1976,* **Station to Station** *(RCA APL1 1327, UK #5, US #3).* ***Broadcast****: 15 December 1979, Saturday Night Live.* ***Live****: 1976, 1978, 1983, 1985, 1990.*

Inspired by Iggy Pop's dream of a television devouring his girlfriend, the avant-garde novelty song "TVC 15" also hailed from *The Man Who Fell to Earth,* in which Bowie's extraterrestrial Thomas Jerome Newton fills rooms with televisions, each tuned to a different channel. Newton's race had learned about Earth by watching TV but it's been a mistake visiting the set. "The strange thing about television is that it doesn't tell you everything. It ***shows*** you everything about life on Earth, but the true mysteries remain. Perhaps it's in the nature of television. Just waves in space."

Television as malevolent artificial intelligence and purveyor of false realities was another staple of postwar science-fiction—take the four-wall TV "parlors" of Ray Bradbury's *Fahrenheit 451* or the demagogic talk show hosts/TV priests who populate Norman Spinrad's *Bug Jack Barron* and Philip K. Dick's *Do Androids Dream of Electric Sheep?* Far from being a modest evolution from radio and film, TV had rewired the human brain (though TV seems, in retrospect, to have been pre-op for the Internet's aggressive surgery). It eroded old verities and remade society in its own funhouse image: a transformation that the human race apparently had always wanted, like our age-old dreams of flying. "The television was an open funnel, with its other end stuck in the middle of everything," wrote Geoffrey O'Brien, recalling his Sixties youth.

Bowie had seen television go from the genteel incarnation of his childhood, TV as a glorified wireless set showing a single government-run channel a few hours a day, to become a lightbox in every home and hotel room, a unblinking electric eye, a compost of old Hollywood movies, riot footage, wildlife documentaries, kung-fu exhibitions and breakfast cereal ads. He contributed to the mix his own bizarre televised performances of the Seventies, including a version of "TVC 15" he sang with Klaus Nomi and Joey Arias on *Saturday Night Live* in late 1979, where he wore a pencil skirt and high heels while a stuffed pink poodle behind him held a video monitor in its mouth.

Yet despite its quadraphonic sound and hologramic televisions, "TVC 15" was at heart a Fifties teenage death ballad, like "Teen Angel," "Endless Sleep" or "Last Kiss," where the singer recalls how his girl perished and wonders whether to join her in death. The catastrophe of "TVC 15" starts when Bowie brings his girlfriend home to see his new hologramic set. She's bored, transfixed, consumed (she's the "Life On Mars?" girl again, or the girl eaten by the Braque painting in "Unwashed and Somewhat

Slightly Dazed"): she crawls in through the screen, leaving him to mourn her and consider leaping "down that rainbow way" himself. The teenage death ballad gave some assurance from the afterlife; the dead girl wailed the boy's name in a graveyard. But here the TVC 15 just stares back, a void in a box. "My baby's in there someplace"is all he can muster.

Fresh from playing the revivalist on "Golden Years," Bowie outfitted "TVC 15" in rock 'n' roll trappings, from the C major blues progression of its verses (with an F minor shuffled in at the turnaround) to Roy Bittan's piano, seemingly airlifted from Fifties New Orleans, to the opening "oh-OH-oh-OH-OH" line nicked from the Yardbirds' "Good Morning Little Schoolgirl." The swaying attack of its verse melodies and the marginal commentaries of guitars and saxophones had some of Otis Redding's "The Hucklebuck" in them, apparently Alomar's contribution. Bowie said Elvis Presley's "The Girl Next Door Went a-Walkin'" (instead of being swallowed by the TV, the girl next door throws herself into marriage) got diced up in the song as well.

As with "Golden Years" there was a "German" abrasiveness to corrode the Fifties references. The 16-bar verses were noise experiments in miniature. Bowie starts each bar holding on one note while three distorted guitar tracks grind together like an engine failing to get into second gear. Carlos Alomar described his and Earl Slick's guitars as a drone: "the music would stay in one place and just keep going." Yet Bowie's vocal becomes buoyant, loopy, as if he's telling you the best story he's ever heard, and maybe he is. The song moves into an F7/A7 bridge, a Kraftwerk-inspired "*trans*-ition! *trans*-mission!" sequence tugged along by Alomar nervously picking at his open B string. Back home in C major, a"Oh my TVC 15!" refrain begins, half mantra, half-jingle, set against a vicious guitar riff and chased by a Roy Bittan piano figure. It erases the lost girl, making the singer a fanatic advertisement for her captor.

With the standard *Station to Station* layout of two guitars in opposing channels, the dense mix suggests radio signals eating into each other's frequencies. ("TVC 15" quickly outgrew the 24-track console, requiring Maslin to keep bouncing down guitar and vocal dubs). The backing singers echo Bowie a beat late; sometimes they hum a different tune or whisper a barely-audible line. The stack of saxophone overdubs (Bowie and Harry Maslin) bay through later refrains like foghorns. It's as if Bowie's recounting his tale after being swallowed by his television: the last testament of his terrestrial life, delivered in flux.

Wild Is the Wind

(Tiomkin/Washington). ***Recorded:*** *ca. 22 September-late November 1975, Cherokee Studios. Bowie: lead vocal, 12-string acoustic guitar?; Alomar: rhythm guitar, acoustic guitar?; Slick: lead guitar?; Murray: bass; Davis: drums. Produced: Bowie, Maslin.*

First release*: 23 January 1976,* **Station to Station***.* ***Broadcast****: 23 June 2000, TFI Friday; 27 June 2000, An Evening With David Bowie.* ***Live****: 1983, 2000, 2006.*

Station to Station, as legend has it, is the work of a Howard Hughes-esque recluse and obsessive, with Bowie locking himself in the studio and, fueled by cocaine, driving his musicians to play for days on end. While that much is true, *Station* wasn't any sort of secret black mass. The album was a typical Hollywood rock star production, with in-studio interviews by *Rolling Stone*'s Cameron Crowe and visits from, and obligatory jams with, the likes of Ron Wood and Bobby Womack. Rod Stewart was in an adjacent studio, as was, at times, Frank Sinatra.

Upon learning that Sinatra was at Cherokee, Bowie was star-struck, pestering the studio owners for Sinatra's session times. The two reportedly got on well enough for Sinatra to listen to some *Station* playbacks, and his alleged approval of Bowie's version of Dimitri Tiomkin and Ned Washington's "Wild Is the Wind" helped ensure its inclusion on the album. But Bowie already was proud of his performance. He'd wanted to record "Wild Is the Wind" since 1972, he told Crowe. "This has a good European feel," he said, listening to the completed track. "It feels like a bridge to the future."

"Wild Is the Wind" was a Johnny Mathis song, crooned over the opening credits of the 1957 Anthony Quinn sheep ranch melodrama it titled. Mathis tumbled through the verses, his voice a warm presence kept aloft on languorous waves of strings, and left the song with untapped potential, in the scarlet gloom of Tiomkin's music, a melancholy journey in A minor with glimpses of sunlight via the occasional E major chord, and in Washington's words, which beg to be savored ("one caress," "HUN-gri-ness"). Nina Simone soon claimed the song. A solo piano performance at New York's Town Hall in September 1959 was a warm-up for her studio take, double the length of the Mathis original. She snaked and burrowed through the song, dousing seemingly every syllable in vibrato, boring through phrases.

Bowie picked up the gauntlet a decade later. At first he followed Simone's lead, making a taffy of vowels (the three-bar "you—ooo—ahhhoooh—ooh kiss me") and turning consonants into trills. He tended to stress words Simone had left untouched, as if avoiding her conquered territories. Take the opening line, which Simone had sung in a giddy rush—*lovemelovemelooovemeee saaaay you doooooooooo*—and which Bowie instead let slowly build—*love me...love me..love me love me SAY you do*. But as he went on, Bowie moved away from Simone, his phrasings becoming grand contortions, his descending lines plunges into the depths (the vampiric "yoooooooooou kiss me" starting at 3:49). His increasingly manic repetitions of the title line concluded with a strangled "wiiiiild" and a sustained high B on "wind" that sinks down a tone, sunrise and sunset in one. No human being seems deserving of Bowie's efforts: it's a monumental performance for a monument.

He and Maslin cut seven lead vocal takes but wound up going

with the first, perhaps because it was the least self-conscious of the lot, Bowie finding his way into the song with Simone's voice in his head as a guide. "What's the difference anyway? I'm not a singer," Bowie joked in the vocal booth. He'd become near-flawless at intonation, able to strike whichever note he wanted, so that "phrasing, mostly, is what he worries about," Maslin recalled. His phrasing on "Wild Is the Wind" wasn't far from his evisceration of "Across the Universe" or his arson-job on "God Only Knows" in the Eighties. But it worked far better here. Perhaps because Bowie used Simone as a guidebook, or maybe it was the abstractness of the song, its gleaming coldness, its sense of having been bred to be ridden.

There was also the accompaniment, restrained where Bowie was excessive. Discarding the strings and piano of Mathis and Simone's takes, the track was built on three guitars, electric and acoustic, panned across the stereo spectrum (reminiscent of "Quicksand"), with an elegant lead (most likely Earl Slick, possibly Alomar) playing golden arpeggios. It was given brisk life by George Murray, whose bass is a secondary vocal in the shadows, and Dennis Davis, whose stereo-panned tom fill after Bowie's"don't you know you're *life itself*?" ignites a last round of fireworks.

Stay

Recorded: *ca. October-late November 1975, Cherokee Studios. Bowie: lead and backing vocal, Chamberlin; Alomar: lead, rhythm guitar; Slick: lead guitar; Murray: bass; Davis: drums, cowbell, shaker?; MacCormack: congas? Produced: Bowie, Maslin.*

First release*: 23 January 1976,* ***Station to Station. Broadcast****: ca. 8-12 February 1976, Dinah!; 22 November 1999, Musique Plus; 27 June 2000, An Evening With David Bowie.* ***Live****: 1976, 1978, 1983, 1990, 1997, 2000, 2002.*

Each *Station to Station* track has a counterpart. If "Golden Years" and "TVC 15" were sister future nostalgics, the icy "Stay" stood in opposition to the lush romance "Wild Is the Wind." In "Stay," Bowie recites lines from the pick-up scene as if he's reading off a cue-card (see the slowly-intoned triplets: "*change-in-the* weather," "*hap-pened-to* you"). His refrains autopsy his failed connections: he sounds like a man flicking a toggle on a broken machine. He sings a disjunctive, barely-there melody, marked by wide intervals (a jump of a seventh in "what I never say is stay this time") and random emphases. It ends with a line that Bowie sings in knots: "never real/ly tell...when/**some**..*bo-dy*/wants…something../you want too/ooo."

He gave his android impression over his musicians' frenzies. Like the title track of *Station to Station,* "Stay" was pieced together over months, with Bowie and his band using amphetamines and cocaine to hammer through three- or four-day jags at Cherokee, playing from midnight to morning, constantly overdubbing. It was a sign of Bowie's depleted creative state at the time—having written few songs and in no condition to compose new ones, Bowie instead offered a few seeds and zealously tended his gardeners' efforts. So "Stay" began as yet another attempt at "John, I'm Only Dancing (Again)," Bowie having Slick and Alomar work up a fresh arrangement for the song with a new opening lick and just slightly altering the "Dancing (Again)" chord progression. After days, if not weeks, of studio jamming, the band "gave [the song] back to him," Alomar said.

Bowie pitted his guitarists against each other, as he had on the Soul Dogs tour. "He had polar opposites, and he allowed those differences to shape the guitar sound on the album," Slick recalled in 2014. With the rhythm section fully in his corner, Alomar knew he was in position to become Bowie's musical foil; Slick, who'd been resentful of Alomar since the tour, fought a rear-guard action (he was gone before the 1976 tour, a victim of Bowie parting company from his manager, who was representing Slick in a solo career bid). Slick would cut a solo, Alomar would overdub a competing line, Slick would cut another dub. The final mix of "Stay" is the record of their war, underpinned by a George Murray bassline that could support a Buick.

The intro assembles the group in formation. First Slick's coiled spring of a riff on his Stratocaster, mixed right and echoed left: he needles his guitar's D string until breaking off with two viciously-sounded G9 chords. Dennis Davis and Murray peg in a foundation, soon joined by congas, cowbell, shakers and an airy keyboard (most likely Bowie on his Chamberlin M1) that sways between two chords like the Stylophone of "Space Oddity." A second Slick track, perched center in the mix, dominates in roars and waves (Murray's bass now paralleling Slick's opening riff) while Alomar makes tart interjections. If Slick ruled the intro, the verses and refrains fell to Alomar, whose jaunty rhythm guitar paces the track, leaving Slick to bluntly echo his moves. At last in the closing solo the two fully go at it, Alomar lightly sparring and dodging while Slick plays variations of his opening riff and breaks into long, searing runs. In the refrains Bowie's vocal paralleled their interplay, with a low-sung "voice of reason" doubled at the octave by a more desperate plea.

It can seem as though Bowie's guesting on his own record, as he disappears by the four-minute mark (he quickly rethought this move live, instead offering a wailed "stay" during the outros and a "stay—why don't you" tag with Gail Ann Dorsey in the late Nineties). "Stay" became a constant of Bowie tours, giving guitarists from Stacey Heydon to Adrian Belew (who ran through everything from finger taps to bottleneck slide) to Slick to Reeves Gabrels an excuse to show off their chops. On stage, Bowie sometimes would stand and watch his players, looking bemused, as removed from the performance as his character in "Stay" was from human life.

Word On a Wing

Recorded: *ca. October-late November 1975, Cherokee Studios. Bowie:*

lead vocal, Chamberlin, vibraphone?; Slick: lead guitar; Alomar: rhythm guitar; Bittan: piano; Murray: bass; Davis: drums, shaker; MacCormack: backing vocal, congas, vibraphone?. Produced: Bowie, Maslin.

***Released:** 23 January 1976, **Station to Station**. **Broadcast**: 23 August 1999, VH1 Storytellers. **Live:** 1976, 1999.*

The heart and hymn of *Station to Station*, "Word On a Wing" is a petition to God, though as prayers go it's more of an opening negotiation, Bowie attempting to use God as leverage in some larger scheme. Hence the song's warring moods, both suppliant and audacious (see Bowie offering his own "word" against the received Word of Christ or the petulant tone of lines like "just *because* I believe don't mean I *don't* think as well"). As in the love-as-confusion "Stay," Bowie denies himself from achieving any connection, no matter how desperately he wants it. Here, he's playing for greater stakes.

He was only nominally Christian. When John Lennon said the Beatles had meant more to British kids than Jesus Christ did, it was the likes of Bowie he was talking about. This didn't mean Bowie was spiritually empty: he'd spent his twenties looking for some sort of God figure that met his high standards, a path that took him from Beat existentialism to Tibetan Buddhism to whatever brew of cabbalist Gnosticism he was imbibing in 1975 (see "Station to Station"). "I had this religious fervor," Bowie recalled in 1993. "I was just looking for some answers. Some secret. Some life force."

"Word On a Wing," closing the first side of *Station to Station*, was Bowie's (apparently) open plea for salvation from God. He'd been tempted at the time by some sort of evangelical Protestantism, which Bob Dylan would dive into headfirst a few years later. As Bowie began writing "Word On a Wing" while filming *The Man Who Fell to Earth*, there was a parallel to Lennon's "Help!"—both songs are pleas for deliverance written while their composers were stuck on a movie set, paranoid and depressed, wondering what they'd become. In an *NME* interview in 1980, he regarded his dalliance with Christianity as a nearly-consummated romance: "There was a point when I very nearly got suckered into that narrow sort of looking…finding the cross as the salvation of mankind."

This revulsion sounded similar to how he'd described past relationships to journalists at the time: as an all-consuming passion that had threatened his sense of self. To bend the knee to God, to accept Jesus Christ as one's personal savior, required humility, an acceptance that there are higher powers beyond your ken, to have faith and to not try to learn the trade secrets of the cosmos. Ultimately this wasn't enough for Bowie; it was taking the sucker's bet.

So like his reference to the Stations of the Cross in "Station to Station," there was a touch of blasphemy in "Word On a Wing," with Bowie using the imagery and musical trappings of Christian art for occult ends. Bowie crafted the song as white magic to set against the dark "Station to Station," the two tracks spinning in parallel on an LP side, yin and yang in grooves ("Golden Years," an ambiguous utopia, keeps them apart). The song was a "protection…something I needed to produce from within myself to safeguard myself against some of the situations that I felt were happening on the film set."

He felt he needed protection. He'd been under siege by "dark forces" since 1974 (once throwing away a doll his cousin had given him for fear it was a Satanic totem), a predicament worsened upon moving to Los Angeles. When his wife Angela found a house on North Doheny Drive, Bowie wanted it cleansed. Following the instructions of the New York witch Walli Elmlark (which required "a few hundred dollars' worth of books, talismans and assorted items from Hollywood's comprehensive selection of fine occult emporia"), Angela performed an exorcism on the house, including the indoor swimming pool, a natural repository for demons.

Bowie was using Dion Fortune's *Psychic Self-Defense* as a bulwark. Fortune, a British mystic of the early 20th Century, wrote that man had two Angels, a Dark Angel (which she likened to the subconscious, "a dark temptation from the depths of our lower selves...we think thoughts, or even do deeds, of which we never would have believed ourselves capable") and a Bright Angel. The mystic's goal is to summon the latter angel in times of "spiritual crisis, when the very self is being swept away," she wrote. "The Higher Self comes to the rescue, 'terrible as an army with banners'." If successful, one has an expanded consciousness, a sense of calm, "like a ship hove-to, securely riding out the storm."

So compare this to Bowie's various public statements about "Word On a Wing," that it was "something I needed to produce from within myself to safeguard myself" or "I wrote [it] when I felt very much at peace with the world....I wrote the whole thing as a hymn. What better way can a man give thanks for achieving something that he had dreamed of achieving, than doing it with a hymn?" "Word on a Wing" was his protective talisman encased in a song, much like the small crucifix he'd wear around his neck for decades.

"Word On a Wing" starts in somber opening verses, which Bowie sings in his low register (on stage in 1976, he sang-spoke the lines, sounding like Lou Reed); it's in B major, an unusual and remote key for a rock song. He cradles the words "sweet name, you're born once again" as if he's consoling God. All at once comes a jolting move to D-flat major (on "Lord, I kneel and offer you…") which continues for over a dozen unsettled bars until the song steadies in D ("Lord! Lord, my prayer flies…"). The latter section builds to the ornate rise-and-fall phrase that closes the refrain, with Bowie and Geoff MacCormack sounding like woodwinds. And then a swift fall down to earth, back to B major to start another verse. Only after further struggle is "Word On a Wing" content to stay in D major, concluding on the home chord as a celestial soprano bears the song away from its fallen creator .

This voice was generated by the Chamberlin, the precursor to the Mellotron, whose appearance here is similar to its role on the instrumentals of Bowie's next two albums, *Low* and *"Heroes."* In particular "Sense of Doubt" on the latter, a track that ends ambiguously, either to "resolve itself via faith into religious commitment or be left unresolved, freestanding and wordless." It would be a wary response to "Word On a Wing."

The Chamberlin's just one of the gorgeous touches, along with the left-mixed vibraphone that's a counterpart to Roy Bittan's piano or the acoustic guitar fills. The heart of the song, however, is a work for voice—see the astonishing harmonies by Bowie and MacCormack in the refrains—and piano. Whatever led to Bittan playing on *Station to Station,* his presence on "Word On a Wing" seems ordained. There are the child's steps of melody Bittan plays in the intro, his steady chording in the verses, the cascading notes under the "sweet name" section, the sprightly two-note punctuation of the "word on a wing" prayer. A fellow pilgrim, Bittan's piano has a grace that Bowie desperately craves, much as he spurns it.

Station to Station

***Recorded**: ca. October-late November 1975, Cherokee. Bowie: lead and backing vocal, sound effects, lead guitar, organ?, melodica?; Alomar: rhythm guitar; Slick: lead guitar, rhythm guitar; Bittan: piano, organ?; Murray: bass; Davis: drums, tambourine, shaker, ratchet?; MacCormack: backing vocal; Maslin: sound effects. Produced: Bowie, Maslin.*

***First release**: 23 January 1976, **Station to Station**. **Live**: 1976, 1978, 1983, 1990, 2000, 2003-2004.*

1.

One of the many lies we tell children is that there's no limit to the imagination. Of course there is. Even the most consuming of minds reaches its borders. Expanding the mind is dog's work; few attempt it, fewer succeed at it, those who do come out twisted and torn. In 1975, existing on milk and drugs, living in paranoid isolation and making a rock record, David Bowie succeeded.

Not sleeping for days, unable to turn off his mind, he read book after book: on the occult, on the Tarot and defensive magic, on mythical obsessions of the Nazis, on numerology, on secret histories of Christianity, on Atlantis, on UFOs, on the Kabbalah, on millennial political conspiracies. He supplemented his diet with Krautrock records and German Expressionist films.

So by the time he wrote "Station to Station," mainly in the studio, Bowie's mind was like a swath of exposed film in a camera whose shutter was stuck open. "Station to Station" inventoried his obsessions, made a mandala of loose thoughts. The lyric reads like grandiose gibberish and hits upon the sublime. "Station to Station" is the culmination of Bowie's musical life; it's his masterpiece, for better or worse. His previous work was its prelude, his subsequent music lies in its shadow.

2.

As a child in Bromley, he'd wanted to be an American. This was a common aspiration for his generation who, in their mid-teens, already stood "a head taller than the middle aged...[and were] looking like Americans." He soon developed a hipster's severity of taste. It wasn't enough to like Westerns and rock 'n' roll. At age 13 he became the only American football fan in his neighborhood, having received shoulder pads and a helmet from the US Embassy, and he walked around his playground in battle armor. He found America through Jack Kerouac and Richard Wright, went through stacks of modern jazz records that he later admitted made no sense to him. His was a United States of the imagination. "It was the image of the people behind the music, because people like [Charles] Mingus are quite characters," his friend George Underwood recalled. He and Bowie would walk around Bromley pretending they were Yanks in the hopes of having better luck with girls. Bowie's first singles were fumbled attempts at code cracking ("Liza Jane," "I Pity the Fool"). Even his stage name was an Americanism.

Now in 1975 Bowie was living in America, a regular guest on American TV. He was in Hollywood, in the westernmost reaches of an ungovernable, adolescent country. To get there, he'd left behind everyone who had formed him—his wife, his half-brother Terry, his mother, his old manager Kenneth Pitt, the mime Lindsay Kemp, even Tony Defries. His old fellow players: Underwood, Hutch, Visconti, Ronson. Even Geoff MacCormack was becoming estranged from him now. To live in America was to live like an original Christian: divesting yourself of everything you'd ever owned or loved. As Ian MacDonald wrote, "uprooted from his native context in the cultural artifice of Europe, isolated in a largely unironic and cultureless alien land, Bowie was forced back on himself, a self he didn't much like."

In the first lines of "Station to Station," Bowie paints himself as a Prospero in an exile of his own devising. As wonderfully weird as these first incantatory lines are, they suggest a diminished figure, a man reduced to his shadow. He'd once sung about exploring space, transcending time, becoming a god. Now he was confined to a room, casting spells that flashed back on him, trapped in his circle.

3.

In the spring and summer of 1975, Bowie was a guest in, variously, Deep Purple bassist Glenn Hughes' house in Benedict Canyon, his manager Michael Lippman's house and the actress Claudia Jennings' apartment, plus the occasional random hotel. Then he found a haunted house of his own, on North Doheny Drive. The stories from this era have piled up over the years; they make the fleshy center of most Bowie biographies. You may recall some. Bowie saw UFOs at sunset. Looking out his window, he saw a body drop. He traced swastikas on walls and windowpanes. He drew pentagrams on the floor. He thought the CIA was sending undercover agents into his home in the guise of aspiring scriptwriters. He believed a pair of witches were trying to steal his semen to breed a Satanic child (the perils of watching *Rosemary's Baby* on cocaine). He stored his piss in jars in the refrigerator. He was convinced the Rolling Stones were communicating via their LP covers. He was in a magic duel with Jimmy Page to become chief Aleister Crowley acolyte.

Most of these tales weren't true; any could have been. Bowie was holding court in a circle of vampires. "Real life" was far more dispiriting: Bowie and Glenn Hughes, nodding out on a couch for hours; Bowie watching Nazi documentaries again and again, Hughes trying to write a song, both itching for the next delivery of coke. As his wife recalled, Bowie would stake out a corner of whichever house he was in and make it his cave, moving about only at night, talking to no one but his dealers and fellow addicts.

He was lost in old heresies, moonlit religions, millennial sects, tales from the plague years. The Sixties had churned these things up: they'd risen to the surface in the wake of the lost revolutions, reborn in airport paperbacks and newspaper astrology columns, whispered about on radio call-in shows. "Station to Station" is filled with the wrack of a dozen religions and cults.

Flashing no color—the Order of the Golden Dawn's Tattwa meditational system. *Does my face show some kind of glow?*—Kirlian photography, a process with which Bowie was enamored, photographing his fingertips before and after taking cocaine to see if it altered his life essence. *The European canon*—a play on the Pāli Canon, a set of Theravadan Buddhist scriptures. *White stains*—a collection of erotic Aleister Crowley poems. *The men who protect you and I*—fascist icons, or the seven world-bringing

Archons of the Gnostics, or Tibetan lamas in exile in London. *Station to station*: stations of the Cross, or stops on the train trip he'd made from Siberia to Paris in 1973. Most of all, the 10 *sefirot* of the Kabbalist Tree of Life, descending from *kether*, the godhead, to *malkuth*, the sphere at the greatest remove from God.

"Station to Station" seemed like another "Quicksand," another obsession inventory, another dalliance with Crowley and Nazi imagery. But the singer of "Quicksand" was terrified of drowning in his useless knowledge. The man singing "Station to Station" wants more, having expanded so much as to become inhuman. "At the time, I had this insatiable appetite for magic, mysticism, alchemy—fired by my ever-increasing use of drugs," Bowie said in 1999. "I think that I'd replaced a real existence with a parallel mystical one in my mind. I was slipping into the fantastical all the time."

4.

A footnote. Landing home in Dover in May 1973 after his trek through Russia and Europe, Bowie signed an autograph as "Edmund Gosse." A reporter noted this but made nothing of it. Why should he? It was an obscure reference, just a book Bowie had read on the train.

Edmund Gosse wrote *Father and Son* (1907), a curse on Victorian England (like Samuel Butler's *The Way of All Flesh*) by one of its children. *Father and Son* concerns parents who impose their will upon their child, who cultivate him and check his growth as if he were a garden plant, and the child's struggle to secure his own mind, to forge his own identity. Gosse was the only son of two devout Presbyterian Brethren members, a couple who lived entirely for God and who expected Gosse to spend his life in service to Him. He rejected them, escaped from their confines, and mourned his liberation. "Of the two human beings here described, one was born to fly backward, the other could not help being carried forward," Gosse wrote, of his father and himself.

This was nothing like Bowie's childhood, of course. He'd been a boy who lacked for little, who'd been allowed by his parents to chase after his dreams. But the idea of having to create oneself through an opposition of forces, that the face you wear in public has to be tempered and weathered, that the biggest threat to one's freedom are those who love you: perhaps these resounded. He was a shy songwriter who'd never felt comfortable on stage, so he'd built another self. "It's the policy of the self-invented man," he told Dinah Shore. "You strip down all the things you don't like about yourself. One thing I didn't like was being shy. So if I gave myself an alarming reputation, then I'd be forced to defend it."

So David Jones kept backstage, or was left back in Bromley, maybe reading Edmund Gosse again. David Bowie was the moon god of *Top of the Pops*, David Bowie "transcends our gloomy coal-fire existence," as Morrissey recalled. David Bowie sang about the end of the world and queen bitches, diamond dogs and the National People's Gang and the Kabbalah. David Bowie had, by 1975, become monstrous. So why not go further?

5.

The return of the Thin White Duke. His agent of liberation was a wastrel aristocrat who roamed from city to city, leaving behind a string of rent boys and unpaid hotel bills. (A "thin white duke" was also a line of cocaine, but every line in "Station to Station" could double as a coke metaphor.) Visual inspiration for Bowie's Thin White Duke character—emaciated, ghoulish, dapper—partly came from Joel Grey's Emcee from *Cabaret*. But the Duke also was a disco-era King Edward VIII. Like Edward (who became a Duke after abdicating in 1938), the Duke's frayed gentility barely disguised his fascist sympathies, his cool manners masking an amoral heart.

So Bowie spent the spring of America's bicentennial year

touring the country in the guise of some rotten offspring of Junkers and counts, some walking revenge from the Old World. The music he performed was merciless in its power, loud and sprawling. He opened shows by playing selections from Kraftwerk's album *Radio-Activity* and screening Dali and Bunuel's surrealist *Un Chien Andalou* (its eyeball-slicing scene revolted and wowed fans—it was Bowie's dig at the bloody theatrics of Alice Cooper and Kiss: "Here, top an actual eyeball being gouged open, you clowns") and then led into "Station to Station" His audiences were witnesses to a nightly exorcism.

That said, the Thin White Duke was more a press creation than a stage one. Tapes of the 1976 shows document an energetic, if sometimes audibly drunk, man who's happy to let his band run away with his songs ("I'm doing it for the money," he'd tell interviewers about why he was touring). He introduced his band by name; they played drum solos, multiple guitar solos, even bass solos. "I didn't much care for the band: too loud, too funky, too much bottom," the critic Lisa Robinson wrote, seeing one of Bowie's LA concerts. "These people have nothing to do with Bowie."

Yet from the start of the tour, he was bringing up Nazis in interviews. Part of this was method acting. He was planning to co-star in *The Eagle Has Landed* with Donald Sutherland and Michael Caine, a film about a Nazi plot to kidnap Churchill (Bowie's character, Oberst Radl, was "a Nazi with a conscience, and I rather wanted him to be totally fascist and die saying "Heil Hitler!"). He didn't get the part due to a scheduling conflict, but it had been an excuse to further his already-heady interest in Nazi memorabilia and occult histories. ("I'm getting into my Nazi bit for this one," as he told the *NME*.)

By the time he returned to "grey" England in May 1976, he'd given several interviews intimating some fascist power was on the rise ("I believe Britain could benefit from a fascist leader") and had called Hitler the first rock star. In East Berlin in April, he'd toured Hitler's bunker, posed like Rodin's Thinker next to a bust of the Fuehrer and his photographer Andy Kent had shot him impishly making a Nazi salute. Now rumors spread that Bowie had given a Nazi salute upon his arrival in Victoria Station.

He'd been going on about Nazism for years, since the airy conversations of his Arts Lab days, just part of his musings about UFOs and Holy Grail conspiracies. The difference was that in 1969 he'd been an obscure folkie talking to friends and sympathetic underground newspapers, and in 1975 he was a global pop star who'd recently done a song-and-dance number with Cher. A press-savvy cynic, he was making deliberately outrageous statements meant to shock credulous interviewers and get headlines, and doing so while he weaning himself off cocaine by drinking brandy.

Like other postwar children, Bowie used fascist imagery as a way to shock/shame his parents' generation. Those whose parents had buried their crimes and collaborations found an "outlaw" allure in fascism (often mixed in with sadism). In Seventies film alone there was Bernardo Bertolucci's *The Conformist,* Liliana Cavani's *The Night Porter* and Louis Malle's *Lacombe Lucien,* all of which treated fascists or collaborators with sympathy. There was Pier Paolo Pasolini's repellent fascist nightmare, *Salo,* which premiered at the same time Bowie was cutting *Station to Station*. British punks would soon start wearing swastikas on their clothing for a ready-made outrage.

Still, Bowie's interviews proved too outrageous even for its time (the Rock Against Racism coalition would cite him as a main offender, and his ravings were taken seriously by right-wing groups like the National Front). He'd spend the next decade publicly repenting. Far from having escaped from the black magic he'd left behind in Los Angeles, he turned out to be an infected host, bringing his cocaine-fueled necromancy back to Europe.

6.

What was all of this? How had he wound up here?

Since the mid-Sixties, Bowie had been moving towards Gnosticism—the belief that we have fallen into this world, conquered by what a nameless Gnostic prophet called "love and sleep," with only the self-elected few aware of the true nature of things. The God who created this false world is a false god, the Demiurge, and the real God is above and beyond him: perfect and infinite. Gnosticism often posits a duality of life, a war between light and dark, white and black magic. It's there in Bowie's Tibetan songs ("Karma Man," "Wild Eyed Boy From Freecloud"), in his generational changing-of-the-guard songs like "Oh! You Pretty Things," in the Aryan cod-myths of "The Supermen," the dream journal "Quicksand" and its monolithic successor.

Yet "Station to Station" was also an end to this cycle. The cold grandeur of Bowie's voice, the song's sense of escaping confinement by renouncing magic and high-tailing it out of LA, suggests that the Gnostic promise—that somewhere within us is a fragment of the true God, that the material world is a prison without a lock, that one can climb to the top of the Tree of Life—hadn't panned out or, worse, wasn't enough.

His favorite Nazi occult books, lurid tomes like Trevor Ravenscroft's *The Spear of Destiny* and J.H. Brennan's *Occult Reich,* argued that the rise of the Nazis had come about via arcane powers and black magic. It wasn't the fear, venality and pettiness of common people who had brought a Mussolini or Hitler into power. No, it was the doing of international cabals with ties to secret priesthoods and blood sacrifices. Delving into these books, Bowie found that his obsessions were all knotted together. There were hidden monastic orders in Tibetan caves ("Karma Man"), which the Nazis had tried to contact via radio links, and secret Tibetan cadres in Nazi Berlin. Aleister Crowley was tied up in it somehow. A Berlin-based Nazi occult order had worked to discover the secret of "vril," the superhuman electric life-force of Edward Bulwer-Lytton's *The Coming Race* ("Oh! You Pretty Things"). The Thune Society, a dark secretive order, had recruited Hitler as the first of the coming race.

None of it was true. "Vril" was the fancy of a novelist, the Tibetan secret monasteries a fiction of the spiritualist Madame Helena Blavatsky, the Thune Society a group of pathetic fantasists with a very remote influence on the Nazi Party and utterly none on Hitler. Ravenscroft had met a German expatriate who said he'd found Hitler's copy of *Parzival* and had learned Hitler was an occultist, peyote user and Holy Grail obsessive. It was a fabrication, in part stolen from another Bulwer-Lytton novel. Even the medieval Kabbalists, the planters of the Tree of Life, may have fabricated some of their legends.

But even if Bowie had known this, would it have mattered? It was all just grist for the mill, all information to be stored, to put to use, to be reconciled, to be gathered for some purpose, somewhere. He'd unlocked doors that led to further doors, he translated symbols into further symbols, he'd cast his life in throws of dice and plays of tarot cards, and he was just as lost as when he'd begun. If only the world was the realm of great dark and light forces, if it only was being run by plots and counterplots of secret figures, if it wasn't just the world.

All he truly knew was work. However outlandish his imagination, however much he punished his body, he was still able to make his music. "Station to Station," even if it was recorded by a man entertaining madness, was still the quadraphonic lead-off track of a Top 3 pop album cut at Frank Sinatra's studio. Most crack-ups happen off screen, with studio roughs or half-written manuscripts their only evidence. Bowie's was immaculate, and you could buy it at Woolworths.

7.

"Station to Station" opens with a minute of train noises,

juddering and whistling from right to left speaker. It was his tribute to Kraftwerk's *Autobahn,* which had begun with a car revving to life (he also may have taken the idea from Kevin Ayers' "Like a Train"). It was an ironic homage. Rather than the sound of a German car on the sparkling Autobahn, driving through the Ruhr valley in purring bliss, it's a locomotive, the iron sound of troop movements and mass deportations. The train noises came from a sound-effects LP, with Harry Maslin and Bowie doctoring the recording with an equalizer and "unconventional phasing methods." (Bowie "was like a child playing with the sound," Maslin said in 1976).

As the train fades, a note played on Earl Slick's guitar turns into gales of feedback. "It was me and David going through two sets of Marshall stacks in the live room at Cherokee Studios. It was two in the morning, and we were just feeding back like two crazy guys," Slick recalled. He'd tried to hold the note for two minutes or more, but was unable to sustain it that long. The solution, Alomar recalled, was "Plug in another amplifier! Just keep the chain of amplifiers going until the sound just keeps going." So Slick and Bowie used a row of amps chained together, six in all, each amp with a different effect, with Maslin using just a single microphone to capture the din. For the final mix, Maslin took Bowie and Slick's various guitar tracks and merged them into a vast bend of sound.

Under Slick and Bowie's feedback concerto, a rhythm assembles: four almost inaudible beats, a metronomic two-note piano, a trio of bass notes. Alomar plays a spidery line on his guitar's B string, a ghostly organ plays some chords, a melodica appears to work the turnarounds. With four kicks of Dennis Davis' bass drum, the song lurches to life. The intro is the same structure as the opening section: a 6/4 A minor measure ("here am I, flashing no color") followed by a 4/4 measure over F and G ("tall in this room overlooking the oh-") and back to 6/4 ("-cean"). Bowie flows through bars, ends phrases harshly (a dental fricative like "mal-*kuth*") or with a caress ("*woh*-ven," "*ohh*-cean"), acts out his lines (the wavering, fifth-dropping "beeeending sound").

Before this, however, was "the return of the thin white duke," both introduction and conclusion, sung over a stream of chords (Cm-G-Gb-D) of no recognizable key, more a loose affiliation of tones. Even the D major chord, apparently marking the "end" of the sequence, is a feint—while it suggests what's to come (the "once there were mountains" section will be in D major) it's diverted by the A minor opening section.

"Station to Station," like "Cygnet Committee," reveals itself as a few scattered ideas welded together. Maslin believes there were two main songs that Bowie joined, while Alomar, who was listening to Jethro Tull at the time, enjoyed the chance to do a multi-movement progressive rock jam, particularly as he got paid more as a session musician the longer the track was.

The first join is prepared for by Bowie quietly singing "white stains" as a guitar plays a dancing figure. At last it's the long-delayed move to D major (the prayer key of "Word on a Wing"): there's an audible sense of escape in this section, with its romping piano (the two-note water torture finally over) and Bowie's soaring, waltzing vocal of almost entirely triplets: "once-there-were *moun-tains-on*...sun-birds-to *soar-with-and*..." A two-bar break (drum fills, a dash of piano, a tongue-twister) and Bowie, staking himself upstage, offers a question, a toast, a command. This was West End theatre, shameless Andrew Lloyd Webber hokum (it's also a bit like Mario Lanza's "drink! drink! let every true lover salute his sweetheart!" ode from *The Student Prince),* with each toast followed by a rapid-shot chord progression over six beats, C/D/E/A/E/F#m, leading back to a G chord to start the next phrase, and so playing games of shuffle with the old composition standby, the "circle of fifths."

And the closing section (only a bar of 5/4 lets on that another set change is coming) opens with the best lines in the song, if not his life. You could have heard it on a Brighton music hall stage in 1902. *It's not the side-effects of the cocaine! I'm thinking that it must be* ***lurve...***

8.

On stage, Bowie hurled out these lines—as a joke, a defiance, a mockery of romance. But the way he sang them on the record is the song's first human moment. His voice hiccups down a fifth on "cocaine" and he croaks out "love" as if he can't conceive how to properly say the word.

You can see what he's done here—he's bridged three of his selves in a single song, going from *Diamond Dogs* occultism through the cracked stagecraft of his life with Ken Pitt and Deram and now, slamming into this monster of a vamp section, being carried off on American rock 'n' roll (Slick), funk (Murray and Alomar) and disco (Davis). It's everything he'd ever wanted from America, played for him by a set of Americans that he'd made work like factory hands. "It starts off with a Chuck Berry kind of lick, and then we just sat there with two guitars, banging around on things I came up with and working up the solo," Slick recalled. "So it wasn't comp'd—we composed it, which is something we rarely did to that extent. I remember very clearly sitting there together and composing it."

Bowie, of course, wouldn't let it end that easily. First the snaky chord sequence, a bumpy journey in B minor with a tilt towards the former key of D, with chord changes landing on the last beat of every bar ("too *late*!" "*hate*-ful!" "*grate*-ful!") and a would-be cadential closing tag that instead slinks back to B minor. And the vamp itself is sometimes twelve bars long, other times thirteen. It's a rock 'n' roll song transplanted into a foreign soil: for Bowie, his idea of Continental Europe. What did he most admire from Kraftwerk? "Their determination to stand apart from stereotypical American chord sequences and their wholehearted embrace of a European sensibility displayed through their music."

The more resigned the lyric—it's too late for hate, for gratitude, for anything, really—the more elated the music. Roy Bittan's piano dances, Davis and Murray slam down, Slick and Alomar drag race. Bowie rushes through his lines, savors the locomotion of "Eur-o-pean-canon-is *here*." He was free, at least in this closing vamp, as if he'd exorcised himself. "He told me he felt his demon had caught up with him," Glenn Hughes recalled years later. "He had to sort himself out...Because that stuff did have its way with him. It twisted and turned him out."

9.

Center Coliseum, Seattle, 3 February 1976. The earliest extant live recording of "Station to Station." The album had come out only two weeks earlier. Primed for weirdness via Kraftwerk on the PA and a screening of *Un Chien Andalou*, the crowd now watches a guitarist in spotlight with his back to them, wringing feedback from his amp for what seems like the entire duration of the concert.

Nassau Coliseum, Uniondale, 23 March 1976. Stacy Heydon's guitar fusillade, part "Flight of the Bumblebee," part surf music, part heavy metal, ends upon the Thin White Duke's belated appearance. The band aims for power and subjugation. Bowie delivers the "side effects of the cocaine" line with bravado. The Duke returns in the outro, as he does in every subsequent live version.

Deutschlandhalle, West Berlin, 10 April 1976. A 14-year-old girl from Neukölln, West Berlin, attends with a friend. They take hits off a pipe offered by American soldiers in nearby seats. "The overall atmosphere was amazing: It was like falling into a different—and better—universe," she recalls. But when Bowie sings "Station to Station," she crashes, feels the world fall in around her. "It was just too close to reality for me," she says of the song, of the notice that it's already too late for her. "I could've really used some Valium then."

Two years later, after Vera Christiane Felscherinow has become a heroin addict and a prostitute, she's interviewed by West German journalists. Her young life is written up as *Christiane F* and soon becomes a film. In late 1980, while Bowie is performing *The Elephant Man* in New York, the director Uli Edel turns the Upper West Side club Hurrah into the Deutschlandhalle for a night. The audience are kids coming off bad highs. The enigmatic Christiane, played by Natja Brunckhorst, makes her way to front of the stage and stares at Bowie, as if she's far older than he is. His performance is time travel: his 1980 band mimes the Philadelphia 1978 recording of a song that had crushed Christiane F. in 1976.

Spectrum Arena, Philadelphia, 28 or 29 May 1978. From a mammoth synthesizer train reproduction to the young Adrian Belew setting fire to the song, from Carlos Alomar making his guitar sound like a koto to Bowie revising his phrasing to make grander and wilder gestures, it's the song's finest performance (it later appeared on *Stage*, possibly with some studio work done). The band takes the key change as a signal to rocket off: there's a communal joy in this music.

Pacific National Exhibition Coliseum, Vancouver, 12 September 1983. The Thin White Duke, drained of menace, is now part of the official Bowie personae, a Super Friends contingent of sorts. Filmed for the *Serious Moonlight* video, this is the least essential version of "Station to Station" ever performed, with twinkling keyboard fills, a superfluous brass section, a healthy-looking Earl Slick and a Bowie vocal with a vicious case of the Anthony Newley-isms.

Tokyo Dome, 19 May 1990. For the greatest-hits tour, it's Belew again, with a decade under his belt. A faded photocopy of the 1978 performance, carried through with brute force. Bowie comes in on rhythm guitar towards the end.

Civic Center, Hartford, 23 July 1990. Bowie played "Station to

Station" that night, according to the bootleg. I have no memory of it.

Roseland Ballroom, 19 June 2000. The train noises begin and Bowie looks off stage right, peers upward. He keeps a hand on his throat and slowly gyrates his body: it's as if he's about to perform "The Mask" again. He turns to face the audience, wanly waves goodbye. Earl Slick, puffing on a cigarette, announces with sheets of feedback that the song's his property again.

Jones Beach Theatre, Wantagh, NY, 4 June 2004. Bowie's second-to-last (to date) American concert, the night before he revived "Liza Jane." This may well be one of the last times Bowie ever performed "Station to Station," and it's a youthful-sounding performance, with no claims made and no debts collected. Three weeks later, at a festival in Germany, he had a heart attack and collapsed backstage. He's never toured again. For almost a decade, he even stopped being David Bowie.

10.

Sephirah Kether. The Crown, The Summit, 1.*The tree-top at last! Here we are at the very apex of the Middle Pillar where we can make no further progress on the Tree of Life unless we leave it altogether into the Nothing above, or fall back to Malkuth and start all over again.*

William G. Gray, *The Ladder of Lights.*

In mid-February 1976, during his tour's stop in Los Angeles, Bowie had a freighting company pack up his things and ship them to Switzerland. He was going to live there, because his accountants needed him to go into tax exile and because he wanted to get as far away from Los Angeles as humanly possible. On 28 March, he left New York via ocean liner, heading for Italy. He was going back to the Old World, he was done with being an American. Of course Bowie would come back to the US, and he's lived in New York for most of the present century. His returns have seemed as if he was honoring the terms of some divorce settlement.

John Lennon had said the Sixties dream was over in 1970 but Bowie had, in his crooked way, remained a believer. He "took it for granted that the music would always be consequential and associated with radical impulses towards change," as Tom Carson wrote. "Even his most revisionist Seventies work depended for its point and urgency on having those Sixties assumptions constant in the background."

So there's a pain, a grand disillusion, in "Station to Station," an abdication in a song, an imaginative disarmament. Retreating to Europe and a longed-for anonymity, Bowie would spend the next few years breaking apart his music and trying to twine himself back together again. He would make some of his finest records, certainly some of his most popular. But "Station to Station" is the terminus, if not of some utopian or Gnostic dream, of the belief that such dreams were possible. The world that had made him was gone, leaving him an orphan. Draft a map of Bowie's collected songs, plot "Station to Station" somewhere near the margin and mark it: *here he went no further*.

Appendix:
The Unheard Music

There are dozens of songs performed or composed by David Bowie which remain unavailable to the public or which were never recorded. Some were unrecorded live performances; some are documented tracks that lie in a vault or a cardboard box somewhere and perhaps will surface one day. Others are the hazy recollections of aging men and likely will remain rumors (some of these songs are likely working titles of other, existing tracks). Here's an incomplete list, in any event:

1958

"Cumberland Gap," "Gamblin' Man," "Putting on the Style," "Tom Dooley." The first public musical performance of David Jones, age 11, was on the Isle of Wight, August 1958. He and George Underwood had gone on holiday with the 18th Bromley Scouts and formed a skiffle group. The group had the requisite tea chest/broom handle as double bass and some unknown Scout played ukulele. The repertoire, mainly Lonnie Donegan songs, was the same as any skiffle group in Britain, including the Quarrymen up in Liverpool. "I remember we went down well," Underwood recalled in a radio interview.

1962

"A Night at Daddy Gee's," "A Picture of You," "Let's Dance." Bowie joined the Kon-Rads in early 1962, mainly playing tenor saxophone but singing on the likes of Curtis Lee's "A Night at Daddy Gee's" and Joe Brown's "A Picture of You." By the fall he was singing at least half the band's set, including Chris Montez's "Let's Dance," which would inspire Bowie's own #1 single in 1983.

1963

"I Never Dreamed," "I Thought of You Last Night(?)" A Bowie co-composition, "I Never Dreamed" was recorded with the Kon-Rads at a 29 August 1963 audition in Decca's West Hampstead studio (see "Liza Jane").

Bob Knight, an assistant to the Rolling Stones' manager Eric Easton, brought the Kon-Rads to Easton's attention after catching them play the Orpington Civic Hall in the summer. Easton arranged an audition for the Stones' label, Decca. (Easton had no idea that the Rolling Stones existed until he was recruited to manage them: he was brought on by the ambitious Andrew Oldham because Oldham was too young to have an agent's license. So Easton agreeing to hear a band as green as the Kon-Rads suggested he was looking to have his "own" bands to run. He was unceremoniously dumped from the Stones as soon as Oldham came of age.)

The Kon-Rads debated whether to play R&B and pop covers or to do one of Bowie's compositions, few of which had been received well on stage. They chose "I Never Dreamed," in part because their drummer/leader David Hadfield said it would show Decca the Kon-Rads were "future-oriented."

"I Never Dreamed" has been described as both being morbid, its Bowie-penned lyric allegedly inspired by a newspaper report of an airplane crash, and as a "typical upbeat love song of the era," as per its co-composer, Roger Ferris. Perhaps it was both. In any case the Kon-Rads mainly chose "I Never Dreamed" for its "strong refrain...chorus-verse, chorus-verse, fade after two minutes," Hadfield later told the Gilmans. At Decca's studio, an intimidated Kon-Rads (Hadfield: "we were literally shaking and I was almost physically sick") cut "I Never Dreamed," with Bowie and Ferris singing lead, and three other tracks, possibly including a cover of Ralph Freed's "I Thought of You Last Night" (likely inspired by Jeri Southern's version).

Easton was unimpressed and gave the band the brush-off,

praising them for their potential (they were a bit too future-oriented). Bowie was crushed, having assumed his band would get a record deal. This failure "sparked the point where he realized he wasn't going to get anywhere with us," Hadfield said. The last gig Bowie played with the Kon-Rads was on New Year's Eve, 1963. Decca later scrapped their audition tape, although an acetate of a rehearsal performance exists.

"Good Morning Little Schoolgirl," "Tupelo Blues," "House of the Rising Sun." Songs performed by the Hooker Brothers (Bowie, Underwood and, according to Cann, a percussionist known only as "Viv"), a brief-lived blues trio that performed in the summer of 1963. The repertoire was mainly blues standards, including John Lee Hooker's "Tupelo Blues," as well as a cover of "House of the Rising Sun" from the first Bob Dylan LP, well before the Animals' single was cut.

1964

"Don't Try to Stop Me." Bowie composition, allegedly in the style of Marvin Gaye, that Bowie sang, *a cappella,* at his audition with the Manish Boys in 1964. Included in live sets but apparently no recording made.

"Last Night" (the Mar-Keys),**"I Ain't Got You**," (Yardbirds), "**Stupidity**," (Solomon Burke), "**Watermelon Man**," (Herbie Hancock, possibly the Mongo Santamaria version), "**I'm Ready**," "**Hoochie Coochie Man**," (Muddy Waters), "**Green Onions**," (Booker T. and the MGs), "**Little Egypt**," (the Coasters), "**If You Don't Come Back**," (the Drifters), "**You Can't Sit Down**," (Phil Upchurch Combo), "**You Really Got Me**," "**All Day and All of the Night**," (the Kinks), "**Big Boss Man**," (Jimmy Reed), "**Try Me**," **Night Train**," "**James Brown Medley**," (James Brown), "**I'mTalking About You**" (Chuck Berry, but possibly the Ray Charles song), "**Can't Nobody Love You**," "**I Believe to My Soul**," "**What'd I Say**," "**Mary Ann**" (Ray Charles). Songs performed by the Manish Boys with Bowie during the latter half of 1964. "Last Night," an instrumental, was the usual set-opener, Also in sets were the trio of songs below:

"Hello Stranger," (Barbara Lewis), **"Duke of Earl,"** (Earl Chandler), **"Love Is Strange."** (Mickey and Sylvia). The first Bowie/Manish Boys session, recorded 6 October 1964 in yet another Decca audition, this one produced by Mike Smith for Mickie Most. Poor harmony vocals allegedly soured this session, which merited a second attempt on 12 October that did nothing to improve anyone's opinion of the band. Bowie recommended the Manish Boys attempt the Chandler and Mickey and Sylvia songs and appears to have not suggested his own songs. The tapes were scrapped as per routine and no acetates have surfaced. "Hello Stranger" was optimistically cited as an upcoming Manish Boys Decca single by their self-penned fanzine, *Beat 64*, in November 1964.

"So Near to Loving You." Manish Boys composition by Bowie (lyric), Rodriguez and Solly (music), ca. November 1964. Not recorded but a chord sheet shows a three-part song structure in C major, moving to G major. Another "builder" like "I Pity the Fool," according to Solly.

1965

"It's a Lie," "Youthquake." Radio jingles recorded for the shirt manufacturer Puritan by the Lower Third at R.G. Jones Studio on 20 May 1965.

"Born of the Night." Bowie composition played live with the Lower Third and recorded in a May 1965 session at Central Sound Studios, a small demo studio located above a shop on Denmark Street (regularly frequented by aspiring songwriter Reginald Dwight). Shel Talmy rejected "Born" in favor of another song Bowie had written around the same time, "You've Got a Habit of Leaving."

"I Lost My Confidence." Rehearsed and rejected by the Lower Third, this aptly-named Bowie composition was soon forgotten.

"**Chim Chim Cheree,**" "**Mars—the Bringer of War**." Instrumentals performed by the Lower Third on stage. "Chim Chim Cheree," though hailing from *Mary Poppins,* was more likely inspired by John Coltrane's version on *Coltrane Quartet Plays* (which also included "Nature Boy," see book 2). The band played it at their 2 November 1965 (failed) audition for the BBC, along with "Baby, That's a Promise" and "Out of Sight." Holst's "Mars," part of *The Planets* suite, was better known among Bowie's generation as the theme song of the *Quatermass* serials.

"**Out of Sight.**" James Brown song performed by the Lower Third at their BBC audition on 2 November 1965 and presumably played on stage at the time.

"It's Lovely to Talk to You." Cited by Trynka as a song Bowie wrote in late 1965 at his manager Ralph Horton's flat. Considered for Bowie's first album but not recorded.

1966

"Dance Dance Dance." Song performed by the Buzz in 1966. Bowie, in an internet chat in 1999, said he thought the song was his, not a cover of the Beach Boys.

"**Breakout,**" **"Jenny Take a Ride**"[Mitch Ryder], "**One More Heartache**" [Marvin Gaye]. "**Land of a Thousand Dances** [Cannibal and the Headhunters], "**Come See About Me**"[The Supremes],""**Harlem Shuffle** [Bob and Earl]," "**Hold On I'm Coming** [Sam and Dave]," "**It Doesn't Matter Anymore** [Buddy Holly]," "**Monday Monday** [The Mamas and the Papas]," "**Nobody Needs Your Love** [Gene Pitney (Randy Newman, composer)], "**You'll Never Walk Alone** [Judy Garland]."Songs played live by the Buzz in 1966.

"Hung Up On This Girl." Also known as "Hung Up." Bowie composition played with the Buzz in 1966. Registered with BMI.

"It's Getting Back to Me," "Take It With Soul," "Send You Money," "The Fairground," "The Girl From Minnesota," "You

Better Tell Her." Other Bowie compositions from this period, some played in a few Buzz gigs, most registered with Sparta Music.

"Whistling," "You've Got It Made." Songs registered with BMI/Embassy Music roughly around this time; unknown if demoed.

"Cobbled Streets and Baggy Trousers." Bowie composition offered to the Decca group Love Affair, who turned it down. Demo likely exists, or once did.

"Flower Song." Song proposed for a film written by Michael Armstrong, *A Floral Tale,* for which Bowie was to play a modern-day Orpheus. The project was vetoed by the British Board of Film Censors, allegedly for a scene in which two men kiss.

"Say Goodbye To Mr. Mind," "Lincoln House." Songs considered for Bowie's first album, in autumn 1966 but apparently not recorded. Bowie registered "Mr. Mind" with his publisher in February 1967.

"Your Funny Smile." Bowie composition recorded for Bowie's first LP in fall 1966; it made the initial LP sequencing (on an acetate of December 1966) but was subsequently cut. Described by Cann as being in the Mod soul style of Bowie's Pye singles.

"Bunny Thing." Bowie composition recorded for Bowie's first LP, with Bowie and John Renbourn on acoustic guitars (during the same session, 14 December, as "Come and Buy My Toys"). Pressed on an early acetate but subsequently deleted from the album sequence (like "Your Funny Smile," it was cut to make room for the 1967 tracks "Sell Me a Coat" and "Love Me Till Tuesday"). Described by Cann as being a parody of a beatnik poetry reading, with drug jokes and Bowie attempting a Germanic accent.

1967

"Pussy Cat." Cover of a Jess Conrad track, recorded at the final "Laughing Gnome" session on 8 March 1967 (Cann).

"**It Can't Happen Here** (Mothers of Invention)"**Dirty Old Man** (the Fugs)." Songs performed live during Bowie's brief stint with the Riot Squad in spring 1967.

"Something I Would Like To Be." Acetate sent in December 1967 as a prospective song to John Maus, one of the Walker Brothers, who was a fellow guest with Bowie on the Dutch TV show *Fanclub* around this time.

"You Gotta Know."An early effort in his translation sideline, "You Gotta Know" was a Bowie lyric intended for a composition in some unknown language.

"Home By Six," "Now That You Want Me," "A Picture of You," "Silver Sunday." Bowie compositions from 1967, of which nothing else is known.

"Going Down," song composed and demoed in 1967 and later compiled on the *Ernie Johnson* tape.

"Maids of Mayfair." Song allegedly composed for *Pierrot in Turquoise* but scrapped during rehearsals, as per Trynka. I agree with Pegg it was likely a rewrite of "Maid of Bond Street."

1968

***Ernie Johnson*: "Tiny Tim (You're Smart, You're Pretty Tiny Tim)," "Where's the Loo?," "Season Folk," "Just One Moment Sir," "Various Times of Day," "Early Morning," "Noon, Lunch-Time," "Evening," "Ernie Boy," "This Is My Day," "Untitled."**

These songs all were composed for a rock opera, *Ernie Johnson,* for which Bowie wrote a four-page synopsis, including proposed stage directions and camera angles (he thought it could be televised). The overall "narrative" was partially inspired by Anthony Newley's *Gurney Slade,* though Cann wrote that some of *Ernie* was recycled from a play Bowie wrote in 1966 called *Peacock's Farm*. By far the largest single collection of unreleased Bowie compositions of the Sixties, *Ernie Johnson* survived as a four-track tape (with Bowie vocal overdubs, his own electric and acoustic guitar work, and percussion dubs) that was auctioned to a collector in 1996.

The premise is that Londoner Ernie Johnson, age 19, plans to commit suicide at a party he's throwing for himself. "Tiny Tim" (see "There Is a Happy Land") is one of the guests, and his opening song is reportedly based on the Searchers' "Sweets for My Sweet." "Where's the Loo?," whose lyric Kenneth Pitt reprinted in his memoir, finds party guests arriving and bitching at each other ("Where's the loo? What crappy chairs! What fabby clothes! Is it true? That after tonight there's no more you? And can we watch?"). As such it's a precursor of "Queen Bitch" and Lou Reed's "New York Telephone Conversation."

"Season Folk" is reportedly "Jimmy Webb influenced," with Ernie mourning past loves; "Just One Moment Sir" finds Ernie having a racist conversation with a tramp; "Ernie Boy" is a monologue in which Ernie talks to the mirror and smokes a joint. The "Various Times of Day" four-song suite, which seems tentatively linked to the Ernie suicide storyline, reportedly features elaborate multi-tracked Bowie vocals. (The "morning, noon and night" idea came from fellow Deram act the Moody Blues, whose *Days of Future Passed* had the same organizing concept.) "This is My Day (A Song of the Morning)" is the climactic number, where Ernie runs to Carnaby Street to buy a tie for his suicide party, while a final untitled track is described as chaotic.

This is the most tantalizing of the unheard Bowie recordings (by most—*Record Collector*'s Peter Doggett was allowed to listen to it in 1996 when the tape was auctioned and is the source of much of the above description), as it could be a storehouse of his future compositions. *Ernie Johnson* is also the end of Bowie's Mod London period. It's telling that none of Bowie's other rock concept albums had anywhere near this degree of narrative structure.

"Angel Angel Grubby Face." Provisionally slated for the second Deram album and possibly recorded in the same session as "London Bye Ta-Ta." A demo version was sold at a Christie's auction in 1993 but hasn't circulated. Ken Pitt told Cann in 1981 that he still had a copy.

"The Reverend Raymond Brown (Attends the Garden Fete on Thatwick Green)," "Threepenny Joe." Other songs slated for Bowie's second Deram album. The latter was likely an early version of his "London Bye Ta-Ta" rewrite "Threepenny Pierrot."

"**Back to Where I've Never Been."** Tony Hill composition recorded with Turquoise on the same 24 October 1968 date as "Ching-a-Ling." Discarded once Hill left Turquoise, possibly a day or so later. Presumably Bowie sang harmony and played 12-string acoustic.

"The Princes' Parties": Bowie composition played at a few Feathers performances in late 1968, unrecorded.

"Strawberry Fields Forever,""Lady Midnight [Leonard Cohen],""**Next** [Jacques Brel/Scott Walker],"**One Hundred Years From Today**": other covers in the Feathers repertoire.

1969

"Graffiti." "Sound collage" intended for a segment of the *Love You Till Tuesday* film in January 1969, apparently not recorded.

"No One Someone." During the Malta International Song Festival, Bowie (along with the rest of the contestants) was asked to provide an English lyric for a Maltese song. He performed his version, "No One Someone," at the festival on 27 July 1969.

"**Don't Think Twice It's Alright**," "**She Belongs To Me**" [Bob Dylan], "**I'm So Glad** [Skip James » Cream]." Covers sung during Bowie's few solo acoustic performances in late 1969 and early 1970.

"Hole In the Ground," "Bump In the Hill." "Hole in the Ground" was a proposed single for Bowie's friend and former bandmate George Underwood, produced by Tony Visconti at Trident Studios in late December 1969. Underwood and Bowie sang while the rhythm section was a "Space Oddity" reunion: Terry Cox on drums, Tim Renwick on guitar and Herbie Flowers on bass. For the B-side, the band cut an extended jam instrumental version of the track, provisionally titled "Bump In the Hill." The single went nowhere and Bowie remade "Hole In the Ground" in 2000 for *Toy* (see entry on blog & in next book).

1970

"Instant Karma!" "Madame George." Bowie covered John Lennon's new single and Van Morrison's "Madame George" during some of the early Hype shows in the spring of 1970. (He may have sung the latter in his 1969 solo act as well.)

1971

"I'd Like a Big Girl With a Couple of Melons." A Bonzo Doo Dah Band-esque song that served as a lead-in to "Oh! You Pretty Things" during Bowie's set at the Glastonbury Festival, 1971, as per Pegg.

"It's Gonna Rain Again." A song whose title was allegedly inspired by Steve Reich's composition "It's Gonna Rain." Bowie played it live at least once, at Glastonbury in 1971. Pegg, who's heard the *Ziggy Stardust*-era studio take, described it as a dull Bob Dylan-inspired song that doesn't merit its legendary reputation.

"Black Hole Kids." A track recorded but not finished during the *Ziggy Stardust* sessions. Reportedly considered for release on Ryko's reissue of that album and later mentioned by Bowie as a song he was considering remaking for an ill-fated 30th anniversary *Ziggy Stardust* album/movie.

"Only One Paper Left." First demoed by the post-Bowie Hype, "Only One Paper Left" (a smoker's lament—see Nick Drake's *Five Leaves Left*) was also tried out during *Ziggy Stardust*.

"King of the City." Title included in a list of songs written along the left margin of the "Lady Stardust" lyric sheet (as displayed in the *David Bowie Is* exhibit), dating to ca.-mid 1971 (it's apparent the list of songs came after, perhaps a while after, the lyric). The title is the last of the list, and is in a different handwriting from the rest. As it's listed after "Here She Comes" (the original title of "Andy Warhol") and "We Should Be On By Now" ("Time"), it's possible "King of the City" was a working title for another song. It also could be a completely unknown composition.

1973

"Ladytron." Roxy Music classic from their debut album, rumored to have been attempted during the *Pin Ups* sessions. This rumor derives from Bowie calling Bryan Ferry to ask permission to perform a Roxy song on the album, though this possibly was just a bluff on Bowie's part (see "Sorrow").

"Star." Song composed and demoed for Amanda Lear to sing in a proposed (and soon abandoned) musical adaptation of *Octobriana*. Apparently no relation to the earlier "Star."

1974

"Are You Coming? Are You Coming?" Cited by the *NME* in January 1974 as a title of a song recorded at Olympic Studios for *Diamond Dogs*. Quite possibly a working title of a subsequently-released song.

"Do the Ruby." Allegedly written for Bette Midler (who did cover "Young Americans" in the sessions for her *Songs from the New Depression*). As the only source ever to mention it was a Cherry Vanilla-penned "Bowie Diary" in the 21 December 1974 *Mirabelle*, there's a strong chance the song never existed.

1975

"Too Fat Polka (I Don't Want Her—You Can Have Her—She's Too Fat For Me)." Tasteful song written by Ross McLean and Arthur Richardson and first recorded by Arthur Godfrey in 1947 (the Andrews Sisters evened the scales with their version, about being repulsed by a fat man). Bowie's take on the song was allegedly cut either during the first Sigma Sound sessions in August 1974 or, more likely, at the Electric Lady with John Lennon in January 1975. There's no actual evidence that this song was recorded but if the take exists, it was more likely a part of a Lennon/Carlos Alomar studio jam that went through old soul and funk songs (see "Fame"). According to fan legend, Bowie burned the tape at the end of the session, which is almost certainly nonsense.

"Turn Blue," "Drink to Me," "Moving On," "Sell Your Love." In Los Angeles in mid-March 1975, Bowie phoned Iggy Pop "out of the blue," according to the writer Nick Kent, who was in LA with Pop at the time. (Another version of the story has Bowie spying Pop walking on Sunset Boulevard and yelling at him to get in his limo. Some also argue the date is more likely mid-May 1975). Bowie invited Pop to work with him on some new songs he was demoing at Oz Studio. Upon arriving, Pop found Bowie alone in the studio with an engineer and *Rolling Stone*'s Cameron Crowe. Bowie and Pop snorted some cocaine and quickly went to work, Bowie laying down all instrumental tracks, Pop coming up with lyrics.

Songs included an early version of "Turn Blue" (later on *Lust For Life*, see Book 2) and a go at "Sell Your Love," which Pop had recently recorded with James Williamson and which would turn up on *Kill City* in 1977. The centerpiece of the session was "Drink to Me" (a provisional title—it has no official one), described by Crowe as an "ominous, dirgelike instrumental track" that Bowie had spent nine hours recording. Pop improvised a verse ("I can't believe that you don't know you look ugly...you're just dumb—straight out of the cradle and into the hole with you") and a refrain ("when I walk through the do-wa/I'm your new breed of ho-wa/We will noooow drink to meeee"). Bowie approved, calling Pop the heir to Lenny Bruce ("It's verbal jazz, man!" he told Crowe).

While this is essentially what Bowie and Pop would do in 1976 on *The Idiot*, the timing, the setting and their various mental/physical conditions weren't right. There was some tension in the studio (Bowie told Pop he was coming off like Mick Jagger, to which Pop replied "I don't sound like fuckin' Mick") and Pop missed the following session, having overslept and then phoning his apologies while drunk. The sessions never resumed.

"Fish?" "Shady?" There are allegedly three outtakes from *Station to Station*. Two titles, "Fish" and "Shady," were listed in a 2010 article in *Liberation*, though with no reference as to who mentioned them. These possibly were working titles for released songs.

The Man Who Fell to Earth. Bowie's performance in *The Man Who Fell to Earth* was "non-acting," in his words, but it's far more a movie-length mime. Take the first shot of his character, Thomas Jerome Newton, filmed in medium shot stumbling down a New Mexican hillside with an exaggerated gait, his arms stiffly swinging. The DJ John Peel, upon first hearing Elvis Presley, said the effect on him was that "of a naked extraterrestrial walking through the door and announcing that he/she was going to live with me for the rest of my life." Now two decades later Bowie offered the British response: a sexless, ageless British extraterrestrial who is consumed and spat out by America.

Bowie's score for Nicolas Roeg's film remains his most legendary lost work. How much of it was actually composed and recorded is unknown. The soundtrack began soon after (if not during) the *Station to Station* sessions, and was recorded at the same Los Angeles studio, Cherokee, with Harry Maslin producing and David Hines as engineer. Paul Buckmaster was recruited as co-composer and arranger by the film's producer, Michael Deeley.

Buckmaster and Bowie first recorded demos on Bowie's four-track TEAC deck, using early-model drum machines for percussion, with Bowie playing Fender Rhodes and Buckmaster cello. For inspiration, they listened to Richard Strauss, Miles Davis (especially *Bitches Brew* and *Get Up With It*) and Kraftwerk albums. "We kind of took them seriously but we kind of laughed as well...because the music had a kind of innocent quality which was very fetching and a deadpan humor as well," Buckmaster said of Kraftwerk (Buckley, 241). As both were heavy cocaine users, the sessions (demos and subsequent Cherokee dates) were a blur. Buckmaster recalled the soundtrack including a) "a couple of medium-tempo rock instrumental pieces with simple motifs and riffy kinds of grooves," b) some "more slow and spacey cues with synthesizer, Rhodes and cello" and c) a "couple weirder, atonal cues using synths and percussions."There were a few recognizable songs, including a piece that would become "Subterraneans" on *Low* and a song called "Wheels," (little green ones, perhaps) "which had a gentle sort of melancholy mood to it," Buckmaster told *Mojo*. The backing band was most of the *Station to Station* lineup (Carlos Alomar, George Murray, Dennis Davis) with J. Peter Robinson recruited to play the Fender Rhodes. Synthesizers included the ARP Odyssey and Solina.

Moving directly into making the soundtrack after finishing *Station to Station* proved too taxing for Bowie, particularly as he had to finish the soundtrack before going on tour in February 1976. Maslin recalled Bowie was having a hard time "doing movie cues," stalling out at nine when 60 were needed. "David couldn't work because he was so tired. He had no concentration on the music." Bowie's cocaine use had gotten to the point where he simply couldn't focus on a single task for long, let alone one as tedious as doing soundtrack cues ("he'd sit and talk about Ziggy for two hours and then we'd get back to the music and then he'd go off and start talking about something else," Maslin said (Hopkins, 158)). It was while making the soundtrack, not *Station to Station*, that Bowie fell apart: hallucinating, babbling and collapsing in the studio. He was at rock bottom, and soon he finally began to wean himself off his favorite drug.

Studio and managerial politics took care of the rest. Deeley reportedly tried to get Bowie to take a lesser deal for the soundtrack, and Bowie recalled being asked to submit his work "along with other people's...and I just said, 'Shit, you're not getting any of it." (Mackinnon, *NME*, 1980). Buckmaster believed that Roeg, though he never said this to Bowie, was disappointed in the music, believing it was underdeveloped and "not up to the standard of composing and performance needed for a good movie score."

So Roeg went with music by John Phillips (leading a band that included ex-Rolling Stone Mick Taylor) and Stomu Yamashta, along with a set of American standards: "Blueberry Hill," "Hello Mary Lou," "Stardust," "Blue Bayou." In 1980, Bowie admitted losing the soundtrack was "probably just as well; my music would have cast a completely different reflection on it all." He credited the soundtrack sessions, chaotic and fruitless as they were, with making him more confident in his instrumental capabilities. "That's where I got the first inklings of trying to work with [Brian] Eno at some point."

It's fitting that Thomas Jerome Newton records an album in the film (released by "The Visitor") whose music we never hear. *The Man Who Fell to Earth* is Bowie's anti-Elvis movie, a film whose rock star lead doesn't sing a note. "I didn't make it for you...[it's] for my wife," Newton says of the album. "She'll get to hear it one day on the radio." Perhaps one day she will.

Producer/Contributor

Dana Gillespie, ***Weren't Born a Man***, 22 March 1974. "**Andy Warhol,**" "**Backed a Loser,**" "**Mother, Don't Be Frightened.**"

In summer 1971, Bowie produced three tracks for his friend Gillespie, which MainMan sat on until releasing them on the ill-received *Weren't Born a Man* in 1974 (Mick Ronson and Robin Cable produced and arranged other tracks). Bowie had written "Andy Warhol" with Gillespie in mind. The authorship of

"Backed a Loser" remains in doubt—it's been cited as a sole Gillespie composition but its inclusion on the 2006 *Oh You Pretty Things: The Songs of David Bowie* suggests some Bowie credit. Its string arrangement is similar to T. Rex's "Children of the Revolution," arguing for it post-dating 1971. "Mother, Don't Be Frightened" is a sole Gillespie composition.

Mott the Hoople, ***All the Young Dudes***, 8 September 1972. **"Sweet Jane"/ "Momma's Little Jewel"/ "All the Young Dudes" / "Sucker"/ "Jerkin' Crocus"/ "One of the Boys"/ "Soft Ground"/ "Ready for Love-After Lights"/ "Sea Diver."**

Though Bowie's "All the Young Dudes" saved Mott the Hoople and was one of his most evocative songs, his work producing their subsequent album, over 20 sessions in June-July 1972, was fairly anonymous. Only "Sweet Jane," for which Lou Reed provided Ian Hunter a guide vocal, stands out as under his influence. Little distinguishes the rest of the tracks from those on earlier Mott records like *Brain Capers*.

Lou Reed, ***Transformer***, 8 November 1972. **"Vicious"/ "Andy's Chest"/ "Hangin' Round"/ "Walk on the Wild Side"/ "Make Up"/ "Satellite of Love"/ "Wagon Wheel"/ "New York Telephone Conversation"/ "I'm So Free"/ "Goodnight Ladies."**

For more details, see the "John, I'm Only Dancing" entry. Bowie likely contributed some lines to "Wagon Wheel." Decades later, he'd sing two lines on a collective "Perfect Day" that was cut for a BBC advertisement. It would be, as of this writing, his last UK #1 single.

Iggy and the Stooges, ***Raw Power***, 1 June 1973. **"Search and Destroy"/ "Gimme Danger"/ "Your Pretty Face Is Going To Hell"/ "Penetration"/ "Raw Power"/ "I Need Somebody"/ "Shake Appeal"/ "Death Trip."**

Brought in to salvage a raw set of tapes (allegedly Iggy Pop had put vocals on one track of a 24-track tape, lead guitar on another, and dumped all other instruments on a third, but this likely was an exaggeration on Bowie's part), Bowie managed to get a commercially-releasable mix that would earn scorn from Pop and James Williamson (both of whom later made their peace with Bowie's mix).

Steeleye Span, ***Now We Are Six***, March 1974. **"To Know Him Is to Love Him."**

In December 1973, during the *Diamond Dogs* and Astronettes sessions, Bowie played alto saxophone on the neo-traditionalist folk outfit Steeleye Span's cover of Phil Spector's "To Know Him Is to Love Him." Recruited by producer Ian Anderson, he turned in an abrasive, honking, occasionally off-key performance that came off as if an inebriated Bowie was playing along to the record at home.

Keith Moon,"The Clover Masters," September 1975. **"Real Emotion."**

An acquaintance of Keith Moon's in Los Angeles, at a time when Moon was a sad, drunken fixture in Sunset Strip night-clubs, Bowie agreed to sing harmonies on "Real Emotion," a Steve Cropper song intended for Moon's second, and never released, solo album (though later included on a reissue of Moon's *Two Sides of the Moon*, the track post-dates that album). Engineer Barry Rudolph described the night the Bowie entourage came to Clover Studios as "a casting call for a circus movie—a pretty freaky crowd that filled up the entire control room." Bowie was fast on his feet, offering vocal harmony ideas (like a counter-melody for the second verse), and he asked Rudolph to use automatic double-tracking for his vocals (Rudolph, unfamiliar with ADT (a Beatles innovation) had to create a "faux version" with an old Revox reel-to-reel). A Harry Nilsson-esque song, "Real Emotion," with Moon regretting a life spent watching television in lieu of "real" human interaction, is a secret prequel to "TVC 15" and "Stay."

Bowipocrypha

"The Better I Know"/ "Now I'm On My Way"/ "Baby It's Too

Late"/ "I'm Over You" / "Judgment Day"/ "I Don't Know How Much"/ "I Thought Of You Last Night." Songs allegedly hailing from a rehearsal tape made by Bowie and the Kon-Rads in July-August 1963. But as the Illustrated DB Guide notes, "With the inclusion of four songs that were released in 1965, it is clear that these songs were recorded during a 1965 studio session without Bowie."

"Penny Lane," "A Little Bit Me, A Little Bit You." Some fans have long claimed the knock-off Beatles and Monkees recordings on a compilation called *Hits '67* (released by the Music For Pleasure label in May 1967) were sung by Bowie, but it's the work of session singer Tony Stephen.

"Day Tripper." The original notes for Ryko's *Jimi Hendrix Experience: Radio One* said it's "generally agreed" that Bowie had sung backing vocals for a Hendrix recording of "Day Tripper" on 15 December 1967. Asked about this decades later, Bowie reportedly said: "Rubbish. Wish it were true, though."

"Don't Be Afraid (Oh Darling).""Don't Be Afraid" was a studio demo said to hail from the period of the Arnold Corns sessions and "Rupert the Riley." It turned out to be a demo by the UK prog/early metal band Czar, included on a reissue of their self-titled 1970 album.

"Something Happens." Also said to come from the *Hunky Dory* era, this was actually a song Colin Blunstone recorded for a 1970 BBC session. As with "Don't Be Afraid," the confusion likely began when a legitimate Bowie recording (a radio interview or a live performance) was put on a tape with the Czar and Blunstone outtakes.

"Let's Twist Again." An alleged reggae version of Chubby Checker's "Let's Twist Again" recorded by Bowie and John Lennon from the "Fame" sessions. Bootlegs reveal a possibly late Seventies-early Eighties recording by someone who sounds neither like Lennon nor Bowie.

List of Songs

Partial Discography

"Liza Jane"/ "Louie Louie Go Home." Released: 5 June 1964 (Vocalion Pop V.9221).

"I Pity the Fool"/ "Take My Tip." 5 March 1965 (Parlophone R 5250).

"You've Got a Habit of Leaving"/ "Baby Loves That Way." 20 August 1965 (Parlophone R 5315).

"Can't Help Thinking About Me"/ "And I Say to Myself." 14 January 1966 (Pye 7N 17020).

"Do Anything You Say"/ "Good Morning Girl." 1 April 1966 (Pye 7N 17079).

"I Dig Everything" / "I'm Not Losing Sleep." 19 August 1966 (Pye 7N 17157).

[All of the above, plus "Bars of the County Jail," "I Want My Baby Back," "That's Where My Heart Is," "I'll Follow You" and "Glad I've Got Nobody" can be found on *Early On: 1964-1966* (Rhino R2 705260).]

"Rubber Band"/ "The London Boys." 2 December 1966 (Deram DM 107).

"The Laughing Gnome"/ "The Gospel According to Tony Day." 14 April 1967 (Deram DM 123).

David Bowie, 1 June 1967. Side 1: Uncle Arthur/ Sell Me a Coat/ Rubber Band (album remake)/ Love You Till Tuesday (album version)/ There Is a Happy Land/ We Are Hungry Men/ When I Live My Dream. Side 2: Little Bombardier/ Silly Boy Blue/ Come and Buy My Toys/ Join the Gang/ She's Got Medals/ Maid of Bond Street/ Please Mr. Gravedigger. [The 2010 reissue has mono/stereo versions of the above, the "Rubber Band," "Laughing Gnome" and "Love You Till Tuesday" singles and the following: "Let Me Sleep Beside You," "Karma Man," "In the Heat of the Morning," "London Bye Ta-Ta" (alternate 1968 take), "When I'm Five" (1968 BBC recording) and "Ching-a-Ling."]

"Love You Till Tuesday"/ "Did You Ever Have a Dream." 14 July 1967 (Deram DM 135).

"Space Oddity"/ "Wild Eyed Boy From Freecloud." 11 July 1969 (Philips BF 1801).

David Bowie (aka ***Space Oddity***), 14 November 1969. Side 1: Space Oddity/ Unwashed and Somewhat Slightly Dazed/ Don't Sit Down/ Letter to Hermione/ Cygnet Committee. Side 2: Janine/ An Occasional Dream/ Wild Eyed Boy From Freecloud (album remake)/ God Knows I'm Good/ Memory of a Free Festival. [2009 reissue has the above and additional disc with the following: Space Oddity (demo)/ An Occasional Dream (demo)/ Wild Eyed Boy From Freecloud (B-side)/ Let Me Sleep Beside You/ Unwashed and Somewhat Slightly Dazed/ Janine (BBC performances)/London Bye Ta-Ta (1970 remake)/ The Prettiest Star/ Conversation Piece/ Memory of a Free Festival Pts. 1 and 2/ Wild Eyed Boy From Freecloud (alt. album mix)/ Memory of a Free Festival (alt. album mix)/ London Bye Ta-Ta (alt. stereo mix)/ Ragazzo Solo, Ragazza Sola.]

"The Prettiest Star"/ "Conversation Piece." 6 March 1970 (Mercury MF 1135).

"Memory of a Free Festival Pt. 1"/ "Memory of a Free Festival Pt. 2." 26 June 1970 (Mercury 6052 026).

The Man Who Sold the World, 4 November 1970 [10 April 1971, UK]. Side 1: The Width of a Circle/ All the Madmen/ Black Country Rock/ After All. Side 2: Running Gun Blues/ Saviour Machine/ She Shook Me Cold/ The Man Who Sold the World/ The Supermen. [1990 Ryko CD issue included: Lightning Frightening/ Holy Holy (1971 remake)/ Moonage Daydream (Arnold Corns version)/ Hang Onto Yourself (Arnold Corns version)].

"Holy Holy"/ "Black Country Rock." 15 January 1971 (Mercury 6052 049).

"Moonage Daydream"/ "Hang Onto Yourself" (Arnold Corns). 7 May 1971 (B&C CB 149).

Hunky Dory, 17 December 1971. Side 1: Changes/ Oh! You Pretty Things/ Eight Line Poem/ Life On Mars?/ Kooks/ Quicksand. Side 2: Fill Your Heart/ Andy Warhol/ Song for Bob Dylan/ Queen Bitch/ The Bewlay Brothers. [1990 Ryko CD issue included: Bombers/ The Supermen (1971 remake)/ Quicksand (demo)/ The Bewlay Brothers (alternate mix).]

"Changes"/ "Andy Warhol." 7 January 1972 (RCA 2160).

"Starman"/ "Suffragette City." 28 April 1972 (RCA 2199).

The Rise and Fall of Ziggy Stardust and the Spiders From Mars, 6 June 1972. Side 1: Five Years/ Soul Love/ Moonage Daydream/ Starman/ It Ain't Easy. Side 2: Lady Stardust/ Star/ Hang Onto Yourself/ Ziggy Stardust/ Suffragette City/ Rock 'n' Roll Suicide. [1990 Ryko CD issue included: John, I'm Only Dancing (unreleased mix)/ Velvet Goldmine/ Sweet Head/ Ziggy Stardust (demo)/ Lady Stardust (demo)/ John, I'm Only Dancing (remix). 2002 30th Anniversary issue includes all of the above plus: Holy Holy (remake)/ Amsterdam/ The Supermen (remake)/ Round and Round/ Moonage Daydream (new mix)].

"John, I'm Only Dancing"/ "Hang Onto Yourself." 1 September 1972 (RCA 2263).

"The Jean Genie"/ "Ziggy Stardust." 24 November 1972 (RCA 2302).

"Drive-In Saturday" / "Round and Round." 6 April 1973 (RCA 2352).

Aladdin Sane, 13 April 1973. Side 1: Watch That Man/ Aladdin Sane/ Drive-In Saturday/ Panic In Detroit/ Cracked Actor. Side 2: Time/ The Prettiest Star (remake)/ Let's Spend the Night Together/ The Jean Genie/ Lady Grinning Soul. [30th Anniversary disc includes: John, I'm Only Dancing ("sax" remake), Jean Genie , Time (single mixes), All the Young Dudes (Bowie vocal), Changes, The Supermen, Life On Mars?,

John, I'm Only Dancing (live, Boston, 1 October 1972), Jean Genie (live, Santa Monica, 20 October 1972), Drive-In Saturday (live, Cleveland, 25 November 1972)].

"Life On Mars?"/ "The Man Who Sold the World." 23 June 1973 (RCA 2316).

"Sorrow"/ "Amsterdam." 12 October 1973 (RCA 2424).

Pin Ups, 19 October 1973. Side 1: Rosalyn/ Here Comes the Night/ I Wish You Would/ See Emily Play/ Everything's Alright/ I Can't Explain. Side 2: Friday On My Mind/ Sorrow/ Don't Bring Me Down/ Shapes of Things/ Anyway, Anyhow, Anywhere/ Where Have All the Good Times Gone? (Ryko reissue included "Growin' Up" and "Amsterdam").

"Rebel Rebel"/ "Queen Bitch." 15 February 1974 (RCA LPB 5009).

Diamond Dogs, 24 April 1974. Side 1: Future Legend/ Diamond Dogs/ Sweet Thing-Candidate-Sweet Thing (Reprise)/ Rebel Rebel. Side 2: Rock 'n' Roll With Me/ We Are the Dead/ 1984/ Big Brother/ Chant of the Ever Circling Skeletal Family. [Ryko reissue included Dodo and Alternative Candidate. 2004 reissue includes those plus 1984/Dodo, Rebel Rebel (US single mix), Diamond Dogs (K-Tel promo edit), Growin' Up, Candidate (Intimacy Mix) and Rebel Rebel (2003 remake).]

"Diamond Dogs"/ "Holy Holy (remake)." 14 June 1974 (RCA APBO-0293).

"Knock On Wood"/ "Panic In Detroit." 13 September 1974 (RCA 2466).

David Live, 29 October 1974. Side 1: 1984/ Rebel Rebel/ Moonage Daydream/ Sweet Thing-Candidate-Sweet Thing (Reprise). Side 2: Changes/ Suffragette City/ Aladdin Sane/ All the Young Dudes/ Cracked Actor. Side 3: Rock 'n' Roll With Me/ Watch That Man/ Knock On Wood/ Diamond Dogs. Side 4: Big Brother/ Width Of a Circle/ Jean Genie/ Rock 'n' Roll Suicide. [1990 Ryko CD includes Here Today, Gone Tomorrow and Time; 2005 issue added to those Space Oddity and Panic In Detroit and placed all bonus tracks into "concert" sequence.]

"Young Americans"/ "Suffragette City." 21 February 1975 (RCA 2523).

Young Americans, 7 March 1975. Side 1: Young Americans/ Win/ Fascination/ Right. Side 2: Somebody Up There Likes Me/ Across the Universe/ Can You Hear Me/ Fame. [1991 Ryko reissue included Who Can I Be Now?, It's Gonna Be Me and John, I'm Only Dancing (Again), all included on later reissues.]

"Fame"/ "Right." 25 July 1975 (RCA 2579).

"Space Oddity"/ "Changes"/ "Velvet Goldmine." 26 September 1975 (RCA 2593).

"Golden Years"/ "Can You Hear Me." 21 November 1975 (RCA 2640).

Station to Station, 23 January 1976. Side 1: Station to Station/ Golden Years/ Word On a Wing. Side 2: TVC 15/ Stay/ Wild Is the Wind. [2010 reissue includes the complete Nassau Coliseum concert, 23 March 1976: Station to Station/ Suffragette City/ Fame/ Word On a Wing/ Stay/ Waiting For the Man/ Queen Bitch/ Life On Mars?/ Five Years/ Panic In Detroit/ Changes/ TVC 15/ Diamond Dogs/ Rebel Rebel/ The Jean Genie.]

"TVC 15"/ "We Are the Dead." 30 April 1976 (RCA 2682).

Subsequently-issued live recordings of the 1964-1976 period. For the sake of brevity, I'll use the tracklistings from the most recent issue. Date of recording in brackets.

Bowie At the Beeb, 26 September 2000. Disc 1:[13 May 1968] In the Heat of the Morning/ London Bye Ta-Ta/ Karma Man/ Silly Boy Blue/ [20 October 1969] Let Me Sleep Beside You/ Janine/ [5 February 1970] Amsterdam/ God Knows I'm Good/ The Width of a Circle/ Unwashed and Somewhat Slightly Dazed/ Cygnet Committee/ Memory of a Free Festival/ [25 March 1970] Wild Eyed Boy From Freecloud/ [3 June 1971] Bombers/ Looking For a Friend/ Almost Grown/ Kooks/ It Ain't Easy. Disc 2: [21 September 1971] The Supermen/ Oh!

You Pretty Things (only available on the Japanese issue)/ Eight Line Poem/ [18 January 1972] Hang Onto Yourself/ Ziggy Stardust/ Queen Bitch/ Waiting For the Man/ Five Years/ [16 May 1972] White Light-White Heat/ Moonage Daydream/ Hang Onto Yourself/ Suffragette City/ Ziggy Stardust/ [22 May 1972] Starman/ Space Oddity/ Changes/ Oh! You Pretty Things/ [23 May 1972] Andy Warhol/ Lady Stardust/ Rock 'n' Roll Suicide. (Disc 3 is the complete 27 June 2000 concert.)

Live Santa Monica '72, 30 June 2008. [20 October 1972]. Introduction/ Hang Onto Yourself/ Ziggy Stardust/ Changes/ The Supermen/ Life On Mars?/ Five Years/ Space Oddity/ Andy Warhol/ My Death/ The Width Of a Circle/ Queen Bitch/ Moonage Daydream/ John, I'm Only Dancing/ Waiting For the Man/ The Jean Genie/ Suffragette City/ Rock 'n' Roll Suicide.

Ziggy Stardust: The Motion Picture, 1 April 2003. [3 July 1973] Intro/Hang Onto Yourself/ Ziggy Stardust/ Watch That Man/ Wild Eyed Boy From Freecloud/ All the Young Dudes/ Oh! You Pretty Things/ Moonage Daydream/ Changes/ Space Oddity/ My Death. Disc 2: Intro/ Cracked Actor/ Time/ Width of a Circle/ Let's Spend the Night Together/ Suffragette City/ White Light-White Heat/ Farewell Speech/ Rock 'n' Roll Suicide.

Bibliography

Bowie: life, music, collaborators

Aladdin Sane: Off the Record. EMI Music Publishing Ltd.: 1993.

Bowie, Angela, *Free Spirit*. Mushroom Press: 1981.

Bowie, Angela with Patrick Carr, *Backstage Passes*. Cooper Square Press: 1993.

Bowie, David and Mick Rock, *Moonage Daydream: The Life and Times of Ziggy Stardust*. Genesis Publications: 2002.

Broackes, Victoria and Geoffrey Marsh, eds., *David Bowie Is*. V&A Publishing: 2013.

Buckley, David, *Aladdin Sane* (2003 reissue notes).

— *Diamond Dogs* (2004 reissue notes).

— *Strange Fascination: David Bowie: The Definitive Story*. Virgin Books: 2005.

— *Young Americans* (2007 reissue notes).

Cann, Kevin, *Any Day Now: David Bowie The London Years (1947-1974)*. Adelita: 2010.

— *David Bowie: A Chronology*. Hutchinson Publishing Group: 1983.

— *David Bowie* (2010 reissue notes).

— *Space Oddity* (2009 reissue notes).

— *Station to Station* (2010 reissue notes).

Carr, Roy and Charles Shaar Murray, *Bowie: An Illustrated Record*. Eel Pie Publishing: 1981.

Crowe, Cameron, *Station to Station* (2010 reissue notes).

Currie, David, ed., *David Bowie: The Starzone Interviews*. Omnibus Press: 1985.

De la Parra, Pimm Jal, *David Bowie: The Concert Tapes*. PJ Publishing: 1985.

Diamond Dogs (songbook). Warner Bros. Publications: 1974.

Edwards, Henry and Tony Zanetta, *Stardust: The David Bowie Story*. Bantam: 1986.

Gillman, Peter and Leni, *Alias David Bowie*. Henry Holt & Co.: 1987.

Hopkins, Jerry, *Bowie*. Elm Tree Books: 1985.

Hunky Dory: Off the Record. EMI Music Publishing Ltd.: 1992.

Juby, Kerry, ed., *In Other Words, David Bowie*. Omnibus Press: 1986.

Koenig, Peter-R., "The Laughing Gnostic: David Bowie and the Occult," 1996/2013. (http://www.parareligion.ch/bowie.htm).

LeRoy, Dan, *The Greatest Music Never Sold: Secrets of Legendary Lost Albums By David Bowie* [*et al*]. Backbeat Books: 2007.

The Man Who Sold the World: Off the Record. EMI Music Publishing Ltd.: 1992.

Matthew-Walker, Robert, *David Bowie:Theatre of Music*. The Kensal Press: 1985.

Miles, Barry, ed., *In His Own Words...David Bowie*. Omnibus Press: 1980.

Paytress, Mark, *Classic Rock Albums: Ziggy Stardust*. Schirmer Books: 1998.

Paytress, Mark and Steve Pafford, *Bowiestyle*. Omnibus Press: 2000.

Pegg, Nicholas, *The Complete David Bowie* (4th and 5th editions). Reynolds & Hearn Ltd.: 2006, 2012.

Perone, James, *The Words and Music of David Bowie*. Praeger: 2007.

Pin-Ups: Off the Record. EMI Music Publishing Ltd.: 1993.

Pitt, Kenneth, *The Pitt Report*. Omnibus Press Ltd.: 1983.

The Rise and Fall of Ziggy Stardust and the Spiders From Mars: Off The Record. International Music Publications Ltd.: 1992.

Sandford, Christopher, *Loving the Alien*. Da Capo: 1996.

Scott, Ken, with Bobby Owsinski, *Abbey Road to Ziggy Stardust: Off the Record with the Beatles, Bowie, Elton and So Much More*. Alfred Music Publishing Co.: 2012.

Space Oddity and Other Songs by David Bowie. TRO Essex Music Inc.: 1972.

Space Oddity: Off the Record. EMI Music Publishing Ltd.: 1992.

Spitz, Marc, *Bowie*. Crown Publishers: 2009.

Station to Station/Low (songbook), Warner Bros. Publications: 1977.

Thompson, Dave, *David Bowie: Moonage Daydream*. Plexus: 1987.

Thomson, Elizabeth and David Gutman, eds., *The Bowie Companion*. Da Capo Press: 1996.

Tremlett, George, *David Bowie: Living on the Brink*. Carol & Graff: 1997.

Trynka, Paul, *Starman*. Sphere: 2010.

The Vintage David Bowie. Wise Publications: 1983.

Visconti, Tony, *Bowie, Bolan and the Brooklyn Boy*. Harper-Collins: 2007.

Weird and Gilly, *Mick Ronson: The Spider With the Platinum Hair*. Independent Music Press: 2003.

[A note. Peter Doggett's *The Man Who Sold the World*, a song-by-song guide to Bowie's Seventies, was published in 2011 (for the record, this was after I wrote all of the blog entries revised in this book). For fear of being influenced or trumped in my revisions, I chose not to read his book, with much regret. I've little doubt that he and I came to similar conclusions on various songs, but hopefully we did so from different angles.]

Popular Music and Culture, Britain and the US, 1947-1976

The following either directly contributed to this book or provided a backdrop for periods discussed.

Ackroyd, Peter, *Albion: The Origins of the English Imagination*. Anchor: 2004.

The Age of Paranoia: How the Sixties Ended (editors of *Rolling Stone*). Pocket Books: 1972.

Altman, Dennis, *Homosexual: Oppression and Liberation*. Outerbridge and Dienstfrey: 1971.

Antonia, Nina, *The New York Dolls: Too Much Too Soon*. Omnibus Press: 1988.

Bacon, Tony, *London Live: From the Yardbirds to Pink Floyd to the Sex Pistols*. Balafon: 1999.

Ballard, J.G., *High-Rise*. Jonathan Cape: 1975.

Bangs, Lester, *Psychotic Reactions and Carburetor Dung* (Greil Marcus, ed.). Vintage: 1987.

Barber, Richard, *The Holy Grail: Imagination and Belief*. Harvard University Press: 2006.

Bardsley, Garth, *Stop the World: The Biography of Anthony Newley*. Oberon: 2003.

Barker, Hugh, and Yuval Taylor, *Faking It: The Quest for Authenticity in Popular Music*. WW Norton: 2007.

Barker, Paul, *The Freedoms of Suburbia*. Frances Lincoln: 2009.

Barnes, Richard, *Mods!* Eel Pie Publishing: 1979.

Baudelaire, Charles, *The Painter of Modern Life and Other Essays* (trans. Jonathan Mayne). Phaidon Press: 1964 (1863).

Beckett, Andy, *When The Lights Went Out: Britain in the Seventies*. Faber & Faber: 2009.

Benarde, Scott R., *Stars of David: Rock 'n' Roll's Jewish Stories*. Brandeis University Press: 2003.

Berman, Marshall, *The Politics of Authenticity* (2nd ed.). Verso: 2009 (1970).

Berry, Chuck, *The Autobiography*. Simon and Schuster: 1987.

Binkley, Sam, *Getting Loose: Lifestyle Consumption in the '70s*. Duke University Press: 2009.

Bloom, Harold, *The Anxiety of Influence: A Theory of Poetry*. Oxford University Press: 1973.

—*Omens of Millennium: The Gnosis of Dreams, Angels and Resurrection*. Riverhead Books: 1996.

Bockris, Victor, *Transformer: The Lou Reed Story*. Simon & Schuster: 1995.

Booker, Christopher, *The Neophiliacs: A Study of the Revolution in English Life in the Fifties and Sixties*. Collins: 1969.

Boorstin, Daniel J., *The Image, or What Happened To the American Dream*. Athaneum: 1962.

Booth, Stanley, *The True Adventures of the Rolling Stones* (revised ed.). A Cappella Books: 2000 (1984).

Bowman, Rob, *Soulsville, U.S.A.: The Story of Stax Records*. Schirmer Trade Books: 2003.

Bracewell, Michael, *Remake/Remodel: Becoming Roxy Music*. Da Capo: 2008

Bradley, Dick, *Understanding Rock 'n' Roll: Popular Music in Britain 1955-1964*. Open University Press: 1992.

Brennan, J.H., *The Occult Reich*. Signet: 1974.

The British Imagination: Twentieth-Century Paintings, Sculpture and Drawings (Edward Lucie-Smith, introduction). Hirschl & Adler Galleries: 1990.

Buckley, David, *The Thrill of It All: The Story of Bryan Ferry and Roxy Music*. Carlton Books: 2004.

Bulwer-Lytton, Edward, *The Coming Race*. Estes and Lauriat: 1892 (1871).

— *Zanoni*. Estes and Lauriat: 1892 (1842).

Burroughs, William S., *The Naked Lunch*. Grove Press: 1962 (1959).

— *Nova Express*. Grove Press: 1964.

— *The Wild Boys*. Grove Press: 1971.

Cannandine, David, *Class in Britain*. Yale University Press: 1998.

Carr, Roy, Brian Case and Fred Dellar, *The Hip: Hipsters, Jazz and the Beat Generation*. Faber & Faber: 1986.

Caputo, Philip, *A Rumor of War*. Holt, Rinehart, Winston: 1977.

Carlin, Marcello and Lena Friesen, "Then Play Long." (http://nobilliards.blogspot.com).

Cavendish, Richard, *The Black Arts*. Capricorn: 1967.

Chambers, Iain, *Urban Rhythms: Pop Music and Popular Culture*. Basinstoke: 1985.

Chapman, Rob, *A Very Irregular Head: The Life of Syd Barrett*. Da Capo: 2010.

Christgau, Robert, *Rock Albums of the '70s: A Critical Guide*. Da Capo: 1981.

Churchill, R.C., *The English Sunday*. Watts & Co.: 1954.

Clapton, Eric, *Autobiography*. Century: 2007.

Clarke, Arthur C., *Childhood's End*. Ballantine: 1953.

Clayson, Alan, *Beat Merchants: The Origins, History, Impact and Rock Legacy of the 1960s British Pop Groups*. Blandford: 1995.

Clutterbuck, Richard, *Guerrillas and Terrorists*. Faber & Faber: 1977.

Cohn, Nik, *Awopbopaloobop Alopbamboom: Pop From the Beginning*. Granada Publishing Ltd.: 1970.

— *I Am Still the Greatest Says Johnny Angelo*. Martin, Secker & Warburg: 1967.

Crouch, Colin, *The Students' Revolt*. Bodley Head: 1970.

Crowley, Aleister, *Confessions of Aleister Crowley: An Autohagiography* (John Symons and Kenneth Grant, eds.). Hill and Wang: 1969 (1929, first two volumes)

—*White Stains*. Leonard Smithers: 1898.

Crowley, John, *Aegypt* (later *The Solitudes*). Bantam: 1987.

Dan, Joseph, *Kabbalah: A Very Short Introduction*. Oxford University Press: 2006.

Davies, Andrew, *Other Theaters: The Development of Alternative and Experimental Theatre in Britain*. Macmillan: 1987.

Davies, Dave, *Kink: An Autobiography*. Hyperion: 1997.

Davies, Ray, *X-Ray*. Overlook Duckworth: 1994.

DeCurtis, Anthony, James Henke with Holly George-Warren, eds., *The Rolling Stone Illustrated History of Rock & Roll* (new ed.) Random House: 1992.

De Groot, Gerard, *The Seventies Unplugged: A Kaleidoscopic History of a Violent Decade*. Macmillan: 2010.

Dick, Philip K., *Dr. Bloodmoney*. Ace: 1965.

— *The Three Stigmata of Palmer Eldritch*. Doubleday: 1965.

Dinn, Freda, *The Observer's Book of Music*. Frederick Warne & Co.: 1953.

Disch, Thomas M., *Camp Concentration*. Rupert Hart-Davis: 1968.

— *334*. MacGibbon & Kee: 1972.

Draper, Robert, *Rolling Stone Magazine: The Uncensored History*. Doubleday: 1990.

Duncan, Robert, *The Noise: Notes From a Rock 'n' Roll Era*. Ticknor & Fields: 1984.

Du Noyer, Paul, *Liverpool—Wondrous Place: From the Cavern to the Capital of Culture*. Virgin Books: 2002.

Dylan, Bob, *Chronicles: Volume One*. Simon and Schuster: 2004.

Edwards, Frank. *Strange People*. Citadel Press: 1961.

Eisen, Jonathan, ed., *The Age of Rock*. Random House: 1970.

Ewing, Tom, "Popular." (http://freakytrigger.co.uk).

Faithfull, Marianne and David Dalton, *Faithfull: An Autobiography*. Little, Brown: 1994.

Farren, Mick, *Elvis Died for Somebody's Sins But Not Mine: A Lifetime's Collected Writing*. Headpress: 2013.

Fortune, Dion, *Psychic Self-Defense*. Rider & Co.: 1930.

Foucault, Michel, *Madness and Civilization: A History of Insanity in the Age of Reason* (trans. Richard Howard). Pantheon Books: 1965 (1961).

Geiger, John, *Nothing Is True, Everything Is Permitted: the Life of Brion Gysin*. Disinformation: 2005.

Gibran, Khalil, *The Prophet*. Knopf: 1923.

Gill, John, *Queer Noises: Male and Female Homosexuality in Twentieth-Century Music*. University of Minnesota Press: 1995.

Ginzburg, Eugenia Semyonovna, *Journey Into the Whirlwind* (trans. Paul Stevenson and Max Hayward). Harcourt, Brace & World: 1967.

Goodrick-Clarke, Nicholas, *The Occult Roots of Nazism: The Ariosophists of Austria and Germany, 1890-1935.* The Aquarian Press: 1985.

Gorer, Geoffrey, *Exploring English Character*. Criterion: 1955.

Gosling, Ray, *Sum Total*. Faber & Faber: 1962.

Gosse, Edmund, *Father and Son*. William Heinemann Ltd.: 1932 (1907).

Gould, Jonathan, *Can't Buy Me Love: The Beatles, Britain and America*. Harmony Books: 2007.

Green, Martin, *Transatlantic Patterns: Cultural Comparisons of*

England With America. Basic Books: 1977.

Greenland, Colin, *The Entropy Exhibition: Michael Moorcock and the British New Wave in Science Fiction*. Routledge and Kegan Paul: 1983.

Harrison, Harry, *Make Room! Make Room!* Doubleday: 1966.

Hatherley, Owen, *Militant Modernism*. Zer0 Books: 2008.

Harrer, Heinrich, *Seven Years in Tibet* (trans. Richard Graves). Rupert Davis: 1953.

Heague, Anthony, "Pismotality" ("Gnome Thoughts" series), 2010-2011. (http://sweetwordsofpismotality.blogspot.com)

Hebdidge, Dick, *Subculture: The Meaning of Style*. Methuen: 1979.

Heinlein, Robert, *Stranger In a Strange Land*. Putnam: 1961.

Hennessy, Peter, *Having It So Good: Britain In the Fifties*. Allen Lane: 2006.

Hermann, Kai and Horst Rieck, *Christiane F.: Autobiography of a Girl of the Streets [Wir Kinder vom Bahnhof Zoo]* (trans.: Susanne Flatauer). Bantam: 1982 (1979).

Hewison, Robert, *In Anger: British Culture in the Cold War, 1945-1960*. Oxford University Press: 1981.

— *Too Much: Art and Society in the Sixties, 1960-1975*. Methuen: 1986.

Hewitt, Paolo, ed., *The Sharper Word: A Mod Anthology. Helter Skelter Publishing: 2010.*

Heylin, Clinton, *All the Madmen: Barrett, Bowie, Drake* [et al]. Constable: 2012.

— *Can You Feel the Silence?* Chicago Review Press: 2003.

Hoberman, J., *The Dream Life: Movies, Media and the Mythology of the Sixties*. The New Press: 2005.

Hoggart, Richard, *The Uses of Literacy*. Hammersmith: 1958.

Hoskyns, Barney, *Glam! Bowie, Bolan and the Glitter Rock Revolution*. Faber & Faber: 1998.

Hughes, Glenn, with Joel McIver, *Glenn Hughes: The Autobiography*. Jawbone: 2011.

Hunter, Ian, *Diary of a Rock 'n' Roll Star*. Panther: 1974.

Jackson, John A., *A House on Fire: The Rise and Fall of Philadelphia Soul*. Oxford University Press: 2004.

Jacobs, Paul and Saul Landau, eds.,*The New Radicals: A Report With Documents*. Random House: 1966.

Judt, Tony, *Postwar: A History of Europe Since 1945*. Penguin Press: 2005.

Kael, Pauline, *For Keeps*. Dutton: 1994.

Kennan, Kent Wheeler. *The Techniques of Orchestration*. Prentice-Hall: 1970.

Kent, Nick, *Apathy For the Devil: A Seventies Memoir.* Da Capo: 2010.

Kerouac, Jack, *On the Road*. Viking Press: 1957.

— *The Subterraneans*. Grove Press: 1958.

Kynaston, David, *Austerity Britain: 1945-1951*. Bloomsbury: 2007.

— *Family Britain: 1951-1957*. Bloomsbury: 2009.

— *Modernity Britain: 1957-1959*. Bloomsbury: 2013.

Laing, R.D., *The Divided Self: An Existential Study In Sanity and Madness*. Tavistock: 1959.

—*The Politics of Experience and the Bird of Paradise*. Penguin: 1966.

Lasch, Christopher, *The Culture of Narcissism: American Life In an Age of Diminishing Expectations*. W.W. Norton & Co.: 1978.

Lawrence, Tim, *Love Saves the Day: A History of American Dance Music Culture, 1970-1979*. Duke University Press: 2003.

Lawson, Twiggy, *Twiggy in Black and White: An Autobiography*. Simon and Schuster: 1997.

Lewisohn, Mark, *All These Years: Tune In*. Little, Brown: 2013.

— *The Complete Beatles Recording Sessions*. Hamlyn Publishing: 1988.

Levy, Shawn, *Ready, Steady, Go: The Smashing Rise and Giddy Fall of Swinging London*. Doubleday: 2002.

Lindholm, Charles, *Charisma*. Basil Blackwell: 1993.

Lulu, *I Don't Want to Fight*. Time Warner Books: 2002.

MacDonald, Ian, *Revolution in the Head* (3rd edition). Pimlico:

2003 (1994).

— *The People's Music* (esp. "White Lines, Black Magic" (1999)). Pimlico: 2003.

MacInnes, Colin, *Absolute Beginners*. MacGibbon & Kee: 1959.

— *City of Spades*. MacGibbon & Kee: 1957.

Matt, Susan J., *Homesickness: an American History*. Oxford University Press: 2011.

Mailer, Norman, *Of a Fire On the Moon*. Little, Brown & Co.: 1970.

Mairowitz, Daniel Zane, *The Radical Soap Opera*. Wildwood House: 1974.

Maitland, Sara, ed., *Very Heaven: Looking Back at the 1960's*. Virago Press: 1988.

Malson, Lucien, *Wolf Children and the Problem of Human Nature* (inc. translation of Jean Marc Gaspard Itard's *The Wild Boy of Aveyron*). New Left Books: 1972.

Marsh, Dave, *The Heart of Rock & Soul: The 1001 Greatest Singles Ever Made*. New American: 1989.

Martin, Bernice, *A Sociology of Contemporary Cultural Change*. Blackwell: 1981.

Marwick, Arthur, *British Society Since 1945*. Penguin: 1982.

— *The Sixties: Cultural Revolution in Britain, France, Italy, and the United States, c.1958-c.1974*. Oxford University Press: 1998.

McKinney, Devin. *Magic Circles: The Beatles in Dream and History*. Harvard University Press: 2003.

McKee, Margaret and Fred Chisenhall, *Beale Black & Blue*. Louisiana State University Press: 1981.

Mehta, Gita, *Karma Cola: Marketing the Mystic East*. Simon & Schuster: 1979.

Melly, George, *Revolt Into Style: Pop Arts in Britain*. Allen Lane: 1970.

Middleton, Richard, *Pop Music and the Blues: A Study of the Relationship and Its Significance*. Gollancz: 1972.

Millard, A.J., *Beatlemania: Technology, Business and Teen Culture in America*. John Hopkins University Press: 2012.

Miles, Barry, *Paul McCartney: Many Years From Now*. Secker & Warburg: 1997.

Miles, Lawrence and Tat Wood, *About Time 1*. Mad Norwegian Press: 2006.

— *About Time 2*. Mad Norwegian Press: 2006.

— *About Time 3* (2nd edition). Mad Norwegian Press: 2009.

Miller, Andy, *The Kinks Are the Village Green Preservation Society*. Continuum: 2003.

Miller, James, ed., *The Rolling Stone Illustrated History of Rock & Roll 1950-1980*. Random House: 1980.

Moorcock, Michael, *The Cornelius Chronicles*. Avon: 1977 (1968, 1971, 1972)

Morrissey, *Autobiography*. Penguin Classics: 2013.

Moss, Walter, *The Immortal*. Simon & Schuster: 1958.

Needleman, Jacob, *The New Religions*. Doubleday: 1970.

Needs, Kris and Dick Porter, *Trash! The Complete New York Dolls*. Plexus Publishing: 2005.

Neville, Richard, *Play Power*. Paladin: 1971.

O'Brien, Geoffrey. *Dream Time: Chapters From the Sixties*. Viking: 1988.

Oldham, Andrew Loog, *Stoned: A Memoir of London in the 1960s*. St. Martin's Press: 2000.

Orwell, George, *Nineteen Eighty-Four*. Harcourt Brace & Co.: 1949.

Packard, Vance, *The Hidden Persuaders*. David McKay: 1957.

Palacios, Julian, *Syd Barrett and Pink Floyd: Dark Globe*. Plexus Publishing: 2010.

Pauwels, Louis and Jacques Bergier, *The Eternal Man*. Souvenir Press: 1972 (1970).

— *The Morning of the Magicians*. Stein & Day: 1964 (1960).

Peach, Edward (Ophiel), *The Art and Practice of Astral Projection*. Weiser Books: 1974 (1961).

Peel, John and Sheila Ravenscroft, *Margrave of the Marshes*. Corgi: 2005.

Peelleart, Guy and Nik Cohn, *Rock Dreams*. Popular Books: 1973.

Perlstein, Rick, *Nixonland: The Rise of a President and the Fracturing of America*. Scribner: 2008.

Pessoa, Fernando, *A Centenary Pessoa* (Eugenio Lisboa, L.C. Taylor, eds.) (esp. "The Heteronyms," "Occult Experiences" and "Occult Beliefs"). Carcanet: 1995.

Poirier, Richard, *The Performing Self*. Oxford University Press: 1971.

Raban, Jonathan, *Soft City*. Hamish Hamilton Ltd.: 1974.

Randolph, Vance, *Roll Me In Your Arms: "Unprintable" Ozark Folksongs and Folklore, Vol. 1*. University of Arkansas Press: 1992.

Ravenscroft, Trevor, *The Spear of Destiny: The Occult Power Behind the Spear Which Pierced the Side of Christ*. G.P. Putnam & Sons: 1973.

Rechy, Keith, *City of Night*. Grove Press: 1963.

Redding, J. Saunders, *On Being Negro in America*. Bobbs Merrill: 1951.

Regardie, Israel, *The Golden Dawn* (6th Corrected Edition). Llewellyn Publications: 1971, 1989.

— *The Tree of Life* (3rd edition). Llewellyn Publications: 2001 (1932).

Reynolds, Anthony, *The Impossible Dream: The Story of Scott Walker and the Walker Brothers*. Jawbone: 2009.

Richards, Keith, *Life*. Little Brown & Co.: 2010.

Rogan, Johnny, *Starmakers and Svengalis: The History of British Pop Management*. London, 1988.

— *Van Morrison: No Surrender*. Secker & Warburg: 2005.

Roszak, Theodore, *The Making of a Counter Culture*. Faber: 1970.

Sadecky, Peter, *Octobriana and the Russian Underground*. Harper & Row: 1971.

Sampson, Anthony, *Anatomy of Britain*. Hodder & Stoughton: 1962.

Sandbrook, Dominic, *Never Had It So Good: A History of Britain from Suez to the Beatles*. Little, Brown: 2005.

— *State of Emergency: The Way We Were: Britain 1970-1974*. Allen Lane: 2010.

— *White Heat: A History of Britain in the Swinging Sixties*. Little, Brown: 2006.

Sandford, Christopher, *Springsteen: Point Blank*. Little, Brown & Co.: 1999.

Sandifer, Philip, *TARDIS Eruditorum: An Unofficial Critical History of Doctor Who, Volume 2*. Eruditorum Press: 2013.

— *TARDIS Eruditorum, Volume 3*. Eruditorum Press: 2013.

Selvin, Joel, *Here Comes the Night: The Dark Soul of Bert Berns and the Dirty Business of Rhythm & Blues*. Counterpoint: 2014.

Seymour, Craig, *Luther: the Life and Longing of Luther Vandross*. Harper Collins: 2004.

Shaar Murray, Charles, *Crosstown Traffic: Jimi Hendrix and Post-War Pop*. Faber & Faber: 1989.

Shattuck, Roger, *The Forbidden Experiment: The Story of the Wild Boy of Aveyron*. Farrar Straus Giroux: 1980.

Sheidlower, Jesse, *The F Word*. Random House: 1995.

Sheff, David, *The Playboy Interviews With John Lennon and Yoko Ono*. Playboy Press: 1981.

Sillitoe, Alan, *The Loneliness of the Long Distance Runner*. W.H. Allen: 1959.

Sklar, Dusty, *Gods and Beasts: The Nazis and the Occult*. Thomas Y. Crowell: 1977.

Sounes, Howard, *Seventies*. Simon & Schuster: 2006.

Spelman, Nicola, *Popular Music and the Myths of Madness*. Ashgate Publishing Ltd.: 2012.

Spurling, Hilary, *The Girl From the Fiction Department: a Portrait of Sonia Orwell*. Hamish Hamilton: 2002.

Stanley, Bob, *Yeah Yeah Yeah*. Faber & Faber: 2013.

St. Denis, Ruth, *An Unfinished Life*. Harper and Bros.: 1939.

Tevis, Walter, *The Man Who Fell to Earth*. Gold Medal Books: 1963.

Thomson, David, *Have You Seen...?: A Personal Introduction to*

1,000 Films. Alfred A. Knopf: 2008.

— *Movie Man*. Stein & Day: 1967.

Thomson, Gordon, *Please Please Me: Sixties British Pop, Inside Out.* Oxford University Press: 2008.

Thurlow, Richard, *Fascism In Britain: A History, 1918-1985.* Olympic: 1987.

Townshend, Pete, *Who I Am: An Autobiography*. Harper: 2012.

Trow, George W.S., *Within the Context of No Context*. Little, Brown & Co.: 1981.

Trynka, Paul, *Iggy Pop: Open Up and Bleed*. Broadway Books: 2007.

Unterberger, Richie, *Urban Spacemen and Wayfaring Strangers: Overlooked Innovators and Eccentric Visionaries of '60s Rock.* Miller Freeman Books: 2000

— *White Light/White Heat: The Velvet Underground Day by Day.* Jawbone Press: 2009.

Vanilla, Cherry, *Lick Me: How I Became Cherry Vanilla.* Chicago Review Press: 2010.

Walker, John V., *Framing Dionysus: The Gutter-Dandy in Western Culture From Diogenes to Lou Reed,* dissertation, University of Toronto, 1999.

Wall, Mick, *When Giants Walked the Earth: a Biography of Led Zeppelin*. Orion Books: 2008

Warhol, Andy and Pat Hackett, *POPism: the Warhol '60s*. Harcourt Brace Jovanovich: 1980.

Waterhouse, Keith, *Billy Liar*. Michael Joseph: 1959.

— *There Is a Happy Land*. Michael Joseph: 1957.

Watkinson, Mike and Pete Anderson, *Crazy Diamond: Syd Barrett and the Dawn of Pink Floyd* (revised ed.). Omnibus Press: 2007.

Waugh, Evelyn, *Labels: A Mediterranean Journal*. Duckworth: 1930.

— *Vile Bodies*. Chapman & Hall: 1930.

Waugh, Patricia, *The Harvest of the Sixties: English Literature and its Background*. Oxford: 1995.

Webb, James, *The Occult Establishment*. Open Court Publishing: 1976.

Weeks, Jeffrey. *Sex, Politics and Society: The Regulation of Sexuality Since 1800* (3rd edition). Routledge: 2012.

Wheen, Francis, *Strange Days Indeed: The 1970s: The Golden Age of Paranoia*. Fourth Estate: 2009.

Williams, Francis, *The American Invasion*. Anthony Blond Ltd.: 1962.

Wilson, Colin, *Aleister Crowley: The Nature of the Beast*. HarperCollins: 1993.

— *The Occult: A History*. Random House: 1971.

— *The Outsider*. Gollancz: 1956.

Wirt, John, *Huey "Piano" Smith and the Rocking Pneumonia Blues.* Louisiana State University Press: 2014.

Wolk, Douglas, *James Brown's Live at the Apollo*. Continuum Books: 2004.

Wyndham, John, *The Midwich Cuckoos*. Michael Joseph: 1957.

Young, Rob, *Electric Eden*. Faber & Faber: 2010.

Essential Bowie Websites

Bowie Wonderworld (http://www.bowiewonderworld.com)

Golden Years (http://www.bowiegoldenyears.com)

Helden (http://www.helden.org.uk)

Illustrated DB Discography (http://www.illustrated-db-discography.nl)

Teenage Wildlife (http://www.teenagewildlife.com)

The Young American (http://homepage.ntlworld.com/gouster)

The Ziggy Stardust Companion (http://www.5years.com)

Film/radio/TV interviews/documentaries:

Arena (Bowie interview). Dir: Alan Yentob. BBC 2: 1978.

Billy Liar. Dir: John Schlesinger. Anglo-Amalgamated: 1963.

"Changes at Fifty." Dir: Yentob. BBC 2: 1997.

Christiane F.— Wir Kinder vom Bahnhof Zoo. Dir: Ulrich Edel. Solaris Film: 1981.

A Clockwork Orange. Dir: Stanley Kubrick. Warner Bros.: 1971.

Cracked Actor. Dir: Yentob.BBC: 1975.

Crossfire Hurricane. Dir: Brett Morgen. Milkwood Films, Tremolo

Productions: 2012.

David Bowie: Five Years. Dir: Francis Whately. BBC: 2013.

"The David Bowie Story." BBC Radio One (Stuart Grundy): 1976, updated 1993 (Paul Gambaccini, John Tobler).

David Bowie: The Plastic Soul Review. E1 Entertainment: 2007.

"Golden Years: The David Bowie Story," BBC Radio 2 (Mark Goodier): 2000.

The Image. Dir: Michael Armstrong. Border Film Productions: 1969 (filmed 1967).

Inside Bowie and the Spiders: 1969-1974. Classic Rock Productions: 2005.

Legends: David Bowie. Produced: Mary Wharton. VH1: 1998.

Love You Till Tuesday. Dir: Malcolm J. Thomson. Thomasso Film: 1984 (filmed 1969).

The Man Who Fell to Earth. Dir: Nicolas Roeg. British Lion Films: 1976.

Nationwide (Bowie interview and feature). BBC: aired 5 June 1973.

The 1980 Floor Show. (Aired on *The Midnight Special,* 1973).

Privilege. Dir: Peter Watkins. Universal: 1967.

Rock and Roll (ep. 7, "The Wild Side," dir.: Hugh Thompson). BBC/WGBH: 1995.

The Strange World of Gurney Slade. ATV (for ITV): 1960 (six episodes).

Ziggy Stardust: The Motion Picture. Dir: D.A. Pennebaker. MainMan, Pennebaker Productions, Bewlay Brothers: 1973.

2001: A Space Odyssey. Dir: Kubrick. MGM: 1968

Notes

Introduction

1 "**kinda like an actor**": Barker, Taylor, *Faking It*, 225; "**another face**": *Crossfire Hurricane*.

2 "**exaggerated camp accent**": Kent, *Apathy*, 59.

4 "**largeness and glory**": *David Bowie Is*, 104.

Chapter 1

9 **Broadcast**: For all references to broadcasts (radio and TV) in this book, the date listed is that of taping, not of broadcast; **David Bowie**: Although David Jones didn't acquire his stage name until 1965, all references to him will be as "Bowie." Purists are welcome to write "Jones" in place of "Bowie" in the first ten entries.

10 **John Bloom**: Born in the East End, his father a tailor, Bloom hit upon selling cheap washing machines made in Holland to working-class British families to purchase on layaway, using full-page advertorials in the *Daily Mirror*. By age 30 he was a millionaire and part of the London scene, his lavish parties written up in the press, which is how Bowie and his father learned his name. Bloom's company went into voluntary liquidation later in 1964, felled by aggressive competitors and a postal strike.

11 **Vocalion**: Having purchased France's Vogue Records' UK subsidiary, Decca in 1962 revived its dormant Vocalion label for UK Vogue releases. These were mainly American blues and country sides and UK knock-offs (*e.g.*, "I'll Let You Hold My Hand" by The Bootles). Conn got Decca to let him use a studio one afternoon (likely a weekend, when labels let independent producers buy studio time) by giving them first dibs on releasing the single; **Marshal Butler**: testimony in *Slave Narratives From the Federal Writers' Project: 1936-1938*; "**holler it out in the fields**": McKee, *Beale Black & Blue*, 189.

12 **Countess Ada de Lachau:** A Victorian aesthete—poet, composer, dancer, spiritualist—who had the misfortune to live in Woodrow Wilson's America. Friend of dancer Ruth St. Denis and an impoverished patron of the arts, de Lachau suffered "somewhat evil days," St. Denis recalled in her autobiography, with De Lachau's young daughter at times supporting the family by singing French songs at society parties. Later in life she was living in New Rochelle, NY, and composing a "Wagnerian" ballet called *The Tigress.*; **Vance Randolph**: Venereal disease was naturally of interest to soldiers. Another "Little Liza Jane" from this era is even more blunt ("my old tool is red and sore, Little Liza Jane!")(Randolph, 455).

13 **five teenagers**: The King Bees most likely learned the song from Smith's single, but there are other possible sources: Donegan's version, which Bowie and Underwood could have picked up when playing skiffle in 1958, or Nina Simone's live recording on *Nina at Newport*, which the future Band (the Hawks) used as the template of their "Go Go Liza Jane" in 1965.

16 **"white-bread kids":** Miles, *British Invasion*, 228. The Raiders revisited "Louie Go Home" on *Midnight Ride* (1966), wrapping the song in current British fashions: fuzz-distorted guitars, an organ intro that all but plays the "Satisfaction" riff and the vocal harmonies of the Yardbirds' "For Your Love." Bowie later used the refrain in his "She'll Drive the Big Car" on *Reality*; **Malone**: Copyrighted by Bland's manager Don Robey under the pseudonym Deadric Malone, "I Pity the Fool" was the work of Robey's house songwriter Joe Medwick and arranger Joe Scott. It hit #1 in the R&B charts in 1961.

17 **Parlophone 5250:** As with its B-side, an alternate take of "I Pity the Fool" was issued on the 1991 compilation *Early On* (it's possible Talmy/Rhino had access only to alternate takes,

not the masters). The alternate take has Bowie reversing the order of Bland's verses and a lesser Page guitar solo; "**Belsen-like refugee"**: Gilmans, 89. The confusion owed to the band confusing Bromley's David Jones with a black American singer of the same name who was working the European nightclub circuit and recording for Pye.

19 **best shtick**: They promoted "I Pity the Fool" by ginning up a controversy about Bowie being barred from television due to the length of his hair. While this was a hit with the London press, it did nothing to move the single; **Parlophone 5250**: An alternate take (the single had "bider" instead of "tiger" in the second verse) is on *Early On*; **distorted bass**: Watson had blown out his amp before the session. Bowie sang the bassline to him, as he would to John Deacon while making "Under Pressure" and Laurent Thibault when cutting the original "China Girl."

20 **Talmy**: He gave "Take My Tip" to fellow American expatriate Kenny Miller, whose blunt version was released in April 1965 as a B-side; "**couldn't play it**": Paytress, "Manish Bowie," *Record Collector*, May 2000; **scant musical training**: Bowie took saxophone lessons from Ronnie Ross for six months in 1963, learning scales, chords and some rudimentary music reading. Upon hearing Lulu's "Man Who Sold the World," Ross said Bowie hadn't improved in a decade; "**dripping with chords**": Chris Roberts, "Lennon and McCartney Tell You How to Write a Hit!," *Melody Maker*, 1 February 1964.

21 ***Early On***: In 1985, Talmy said there were up to eight unreleased Bowie tracks. Rhino issued five (three songwriter demos and two full-band recordings) and another was bootlegged ("That's a Promise").

22 **"I Want My Baby Back"**: Bowie likely took the title from favorites the Downliners Sect, who'd just cut a version of Jimmy Cross' teenage car-crash death ballad on their EP *The*

Sect Sing Sick Songs.

25 **press release to apologize for it**: Whoever wrote it assured reporters that Bowie, despite having a "baby singing voice" on the single, "is a versatile singer, which will be seen in later records." Bowie told Chris Farlowe not to bother buying the single.

29 **recorded**: Cann's vague about when "Can't Help" was recorded but Trynka notes 10 December 1965. If correct, Bowie and the Lower Third also played a show at the Marquee the day they cut the single; **engineered**: There are no engineering credits on any of the Pye singles. One candidate is Ray Prickett, who ran most of Hatch's Petula Clark and Jackie Trent productions; **lower reaches of some charts**: Thanks to judicious payola, "Can't Help" reached 34 on the *Melody Maker* singles chart but the single didn't make *Record Retailer*, the UK's standard. It got airplay on the pirate Radio London: at Charterhouse public school, Tony Banks became a fan and soon turned his classmates Peter Gabriel and Mike Rutherford onto Bowie.

30 "**too long to get going**": Trynka, 57; **disapproving mother**: During performances in 1999, Bowie sang "*Dad* says I brought dishonor" in the opening verse; **C major into F minor**: beginning in C, the verses shade into Fm midway through, with the rise of the new tonic Fm chord abetted by D-flat and A-flat chords; the refrains are built on a IV-I-V sequence (Bb-F-C).

31 **tambourine player:** An endlessly-recalled anecdote has that before recording "Can't Help," Hatch handed Bowie the "lucky" tambourine used in the session that produced Petula Clark's "Downtown." Hatch later denied having any such tambourine. Moreover there's no tambourine on "Downtown."; **factory-setting progression**: I-vi-IV-V, aka the "doo wop" or "Stand By Me" progression (established further here by Rivens playing the "Stand By Me" bassline

at times).

32 "**Do Anything You Say**": The first single to be released under Bowie's name. Its reissue on the 1999 compilation *The Pye Singles* had a different mix with less prominent piano; **bloodletting**: Audience members at a show at the Marquee that afternoon noticed visible discomfort between Bowie and the Lower Third, in part because the show had been billed solely as "David Bowie." Horton had told Taylor he was broke, despite having received £300 the day before. According to the band, he'd singled out Taylor as the means "to bring the rest of us to heel." (Trynka, 60).

33 "**so not part of everyone else**": *A&E Biography*; "**he wanted to get away from home**": Trynka, 63; **thrown on stage**: "We were more meek...we acted like a backing band," Hutchinson told Trynka, while Fearnley added "you can't just put four blokes together and expect them to jell." Fearnley was cribbing chord changes from a piece of paper while playing his first Marquee gig with Bowie.

34 **glimmers of life**: Dusty Springfield, reviewing the single, rightly called its production "messy," suggesting the Bowie sessions were an afterthought for Hatch. Compare the arrangements and sound balance of his Petula Clark singles.

35 **BBC**: Along with "London Boys," this performance wasn't included on the concert CD. "I Dig Everything" had one of the more radical revisions on Bowie's *Toy*: a Swinging London song reborn as a Cool Britannia one, the Hammond riff replaced by layers of distorted guitars, the "Latin" percussion by Sterling Campbell thrashing his ride cymbals.

36 **time-check girl:** *Cf.* Dylan's "Talkin' World War III Blues": "I called up the operator of time/just to hear a voice of some kind."; **singers**: All had sung with Dusty Springfield. Dee later duetted on Elton John's "Don't Go Breaking My Heart" while John recorded Duncan's "Love Song" on his

Tumbleweed Connection (as did Bowie, see Ch. 3).Bell sang with Serge Gainsbourg on "Ford Mustang" (see "Young Americans") and on Blue Mink's "Melting Pot," later immortalized by Alan Partridge; **London musos**: Jimmy Page, John McLaughlin and/or "Big Jim" Sullivan on guitar, Alan Hawkshaw or Roger Coulam on Hammond, Herbie Flowers or John Paul Jones on bass and Bobby Graham or Tony Newman on drums. The guiro/congas percussion line is similar to *A Latin Happening*, an instrumental album Hatch released in 1967; "**one great octave**": Glenn Gould, "The Search for Petula Clark."

37 "**getting further away**": Trynka, 66. Hatch said he'd wished he'd had one more year with Bowie, that they may have jelled by then.

Chapter 2

40 **unknown musicians**: Kevin Cann said the single was recorded with only the Buzz (reduced to a trio of Boyes, Fearnley and Eager) and two session musicians, but there are three instruments (trumpet, tuba, oboe) in the arrangement. There's also acoustic guitar audible towards the end of the trumpet solo; "**electric state**": *Life*, 29 November 1963; "**I could afford to be silly**": Leigh and Firminger, *Halfway to Paradise*. Bowie, interviewed by *20/20* in 1980, said "I always found it sort of embarrassing to sing my own songs as me."

41 "**I love old things**": "Take a Look at This New Face—It Belongs to 1966," *Daily Telegraph*, 27 October 1965; "**cool, if deep chauvinism**": Melly, *Revolt Into Style*, 7. Melly scripted the 1967 film *Smashing Time*, which contrasted two Northern girls in London: one (Rita Tushingham) is cold bedsits and make-do drudgery, the other (Lynn Redgrave) is swept up in the whirl of Carnaby Street. See "Maid of Bond Street" and "Join the Gang."

42 ***Sgt. Pepper's***: The New Vaudeville Band-esque "When I'm 64" was one of the first tracks recorded for it, in December 1966. "Winchester Cathedral" came out two weeks before Bowie cut "Rubber Band." The mock-Twenties singles of the Bonzo Dog Doo-Dah Band like "I'm Going to Bring a Watermelon to My Girl Tonight" were also an influence, as later Bonzos tracks would be (see "Big Brother").

43 **Deram**: the first new domestic label Decca had launched since the Twenties, it was intended to simplify marketing. It would be a single globally-distributed label, in contrast to the warring fiefdoms of US Decca and UK Decca. Deram would also double as an ad for Decca's engineering and its hardware.

44 **broadcast**: Appearing on *Für Jeden Etwas Musik* in November 1968, Bowie performed a mime routine and an unidentified song. Claims this was "London Boys" are dubious (it was most likely "When I Live My Dream"); "**died of junk**": unpublished interview for *The Kinks: The Official Biography*, cited by Andy Miller (*Village Green*, 150); "**You Just Can't Win**": A track off *The Angry Young Them*, released June 1965. Their opening verses are in a similar vein: Them ("one more coffee, one more cigarette/ one more morning trying to forget"); Bowie ("you've bought some coffee, butter and bread..").

45 ***Toy***: "London Boys" seemed intended as the closer of *Toy* (and inspired its title). Excerpts were released on Bowie's website in 2002. There are two different *Toy* versions: one circulating has Visconti-scored strings while the other, which leaked on the "official" *Toy* bootleg, is likely an earlier mix with a brass/woodwind accompaniment.

46 **Beuselinck**: Known as "Oscar" at the time, he'd also recorded Pete Townshend's "Join My Gang." He later changed his stage name to Paul Nicholas and had a run of stage shows and mid-chart hits in the Seventies;

"**Wormwood Scrubs Tango**": Teague, "Gnome Thoughts 37."

47 "**thought it was original**": Lenny Kaye, "David Bowie: Freak Out in a Moonage Daydream," *Cavalier*, January 1973. (In 1969, Bowie claimed his first LP "was [made] in about 15 minutes for 5s 6d.")

48 "**weird list of instruments**," Juby, 16; "**writing sort of short stories**":"David Bowie Story," 1976; **portrait of Dek Fearnley**: Trynka, 67. Bowie loved Batman too, asking Pitt to get comics and posters when the latter was in New York.

49 **more surreal**: In Sillitoe's story, the equivalent to "Sally" is a "posh" pseudo-Marxist intellectual who marries Jim out of class solidarity; **Arthur and Sally go bust**: Another reading of the song is that Arthur is a closeted gay man who's married a woman, with the excitement in the last verse (the rising vocal line that peaks with Arthur going home to mother) suggesting Arthur's happily escaped that fate. (See Elton John's "Someone Saved My Life Tonight.").

50 "**Hey Joe**": F-C-G-D-A. Bowie also may have known in the Leaves' version (Jimi Hendrix's was issued after Bowie cut this track), but again this progression was as common as dirt in the mid-Sixties.

51 "**everything slowed down**": *Awopbopaloobop*, 228; "**Join the Gang**": Pete Townshend wrote "Join My Gang" around October 1966. Bowie heard a demo as he and Townshend shared publishers and he stopped Townshend on the street to compliment him on the song, which Townshend had given to Oscar Beuselinck (see "Over the Wall We Go."); **Sibylla's**: George Harrison was an investor. It got to the point where even Julie Christie felt intimidated. "There was definitely status within that apparently no-status, "classless" society...and it hung on how much drugs you took or how you dressed or just how freaky you were. I know I always felt I was on the outside looking in. I think

the majority of people did…I felt like a country bumpkin who had for some reason found herself in this elevated society and had no idea how to handle it." (quoted in *Very Heaven*). The co-founder of Sibylla's threw himself off a Chelsea rooftop a few months after it opened in June 1966; **manic sitar**: The comical use of the sitar (played by "Big Jim" Sullivan, one of the few musicians in London who could actually play it instead of treating it like an oversized guitar) showed how the instrument had gone from object of exotica to wincing cliché in a year. Deram would soon release a "music hall sitar" single by Chim Kothari ("Sitar 'n' Spice").

52 **changed keys**: most verses keep on the tonic chord, shifting only to flatted VII chords (*e.g.*, the F major on "beam went wrong") before closing back on the tonic; **buried as the B-side**: it was slated for *David Bowie*'s first side, between "Your Funny Smile" (see appendix) and "There Is a Happy Land," until Bowie recorded more tracks in early 1967; **astral projection**: entails the sleeping or meditating person "seeing" themselves asleep and then, as they hone their skills, traveling outside the body. During Bowie's immersion in Mahayana Buddhism, he recalled getting "three or four feet, maybe even further, outside my body" during meditations. He possibly used Ophiel's *The Art and Practice of Astral Projection* as a primer, as his lyric shares Ophiel's flattering tone: "to practice Astral Projection, and/or the Occult Arts, you have to have...something of the Soul of an Artist in you and then be able to let it out in expression." Some forms of astral projection involve the "flashing" Tattwa colors, later referenced in "Station to Station."

54 "**every child is an only child**": introduction to *There Is a Happy Land*. Waterhouse got into the frame of mind to write the novel by crouching on his knees on the street for a

child's eye view of houses and shops, which restored to him the sense of mystery and powerlessness that a child has when engaged with the greater world; **same title**: it came from a hymn—"There is a happy land, far far away/Where saints in glory stand, bright bright as day"—defaced by generations of children (*e.g.*, "where they have jam and bread three times a day."); **rapid harmonic rhythms**: G major seems the stronger candidate, but the verses establish it in a roundabout way: F added 9th/G/A7 sus/D/Am/Em/F/C and finally closing on G.

55 **overpopulating**: After running through London, New York and China's population totals, Dudgeon ends with: "Bridlington Spa: lots!" Bowie's first line is "our studies include exophagy," a trait of cannibal tribes to restrict their eating to outside the tribe, which one hopes is the only time "exophagy" has been used in a pop lyric; **can-do positivism:** Even holocausts had upsides. Pat Frank's *Alas, Babylon* had nuclear war restore America's pioneer spirit.

56 ***Population Bomb***: Ehrlich's theories came from a 1954 pamphlet by Hugh Everett Moore. Images of humans packed like sardines into teeming high rises were constant in SF: take the *Star Trek* episode "The Mark of Gideon" and John Brunner's *Stand on Zanzibar*. The idea reached mass saturation by the early Seventies, referenced in everything from Gore Vidal's *Myra Breckenridge* to the "no population boom" of the Stylistics' "I'm Stone In Love With You" to Genesis' "Get 'Em Out by Friday." When *Make Room!* was filmed as *Soylent Green* in 1973, the adaptation introduced the dead-processed-as-food concept; **Caldecott**: Cann, *DB* notes.

57 **cello**: The sessions seem to have been arranged around whichever musicians were needed—this session (Dec. 8-9) was the first to feature string players; **mixed their vocals**: Weston bounced the four-track Deram master down to

three, freeing up a new track for the harmony vocals and diminishing the sound of the original tracks.

58 **Top Gear**: "Bombardier" was played at the behest of producer Bernie Andrews and on the 2010 reissue of *David Bowie*. With accompaniment by the Arthur Greenslade Orchestra, it had a more exacting waltz tempo, with a prominent bass serving as dancing master; **Alan Sillitoe**: Bowie reportedly took his character's name from the three-year-old son of the Beatstalkers' Alan Mair, though another likely source was Sillitoe's "The Decline and Fall of Frankie Buller." Also Sillitoe's "Disgrace of Jim Scarfedale" ended with Jim arrested for exposing himself to children; "**Maid of Bond St.**": As with "We Are Hungry Men," "Maid" was cut from the American *David Bowie*, likely owed to the American practice of reducing UK LP tracks to lower publishing royalties. Bowie's advertising job in 1964 was on Bond Street. Some lines may come from an early narrative concept for the LP, which was to be about a boy who works in an art gallery.

60 **prospective covers**: Billy Fury would cover it in 1968 as a B-side.

61 ***Seven Years in Tibet***: "Religion is the heart of the fabric of the State...the life of the people is regulated by the divine Will, whose interpreters the lamas are...The gods must be unceasingly entreated, placated or thanked. Earthly existence has little worth in Tibet and death has no terrors." (Harrer, 168). Bowie's "Seven Years In Tibet" was a sequel of sorts, the perspective of a monk in Chinese-controlled Tibet at century's end. While Harrer depicted China's takeover of Tibet in 1950 as tragic, he noted Tibet was a chaotic place, with routine monk riots and attempted coups, one of which was put down with howitzers that leveled buildings in Lhasa; **extremely unorthodox**: While there are images of the "starving Buddha," this was from an early period of his life,

when he almost died of starvation until realizing physical austerities wouldn't lead to salvation. Hence the Buddha's move toward moderation or the "Middle Way." (Janna Rose White). By contrast Bowie favored an "extreme" version of Buddhism (see "Karma Man").

62 "**process of self-discovery**": Tremlett, 74. Bowie offered a metaphor for Tremlett, using the image of a cigarette lighter (your mind) and cigarettes arrayed in a circle around it (your experiences). The aim of the Buddhist novitiate is to remove the cigarettes and leave the lighter, he said.

63 **first female singer**: Marion Constable was a friend of Eager's who visited the studio when they were taping "Silly Boy Blue." Reportedly studio tapes document that Bowie spent much of the vocal session trying to pick her up; "**on the fours**": As on Spector tracks like "Be My Baby," with Eager cracking his snare on the last beat of each measure—it's also the beat of the contemporary Walker Brothers hit "The Sun Ain't Gonna Shine Anymore." Eager plays some Blaine-style quarter-note triplet fills as well, some of which are a bit shaky towards the close.

64 **Renbourn**: Renbourn had become a renowned folk guitarist by the mid-Sixties. He once lived, in high bohemian style, on a barge in the Thames. The guitar riff in Madonna's "Don't Tell Me" is very close to Renbourn's here: the pieces have a near-identical opening chord sequence (D/Am/C/G for Madonna, D/Am/C/G6 for Bowie); **nursery rhyme**: "Smiling Girls, Rosy Boys," while the ballad's better known as "Scarborough Fair"; **Jansch**: His finger-picked playing style had inspired Donovan, of whom this song seems a parody (compare Bowie's "kiss the wind" to Donovan's "Catch the Wind").

65 "**box of gravel**": Using sandboxes was an old trick: the producer Joe Meek shook one to create a "marching" sound for Anne Shelton's "Lay Down Your Arms."; **Lesley Ann**

Downey: Trynka, 71.

66 **more isolated**: an insight from Steve Harvey. The song apparently had a set of chords, as the original demo was Bowie singing while playing organ; **Boris Yeltsin**: As recounted by Pres. Bill Clinton to Taylor Branch, *The Clinton Tapes*. Asked how the Secret Service handled Yeltsin, Clinton said "well, he got his pizza." Yeltsin also got drunk and eluded security the following night; he was caught when a guard mistook him for an intruder; "**chipmunk-voiced**": "Stardust Memories," *Las Vegas Weekly*, 16 December 2009; "**this is the man**," *Trouser Press*, 1984.

67 ***NME***: Bowie considered returning "Gnome" to its origins by playing it VU-style but he balked out of irritation with the *NME*'s heavy-handed campaign; "**The Gnome**": Barrett's gnome is named Grimble Gromble and is more of a stay-at-home than Bowie's. However, both gnomes like their booze and are color-coordinated: Grimble wears a "scarlet tunic [and] a blue-green hood" while the Laughing Gnome sports scarlet and grey.

68 **weeks writing and scrapping**: There were likely dozens of versions made, including a Gnome-only song. Two alternate mixes on acetate sold on eBay. The obsessive redubbing made for a messy master: a stereo mix made for the *David Bowie* reissue has several half-erased "gnome" voices audible in the left channel. ("Gnome" works because its players are as poker-faced as Buster Keaton. For an excruciating alternative, listen to Ronnie Hilton's 1967 cover, where Hilton hams it up mercilessly.); **critical pasting**: In a laudatory review of *Sgt. Pepper* in *The Times*, William Mann took a swipe at "Laughing Gnome" as the sort of pop garbage the Beatles had transcended; **piano**: Cann claimed Bob Michaels, the Hammond organist of Dave Antony's Moods, plays on this track, but I don't hear organ. Was Michaels the pianist?

69 **10-bar blues**: Leave it to Bowie to write an A minor blues with five chords (including a G13). The progression's also not really a blues: Am-D7 (x2)-Am-F-G13-Am-Em; **4-verse lyric**: outtakes from the session have a scrapped verse that lampoons Decca A&R head Dick Rowe, in keeping with how Bowie's characters in "Tony Day" are tight-fists and scam artists; **remake**: Another version of the proposed single remake, with a slightly different Bowie vocal, is on bootlegs.

70 **F to Ab**: Transitioned via an odd move to an A major suspended chord ("tell them that I've got") and using a G major as a pivot chord ("starring role"). And the song concludes back on the original tonic chord, F.

71 **last gasp**: It fared better in films: Leos Carax used it well in his *Boy Meets Girl*, as did Seu Jorge in *The Life Aquatic*, the latter aided by Jorge singing the lyric in Portuguese.

72 **best reviews**: Except for Syd Barrett, who knocked it in a *Melody* Maker interview, in what Chris Welch recalled as "a cold, angry diatribe." Comments like "Yeah, it's a joke number. Jokes are good. Everybody likes jokes. The Pink Floyd like jokes. If you play it a second time it might be even more of a joke" more suggest Barrett's growing estrangement from the pop music world than any condemnation of Bowie; **obvious quotations**: Most notably the end tag of "Hearts and Flowers," a song taken from the introduction of Alphons Czibulka's *Wintermärchen* Waltzes that, by 1967, had become the cliché theme for melancholy, used when the likes of Elmer Fudd moped in a Looney Tunes cartoon; **demoed**: Cann and Pegg differ on when (1965, 1966, respectively). For me "Tuesday" seems more in line with Bowie's '66 Deram songs. (It's also hard to imagine Tony Hatch not attempting "Tuesday" had it been in Bowie's catalog during the Pye period.); **Bb major**: Bowie backs into establishing the key in the verse: F7-Eb7-Bb (V7-IV7-I). He changes key briefly (D-flat) in the coda before landing back

on the original home chord to close (as he did with "When I Live My Dream").

73 **first release**: Its official release sounds worse than bootlegs, plus it has a spliced-in harmonica/bass intro; **didn't come to much**: Pitt made some effort to bring the VU to Britain but a proposed show at the Roundhouse fell through when the venue's owners refused to pay enough to justify the trip.

74 "**essence of Mod**": *Vanity Fair*, 2003; **down-tuned**: Reed's guitar was tuned D-A-F-C-G-D, possibly to be in tune with Cale's piano at the session. Bowie/Ronson typically played the "Lexington-125" chords (E-G#-A-F#) as E-G-A-B. In some Nineties performances (including his duet with Reed in 1997), Bowie played the song in its original D major key.

75 **first release**: This compilation includes two versions of "Toy Soldier," the oft-bootlegged Decca take and a demo likely from a few weeks earlier.

79 **boarding school**: Said to be Lancing College, which expelled four students for "drug trafficking" in October 1967. However, that doesn't fit the chronology of the song, written earlier that year; **time with the Riot Squad**: A nine-minute jam version was released in 2012. The Riot Squad kept it in their sets after Bowie had left; **Slender Plenty**: They were Bob Bardwell (vocals), Colin Charles (guitar), Barry Parfit (keyboards), Peter Burford (bass) and Barry Digby (drums), as per Burford's daughter, Charlotte Burford.

80 "**Autumn Almanac**": If this was an inspiration, it would date "April's Tooth" to after October 1967, when the Kinks single was released; **first release**: Another mix of "Sleep Beside You," with different vocals and missing guitar overdubs, is on bootlegs.

81 "**Top 10 Rubbish**": Pitt, 83. The conversation continued: P: I don't think you could ever knowingly write rubbish of any kind. B: Wanna bet? You've seen nothing yet.

82 **C major progression**: C-Bb-F-C, (or I-VIIb-IV-I) is a storied "classic rock" progression, found in everything from "Magic Carpet Ride" to "Won't Get Fooled Again" to "Sweet Child 'O Mine." The use of the flatted VII chord (B-flat here) gives it a bluesy feel. The only other chords are a G minor to start the four-bar pre-chorus ("I will show you games..") and an E-flat chord subbing for C ("ima-*gine that*") in the bridge.

83 **Deram rejected**: Pitt depicted Decca's music review panel as a group of old men in suits, meeting each Monday morning to vote on the latest "jangles" while reading newspapers and falling asleep. One imagines it being something like the "Circus" meetings in *Tinker Tailor Soldier Spy*. Bowie told Dave Travis in 1969 that he didn't think the lyrics were "dirty" but rather "ethereal"; **transcendental meditation**: The Beatles' time with the Maharishi marked the breaking point for some. "The unfortunate Beatles...are in grave danger of coming into contact with the Spirit of Universal Truth, an unhelpful tipple which has in the past turned the great mind of Aldous Huxley to mystical blotting paper," John Mortimer, *The New Statesman*, 29 September 1967. Theodore Roszak cuttingly described the ideal swami for Westerners as being "a kindly orientalized version of an Irish Jesuit priest in charge of a pleasant retreat."

84 "**all limits magically removed**": Martin, 156; **Pop religion**: "Maybe it sounds like Eastern religion, but I'm trying to truly live in the moment," former Gov. Mark Sanford, *New York Times*, 5 August 2011; **heckled by American Maoist**: A clash of utopias. Mao's China, for some radicals, was as pure as Tibet was for Western Buddhists. "There isn't a trace of alienation in China, nor of those neuroses or that inner disintegration of the individual found in those parts of the world dominated by consumerism," wrote the Italian Marxist Maria-Antonietta Macciocchi in her *Daily Life in Revolutionary China* (1972).

85 "**spends his days sitting lotus fashioned**": O'Brien, *Dream Time*, 79. See the "Tribute to Doctor Strange" dance, one of the first San Francisco happenings, or T. Rex's "Mambo Sun": "On a mountain range/I'm Doctor Strange"; **D major verses**: With occasional 2/4 bars ("hole in the fence," "only dig now"), a trick Bowie would use repeatedly on *Ziggy Stardust*.

86 **eight versions**: Cann, *ADN*, 116; "**David is contented**": This inertia frustrated Pitt, who by the end of 1967 commiserated with Bowie's father that "it [is] impossible for David to make any money the way he want[s] to, sitting on his backside strumming a guitar." (Pitt, 99); **recorded**: Bowie's demo tape had him singing his lyric as the original acetate played on a turntable. He only sang his version publicly once, for a cabaret audition in August 1968.

87 **rejected Bowie**: The French publishers "wanted a star to record the song, not this yobbo from Bromley," Heath later said; **second album**: A provisional sequence included "C'est la Vie," "Silver Tree Top School For Boys," "When I'm Five," "Everything Is You," "Angel Angel Grubby Face," "Threepenny Joe," "Tiny Tim" and "The Reverend Raymond Brown" (for the latter four, see appendix).

88 **discarded demos**: Pitt sent songs to Peter, Paul & Mary, Big Brother and the Holding Company and Judy Collins, with no luck; **lyric full of soldiers**: Bowie thoroughly revised his lyric after debuting the song in a December 1967 BBC session (wisely—an original line was "where cunning magpies steal your name"); **organ hook**: According to the sleeve notes of *World of David Bowie*, Tyrannosaurus Rex's Steve "Peregrin" Took was credited with playing "pixiphone" (a nickname for the Sooty Pixie Xylophone) on the track, with some sources claiming Visconti mixed the pixiphone with electric guitar. I hear only organ and guitar and it seems likely that Took's only involvement with the

song was singing on its May 1968 BBC performance; **Deram in internal disarray**: they'd never recovered from the mid-1967 departure of the Move and Procol Harum, while a disgruntled Cat Stevens would soon leave for Island. The label staggered through the Seventies. After Decca was bought by PolyGram in 1980, Deram briefly became an imprint label for new wave bands (Bananarama, the Mo-dettes).

89 **Powell**: Bowie, to *Music Now!* in 1969, said "the only person who is coming through with any strength is Enoch Powell. He is the only one with a following. Whether it's good or bad is not the point, the fact is he had."

90 "**curry for a pound**": rather expensive for the time. The poet's a "pirate" in the alternate 1968 take; **acoustic guitar**: Moving from D major to Dsus2 or Dsus4 and back to D again, just by keeping the D chord shape and either lifting a finger or moving it down a fret. The opening verse melody, four notes down and four notes up, suggests Bowie was inspired by arpeggiating the D chord; **ill-fated song:** The original master has circulated on bootleg while an alternate take of the '68 recording, with a different Bowie vocal and no sound effects (the master has hoofbeats at the end), is on the *David Bowie* reissue. Alternate stereo mixes of the remake are on the *Space Oddity* reissue.

91 **first release**: Allegedly issued as single in the Philippines in late 1968; **weird vocal**: Particularly on the BBC performance of May 1968, the closest "Five" ever had to an official take. The demo had Bowie singing down an octave, with a halting phrasing. By contrast the BBC take is well-sung, with Bowie solving a breath control issue in the bridge by incorporating a loud gasp into the last line; **Beatstalkers**: as the B-side of the appropriately-titled "Little Boy" (CBS 3936). The single marked the end of the band's connection to Bowie and, soon enough, of the band itself.

92 **Farthingale**: "She played a little bit of bedsitting-room guitar, that kind of folk guitar that every girl that looked beautiful could play in those [days]...they all did Joan Baez numbers," Bowie, "David Bowie Story," 1993; "**into softer things,"** Spitz, 96; **meager circuit**: While Pitt listed Feathers as having only played three gigs, they likely played more shows at clubs like the Middle Earth "under the table" without telling him.

93 "**ghastly**," Spitz, 97; **at Trident Studios**: The proposed B-side was Tony Hill's "Back to Where You've Never Been." The session was financed by David Platz at Essex Music and approved by Kenneth Pitt, but Visconti in his autobiography claims he had to record it on the sly or he would've caught flak from his employer, Denny Cordell. While no one's credited, there are obviously drums and bass on the released track, possibly Herbie Flowers and Barry Morgan, who Visconti used for Bowie's BBC dates in the same period, though Visconti could have played bass himself.

94 "**simple family game**": Mick Brown, "A Star Comes Back to Earth After a Lifetime of Identity Crises," *Daily Telegraph*, 14 December 1996.

95 "**joined the circus**," "Bowie Story"; ***Pierrot in Turquoise***: The songs performed in the first run (28 December 1967, 3-5 January 1968, 5-16, 26-30 March 1968) were all from the Deram LP: "Sell Me a Coat," "When I Live My Dream," "Come and Buy My Toys," "Silly Boy Blue," "There Is a Happy Land," "Love You Till Tuesday" and "Maid of Bond Street." Bowie later wrote three original songs for a 1970 TV production of *Pierrot* (see Ch. 4).

96 **blood-stained Pierrot costume**: While some sources have Korniloff also attempting suicide via sleeping pills, she later took pains to note that she had been exhausted and had accidentally overdosed; "**invisible telephone kiosk**," Buckley, 45. Ward attended a 22 February 1969 show at the

Manchester Free Trade Hall.

Chapter 3

99 **demo 2**: Cann claims that Bowie and Hutchinson recorded their 10-song demo at the London office of Mercury Records; Pegg counters that the amateur-sounding demo was more likely recorded at Bowie's room in Mary Finnigan's flat in Beckenham, a sounder argument for me. The first demo (taped either in Bowie's room in South Kensington, Kenneth Pitt's home on Manchester Street (my guess) or Bowie's publisher's office) seems intended as a guide for the *LYTT* recording but there's a chance it post-dates *LYTT*; **single**: "Space Oddity" was cut on 20 June, but another session was needed for vocal overdubs a few days later, the slight delay due to Bowie having come down with conjunctivitis.

100 "**Ernie the Milkman**," DB Story, 1993. (A reference to Benny Hill's #1 "Ernie (The Fastest Milkman in the West)"); **Bee Gees**: Gilmans, 160. When he was writing "Oddity," Bowie called it "the Bee Gees thing," Hutchinson said. The Bee Gees' *1st* was often on Bowie's turntable; **Clareville Grove:** *LYTT*'s producer Malcolm Thomson claimed some of "Oddity" was communally written over a few nights when he and his assistant Susie Mercer visited. "We all produced lines. It was very much a spontaneous thing among a group of people." (Gilmans, 159). There were several such claimants: Marc Bolan told Spencer Leigh he'd written "part" of "Oddity" and suggested Bowie sing it like Robin Gibb; "**out of my gourd**": *Performing Songwriter*, September 2003; **Bradbury, Walter, Pratchett**: In *The Illustrated Man*, *New Worlds* 161 (April 1966) and *New Worlds* 156 (November 1965), respectively.

101 "**vending space**," *Life*, 14 November 1969; **seemed in questionable taste**: "Space Oddity" was allegedly black-

listed in parts of the US. Pitt got a letter from a woman in Texas who said her local radio stations wouldn't take her requests for the song (Pitt, 175).

102 **drift into the void**: As Bowie once said he had "a flirtation with smack" in 1968, some have interpreted "Space Oddity" as a junkie song, the "liftoff" marking when the needle hits the vein. Many Bowie contemporaries (Visconti, Mary Finnigan, Hutchinson) say the idea Bowie was doing heroin in '68 is preposterous, as he rarely even smoked pot (Bowie and Farthingale "were [more] into white wine," Hutchinson told Trynka). Bowie even presented a few anti-drug lectures at the Arts Lab in late 1969; **"Over the Rainbow":** Compare "someday I'll wish upon a star..." to "take your protein pills..."; **kid's word over the bureaucrat's**: Buckley, 61; **on such a scale**: Hutchinson said Bowie recycled a Lower Third riff for the intro and some of "There is a Happy Land." The psychedelic outro replaced what the demos show was yet another use of the Bo Diddley guitar riff. Bowie worked the whole song out, barring the solos, before entering the studio. "His songs have a structure he dreams up for himself," Hutchinson told Trynka; "**some kind of rock musical**": Radio 4 *Front Row* (with John Wilson), June 2002.

103 **C-F-G-A-A**: Bowie follows the basic progression of a C major key—C, F, G—with an A major, making a power chord move (a la the Kinks' "Lola") more unstable—is it still in C or now shifting into A?; **fret shapes**: Trynka, 88. Hutchinson "changed some chord shapes" and contributed the Fmaj7th, a chord Bowie wanted but didn't know how to play. Hutch's also responsible for the run of added ninth chords in the bridge; **E7**: an E chord (E-G#-B) augmented with a D note; **bridge**: This still keeps the song in C if you consider Bb the flat VII chord of C mixolydian (a scale popular with folk musicians, in which the seventh degree is flatted, so C (I), Bb (flat VII)).

104 **goal not quite reached**: via Larry Hardesty; **Stylophone**: nearly inaudible in the *LYTT* mix until it honks in the coda. Its manufacturer, Dubreq, had sent a promo model to Ken Pitt, though Marc Bolan once claimed he'd given it to Bowie. Bowie soon tired of the instrument: "that thing...daren't you mention it," he said on a BBC session, though he'd reclaim it in the early 2000s; **futurist police siren**: similar to the electric piano opening of "I Am the Walrus."

105 **eight tracks**: While 8-track was an advanced console for the time (it's the most the Beatles ever had), Visconti wrangled a 16-track for the *Space Oddity* LP. Dudgeon allotted one track for higher-pitched strings, another for celli and flutes. The Mellotron had its own track; **takeoff sequence**: the idea came from Hutchinson. In Feathers shows, he'd scrape his guitar strings for effect during poetry readings. (You can hear this in the first demo). **his two solos**: Wayne's lead guitar chart is heavily visual, with notes written as shimmering upward in clumps; "**which meant octaves**" Trynka, 97; Cann, 154; **Cox**: he recalled the session as being "loose," with Bowie and Dudgeon letting players improvise much of their parts. The only instructions Bowie gave Cox was to have him put a blanket on his drums.

106 **barely charted**: It peaked at #48. In late 1969, Bowie recorded an Italian vocal, "Ragazzo Solo, Ragazza Sola," which was a minor hit in Europe. The translation (by Mogol) had nothing to do with Major Tom: the "lonely boy, lonely girl" of the title met on a mountaintop. (Allegedly the Italians wouldn't have gone for Bowie's SF scenario). Bowie returned the favor by utterly mistranslating Mogol's "Io vorrei...non vorrei...ma se vuoi" for Mick Ronson (see "Music Is Lethal").

107 **Hadfield**: He had to remove his video from YouTube after a year, not because of Bowie (who said he'd waive his royalties) but as part of his negotiation with Bucks Music,

the song's publisher.

108 **quiet influence**: Duncan and Bowie shared composing styles. She'd write songs in her head while sitting in cafes, then have an arranger play chords on piano until she heard what she wanted. (Ian Chapman, 1987 interview.) They were on similar trajectories in 1969, each getting new record deals and press at last. Her dislike of touring kept her an obscure figure, if one celebrated in music industry circles (she sings on Pink Floyd's *Dark Side of the Moon*). She died of cerebro-vascular disease in 2010.

109 **Djinn rejected**: Cann, 140. Bunn's "Life Is a Circus" wasn't released until 2005, when it appeared as a bonus track on a *Piece of Mind* (1970) reissue; **engineered**: Scott, Toft and Sheffield all worked at Trident; all received credit on the LP. Toft once claimed he recorded one side and Sheffield the other; Scott said he cut all *Space Oddity* songs except the single; ***Space Oddity***: To reduce confusion, all subsequent references to this record, first released as the second *David Bowie*, will be as *Space Oddity*, which RCA renamed it in 1972 upon acquiring Bowie's Philips/Mercury catalogue; **last day as a couple**: Farthingale danced in films including *Tales of Hoffman*. Bowie later said he met her once more during the Ziggy Stardust era and that she'd become a cartographer and South American explorer. If true (doubtful), she lived the life of a Wes Anderson heroine.

110 "**could have gotten back together**": "Golden Years," 2000.

111 **E7sus4**: Some transcribers have this as an E minor 11, but this would have been difficult to play on 12-string as opposed to the E7sus4, which Bowie could have gotten simply via a slip of a finger while playing E minor; **wistful scatting**: Possibly inspired by Simon & Garfunkel's "Mrs. Robinson." Hutchinson sang the intro and outro scats in the demo, suggesting he'd come up with the idea after having worked out the guitar line.

112 "**Occasional Dream**": Farthingale told Trynka she found this song "more moving" than the one named after her because of its more specific details about their life at Clareville Grove; **byzantine chord sequence**: Beginning in B minor, it veers through Bb major in the verses, C major in the pre-chorus and closes with an eleventh-hour push into D minor (on the very last "dream").

114 "**Janine**": An inspiration was George Underwood's Mauritian girlfriend. On the demo, Bowie said the song was about how Underwood "should see her." Underwood later said he was baffled by this; **Polish wanderer**: reference to a stock figure of the Romantic era, the dispossessed Pole (his country parceled up by Russia and other powers), sometimes conflated with the Wandering Jew; **open-D tuned**: D-A-D-F#-A-D: a folk tuning used by Joni Mitchell, Richie Havens and Bob Dylan on *Blood on the Tracks*.

115 "**Conversation Piece**": One of the *Ernie Johnson* songs is a "conversation piece" between Ernie and a racist tramp (Appendix).

116 **key shifts**: The closing sequence hovers between A minor and major, leaving the singer's fate a question mark; "**rips your heart out**": LeRoy, 44; **scrapped from the album**: Included on the master (sequenced on Side 2) but scratched off the tape box. Another remake was rumored from the *Aladdin Sane* sessions, though this seems dubious.

117 **Mick Ronson**: Tony Visconti says Ronson contributed guitar and handclaps during a "Frecloud" overdub session. Others like Cann and several biographers refute this, claiming Bowie and Ronson first met in early 1970 and that Ronson's first appearance on a Bowie record is the "Memory of a Free Festival" single. Visconti's claim is odd: why would a guitarist whom he or Bowie had never met get overdubbed onto a key song on the LP? That said, the *Oddity* sessions were lengthy and chaotic, and there are instances of people

showing up in the studio and winding up on the record, such as the singers on "Free Festival." So if Ronson visited his friend John Cambridge when Visconti needed a guitar dub, it's easy to see how Visconti could've put Ronson to work. In a compromising spirit, I offer this: if you want Ronson to be on this track, he is.

118 **outsider figure**: The Wild Boy had a revival in the late Sixties as part of a vogue for hippie Christs and "natural" rustics. A set of noble savages as the court jesters of the jet age. Francois Truffaut turned Itard's book into a film, *L'Enfant Sauvage* (1970) while Werner Herzog took another "feral" 19th Century boy, Kaspar Hauser, as his subject. See also Henry David Thoreau resurrected as ur-hippie and draft dodger in Lee and Lawrence's play *The Night Thoreau Spent in Jail* (1970); "**beautiful way of life**": *Disc & Music Echo,* October 1969. Bowie also said the Boy's crime was his "unnatural" relationship with the mountain; **chromatic bassline**: The song discloses its birth on guitar, as its central chord sequence (D, D/C#, D/C, Bm7/F#) is derived by keeping the D fret shape while moving a finger down the G string to play the bassline.

119 "**Wagnerian orchestra**": Visconti, *Brooklyn Boy,* 139. He may have been inspired by the descending progression in the verses, whose Bm7 suggested the 'Tristan Chord' from the prelude of Wagner's *Tristan und Isolde;* "**really you**": A steal from Biff Rose's "The Man," as discovered by Pegg; **time for only one take**: As Trident had only just gotten its 16-track console, engineers spent much of the "Freecloud" session frantically trying to calibrate sound levels, with test takes overwhelmed by hiss. Visconti couldn't afford to have the musicians go into overtime so he eked out a releasable take five minutes before call time. He said the track was "hell to mix."

121 **recorded**: While the "God Knows I'm Good" master take

was cut on 16 September, Bowie was working on the song on 5 August when he learned his father had died. An 11 September 1969 recording was taped at Advision Studios; **soulless modern supermarket**: By the late Sixties, the likes of Tesco were supplanting the neighborhood market, a victory for the "greater and greater emphasis placed on packaging and advertising" in Britain (Marwick, *Sixties*, 116).

123 **chords**: It hints that the song's battle will be between A's parallel minors/majors, distracting from the real struggle, later in the song, between Am and C major; **shifting times**: Including 2/4 ("look down so far from your") and 3/4 ("[Uto]pia dream"); **street figure**: Bowie told Tremlett that an inspiration for the title had come from the "funny stares" he got on the street; **rich girl**: Farthingale, a doctor's daughter, was of a higher class than Bowie, son of a charity home publicist, continuing the class friction of Bowie's earlier relationship with the aristocrat Dana Gillespie. The "earthy" musician/ "snob" girl pairing is wearily eternal in British pop, from the Stones' "Play With Fire" to Pulp's "Common People."

124 **scattered album sessions**: *Space Oddity* was recorded in fits and starts over nearly three months, with Bowie introducing new material by sitting on a stool, running through the song on his guitar and asking the players to get on with it. Described as being indecisive and reserved in the sessions, Visconti later admitted he "didn't know what he was doing yet"'; **Benny Marshall**: The lead singer of the Rats, the source of 2/3rds of the Spiders From Mars. Visiting John Cambridge in the studio, Cambridge said Bowie thought the track needed harmonica, which Marshall offered to play. Bowie, who ran out to purchase a harmonica for Marshall, nervously watched him during the overdub session ("I felt he was worried I would ruin his track and his album,"

Marshall later said, as per "the Hype" on the Illustrated DB board, 12 December 2011).

125 **Arts Lab**: The first Arts Lab was formed by Jim Haynes in 1967 in Covent Garden. It featured music, dances, theater and served as a dormitory for 15-20 people. It folded in late 1969, Haynes blaming its demise on "puritan elements" because "the ecstasy count, the sensuality count, was very high" at his Lab (Hewison,123); "**nothing in Beckenham**": "Bowie's Great Love is His Arts Lab," *Het Parool*, 30 August 1969; "**heads and skinheads alike**": *International Times*, 15 August 1969; "**bit of a twerp**": Sandford, 74.

126 "**one of the other people**": Juby, 27; **most talented figure**: Bowie once was blown off the stage by an opening act, Comus (Young, 509). Marc Bolan, Lionel Bart and Chime Rinpoche were among those who performed at the Lab; **harmonically free**: While EMI transcribers propose shifts of B minor to B-flat minor to C major, "Committee" is more in a state of harmonic instability, with various possible keys (you could argue the progression's more D to Db to C). That said, Matthew-Walker's claim "there is hardly one bar in the whole of this nine-and-a-half minute work which can be said to be in any one particular key" (68) is rather an overstatement; "**fellow man I do love you**": Salvo, *Interview*, March 1973; **bassline**: D-C-B-Bb, the last tone signaling the B-flat minor section (it's close to the bassline of "Wild Eyed Boy From Freecloud"); **cult leaders**: See Bill Fay's *Time of the Last Persecution* (1971), a record full of warnings about, in Rob Young's words, "false leaders, messiahs and prophets."

127 "**trailer for the promised land**": Crouch, 55-56. See *Black Dwarf* editorial, 15 October 1967: "We are the only major capitalist country which has not produced a comparable student movement." That said, there were a few student takeovers at the LSE and various arts colleges in 1968-1969;

"**laziest people I've met in my life**": Kate Simpson, *Music Now*, 20 December 1969; **underground's slide into criminality**: See the Notting Hill-based community agency Bit, which fell "into the hands of a bunch of petty crooks, speed freaks, con-artists and jaded hypocrites mouthing meaningless platitudes about 'The Alternative Society' while they dealt barbiturates and stole from their friends," the *IT* recalled in 1980.

129 **release:** A ragged 9:22 edit is on the 2009 reissue; **groups like the Strawbs**: Bowie tried to get Noel Redding, late of the Jimi Hendrix Experience, to play the show, only to be told by the latter's manager that "Noel Redding is a superstar and doesn't play free festivals"; **success**: "We all grooved in the sun and even made a profit for Growth, which seemed too much to expect," the post-Festival *Growth* newsletter beamed.

130 "**triple-priced Lyon's**": *Play Power*, 120. "Pop's own institutions become like Buckingham Palace without the efficiency"; **free festival as fault line**: The free festival held on through the early Seventies, with Phun City (which in 1970 had William S. Burroughs, Morris dancers, pinball tournaments and the MC5), the Glastonbury Fayre (co-founded by Churchill's granddaughter) and the Windsor People's Free Festival, whose organizer advocated replacing "the family with the commune" and "to bring God down out of the sky and put him where he belongs—the human heart"; **Rosedale electric chord organ**: It had 12 buttons that the left hand pressed to sound a chord (A, Bb, C, D, F and G, all both major and minor), while the right hand had a three-octave keyboard to play. Similar in tone and range to the accordion, it was a tribute to a Bowie favorite at the time, the eccentric singer/accordionist Ivor Cutler.

131 "**Hey Jude**": Bowie shouts "here comes the sun!" at one point. The backing singers, who Visconti repeatedly tracked

until they sounded massive, were future Sony VP Tony Woollcott, DJ "Whispering" Bob Harris and his wife Susan. Marc Bolan and a performer known only as "Girl" (it was 1969) were overdubbed in a later session; **get to the refrain faster**: By extracting the "sun machine" chant and putting it to a beat, you had a dance record. E-Zee Possee's "The Sun Machine" (1990) put the chant over house piano while Dario G's 1998 "Sunmachine" featured Visconti playing recorder and a sampled Bowie vocal; **psychedelic interlude deep-sixed**: Instead John Cambridge welded verse and refrain by using a scene-change trick he'd picked up from the Rats: he struck a cymbal with a mallet, which Visconti slowed and reversed on tape (Cann, *SO*); **Ralph Mace**: A former Philips executive, Mace visited the studio to find Bowie and Visconti flummoxed by the Moog, which they'd intended to replace the original track's saxophone line (the part "required more supple fingers than any of David's band could provide," Mace said). Cutting his part in a few takes, Mace was hailed as a Moog wizard and soon recruited for *The Man Who Sold the World*. The stray high note heard at 1:29 on "Part 1" was Ronson's doing, as he pressed a key by accident during a run-through. (Cann, *SO*.)

Chapter 4

134 "**London Bye Ta-Ta**": It was earmarked for the A-side, which Kenneth Pitt thought was the right choice. So he was surprised to find, receiving an advance pressing, that "Prettiest Star" was the A-side and "Ta-Ta" cut entirely. The last-minute change was Bowie and Angela's doing; **declined to promote it**: There was also the chaotic state of Bowie's management (working up the nerve to leave Pitt, he cut Pitt out of decisions) and the meager promotional resources of his label, which had exhausted itself flogging

"Space Oddity"; **SF-themed sequel**: Calling "Prettiest Star" "one of the best things [Bowie's] ever done," Marc Bolan said it "was daring at the time because after 'Space Oddity' it would have been easier to put [out] something with a string Mellotron sound." One could make the case "Prettiest Star" was an ode to Bolan, about to become the prettiest new pop idol; **professional ambition**: Tellingly, Bowie changed this to "*you and I* will rise.." on the *Aladdin Sane* remake. Nicholas Pegg credits Biff Rose's "Angel Tension" as a likely source for the arrangement and lyric (*cf.* Rose's "going baaaack in memory" with Bowie's "staying back in your memory"); **occasional spices**: An A7 ("peace child," "see wide"), a B-flat minor ("when I loved") and a VII chord with an added ninth, which makes a swoon out of the return to the F major tonic: "(Ebadd9) movies in the (F) dark"; "**naive approach**": "David Bowie Story."

137 **original's piano melody**: He possibly also rewrote "London Bye Ta-Ta" as a potential Deram track, "Threepenny Joe" (see appendix).

138 "**acceptable middle-class hippie**": Rose played "Buzz" on his first appearance on the *Tonight Show* in December 1968. He was a regular guest for a year, serving as Johnny Carson's hippie court jester. After years being ripped off by the music business, Rose returned to New Orleans near-destitute. He's spent the last two decades with no fixed address but a tart Internet presence (Chris Rose, "60s Folk Singer Biff Rose Is a Man Without a Country," *New Orleans Times-Picayune*, 8 November 1997); **bungled jokes**: Bowie's Buzz shoves his gun into Alice's back and says "this is a bust!": it's supposed to be her chest (rim shot); **recorded**: The "Amsterdam" issued as the B-side of "Sorrow" was apparently from the *Ziggy Stardust* sessions of late 1971. However, Cann claims this take was cut during the *Pin Ups* sessions of summer 1973, which doesn't seem right. A demo (cut in

early 1971?), similar in vocal phrasing to the studio cut, is also circulating; "**disconcertingly loud hush**": Guillaume, *A Life*, 125.

139 **engineered**: Depending on the studio: Trident (Scott), Advision (Chevin); **first release**: Due to the near-independence of Mercury's US and UK arms, *The Man Who Sold the World* was released far earlier in America (4 November 1970) than it was in Britain (10 April 1971). It charted (UK #26) in 1972.

140 **violin case**: Ronson hated the violin so much he'd play it like a guitar. He was also a solid drummer (Cann, 214); **London**: Ronson played on Michael Chapman's *Fully Qualified Survivor* in 1969, whose producer, Gus Dudgeon, considered him for Elton John's guitarist, and he played on an early take of "Madman Across the Water" during *Tumbleweed Connection* sessions in March 1970, just after his arrival in London to meet Bowie. There's an alternate Earth where Ronno plays on "Saturday Night's All Right For Fighting"; "**all turned to 10**": "David Bowie Story"; **notched fingernail**: Mike Garson told *Mojo* in 1997 that Ronson "would just milk one note to death—I loved it"; **read music**: Raised on classical piano, Ronson was a dyed-in-the-wool tonalist ("in classical music everything has to be relative [e.g.] the relative minor to a C chord is A minor...when you're brought up in classical rules you tend to follow them...it still affects the way I think now," *Starzone*, 63) and he could make harmonic order out of the most outré Bowie chord progressions.

141 **first met**: Bowie had been quietly auditioning lead guitarists. Mick Wayne reportedly didn't make the cut because of his drug use, copious even for the time. Tim Renwick, the other guitarist on *Space Oddity*, seemed the likely choice until Ronson offered to work for free until Bowie got some gigs; "**Width of a Circle**": Bowie first used

the title for a George Underwood drawing on the *Space Oddity* LP; **The Hype**: Ken Pitt claimed the name was his coining. "There wasn't a nice feeling there, something was wrong," he said of the first Hype show. The name reflected its era. The guitarist Mike Bloomfield, recalling the Electric Flag's performance at Monterey Pop, said "We played rotten, man...And the people loved it—oh my God, the hype, the image, the shuck, the jive." Symbolically, Bowie skipped an Arts Lab performance to play the first Hype show; **extended set-pieces:** George Tremlett, catching some Hype shows, noted Bowie often took a riff or a verse and "semi-spontaneously [expanded] it to maybe two or three times its original length, playing to the mood of his audiences (111).

142 **debut performance**: Despite a few missed cues and fluffed notes, the band felt the first BBC "Width" was a breakthrough. "It was raw as fuck…You could see it was a lot better. Mick lifted it," Cambridge said (Trynka, 112). Its second BBC recording on 25 March 1970 was a dress rehearsal for the studio cut. The staggered opening riff's in place and the Ronson/Visconti "boogie riff," still just an instrumental jam, now closes the performance; **drums bleeding**: One of the first to liberate his drummer from the booth was Jimmy Page, who recorded the first Led Zeppelin record in late 1968 with this set-up.

143 **tempo slows**: Starting at 92 bpm, the song slows to 60 bpm here, tears off to 136 bpm when the "boogie riff" starts and closes exhausted at around 70 bpm; "**turn around**": There are some good jokes, too. "You'll never go down to the Gods again!" the demon lover says, punning on a line from "The Teddy Bears' Picnic" ("if you go down to the woods today") and "the Gods," the cheapest balcony seats in a theater and as such a favorite place for hook-ups.

145 **overmen**: In the same 1972 *NME* interview in which he

"came out," Bowie talked up this idea. Michael Watts: "He has a great need to believe in the legends of the past, particularly those of Atlantis; and for the same need he has crafted a myth of the future, a belief in an imminent race of supermen called ***homo superior***. It's his only glimpse of hope, he says—'all the things that we can't do they will.'"; ***More Than Human:*** Sturgeon's novel (1953) concerned a group of mutant children who together form a new entity, *homo gestalt*, a plural human being (see Bowie's "where all were minds in uni-thought."); "**liked the cover**": "David Bowie Story"; "**one Sunday afternoon**": Trynka, 121.

146 "**period piece**": CSM, *NME*, 24 February 1973; **main riff**: Offered during the "I Pity the Fool" session in 1965. Bowie and Reeves Gabrels later reused it for "Dead Man Walking"; **drums**: Bowie first attempted "Supermen" during the "Memory of a Free Festival" remake session on 23 March 1970. Cambridge allegedly had trouble mastering the beat, particularly a "skipping" bass drum part (as played by Woodmansey, this entailed hitting an eighth note and two 16th notes on kick drum between snare hits). (Cambridge was a blunter presence on "Width of a Circle" than Woodmansey; see the 25 March BBC session for evidence.) Many sources agree Ronson was influential in the push to fire Cambridge; **C major**: The refrain, opening in F major, has a shift to F minor ("life...rolls into one for them") and after a sharp turn via A major ("supergod") it ends on C major ("CRIES!"), the dominant (V) chord of F. Yet the C feels like such a slam "home" (plus the fact it eventually ends the song) that it doesn't seem to want to resolve to F but supplant it. It's another warring god in a song full of them.

147 **outrageous vocal**: The argument that "Supermen" is secretly a joke song is bolstered by another influence discovered by Pegg, Biff Rose's recording of Joseph Simon

Newman's "Paradise Almost Lost." This poem, set at the dawn of history, blames the Fall of Man on two horny protozoa. As Pegg noted, Bowie's verse matches Newman's iambic tetrameter ("*all* the *world* was *ve*-ry *young*"). Newman, uncle of actor Paul, was a co-founder of the educational toymaker Electro-Set Co. "Paradise Almost Lost" was from his 1948 collection *It Could Be Verse!*

148 **live, 1971**: Its only live performances in 1971 were during Bowie's promotional tour of the US, including a private party at the home of attorney Paul Feigen in Los Angeles. A snippet of this performance is on the soundtrack of *Mayor of the Sunset Strip*; **ward of Cane Hill**: Bowie would introduce himself to Haddon Hall newcomers by saying he was "Terry's brother." To *Sounds* in January 1972, he said "there's a schizoid streak within the family anyway so I dare say that I'm affected by that. The majority of the people in my family have been in some kind of mental institution, as for my brother he doesn't want to leave. He likes it very much...He'd be happy to spend the rest of his life there—mainly because most of the people are on the same wavelength as him. And he's not a freak, he's a very straight person"; "**threat of insanity**":"David Bowie Story."

149 "**unlivable situation**": *Politics*, 11-12. "What we call 'normal' is a product of repression, denial, splitting, projection, introjection and other forms of destructive action and experience. It is radically estranged from the structure of being...The 'normally' alienated person, by reason of the fact that he acts more or less like everyone else, is taken to be sane"; **anti-psychiatry movement**: For a cultural shift, compare Hitchcock's *Spellbound* (1945), where an asylum is a stately Vermont manor and the face of psychiatry is Ingrid Bergman in a lab coat, with Milos Forman's *One Flew Over the Cuckoo's Nest* (1975), where the asylum's a shabby jail and patients are at the mercy of the sadistic bureaucrat Nurse

Ratched. Sympathetic portraits of the insane were common in Sixties SF as well, "a whole harlequinade of the naturally or chemically crazed," like the political prisoners of Thomas M. Disch's *Camp Concentration*. (Greenland, 174.); **yearns for transcendence**: Carl Jung in a 1935 lecture: "that young man is striving to identify with Zarathustra, to be a dweller on the heights...but if he escapes the law of the earth he becomes an inhuman spirit: he will be struck by lightning and destroyed."

150 **two spheres of influence**: The D minor in the verse ("thin men walk the streets") is the relative minor of F. The E minor ("while the sane") is both parallel minor of E and VI chord of the impending G in the refrain. The refrain introduces more major triads: A and C#. The A major advances the "narrative": after having gone through E, F and G, the subsequent move to A has a cadential feel (E's also the dominant (V) chord in the key of A). And while the C# first seems like the dominant chord of F#m (A's relative minor), that theory collapses once Bowie substitutes a Bm for it in the second half of the refrain. Instead the C# is just standing there making trouble in the song; **conflict never resolved**: If the refrain's in A, it ends by coming home: "sane as me"; if it's in E, its sympathies instead lie with "all the madmen" and the refrain ends on the dominant, leaving a feeling of unease. (Hardesty); **first recorded**: It was the first song taped in the first session at Trident, starting at 1 AM on 17 April 1970; **spoken interlude**: The newscaster voice calls back to "We Are Hungry Men" while the distorted "girl" voice is a varisped Bowie (*cf.* "Segue: Baby Grace" on *1. Outside*). Some early mixes omitted the interlude.

152 **guitars**: The latter sounds like a mandolin, but it's Ronson (most likely) rapidly picking sixteenth notes on the two highest courses of a 12-string acoustic; "**oh by jingo**": Likely taken from the Twenties pop hit of the same name,

sung by Billy Murray and Spike Jones, among others.

153 "**maybe write a bridge**": "David Bowie Story"; **Ronson and Visconti**: To *Mojo* in 1997, Visconti said "the songs were written by all four of us," though he was a bit cagier in his subsequent autobiography. Bowie's tart response was say "no one writes chord progressions like that." Ralph Mace, interviewed by the Gilmans, said while Bowie was absent at times, he was there just as often to run sessions and direct his players. Bowie has publicly regretted turning over so much of *MWSTW* to Visconti and Ronson. "I'd never done an album with that kind of professionalism...I felt invalid somehow," he said in 1976. He also said he wished he hadn't used eight-track, as the sound was "too glossy" (had he listened to the album since 1970?); **homage to Cream**: Watching Led Zeppelin on TV one night in Haddon Hall, Angela Bowie challenged Ronson to "do a better blues song than that"; "**nuance for noise**": *Revolution*, 298; **Ronson**: "She Shook Me Cold" was "completely a Ronson composition—Bowie didn't add his lyrics until much later" Visconti said in 1997. Compared with the intricate guitar dubs of "Black Country Rock," "She Shook Me Cold" is minimalist, just one guitar w/Wah-Wah, with a second guitar only tracked in the "moaning" verse.

154 "**Saviour Machine**": Originally titled "The Man Who Sold the World" and, at the time of the rhythm track's recording, as "Invader"; **a few cranks**: These included Bowie's manager Tony Defries, who reportedly predicted everyone would have "laptop computers" at home one day; **mega-computers**: See *Colossus: The Forbin Project*, in which American and Soviet supercomputers unite to control Earth ("freedom is an illusion," the Colossus computer says at the end), which seems an obvious inspiration for Bowie's lyric. The timing's very tight, though. *Forbin* came out in the US in late April 1970, when Bowie had begun *MWSTW*, and it's

unknown when it was released in London. But if the film came out in May, it's conceivable Bowie saw it and used it for his lyric (thanks: Richard Lesses).

155 **12/8**: With bars of 6/8 and 9/8 to round out the bridges and choruses, respectively.

156 **My Lai**: The massacre had just gone public, the story broken by Seymour Hersh in November 1969 (the US army had covered it up until then; the trial of Lt. William Calley wouldn't take place until November 1970). The UT shootings fascinated Bowie, who'd describe America as being full of "snipers on rooftops" as late as 1990; "**plug a few civilians**": A filler lyric for the end of the refrain was "Humpty Dumpty sat on a wall." As the track was originally called "Cyclops," it's possible that Bowie envisioned his killer as a modern-day Polyphemos with corpses stacked around him; **leads off 2nd side**: Much as how the end of "After All" calls back to the start of "Width of a Circle," the harmonies in the outro of "Running Gun Blues" mirror those of its side closer, "The Supermen," the harmonies descending here where those on "Supermen" ascend.

157 **first release**: Its first appearance in Britain was as the B-side of "Holy Holy" in January 1971; "**Black Country Rock**": It's well-sequenced as the light "scherzo" movement of an otherwise brooding side-long suite of "Width of a Circle," "All the Madmen" and "After All." (Matthew-Walker, 73); **bass**: The first riff likely began as a Visconti bass line, given that Visconti plays it note-for-note and Ronson plays most of it on his low E string.

158 **live performances**: That said, most of the album (six of nine tracks) wasn't played live at the time; five songs never have been; **heavier sound**: Robert Plant, born in West Bromwich and schooled in Stourbridge, called himself a "Black Country hippy full of high ideals and low cost living" (Wall,

170). Zeppelin's "Black Country Woman" was on *Physical Graffiti*; **Bolan imitation**: Some 40 seconds of Bolanisms were cut from the final mix.

159 **Mike Weller**: He access to some early mixes, as he based his illustration primarily on "Running Gun Blues" (which might explain why Bowie kept that song on the record); **changes to the record**: This irritated Bowie, along with Mercury scrapping a proposed gatefold with Bowie in a dress (which would be the UK version's cover). But he didn't seem that invested in the name *Metrobolist* as he and Tony Defries considered calling the UK edition *Holy Holy*, which presumably would've included that single in a new sequencing. When RCA reissued *MWSTW*, it changed the cover to an action shot of an early Ziggy Stardust.

161 **starting most of his phrases**: To give a sting to these words, Bowie typically sings the subtonic (VII) note of the chord: e.g. "spoke" is a G note in an A7 chord. For extra oomph, he'll sing a word as a dominant note ("gazed" is a C in F); **percussive colors**: Woodmansey had injured a finger during the *MWSTW* sessions: was this why there's no drum track, just percussion that a man with a bandaged hand could play? The guiro beat is short-short-long, the woodblock's hit on the third beat of each bar. They join the maracas in later refrains and outro; **first guitar lesson**: Ronson holds his G string down at the second fret, plays three notes, lifts up his finger to sound the open string, slides to the third fret and back again, lifts his finger to close the loop; **moving landscape**: Chet Williamson: "The melody of the riff is unchangeable. It seems to owe nothing to any key, and stands alone, adapting itself to the darkness of D minor, the brightness of F, and the intermediary and transitory character of A." (http://www.myspace.com/chet_etown/blog/268275361); **D minor**: It supplants A major as the verse key via a conspiracy of F and C major chords, much as how

the opening C major of the refrain winds up in the thrall of F major. In the coda, Bowie first sings the dominant note of each chord he's in (so moving from E (in A) to A (in Dm) and then the root notes of F and Dm).

162 **Chad Channing**: He left Nirvana in 1990, though the sound of "classic" Nirvana is partly his doing: the drum pattern of "In Bloom" was mostly his work, for instance; **Cobain**: He misheard "all the millions here" as "and climbed a million hills"; **Lulu**: Bowie told her the song concerned "devils and angels" within himself (Gilmans, 222).

163 ***Saturday Night Live***: The performance was inspired by the Dadaist Hugo Ball, who was once carried onstage in a tube; Bowie's costume was based on Sonia Delaunay's designs for a 1923 Tristan Tzara play, *Le Coeur à Gaz*; **Bowie made his move**: He sang the revised version live in 1995-1996. A Brian Eno-mixed studio take, misleadingly labeled a live version, was included on the CD single of "Strangers When We Meet."

164 **"Holy Holy"**: It could parody Neil Diamond's "Holly Holy," though the 1969 Diamond single was fairly obscure in Britain.

165 **split with Visconti**: Visconti didn't trust Tony Defries, who had wanted him to sign a managerial contract, and he'd also had enough of what Bowie's scattered work ethic, which he thought was hindering his ability to improve in the studio; **Blue Mink**: Another member was guitarist Alan Parker ("Hurdy Gurdy Man") who'd later play on *Diamond Dogs*; **half-written song**: Flowers, looking to beef up the song, proposed a bridge that Bowie vetoed; **"pure silk shirts"..."a man's prowess"**: Crowley, *Confessions*, 15, 463. Crowley's everywhere in Sixties-Seventies pop. *The Book of the Law*'s "every man and every woman is a star" leads to Sly Stone's "Everybody Is a Star" or see the Only Ones' "The Whole of the Law."

166 **dark prosperity gospel**: "When you've discovered your true will, you should just forge ahead like a steam train. If you put all your energies into it there's no doubt you'll succeed," Page said in 1977. For Bowie, "Holy" paid quick dividends: Chrysalis' publishing head loved it so much that he signed Bowie to a £5,000 deal based on it. It was the biggest cash advance he'd ever received and ended the money troubles that had plagued him in 1970, settling Bowie enough so he could work on improving his songs; "**sexual athlete**": Wilson, *Crowley*, 103; "**the illumination**"; Wilson, *Occult*, 140; "**charlatan**": Jay Matthews, "Drum 'n' Bass Oddity," *NME*, February 1997.

Chapter 5

169 **first release**: *Hunky Dory* was released a touch earlier in the US, though one cited date of a Saturday, 4 December 1971, is questionable (it's the date of the *Billboard* mentioning the LP release). *HD* came out on 17 December in the UK, the date I'll use for simplicity's sake instead of some monstrosity like "4?/17 December"; **F# major**: The track's likely a semitone lower than it was recorded—the piano sounds slightly flat. Transcribers have the key change as being either F# major to G major or F major to G-flat major: the former seems more accurate, as Peter Noone recalled Bowie being in F# when he played piano on Noone's single; **quaver chords**: There's a bit of Andy "Thunderclap" Newman's barrelhouse solo in his namesake band's "Something In the Air"; **chaise lounge:** Bowie, "I Went to Buy Some Shoes...," *Daily Mail*, 28 June 2008; **foxing run of chords**: A progression of G#dim/D/D#dim/E/B-F#/F#sus4/F# and bam!, back to G major to start another verse.

170 **composer's piano**: Playing piano was a challenge for Bowie in the Noone session; Most had to edit his track together from various takes. "I knew all the chords but I couldn't play

them in succession. I could play three or four at a time and then my fingers would hurt," Bowie, "David Bowie Story"; **recorded dryly**: An early mix (for a promotional release) has a more centrally-placed Bowie's vocal, with generous reverb applied to it and the backing vocals. The piano's also set back in the mix; **cello**: The sole cello was another minimalist response to the Noone single, which had violins play lilting countermelodies throughout. The cello has some distortion applied to it, possibly a flanger or routed through a Leslie speaker; "**plodalong bassline**": "David Bowie Story." See "Martha My Dear" in particular. "An old-fashioned poignant sentimentality," Bowie said.

171 ***Childhood's End***: Clarke's novel was a touchstone of the time: see Pink Floyd's "Childhood's End," Genesis' "Watcher of the Skies" and Led Zeppelin's *Houses of the Holy*, whose cover is the novel's climactic scene of naked super-children ascending a mountain. Other sources were John Wyndham's *The Midwich Cuckoos*, with its alien-seeded Children, Edward Bulwer-Lytton's *The Coming Race*, which Bowie name-checks (subterranean super-folk plan to take over the earth's surface) and Biff Rose's "Children of Light," who "will be given a means of escape/from a world wrapped in flame." Bowie may have taken "homo superior" from a conversation with Roger Damon Price during a taping of *Six On One: Newsday*, in which Price mentioned his upcoming TV show *The Tomorrow People* (Cann, 202).; **beautiful boys and girls**: See Michael Moorcock's *The Final Programme* (1968): "The true aristocracy who would rule the seventies were out in force: the queers and the lesbians and the bisexuals, already half-aware of their great destiny...the terms male and female would become all but meaningless."

172 "**Miss Peculiar**": There are two circulating versions: one's a piano demo with bass and drums, the other a King-(appar-

ently) sung take with horns. The former appears to be the demo sent to Tom Jones in January 1971, Pegg lists this take as having been cut in April; he claims a later take is from the *Hunky Dory* sessions and features Rick Wakeman on piano.

173 **dud single**: Released 15 October 1971, as a double-A side with "Walnut Whirl" (RAK 121); **engineered**: *Ziggy Stardust* has no engineering credit. Cann credits Stone as engineer, while MacKay was interviewed by *Uncut* in 2012 and spoke in detail about the sessions. Did both work on the record at different stages?; "**Universal Witness blue fur coat**": Cann, 203. Sandford describes the outfit as "a purple maxi-coat and a white chiffon scarf" (73). I'm sure it was striking in any regard.

174 **drew a gun**: Sandford, 73; "**Hang Onto Yourself**": It's listed as "Hang Onto Yourself" on the Corns single, "Hang On To Yourself" on the first *Ziggy* LP pressing, "Hang Onto Yourself" on the Ryko CD reissue, "Hang On To Yourself" on the 40th anniversary CD. I went with the first.

175 **Gene Vincent**: Reports that Vincent played on the "Hang Onto Yourself" demo are unconfirmed, although Bowie had wanted him to record the song. Vincent died of a stomach ulcer eight months after meeting Bowie, who used one of Vincent's signature stage moves—crouching at the mike with his injured leg jutting behind him—for Spiders shows. Bowie also recorded demos at Ayres' house with a Texas bluegrass quartet called the Boneshakers (Cann, 205); **unable to record**: Bowie had spent so much time making demos in early 1971 that his publisher leased four of them to the indie label B&C "simply to try to get some money back," Bob Grace told Dave Thompson; **Rungk**: Swedish for "wank," Broadbent told Trynka. "When you're 14, that's pretty funny."

176 "**Moonage Daydream**": A recording from Birmingham, 13 December 1995, was issued as a B-side of "Hallo Spaceboy"

in February 1996; "**TV Eye**": A lyrical nod, too: "She got a TV eye on me, oh" = "keep your 'lectric eye on me babe"; **12-string acoustic**: Bowie's Hagström is triple-tracked to pan across the stereo spectrum, with the center-mixed guitar being high-frequency tones audible only when sustained chords from the other two tracks fade.

177 **piccolo/baritone sax**: This was a guitar solo on the Corns single (Bowie sang the melody note for note to Pritchett). Bowie rewrote it as a wind solo, inspired by "Sho' Know a Lot About Love," the B-side of the Hollywood Argyles' "Alley Oop," which had a fife and baritone sax duet. "That's the greatest combination of instruments. It's so ludicrous—you've got this tiny sparrow of a voice on top and a huge grunting pig-ox of a thing at the bottom," Bowie said in 1997. On "Moonage" the winds, set three octaves apart, play the same chromatic descending line (the saxes are doubled in the latter half of the solo). While played as a guitar solo with the Spiders and with Reeves Gabrels in 1995 and 1997, it was a saxophone/keyboard break in 1974 and a Mike Garson keyboard solo in 1996; "**funfair**": Trynka, 133; **Thomas Paine**: In post-revolutionary France Paine had advocated for a new "Church of God, Love and Man" (saint's days would honor George Washington and Voltaire). He was granted 10 disestablished parish churches but once Napoleon took power, Paine's charter was revoked (not that he'd had much luck finding parishioners). So "Church of Man-Love" is a glam revival, a spiritual assembly of homosexuals/bisexuals. It's also a pun, as Bowie saying "church of man, lurve" as he says "space-face close to mine, lurve" in the refrain; "**constructed to be seen**": Hoskyns, *Glam!*, 41; "**fat megaphone shape**": Buckley, 118. The solo's descending chord sequence (Bm7/A/G/F#) was a favorite Bowie progression ("Bewlay Brothers," "China Girl"). Known as the "Andalusian

cadence," it's the backbone of the likes of "Good Vibrations," "Hey Joe" and "Walk Don't Run."

178 **Les Paul's tone**: Some of Ronson's tone was owed to his relatively rare amp, a Marshall 200W; **bass**: Bolder used a Fender Mustang and a Gibson EB3 during his time with Bowie, with a Carlsbro cabinet and a Selmer 100W amp; "**really lifted**": "David Bowie Story"; **Bowie's cars**: Bowie owned three Rileys in quick succession, his prize being a 1100cc Riley Gamecock from the Thirties. He was a disaster as a motorist: the Riley's crankshaft handle once impaled his leg, nearly severing an artery; a year later, he got into a head-on crash while driving in Cyprus; **sound effects**: He used his Revox tape recorder to capture his neighbor revving up the Riley and driving it away from Haddon Hall in a spray of gravel. (Cann, 209).

179 "**club boy**": BowieNet chat, 1998 (quoted in Buckley, 92); **bonus track**: The Ryko reissues could be wildly off-base about the provenance of their outtakes. Ryko claimed "Lightning" predated the *MWSTW* sessions and featured Tim Renwick, John Cambridge and Tony Visconti, though Visconti obviously isn't playing on it. Ryko's "Lightning" is also in mono, cut by a minute and faded-in; a complete stereo take is circulating.

180 **Arnold Corns single**: B&C released the single in summer 1972 to cash in on *Ziggy Stardust*; co-written: Pritchett was possibly given full credit as a publishing dodge; **Factory**: Some of this stable was absorbed by Tony Defries' management company MainMan, whose London and New York branches hired many "former actors," in Iggy Pop's recollection.

181 **studio takes**: One's more in line with the BBC take, with Bowie and Pritchett alternating on verses; the other, mentioned above, has a more free-for-all vocal; "**Almost Grown**": Released by Berry in March 1959, "Almost Grown"

only hit #32 on the Hot 100 (Berry's pianist Johnnie Johnson said it showed the formula was played out: "I was gettin' tired of rock 'n' roll.").

182 **Bolder**: A last-minute substitute for Herbie Flowers, Bolder had to learn a dozen songs in two hours, he recalled; **Ralph J. Gleason**: He'd co-founded *Rolling Stone* in 1967. He once wrote that American children were "sleep learning" by listening to Doors and Traffic records as they slumbered, which explains the Seventies as much as anything else. Quotes from *RS*, 5 April 1969.

183 "**nauseating me**": Dylan, *Chronicles*, 109; "**Song For Woody**": "Hey hey Woody Guthrie I wrote you a song" A "hear this Robert Zimmerman, I wrote a song for you." Bowie's top melody is also reminiscent of Dylan's "My Back Pages."; "**leadership void**": Robert Hilburn, "Bowie: Now I'm a Businessman," *Melody Maker*, 28 February 1976.

184 **Lennon**: "Dylan is bullshit. Zimmerman is his name. You see, I don't believe in Dylan and I don't believe in Tom Jones either, in that way. Zimmerman is his name. My name isn't John Beatle. It's John Lennon," "Lennon Remembers," *Rolling Stone*, 21 January 1971; **different songs**: As John Peel introduced the song as "Here She Comes," the refrain may have started as one of Bowie's Velvet Underground tributes. He also recycled a few pieces of "Looking for a Friend"; **hated *Young Americans***: Sandford, 114. Bob Neuwirth said Ronson was hazed upon joining Dylan's Rolling Thunder tour by everyone on the bus ridiculing Bowie.

185 **Warhol**: Bowie, giving a book on Warhol to Mark Pritchett, said "here's where it all started." (Cann, 153). Bowie was at his most Warholian in a 1971 interview with *Sounds*: "I'm not writing deeply at the moment...I'm just picking up on what people say, writing it down and making songs out of it"; "**court painter**": Robert Rosenblum,1979, essay collected in *On Modern American Art*, 1999; **Dana Gillespie**: George

Underwood also demoed it. Gillespie's recording, cut with Bowie and a Ronson-arranged string section, was released on her 1974 *Weren't Born a Man*.

186 **art is boring**: Warhol disliked TV action shows because they varied the plots and characters. Instead he preferred to watch the exact same thing over and over again. "Because the more you look at the exact same thing, the more the meaning goes away and the better and emptier you feel." (Warhol, *POPism*, 50); **whip**: Not an actual whip but a percussion instrument that looks like a small pair of paddles hinged together; **his take**: The E minor verses soon fall under the sway of A major, which dominates the choruses; "**War-hol**": As a commenter "familiar with the Estuary accent" noted, Bowie's doing some punning: on "hols," slang for vacation, and "Hull," the home of the man in the studio with him.

187 **it concluded**: In live performances in 1972, Ronson played a closing solo, first a run of harmonics, then a series of fast arpeggios on his high strings, while Bowie sang along with what sounded like the "do de-do" vocal hook of Lou Reed's "Walk on the Wild Side."

188 "**Sister Flo**": Also poss. a reference to Flo (Mark Volman), former Turtle and session singer (*Electric Warrior*), whose voice many listeners assumed was a woman's; **the riff**: While varied throughout, his most common pattern is eight strums per bar, the fourth and sixth muted.

189 "**Bombers**": The BBC performance ends with the old man resembling "how you used to look/in my holy book." Its chorus melody is close to Bullet's "White Lies, Blue Eyes," a 1971 single, suggesting "Bombers" was another blatant pilfering like "Lightning Frightening." However "White Lies" wasn't issued until August and didn't chart until Christmas. So either a) Bowie heard an advance pressing of "White Lies" or b) Bullet somehow heard "Bombers" and

ripped *Bowie* off or c) the whole thing's a weird coincidence.

190 **Bowpromo**: A Bowie/Dana Gillespie disc that Tony Defries sent to prospective record labels in summer 1971; on Bowie's side, "Bombers" segued into the ARP synthesizer intro of "Andy Warhol."

191 "**It Ain't Easy**": Three Dog Night's version, which titled their third LP, pre-dated Davies' LP release by five months, so apparently the song was around in demo form in 1969. Baldry's take, again the title song of his LP, had just come out in June 1971 when Bowie sang "Easy" at the BBC session; **considered for *Hunky Dory***: It was included on the Bowpromo disc with other *Hunky Dory* songs, it flitted in and out of *Ziggy*'s running order. Bowie reportedly was "adamant" that the track make the final sequence; **A major**: Bowie's take has a drone feel, with he, Bolder and Wakeman sounding steady A root bass notes throughout the shifts from A to D major in the verses.

192 **would-be Americanisms**: "Hoochie coochie woman" seems a mishearing of Davies singing "Whooo! she take it"; **first release**: The promo version of "Kooks" has a notably different mix, with stereo-separated acoustic guitar tracks in the intro. The acoustic guitar is also audible throughout the verses while faded down on the album mix; **Neil Young**: His "I Believe In You" gets a call-out in the chorus.

193 "**Wonderboy**": Ray Davies wrote it when his wife Rasa was pregnant with his second daughter, later calling it being "about looking at a child for the first time and wondering what's going to happen in its life, how fucked-up it's going to be when it gets into the world"; **D major**: The verses are I-V or I-IV progressions in D major (a reverse of the A-D progressions in "It Ain't Easy"), while the chorus falls under the sway of A minor in its latter half ("soon you'll grow"); **trumpet**: As a child, Bolder had played trumpet and cornet in a few Hull brass bands; **mediant notes**: The

"middle" note in each chord. So either F# (in D major: D-F#-A) or G in Dsus4 (D-G-A),though Ronson hits a high root A right as the intro ends in A minor; **school disaster**: Morrissey paid tribute to "Kooks" with "throw your homework onto the fire" on the Smiths' "Sheila Take a Bow"; **Bowie sings**: He closes refrains by savoring the consonance of "couple of kooks," then darts up in a bar of 6/8 ("up on ro-") only to slide back down to the dominant note ("-man-CING")—it's a whim inflated and deflated in a breath.

194 **Biff Rose**: During his LA visit in1971, Bowie saw Rose perform, furthering his desire to cover Rose's songs on record. Bowie also drew from Tiny Tim's cover, the B-side of "Tiptoe Through the Tulips." Tim had sung it with glee and amazement, as if he'd finally found a song worthy of his persona; "**fear is in your head**": Paul Williams' answer to "White Rabbit"? There's also Frank Herbert's *Dune* ("fear is the mind-killer").

195 "**he's an imitation**": Rose, 2009 (http://wascals.com/biff/dotcom/kansascity.html).

196 "**my knowledge**": Chris Roberts, *Uncut*, October 1999; "**collection of other people's ideas**": Barbara Staib, "That Strange Glitter," *Ingenue*, March 1973. In his notes for the *Hunky Dory* press release, Bowie wrote: "There is a time and space level just before you go to sleep when all about you are losing theirs and whoosh! [the] void gets you with its cacophony of thought—that's when I like to write my songs"; **Order of the Golden Dawn**: A British society, founded in 1887, whose members were "taught the principles of Occult Science and the Magic of Hermes" (Regardie, *Golden Dawn*, 15). A dramatic evolution of Victorian table-rappers and spiritualists, the Society was credited with helping to revive magic in the 20th Century. One of its disciplines concerned the Kabbalah and the Tree

of Life (see "Station to Station"). Its adepts pledged to apply themselves to "the Great Work...to purify and exalt my spiritual nature that with Divine aid I may at length attain to be more than human and thus gradually raise and unite myself to my higher and divine Genius." (37) Aleister Crowley joined them in 1898 but left after a schism between the society and its founder; "**uniform of imagery**": A pun: "uniform" as in Himmler's dress uniform but also "uni-form" (see "The Supermen": "all were minds in uni-thought"); "**silent film**": While the "Garbo" of the lyric could be Greta, it could also be the WWII British double-agent Joan Pujol Garcia, code-named Garbo ("after the greatest actor"). Sefton Delmer's *The Counterfeit Spy*, which detailed the Garbo operation, was published in 1971. If the latter was the inspiration, it's a contender for the most obscure reference in the Bowie catalog.

197 **Ken Scott**: *Hunky Dory* was Scott's first record as a solo producer. One reason he took the job is that he figured few people would hear Bowie's album, so he felt under less pressure. Along with Alan Parsons, Geoff Emerick and Chris Thomas, he'd cut his teeth at Abbey Road with the Beatles and George Martin.

198 **Ronson's arrangement**: Scott said that Ronson, because he wasn't a "proper" arranger, was freer in his instrumentation: he'd use a single violin or cello where a more conventional arranger would have massed strings. Ronson took a few refresher sessions on music theory with his sister's piano teacher before *Hunky Dory*. Further sweetening occurred at the final mixing stage, as the promo mix lacks strings at 3:20 ("if I don't explain"). Oddly the promo's in stereo throughout while the album cut is in mono until Bowie's vocal starts; **home chord**: The first verse ends with an A minor 7th shifting to A major. It seems at first as if Bowie's lightening the song by with a quick move to the

parallel major, but A major soon establishes itself as the new tonic; **acoustic guitar**: I asked the musician Dave Depper to play "Quicksand." "Those diminished chords are just so chunky and satisfying under the fingers!" he said. Bowie likely came up with progressions by trying out chord shapes on various frets, as the same shape that makes D# dim, shifted up two frets, is now Bb dim.

199 **first release**: It was also the LP's first single, released 7 January 1972 (RCA 2160/ 45-0605).

200 "**near anarchic**": "Still Hunky Dory After All These Years," reprinted in *Bowie Companion*; **expands and contracts**: There's a general compression in the verse: Bowie sings four phrases in the first four bars, three in the next four, two phrases in the last set.

202 "**Eight Line Poem**": Its only live performance was at the Friars Club in Aylesbury, 25 September 1971; **treated piano**: A flanger was likely applied. In the promo mix, the piano sounds more "natural." The promo also plays stereo games with Ronson's guitar, batting it from right to left channel, and has a different vocal: the album vocal's more closely cut to fit the melody (*e.g.*, the promo has "They've opened shops" where the album has "opened shops"); **competing chords**: As F major is the subdominant chord of C, the former chord sounds like it's pushing "away" from the latter, giving Ronson and Bowie a clear separation of roles. "Eight Line Poem" was also wonderfully sequenced: the last chord of the preceding "Oh! You Pretty Things" was (originally) a C major and the first chord of "ELP" is an F major (the battle already underway). The last chord of "ELP" is a C; the first chord of the following "Life On Mars?" is an F.

203 **blank verse**: In their 1973 co-interview, William S. Burroughs told Bowie "I read this 'Eight Line Poem' of yours and it is very reminiscent of T.S. Eliot." "Never read him," Bowie replied, which was a fib: Eliot's such an obvious

influence here that the track could've been titled "One Duet." Bowie uses a prepositional phrase as the hinge of each line ("*to* your window," "*of* your room") until line six; "**Bewlay Brothers**": An alternate mix appeared on Ryko's 1990 *Hunky Dory*. Its minor differences were in stereo separation, less guitar reverb and higher-mixed vocals, especially in the coda.

204 "**wad of words**": Bowie, *Daily Mail*, 2008; **protracted feint**: A sign of the song's significance to Bowie was that he named his publishing company after it.

205 "**another part of me**": "Golden Years", 2000; "**gave me the energy**": "David Bowie Story"; **programmed David Bowie**: "My brother was one of the bigger influences of my life in as much as he told me that I didn't have to listen to the choice of books that were recommended at school, and that I could go to a library and choose my own, and he introduced me to authors that I wouldn't have read, probably. The usual sort of things like the Jack Kerouacs and Ginsbergs and ee cummings and stuff." Capitol One interview, October 1977.

206 **his vocal**: The first verse alone is a shower of descending phrases ("said the things to make it seem" a set of second-interval drops) whose movement is halted by a five-note, four-beat word ("improbable") that signals a run of rising phrases. It ends with an octave-tumbling line ("Sighing the swirl..."); **chord progressions**: Verses are D-Em-A-D (I-ii-IV-I). The refrain starts in B minor (vi) and ends with the ii chord (E minor) and a flattened VII chord, C, that resolves to D major.

207 ***Blood on Satan's Claw***: A find by David Dent; **starting point**: The chords of the two songs are hardly similar: a shared use of C minor and G minor, that's about it. Bowie said he'd used "clutches of melody" and "definite parodies" of "My Way."

208 "**doldrums of reality**": "Changes: Bowie at Fifty," 1997; **esoteric references**: The lyric sheet, included in the *David Bowie Is* exhibit, showed that the original second verse (and a scrapped third verse) were vastly different, much in the vein of "Quicksand," with lines like "a great Lord sighs in vain" and "a kiss in the face of a sub-human race."

210 "**Hey Jude**": Trident's 100-year old Bechstein grand piano, which had a crack in it that contributed to its tone, was a colossus—Wakeman guessed it hadn't been moved from its spot in the studio for years. It was auctioned off on eBay in 2001; "***2001*** **tympani**": A Bowie perennial by this point (see "Width of a Circle" and "The Supermen"); **phone rings**: This tag was left over from an earlier take spoiled by a public phone ringing in the studio. Scott recorded over this scrapped take, but as the subsequent take was slightly shorter, the last seconds of the scrapped take remained. Liking how this sounded, Scott and Bowie kept the fragment, which has become such a part of "Life On Mars?" that the Bad Plus included it in their 2007 jazz version. As to what's being mumbled, Scott said it's Ronson cursing the spoiled take. An attempted transcription: Ronson: "Bollocks! Well I think that's the one. Fooking—"; "**Shadow Man**": It made the short list for the *Sound + Vision* set but was apparently rejected by Bowie.

211 **Biff Rose's "The Man"**: A wonderful Pegg discovery. For example, compare Rose's "His name might be John, his name might be Christ" to Bowie's "you can call him Joe, you can call him Sam"; **B-side**: The released "Shadow Man" was slightly different from the *Toy* outtake. It was longer and had an altered string arrangement, suggesting that Visconti had remixed it post-*Toy* in 2001-2002.

212 **another actor**: Tony Defries and Angela Bowie were intrigued by the idea of merchandising Ziggy Stardust dolls that would say "wham bam thank you ma'am!" when you

pulled a string.

213 ***Stranger In a Strange Land***: Bowie told William Burroughs he disliked Heinlein's book as it was "too flower powery"; **Spiders From Mars**: Ziggy's band's name most likely came from a line about the mad ones who "explod[e] like spiders across the stars" from Kerouac's *On the Road,* though there were a number of Fifties SF films about invading spiders from Mars, including *Earth vs. the Spider* and *The Angry Red Planet*; **Michael Moorcock**: Moorcock's conceit was that an "Eternal Champion" figure reoccurred throughout time and space, undergoing the same adventures and meeting the same characters in different personae; he was "a latter-day Pierrot, Harlequin and Columbine." One incarnation was Jerry Cornelius, a millionaire rogue rock musician who used a needle gun to dispatch foes and siblings. Cornelius first appeared in *The Final Programme* (1968) and was played in a 1973 film adaptation by Peter Finch; ***Rise and Fall of Ziggy***: The title was possibly a nick of the Ronson-era Rats' 1967 "The Rise and Fall of Bernie Gripplestone."

214 "**out-hip those queens**": *David Bowie Is,* 181; **Lord Buckley**: He would dress as an aristocrat (sometimes in tuxedo, sometimes with pith helmet) while conversing in pseudo-beatnik jargon and giving historical figures nicknames: Gandhi was "The Hip Gahn," Einstein "The Hip Einie," Christ "The Nazz."

215 "**the kids are fed up**": Tom Hibbert, "Slade: Feel the Noize," *History of Rock,* 1983.

216 **the riff**: Played on two Ronson electric guitar tracks—in the first bar, they parallel each other but in the second they split: one establishes the chords as the other plays arpeggios (Bowie's acoustic is also low in the mix); **chromatic bass figure**: The progression's a quick shuffle, G-C-A7-D, whose bassline is a rising B-C-C#-D; **his band**: While some thought "Weird and Gilly" were nicknames for Woodmansey and

Bolder, "Gilly" at least was a former Bowie classmate at Bromley Grammar ("a rebel who told off the head," as per George Underwood). Cann, 253;

217 **Chameleon**: They cut a version in May 1971 that Pegg describes as "bass heavy and prog-inflected." It was never released; **sequencing**: "Star" and "Hang Onto Yourself" share the same G major key and, initially, the same C/G chord sequence.

218 **2/4 bar**: Often used for effect on *Ziggy Stardust* ("Hang Onto Yourself," "Rock 'n' Roll Suicide," "Soul Love").

219 "**too provocative**": ca. spring 1972 US radio interview.

220 "**oral sex**": *Musician*, July 1990; "**99 years**": could be "99 tears" or "99 days"—all of them work.

221 "**Round and Round**": There are three mixes, all of which have the same vocal take—the original B-side, the original *Sound + Vision* set and the reissued *Sound + Vision*. A fine example of diminishing returns; **almost titled album**: Worked as a pun on how an LP goes, like the Beatles' *Revolver*.

223 "**Song For Marc**": In his performances of "Lady Stardust" at the Rainbow Theater in August 1972, Bowie sang with Bolan's face projected on a screen behind him. Bowie demoed it just before T. Rex's first UK #1, "Hot Love"; **discreet backdrop**: Woodmansey's rationed to one cymbal crash for each verse. Otherwise he just marks the third beat of each bar on his snare, joined by a tambourine shake in refrains; **E major/minor**: Also a reverse move from "Soul Love" (which replaced Em with E in refrains); "**drag transgresses**": Sandifer, *3*, 212; **Oscar Wilde**: Pegg, 133. Referencing "the Love that dare not speak its name" from his 1894 poem "Two Loves," introduced as evidence at Wilde's indecency trials of the following year.

224 **Ronson translated**: So instead of playing an A chord, Ronson plays an A#11 and an A bass note doubled by

Bolder. Coming full circle, Bowie sang the intro melody again on a 1997 BBC broadcast, the only time he performed "Lady Stardust" without piano; **fleeting notes**: Tellingly he double-tracked these lines to shore them up. The highest note in the song is the C that opens the bridge ("*Oh!* how I sighed"); **infestation**: "I was in love once, maybe, and it was an awful experience. It rotted me, drained me, and it was a disease. Hateful thing, it was," Bowie, *Playboy*, September 1976.

225 **harmonies**: So on "eyes" or "sleep" it's a high G (backing vocals: "soul"), a D (Bowie's "eyes") and Ronson (and Trevor Bolder) playing a root G note; **progression**: "Soul Love" compresses the "Five Years" Gm-Em-A-C sequence, the verses G-Em-C until closing with a shuffle of Bm-Amsus4-D; **bassline**: Close to the baión bassline of "Stand By Me." The rhythm proved too subtle to replicate live, with a rhythm guitar typically playing a supplementary riff; **saxophone**: Bowie's saxophone shifts in and out of being double-tracked, sometimes in the same bar. While gamely playing the solo live in 1973, he gave it to Roger Powell's synthesizer for his 1978 tour; **Ronson**: His 1975 country-ska remake, "Stone Love," was included on reissues of his *Play Don't Worry*.

226 **terminal prognosis**: Bowie dispelled some of the mystery in a 1973 *Rolling Stone* interview, where he said the world was ending because of "a lack of natural resources"; "**hopelessness**": *Inside Bowie and the Spiders*. Bowie typically had Woodmansey come up with drum patterns but here he told him to avoid using toms, likely inspired by the snare-kick intro of Sweet Thursday's "Gilbert Street" (1969). When Dennis Davis played "Five Years" live with Bowie in 1976 and 1978, he loosened the pattern with scads of tom fills; ***Doomwatch***: An episode that aired on 22 March 1971, "Public Enemy," had as its tagline in the *Radio Times*: "at the

rate we're going...at the rate we're polluting...we've got 30 years. 30 years of slow, dirty dying."

227 **Khmer Rouge**; *The Ecologist*, July 1975; "**mocking angle**," CSM, *NME*, 22 July 1972: **poem**: Some T.S. Eliot, too ("A crowd flowed over London Bridge, so many/ I had not thought death had undone so many" to Bowie's "I never thought I'd need so many people"); **jazz/pop sequence**: The "Heart and Soul" progression's usually I-vi-ii-V, "Five Years" is I-vi-II-IV. Bowie's using a major II chord (A) and closing with the IV chord (C), adding a bit more shadow and tentativeness. The V chord (D) barely appears in his verse/refrains and then as a quick means to get home to G major ("I (D) saw/(G)boys!") (thanks: Mark Milano).

228 **autoharp**: Live in 1972, Bowie replicated this by making a slow upstroke on his 12-string acoustic.

229 "**Wham Bam Thank You Man**": The B-side of the last Small Faces single. As Laird Galbraith noted, one line in the Faces' song ("she was good to those who took off all their clothes and played guitar") is yet another Ziggy Stardust influence, as the line sounds like as "put on holy clothes and played guitar."

230 **structure**: A strut in A major, the song's built on ascending major chord sequences (A-F-G in the verses, A-D-F, C-G in the refrain), with the E major dominant chord only appearing to tease out the fake ending; "**piece of sponge**": Scott, 155; "**terrorist**": "David Bowie Story." Bowie opened most "Ziggy Stardust" shows with *ACO*'s Moog Beethoven's 9th, arranged by Wendy Carlos.

231 **Fifties ballad**: "It wasn't obviously a '50s pastiche, even though it had that rhythm that said total '50s. But it actually ends up as being a French chanson. That was purposeful. I wanted that blend, to see if that would be interesting." Bowie, *Performing Songwriter*, Sept. 2003; **inspired lines**: Edith Piaf's "Non, Je Ne Regrette Rien" is also in the refrain.

The opening lines, in which time takes cigarettes and tugs on your fingers, is possibly from the Spanish poet Manuel Machado's *"Tonás y livianas"*:"Life is a cigarette…some smoke it in a hurry." (Pegg),

232 **saxophones**: Scott said the ARP also was used on this track (see "Suffragette City"), possibly mixed with the saxophones.

233 **wrenching move**: An A major ("make you care") collides into a D-flat minor ("no, love!"). The next modulation's smoother, a Db (VII) chord ("the pain") converts into the tonic of the next key, Db major**; D-flat**: A chord far, in terms of distance on the "circle of fifths," from the first chord heard on the album, the autoharp/piano G major that opened "Five Years." (Matthew-Walker.)

234 "**all worthwhile**": "Let the children lose it...let all the children boogie" parodies Christ's allowance to "suffer the little children, and forbid them not, to come unto me" (Matthew 19:14, often translated as "Let the children come to me"). It furthers the sense *Ziggy Stardust*'s mocking "hippie Christ" musicals; **Von Däniken**: His most popular book was *Chariots of the Gods*? (1968), source waters of documentaries like *In Search of Ancient Astronauts* (1973). Many of his claims first appeared in another Bowie favorite, *The Morning of the Magicians* (1960) and in the works of H.P. Lovecraft.

235 "**Starman in Ward 7**": *New Worlds* 146, January 1965; **guitar/piano hook**: A piano and electric guitar mixed together, then run through a Countryman phaser. Each plays runs of A octaves. There were two mixes made of "Starman," one of which (used in British pressings) is much louder on the "telegraph" sections. Other inspirations include Blue Mink's "Melting Pot" and the Five Americans' "Western Union"; **major sevenths**: The subdominant (IV) and home chords of the F major key; **Ronson's solo**: Jesse

Gress, "10 Things You Gotta Do to Play Like Mick Ronson," *Guitar Player*, December 2008.

236 "**detached from everything**": *Autobiography*, 62.

Chapter 6

238 **Nicky Graham**: The pianist of the first leg of the Ziggy Stardust tour, although it sounds like he's taken five on circulating recordings of "Got to Have a Job"; **Toby Jug**: Described as "a gaunt fortress of a pub" by the Gilmans (342), though period photographs of it document a rather stately-looking establishment. Located just off the A3, it was leveled a decade ago, its site now being considered for development by Tesco.

239 "**no drag act**": *MM*, 19 Feb 1972; "**Around and Around**": The Imperial College gig review listed a cover of Berry's "Reelin' and Rockin'" but I'd venture this was a misidentified "Around and Around" as there's no record of Bowie ever playing "Reelin'" again; **James Crawford**: His single (Mercury 72441), titled "If You Don't Work, You Can't Eat," was credited to Nat Jones, Brown's band director, and "Ted Wright," Brown's regular pseudonym. The remake was credited to Brown and his trumpeter Waymon Reed; **James Brown**: A Parisian newspaper called Bowie and the Lower Third "des disciples de James Brown" in a preview of their Golf Drouot shows in December 1965.

240 "**I Feel Free**": A concert recording from Kingston Polytechnic appeared on *RarestOneBowie*, a semi-official 1995 release by Bowie's former management company MainMan; **live**: Bowie's recollection in 1993 that the Spiders had only played the song "once" is inaccurate, however, as several 1972 concert recordings feature it, the latest extant being Preston, 6 June.

241 **Ronson's solo**: Apparently a late inclusion, as Bowie's then-current guitarist Reeves Gabrels had originally cut a solo for

"I Feel Free," which was erased in favor of Ronson's.

242 ***Treatise on White Magic***: Reed mentioned the book in a November 1969 interview with KVAN. He'd been exploring a Japanese form of healing in Los Angeles that's "a way of giving off white light…I've been involved and interested in what they call white light for a long time." Rob Norris, a post-Reed member of the VU, recalled Reed "being a member of the Church Of Light in New York, which studied Bailey's work as part of its theosophical teachings." (Unterberger, *WL/WH,* 161). Dave Davies also was a Bailey advocate, quoting from *White Magic* in his autobiography.

243 **Reed into his sphere**: A Bowie roadie recalled seeing Reed in tears after a Rainbow gig, saying "I've never heard my music played so beautifully before"; "**Boy, Ronson's good**": *Classic Albums: Transformer.* Bowie was rumored to have co-written *Transformer*'s "Wagon Wheel," yet as a tape exists of Reed playing an instrumental "Wagon Wheel" in New York in 1971, a time when he'd only met Bowie once at a nightclub, Bowie's contributions may have just been secondary touches, like the "spoke-spoke" backing vocals.

245 **heckler**: After Bowie said "it's a bit boring at the end: it needs something else," Hunter recalled some things he'd said while pouring beer over a heckler's head at the Rainbow Theatre. (*Uncut,* January 2008); **secession**: Marc Bolan was allegedly irritated by "who needs TV when I got T. Rex," while Tony Visconti once wondered whether the initials were a dig at him (as Bowie would've normally said "telly"); **last great album**: *Mott,* 1973. Aptly described as being "as split-prone as some late-'70s left faction" by Charles Shaar Murray, Mott cracked up soon afterward; **soon sinks**: The refrain, initially in D major, falls to C major. For his take, Bowie lowered the key, moving the refrain to B-flat major, a move triggered by a G minor chord (the first "news"), followed by a new tonic, B-flat ("boogaloo").

Bowie fights his way back to C major via a 3/4 bar of F-Bb-G.

246 **the single**: Bowie quickly came up with a replacement line for "Marks and Sparks" (slang for the retailer Marks & Spencer) once it was clear the BBC wouldn't play the song due to the line possibly being construed as an advertisement.

247 "**I'm gay**": *MM*, 22 January 1972. Chris Charlesworth, *MM*'s news editor at the time, told Spitz that "the gayness didn't put us off [Bowie]. We covered him fairly intensely because having him on the front page sold papers"; "**the spice**": "David Bowie: The Gender Bender," *The Face*, November 1980; "**Gay liberation**": Bowie expanded on this point to CSM (*NME*, 24 Feb 1973), saying he feared that "so many [gay] people all together at once is perfect, *perfect* meat for the papers to pick upon and ridicule" and that gays risked losing their individuality by being defined as an interest bloc. "With a bit of luck [being gay] will become part of society."

248 "**the one taboo**": Tony Parsons, *Arena*, May/June 1993; "**All the Young Dudes**": "The song made us instant gays: we were tranny magnets when we played in the US. Touring with Bette Midler probably helped add to that reputation," Ian Hunter recalled (*Uncut*, 2008); **not released in US**: "Jean Genie" was written expressly as a replacement single for America.

249 **bassline**: Bolder recently had switched from a Fender Mustang to a Gibson EB-3; **recorded twice**: One take was cut at Trident on 24 June and another at Olympic two days later. Ken Scott didn't produce the latter. It's unknown from which session the single master came. Neither Scott nor Bolder knew for sure, though there's some consensus it's the Olympic take, for which members of the Faces provided handclaps (recorded in Olympic's entrance hall). The

violinist Lindsay Scott reportedly played on one take, though there's no audible violin on the single mix. The original single's identifiable by the opening acoustic guitar confined to the left channel, its remix has acoustic guitar in both channels.

250 **sax section**: Bowie told his players to think in terms of art styles ("renaissance" and "Impressionist") (Trynka, 179). "The "brass" remake, intended as an album closer for *Aladdin Sane*, was released as a single in April 1973, given the same serial number as the original single and with no indication it was a different take. This take appeared on the first pressing of *ChangesOneBowie*; "**Bowie was seismic**": Buckley, *SF*, 106; "**Queer David**": Gill, *Queer Noises*, 110; **refused to fly**: Defries exploited Bowie's legitimate fear of flying in the press to further Bowie's Garbo-esque eccentric image. In 1973, Bowie told a reporter "I won't fly because I've had a premonition I'll be killed an airplane crash if I do. If nothing happens by 1976, I'll start to fly again." His first flight post-Cyprus was in 1977.

251 **Rainbow Theatre**: Titled "The Ziggy Stardust Show," it was the only proper live production of Ziggy Stardust, as per Bowie, and an "expensive experiment" as per Tony Defries, who vetoed the dancers and stage set for Bowie's first US tour. "He wanted to break us in America as a band, rather than a dance routine," Bolder said; "**dark images**": Reynolds, *Impossible Dream*, 177; "**La Mort**": Recorded for his 1959 *La Valse à Mille Temps*, Brel's "La Mort" is a loose march with a brass arrangement. Brel's taken death's measure and is sporting with him; **strum patterns**: He also uses quick-shuffle chord changes similar to those of "Space Oddity" to move into a fresh verse. He'd revive "My Death" with Mike Garson in the mid-Nineties, with luxuriant full band accompaniment.

253 **one take**: Ken Scott remixed "Jean Genie" for *Aladdin Sane*

(the Bowie-produced single was in mono); "**I'm a Man**": The tempo of "Jean Genie" is loser to the Shadows of Knight's 1966 "Oh Yeah" (itself an "I'm the Man" rip). Ronson's opening guitar salvo was close to that of the Beatles' "Revolution," his closer was from "Smokestack Lightnin'"; power chords: Ronson's often just keeping to his two lowest strings, the low E open; **Esus4**: An E major chord with a fourth interval instead of a fifth, so it's E-G#-A instead of the typical E-G#-B. The "suspense" ends typically by moving home to the E chord or finding another way to bring in the dominant tone (B, here: it's why the B major chorus packs a wallop). Progressions of alternating suspended chords with major counterparts are common: *e.g.*, "Pinball Wizard." Here the Esus4's established by one rhythm guitar playing an A power chord and Bolder an A bass note; **squalling harmonica**: Though derided by critics for his harp playing, Bowie kept at it, soloing on "Jean Genie" as late as 2003.

254 "**American primitive**": "Golden Years." Another (conscious/subconscious) inspiration was Eddie Cochran's "Jeannie Jeannie Jeannie," a 1961 UK hit.

255 **UK #1 albums of 1972**: *20 All Time Hits of the 50s* and *25 Rockin' and Rollin' Greats* ruled the top of the album charts for the last three months, holding off *The Slider* and *Ziggy Stardust*, among others; "**unfit for life**": Matt, *Homesickness*, 7.

256 **overnight train ride**: Hence its "Seattle-Phoenix" parenthetical. When Bowie debuted the song live he said he'd written it on a train ride from "LA to Chicago" and "Chicago to here (Miami)." If so, he may have had his vision while sitting in the "Vista-Dome" viewing car, a carriage of the California Zephyr train with a Plexiglas roof. Bowie and friends had spent much of the evening there when traveling by rail to California; **silver domes**: They may have been civilian domes. Domes were popular in the counterculture

as ecological-friendly communal housing, inspired by Buckminster Fuller's designs (175,000 copies were sold of *Domebook II,* a 1971 instructional manual). The dome vogue quickly faded once dome-dwellers discovered the structures were "hot in summer, cold in winter and prone to leaking" (Binkley, 191); "**year 2033**:" Miami concert, 17 November 1972; "**reproductive organs**": Howard Bloom, *Circus,* July 1973; "**strange ones**": The 1972 British film *ZPG (Zero Population Growth)* features a polluted, overpopulated Earth that's barred breeding for a generation, with women given mechanical baby dolls in lieu of children. (David Dent); "**ravers**": Mick Farren: "Ravers were...vicarious quasi-Bohemians who wore bowler hats and baggy black sweaters and danced to bad Dixieland jazz with a peculiar skipping motion...they were beneath our contempt"; "**orgy**": Coward, *Diaries,* 4 July 1965 (Coward saw the Beatles in Rome on 28 June); **glum versions**: Bowie sang it as an acoustic guitar ballad in a few of his 1974 concerts.

257 "**If There Is Something**": Bowie considered covering it and "Ladytron" on *Pin Ups,* later recording the former with Tin Machine in 1989; **A major**: While the verses have an altered "doo-wop" progression (A-F#m-Amaj7-E, or I-vi-Imaj7-V) and the IV chord, D major, rules the pre-chorus, the refrain could be in G major, C major or a muddle of the two keys, a situation further complicated by the occasional C major chord with a G root note; **"Jung the foreman**": A play on Carl Jung but also a possible nod to Thomas Pynchon's *V,* where "Bung the foreman" is the despised supervisor of the Alligator Patrol. Other lyrical references include the New York Dolls' Sylvain Sylvain (Bowie in turn inspiring David Sylvian's stage name) and the Astronettes, the name Bowie gave Lindsay Kemp's dance troupe and which he'd soon bestow on Ava Cherry's soul trio; **Ronson's guitars**: One of which is in drop D tuning (*i.e.,* the guitar's lowest string is

tuned to D instead of E). The 12-string acoustic in the refrain is capoed at the 12th fret.

258 **live record**: A few US shows were taped with this intention, including Boston and the oft-bootlegged Santa Monica gig, with the latter released in 1994. The idea went far enough along for George Underwood to draft an LP cover; **erratic itinerary**: While Bowie could sell out NYC and LA, shows in "second tier" cities sold poorly, mainly because Defries had shunned the established method of breaking UK acts in America: opening for larger acts to build a national rep. Defries said Bowie would only headline shows, which was a problem when no one in Kansas City knew who he was. By November, Defries had cancelled Dallas and Houston gigs due to weak ticket sales and couldn't attract other promoters. This created a half-month gap in the tour schedule and left Bowie stuck in Phoenix for six days; "**drum sound**": Buckley, *AS*; **New York Dolls**: The band had a Tuesday and Sunday residency at the Mercer Arts Center. Bowie saw them there on 19 September and likely the following Tuesday, the 26th, when he was back in town after his Memphis gig. While the party in question was reportedly after his Carnegie Hall show on 28 September, several contemporary reports have Bowie sick as a dog with flu then, so it may have been another night.

259 "**hard to tell**": Hoskyns, *Glam!*, 71. ("Everybody was festively dressed and having sex with each other": Bebe Buell's description of early Dolls concerts); "**more power**": Scott, 172. ("Hearing it today I feel that I went overboard"); ***Goats Head Soup***: Things were catching up to the Stones—during the *Soup* sessions, the producer Jimmy Miller was barely functional, spending his time carving swastikas onto the recording console, while Keith Richards once tried to play a guitar solo on a bass and didn't realize his mistake for 15 minutes; **volatile marriage**: The verse progression is I-IV-

V-vi (A-D-E-F#m); the "deception" is the move to the submediant (vi) chord (F#m) instead of the return to the expected tonic chord (A).

260 "**Reverend Alabaster**": Likely a joke at Bowie's skeletal/ghost-white appearance, with "alabaster" a common reference in occult books (Aleister Crowley once described Victorian Britain as "an aristocracy of alabaster").

261 **Jerry Cornelius**: "You were a guerilla. An assassin." "I've always been in show business. All my life. Promotions. Management." Moorcock, *The English Assassin*, 1972. At the 1972 Democratic National Convention, Jerry Rubin and Abbie Hoffman were tailed by policemen who'd heard rumors that a Warner Bros. camera crew was filming their adventures in Miami. Each cop wanted to be the one in the film bashing in Hoffman's head with a club. As there was no movie crew, it was a peaceful convention. Also see Camper Van Beethoven's "Tania"; **Che poster**: Gisele Bündchen wore a Che-print bikini on a Brazilian runway in 2002 and Magnum offered the "Cherry Guevara" ice cream bar in 2003 These likely have been topped in absurdity in the decade since; "**wholly intellectual**": Clutterbuck, 20; **National People's Gang**: note-perfect name, possibly derived from Maoist China's National People's Congress.

262 "**snipers**": *Musician,* 1990. Bowie recalled Pop's stories about snipers during the Detroit riots (though several identified as "snipers" in the local press turned out to be unarmed people shot on rooftops by the police). He may have conflated them with the UT shootings of 1966 ("Running Gun Blues") and the sniper killer "Scorpio" in *Dirty Harry*; **bombing runs**: Ronson's scalar drop (tracked up an octave by another guitar and down an octave by Bolder's bass) is set against two other tracks of guitar chords; the latter get the spotlight in alternating bars; **B minor**: Intro and solo are in B minor, each closes on an A

major chord to pivot to D major for verses/choruses; "**Panic In Detroit**": Bowie remade it in 1979 for the *Kenny Everett Show*. It's one of his more bizarre revisions. He sings much of it in an affected accent ("panic-innnnn..Dee-TROIT!") and plays a Speak-and-Spell in place of a guitar solo.

263 "**back room**": Edwards/Zanetta, 188; **Scientology**: Garson even tried to convert Bowie, which proved a futile effort. Mick Farren: "What a ludicrous idea, expecting David to sublimate his ego to L. Ron Hubbard's" (Trynka, 174); **hotel bill**: Estimated at $100,000 by the Gilmans but that seems too colossal a tab (half a million dollars, inflation-adjusted).

264 **Marshall amp**: A move due to "Ronson [being] particularly loud and distorted on that track and the harmonica sounded smaller than everything else," Scott, 172; **loose alliance**: Verses (F-Am-E5-D) suggest an A minor key possibly shifting to A major midway through.

265 **rainbow-haired men**: Benarde, *Stars of David: Rock 'n' Roll's Jewish Stories,* 211; **George Underwood**: He cut a demo at Advision Studios in the summer of 1971 (Cann, 219); "**senseless things**": Cann, 294; **Chuck Berry quote**: From "Reelin' and Rockin'" ("..it was 10:05/man, I didn't know if I was dead or alive").

266 **Billy Murcia**: He had an awful death, asphyxiating after being force-served coffee and plunged into a cold bath. Friends were trying to revive him after he'd chased barbiturates with champagne; "**traveling artist**": Carlin, TPL #125, *Aladdin Sane* (http://nobilliards.blogspot.com/2011/06/david-bowie-aladdin-sane.html).

267 "**left field**": Buckley, *AS*. Stride was an outgrowth of ragtime piano, in which a pianist repeated sets of bass octaves and chords with his left hand while improvising melodies and playing syncopated fills with his right, as exemplified by James P. Johnson; **foggy transition**: An opening C# diminished chord ("Time...in Quaaludes")

quickly shifts to C major as if to emphasize "demanding." A D minor ("wine") is answered by a D major ("mine"), which, serving as the secondary dominant chord of C major (it's the V chord of G, C's V chord), tugs the song into that key; **Scott's mix**: He was responsible for bringing up in the mix two bars of heavy Bowie breathing in the second verse (2:10). Bowie would gasp into his mike during live performances; **Ronson**: In the post-Ronson 1974 tour, Garson replaced the "whinnying" guitar solo and tried to top Ronson in classical quotations.

268 "**walking messes**": Bockris, *Transformer*, 204; "**absurd little jumble**": *Labels*, 40.

269 **mayfly slang**: Bryan Ferry was working the same field: see "The Bogus Man" (a phrase used repeatedly in *Vile Bodies*); "**Tale of Archais**": Crowley poem dating to 1899, just after he left university.

270 **sense of unease**: This only deepens in the verse, when the C major 9th becomes a C major 13th with a sharpened 11th, and the E suspended 2nd chord become an E minor 11th; **rhythm track**: It's unknown whether Ronson's lead guitar track, an improvised performance with heaps of fuzz, feedback and Wah-Wah, was recorded before or after Garson's solo. According to Ian Hunter's diary, Bowie played on 10 December 1972 in New York a vocal-less "Aladdin Sane," which was likely just the rhythm tracks but possibly had Ronson's solo on it; "**avant-garde artefact**": MacDonald, *Revolution*, 230.

271 **dodecuplets**: Twelve notes played in the space of eight. *Aladdin Sane: Off the Record* gamely lists the last run of notes as being in a 28:21 ratio.

272 "**On Broadway**": The 1981 compilation *ChangesTwoBowie* appends "On Broadway" and its composers to the credits of "Aladdin Sane," suggesting a copyright settlement, but the credit's never appeared again, including the 30th and 40th

anniversary editions of *Aladdin Sane*; "**Let's Spend the Night Together**": Given its live performances in late December 1972, Bowie may have cut it during the New York sessions earlier that month; **Olympic Studios**: Often said to be a drug raid, the visit was far more innocuous: Glyn Johns recalled the policemen came into the studio just to make sure everything was okay, as they'd noticed the front door left open. They wound up clacking their sticks to replace a finger-snap track. Most of the piano was likely Jack Nitzsche, with Richards playing the higher octaves.

274 ***Gone With the Wind***: Perone, 37. Ian McCulloch's "belongs to HIM" refrains on "The Killing Moon" seem a homage to "Lady Grinning Soul"; **Amanda Lear/Claudia Lennear**: Lennear's only public connection with Bowie were newspaper rumors that she'd tour with him (she never did). Bowie was so besotted by Lear that he planned a film adaptation of the Czech comic strip *Octobriana* as a starring vehicle for her. He demurred identifying his muse, writing in 2008 that the song "was written for a wonderful young girl whom I've not seen for more than 30 years. When I hear this song she's still in her 20s, of course"; Lear: Andrew Anthony, "At the Court of Queen Lear," *Observer*, 3 December 2000. Lear suggestion from Anna Bo; Paglia: *David Bowie Is*, 83; **weak LP side**: The first sequence had two remakes of older Bowie songs ("Prettiest Star," "John"), a Rolling Stones cover and the already-released "Jean Genie."

275 **progression**: It's B major if you take F# minor as a minor v chord, and G and A majors as flat VI and VIIs, respectively; "**Liszt**": Buckley, *SF*, 162.

276 **highest note**: It's mixed into electric guitar in places, possibly to cover a flaw.

277 "**total sensory overload**": CSM, *NME*, 26 May 1973; "**can't sing**": Ray Fox-Cumming, *Disc & Music Echo*, 2 June 1973.

Chapter 7

279 **Denis Blackeye**: As credited on the sleeve. Presumably the engineer Dennis MacKay. Martin Hayman noted Andy Scott engineering at least one *Pin Ups* session; **Château d'Hérouville**: A Louis XV-era castle whose owner, the composer Michel Magne, had converted it into a recording studio in 1969. Elton John, T. Rex and Pink Floyd recorded there in 1972, with both John and Marc Bolan recommending it to Bowie. One of its appeals was that recording in France was a tax loophole for British artists. Bowie would cut *Low* there in 1976.

280 **solution was obvious**: Wayne County, who had signed with MainMan, claimed he was the inspiration. In a 1993 interview with *Seconds*: "I told David I had the best idea in the world. I told him I wanted to do a whole album of all British Invasion hits. Six months later he comes out with *Pin Ups*. I was flabbergasted! When I would say anything to anyone, they would just laugh and say I was paranoid"; ***Pin Ups***: The title's one word on the original LP cover and inner sleeve, hyphenated on the original LP label, two words on the 1984 CD and 1990 Ryko CD and one word on the 1999 EMI CD reissue. Your call; ***Box of Pin-Ups***: Most of Bailey's 36 photo subjects were male (Marwick, 409: "in the age of Mick Jagger, it is the boys who are the pin-ups"), including the London gangster twins the Krays; "**an audience**": CSM, *NME*, 14 August 1973. "They dressed weeks out of date but they did all the right stuff," Bowie recalled of the Who on a 1973 promo recording made for *Pin Ups*; **British (mostly)**: Australia's Easybeats were the ringer. Bowie intended a sequel in which he would cover US bands (provisionally titled *Bowie-ing Out*).

281 **Scott Richardson**: Edwards/Zanetta, 211. Richardson was a Bowie prospect (Bowie toyed with producing a Richardson album as an American Ziggy Stardust), an old friend of the

Stooges and Angela Bowie's occasional lover; for America: Only "Friday on My Mind," "Here Comes the Night" and "Shapes of Things," and none broke the Top 10.

282 **Ken Scott was distracted**: That said, it's Scott's best Bowie production—the liveliest, brightest Bowie recording of the early Seventies. Scott wouldn't get paid until Bowie bought out Tony Defries via the "Bowie Bonds" in 1997; "**and they were gone**": Trynka, 193; "**Everything's Alright**": Released as "Everything's Al'Right," (Decca F11853), c/w "Give Your Lovin' to Me." It peaked the week of 2 May 1964; "**this thing was actually happening**": Du Noyer, *Liverpool Wondrous Place* (pp. 88-91).

283 **national hit**: It was actually the Mojos' second single. Their debut was the envy-riddled "They Say You've Found a New Baby": "they say he's got eyes like a tiger!" the singer wails about his rival, who may not exist. They could never follow it up. "[We] didn't know what it was about ["Alright"] that everyone loved. It had been so spontaneous. Now we sat around analyzing our own song." (James to Du Noyer, 91). Editions of the band (one of which had Dunbar on drums) persisted until 1967; **Bowie's cover**: Adding to the sense of *Pin Ups* being a bunch of Sixties pop fragments, "Alright" ended with an "ooooh!" and concluding major sixth that mashed up the Beatles' "It Won't Be Long" and "She Loves You."

284 **Arnold as a bluesman**: "I didn't want to be capitalizing on no Bo Diddley type of thing. But once you do something, you're stuck." Interview, Richie Unterberger (http://www.richieunterberger.com/arnold.html); "**I Wish You Would**": Vee-Jay 146, c/w "I Was Fooled," released June 1955. The Yardbirds' cover was Columbia DB 7283 c/w "A Certain Girl," released 1 May 1964.

285 "**young and white**": Clapton, *Autobiography*, 48. "In the studio, my own personal inadequacy was there for all to

see."; **Yardbirds**: Bowie did a letter-perfect imitation of Relf singing "I Wish You Would" in his audition for the Manish Boys and the song was often in their sets in 1964-65; **key shift**: The same (G to A) recently done to "Let's Spend the Night Together"; **replaced the harp riff**: The left-mixed guitar seems a replacement for a wiped harmonica track: the harp's heard once instead of guitar (1:41) in the second verse and there's a trace of it in what sounds like a botched edit at 1:55; **Michel Ripoche**: He also played trombone and tenor saxophone, and co-founded the French avant-garde jazz-pop Zoo in 1968; **dervish**: The Yardbirds liked to play out the song. See the double-rave-up version taped at the Crawdaddy Club in 1963 or one of their last concerts in 1968 with a massive Page solo that segued into Donovan's "Hey Gyp"; **Pretty Things**: Bowie was a regular at their shows in 1964-66. Their "Trippin'" (1967), with its stutter title hook, likely influenced "Changes"; "**Rosalyn**": Fontana TF 469 c/w "Big Boss Man" (UK #41), released 8 May 1964; **Viv Prince**: May said Prince, who sometimes went through a bottle of whiskey in a recording session, would "hit anything—a mike stand, a fire bucket..Drummed on the floor, on the guitars themselves." (Unterberger, *Urban Spacemen*, 16.).

286 **Johnny Dee**: May described Dee as a would-be P.J. Proby. "He was a little like Buffalo Bill, weird guy. And he swore he was half Indian, Cherokee or something." (Unterberger, *US*, 18). Bowie had met Dee in 1965, as they were both regulars at the Giaconda cafe; "**Don't Bring Me Down**": Fontana TF 509 c/w "Don't Lie to Me" (a concept single!). Peaked at #10 on 22 October 1964.

287 "**down, man**": *Cf.* "we mean it, MAN" in the Sex Pistols' "God Save the Queen." And recall John Lydon had gone to Pretty Things shows when he was 12; **in Bowie's care:** Townshend, *Who I Am*, 176. "After the show, they both said

the same thing: 'I am going to do this.' David meant he would create conceptual albums, Simon meant he was going to be a rock musician."

288 "**terribly badly**": 1966 interview clip, *The Kids Are Alright*; **universal note**: He'd taken the idea from Henry Purcell's *Fantasia Upon One Note*; Townshend's "Pure and Easy" was another response; "**I'm very selfish**": *60 Minutes* interview, 28 June 2002.

289 "**I Can't Explain**": Brunswick 05926, c/w "Bald Headed Woman," (UK # 8, US #93), released 15 January 1965; **halved in tempo**: Bowie's version is still longer than the Who's despite having cut a guitar solo, a verse and a chorus. During mixing Bowie and Scott slowed the master take down and re-recorded some instruments in the new key. Where the Who single opens E-D-A-E, Bowie's is C-Bb-F-C; **songs were doing to him**: Townshend wrote it after immersing himself in Booker T's "Green Onions," John Lee Hooker's "Devil's Jump" and Bob Dylan's *Freewheelin'*, among others. "I tried to divine what it was I was actually feeling as a result...one notion came into my head: I can't explain, I can't explain." (Townshend, 75); "**Anyway Anyhow Anywhere**": On the single (Brunswick 05935 c/w "Daddy Rolling Stone," UK #10) the title was printed without commas: very Mod. It was punctuated on *Meaty, Beaty, Big & Bouncy* and subsequent Who compilations. While appearing as one word on the sleeve of *Pin Ups*, on the LP label its title not only had commas, it now ended in a question mark.

290 "**guitar sounds like a machine gun**": *Guitar World*, October 1994.

291 **taste for recycling**: Berns didn't just steal from his own records—he loved to reuse the chords of "Guantanamera"; "**Here Comes the Night**": Issued as Decca F 12094, c/w "All For Myself." Lulu's was Decca F 12017 (credited to

"Russell," one of Berns' pseudonyms).

292 **without his producer**: Due to the ongoing royalty fight with Ken Scott, the Lulu single was a sole MainMan production. So Scott had to set the recording levels and leave the studio before anyone played a note.

293 "**Where Have All the Good Times Gone**": Pye 7N 15981, released November 1965 (UK #8). Bowie added the question mark; **broke, feuding and blacklisted**: Davies felt he was being ripped off by his managers and producers: he'd "written five major hit singles...but apart from a salary of £40 a week, I had no real money." (*X-Ray*, 261). Bowie would soon empathize. The Kinks were unofficially banned from playing the US after they'd appeared on TV without paying dues to the American Federation of Television and Recording Artists. They were blacklisted by the union for the rest of the decade; "**Tired of Waiting for You**": Van Halen covered "Where Have All the Good Times Gone?" on their 1982 *Diver Down*, where David Lee Roth sounded like a malicious wedding toastmaster—onstage, he'd roll his eyes while singing "will this depression last for long." They were as much inspired by Bowie's take as the Kinks original, using Bowie's edits (trimming a refrain after the second verse) while Eddie Van Halen took up Ronson's use of the "Tired" riff.

294 "**Friday On My Mind**": Released as UP 1157, c/w "Made My Bed; Gonna Lie In It," peaked the week of 17 December 1966. Hit #16 in the US; **scribbles in the margins**: there's one unmistakable "feel like fucking you" in Bowie's best Dracula voice. He also gasps out "poor man, beggarman, thief!" after "working for the rich man."

295 **arrangement**: While there's a low-mixed keyboard on the Easybeats single, Bowie didn't use Mike Garson for this track; "**heard I was doing this thing**": Buckley, *Thrill of It All*, 145. Sandford is the source of the "rip off" and possible

injunction, while Edwards/Zanetta claimed Bowie told Scott Richardson he wanted "to get a jump on Ferry." An apparent compromise was that *These Foolish Things* came out two weeks before *Pin Ups* (5 October and 19 October 1973, respectively).

296 **ready-mades**: A term coined by Marcel Duchamp ca. 1916 for a mass-produced object on which an observer bestows the title of art, whether by displaying it formally or by giving it a new name (*e.g.*, Duchamp's repurposed urinals); "**grand camp gestures**": "Bryan Looks Back," *The Monthly*, May 2007; **Goldstein**: They'd written "My Boyfriend's Back" and, as their fake Australian group the Strangeloves, "I Want Candy"; **three chords**: "Sorrow" mostly clings to its tonic G major, only venturing to the IV chord, C, on the title line, while the V chord (D) only appears on the first "oh!" in the miniscule bridge; **Merseys**: Fontana TF 694 (UK #4). The Merseys were a reduction of their earlier group, the Merseybeats. An earlier version of the Merseys' "Sorrow" was performed by a hard-rock supergroup: Jack Bruce, Jimmy Page and John Paul Jones.

297 "**Shapes of Things**": Columbia DB 7848, c/w "You're a Better Man Than I" (UK #3, US #11), released 25 February 1966.

298 **violin line**: It's likely Michel Ripoche was one of the violin players; particularly the lead violinist in the first verse.

299 "**See Emily Play**": Columbia DB 8214 c/w "Scarecrow" (UK #6), released Bloomsday 1967. Syd Barrett had intended the song to commemorate the Floyd's May 1967 "Games For May" concert but he altered the lyric upon meeting 15-year-old Emily Young, a student at the Holland Park Comprehensive School who frequented "underground" concerts; "**a warning to himself**": Palacios, *Dark Globe*, 230. Barrett's lyric also referenced Shelley's "The Song of Asia"; **creative predecessor**: Bowie had been inspired by Barrett's

singing voice, with its uncloaked English accent, and his shambling stage appearances, which became the germ of glam (Barrett was the first man Bowie ever saw wearing make-up on stage).

300 **analog trickery**: The "Hawaiian" guitar appearing midway through the verses in the Floyd single was just Barrett playing bottleneck guitar, with a bit of echo and distortion, and speeding it up an octave. Barrett also scraped a plastic ruler on his fretboard for one overdub.

301 "**just my la-la-ing,**" Hayman, *Rock*, 8 October 1973; "**incomplete track called 'Zion'**": CSM, *NME*, 14 April 1973. He was possibly referring to another track, as it wasn't unusual for Bowie to swap provisional titles around (*cf.* "The Man Who Sold the World").

302 "**when we split**": Ben Fisher, "But Boy Could He Play Guitar," *Mojo*, October 1997.

303 "**great technician**": Mick Rock, *Music Scene*, September 1973; "**Stockhausen or whoever,**" *Mojo*, 1997; "**I don't want a band**": Michael Benson, "This Band Will Be a World Beater," *Disc*, 20 October 1973.

304 "**He got too flummoxed**": *Mojo*, 1997; "**Io vorrei...**": It was from Battisti's *Il Mio Canto Libero*, a top-selling Italian pop album in late 1972. Ronson covered another Italian song, "Io Me Ne Andrei," on *Play Don't Worry* (as "Empty Bed"); "**guy in the 1980s**": CSM, *NME*, 29 September 1973.

Chapter 8

308 **extraterrestrial on TV**: In a 1993 interview, Bowie said that for his *Cher* appearance he'd desperately wanted not to seem theatrical, instead wanting what "people in the street wear." So he went to Sears before the taping to buy a "regular" suit; ***Midnight Special***: MainMan convinced its producer Burt Sugarman to devote the entire broadcast to Bowie. The UK didn't get the program: for British fans, it

was the start of Bowie seemingly abandoning the UK for America.

309 **Marianne Faithfull**: Bowie considered Faithfull, who was starring in the play *Mad Dog* in London in fall 1973, for his *Nineteen Eighty-Four* musical (presumably as the female lead, Julia). She also sang a blissed-out "As Tears Go By" and "20th Century Blues" during the *Floor Show*. A heroin addict and suffering from anorexia, Faithfull lived on the Soho streets for a time in the early Seventies; "**love redeems everything**": Marsh, *Heart of Rock 'n' Soul*, 160.

310 "**Growin' Up**": Ryko claimed "Growin' Up" was from the *Pin Ups* sessions, almost certainly an error. It's possible Ron Wood's lead guitar and other overdubs were recorded in January-February 1974 at Studio L Ludolf Machineweg, Hilversum, Netherlands, where both Bowie and the Stones were recording; **"so cringe-making"**: Scott Isler, "David Bowie Opens Up a Little," *Musician*, August 1987.

311 "**It's Hard to be a Saint**": Rykodisc listed the track as from the *Station to Station* sessions of late 1975 but much of the recording is likely from two years earlier. Members of the Illustrated DB board confirmed the track was a) not recorded for *Station to Station*, as per producer Harry Maslin and b) doesn't have Carlos Alomar on it and wasn't cut in the *Young Americans* sessions of August 1974, as per Alomar. The only viable period remaining is the Astronettes/*Diamond Dogs* era of late 1973, when Bowie was obsessed with Springsteen's debut LP (cutting two other songs from it at the time). The piano is unmistakably Mike Garson and the guitars are most likely Bowie and/or Mark Pritchett (with a chance that Earl Slick cut overdubs in 1974). Visconti, interviewed by Pegg, said that while a new backing track for "Saint" was indeed cut in the November 1974 sessions, the released take is earlier, likely with the "Astronettes" rhythm section of Herbie Flowers and Aynsley Dunbar. Bowie's

vocal is the last piece of the puzzle: was it recorded during *Young Americans* or, to close the loop, around the time of *Station to Station*?

312 "**mythic urban grease scene**": In Sinclair's vicious pan of *Born to Run* (Sanford, *Point Blank*, 78). "After I heard this track I never rode the subway again… it's called 'Saint In the City.' That really scared the living ones out of me, that," Bowie said on Radio One, May 1979. He also said he didn't care for Springsteen's new record at the time, *Darkness at the Edge of Town*; **strings**: The strings on Bowie's bridge are close to those on the bridge of "Born to Run" ("beyond the palace, hemi-powered drones..."). Was Bowie's string arrangement done after *Born to Run*'s release in August 1975, or did Bowie and Visconti predict Springsteen's? The latter's possible, as the strings could be adapting the piano line on Springsteen's original "Saint"; **living out his myths**: "Bruce is stylishly attired in a stained brown leather jacket with about seventeen zippers and a pair of hoodlum jeans. He looked like he just fell out of a bus station, which he had," Mike McGrath, *The Drummer*, Nov. 1974.

313 "**what do I say to normal people?..chickening out**": *Musician*, 1987; **Roxy Theatre**: The BBC's Bob Harris noticed Bowie and George Harrison talking during Springsteen's opening number but "three songs in they were hooting and hollering along...Bruce left that gig a superstar. We knew it, he knew it and from their faces, Bowie and Harrison knew it too." Sandford, *Point Blank*, 108.

314 **Astronettes**: From a line in "Drive-In Saturday": **Jason Guess**: Little's known about him, not even if that was his real surname (he's also been listed as Jason Guest, Carter and Cross). He and Bowie had a mutual friend who "ran a soul food restaurant," as per Ava Cherry; **Astronettes material**: By mid-January it was made clear to Bowie that his time at Olympic was limited (he risked a permanent

ban) due to the studio's ongoing struggle to get paid by MainMan. So he pulled the plug on the Astronettes and got down most of the basic tracks of *Diamond Dogs* in a few days; **later albums**: 12 rough mixes of Astronettes tracks were issued on a MainMan CD in 1995.

315 ***Freak Out***: The Astronettes version is based on the *Freak Out* original, not Zappa's remake on *Ruben & the Jets*; **Astronettes compositions**: Bowie's credited as songwriter on four Astronettes songs. "Having a Good Time" and "Only Me" have no listed composer, falling under Copyright Control. Ava Cherry recalled singing a developing version of "Having a Good Time" for Mick and Bianca Jagger, so was it a Bowie/Cherry composition? I'm comfortable assigning some of it to Bowie. The MacCormack-sung "Only Me," reminiscent of a Todd Rundgren Sixties homage, is a tougher call: it could well be a sole MacCormack composition; **Joe Cuba**: Bowie loved Cuba's early Seventies records, especially *Bustin' Out*. Both Cuba and Santana had recorded "Oye Como Va," an obvious influence on "Things to Do."

316 **string arrangement**: Though credited to Luis Ramirez on the 1995 CD, the arrangement sounds like Visconti's work (and Visconti had scored the Astronettes' "God Only Knows"); **worst excuses for a lyric**: Some of its clunky tastelessness was owed to Bowie's promiscuous use of cut-up, here done to William Burroughs' *The Wild Boys*, as "driving in my Duesenberg" likely references the Duesenberg the Boys drive around in the novel's "And Bury the Bread Deep In the Sty" section; **Sigma Sound**: The version of "Laser" described here was recorded at Sigma on 13 August 1974; it's unknown if there were other takes made. *The Gouster* was one of the working titles for *Young Americans*, suggesting that "Laser" was in contention for making the LP at one point.

318 **first release**: The date of release is 24 April 1974 as per most Bowie references but Cann's *Any Day Now* shifts it to 31 May 1974. As there's a front-page ad in the 11 May 1974 issue of *Billboard* noting *Diamond Dogs* is "on record now" and the LP's reviewed in the 25 May 1974 *Billboard*, this argues for a mid-May release, at least in the US. Given this vagueness, I'll stick with the traditional release date; "**Socialist with communist leanings**": Edmonds, *Circus*, 27 April 1976; "**stone cold version...out of your gourd**": "David Bowie Story," 1993.

319 **Sonia Brownell Orwell**: Disparaged by some in the UK literary world (and later in the rock 'n' roll world), Brownell had run several literary journals, including Cyril Connolly's *Horizon*, and was greatly responsible for Orwell's postwar reputation, editing his *Collected Essays*, among a host of other things. She died almost penniless in 1980 after a legal battle. (The book to read is Hilary Spurling's *The Girl From the Fiction Department*.) Soon after her death the Eurythmics wrote "Sexcrime (1984)" for Michael Radford's film adaptation of the novel, both of which probably would have appalled her.

320 "**staring at us**": Musel, "Rail Journey Through Siberia," UPI, 1973; "**who's controlling this damned world**": Roy Hollingworth, *MM*, 12 May 1973.

321 "**chain smoking**": Wheen, *Strange Days*, 61. A few weeks later, the *Spectator* editorialized that "Britain is on a Chilean brink." Other alarmists included Secretary of State for the Environment Geoffrey Rippon, who said Britain was on course to be a new Weimar Germany, and Tony Benn, who speculated whether an army exercise at Heathrow "[w]as a way to get people used to tanks and armed patrols on the streets of London"; "**Dodo**": Its working title was "You Didn't Hear It From Me."

322 **knotty progression**: Bridges include a Bb chord (pivoting

between being the VI chord of D minor and the V chord of Eb) and a G minor chord that closes the Eb bridge and swings the song back into D minor (it's the IV chord of the latter); "**black funky**": Trynka, 197.

324 "**please savior**": A reference to Orwell's novel, in which a woman swoons "My Saviour!" upon seeing Big Brother; **D major refrains**: Accomplished simply by altering the Bm-F#m-A sequence of the verse (i-v-VII in B minor) to Bm-G-A in the refrains (vi-IV-V in D major).

325 "**Mr. Apollo**": "Follow!/Mr. Apollo!/Everybody knows he's the greatest benefactor of mankind!"

326 "**naked feet and tom-toms**": Orwell, *Nineteen Eighty-Four,* 11-17; **12-bar sequence**: You could also read this as 6/4, 5/4, 5/4, 6/4, 5/4, 6/4. There's a harmonic logic to the shifting time signatures: the 2/4 bar (or the start of each 5/4 bar) is always on the home chord, A major, while the 3/4 bars shuffle chords, like the opening E-D-G-D run or the concluding E-C-A-D-G, the latter sequence ending on a flatted VII chord (G major) to hook into the next repeat. When covering "Chant," the Wedding Present moved to 4/4 with a 2/4 transition bar between sequence repeats.

327 **title**: Just before Winston Smith and Julia are arrested, Smith has a vision of the "proles" (the working class of the novel) being the "immortals" of history while the failed revolutionaries like him are the dead; **Brion Gysin**: An American poet who lived in Paris, he said the inspiration for his "First Cut-Ups" (1960) came when he used a Stanley blade to cut through a pile of newspapers, then pieced together the "raw words" he found.

328 **cut-up**: another of Bowie's borrows from Mick Jagger, who'd used cut-up in 1971 for *Exile on Main St.* lyrics (*e.g.*, "Casino Boogie"); "**first thought**": Ginsberg took the phrase from his talks with the poet Chogyam Trungpa; "**fuck-me pumps**": One of the first recorded usages (originally referring to a

style of strapped, wedge-heeled shoe favored by Joan Crawford) in the English language. (Sheidlower, *The F-Word*, 151); **I Ching**: Bowie would throw the I Ching while making *Tonight* in 1984 as a way to determine if a mix was done. Burroughs, in a 1976 lecture, said "when you experiment with cut-ups over a period of time, you find that some of the cut-ups and rearranged texts seem to refer to future events...when you cut into the present, the future leaks out."; **nebulous key**: The sequence is Fm/Gb/F/Ab/Gm, suggesting a key of F minor or a C minor sequence governed by an absent tonic chord.

329 **chords**: MacCormack had been toying with a progression on Bowie's piano at Oakley St.; Bowie took it from there. The verse progression is a pinball-like movement from a major VI chord (A, "always wanted") to the ii chord (Dm, "surroundings") to the dominant (G7, "room to rent") before finally falling home to C ("lizards lay"). The pre-chorus shades into A minor with a climactic collision of D minor and major ("tens of thousands found me in demand"). Bowie's refrain, C-Em-F-C (I-iii-IV-I) is a salt-of-the-earth diatonic progression (same as the Band's "The Weight"); "**change every night**": Craig Copetas, "Beat Godfather Meets Glitter Mainman," *Rolling Stone*, 28 February 1974.

330 "**doing it to me. Stop it**.": Robert Hilburn, *MM*, 14 September 1974; **on stage**: A version of "Rock 'n' Roll With Me" recorded in Philadelphia and included on *David Live* was released as a North American single (PB 10105) in September 1974, rushed out to compete with Donovan's cover. Neither single charted.

331 **Queen**: Their first appearance on *Top of the Pops* in February 1974 occurred because Bowie's promo film for "Rebel Rebel" didn't reach the BBC in time for broadcast; "**great scenes die**": Hoskyns, 101. The last nail in glam's coffin was

in summer 1975, when the production team of Mike Chapman and Nicky Chinn split (Chapman moving, like Bowie, to seek his fortune in the US).

332 **progression**: Bowie backs into establishing the A major key, keeping on the IV and V chords (D and E) and withholding the tonic (A) until a minute into the song. In the bridge, a B minor ("you tacky thing") adds a slight wrinkle; **lead riff**: For the last segment, move from an open low E string to the B string on the 2nd fret. The riff chords? The 1974 sheet music has D/D-A-E for every two bars; *Definitive Collection For Guitar* has it Dadd9-A-E/E. Other guitarists suggest Dsus2 (or Dsus4)-E-E6 as the sequence; "**want it to sound like the Stones**": Buckley, *DD*. Parker told Trynka he added a "particular chord shape" (possibly the first, shortened E chord) as well as the "beeong" bend at the end of the chorus. Bowie also credited Parker with the last three notes of the riff. "I've got this riff and it's a bit Rolling Stonesy—I just want to piss Mick off a bit," Parker recalled Bowie saying (*Uncut*, April 2014).

333 **Bowie's voice**: On the handwritten lyric sheet, you can see Bowie decide on perspectives: "they put you down" was crossed out for "put *me* down," which in turn was crossed out, Bowie going back to "put you down"; **4 1/2 minutes**: The original UK single was shorter (4:22) than the LP version, with a slightly different mix: it wasn't reissued until a Record Store Day promo 7" in 2014 (it's this mix, whose master tape was lost, that bootlegs have misidentified as "Mix 1" or an acetate). An Australian EP had a shorter edit (4:06) and then there's the US/Canada remake single described in the entry.

334 **Burroughs**: "screams of pain and pathos and screams plain pathetic, copulating cats and outraged squawk of the displaced bullhead, prophetic mutterings of brujo in nutmeg trance, snapping necks and screaming

mandrakes..." (*Naked Lunch*, 191).

335 **"worked 'cos we said it worked"**: Sheff, 197; ***Something Wicked This Way Comes***: p. 92. Noted by a commenter known as "ledge."

336 **least-successful single**: Released (RCA APBO 0293, c/w "Holy Holy") in June 1974; **"It's Only Rock 'n' Roll"**: A locus of speculation. Bowie's been rumored to have sung on the Stones track and also to have co-written it with Ron Wood, though there's no concrete evidence he had anything to do with it.

337 "**glitter apocalypse**": Sandford, 120. Bowie may coined "diamond dogs" via reading the novel: "wild boys in the streets whole packs of them vicious as famished dogs" (*Wild Boys*, 50.); **packs of feral kids**: "They'd taken over this barren city, this city that was falling apart...They had snaggle-teeth, really filthy, kind of like vicious Oliver Twists. It was a take on, what if those guys had gone malicious, if Fagin's gang had gone absolutely ape-shit?…they were all little Johnny Rottens and Sid Viciouses, really," "David Bowie Story," 1993; "**paranoid refugee of New York**": Charlesworth, *MM*, 13 March 1976. See any random viewing of films from the early Seventies. The locations of Hal Ashby's *The Last Detail* (1973), a guided tour of a blighted East Coast, don't look that much different than the zombie-plagued Los Angeles of *The Omega Man* (1971).

338 **Dylan**: The most Dylanesque phrasings are in the verse ("silicone HUUMP and your ten-inch STUUMP"); **no-frills progression**: The intro (A5-C5-Eb5-Bb5-F) feints at being in F major but an A bass note in the F chord grounds the song in A. The refrain (D5-A5-B5-A5) throws a curveball with a B5 chord (the V chord of A major's dominant, E); **1 &3s**: See Ginger Baker's drums on "Sunshine of Your Love" for another example; **distorted**: Visconti used a Keypex, a device that allowed you to open and close an audible signal,

to make Bowie "sound[] like he's gargling" in the intro, using it to "key the vocal to a 20-cycle-per-second oscillator tone, which created a quavering effect." (*Circus*, December 1974); "**Alternative Candidate**": Much of this entry is inspired by Momus' suggestions and speculations.

339 **detuned snare**: See the detuned bass drum on "1984," an ancestor of the Harmonized snare drum on *Low*; ***1984* musical**: On the 2004 CD reissue, its title was appended with "Demo for a Proposed Musical of 1984"; **chords**: Mainly a straight B minor sequence with a few steals from the parallel major (*e.g.*, the F# in the refrain); **Tommy Tinker**: An old nursery rhyme character ("poor little innocent guy!").

343 "**backwards and forwards**": *Uncut*, April 2014; **the suite:** The verse structure (C-D-C-D-C etc. with an E minor popping up on occasion ("from the DOOR," "trails on a LEASH") is similar to "Rebel Rebel"—two warring major chords in the eventual thrall of a minor tonic, with a B minor at the close ("center of THINGS") securing the E minor key (it's the V chord of Em); **John Rechy**: See also the Doors' "L.A. Woman": "City of night!"

Chapter 9

345 "**Knock on Wood**": A UK and European single. In the US, it was the B-side of "Young Americans."

346 ***Zinc Alloy***: When Bolan and Jones visited Bowie in LA in 1974, Bowie lectured them that American audiences needed "a Hollywood style to which they could relate" and that Bolan should consider R&B; "**it honestly**": Du Noyer, *Mojo*, July 2002.

348 **through glass**: *Young Americans* was by "somebody who watches more from outside than actually getting involved with it inside," Bowie, *ZigZag*,1978.

349 **a month later**: Possibly in late June, Bowie, Slick and Mike Garson went to Star Studios in Milwaukee to overdub D.A.

Pennebaker's film of the last Ziggy Stardust concert. Bowie had Slick recut Jeff Beck's guitar solo on "Jean Genie"; "**last big production**": *Rock,* 1974; "**rabbit foots**": Bowman, *Soulsville U.S.A.*, 99.

351 **Harwood**: The original *David Live* mix was by Eddie Kramer at Electric Ladyland. Visconti recalled Kramer "conducting" the mixing desk, throwing back his head as he moved levers on the console. Visconti improved the low end (Flowers' bass is now audible on "Rebel Rebel") and brightened the presence of instruments like the baritone saxophone on "Knock On Wood." Slick got the raw end of the deal, his guitar now sometimes confined to the margins; "**Here Today**": Bowie apparently only sang it in Philadelphia: it's possible the track was actually recorded during a soundcheck. On the 1990 reissue where it first appeared, "Here Today" was at the end of the second CD.

352 **produced**: Harry Maslin remixed all but the title track of *Young Americans* in New York in January 1975 and got a production credit for three songs ("Across the Universe," "Fame" and "Can You Hear Me"). Visconti, in his autobiography, claimed Maslin hardly altered his original mixes.

353 **session player**: Main Ingredient co-founder Tony Silvester recommended Alomar for the session. Alomar played on the Main Ingredient's *Aphrodisiac* (1973), whose "You Can Call Me Rover" has some early traces of his "Fame" riff; "**fuckin' vampire**": Buckley, *SF,* 193; **touring guitarist**: Alomar turned him down because the wage Tony Defries offered, $250 a week, was a substantial pay cut; **"every British musician"**: Ron Ross, *Circus Raves,* February 1975; ***On Being Negro***: A fascinating autobiography/cultural study (1951) of white supremacist America. "I have done what I have, not because I wanted to, but because, driven by a daemonic force, I had to. The necessity has always been a galling affliction to me and the root of my personal

grievance with American life"; "**Carlos**": *Rock*, 1974; **Sigma Sound**: Joe Tarsia was a stickler for economy. Rather than hiring a full string ensemble, "I would use two mics on the six violins, a microphone on the [two] violas and a microphone on the cello...We always doubled the strings. Nobody moved, I threw all the phase reversal switches; we recorded the strings again, the speakers are now out of phase and the leakage cancels," he told Toby Seay. By 1974, Sigma was triple-tracking string players.

354 "**he met the guys**": Gilmans, 388; **didn't use MFSB**: There was scheduling conflict for most of the band. However, according to one source, some Sigma regulars also had reservations about working with Bowie, who they considered something of a carpetbagger. Deep Purple's Glenn Hughes, whom Bowie recently had befriended, recalled that Bowie asked him to come to Philadelphia to sing on *Young Americans* but Richie Blackmore demanded that Hughes decline; **little reverb**: This process was a relic from the Sixties, when UK studios had four-track mono consoles and engineers essentially had to produce records "live." Visconti said he tweaked the sound at Sigma to satisfy Bowie, setting up a dual-mike system to reduce instrumental spill. That said, Bowie had recorded at RCA Studios in New York in 1972 without any complaints; "**my drug problems**," Buckley, *YA*.

355 **slurred nasal phrasing**: On earlier takes, Bowie sang this line in the same tone he used for the rest of the vocal; **C major**: The verse is F-Bbmaj7-C (i-IV-V), then F-Bbmaj7-Am7-Gm7-C (I-IV-iii-ii-V). The refrain progression includes Fmaj7-G-Ab and the triumphant push to reach C major: Gm-Bb-F-C (ii-IV-I-V).

356 **on piano**: On early takes, Garson played Fender Rhodes; **David Sanborn**: On an early take of "Dancin'," possibly its first (13 August), Sanborn isn't on the track, suggesting he

was holding back while learning the song. He warmed up quickly. The outro of a 14 August take is a duel between Sanborn, Alomar and Garson on clavinet.

357 **five verses**: Bowie tweaked lines during takes: "Boogie down with Davey now" was formerly "boogie down with Eddie." He also quoted "Bang a Gong" on a 14 August take.

358 "**get on that, G!**": On the 13 August take, Garson, worked up during the outro, spun back to play Fender Rhodes for a bar and fumbled his return to clavinet; **US #28**: The US single, a brutal 3:11 edit, guts the second and fourth verses and the breakdown sequence; "**no story**": O'Grady, *NME,* August 1975.

359 "**loneliest person**": Howard Bloom, *Circus,* July 1973; ***Behind the Fridge***: Bowie had attended a performance in March 1973 (in keeping with the homonymic confusion, Peter Cook took the name of the show from an Italian waiter's malapropism of his earlier revue, *Behind the Fringe*). It was a dark show: a highlight was a skit in which Cook played a chauffeur who might be a serial killer. In some live versions, especially during the Serious Moonlight tour, Bowie would sing "bridge."

360 **White House**: Nixon had resigned the presidency a few days before Bowie recorded "Young Americans." In later live versions, Bowie changed the line to "President Reagan" and, in some performances in 1990, "President Bush" (the latter didn't scan but the crowd cheered anyway, at least in Hartford).

361 "**I peered**": *Creem,* January 1975; **first takes**: Sources including Visconti claim "Young Americans" was completed on the first night of the Sigma sessions (either August 11 or 13) but the tapes don't back this up. There were at least two takes cut on the 13th, neither of which is close to the released version (no Sanborn, no backing singers, unfinished lyric, slower tempo). A take cut on the

14th is sluggish, Bowie misses a vocal cue and the band has to get up to speed (Sanborn now joins in, developing his saxophone hook midway through); **bridge section**: This begins with Sanborn soloing over a chord progression close to the verse (Am/C, Dm7, Fmaj7, G/F). Things go askew with the bridge ("do you remember?"), which takes the A minor from the sax solo, swaps the G for an Em7 (a G chord with an E on the bottom), feints back to the verse key with a C major and then closes with an out-of-nowhere E major ("yesterday"). Thanks: Jeff Norman; "**Latin feel**," Buckley, *YA*.

362 "**go into harmony**": Barry Walters, "Soul God," *Spin*, April 1987; "**break it down**": Lawrence, *Love Saves the Day*, 113; **break**: Rather than opening with the now-expected move to A minor (it's how the sax solo and bridge began, plus the G# note in the bridge's closing E chord (E-G#-B) leads the ear to expect a move "upward" to A), the break opens with a D major chord, then veers off into E minor and ends with Alomar readying for the modulation to D major via a closing Amaj9, D's dominant chord.

363 **his rant**: In early takes, Bowie sang the last two verses in a deadpan tone, reminiscent of Lou Reed; **eBay**: Having claimed to have bought the reel in a yard sale, the seller used a Philadelphia studio to digitally convert the tape (leaked snippets were from MP3s for prospective buyers). The reel in question had "gone missing" during the transfer of tapes from Sigma Sound studio to Drexel University, which archives the Sigma tapes. Bowie's staff squelched the sale and the reel returned to Drexel, who sent it on to Bowie. Most Sigma reels have vanished, likely into the hands of collectors. *Young Americans* is one of two albums of which Bowie doesn't possess the session tapes and masters (*Station to Station* is allegedly the other).

365 **reissue**: The mix issued on Ryko's *Young Americans* CD

lacked Visconti's string arrangement. The strings mix didn't appear until a CD/DVD reissue in 2007; "**young girl**": The identification with groupies was more explicit in an earlier take, where the girl's "wearing a little glitter"; "**I'd immerse myself**": Chris Roberts, *Uncut,* October 1999.

366 **long ramble**: After appearing at the start of the verse ("Hey Jack..") and once midway through ("tried so many, many...ways"), the C major chord doesn't appear again until the final bars of the refrain, on the title phrase. Until then the song's mainly a run of IV, V and vi chords (F, G, A minor), which heightens a sense of longing and exile; **Garson**: In two takes of "It's Gonna Be Me" on 13 August, Garson's piano was recorded on a single track, where typically pianos have two tracks to cover high and low end. This suggests Garson had been on the mono Fender Rhodes for rehearsals and/or earlier takes and then switched to piano, with the engineer not catching the change at first.

367 ***Sound + Vision***: The 14 August take is marred by rocky transitions between refrains and verses and a few flubbed bass notes. My guess is the *S&V* take (chosen by Ryko over a ballad take) was cut after this one.

368 **Andy Newmark**: He once described his sound as being "either super low or super high—super bottom or super top. Everything cuts through the band. The bass drum and the floor tom are like volcanoes." *Modern Drummer,* February 1984.

369 **backing vocals**: Vandross built the arrangement piece by piece at Sigma, with Visconti offering suggestions from the control room. Vandross often brought Clark and Cherry into a free studio to work on a particular phrase or section.

370 ***Sirens of Titan***: The journey of Malachi Constant, the world's richest man and "luckiest man who ever lived," has some parallels to Bowie's Major Tom. (Thanks: Ian McDuffie); "**bundles of daydreams**": Packard, 7; "**they're**

killers": *Creem*, February 1975. Bowie credited his few months of working in advertising in 1963, which he treated as if it was a flirtation with Freemasonry, as the basis for his insights; **base cravings**: Examples included a report of subliminal images of ice cream inserted into films at a New Jersey cinema in 1956 and campaigns keyed for women at various stages of their menstrual cycles.

371 ***Privilege***: Jones' concerts start with him being locked in a cage and then freed at the show's climax, upon which the frenzied teenage audience rushes the stage to attack the police. His tours are meant to "channel the violence of youth—keep them off the streets and out of politics." Jones is later made to "convert" to the church as part of his career arc. "You can lead them into a better way of life—a fruitful conformity"; "**never see his like**": Crowe, *Playboy*, Sept. 1976. See also Steely Dan's "Chain Lightning," Nazi rally as pop concert. "Some turnout: a hundred grand!"

372 ***The Immortal***: Bowie displayed the book in *Diamond Dogs* promotional photos; "**watch out mate**": O'Grady, *NME*, 26 July 1975; **avoid any move home**: It's a run of the IV, V and secondary dominant (v-of-V) chords of A major (D, E, B). The 12-bar refrain plays a similar game. After descending twice from D to A major, a move to an F major chord (on the title phrase) kicks off eight bars' worth of avoiding A major, first via repeating the saxophone intro; "**laundromat**": *Love Train* review, Pitchfork, 26 November 2008.

374 **structure**: Bowie had sung higher in an earlier, circulating take, which also shows how he altered the structure to lessen monotony, moving the breakdown to come after the second refrain (in the earlier take, it's after three refrains) and shifting Alomar's solo to break up the third and fourth refrains.

375 **drums**: In later sessions at Sigma and the Record Plant, Ksasan replaced Weeks, while Newmark apparently

continued on drums for the last Sigma session. With no accessible studio records of these sessions, it's unknown exactly who the rhythm section is on this track, "Fascination" and "Win."; **five songs**: By 10 October, Bowie was performing "Young Americans," "John I'm Only Dancing (Again)," "Somebody Up There Likes Me," "It's Gonna Be Me," and "Can You Hear Me"; "**third rate gospel**": Gilmans, 486; **Slick**: He feared he was being edged out of a job and was only kept on because Bowie still "needed me for the rock material." Alomar adapted on stage by playing "on the top half of the guitar." Thanks to his time at the Apollo, he was used to having to fit in with three or four other guitarists. (Buckley, 212-213.); "**crazed Funkadelic**": Trynka, 221; "**I like devising shows**": CNN interview, 30 November 2002.

376 **medley**: He may have hit upon using "Sister Kate" via the line "sister May" in "Foot Stomping." Bowie also allegedly cut a take of the Forties novelty song "Too Fat Polka" (see Appendix); ***Dick Cavett***: Audio of the *Cavett* performance was released on *RarestOneBowie*, though it wasn't included in the *Cavett* footage on the *Young Americans* CD/DVD reissue. Its earliest extant live recording is from a 28 October 1974 concert at Radio City.

377 **Louis Armstrong**: Sidney Bechet and Kid Ory backed his claim. When asked about Armstrong's accusation, Piron said "that tune is older than all of us" and that Armstrong was trying to take credit for a traditional blues song (which, of course, Piron had done); **first release**: "Fascination," "Right" and "Win" were released in alternate stereo mixes on the Ryko CD reissue. A tell for the "Win" alternative mix, for example, is its intro, where Sanborn's saxophone is panned right to left.

378 "**living in the Bronx**": Seymour, *Luther*, 67; **black magic**: Bowie likely took "Fascination" from Rechy's *City of Night*,

where the word's flashing on a sign in Times Square, but he was also playing with the occult meaning of the verb: to entrance someone with your voice.

379 **progression**: Likely in E minor (i-VII-VI) but it could be in an implied G major key (vi-V-IV); **live**: Only one live recording of "Win" exists: 1 December 1974 at the Omni Theater in Atlanta, the last night of the tour. It's unknown whether it debuted there or in Nashville or Memphis gigs in late November, neither of which were taped. Bowie hummed and sang the first line of "Win" after a performance of "Station to Station" in Jones Beach, 4 June 2004, then cruelly yelled "enough!" to his band (most of the audience seemed oblivious); **6ths and maj7ths**: 6ths, maj7ths and 9ths are a way of giving a standard chord "color" (so where a C chord is C-E-G, a C6 is C-E-G-A). They're a staple of soul and blues records: see Steve Cropper on "Soul Man," for instance.

380 "**whole chord structure**": Buckley, *Mojo*, May 2014; **modulation**: "Win" is in G mixolydian (the G major scale with a flattened VII chord, here the song's "rival" chord, F major). The verse sequence of G-G6-A-A6-G-G6-Fmaj7-F6 is odd, as the A major, instead of the expected A minor, seems as though it should have a "purpose." But it doesn't change the key: you go right back to G major and then move to the flatted VII chord, F. Bowie just uses A major as a strong flavor in his soup; **hiccup**: compared "all you've-got-to-do-is-win" with the bridge of "Hello It's Me," "I'd nev-er-want-to-make-you-change" (Jeff Norman); "**hitting every line**": Steve Volk, "David Bowie's Young Americans," *Philadelphia Inquirer*, 24 July 2002.

381 "**at the floor**": Visconti, 222.

383 **irregular meter**: The verses of the original "Universe" had bars of 5/4 and 2/4; **backing vocals**: Jean Millington was a member of Fanny, "one of the most important female bands

in American rock," as per Bowie. She would marry Earl Slick. Jean Fineberg, a flutist and saxophonist, played in all-female bands like Godmother and ISIS. Though credited as singers on this and "Fame," I don't hear them, suggesting their vocals could have been wiped. Fineberg also apparently played a flute overdub, which you can hear in one circulating "Fame" mix.

384 **first release**: released as a single on 15 August 1975 (RCA 2579/ PB 10320, US #1, UK #17). It's the only time a Bowie single charted higher in the US than in the UK; "**just a vamp**": *Bowie: Plastic Soul Review*; "**shit**": *Mojo*, May 2014; **drum quota**: Take how Davis only plays a snare fill once in the verses, otherwise keeping to his hi-hat.

385 **oldies album**: On a recording of a drink/drug-fueled session in LA in May 1974, at which Lennon jammed with Stevie Wonder and the McCartneys, Lennon yelled that all songs "have gotta be something done around the Fifties, or no later than '63, or we ain't gonna know it"; "**Shame Shame Shame**": Both Zanetta/Edwards and Trynka's source was May Pang, who recalled Lennon playing the Shirley & Co. riff and Bowie leaving the room, soon to return with a complete lyric. Alomar denies this happened. A point in his favor is that "Shame Shame Shame" had only started getting airplay in late December 1974 and it's odd Lennon would be *that* up to date on new disco. Points against: Lennon's squeaky vocal contributions and the final descending "fame" vocal hook do seem derived from Shirley & Co.

386 **Bowie Bonds**: MainMan got 50% of all future royalties from *Space Oddity* through *David Live*, 17% of royalties from *Young Americans* to *Baal*, 25% of Bowie's publishing and 5% of live earnings until 1982. (Gilmans, 407; E/Z, 340); **Lennon's opposite move**: He sings "fame" (G#) on Bowie's second (Eb), then sings a second "fame" (A) on Bowie's

"makes" or "what" (D), a fifth interval, so that the two sound like they're peeling away from each other. **mistaken mastermind**: See Philip Norman's *Lennon*: "John attended the session at Electric Lady studio and improvised a three-note riff around the single word "fame"; "**plain, stupid old rock 'n' roll song**": Buckley, *SF*, 215; "very much in charge": Trynka, 224; **guitars**: Alomar claimed he cut more overdubs after Bowie left the studio, which Bowie denied.

387 **percussion**: For Ryko's CD reissue campaign, Bowie reworked "Fame" in 1990. The new mix was larded with gewgaws like a synthetic vocal "stutter," the rhythm was on steroids. Bowie then turned over his sins to other parties to amplify. Though "Fame" was ideal for a hip-hop revision, Bowie wound up with a Queen Latifah performance that's mediocre in its better moments; **topped US charts**: The British, in a nostalgic contrarian mood, sent a "Space Oddity" reissue to #1 in November 1975.

Chapter 10

390 **Cherokee**: There's no engineering credit on *Station* but one of Cherokee's owners, Dee Robb, recorded some sessions. The three Robb brothers had made their name with a studio they'd built on a horse ranch in Chatsworth, where Steely Dan cut *Pretzel Logic*. Liking the British sound, the Robbs imported a custom-made Trident 80-input A range desk just in time for *Station*. (Maureen Droney, *Mix*, 1 March 2002.); **live**: claims Bowie sang "Golden Years" in Evansville, Indiana on 22 February 1976 are dubious; no recordings exist, there's no mention of the song (a then-current hit single) in local newspaper reviews of the concert and no other evidence of Bowie singing "Golden Years" in 1976. Not having MacCormack on tour was likely one reason, although Bowie had Carlos Alomar sing high harmonies on "Stay," for instance.

391 **filling in for Bowie**: MacCormack said Bowie's voice gave out halfway through. The fact that Bowie didn't recut his backing vocal later, while doing countless overdubs and retakes for the rest of *Station*, suggests a rush to get the single out; "**Happy Years**": mainly in a similar vocal tag—"ah-ooh cha-cha-cha"—and title; "**Funky Broadway**," "**On Broadway**": It's also possible Alomar and Slick, both of whom have admitted to not remembering much of the sessions, confused their respective "Broadway" songs. Alomar also raided Cliff Noble's "The Horse" for ideas; **F# chord**: "Golden Years" is in the mixolydian mode, with E major the flatted VII chord of F# major; "**this incredible sound**": promo flexi-disc, 1983; **issued as a single**: It would be Bowie's last US Top 10 hit until 1983.

392 "**round sounding**": Richard Cromelin, "The Return of the Thin White Duke," *Circus*, March 1976; **real progression**: some transcriptions have the B minor 7th as an A-sharp diminished 7th; **down in pitch**: there's a subtle compression in the verse: the first phrase ("don't let me hear...") falls a fourth, the second ("taking you..") by a third, the up-an-octave "AN-gel!" falls by a second.

393 **US #3**: The only time a Bowie album's charted higher in the US than in the UK. "TVC 15" was released, in a 3:29 edit, as a single on 30 April 1976 (RCA 2682/ PB 10664, UK #33); **fills rooms with televisions**: starting with four and ending with a dozen. An image lifted by Alan Moore for *Watchmen* a decade later.

394 **Philip K. Dick**: Often associated TV with grotesque evil. Take his *Lies, Inc.* where a politician on TV transforms into a monster who consumes eyeballs; **quadraphonic sound**: 4-channel sound, favored by Seventies audiophiles. *Station* was mixed with this process in mind. When Walter Tevis revised *The Man Who Fell to Earth* upon the film's release, he changed "LP albums" to "quadraphonic" albums.

395 **void in a box**: "TVC 15" would inspire, if subconsciously, two films of the following decade: David Cronenberg's *Videodrome*, in which James Woods makes out with Deborah Harry through a pulsating screen, and Tobe Hooper/Steven Spielberg's *Poltergeist*, where a girl is stolen by a TV set; **16-bar verses**; live, Bowie broke up the long run of verses, moving the first bridge/refrain to come after the first verse; **distorted guitar tracks**: in its 2010 reissue, "TVC 15" appears to have had guitar tracks down-mixed in the verses.

396 **first release:** later released as a single in November 1981 (RCA BOW T 10, UK #24); **Sinatra**: While Dee Robb said Bowie and Sinatra regularly hung out at the studio together, the only documented Sinatra visit to Cherokee in the period was a 24 October 1975 session, when the Chairman recorded a John Denver Christmas song. Claims that Sinatra was recording his album *Trilogy* in these sessions are wrong; claims that Bowie sang harmony on a Sinatra track are very dubious; **Tiomkin**: A Russian émigré who had studied under Prokofiev, Tiomkin became a renowned Hollywood composer. He and Washington (lyricist of "When You Wish Upon a Star," "Stella By Starlight," "The Nearness of You" and other standards) also collaborated on "Town Without Pity" and "Rawhide."

397 "**good European feel**": Crowe, *Station*; **Nina Simone**: Simone cut her take on 21 March 1964 but it wasn't released until the album it titled, a grab-bag of various mid-Sixties sessions, was issued in late 1966; **lead vocal takes**: By contrast Rod Stewart, recording *A Night On the Town* during the same period at Cherokee, said he didn't cut a single useable vocal there. "I couldn't sing. I just couldn't hit a note. The reason, if you ask me, is the fucking smog. It cuts the shit out of your voice." (*Rolling Stone* 211, 1976).

399 **no condition to compose**: Maslin said Bowie only had two songs when he went into the studio, "Golden Years" being

one. Other likely candidates are "Word On a Wing" and "TVC 15," as the latter was cut early in the sessions, as per Crowe; **another attempt at "John"**: he just turned 7th chords into 9th chords ("The 9th chord belongs to James Brown. Rock and roll is not about the 9th chord," Alomar said). The refrain chords of each song are identical but for an A minor 9 ("staaay") where "John" had an A9sus4 ("Jooohn"); "**gave it back to him**": Buckley, *SF,* 238; "**polar opposites**": Michael Molenda, "Earl Slick's Street Rock Odyssey," *Guitar Player*, 30 January 2014.

400 **guitar track**: Slick recalled the rhythm guitar being "an early '70s black Les Paul [run] through a late-'60s 100-watt Marshall stack" while he played lead on his early 1960s Stratocaster. "I only owned one pedal, so there's no effects. Just straight through the amp, no master control. Old school. Just turn it up to 10 and blast away." (Jeff Slate, *Music Radar,* 26 February 2013). Photographs of Bowie at Cherokee show him playing a white Les Paul Custom.

401 **nominally Christian**: The decline of British churchgoers was the subject of national concern and of a heap of books, the wittiest of which was R.C. Churchill's *The English Sunday* (1954): "The Bible itself, however, has ceased in general to be read in England. What, then, do we read instead? Apart from Sunday newspapers a good many people, of course, read nothing at all on Sundays"; "**religious fervor**": Parsons, *Arena,* 1993. Bowie took after his father, who he described as "one of the few I knew who had a lot of understanding of other religions...I think some of that was passed on to me. There was no enforced religion [at home] though he didn't particularly care for English religion—Henry [VIII]'s religion" (CSM, *NME,* 29 September 1984).

402 "**finding the cross...protection**": MacKinnon, *NME,* 13 September 1980; "**few hundred dollars**": *Backstage Passes,*

304.

403 "**needed to produce**": MacKinnon, 1980; "**as a hymn**," Hilburn 1976; **B major:** uncommon for pop composers, given the high number of sharps in the key (the only Beatles songs in B are "For No One," "Penny Lane" and "One After 909"). The verse chord progression is straight I-IV-V while Bowie initially sings the root note, B, in parallel with the bass; **jolting move**: Bowie prepares the ear for the move to D-flat by singing the closing "heaven or hell" as a stepwise rise of C#-D#-E , then going up a half-step with the F note on "Lord!" which is the mediant of the underlying (and new tonic) chord, D-flat (D-F-Ab). He does it again on the move to D major, a half-step rise from "light" (F) to "Lord!" (G, now the root note of a G chord, which is in turn the IV chord of the new D major key).

404 **Chamberlin**: Bowie purchased a Chamberlin M1 during his 1974 tour. "**freestanding and wordless**": Momus; **Roy Bittan**: No one quite remembers how Bittan was recruited for the album. Earl Slick, who'd played with Bittan, said he'd suggested him, while other sources have Bittan happening to be staying in the same LA hotel as Bowie. (Mike Garson got the boot at the end of 1974, likely due to Bowie's paranoia about Scientology.)

405 **book after book**: Including Arthur Edward Waite's *The Book of Black Magic*, Richard Cavendish's *The Black Arts*, Pauwels and Bergier's *The Morning of the Magicians*, J.H. Brennan's *Occult Reich*, Trevor Ravenscroft's *The Spear of Destiny* and various Colin Wilson books like *The Occult* and *Mysterious Powers*; "**looking like Americans**": *Town*, September 1962 (cited by Lewisohn, 1384).

406 **MacDonald**: *People's Music*, 140; **first lines**: Similar to Aleister Crowley's "A Paean in the Springtide" in *White Stains* ("Here in the spring we are free, as the winds that look love at the ocean...").

407 **Tattwa**: A Hindu-derived practice. Draw a card from a 25-card Tattwa deck and visualize the image on the card while regulating your breathing. In the mind, the Tattwa image should have a "flashing color," that is, an opposite color from its printed color (so the blue Vayu image will flash orange in the mind). The goal is to expand this image until it becomes a portal to an astral plane. The Tattwa without color is the "Akasha–Tattwa, the superimposed quintessence of all the others" (Peter-R Koenig)."I thought it was Tibetan," Angela Bowie told Koenig. "When I focused on a spot it became very bright, and when [Bowie] moved toward me the spot turned to black"; **Kirlian photography**: discovered in 1939 by its Russian scientist namesake, is done by placing film upon a metal conducting plate, placing the photo subject on the film, and then briefly applying high-voltage electricity to the plate. This gives off a "corona discharge" as seen in the resulting photograph, in which there's usually a colored glow around the object, which some researchers have claimed is the object's psychic aura. Bowie received a Kirlian machine from Dr. Thelma Moss, head of UCLA's Dept. of Parapsychology, and photographs of his cocaine-enhanced fingers were used in tour productions and the CD booklet of *Earthling*.

408 **Kabbalah**: To explain the Kabbalah in a footnote is rather insane, even by the standards of this book. It's an esoteric Jewish mystical tradition that begins around the 13th Century. The Tree of Life, whose 10 points are known as the *sefirot*, is a Kabbalist invention, possibly derived from the basic numbers. The *sefirot* were stages of divine emanation: *kether* (10) is the divine creative will, funneled through other *sefirot*, to end in *malkuth* (1), the intermediary that transfers divine power to physical creation; "**insatiable appetite**": *Spin*, November 1999.

410 "**too loud**": *Hit Parader*, August 1976. Asked about the band,

Bowie said "they'll all probably wander off after the tour and go back to James Brown or wherever they came from. I really don't know them...I mean, I know Carlos..."; "**Heil Hitler!**" Edmonds, *Circus*, 27 April 1976; "**Nazi bit**": *MM*, 13 March 1976.

411 "**fascist leader**": press conference, Stockholm, 26 April 1976; **Nazi salute**: Video footage convincingly shows that Bowie was just stiffly waving his hand. ("I never felt David was a Nazi sympathizer...It just think it was what I'd call an adolescent attraction," Kent later said (*Uncut*, April 2001); **Bertolucci**: "I realized that making movies is my way to kill my father. In a way I make movies for...the pleasure of guilt," *Guardian*, 21 February 2008.

413 **Bulwer-Lytton**: This scenario (old man in a used occult bookshop reveals to protagonist a secret clue) was taken from *Zanoni*, a book that Bowie recently listed as one of his 100 favorites.

414 ***Autobahn***: Bowie: "I think how Kraftwerk influenced me was attitudinal. It was the stance they took. It's almost like: There's a new universe once can exist in. What would I find if I went to that universe?" *NME*, 2 December 2000; "**like a child**": *Circus*, 1976; "**two crazy guys**": Molenda; "**plug it in!**" Buckley, *SF*, 239.

415 **circle of fifths**: The whole sequence is G-D-F-C-D-E-A-E-F#m. Jeff Norman: "It's as if we have some unholy extended V-of-V thing, with each 2-chord set reversing the order. The whole thing's derived from E-A-D-G-C-F. Antecedents are the turnaround in John Coltrane's "Giant Steps," the intro to the Beatles' "Like Dreamers Do," and (closest to Bowie, since he covered it) the bit just before the chorus of the Easybeats' "Friday on My Mind.:

416 "**Chuck Berry**": J. Slate; **B minor**: "European cannon is here" moves from G to A and you'd expect this to follow with a move to D, but instead it's back to B minor ("does my

face show.."); **"their determination"**: *Uncut*, 2001.

417 **"twisted and turned"**: Trynka, 244.

420 **Carson**: *RS Rock 'n' Roll*, 536.

Contemporary culture has eliminated both the concept of the public and the figure of the intellectual. Former public spaces – both physical and cultural – are now either derelict or colonized by advertising. A cretinous anti-intellectualism presides, cheerled by expensively educated hacks in the pay of multinational corporations who reassure their bored readers that there is no need to rouse themselves from their interpassive stupor. The informal censorship internalized and propagated by the cultural workers of late capitalism generates a banal conformity that the propaganda chiefs of Stalinism could only ever have dreamt of imposing. Zer0 Books knows that another kind of discourse – intellectual without being academic, popular without being populist – is not only possible: it is already flourishing, in the regions beyond the striplit malls of so-called mass media and the neurotically bureaucratic halls of the academy. Zer0 is committed to the idea of publishing as a making public of the intellectual. It is convinced that in the unthinking, blandly consensual culture in which we live, critical and engaged theoretical reflection is more important than ever before.